Seapower

Second Edition

The sea has always been central to human development as a source of resources, and as a means of transportation, information exchange and strategic dominion. It has been the basis for our prosperity and security. This is even more the case, now, in the early twenty-first century, with the emergence of an increasingly globalised world trading system.

Navies have always provided a way of policing, and sometimes exploiting, the system. In contemporary conditions, navies – and other forms of maritime power – are having to adapt, in order to exert the maximum power ashore in the company of others and to expand the range of their interests, activities and responsibilities. Their traditional tasks still apply but new ones are developing fast.

This updated and expanded new edition of Geoffrey Till's acclaimed book is an essential guide for students of naval history and maritime strategy, and anyone interested in the changing and crucial role of seapower in the twenty-first century.

Geoffrey Till is a recognised authority on maritime strategy past and present. Formerly Dean of Academic Studies at the Joint Services Command and Staff College, he is currently Professor of Maritime Studies in the Defence Studies Department and Director of the Corbett Centre for Maritime Policy, King's College London at the UK Joint Services Command and Staff College. He is author of a number of books including *Air Power and the Royal Navy*, *Maritime Strategy and the Nuclear Age* and, most recently, *The Development of British Naval Thinking* (also published by Routledge).

Cass Series: Naval Policy and History
Series Editor: Geoffrey Till

ISSN 1366-9478

This series consists primarily of original manuscripts by research scholars in the general area of naval policy and history, without national or chronological limitations. It will from time to time also include collections of important articles as well as reprints of classic works.

Seapower

A Guide for the Twenty-First Century

Second Edition

Geoffrey Till

Routledge
Taylor & Francis Group

LONDON AND NEW YORK

First published 2004
by Frank Cass Publishers
an imprint of Taylor & Francis Group, an informa business

This edition published 2009
by Routledge
2 Park Square, Milton Park, Abingdon, Oxon OX14 4RN

Simultaneously published in the USA and Canada
by Routledge
270 Madison Ave, New York, NY 10016

Routledge is an imprint of the Taylor & Francis Group, an informa business

© 2004, 2009 Geoffrey Till

Typeset in Times by Wearset Ltd, Boldon, Tyne and Wear
Printed and bound in Great Britain by TJ International Ltd, Padstow, Cornwall

British Library Cataloguing in Publication Data
A catalogue record for this book is available from the British Library

Library of Congress Cataloging in Publication Data
Till, Geoffrey.
Seapower: a guide for the twenty-first century/Geoffrey Till. – 2nd ed.
p. cm.
Includes bibliographical references and index.
1. Sea-power. I. Title.
V25.T55 2009
359'.03–dc22
2008040542

ISBN10: 0-415-48088-4 (hbk)
ISBN10: 0-415-48089-2 (pbk)
ISBN10: 0-203-88048-X (ebk)

ISBN13: 978-0-415-48088-8 (hbk)
ISBN13: 978-0-415-48089-5 (pbk)
ISBN13: 978-0-203-88048-7 (ebk)

Contents

Illustrations

Figures

Tables

Foreword

The Royal Navy, like many other navies, is facing a world of substantial challenges. The international scene is confused and confusing, essentially unpredictable, partly encouraging and partly not. Inevitably this creates real problems for naval planners.

One of these, of course is naval defence inflation. Our problem is part of a universal trend affecting all the world's navies. Individual platforms, sensors and weapons are simply getting more expensive relative to the financial resources available for naval construction. The result, especially in Europe and in much of the Asia-Pacific region too has been quite drastic numerical downsizing. While the increased capability of remaining platforms like the magnificent Type 45 or the Astute submarine is much greater, it remains true that coverage and flexibility suffer from the inescapable fact that, however capable the individual platform, it can only be in one place at one time.

Again, as in most other navies, British naval force planners are torn between the demands of major combat operations on the one hand and, for want of a better word, stabilisation operations on the other. The first calls for such high-intensity sea control naval capabilities as deep-water anti-submarine warfare, anti-air warfare, and ballistic missile defence, together with sea-based nuclear deterrence. This all makes best sense against the 'symmetrical' peer-competitors who might yet re-emerge. The second, really aimed at the asymmetrical threat, calls for the capacity to deliver the range of services required for expeditionary operations (sea based force projection, and the support and sustainment of forces ashore), for maritime security operations (maritime domain awareness, small-ship operations, cooperation with coast guards) and for constructive naval engagement with other countries (surface ships and inclusive naval procedures). The second is not a cheap, or even necessarily a cheaper, option. The hit secured on the well-armed Israeli corvette *Hanit* by a C-802 missile fired by Hezbollah forces in Lebanon showed just how militarily demanding and indeed politically complex some of these operations can be. Our American colleagues have recently been quite candid about the 'tensions … between the requirements for continued peacetime engagement and maintaining proficiency in the critical skills necessary to fighting and winning in combat'.

Allocating scarce resources between these competing sets of commitments is the most difficult conceptual issue facing the world's naval planners.

And then there is the problem of what you might call the 'time squeeze' caused by the natural focus on the demands of long drawn-out operations in Iraq and Afghanistan. What Geoffrey Till calls the 'tyranny of the immediate commitment' means that the media and the political establishment will naturally tend to assign top priority to defence projects that are relevant to current and actual operations, pushing those to do with possible future contingencies on to the back burner. This hits navies in two ways. First, it tends to jeopardise, or at least delay, longer-term projects against remoter threats. Second, it raises issues about the perceived utility of naval power at a time when 'boots on the ground' seem to be the main requirement. Despite a very obvious shift in naval priorities from power *at* sea to power *from* the sea, the critical contribution that navies have made and are making to these operations is generally out of sight and so out of mind. The result of all this is a totally misguided sense that navies do not matter as much as they used to, a matter of salience whenever an expensive naval project is presented to the media or the political establishment.

Although this reaction is perhaps understandable, it is especially bizarre at a time when the whole world system might be fairly said to rest on globalisation, which in turn rests on the container and the modern shipping industry. As this book shows, seaborne commerce produces a mutually dependent international community of industrial production and consumption. The world has increasingly to be seen as a tight, interconnected nexus of countries and regions with high degrees of mutual economic, and therefore political, interdependence. The world's peace and prosperity depend on it. Nonetheless, this is a system under threat. Navies have to do their best to defend it at sea and from the sea, in conjunction with the other services, their allies and in cooperation with other governmental and indeed non-governmental agencies.

But this is all at a time when resources are tight and choices difficult. The need for clarity of thought and informed judgment has never been greater. I join with Geoffrey Till in hoping that this book will help.

Admiral Sir Jonathon Band KCB ADC
Royal Navy. First Sea Lord and
Chief of the Naval Staff

Preface to the second edition

Our navy is addressed, our power collected.

Shakespeare, *Henry IV, Pt 2*, IV/4

In the first edition of this book I used King Henry's comment to make the point that, in fact, all was then far from certain in the naval world. Events over the past few years have confirmed that view and this second edition is an attempt to focus a little more on issues that have become a good deal more important, if not, unfortunately, clearer since that time. Apart from some general updating and textual rearrangements, this volume goes deeper into an international political context that determines the roles of navies, and contains a new chapter that aims to show how the ideas discussed in this book are currently being put into practice by four of the world's navies, in a geographic area of growing interest to everyone else. It makes for a rather longer book, but as anyone studying seapower knows only too well, it has no obvious boundaries. Thinking about the subject holistically requires people to range far and wide.

The thanks extended in the first edition of this book to countless people – active sailors, academics, naval students – around the world still stand although they are not reprinted here for reasons of space. In the several years since then, I have also benefitted from the advice and help of a good many more. I would like to thank the British Academy for their generous support through two grants, SG 33339 and 48492, which made it all possible, and for the assistance of Professor Mike Pugh and Sarah Somers and her team in getting and administering them. During this period I also benefitted from two extended research trips. The first research trip in 2007 was to the Rajaratnam School of International Studies at the Nanyang Technological University, Singapore where I was Senior Visiting Research Fellow for three very productive months. Singapore is as good a maritime watchtower as I have come across and I am grateful to Cdr Joshua Ho in helping to set the arrangements up and for the counsel of the many excellent academics at the RSIS who are too numerous to name individually. I would like to single out Cdr Nigel Race, the RN Liaison Officer to Singapore, Commodore (ret'd) Sam Bateman and Dr Paul Mitchell, Dr Tim Huxley of the Singapore branch of the IISS, Michael Richardson, Drs Ian Storey and Vijay Sakhuja of ISEAS, Yoshiaki Ito of ReCaap and Dr Derek da Cunha for their help. While in Singapore I was fortunate enough to be welcomed into the merchant shipping community through the Shanghai Surveyors Society and its many interesting members, contacts that also led, through the good offices of

Helmut Sohnen and Arthur Bowring, to the Hong Kong Shipowners Association. The analysis in this book of globalisation as a maritime phenomenon owes much to these people.

The second long research trip was another three month stay, this time as the inaugural holder in 2008 of the Sir Howard Kippenberger chair in Strategic Studies at the Victoria University of Wellington, New Zealand, courtesy of the extraordinarily accomplished Peter Cozen and the Weston Foundation. Here I benefitted from discussions with another range of maritime people too numerous to name individually, although again I would like to single out a few, particularly John Mackinnon, Secretary of Defence, Admiral David Ledson, Chief of Navy, Cdre Tony Parr, Cdrs Karl Woodhead and Richard Jackson, Dr Lance Beath and Professor Brian Lynch for being so generous with their time. Since a major strand of my interest concerns the maritime developments of the Asia-Pacific region, these two trips were of very considerable value to me. I am grateful to Admiral Shalders, Chief of Navy and Captain Pete Levey of the RAN for the invitation to join in the discussions of the Seapower 08 conference and to Dr David Stevens for his hospitality during it. Rear-Admiral James Goldrick, as ever, has been very helpful.

One major thrust of this second edition of the book has been a focus on the naval policies of China, Japan, India and the United States as case studies of general naval developments around the world. For China, I relied on the help of colleagues in Singapore, a range of contacts in Hong Kong and the expertise of a number of colleagues in the United States, particularly James R. Homes, Andrew Winner and Toshi Yoshihara.

Through the good offices of Capt Simon Chelton, the British naval attaché to Tokyo, I benefitted from a wide range of contacts and discussions from officers of the JSMDF, retired and present, including Admiral Kaneda Hideaki, Captain Toshihiro Yamamoto, Rear Admiral Yoichi Hirama, Captain Yoshitaka Toui of the JCG and Rear Admiral Sato of the Mikasa Foundation. Professors Tomoyoki Ishizu of the National Defence Academy and Yoshinaga Hayashi of the national Institute for Defence Studies and their colleagues from the two institutions were helpful on the general background. In the UK, Captain Hiro Terada was extremely helpful as were Drs Euan Graham from the FCO, Dr Elizabeth Guran and Alessio Patalano, together with fellow enthusiasts from the Anglo-Japanese Society.

In several trips to India, I was able through the good offices of Brigadier Ian Rees and Captain Charles Ashcroft in New Delhi and Commodore J.A. Singh in London, to engage in useful discussions with a wide range of past and present officers of the increasingly impressive Indian Navy, including Vice Admiral Verna, Deputy Chief of the Naval Staff, Admiral Vohra and his colleagues from the NMF, Commodore Sujeet Samaddar, Captain Ashok Kumar in Singapore and Captain Rajan Vir of the IMF in Pune. The transcript of Admiral Mehta's important address to the IISS in London was made available to me through the good offices of Jason Alderwick.

As ever, the United States is a ferment of interesting ideas about naval developments and I would particularly like to thank Professors Vince Mocini and Richmond Lloyd of the excellent Naval War College at Newport for their good offices in gaining me access to, and the ability to comment on, the debate about the evolving new US naval strategy, 'A Cooperative Strategy for 21st Century Seapower', through a number of visits and conferences held there. Cdre Alan Bennett, the British Naval Attache to Washington, was extremely hospitable during my stay in

Washington. Peter Swartz of the CNA was, as always, extraordinarily helpful both in ideas and in contacts, and again I benefitted from a wide range of discussions. Captain 'Buz' Sorce was particularly forthcoming on US naval construction plans, as were Ron O'Rourke of the CRS, Robert O. Work of the CSBA. For general policy inputs I am grateful to Clifford A. Hart, Loren Thompson, Walter Russell Mead, Donna Hopkins of the State Department and Michael Coulter. The Pacific focus was covered by a couple of trips to Honolulu (always a burden!) and I am grateful to Admiral Robert F. Willard and Dr Bill Morgan and their colleagues from the Pacific Fleet, Dr Mohan Malik for setting up valuable discussions at the Asia-Pacific Centre, to Dr Paul Bratton for doing likewise at the Hawaiian Pacific University and for discussions with Richard Halloran.

A second emerging theme has been a particular focus on what in this book I have called the 'post-modern' preoccupations of today's navies, the maintenance of good order at sea, coalition operations, multilateral counterterrorism and the like. For this I have benefitted from the extensive discussions and help from Captains Bruce Stubbs and Samuel M. Neill past and presently of the splendid US Coast Guard, a number of trips to South America partly through the good offices of Captain Paul Robinson and Cdr Steve Kerchey of the MoD's Defence Sales Organisation. In Peru I was helped particularly by Captains Fernando Luna del Castillo and Garcia Romani. In Brazil I benefitted from discussions with Admiral Ruy de Almeida Silva, Captain Francisco Alves de Almeida and Captain Renato Aguiafreire. A second fascinating trip to Chile was facilitated by Admiral Hugo Desformes who set up a visit to *Exponaval 2006* and a trip with the Chilean Navy to the Antarctic, which was quite literally the experience of a lifetime. A moderately stormy voyage across the Drake Passage in the *Almirante Viel* gave me a brief insight into what real sailoring is all about! Many thanks to Admiral Edmundo Gonzalez Robles, Captains Humberto Senarega and Pelago Castro and Cdr Miguel Marin Zuaznabar. Across the world, Cdre Paul Robinson and his staff in the British headquarters in Bahrain, the British Ambassador and Jed Snyder the US pol-mil representative on site explained the complexities of coalition operations in the Gulf, while Bahria University in Karachi provided much useful information on the problems of maintaining good order in the Arabian Sea, with help from Commodore Asif Saleem and Captain Raja Javed Afzhal.

Finally, for more general help and source of ideas, I have to thank the legions of naval students I have taught, and been taught by, at my own Joint Services Command and Staff College, and in regular teaching sessions over the years at the staff colleges of Bangladesh, Belgium, the Netherlands and Kuwait and Pakistan, plus the countless others met at conferences and workshops. Captain Nick Stanley and Cdr Tim Ash at the JSCSC have also been very helpful. I am particularly grateful for the support of the British First Sea Lord who wrote the foreword to this volume when the Royal Navy was facing some particularly exciting if challenging times.

A negotiated and very welcome change of my circumstances in the Defence Studies Department of King's College London at the UK Command and Staff College provided the opportunity for this effort, and I am grateful to all my colleagues for their forbearance. I have to record the magnificent help, once again of the excellent staff of the magnificent Library at the Joint Services Command and Staff College, part of the UK Defence Academy and the DSD support team throughout. One couldn't hope for better. The task now is to build up the reputation of the new Corbett Centre for Maritime Policy Studies at King's College London, to take such studies on, but it is important to note that the views expressed and the mistakes made in this book are all mine and should not be taken necessarily to reflect the position of the Corbett Centre, King's College London, the UK Defence Academy or any other agency of the British government.

Finally, I would like to thank my wife for her forbearance, for organising and, at considerable personal sacrifice, accompanying me on the many trips this research programme required. She will, however, be pleased to note that this book is dedicated to the two latest ships in the convoy, Barney and Martha Powell. We both hope that the developments analysed in this book will allow them also to enjoy, in due course, a fair wind and a following sea.

Abbreviations

AAW	Anti-air warfare
ACS	(US) 'A Cooperative Strategy for 21st Century Seapower'
AEW	Airborne early warning
AORs	Support ships
ARG	Amphibious ready group
ASW	Anti-submarine warfare
ATO	Air tasking order
BMD	Ballistic missile defence
C^4I	Command, control, communications, computers and information
CAP	Combat air patrol
CARAT	Cooperation afloat readiness and training (exercises)
CASD	Continuous at sea deterrent
CNO	(US) Chief of Naval Operations
CONMAROPS	Concept of Maritime Operations
COTS	Commercial off the shelf
EEZ	Exclusive economic zone
ERGM	Extended range gun munitions
Extac	Exercise tactics
FACs	Fast attack craft
GPS	Global Positioning System
GWOT	Global War on Terror
HADR	Humanitarian assistance and disaster response/relief
ICBM	Intercontinental ballistic missile
IMB	International Maritime Bureau
IMO	International Maritime Organisation
IOMARC	Indian Ocean Marine Affairs Cooperation
IONS	Indian Ocean Nations Symposium
ISPS	International Shipping and Port Facilities security code
IT	Information technology
IWCO	Independent Communion of the World Ocean
JCG	Japan Coast Guard
JFACC	Joint Force Air Component Commander
JMSDF	Japanese Maritime Self Defence Force
JSTARS	Joint surveillance target attack radar system
LCS	Littoral combat ship
LIMO	Low intensity maritime operations

LPG	Liquid propane gas
LPH	Landing platform (helicopter)
MARPOL	International Convention for the Prevention of Pollution by Ships
MCM	Mine counter measures
MDA	Maritime domain awareness
MIOPS	Maritime interception operations
MMS	(Indian) Maritime Military Strategy
MOOTW	Maritime operations other than war
MPA	Maritime patrol aircraft
MTB	Motor torpedo-boats
MTR	Military technical revolution
NATO	North Atlantic Treaty Organisation
NCW	Network-centric Warfare
NDPO	(Japan's) National Defence Programme Outline
NEO	Non combatant evacuation operation
NGO	Non governmental organisation
NGS	Naval gunfire support
NM	Nautical mile
NMD	National missile defence
OGD	Other government departments
OMFTS	Operational manoeuvre from the sea
OMG	Operational manoeuvre group
P & I CLUB	Protection and Indemnity Club (for marine insurance)
PASSEX	Passing exercise
PJHQ	Permanent Joint Force Headquarters
PLA(N)	(China's) People's Liberation Army Navy
PSI	Proliferation Security Initiative
PSOs	Peace support operations
REA	Rapid environment assessment
ReCaap	Regional Cooperation Agreement on Combating Piracy and Armed Robbery against Ships
RMA	Revolution in military affairs
Ro-Ro	Roll-on roll-off (ferry)
RSTA	Reconnaisance, surveillance, targeting and acquisition
SACLANT	(NATO's) Supreme Allied Commander Atlantic
SAR	Search and rescue
SLOCs	Sea lines of communication
SOLAS	Safety of life at sea
SOSUS	(Anti-submarine) sound surveillance system
SPE	Service protected evacuation
SSBN	Ballistic missile firing nuclear powered submarine
SSK	Diesel powered submarine
SSN	Nuclear powered submarine
STOM	Ship to objective manoeuvre
SUA	Suppression of Unlawful Acts at Sea Convention
TBMD	Theatre ballistic missile defence
UAV	Unmanned aerial vehicle

UNCLOS	United Nations Convention on the Law of the Sea
USCG	US Coast Guard
UUV	Unmanned underwater vehicles
WPNS	Western Pacific Naval Symposium
WTO	World Trade Organisation

1 Seapower in a globalised world
Two tendencies

1.1 Introduction: seapower and globalisation

Because of its effect on the state, and state practices, globalisation is the central fact of the strategic environment of the early twenty-first century. Believers, in the traditions of the nineteenth-century British Manchester school, welcome the onset of globalisation hoping that it will usher in an era of peace and plenty by replacing earlier, competitive, aggressive balance-of-power politics with a much greater sense of international community. Unbelievers see globalisation as undermining their way of life, their independence, their beliefs and their future prospects. A third group, the unconvinced, dispute assumptions of globalisation's assumed longevity and ponder the consequences of its prospective if not imminent collapse. Either way, the present and future state of globalisation is and will be a major determinant of the shape and nature of world politics of states. Governmental and indeed social attitudes to globalisation will in turn be a major determinant of strategy and defence and naval policy and therefore of the size, shape, composition and function of navies.

In broad terms, the world's states are often divided into three notional categories, and these are determined more by their economic development than by anything else. Pre-modern states tend to be essentially agricultural, with limited economic interdependence and insufficient surpluses to invest in further development. Because much of the rest of the world has moved on, pre-modern states are often regarded as weak, failing or failed. They are said to be commonly characterised by the poor standards of governance, corruption, lawlessness and communal strife that make economic and social progress difficult. Modern states, by contrast, are shaped by industrial mass production into efficient self-confident entities of the sort usually said to have begun emerging in Europe after the treaty of Westphalia in 1648. They are inherently competitive and driven by 'Realist' expectations that international relations is basically a struggle for who gets what, when and how, the 'what' being a question of resources, territory, influence and power. Post-modern states, on the other hand, are economically and institutionally efficient in different ways; they are moulded by, and for, the contemporary information economy that is such a characteristic of contemporary globalisation. Instinctively collaborative, they aspire to a cooperative world system of openness and mutual dependence.

Pre-modern states are still to be found in the more challenged parts of Africa, the struggling small island states of the South Pacific and Haiti, Somalia and occasionally elsewhere. Most states in the Asia-Pacific are predominantly modern, while most post-modern states are located in North America or, most especially, Western and Northern Europe. Of course, these categories are all matters much more of degree than of kind, and some 'modern' Asia-Pacific states for example have 'post-modern' tendencies, some of them (such as Australia, New Zealand, Singapore and Japan) really quite strongly. Come to that, some of the most post-modern of European states have markedly 'modern' elements to them too!

It would seem to follow from all of this that there are three notional models of naval development, which reflect both the national security perspectives of states and their current view of globalisation in general, and its impact and consequences on naval forces in particular. Post-modern navies are naturally associated with post-modern states, modern navies with modern ones, pre-modern navies with pre-modern states.

But perhaps some clarifications on terminology are called for here. While these three models of state and naval development are labelled pre-modern, modern and post-modern this is largely *faute de mieux*. None of these terms are value judgments implying that one is better or worse than the others. Nor should they be taken as mutually exclusive absolutes for as we shall see both elements commonly co-exist. 'Modern' here means the adaptation of traditional or conventional concepts of naval employment to contemporary circumstances; post-modern means their transformation into something else in some or all respects. Pre-modern navies, on the other hand, verge on being a contradiction in terms since adverse circumstances mean they struggle to exist or to do anything other than symbolise their country and its problems, while perhaps providing at best a sporadic defence of some of its key interests.

These labels are not entirely satisfactory and, if only for the sake of variety, the terms traditional and non-traditional, conventional and non-conventional will often be used instead. In the main, this review will stick to 'modern' and 'post-modern' because the alternatives have their weaknesses too and especially because the terms specifically link the development of navies to the nature of the state they serve and to competing attitudes towards globalisation.[1] And that, really, is the point.

Globalisation: the security implications

Before we look specifically at these naval consequences, however, several points need to be made about the general defence implications of globalisation. First, it encourages the development of a 'borderless world' in which the autarchy of the national units of which it is composed is gradually being whittled away by the development of a variety of transnational economic and technological trends. The focus will increasingly be on the system not its components; military plans and strategy will, the post-modern argument goes, need to serve that system as a whole. It is an essentially system-centred approach to strategy that is substantially different from the conventional, traditional, modern state-centred one that we are more accustomed to. The system reduces both the capacity and the incentive for states to take independent action in defence of their interests. States will become more relaxed about their borders because they have to be.

But this cuts both ways; they will be relaxed about the borders of other nations too. In a globalising world, the post-modern systems approach tends to pull strategists forwards geographically. This forwards leaning approach to the making and implementation of strategy has been a marked characteristic of European and American defence thinking for a decade now. Thus Tony Blair in early 2007:

> The frontiers of our security no longer stop at the Channel. What happens in the Middle East affects us … The new frontiers for our security are global. Our Armed Forces will be deployed in the lands of other nations far from home, with no immediate threat to our territory, in environments and in ways unfamiliar to them.[2]

Or, again, Brendan Nelson, then Australia's Minister for Defence, 'What happens in the Mid-East and more remote parts of the world is no less important to our security and interests than what happens on our borders.'[3]

Second, globalisation is a *dynamic* system since, amongst other things, trade and business produces a constantly changing hierarchy of winners and losers and, historically, conflict seems to be particularly associated with economic volatility.[4] The introduction of fast, refrigerated iron-hulled steamships, the cutting of the Panama canal and the capacity of buyers and sellers to talk to one another more or less instantaneously by telegraph were all excellent for New Zealand meat and dairy producers, and indirectly for British manufacturers (as it reduced food inflation) but it was bad for British sheep farmers and dairy producers. The success of globalisation depends on new players in the game being accommodated, its victims supported and future directions anticipated. An effective all-round defence of the system has therefore to be constant, and proactive rather than merely intermittent and reactive. This calls for continuous, carefully integrated action to 'shape the international security environment in a nice way' through a comprehensive approach that links diplomatic, economic, social and military policies.

Third, globalisation depends absolutely on the free flow of sea-based shipping. For that reason, it is profoundly maritime in nature – something therefore likely to be of particular interest to the world's navies. International shipping, especially in the shape of the container, underpins the prospect of further beneficial growth in world trade. But to have that effect it needs to be predictable, traceable, compliant with detailed pick-up and delivery schedules and secure. This provides both an opportunity and a challenge, not least because sea-based globalisation is potentially vulnerable to disruption. In itself, this is not new, for Mahan warned us of this over a century ago:

> This, with the vast increase in rapidity of communication, has multiplied and strengthened the bonds knitting together the interests of nations to one another, till the whole now forms an articulated system not only of prodigious size and activity, but of excessive sensitiveness, unequalled in former ages.[5]

The 'excessive sensitiveness' that Mahan had in mind derives from the fact that interdependence, and indeed dependency of any sort, inevitably produces targets for the malign to attack. But there is special point in his warnings now, partly because the extraordinary extent and depth of today's version of globalisation depends on a supply-chain philosophy of 'just enough, just in time' that increases the system's vulnerability to disruption, particularly given the lamentably low reserve stocks of life essentials such as oil and food that most countries hold. The marine transportation system's tendency to produce fewer but much larger tankers and container ships and to concentrate on nodal hub-ports intended to supply the needs of regions may also provide the malign with particularly fruitful targets.

Moreover, there have emerged various groups that could exploit or exacerbate that increased vulnerability. Such consequential threats include, obviously, direct attack by groups or states hostile to the values and outcomes that the system encourages. Less obviously, international maritime crime in its manifold forms (piracy, drugs and people smuggling), and the unsustainable plundering of marine resources all threaten to undermine the good order on which the safe and timely passage of shipping depends. Conflict and instability ashore, moreover, can have disruptive effects in neighbouring seas, as was demonstrated all too clearly in the 'tanker war' of the 1980s or, more recently off Somalia, for example. In some cases these threats may be posed against sea-based trade itself; more commonly, the broader conditions, both ashore and at sea, that make that trade possible are at risk.

Paradoxically, some of these threats to the system are also globalising. The menace of international terrorism is the most obvious example of this but various other forms of maritime crime seem to be following the same path. To take just one illustrative example, it was reported in February 2006 that the Russian mafia was involved in large-scale poaching by Norwegian trawlers under a Russian flag from cod reserves in the Barents Sea; the fish were sent to China for filleting and then returned to Grimsby and Hull for sale in the British market. The consortium responsible for this had Swedish, Russian, Norwegian and Hong Kong connections; the consequence was the depletion of cod reserves and considerable financial benefit to Russian mafia and other criminals, whose existence and success threatens good governance, domestic stability and the good order at sea upon which, it is worth repeating, the safe and timely passage of shipping depends.[6]

As already noted, the level of prospective threat encourages some people to conclude that globalisation may prove to be no more than an interlude in normal state-centred business. Thus Jeffrey Frieden:

> As was the case a hundred years ago, many people now take an integrated world economy for granted, regard it as the natural state of things, and expect that it will last forever. Yet the bases on which global capitalism rests today are not very different from what they were in 1900, and the potential for their disruption is as present today as it was then … The apparent stability of the early 1900s was followed by decades of conflicts and upheavals. Today's international economic order also seems secure, but in historical perspective it may be only a brief interlude.[7]

Because, modernists will tend to argue, economic rationality is far from being the only driver of human behaviour, the threats that globalisation faces are serious and may prove fatal. It is worth remembering that the globalisation of the Eurasian land mass brought about by Mongol conquest eventually disintegrated.[8] Further, in many ways the world of the late nineteenth century was, in its own terms, as globalised as ours is today, but this system collapsed in the face of commercial rivalry, the discontent of the disadvantaged and growing nationalism.[9] In some ways, indeed, these problems were actually a by-product of globalisation, especially in regard to the kind of perceived inequality of benefit that bred nationalism. The result of this was a World War which, as Niall Ferguson has observed

> sank globalization – literally. Nearly thirteen million tons of shipping went to the bottom of the sea as a result of German naval action, most of it by U-boats. International trade, investment and emigration all collapsed. In the war's aftermath, revolutionary regimes arose that were fundamentally hostile to international economic integration. Plans replaced the market; autarky and protection took the place of free trade. Flows of goods diminished; flows of people and capital all but dried up.[10]

A Marxist could argue that much of this could come about in consequence of the 'inherent contradictions' of global capitalism and, accordingly, that such crises are historically inevitable.[11] Certainly, deliberate or perhaps inadvertent assaults on the system could prove especially effective if they took place in conjunction with major financial upsets such as the Asian financial crisis of 1997 or worries about a sustained worldwide downturn in economic activity. This would certainly strain the sea-based trading system on which globalisation depends. Shippers point out that we are now passing through the most continuous period of economic growth in history and wonder how long this can go on. Worse still, in some respects, it is possible to argue that our variant of globalisation faces an extra range of threats (most obviously international terrorism, pandemic disease, resource depletion and environmental degradation) that previous ones did not.[12]

But, alternatively, perhaps globalisation's biggest problem is not that it is going too far, but that it hasn't gone far enough – that it 'is not truly global at all' and in effect misses out so many poor, newly independent, arguably pre-modern, countries especially of Africa and the South Pacific. Here the concerns raised range from the view that globalisation's future is at risk because free trade is not free enough at one end of the scale to the notion that it should be constrained from transferring risk from rich countries to poor ones and money from the poor to the rich, at the other.[13] The First World War provides indeed a chilling historical example of the way in which war and serious conflict could result from such strains in globalisation and, to borrow Thomas Friedman's phrase, 'unflatten' the world'.[14]

Differing conclusions

Post-modernists conclude that globalisation, in one form or another, will continue but that the sea-based trading system on which it depends will need to be defended against a variety of threats in a novel and unfamiliar world. They believe that we are indeed living 'on the cusp of a new era ... [one] plagued by uncertainty and change and unrestricted warfare, an era of shifting global threats and challenging new opportunities ... that calls for new skill sets, deeper partnerships, and mutual understanding.'[15] They conclude that the defence of the system will indeed become, and remain, at the heart of naval policy around the world.

By contrast, modernists dispute the cosy assumptions of the Manchester School that with free and increased trade comes increased peace and prosperity. They argue that 'War and warfare will always be with us; war is a permanent feature of the human condition' and conclude that basing defence preparations on the assumption that the era of old-fashioned 'modern' interstate conflict is definitely over demands a level of confidence in one's own capacity to predict the future that verges on the irresponsible.[16]

In short, this argument goes, we should expect the survival, even the revival, of apparently old-fashioned modern concerns for a 'realist' state-centred approach to world behaviour and security-policy formulation. Cautious defence planners might well conclude from much of this that they should not base their planning and preparations simply on post-modern assumptions about the nature of future security. They may well argue for a policy of 'keeping one's powder dry' against the possible resurgence of interstate conflict and the conceivable collapse of globalisation. Given the long lead time in developing the required weaponry, they could well conclude it is necessary to continue to develop such residual capacities now, however remote the contingency that justifies them currently seems to be. 'What is certain', says New Zealand's military doctrine after all, 'is that credible and effective military forces can not be generated instantly to meet a need at the time it is required.'[17]

These competing visions of the world's future in turn produce the two visions of the nature of seapower in the twenty-first century to which we now turn – the post-modern, and the modern.

1.2 The post-modern navy

Seapower is at the heart of the globalisation process in a way in which landpower and airpower are not, simply because the system is based essentially on sea transportation. Accordingly, as Daniel Coulter has observed:

> Maintaining the security of globalization, therefore, is a role from which navies dare not shrink. It is the raison d'etre for navies, and navies that understand that first, the ones that come up with the most coherent, credible and imaginative strategy for pursuing it, are the navies that will justify their existence and be firmly in tune with their master, the public.[18]

The protective function of naval activity will plainly be a significant part of any defensive response because so many of these threats to the system can, and do, take a maritime form or have important maritime consequences that require maritime responses. Indeed, the tanker war mentioned earlier is a particularly clear example of the many ways in which navies 'protect the system' both directly by what they do *at* sea (by defending trade) and indirectly by what they do *from* the sea (by defending the conditions ashore that make that trade possible).

Two quick observations about these system defence naval tasks may need to be made at this point. First, and to repeat the point made earlier, many of these requirements are bound to pull sailors forwards, geographically. This is by no means a new development, for a forwards-leaning policy was a characteristic of *Pax Britannica* – the last great age of globalisation. Thus:

> Britannia needs no bulwarks
>   No towers along the steep;
> Her march is o'er the mountain waves,
>   Her home is on the deep.[19]

Second, system defence also requires not just strategic reach but a range of naval capabilities covering the whole spectrum of conflict, a range that seems to be getting ever wider. Consequently, identifying, and prioritising between, the range of possible naval responses and preparing the platforms, weaponry and skill-sets that will realise those responses becomes the chief task of today's naval planners.

Missions of the post-modern navy

In order to cover this necessary spectrum of risk, threat and conflict, post-modern navies are developing forces and strategies intended to produce four sets of outcomes or deliverables. The first two of these are distinctively different interpretations of traditional maritime aspirations; the second two are, to all intents and purposes, new. The four aspirational deliverables are:

* sea control
* expeditionary operations
* good order at sea
* the maintenance of a maritime consensus.

We need to review all four of these distinctive characteristics of the post-modern navy in turn.

Sea control

To some extent at least, post-modern navies tend to reformulate this traditional element of maritime strategy. In broad terms, sea control remains what it has always been – the grand enabler that allows the sea to be used for whatever purpose that will serve the interests of the power that controls it. It therefore remains at the heart of maritime strategy, both modern and post-modern. For most post-modern navies, however, sea control is much less about open ocean operations against opposing fleets and is much more likely to be taking place in littoral regions where the threats are very different from, and at least as challenging as, those encountered on the open ocean. Moreover the likelihood that such campaigns take place in the course of wars of choice rather than of necessity makes the 'force protection' variant of sea control peculiarly apposite.

The fact that three of the best and most professional navies in the world have all recently been worsted by asymmetrical adversaries (the USS *Cole* incident in Aden, the ambush of a boarding party from the British frigate HMS *Cornwall* by the naval wing of the Iranian Republican Guard and the hit secured on the well-armed Israeli corvette *Hanit* by a C-802 missile fired by Hezbollah forces in Lebanon) show just how demanding post-modern operations can be. Politically, there is ample evidence that contemporary domestic opinion, perhaps especially with an intrusive and unsympathetic media, will not wear the level of attrition common, for example, in Britain's system-defence wars in the third world of the nineteenth century.[20] Sustainable system-defence in the twenty-first century depends on the maintenance of high levels of security for the peacekeepers themselves. And this is as true for sailors operating off the coast as it is for soldiers in the streets of Basra or Baghdad. Forces operating in littoral waters need to be shielded from sea-denial capabilities such as coastal submarines, shore-based artillery and missiles and mines and a variety of novel threats such as 'swarming' attacks from clouds of fast attack craft and terrorists in small boats or on jet skis. Accordingly, less emphasis is placed on high-intensity capabilities aimed at conventional naval forces in open water, and more on low-intensity threats closer to shore.

But there is a second significant post-modern angle on sea control as well. In a globalised world it is now less a question of 'securing' the sea in the sense of appropriating it for one's own use, and more of 'making it secure' for everyone but the enemies of the system to use. This is clearly aligned with the notion that 'freedom of navigation' is a universal requirement, if not a universal right, and ideally should not be restricted to particular flags or cargoes.

When he was still the US Navy's Chief of Naval Operations, Admiral Mullen made the point that:

> Where the old maritime strategy focused on sea control, the new one must recognise that the economic tide of all nations rises not when the seas are controlled by one but rather when they are made safe and free for all.[21]

The language and the rhetoric of maritime strategy seems to be taking a step further away from older, more exclusive concepts of the 'command' of the sea. In short, the second word in the concept of 'sea control' is beginning to transmute into the French version of 'controle', which means, in effect, 'supervision' rather than command. This spirit of the common defence of all legitimate forms of the use of the sea was a significant element in the new cooperative strategy of the United States that was unveiled at the Naval War College in Newport in October 2007.[22]

Expeditionary operations

Of course, it is the land that is the source of most maritime disorder. The security problems in the waters around Indonesia in recent years, for example, have been largely a problem of the lack of governance ashore. At sea, therefore, navies are usually dealing with the symptoms of the problem, more than its causes. To help deal with those causes, navies need to be able to influence events ashore and here they may be at their most strategically effective. Here, also, they are defending the system indirectly by what they do *from* the sea rather than at sea. They are defending the *conditions* for trade rather than trade itself. Because it is the area where most people live, most industries can be found and through which most trade is conducted, the littoral is where the threats are located and so becomes the natural arena for post-modern maritime operations.

In the post Cold war period, there has developed a concept of liberal interventionism in defence of the system that is based on the notion that if we do not go to the crisis, then the crisis will come to us.[23] Best of all, is to be there already, preventing the crisis from arising in the first place. 'The emphasis on expeditionary operations', explains the British Ministry of Defence, 'has enabled the UK to have a key role in shaping the international security environment.'[24] This kind of thinking has produced in Europe and the United States, and in a perhaps surprising number of countries in South America and the Asia-Pacific as well, a strong focus on the conduct of expeditionary operations.

Expeditionary operations, at least as now understood, are inherently different from conventional amphibious operations in that they do not necessarily involve beach assault, they tend to be highly politicised, they are at least intended to be of relatively short duration and they are conducted far from home, usually in the company of others. They are not seen as a precursor to a conventional war, and traditional military or even naval activities may play a relatively small part in the overall campaign of which they are a part. While, ultimately, events do have to be decided on the ground, naval forces, at the strategic, operational and tactical levels of conflict, enable this to happen through a variety of crucial contributions to joint and combined expeditionary operations. These naval contributions rest on the capacity to manoeuvre from the sea and they include the transportation of forces, their supply and sustainment, their support with different kinds of offensive airpower and their protection against all forms of air attack. The expeditionary impulse is an essentially post-modern adaptation of an ancient maritime or amphibious style of war that is best not confused with the original.

The British operation in and off Sierra Leone and the Australian led East Timor operation are both regarded as reasonably successful examples of liberal interventionism. They illustrate the extent to which post-modern navies have accordingly switched their focus away, to some extent, from what they do *at* sea to what they can do *from* it.

Summarising, power projection in an expeditionary mode can therefore be seen as a defence of the trading system against the instabilities and conflicts ashore that might threaten it. These potential shore-based threats include rogue states, inter- or intrastate conflict and the malign effects of a host of newly empowered non-state actors. In certain circumstances these can all be seen as threatening the health of the global sea-based system. By contrast, in earlier ages of course, defence of the trading system was based primarily on the *direct* defence of shipping at sea. Mahan indeed famously observed:

> The necessity of a navy springs from the existence of peaceful shipping and disappears with it, except in the case of a nation which has aggressive tendencies, and keeps up a navy merely as a branch of the military establishment.[25]

But nowadays the defence of the immediate political and strategic *conditions* that make beneficial trading possible has taken its place in naval priorities. There remain sea-based threats to the trading system of course, and these will still need to be dealt with, but in the post-modern world they no longer command the attention that they did in Mahan's day. Instead the system is largely defended by collective expeditionary action against threats ashore.

The current focus on the apparently unending land phase in Afghanistan and Iraq, however, poses a number of real challenges for the navies of the participants. In the short term these conflicts absorb funds and resources that might otherwise go to navies.[26] The tyranny of the immediate commitment is certainly a factor in the longer-term budgetary embarrassments of the US, British and several other European navies,[27] perhaps post-modern ones especially. The problem is exacerbated by the tendency to forget that expeditionary operations are often essentially maritime in the sense that Corbett defined the term, namely relating to operations 'in which the sea is a substantial factor'.[28]

Politically, the costs and disappointments of both campaigns seem likely to make similar forays elsewhere less likely. On the face of it, this could undermine the case for developing expeditionary capabilities. Since expeditionary assumptions underlie, even justify, many of the major acquisitions of Western navies (in the shape of air-craft carriers, amphibious forces and so forth), this would seem to be serious news for post-modern sailors. On the other hand, the limited liability implied by purely sea-based responses to instabilities ashore may commend more 'maritime' conceptions of intervention to politicians, who may be more anxious to avoid casualties and messy long-term commitments ashore.

This vision of a more sea-based conception of expeditionary operations, with much less emphasis given to the commitment of land forces ashore, comes close to the notion of 'good order *from* the sea'. Either way, the future shape of expeditionary operations, and a country's prospective willingness to participate in them will clearly be another major determinant of post-modern naval policy. The interest in the kind of sea-basing that underpins expeditionary operations that is so evident in the US, Europe and parts of the Asia-Pacific is an obvious manifestation of this impulse.[29]

Good order at sea

Globalisation prospers when trade is mutually beneficial and takes place in conditions of order, both on land and at sea. But as the *U.S. Coast Guard Strategy* says, a variety of threats to good order at sea imperil this:

> Weak coastal states often are not able to regulate or provide protection for the legitimate movement and safety of vessels within their waters. They are frequently ill-prepared to safeguard their maritime commerce and energy infrastructure, or protect their marine resources from illegal exploitation and environmental damage. Combined, these vulnerabilities not only threaten their population, resources, and economic development, but can threaten the security of the maritime commons and even the continuity of global commerce.[30]

Such threats, the post-modern argument goes, comprise all forms of transnational crime namely piracy, people, drugs and arms smuggling and international terrorism. In the long run, environmental degradation and the systematic despoliation of marine resources may pose an even greater threat to the health of the international system, even perhaps the physical state of the planet itself. As will be further discussed in Chapter 11, globalisation means that all this is bound to have its 'home' and 'away' dimensions – post-modern navies tending to be more interested in the latter than modern ones.

The maintenance of good order at sea may be down at the softer, more constabulary end of the spectrum of required maritime capability in defence of the system. For all that, it is increasingly seen as a crucial enabler for global peace and security, and therefore something that should command the attention of naval planners everywhere. It is recognised as the third of the four naval necessities of the post-modern age of maritime strategy. This concern for maritime security of this broader kind is not entirely new of course, but the emphasis it is currently being given even by navies such as those of the United States and the United Kingdom, where 'modern' conceptions of maritime strategy run deep, is striking.

Where navies *are* coast guards in all but name, this raises few issues; but it certainly does so for those planners of larger navies grappling with the allocation of resources between the hard and soft variants of maritime security. Here the essential question is the balance to be struck between 'softer' coast guard forces and functions (which are by no means restricted to home waters) and harder, conventional, naval ones. Should navies absorb these functions or hive them off to specialised forces specifically designed for the purpose?[31] There are arguments either way, but little doubt that the function itself is important and becoming increasingly so.

The maintenance of a maritime consensus

Maritime cooperation is increasingly seen as so important to the successful defence of the sea-based trading system that it almost becomes an aim in its own right, and this is an aspiration that is quite novel in many, if not all, ways. While a great deal has been written about 'commanding the global commons', by which is usually meant the sea and the air and space above it,[32] people are recognised as the biggest 'commons' of all. To a post-modernist, securing their support is probably the most crucial single requirement for the defence of the system. Commanding the human commons provides such a level of military and political advantage that it is to be regarded as *the* key enabler for overall success. Accordingly it is hard to exaggerate the importance of the consequent battle for world opinion, whether this finds expression in the parliaments of allies, the editorials of the *Washington Post* or the streets of the Middle East.

The perpetrators of 9/11 were not arguing for a bigger slice of the cake, they were trying to blow up the bakery because they thought globalisation inherently inimical to their aspirations; but they are half-supported by huge numbers of people who *do* want a bigger slice of the cake, and who need to be persuaded away from that level of support by the assurance of a system that seems fairer to them. Hence the importance of the political, social and economic lines of development, in which naval forces are of particular utility because of their flexibility and ubiquity. A forward and sensitive maritime presence can help not only deter malefactors from malign actions or compel them into benign ones; it can also provide a means of signalling interest in a region's affairs, monitoring events at sea and ashore and of contributing to the development of a sense of international community through a policy of active coalition building. The guiding principle throughout is that when preserving national objectives, preventing war is always better than winning it.

This being so, the benign[33] applications of seapower have particular salience in broader operations intended to defend the system through winning the hearts and minds of the populations on which it ultimately depends. The notion of the 'global fleet station' and the conscious use of sustained cruises by hospital ships such as the USS *Mercy* and *Comfort*, and other such humanitarian relief operations are seen by post-modernists to fit the bill exactly.[34] In other circumstances, of course, coercive deployments of carrier battlegroups off a potentially hostile coast may be more appropriate. Either way, naval diplomacy requires the closest coordination between navies and their foreign ministries. Many of these post-modern ideas were originally subsumed within the concept of 'The Thousand Ship Navy', to be discussed in Chapter 10.

The Asian Tsunami relief operation of 2004 in many ways showed the concept in action, since this very necessary task was successfully performed by a loose coalition of the willing that got together, at very short notice, outside fixed agreements, with no one 'in charge'. The international rescue effort from the Lebanon in 2006 was much the same. Both were made possible by the participating navies' developed habit of working together.

Maritime cooperation of this sort both illustrates and assists the creation of institutions that reduce the prospect of conflict, perhaps through confining or constraining national behaviour, and which are also likely to contribute to regional economic growth. Taken together, such developments suggest a shift away from traditional 'realist' conceptions of national security and towards much more cooperative, regional variants. Naval activity of this sort can therefore be seen as exemplifying and encouraging a move away from traditional balance-of-power dynamics of the sort that has characterised European experience until recently.

The post-modern navy: enablers

Post-modern navies are distinctive not only in what they do, but also in the enablers that allow them to do what they do.

Contributory fleets

Recent drastic changes in Scandinavia's navies are interesting not just for a radical change of role from coastal defence to expeditionary missions but also because they so clearly exemplify a *contributory* strategy – the acceptance, in other words, that resource limitations mean no single nation can solve its security problems on its own, and that a *collective* maritime effort is required, with all the loss of operational and political independence in the conduct of the campaign that that implies. 'Many countries have tried to maintain military forces that can independently perform all aspects of a military mission', says New Zealand's Defence Doctrine.

> It is unlikely that New Zealand will ever have the financial capacity to resource such a military force, rather it will seek to resource a force that has the ability to fully integrate with and complement other forces and agencies ... it will most likely result in operations conducted with those (of) other nations in multinational alliance or coalition arrangements, with relationships of increasing complexity.[35]

Post-modern navies do not expect to cover all the colours of the naval rainbow, but, ideally, remain confident that someone else, equally reliable, will. They may not welcome this development, nor the degree of reliance on allies that it implies, but in the face of budgetary realities, they accept its inevitability.

Because it is so heavily influenced by resource constraints, this post-modern characteristic will tend to be particularly evident in the case of smaller navies. For them the real issue might be to decide *how* rather than *whether* they will contribute. Would contributing a stand-alone force that can be integrated as such within a larger coalition organisation on the one hand, or a collection of niche capabilities that may not make much sense when considered as a command on the other, be more or less effective militarily and/or politically?

An open defence market

The same kind of perhaps resigned realism may reinforce market-driven prefer-
ences for laissez-faire attitudes towards the maintenance of a domestic defence
industrial base. This approach may well be characterised by a relaxed naval or governmental attitude to the foreign supply of naval equipment and/or to the acquisition of domestic industry by foreign concerns. Post-modern navies may get what
they need more quickly and more cheaply from foreign suppliers than they could by
relying on domestic industry; they may not be particularly bothered by the theoretical strategic vulnerabilities this reliance on an open defence market may open up
now or in the future. This pragmatic approach fits nicely into the conceptions of an
interdependent, borderless world and an open economy – conceptions that lie at the
very heart of globalisation.

Summarising the post-modern navy

To summarise at this point, globalisation encourages developments within post-
modern states that makes them outward looking in economic, political and military
terms. Much of this was summarised in Singapore's Defence White Paper of the
year 2000 in words that can hardly be bettered:

> The Asian economic crisis has demonstrated how closely intertwined the inter-
> ests of nations have become in a borderless world. A small and open country
> like Singapore is especially susceptible to unpredictable shifts in the inter-
> national environment. This vulnerability will increase as we become more integ-
> rated with the global economy. What happens in another part of the world can
> have immediate and great spill-over effects on our economy and security. But
> we cannot turn back from globalization. We depend on the world economy for a
> living. We will have to work more actively with others to safeguard peace and
> stability in the region and beyond, to promote a peaceful environment con-
> ducive to socio-economic development.[36]

Driven by such ideas, post-modern states are content to open their economies to
others and, if necessary, to see the relocation elsewhere of their manufacturing
industries, especially those of the general metal-bashing type. Their governments
adopt classic laissez-faire attitudes to the defence of national economies, as much as
they think they can, and do not necessarily put strong emphasis on the creation or
maintenance of a totally independent defence industrial base. They do, however,
pride themselves on developing open, accountable forms of government in which
information is freely available as a basis for continuous innovation.

Post-modern states of this sort adopt defence policies that are likely to produce
navies whose focus is on the maintenance of *international* rather than national security. They will embrace inclusive rather than exclusive attitudes towards sea control
in which the priority given peer competition with possible rivals is typically much
lower than it is in modern states. Reflecting a marked predisposition towards liberal
interventionism, their shape, composition and activities reflect high priorities in the
conduct of generally collaborative expeditionary operations. Acutely aware of the
centrality of general maritime security to the efficient operation of a globalised

sea-based trading system, emphasis is given to the maintenance of general maritime security through the protection of good order at sea. Finally, they put a premium on developing good, enduring and constructive maritime relationships with others. These collaborative assumptions often find expression in a 'contributory' attitude towards the development of the naval capability to deal with significant threats to the system. Such navies expect to participate in coalition operations rather than attempt to act on their own.

1.3 The modern navy

Modern states, by contrast with the post-modern ones just described, will be warier about the implications of globalisation for their own security and sovereignty, more protectionist in their economic policy and less inclined to collaborate with others in the maintenance of the world's trading system. They make contingency preparations against the possibility that should globalisation either collapse or enter a period of terminal decline, they would face a bleaker, harder, much less communal world of increased levels of competition in which coercive military force and power politics resume their dominance of the strategic horizon. The world would indeed have a warlike future.

The second traditional, more conventional, more 'modern' paradigm of naval behaviour therefore clearly proceeds on the basis of a rather different set of assumptions about the roles and the necessary capabilities of navies in which national preoccupations prevail over the collaborative. They are, accordingly, in many ways rather different from, and sometimes the complete opposite to, the naval assumptions of the post-modernists.

The first obvious difference is the modernist's tendency to focus on the defence of the country and its immediate interests, rather than on the system. This has a considerable impact on a navy's mission priorities.

Missions of the modern navy

Nuclear deterrence and ballistic missile defence

The maintenance of nuclear deterrent forces at sea, and everything that goes with it, including the various forms of sea-based cruise and ballistic missile defence make most sense in the context of state-on-state conflict, since, normally, only states have the resources required to engage in this kind of conflict. Such events as the Hezbollah attack on the Israeli corvette in 2006 and the periodic firefights between the Sri Lankan Navy and the 'Sea (Tamil) Tigers' suggests that the gap may be narrowing, however. Perhaps for this reason, the number of navies slowly developing such offensive and/or defensive capabilities is slowly increasing

Sea control

The modern navy is distinguished by different, more traditional conceptions of sea control. Essentially, naval preparations are framed by analysis of what other possibly competitive navies are doing. Much more emphasis is placed on more 'Mahanian' concepts of sea control, and all the naval disciplines that contribute to the independence of action that this implies. In the Asia-Pacific region there is indeed a tendency to focus on the preparations of neighbours as much as, or indeed sometimes more than, on those presented by non-state actors of various kinds. This is the preoccupation with like-against-like, symmetrical peer competition of the sort that dominated the twentieth century. It tends to imply an emphasis on preparation for high intensity 'fleet versus fleet' engagements as Admiral Gorshkov used to call them. Relevant capacities are expensive and probably optimised for open ocean operations rather than land attack. Weaponry and sensor mixes emphasise anti-submarine warfare (ASW), anti-air, anti-ship missiles and so on – defence against capabilities that we would not expect to be generally available to non-state actors. Australia's 2000 Defence White Paper, in its discussion of the Royal Australian Navy's (RAN) sea control requirements clearly illustrated this approach: 'The key to defending Australia', it says, 'is to control the air and sea approaches to our continent, so as to deny them to hostile ships and aircraft, and provide maximum freedom of action for our forces. That means we need a fundamentally maritime strategy.'[37]

Although benchmarking against the naval capabilities of other countries, or even explicitly preparing against them, makes professional sense, and may indeed head off conflicts by deterring potential adversaries, it can, unless carefully handled, have consequences that are quite the opposite of this. Arms dynamics where countries may coincidentally be going through simultaneous programmes of naval modernisation can easily turn into more dangerous arms races. Preventing this may require modern navies to engage in sensitive and potentially difficult confidence- and consensus-building measures, at the same time.

Narrower concepts of maritime power projection

Modern states tend to be much less affected by the impulse for liberal interventionism than post-modern states, and the consequent proclivity for expeditionary operations that it leads to. There is nothing new about this debate for and against liberal interventionism. In the last great era of globalisation, for example, the British Prime Minister, Lord Palmerston, thought that liberalism and the world's middle classes 'far more likely than despotism to produce governments stable, pacific and friendly to England and English trade'. Accordingly he advocated, and indeed implemented, acts of liberal interventionism. These assumptions were challenged by the conservative balance-of-power school represented by Lord Melbourne who argued that on the contrary, such assisted powers 'never take our advice ... treat us with the utmost contempt and take every measure hostile to our interests; they are anxious to prove that we have not the least influence on them'.[38] Such interventions, in short, would do no good. Instead the focus should be on the defence of national tranquillity and on those who might threaten it directly. In a world much less determined by the exigencies of a mutually dependent community of production and consumption, the traditional, nationalist views of latter-day Melbournes are likely to prevail. As already noted, expeditionary campaigns ashore may become more difficult politically in any case.

This suggests less of a stress on the prosecution of collective expeditionary campaigns ashore, and more on the maintenance of the more traditional kinds of maritime power projection, including amphibious and maritime strike capabilities, where the putative adversary demands sophisticated and high-intensity weaponry, and where the aspiration is less for the defence of the international trading system against a variety of threats, than for strategic gain against conventional adversaries. This may well include a determination to maintain, or develop, a sea-based nuclear deterrent, something again that at least for the moment, implies a focus on a traditional 'symmetrical' adversary.

Good order at sea

Good order as sea of course is as important to the modern state as it is to the post-modern one, but here it is much more focused on the *exclusive* defence of national interests and sovereignty in home waters. It is a matter of keeping such threats out of home waters, and of defending a maritime frontier against all manner of malign intruders. This approach may be revealed by less practical willingness to cooperate with other states in ways that might undermine political independence, maritime sovereignty or standard operating procedures. Modern navies are likely to exhibit lower levels of effective compliance with international maritime conventions or aspirations such as the information-sharing intentions of Maritime Domain Awareness, either because they do not wish to, or because they do not enjoy the degree of good governance that makes such compliance effective.

In the past, these kinds of constraint have tended to complicate anti-piracy operations in sensitive areas such as the Straits of Malacca. Finally, modern states will tend to be more autarchic and economically self-contained, and so are much less preoccupied by the consequences of distant disorder. Their involvement in, and consequent capability for, the 'away' aspects of maritime security, is accordingly much more limited.

Maritime consensus

For all these reasons, the 'modern' navy will tend to be wary about the maritime consensus aspects of such current ideas as the 'Global Maritime Partnership', because such arrangements will usually require compromises and a willingness to accept less sovereignty of decision at the national level. Multilateral naval cooperation with other countries has a much lower priority and when it does take place is more constrained both politically, and in terms of the practical mechanics of interoperability. Modern navies will therefore exhibit a preference for bilateral arrangements on specific issues, as opposed to general purpose, multilateral ones. In this, naval behaviour reflects a general national scepticism about the utility of institutions and behaviours that purport to contribute to cooperative security at the regional level. Scholars of a realist persuasion tend to share this scepticism and argue instead that the nation state and traditional conceptions of national interest continue to determine the security agenda.

The modern navy: enablers

These differences of approach between the modern and the post-modern also extend into the development of the two major 'enablers' that underpin all naval activity, namely the maintenance of both a balanced fleet and an independent national maritime defence industrial base.

A balanced fleet

Modernists exhibit a preference for the maintenance of the traditional naval fighting disciplines and a balanced, not a specialised, 'contributory' fleet of the post-modern sort. Preferring not to reduce their capacity for independent action, modern navies will try to maintain as wide a set of independent all-round capabilities as their resources will allow in order to keep their options open for an unpredictable and probably challenging future. They will not accordingly be content simply to develop niche specialisations in the expectation that someone else will fill the consequent gaps.

An indigenous defence industrial maritime base

The desire to keep operational options open is closely associated with the last characteristic of the 'modern' approach to maritime strategy – the determination to maintain a secure indigenous maritime base, if necessary at the price of industrial and commercial cooperation with allies. The greater the extent to which this is part of a larger national policy to close, and defend, the economy against external pressure the more it would be at variance with the free trade conceptions that underpin globalisation. Most countries, even markedly post-modern ones, feel such pressures to some extent.[39]

1.4 Modern/post-modern compromises

These modernist and post-modernist paradigms of national state and naval behaviour are very crudely drawn; the differences between them are fuzzy matters of degree and decidedly not pole opposites. Nor do such visions necessarily imply a set of naval roles and capacities that are mutually exclusive alternatives. Indeed, such naval capacities as amphibious warfare ships and load-carrying ship-borne helicopters can be as valuable for humanitarian relief operations as they are for kinetic types of maritime power projection. Because of this and because most expectations for the future seem to lie somewhere between the two extremes of secure globalisation on the one hand, and blood-chilling system collapse on the other, most states exhibit a blend of the two sets of behaviours and characteristics and their navies might therefore be expected to, and indeed do, illustrate the same thing.

Earlier reference was made to the defence policy of Singapore, and the Singapore Navy does exactly this. Singapore is one of the world's most globalised cities and clearly intends to remain so. It is investing heavily in the infrastructure and the institutions needed to sustain an expanding global maritime role, and it also puts a high premium on the kind of multilateralism that it thinks will stabilise relationships in the Asia-Pacific region.[40] Its military forces have operated in combination with others against common threats, such as international terrorism, including Operation Enduring Freedom and it is proud of its achievements in the East Timor crisis and the Asian Tsunami relief operation.

Nevertheless, it 'traditionally viewed its neighbours with caution, even suspicion'. After the traumatic experience of being abandoned by the British, first in defeat in 1942, and then again in their precipitate scuttle from 'East of Suez' announced in 1967, it has developed a strong preference for self-reliance and robust, if notably opaque, national defences.[41] These 'somewhat provocative military plans' have in fact sometimes produced adverse reactions in the region,[42] and are an expression of a determination to defend national interests as well as collective ones.[43]

Like that of Singapore, most navies exhibit a blend of both approaches, and so tend to situate themselves in a spectrum of possibility between modern at one end of the scale and post-modern at the other. Their position on the spectrum is determined by their doctrinal and other policy declarations (what they say), at the structure and nature of the fleet (what they've got) and at the nature of their operations (what they do). Finally, policies towards the country's defence industrial base may well also be generally indicative of a particular navy's place on the modern/post-modern continuum.

The Swedish Navy, for another example, might be considered as being very much towards the post-modern end of the scale. Since the end of the Cold War it has transformed itself utterly from a totally self-reliant, determinedly non-aligned force exclusively concerned with the defence of its own waters, to a navy whose coastal expertise is of decided value in the conduct of coalition expeditionary operations. One of their submarines was loaned to the US Navy for two years. According to Rear Admiral Anders Grensted the naval Chief of Staff this was 'a win–win situation for both navies' since the Swedish Navy learned a good deal about the demands of interoperability and maintaining sustained logistical support at long distance and the Americans of how to deal with 'the sort of stealthy, high tech submarine threat that they can see occurring in the next ten years on the Pacific'. Grensted went on:

> Sweden was isolated in the Cold war; since the collapse of the USSR we have opened to become more international and we are working hard to become more interoperable ... We consider the Baltic Sea our littoral, but we are becoming a navy with global reach; where we can do the same sorts of operations as we do in the Baltic but in other seas. We have watched the Danish navy undergo similar changes.

Swedish defence policy now envisages participation in properly mandated expeditions overseas, and appears content with the acquisition of key industrial capacities such as the submarine-builders Kockums by foreign concerns. 'But on the other hand', Grensted concluded, 'we have to build for an unpredictable world ... [since] ... the high level threats may come back'.[44]

To a considerable extent, such naval assumptions relate to, and indeed are explained by perceptions of the international context. In particular, they reflect the contemporary debate about the extent to which traditional nations, and traditional national perspectives will determine the world's future, and whether those relationships will be conflictual or cooperative. To understand all this, we need to explore the notion of competition a little more deeply. Competition implies that the contestants have much in common as well as things that divide them. Their situation can be explained through the analogy of two slabs of cake laid end to end. The first slab represents the cooperative relations between two states, the second the conflictual. This illustrates a spectrum of varying relationships ranging from pure cooperation at one end to pure conflict at the other, although both extremities are highly unusual. In practice, the particular relationship that two states have with each other will normally involve a cut across both slabs of cake.

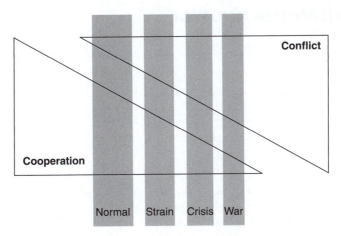

Figure 1.1 The conflict/cooperation spectrum.

Of course, this kind of imagery is grossly simplistic; where the cut comes in one dimension of the relationship of two countries (say trade, or the World Cup) may not be the same in another (fishing agreements, or the future security architecture for the North East Pacific). Moreover the relationship may be changing all the time.

Nevertheless, the notion that there is a spectrum of conflictual and cooperative relations between states, and that most of the time the mixture of the two determines and reflects military and naval behaviour is a useful one to which constant reference will be made in this book. It is one of the keys to a proper understanding of the role of seapower, past, present and future.

2   Defining seapower

You are absolutely correct, we are victims of our syntax ... some of the things we
write in the Navy are not necessarily understandable.
                    Vice Admiral William Crowe US Navy, Deputy Chief of Naval Operations[1]

2.1 Introduction

But first, what is seapower anyway? Perhaps oddly, Mahan himself does not define
the word, or words (!) seapower very explicitly, even though he coined it himself.
What he meant by the phrase has largely to be inferred. Such ambiguity is depressingly common and sometimes impedes communication. People use the same words
but often seem to mean somewhat different things by them. Others use different
words to describe the same things. It is all very confusing and is much lamented by
analysts of seapower.[2]

There seem to be three reasons for the difficulty. The first is purely to do with
English semantics, and that is the limits of the words available to describe sea-
related things. Some of them are adjectives without nouns ('maritime', 'nautical',
'marine'), others are nouns without adjectives ('sea', 'seapower'). Sometimes there
are nouns that have adjectives ('ocean/oceanic', 'navy/naval') but they tend towards
greater specificity. Unfortunately this semantic awkwardness makes the consistent
use of words very difficult.

The second reason is a matter of more substance. The 'power' part of the word
'seapower' itself has generated enormous attention in academic analysis of international politics. What does power actually mean? Some analysts focus on *inputs* –
in other words the characteristics that make countries or people powerful (having
military or economic strength for example). Others concentrate on *outputs* – a
country is powerful because others do what it wants. Power can be either potential,
or consequential – or, commonly, both! To add to the confusion, power can sometimes be applied specifically to particular countries (the 'great powers'). Not surprisingly, there is a tendency to avoid the word if possible.

Third, people *do* actually mean different things by the labels they use – in the sense
that they wish either to include or to exclude various phenomena related to the sea.
'Maritime' activity for example is sometimes taken to concern only navies, sometimes
navies operating in conjunction with the ground and air forces, sometimes navies in
the broader context of all activities relating to the commercial, non-military use the
sea, and sometimes inevitably the word 'maritime' covers all three possibilities!

As a concept 'seapower' combines both difficulties. It is something that particular countries, or sea powers (two words), have. It too has to be seen both as an input and an output.

Seapower as an input

The obvious inputs are navies, coast guards, the marine or civil–maritime industries broadly defined and, where relevant, the contribution of land and air forces. Figure 2.1 shows the constituents of seapower and its place within broader definitions of national power.

Seapower as an output

Seapower is not simply about what it takes to use the sea (although that is obviously a prerequisite). It is also the capacity to influence the behaviour of other people or things by what one does at or from the sea. This approach defines seapower in terms of its consequences, its outputs not the inputs, the ends not the means.

It is, moreover, about the sea-based capacity to determine events both at sea and on land. As that other great master of maritime thought, Sir Julian Corbett, never

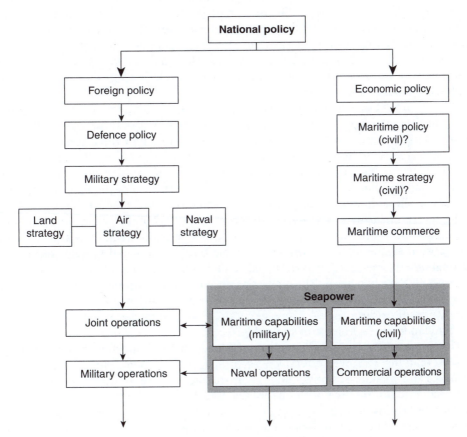

Figure 2.1 Seapower: its setting.

tired of saying, the real point of seapower is not so much what happens at sea, but how that influences the outcome of events on land:

> Since men live upon the land and not upon the sea, great issues between nations at war have always been decided – except in the rarest cases – either by what your army can do against your enemy's territory and national life, or else by fear of what the fleet makes it possible for your army to do.[3]

In recent years, as we have seen, there has been a marked shift in naval attention from power *at* sea, to power *from* the sea.

From this bald summary of the conclusions of Mahan and Corbett, two conclusions can immediately be drawn. First, is the simple point that there is more to seapower than grey painted ships with numbers on the side. Seapower also embraces the contribution that the other services can make to events at sea, and the contribution that navies can make to events on land or in the air.

Seapower also includes the non-military aspects of sea use (merchant shipping, fishing, marine insurance, shipbuilding and repair and so on) since these contribute to naval power and since they can also influence the behaviour of other people in their own right.

Second, seapower is a *relative* concept, something that some countries have more than others. The real issue is the matter of degree. Nearly all countries have a degree of seapower. It may be through their naval strength, or their shipbuilding, or their skills in marine insurance, or their capacity to supply seafarers, or a combination of all of these characteristics and others. But some countries, and this is the point, have more or less than others, and it is that relationship that is strategically significant in peace and in war.

This is a useful conclusion since it provides a way out of dealing with futile questions such as whether, for example, Soviet Russia was a seapower or not. In the sense described here it certainly was. In the Soviet era under the astute guidance of Admiral Sergei Gorshkov, it had a first class navy able to curtail the operations of the US Navy; it had a large merchant marine, one of the world's leading fishing fleets, oceanographic and scientific knowledge about the sea of the first order and an impressive shipbuilding industry. But at the same time the relationship of the navy to the rest of the armed services was different in kind from that which applied in the United States; its operational focus for purposes of war on the narrow seas and local seas more than the open oceans. Its strategic thinking was still largely continental. Throughout its existence, Soviet naval leaders explicitly rejected the notion that they should slavishly use Western practice and thinking as though that were the only true path to success on the oceans. The Soviet Union was a seapower, but a seapower with a difference.[4] More generally, most countries will tend to be both sea- and landpowers, at least to some degree.

The emphasis on the *relative* nature of seapower has important consequences. It follows that the strategic effectiveness of seapower depends importantly on the strengths and weaknesses of whom it is exerted against. Seapower is therefore often best recognised in the eye of the beholder. Because of this, as Colin Gray shows so eloquently, seapower, in some circumstances, merely enables a conflict to be won by air and ground forces; in others (such as the Pacific campaign against Japan) it was the executive and decisive form of war.[5]

Seeing seapower as a relative concept is also a convenient means of closing down the curiously long-lived misapprehension that it is the exclusive property of a handful of largely Western countries. It is not, and never has been, although some of them have certainly been more maritime than most.

Nor is the capacity to operate decisively at sea *necessarily* a function of size. The experience and the strategic functions of the nineteenth century navy of Chile in dealing with first a threat from Spain in the 1860s and then in the conduct of the War of the Pacific (1879–1884) with Peru may have been small scale when compared to the naval side of the similarly named Pacific campaign 60 years later. But in all other respects, exactly the same processes (the pursuit of battle, attacks on shipping, the support of amphibious operations) were at work.[6] The same applies to nearly all countries irrespective of shape, size and period. To some extent, they nearly all are, or were, seapowers.

For all its imperfections and ambiguities it seems best to follow the common practice of using the labels maritime power and seapower interchangeably. Either phrase should be taken to incorporate naval interactions with the civilian/marine dimension on the one hand and with air and ground forces on the other since all of these can have a major impact on the behaviour of others. A final advantage of using the word seapower, even if in this cautious way, is that it is a reminder of the fact that it is a form of power that derives from the attributes of the sea itself.

2.2 The sea: four historic attributes

Nearly three-quarters of the world is now covered by seawater, much more than used to be the case. Britain only became a group of islands 8500 years ago. Although already amounting to a huge 139 million square miles, ocean coverage could increase markedly in the future. It is already by far the single biggest environment on our planet and, in ways that we still do not fully understand, the sea regulates its climate and helps us measure its health. Human life began in the sea and ever since has been dominated by it. It is crucial to our way of life, our very survival as a species.

But it is still a dark, mysterious and dangerous place in which people cannot commonly live – and for the most part decidedly do not want to. Much of it is cold, wet, still largely uncharted and it makes most people sick. Seafarers seem often to live only on the fringe of settled society. The Greek philosopher Diogenes was not sure whether they should be counted amongst the living or the dead. The Bengali word for 'sailor' has strong affinities to that used for 'prisoner' – and so it goes on.[7]

And yet, from earliest times, the sea has been a major focus of mankind's concern. Why is this? Will it continue? And what is the place of navies in all this?

Mankind did not take to the sea for any one single cause but for a variety of reasons that are linked to the four attributes of the sea itself, namely, as a resource, and as a means of transportation, information and dominion. Each of these four attributes is intimately connected, and each also exhibits the same cooperative and conflictual tendencies characteristic of international relations. Since the sea is so important to human development, neither of these points should come as a surprise.

Problems in making the most of these four attributes of the sea largely determine the functions of navies, both directly and indirectly.

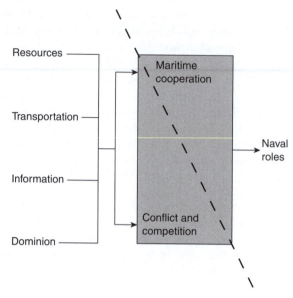

Figure 2.2 Responding to the four attributes of the sea.

The sea as a resource

All around the world, tens of thousands of years ago, mankind began gathering food from the sea, initially in the form of shellfish. From earliest Mesolithic times, in Europe and elsewhere, the sea and the estuaries were seen as 'an unlimited food resource to those with the technology and courage to pursue it in the open sea'. The sophisticated fishhooks and the bones of deep-sea fish like cod, haddock and hake that are frequently found in the rubbish heaps of the coastal communities scattered along Europe's Atlantic fringe from Portugal to Scandinavia show that 7000 years ago early Europeans were able to venture far enough out to sea to catch deep-water fish sometimes up to 1.5 metres long. In their lightly framed hide-covered boats, such early sailors evidently covered considerable distances in pursuit of their catch. It was dangerous no doubt, but it was an easier way to get protein than attempting to hunt it, or later grow it, on land. Moreover the fatty acids to be found in all kinds of seafood were, and are, beneficial to the brain and to human health generally, helping produce better, brighter, healthier people.[8]

The existence of early cemeteries in such settlements with their evidence of collective and continuous burial, show that these rich and varied resources encouraged an increase in the population, the adoption of agriculture and more sedentary habits. People operating on the interface between the sea and the land produced a raw human energy that encouraged innovation and development, playing a major part in kick-starting European civilisation. According to Barry Cunliffe one of Britain's leading archaeologists, these people also soon manifested a maritime, and in this case an Atlantic, mid-set. From the very beginning then, civilisation was heavily influenced by people who 'faced the ocean'.

This was a global phenomenon. As a source of resources, the sea was crucial to the development of world civilisation – and it remains crucial since mankind still harvests some 20 per cent of its daily protein from the oceans. More recently, other marine resources (especially oil and gas) have become economically important too.

Indeed, demand for all these things shows definite signs of outstripping supply. Inevitably, this tends to increase the competitive element in mankind's exploitation of this attribute of the sea. Sadly, acute competition for scarce or valuable sea resources has always played an important and often destructive part in human history.

The sea as a medium of transportation and exchange

Centuries ago, the Makassar peoples came once a year to the inshore waters of northern Australia in search of bêche-de-mer (sea cucumber) for the Chinese soup trade. They developed relations with the first Australians, and inevitably began trading with them. In just the same way European fishermen following shoals of migratory fish far out from shore, came into contact with fishermen from other areas and developed a sense of community. A loose but definite Atlantic community was established in which the sea was a medium for the exchange of goods, news and ideas.

This sense of a distinct maritime community developed very early, by the Neolithic era, and explains the remarkable cultural similarities that can be seen along the Atlantic facing coast from Scandinavia to Portugal. Evidence for this community includes strong similarities in their distinctive burial practices (for example, the characteristic passage tombs of the fourth millennium BC) and their pottery (for example, the so-called bell beakers of the third/second millennium BC). Of course, as time went by these characteristics changed and grew generally more sophisticated and benefitted also from contact with the peoples of the interior. Despite this, it was the sea that linked them together.

There were equivalents to this all over the world – in the Asia-Pacific, the Indian Ocean, the Arabian Sea and the Mediterranean. These local trading systems are increasingly considered by archaeologists to be much older and more sophisticated than originally thought.[9] Arguably, it all started in the Nile 7000–8000 years ago.[10]

The resultant regional, sea-based communities overlapped and indeed interacted at the key, geographic nodal points that separated them geographically. Thus in the later Bronze Age, the Phoenicians based in the central and east Mediterranean, bringing luxuries from the south went through the Straits of Gibraltar and established a big trading centre at Gadir/Huelva in southern Portugal to link up with the Atlantic community in their search for copper and tin. People travelling from one area to another would encounter sub-regional local transportation systems. Thus the Greek Pytheas setting out from Marseilles, either rounded Spain or sailed along the River Garonne to the Bay of Biscay and was then able to make use of an interconnected series of local sailings to complete a remarkable circumnavigation of the British Isles, with an excursion to Scandinavia on the way, in the late fourth century BC.

The Vikings, 1500 years later, inspired by the same spirit of adventure, enterprise, curiosity and greed made their way across the North Atlantic via Iceland, Greenland and Newfoundland to make first contact with the Americas. The Portuguese and Spanish and other West Europeans, followed these early explorers 200 years later, over the Atlantic, felt their way down round Africa (in the opposite direction to the Phoenicians who had come round the other way 2000 years before) and into the Indian Ocean, eventually reaching the Asia-Pacific.

When they got there, they found an area stretching from the shores of the Indian Ocean to the western Pacific that was steeped in the results of centuries of maritime endeavour. From the earliest Mauryan era (324–184 BC) Arab and South Asian traders sailed the waters of South East Asia, established themselves under the Cholas over much of South East Asia and had developed settled communities in China, while Chinese traders did the same in the opposite direction. By the eleventh century, cities in south east China like Quanzhou and Guangdong had developed cosmopolitan Asian trading centres with large permanent settlements of foreign merchants. Such overseas trade when combined with overland commerce from the interior made the China of the Song and early Ming dynasties the world's largest and wealthiest commercial empire of the era, a magnet, therefore, for everyone else.[11]

Indeed, the antiquity and extent of Chinese penetration of the world's oceans and the relative sophistication of their maritime endeavour more generally is only now becoming clear. Maritime artefacts dating back some 8000 years have recently been uncovered. By the end of the Tang dynasty (AD 907) regular commercial routes to South West Asia and Western Africa had been established.[12] Some historians even believe that Zheng He's famous Indian Ocean cruises of the fourteenth century in fact extended to the first circumnavigations of the world and to exploration of the coast of America.[13]

The result of all this maritime trading was a complex web of inter-regional, regional and sub-regional maritime transportation systems that spanned the globe. Technological innovations through the industrial era, especially the advent of steam power, tended to make the connections tighter. The invention of the container has further revolutionised the process. Indeed, '[i]t is no exaggeration to say that the shipping container may have transformed the world, and our daily lives, as fundamentally as any of the other more glamorous or complex inventions of the last 100 years, the internet included'.[14] The arrival in a European port of a container ship like the *Emma Maersk* half a mile long, stacked 200 feet high with containers carrying 45,000 tons of goods, probably mainly from China, which its owners expect to be turned around in 24 hours, illustrates the sheer scale of this revolution. Over 95 per cent of the world's trade is conducted by sea, and the volume of that trade has hugely expanded over the past 30 years or so, from 2.6 billion tons of goods in 1970 to 7.12 billion tons in 2005. In 2005 the world merchant fleet grew by 7.2 per cent over the 2004 total to 960 million deadweight tons. And so the staggering statistics roll on.[15]

Not only does the modern shipping industry make globalisation possible; it is itself profoundly globalised. Over 60 per cent of ships fly flags different from the nationality of their owners. In many cases these owners are in fact multinational corporations. A ship's crew, cargo and itinerary will be totally international and quite possibly insured, brokered and operated in still other countries too.[16]

Accordingly the whole concept of globalisation is profoundly maritime. Low and decreasing seaborne freight rates mean that the shipping costs of a $700 TV set from China to Europe is no more than about $10. This helps keep European costs of living and rates of inflation down, encourages China to industrialise (improving thereby life for its citizens) and makes possible industrial relocation, most obviously from Europe and North America to the Far East, and the diversification of production lines around an increasing number of countries.[17] Seaborne commerce therefore produces a tight mutually dependent community of industrial production and consumption.

Explaining the system

There were two main, interconnected reasons for this most important of human developments. First, at least until the latter stages of the industrial revolution, it was faster, cheaper and safer to travel and to send goods by sea (or by river) than by land.

The advantages of water transport were not, Mahan emphasised, 'accidental or temporary; they are of the nature of things, and permanent'. '[S]o it is upon the sea-coast, and along the banks of navigable rivers', concluded Adam Smith in 1776, 'that industry of every kind naturally begins to subdivide and improve itself.' Water transportation made everything possible, encouraging and stimulating an expansion of trade.[18]

Second, and connectedly, there were enormous profits to be made, despite the ship and crew losses of early trading ventures. The Portuguese in the sixteenth century developing their trade in spices through the Indian Ocean, could lose perhaps a quarter of their ships at sea, and up to half their crew but still turn in a profit. It was said that a merchant could ship six cargoes of spices and lose five, yet still make a profit when the sixth was sold.[19]

...and its consequences

But while the sea was indeed the high road to prosperity, Adam Smith was keen to make another point, namely that the trading system it produced was mutually beneficial. 'What goods could bear the expenses of land-carriage between London and Calcutta?' he asked, rhetorically. Water transport, however, made everything possible. As a result, 'Those two cities, however, at present carry on a very considerable commerce with each other, and by mutually affording a market, give a good deal of encouragement to each other's industry.'[20]

The result was a web of four-way trading links between China, South East Asia, the Indian Ocean and Europe in which everyone participated regardless of religion, race or allegiance and from which everyone benefitted at least to some degree. Although overland trading routes *were* still important, this was largely an oceanic system.[21]

Nineteenth-century Liberal free traders further developed these ideas. They articulated the notion that sea-based trade was a process of mutual benefit and partnership and rested essentially on international peace to which the resultant prosperity and stability would materially contribute. Nowadays, of course, these are the values and assumptions of the World Trade Organisation and contemporary advocates of globalisation. They emphasise, in Mahan's words, the 'commercial interest of the sea powers in the preservation of peace'.[22] As already noted, postmodernists also link globalisation to peace, believing it likely to reduce the likelihood of conflicts between states and to increase levels of international cooperation against anything that seems likely to threaten a system on which all depend.

But there is a darker side to all this as well, namely the mercantilist notion that trade often benefits one party to the transaction much more than it does the other and that one's loss is the other's gain. This could lead to intense commercial rivalry of the sort characteristic of the Dutch and English East India Companies for example. This spilled over into lethal violence and both maintained their own armies and navies to defend their interests. Trade competition could in fact almost be regarded as a form of war between rival suppliers.

The relationship between customer and supplier could be nearly as conflictual. When, for instance, the Portuguese arrived in the Indian Ocean they behaved in an extraordinarily aggressive and combative manner, determined to trade 'with advantage' and to force their terms of trade on others if necessary.

Perhaps the most notorious examples of this approach are the two 'Opium Wars' between China and Britain and other Western powers in the nineteenth century. To buy British manufactures, Indian opium growers and country traders had to export their crop to China, even though this was entirely contrary to the wishes and interests of the Chinese authorities. In their turn, the Chinese would pay for opium by exporting tea to Britain. The expressed purpose of the resultant maritime wars was to force the Chinese to participate in a balanced and global trading system that would, it was widely and genuinely believed, be in their own long-term interest.[23]

The maritime character of the two wars that resulted showed that, in Mahan's words, 'Commerce, the energiser of material civilisation can work to the greatest advantage, and can most certainly receive the support of the military arm of sea power.'[24] Despite the cooperative expectations of liberal free traders then, maritime trade could sometimes become bound up with conflict and war – and this for two distinct reasons. First, simply because it was so central to the prosperity of nations, a nation's share in maritime trade was bound to be the subject of acute competition in peace and attacked in war. Second, and this goes back to Mahan's original point, the global maritime trading system was sensitive and vulnerable,[25] and so needed military protection. The sea's second and fourth attributes as both the means of transportation and of dominion are clearly linked. This was what Sir Walter Raleigh was talking about with his much quoted observation: 'Whosoever commands the sea, commands the trade. Whosoever commands the trade of the world commands the riches of the World, and consequently the world itself.'[26] It is also worth making the point that some of the things that travelled around the world in consequence of the sea's advantages as a means of transportation could be even more malign. Distinctive contagious and deadly diseases developed in various parts of the world, but the world transportation system spread them around before newly exposed populations could develop their immunities. The results were often catastrophic. The Black Death probably came to Europe through shipboard rats. The Europeans brought diseases with them to the Americas that devastated local peoples. As late as the early 1900s, shipping spread bubonic plague around places as separated as Bombay, Sydney, San Francisco and Buenos Aires with awful consequences. These events are a useful reminder that maritime transportation can sometimes have terrible consequences.[27]

The sea as medium for information and the spread of ideas

Consciously and unconsciously spreading ideas

Trade involves talking. It is about the conscious or unconscious exchange of ideas and information as well as goods. Through their maritime interaction, the Mesolithic Europeans picked up ideas about how to construct burial chambers, how to decorate pots and doubtless about much more that has left no specific trace. Maritime trade and the exchange of ideas and information appear inseparable.

Sometimes this exchange of information and values is conscious and deliberate. Early explorers discovered new hitherto unknown crops and brought them home. In this way potatoes, tobacco, bananas, coffee and tea and so forth arrived in Europe. Maritime traders from South East Asia and the Indian Ocean area brought early-maturing rice, sugar cane, jasmin, cotton, pumpkin, cabbage and so on to early China. These all produced green revolutions and major markets. China imported its first sweet potatoes in 1593 and now produces 80 per cent of the world crop.[28]

Some people however, went further and saw the sea as a means by which they could communicate their ideas to the unenlightened in a much more deliberate manner than this. There were strong maritime associations with the spread of Christianity for example. Missionaries of the ninth and tenth centuries AD set out from Ireland across the Irish Sea to the other islands of the north Atlantic, finding their way in due course to America with the express and conscious purpose of bringing Christianity to the heathens and converting them if possible. Whatever their other motives may have been, the Spanish and Portuguese colonists of later centuries also came to America, the Indian Ocean and the Far East in pursuit of souls. Thanks to the sixteenth-century activities of Francis Xavier and others, half a million of Japan's 18 million people were Christian; enough, concluded the Tokugawa shogunate, to threaten the very nature of Japanese culture and society.

Although Christian sea-based proselytisation is the clearest and arguably most successful example of this sort of thing, it is not unique. Islamic rulers spread their faith in much the same way around the Indian Ocean, the Mediterranean and into the Far East. There were complex links too between the spread of Buddhism and sea-based trade.[29] Sadly the desire to spread the faith in this way could itself become a source of international strife.

Very often, though, it was more a question of the *unconscious* transmission of trading values and everything that went with them. We will need to return to this important issue later.

In search of information

> The fair breeze blew, the white foam flew
>> The furrow followed free.
>> We were the first that ever burst
>> Into that silent sea.
>
> Samuel Taylor Coleridge, *The Rime of the Ancient Mariner*

People went not just to spread information but to gain it as well. The urge to explore, to find out what was over the far horizon, and sometimes to reach a better place, was part and parcel of mankind's relationship with the sea. Francis Bacon's *New Atlantis* of 1627 is an early English example of this. It is a mysterious, allegorical, romantic work suffused with the notion of cooperative, scientific endeavour linked with maritime activity. It is about the association of the sea with freedom of travel, open horizons, enquiry, discovery and the pursuit of knowledge and progress, contrasting with the 'ignorant, fearful and foolish' who so limited their destinies by trying to insulate themselves from such maritime endeavour.[30]

This was at least part of the motivation for maritime exploration especially from the sixteenth century onwards. While by no means restricted to the Europeans, the reasons for mankind's urge to find out what was over the far horizon can be summed up best by looking at their example, particularly the case of Captain James Cook and his colleagues and rivals of the eighteenth century. Amongst their motivations were:

- *High-minded scientific enquiry.* This included helping to develop cartography and navigation (specifically by measuring the transit of Venus across the sun from Tahiti) and discovering flora, fauna, peoples and societies unknown to the Europeans (hence the large numbers of naturalists and artists embarked).
- *Commercial interest.* Admiral Byron was sent find *Terra Australis Incognita* 'in latitudes convenient for Navigation and in climates adapted to the product of commodities useful in Commerce'. Since Ptolemy, the existence of a large temperate continent to the south, necessary to counterbalance the Eurasia land mass to the north was thought to exist. If found, it and its people, could be a tremendous market.
- *Strategic interest.* New sea routes might have considerable strategic significance. Norfolk Island pine and Australasian hemp might be a means of reducing Britain's dangerous dependence on the Baltic area.[31]

Not surprisingly, therefore, even the sea's attribute as a means of gaining and transmitting information could be a matter of both cooperation and conflict. On the one hand, the pursuit of knowledge was regarded as a universal good. For that reason, Cook was given immunity from attack by the French and others, even during war, because his activities were considered to be in the common interest.[32] But there was very real rivalry here too. The Europeans tried to keep early route-finders (Rutters) and maps (Waggoners – after Lucas Waghenaer) very much to themselves. Inevitably there was much industrial espionage in which spies sought constantly to uncover their competitors' navigational secrets.

And, most obviously, when Cook and others found 'new' bits of desirable real estate they did not simply record its existence, they claimed it for their countries – whatever the locals might think.

The values of the peoples they discovered were often treated in the same way. On the one hand, many Europeans were surprisingly sensitive to local perceptions and interests. Mariners chancing across Tahiti thought they had discovered paradise and philosophers like Denis Diderot pleaded for the Pacific to be left unexploited and uncorrupted. On the other hand, there were those who strongly disapproved of local social values (which was tyrannically stratified and included human sacrifice and infanticide on a large scale) and sought to reform the benighted for their own good. Mahan, writing much later during the relief expedition to Peking during the

Boxer rebellion, summed it up quite well. He supported the Western maritime right, 'To insist, in the general interest, by force if need be, that China remain open to action by European and American processes of life and thought.'[33] Inevitably, this takes us to the fourth and last attribute of the sea.

The sea as a medium for dominion

The fact that so many coastal communities are fortified both against, and from, the sea shows that the sea is a source of vulnerability to marauders from afar. Ireland itself has over 250 known cliff-top castles acting both as a defence against invaders from the sea, and a springboard for aggressive Irish maritime endeavour, a pattern to be found all round the world.

In Europe and the Near East, the Phoenicians, the Greeks and the Romans demonstrated all too clearly that the sea is a strategic highroad, a medium by which one group of people can come to dominate the affairs of another. Rome conquered Britain, by sea, because it was a refuge to political refugees and asylum seekers always causing trouble on the Roman mainland. The Vikings likewise came by sea, attacked and conquered most of Britain, partly to escape the pressure of other land-based marauders to their east and partly in search of the riches associated with dominion. They went on to the Mediterranean, and across the Atlantic via Iceland to Greenland, Nova Scotia and the Americas. Their Frenchified successors, the Normans, followed suit a few centuries later still.

Later Europeans, initially the Portuguese and the Spanish, followed soon after by the Dutch, the French, the British and most others to some degree came by sea to North and South America, to the Indian Ocean and the Pacific, in tiny numbers overthrowing (often with extreme savagery) huge empires such as the Aztecs and the Incas. The Portuguese are an especially good example of what the Greeks call a 'thalassocracy' an empire founded on mastery of the sea. The Portuguese first fought their way into a new area and then had to protect their investments there. Their soldiers were never sufficiently numerous to engage in major continental campaigns, so their 160-year empire in the Indian Ocean rested on a few garrisons in strategic places and on superior naval forces. When others, especially the Dutch and the English, began to accumulate greater levels of naval force it went into decline.

The British Empire, which succeeded it in this area, was likewise based on seapower. Its strategists conceived of the empire as a huge land mass divided by eight chunks of water (the Dardanelles and Bosphorous, the Caspian Sea, the Tigris–Euphrates rivers, the Nile, the Red Sea, the Aral sea and River Oxus, the Gulf and the Indus/Sutlej). Controlling these water areas assured control of the land. Losing them would result in imperial decline. The security of the empire then rested on a series of defensive and offensive strategies centred on controlling the sea.[34]

For better or worse, the Europeans created new empires and changed the world. And they did it by sea. To make it all possible, they developed navies and a strategy, a set of concepts of how to use them from which all of the classic functions of seapower derived: assuring sea control, projecting power ashore in peace and war, attacking and defending trade, directly and indirectly, and maintaining good order at sea.

Although the Europeans provide perhaps the clearest example of the sea as a means of dominion, they are far from unique. The Islamic world around the Indian Ocean shows another example of the way in which traders are followed by

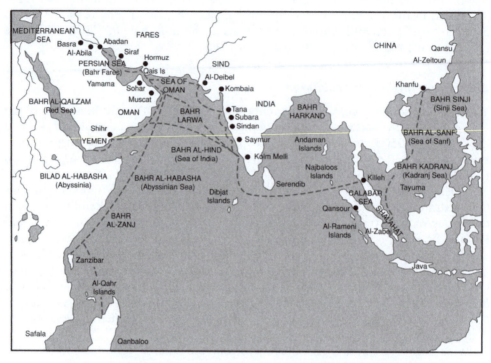

Figure 2.3 Oman's sea routes to the Far East and Africa in the eighth century AD
(source: Casey-Vine, 1995).

missionaries and soldiers, and empires result. The Oman sea-based empire of the seventeenth to nineteenth centuries is another later example of the same kind of thing.

Mixed motivations that span the four attributes of the sea

Motivations for such maritime endeavour were mixed but certainly included a strong economic dimension, in that there was a widespread view (rightly or wrongly) that in order to sustain growth, modern states needed access to other areas, preferably controlled in some way for further resources and markets. It is not only Marxists who conclude that this kind of international competition linking all four attributes of the sea led to imperialism. Mahan was quite clear that colonies offered, 'a foothold in a foreign land, a new outlet for what it [the colonial power] had to sell, a new sphere for its shipping, more employment for its people, more comfort and wealth for itself'.[35] The last and one of the clearest examples of this was the Japanese attack on the US Fleet at Pearl Harbor and European holdings in South East Asia in a desperate attempt to shock them into the acceptance of the establishment of a Greater East Asia Co-prosperity Sphere.

Sometimes, of course, there were 'informal' versions of this, in which a great power exercised great commercial power over an area, perhaps with military power over a distant horizon, but without the formal and costly institutional trappings of empire. British trading strength in South America in the nineteenth century is one example of this; to its modern critics, globalisation is another.

The advantages of seapower

The conclusion to all this seemed obvious. Strength at sea was such a clear path to dominion and power that countries sought to control it for what that control could apparently give them. They sought dominion over the sea itself. Thus the Treaty of Tordesillas of 1494 that divided the oceans of the world into two giving one half to Portugal and the other to Spain; the literally exclusive legal thinking behind John Selden's *Mare Clausum* of 1635; the development of the concept of the territorial sea, of the maritime frontier, of the insistence of tribute and deference from passing seafarers.

Mahan famously concluded, 'Control of the sea by maritime commerce and naval supremacy means predominant influence in the world ... [and] is the chief among the merely material elements in the power and prosperity of nations.'[36] To many, the final collapse of the essentially un-maritime and land-bound Soviet empire at the end of the twentieth century was simply the latest illustration of the relative advantages of seapower. With it, moreover, the revisionist school associated with the historian Paul Kennedy who argued that Mahan had exaggerated the historic effectiveness and future importance of seapower fell to some extent from academic grace.[37]

To the degree that they could profit from the sea as a medium of commercial transportation and trade, the economies of the sea powers would boom; to the extent that could exploit the strategic advantages of deploying decisive military power at sea and then projecting it ashore against the land-bound, their strategies would succeed. Because, therefore, the seapowers would generally prosper in peace and prevail in war, they would inevitably become great. That is, they conclude, the only explanation for the success of small countries with limited land areas, populations and resources such as Portugal, the Netherlands, England and they might have added, Venice, Oman and quite a few others. Thus in Corbett's view only seapower explained how it was, 'that a small country [like Britain] with a weak army should have been able to gather to herself the most desirable regions of the earth, and to gather them at the expense of the greatest military powers'.[38] But even if their continental preoccupations meant that countries like France, Germany or Russia could not go so far in exploiting such maritime opportunities, they would benefit commercially and strategically to the extent that they could follow suit.

2.3 Explaining the secret of maritime success

> There is nothing – absolutely nothing – half so much worth doing as simply messing about in boats.
>
> Kenneth Graham, *The Wind in the Willows*

Seapower is clearly a larger concept than landpower or airpower, neither of which encompasses the geo-economic dimensions of human activity to the extent that seapower does. As a Bangladeshi author has interestingly remarked:

> Unlike the army and the air force, whose size and firepower have to be related to that of potential adversaries, the size of the navy is determined by the quantum of maritime assets and interests that you have to safeguard.[39]

Accordingly, seapower can best be represented as a tight and inseparable system in which naval power protects the maritime assets that are the ultimate source of its effectiveness.

Of course navies that have tended to prevail were generally those with great warships and effective weaponry, with better tactics and more advanced technology, and above all perhaps with first-rate commanders able to wield their fleets with ruthless efficiency. The Portuguese broke into the Indian Ocean because they had all these advantages and so prevailed against the much larger navies they encountered there. If there was a revolution in maritime affairs at this time, it was the combination of the maritime nail and naval artillery of the Portuguese men-of-war. Local vessels, held together by coconut fibre could not stand the shock of heavy artillery. Their practice was to ram and board – fighting, infantry style, at close quarters. At the battle of 1502 off the Malabar Coast a small Portuguese fleet under Vicente Sodre faced a huge local armada in which several hundred Red Sea dhows joined forces with the fleet of the King of Calcutta; the Portuguese simply stood off and battered their adversaries to pieces from a distance.

Such fighting advantages were not, however, the exclusive property or the invention of the Portuguese or of anyone else. After all, many of the navigational advances made towards the end of the European Middle Ages derived from contact with the Islamic world, even down to the use of the word 'Admiral' which in Arabic once meant the 'Prince at Sea'. Across the other side of the world, the Koreans deployed the first armoured warship and, of course, China of the Song dynasty (from AD 1000–1500) boasted 'the world's most powerful and technologically sophisticated navy'.[40]

What *was* distinctive about the European approach to seapower at this time was that like the Chinese and others before them they had discovered the huge advantage to be derived from the close association between the military and the mercantile aspects of seapower. Especially in the hands of the Venetians, the Dutch, the British and, to a lesser extent, the Portuguese, Spanish and French, a virtuous circle was at work.

From maritime trade, the Europeans were able to derive maritime resources that could be diverted to naval purposes when the need arose. Partly it was through having ports, merchant hulls and seamen that could be used to support the navy

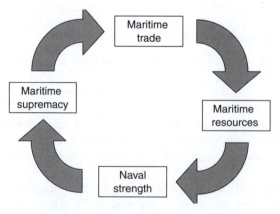

Figure 2.4 The virtuous maritime circle.

directly. Partly it was through having access to the indirect benefits deriving from the kind of sophisticated financial structures that maritime trade encouraged.

All this underpinned naval strength in a whole variety of ways:

- Mercantile finance could be used to fund naval effort. This meant it was much easier for the maritime powers (that is naval powers with a strong mercantile element) to build a navy than it was for the merely naval powers. At the end of the seventeenth century, the French (at this time much less maritime than the British) showed that with a real effort they could out build the British and produce a bigger and indeed very fine fleet – but they could not maintain it. The British simply outlasted them. Maritime powers could devote huge resources to building and maintaining a fleet but at less real cost, and they often had enough left over to support the war effort generally and, in Britain's case, to subsidise allies as well.
- Mercantile finance from the profits of trade also funded access to a mass of industrial and technological developments. The Royal Navy of the eighteenth century and all of its supporting dockyard and manufacturing infrastructure, for example, was the world's biggest industrial enterprise by far.[41]
- This could be translated into specific military advantage. The British industrial lead in coke-smelting techniques and steam machinery, for example, meant it was much easier for the Royal Navy than the French to copper-bottom its ships – making them more nimble and faster than old ships would otherwise have been.

Here the British example has been given, but there were many others – for instance, Oman:

> Most human settlements along Oman's coastline depended primarily on the sea for their livelihood. Omanis were in need of a big mercantile fleet to achieve their goals. The Omani fleet represented, from the outset, the backbone of the country's economic life. It was multifunctional, involved with fishing, transportation, trade and protection of the country and its people [on the land as well as at sea]. It would not be an exaggeration to say that Oman's power depended upon its maritime strength and *vice versa*.[42]

All this made for an approach to war that was uniquely cost-effective, as we shall see later and does much to explain why the maritime powers predominated over the merely naval, and in most cases in the last few centuries over the continental ones too. The interconnections were perfectly summarised by the French Minister of Marine in 1901, J.I. de Lanessan:

> If we wish to become a great commercial democracy, which will necessitate a great development of our mercantile marine and important progress in our Colonial empire, we must possess a fleet of such strength that no other power can dominate to our detriment the European waters on which our harbours are situated, or the oceans where our merchant ships circulate.[43]

The failure of de Lanessan's project to develop France into a great maritime power, however, demonstrates that this virtuous circle was not a closed system – it could be influenced decisively from outside. In this case the overland threat from Germany essentially broke the circle up. Much the same thing happened to Oman and China when their land borders were threatened by neighbours.

But recent studies have taken this argument a little further and sought to explore the workings of this virtuous circle.[44] What kept it going, generally, so well? One key candidate for this role is the association of maritime supremacy with a system of beliefs and of styles of government. The argument is as follows.

Seafaring and trade produce merchants. Merchants accumulate wealth and political power in order to defend and develop it. Often they will prevail in government, and enforce their ideas on others. These are the ideas that encouraged trade in the first place: freedom of information and therefore of opinion, open and responsive government, fair taxation, social enterprise – all the liberal values so familiar today. In the seventeenth century, the English marvelled at the freedoms of the Dutch. Thus Sir William Temple, the English Ambassador reported on that 'Strange freedom that all men took in boats and inns and all other common places, of talking openly whatever they thought upon all public affairs both of their own state, and their neighbours.'[45] A century later the Frenchman, Montesquieu, said much the same thing about England calling it 'the freest country in the world'. That freedom was both a product of commercial enterprise and something that facilitated it. Because of the wealth and the resources it generated these freedoms were at the heart of maritime power. Nicholas Rodger makes the essential point: navies need consensus because they require the maximum involvement of seafarers, shipowners, urban merchants, financiers and investors. Autocracies manage armies well enough, because that is much more a matter of simply mobilising manpower and the equipment it needs.[46]

It would be easy to fall into the trap of concluding that these values were Western values, but they are not. They are *trading* values and have been espoused by other peoples at various times. The China of the 500-year-long Song dynasty was one example of this. Despite overland threats from the north and west, naval power was important to the regime, and had a distinctly mercantile approach. Protecting the merchant fleet against some particularly powerful and well-armed pirates was a high priority. This resulted in the construction of a chain of naval bases along the coast, the development of a convoying system and encouragement of new and sophisticated means of boarding and close engagement, since it was much better to seize or destroy pirate ships than merely to drive them away.[47]

Arguably, the connections between maritime power, liberalism, trade and prosperity are as true now as such authors claim they were then. To judge by current economic performance early in the twenty-first century, free societies seem to have continuing advantages. Democracies are used to the free exchange of information that is at the heart of successful trade and it seems no coincidence that they are also the leaders of the information revolution.

But for many these were, and maybe remain, unsettling thoughts. Some regimes discerning the risks and the challenges inevitably associated with maritime power have deliberately pulled up the drawbridge against its apparent advantages and opportunities. One Chinese Emperor did that quite consciously. After nearly 500 years of deeply impressive and rounded maritime endeavour, the construction of all sea-going ships and foreign travel were banned because China's rulers did not know where it would all end. A little later, in 1639, the Japanese under the Tokugawa shogunate followed suit, turned their back upon the sea and based their system on domestic peace and agricultural taxes. Japan's culture flourished, but the Japanese fell further and further behind global developments until their self-imposed isolation was rudely shattered by the US Navy in 1853.

The Russians, too, have always been ambivalent about the sea. Peter the Great developed and built a navy specifically to attract trade and Western ideas and even moved his capital to St Petersburg in order to accommodate all this. His navy was full of foreigners; he personally learned about shipbuilding in Amsterdam and Deptford. He did everything he could to turn Russia into a trading nation. For many of his subjects and his successors this was all too much. Despite its periodic brilliance (especially at the end of the eighteenth century under the great Admiral Ushakov), the navy was seen by conservatives as basically un-Russian and a source of ideas dangerous to the existing system, which of course it was. When Stalin shot most of his admirals in the late 1930s he was in one sense conforming to an ancient Russian tradition of eliminating possible sources of insurrection; but paradoxically the admirals he spared were exactly those who said that the Soviet Navy needed to modernise and follow the general lines of development set by the British, American and Japanese navies.

In this, Stalin was tacitly acknowledging the difficulty of insulating his regime from the pervasive influences of modern maritime power. The Japanese and Chinese had already discovered this.

2.4 Seapower: qualifications and limitations

All this should not be taken to mean that the maritime powers always prevail, for manifestly they do not. Being maritime brings vulnerabilities as well as opportunities. Sophisticated maritime powers depend on a complex network of shipping that imports raw materials, food and uncompleted goods, and exports finished and manufactured products. This can be a delicate system, and a dangerous source of vulnerability especially when the distracting effect of continental threats, or governmental neglect or the appearance of a stronger maritime adversary produces a navy insufficient to protect the wider maritime system on which it ultimately depends. As the fate of the Netherlands in the late seventeenth century and Japan more dramatically in the mid twentieth century show, not just the interests but the very survival of the maritime power may be at stake.

Many argued at the time of the Cold War, that NATO (the North Atlantic Treaty Organisation) had such dangerous vulnerabilities too. As its name suggests, it was an alliance as much separated by the ocean as it was joined by it. Its strategic coherence and economic survival depended on sea-based transportation, which sometimes seemed dangerously exposed to the burgeoning Soviet Navy and land-based air forces. Accordingly much of NATO's naval resources were directed at the *defence* of those unavoidable maritime vulnerabilities. This, combined with the often remarked superiority of the offence at sea (which will be considered later), meant that much of NATO's maritime effort was devoted to ensuring that NATO did not lose a possible war with the Soviet Union, rather than providing a means by which NATO could win it.

The demanding but essentially protective function that seapowers usually have limits their capacity to impose their will on others, and was seen by the great British geographer, Halford Mackinder, and his followers as a grave, historic and developing weakness. Such geo-politicians pointed out that many long-lasting empires had in fact been based on landpower not seapower (not least the Mongols who had created a massive empire lasting some 500 years that was about as far from the sea as it is geographically possible to get). Mahan and others had made too much of the Columban era, which was in fact the exception to the rule. Further, they argued that the 'world political potential of sea power had been in full retreat long before the first submarine had plunged below the surface and the first plane had taken to the air'.[48] This was because land communications were improving and land powers were developing ever better means of exploiting the vulnerabilities of the maritime powers. They developed naval forces (like the German U-boats of the First and Second World Wars) that had no protective function to distract them and could be wholly devoted to offensive campaigns of sea denial.

Mahan and Corbett were, however, far from the only writers to consider the importance and workings of seapower, a matter to which we should now turn.

3   Who said what and why it matters

There is no smartness about sailors. They waddle like ducks, and can only fight stupid battles that no one can form any idea of. There is no science nor strategem in sea-fights – nothing more than what you see when two rams run their heads together in a field to knock each other down. But in military battles there is such art, and such splendour, and the men are so smart, particularly the horse-soldiers.

Anne, in Thomas Hardy's *The Trumpet Major* (London: Macmillan, 1925), p. 354

3.1 The value of theory in maritime operations

The case against

However sensible her views on other things, Anne was wrong about there being 'no science nor strategem in sea-fights'. There is, but naval officers around the world have traditionally been averse to thinking about it. Mahan lamented the fact that not only were British naval officers not 'instruit' in the French sense, they did not want to be: 'To meet difficulties as they arise, instead of by foresight, to learn by hard experience rather than by reflection or premeditation, are national traits.'[1]

This was partly because the process was and is often quite boring, partly through fear that abstract concepts may damage young or tender minds and partly as Winston Churchill remarked: 'The seafaring and scientific technique of the naval profession makes such severe demands upon the training of naval men, that they have very rarely the time or opportunity to study military history and the art of war in general.'[2]

More seriously there is concern that the consequences of such thinking might prove too prescriptive and deadening for free-ranging operations on the open ocean. Corbett reproduced a seventeenth-century report that pointed out the essential difference between operations at sea and on land:

> it intended to enjoin our fleet to advance and fight at sea much after the manner of an army at land, assigning every ship to a particular division, rank, file and station, which order and regularity was not only improbable but almost impossible to be observed by so great a fleet in so uncertain a place as the sea.[3]

Compared to navies, armies in action disaggregate into much smaller units, (down to platoons and very possibly individual soldiers). A strong sense of common purpose and prescriptive doctrine is the only thing that may bind them together in the confusion of battle. Fleets at sea need it too, but to a much lesser degree, the argument goes. Hence the traditional naval wariness about excessive conceptualisation and prescriptive doctrine; better to rely on an offensive instinct schooled by experience. The pantheon of naval heroes indeed is dominated by people, like Nelson, who are held constructively to have broken 'the rules', whereas 'rat-catchers' like Admiral Jellicoe observed and even invented them. Battles of lost opportunity such as Jutland and the inconclusive line engagements of the British and French in the eighteenth century on the other hand show the ultimate futility of simply 'going by the book'.[4]

The case for

These days such arguments fail to convince. The modern naval view is that the *absence* of theory is far more likely to stultify action than its presence. Navies are still important but they operate in a vastly different strategic environment and face entirely different problems (as well, of course, as many more familiar ones); all these issues need to be seriously thought about and theorised over because they have implications for what navies do and how they do it.

How can the conduct of naval operations in the context of a major war between advanced states continue to be the guiding principle for naval preparations, if such wars are indeed going out of fashion? On what basis other than constructive and continuous theorising can navies safely steer their way through the deluge of new technology, make their investment decisions, determine their fighting techniques and plan and conduct their operations? As so often, Clausewitz makes the essential point:

> Theory cannot equip the mind with formulas for solving problems, nor can it mark the narrow path on which the sole solution is supposed to lie by planting a hedge of principles on either side. But it gives the mind insight into the great mass of phenomena and of their relationships, then leaves it free to rise into higher realms of action...
>
> Theory exists so that one need not start afresh each time sorting out the material and ploughing through it, but will find it ready to hand and in good order. It is meant to educate the mind of the future commander or, more accurately, to guide him in his self-education, not to accompany him to the battlefield.[5]

Clausewitz's point that 'one need not start afresh' is worth emphasising. Since theory is often based on the processing of past experience, history, far from being simply 'a record of exploded ideas' should help us avoid repeating previous errors. History rarely repeats itself but it does point out not just the similarities of past and present but also the essential differences. Studying it and reflecting on the conclusions that previous thinkers have drawn from it helps; at the very least helps to identify the questions that ought to be asked and the issues that need to be thought about in difficult and troubled times.[6]

Musashi's conclusion that 'the warrior's is the twofold way of pen and sword, and he should have a taste for both ways' seems right and applies to naval warriors too.[7]

3.2 On types of theory

Strategy and strategic thinking

Like many other military terms, 'strategy' has been taken over by the business community and has become so watered down as to mean not much more than the way you try to get what you want. This is not very helpful. Instead, it is better to revert to the original use of the term as it relates specifically to the strategic level of war. Robert Osgood reminds us that this level of war is especially characterised by the association between military means and political ends:

> Military strategy must now be understood as nothing less than the overall plan for utilising the capacity for armed coercion – in conjunction with the economic, diplomatic and psychological instruments of power – to support foreign policy most effectively by overt, covert and tacit means.[8]

Three points emerge from this quotation.

*   Clearly Osgood, like Mahan and most other strategists, is taking an unashamedly 'realistic' view of human nature and behaviour.
*   Osgood's is a broad definition, which emphasises that there is much more to strategy than simply killing people efficiently. Strategy is not restricted to the conduct of war, but extends into peacetime as well. Osgood widens the agenda by emphasising other forms of power and differing types of strategy. It may well include using your armed forces to win friends, or to influence their behaviour as much as coercing or deterring possible adversaries.
*   The phrase 'to support foreign policy' makes the point that strategy, war and conflict should be designed to accomplish a political objective. This is what justifies strategic action and, as Clausewitz remarked, this is what determines a consequent conflict's form and character:

> War is nothing but a continuation of political endeavour with altered means. I base the whole of strategy on this tenet, and believe that he who refuses to recognise this necessity does not fully understand what matters. The principle explains the whole history of war, and without it, everything would appear quite absurd.[9]

Liddell Hart made the same point more succinctly, by defining strategy as, 'The art of distributing and applying military means to fulfil the ends of policy.'[10] Strategic theory, obviously, is thinking about strategy, trying to 'put it all together' through the development of a skein of connected thought about the nature, conduct and consequences of naval power. This is what distinguishes the likes of Mahan and Corbett from people like Shakespeare, Hardy and Coleridge, whose stimulating maritime observations may enliven these pages but who are clearly not maritime strategists.

Maritime strategy: five questions to ask

For now these five questions will simply be raised. It is hoped that the answers will emerge in the following pages – that is certainly the intention!

First, does maritime strategy really matter? Sceptics point to the fact that most sailors have to concentrate on the tactical level of war; for them, the focus of books such as Ian Inskip's brilliant *Ordeal by Exocet: HMS Glamorgan and the Falklands War 1982* show what sailors at the sharp end have to bear and do much better than accounts set at the higher levels of war.

Even at these higher levels, it is often difficult to measure the practical influence that people like Mahan and Corbett actually had on naval policy. It is true that John Clerk, in his 1782 *Essay on Naval Tactics*, did discuss the idea of the British making an echeloned approach to their enemy from to-windward in a manner that prefigured Nelson's famous Toulon memorandum and his dispositions at Trafalgar. It is also true that in the absence of Emma Hamilton, one of Nelson's notions of entertainment was to listen to his chaplain reading aloud in the evening from Clerk's work. But trying to establish any closer link between abstract theorising and the conduct of naval operations is usually impossible. Indeed, some would reverse the connections between ideas and events. Mahan is, for example, often held to have benefitted from rather than been responsible for the expansion of the US Navy at the beginning of the twentieth century and its adoption of 'Mahanian' ideas. In which case, 'Why bother?' – some might ask.[11]

Second, the previous quotation from Liddell Hart is also useful in that it raises the perennial issue of whether maritime strategy is an art or a science. There have always been two traditions here. Some maritime strategists focus on the material and quantifiable aspects of war (the disposition of fleets, the physical performance of weapons) and treat it almost as a science. Here the essentials of strategy can be reduced to neat and tidy laws. Others focus instead on the unquantifiable, unpredictable human aspects of war (command, leadership, motivation) and regard strategy as an art, where the commander's judgment is crucial. Of course both traditions apply to all military situations and to nearly all strategic theorists, although the balance struck between them varies. But Mahan spoke for most when he concluded that war is essentially an art and 'it is for the skill of the artist in war rightly to apply the principles and rules in each case'.[12]

Third, are the principles of maritime strategy permanent, true for all time, or do they have to be continually recast, as technology and the strategic environment changes? Colin Gray is quite clear on the matter: 'To understand modern strategy is to understand it in all ages. The purposes for which humans contend will change, but the deadly game endures.' He argues that Mahan is (mainly) right, always has been and always will be. Technology may alter the detail but not the essentials of maritime strategy. John Reeve on the other hand 'reject[s] the view that there are unchanging principles of naval strategy save in all but the very broadest sense, and ... argue[s] that strategy is always evolving within the changing context of history'. Distinctions, however, may be drawn between broad and abiding concepts and the much more ephemeral nature of their application in a way that could lead to the conclusion that the higher the level of warfare being dealt with the more permanent are its essential characteristics. Plainly, this is an issue that strategists need to address; doctrine writers with their concern for the here and now need be less concerned with such metaphysics.[13]

Fourth, are the principles of maritime strategy universal and do they apply to everyone? 'Do second and third class navies', Colin Gray has asked, 'sail in the same waters of theory and military practice as do the navies of the first rank in combat prowess?' and concludes that they do. Ken Booth, on the other hand, disagrees. Mahanian, thinking, for example, was 'relevant only to the United States and Britain. It was not relevant to those states with neither the need nor the inclination to use the seas in such ambitious ways.' At the grand strategic level of what can be done with navies, Colin Gray would seem nearer the mark. It is, for example, very easy to draw comparison between a country like Oman and their ancient adversaries, the Portuguese. Both demonstrate systemic linkages between trade and seapower, the need for a modern fighting fleet, continuous struggles for naval supremacy and the despatch of distant expeditions. Bernard Brodie in his classic review of maritime strategy declared: 'No valid conception of sea power can vary according to the psychology or culture of different nations. A concept of sea power is either correct and conforms with the realities of war, or it is wrong.'[14]

Nonetheless local conditions have a major effect on the manner in which such broad ideas are put into effect. During the Cold War, for example, the maritime approach of both sides was determined in large measure by geographical considerations, the resources available for maritime purposes, the decision-making process, access to current technology, perceptions of the strategic environment and of the maritime behaviour of the putative adversary. A navy that is central to the concerns of a powerful country is obviously likely to be more ambitious in its aspirations than the incidental navy of a small and weak one. This leads to the conclusion that the conceptions of maritime strategy are universal, but the extent to which individual countries can (or even want to) realise them, may be highly particular. Even so, one of the very basic questions that ought to be asked of any maritime strategist is the extent to which their conclusions apply generally.

Fifth, and finally, how distinctive is maritime strategy? To what extent are navies 'different' from the other services? Traditionalists argue that they are different – and that failing to appreciate the distinctive characteristics of maritime operations may lead to major error. In the case of the Soviet Navy, for instance, Stuart Slade has pointed out the

> disastrous effects of trying to impose land-oriented strategic and operational concepts on naval forces. The Soviet navy, in its own eyes and confirmed by its own exercises, was incapable of performing its operational roles until it started to evolve its own distinctive strategies optimised for the unique conditions of naval warfare. The lesson is a salutary one that should be borne in mind by those championing 'joint command' and 'service unification'.[15]

Accordingly, most maritime strategists have been at pains not just to apply general strategic principles to maritime operations but also to explore what is distinctive about them, and what particular benefits maritime success can convey. These differences partly derive from the maritime environment itself. Specifically, the sea is:

- global – the sea is 'all joined-up' so a conflict may rapidly spread and forces may quickly be moved across the great majority of the world's surface;
- largely un-owned and un-ownable – neutrals may well be present in any area of

operation. Possession of the sea is not generally an object of maritime operations. There has never been a maritime 'front line';

- three dimensional – the subsurface, surface and air dimensions of maritime operations may interface at any time, presenting threats and challenges from all azimuths;
- large, opaque, varied and often hostile – finding the enemy is often the main problem. It took Nelson three months of searching to locate the French Fleet at the Nile. For all these reasons the normal ratio of the strength of the defence to the attack (3:1) is often reversed at sea where, Mahan claimed, the defence was the stronger form of waging war. Moreover unpredictably shifting winds, water conditions and the weather may determine naval outcomes and make all the difference between success and failure. The sea itself indeed can be an enemy.[16]

Again, the nature of the forces engaged in maritime operations have their special characteristics too. They are expensive, hard to replace and even the smallest units represent a sizeable investment in human resources whose loss can be sudden and instantaneous and very hard for publics and governments to bear. Because they range over such a huge area of the world's surface and may be 'out of touch', navies have traditionally developed a sense of independent and delegated command only now being challenged by modern technology. Famously, Nelson sent no orders or signals during the battle of Trafalgar.[17]

The issue of the extent to which navies are 'different' is important because the answer has a bearing on what special capabilities they have to offer and on the extent to, and the manner in, which they operate alongside the other services. Effective jointery is a tremendous advantage in military operations, but only if it is based on clear recognition of the differences between the services as well as their similarities.

Nonethless, maritime strategy has evolved, not in a vacuum, but as a subset of general strategic thinking. In many ways, it seeks to apply general strategic principles to maritime operations. Mahan called his dog 'Jomini' not apparently intending any disrespect but in recognition of the debt he owed the great Swiss master of strategy, especially for his use of the concept of 'lines of operation'. Likewise, the debt that Corbett owes Clausewitz, particularly for his stress on the need to relate military means to political ends is obvious from the very first page of his main book.

In just the same way, the concept of 'principles of war' (a short, handy summary of 'broad precepts distilled from experience which influence the conduct of armed conflict and which should inform all strategic and operational decisions')[18] apply as much to maritime operations as to any other. The British list is as follows, the first being the so-called 'master principle', the rest being in no particular order of precedence:

- selection and maintenance of the aim (the commander should only have one aim at any time, and it should determine all actions);
- maintenance of morale (partly sustained through a common sense of purpose);
- offensive action (a state of mind conferring the initiative on the attacker);
- surprise (often leads to levels of success disproportionate to the size of forces employed);
- security (reduces vulnerability to enemy attack, requires only calculated risks);

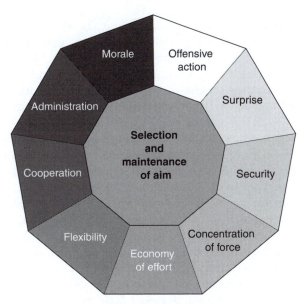

Figure 3.1 The principles of war.

- concentration of force (having more than the adversary at the decisive time and place);
- economy of effort (judicious and cost-effective expenditure or resources);
- flexibility (ability to adapt to the unpredictability of military operations);
- cooperation (team spirit of all units involved, including other services and national forces);
- administration (good staff work, efficient logistics).

This could lead to the conclusion that there is nothing distinctive about maritime strategy and maritime operations, a conclusion that Russian naval thinkers seemed closely to approach in the Soviet era. Thus Admiral Chernavin, the last Commander-in-Chief of the Soviet Navy:

> Today ... there is no purely specific realm of warfare. Victory is achieved by the combined efforts of [all branches of the armed forces] which brings about the need to integrate all knowledge of warfare within the framework of a united military science.[19]

The general issue of the distinctiveness of maritime operations has long been of interest to strategists, but it has a particular salience for the twenty-first century. The extent to which the concepts of sea, air and land warfare coincide or differ helps determine the way in which they can be brought together in joint operations. Modern preoccupations with jointery accordingly make this an important issue nowadays – not least in the writing of doctrine.

Doctrine

Maritime doctrine is the application of maritime theory in a particular time and place. If maritime theories are about the art of cookery, doctrine is concerned with today's menus. Both are essential. Without strategic theory, doctrine writers would not know where they have been, where they should start and are less likely to be able to work out where they should go; without doctrine, sailors would have either to rely on luck and blind instinct or to convene a seminar to decide what to do when a hostile fleet appears on the horizon.

Doctrine comes at various levels, and tends to be least prescriptive at the higher levels, and most prescriptive when it takes the form of 'Fighting Instructions' and 'Tactical Procedures' and where the emphasis is much more on how to think and do things rather than on what to do and what to think about. Doctrine is based on processing historical experience and discovering what the Russians call the 'norms' – or what usually works. But merely having experience is not enough. Sailors need to think about it – otherwise, as Frederick the Great famously observed, quite a few of his pack mules would deserve to be field marshals.

The particular aim of doctrine is to give everyone a sense of common purpose, so that they can sustain the attacks of hostile forces (opposing fleets, the other services, treasuries and sceptical politicians) and play their proper part in defeating them. Four things make this particularly important:

- The ever increasing development of professional specialisations within navies could lead to institutional fragmentation, even in-fighting, if all the diverse tribes are not bound together by a clear sense of purpose and direction. Doctrine, in other words, helps re-aggregate necessarily diversified navies.
- There is growing emphasis on cooperation with the other services, especially in the conduct of expeditionary operations. This requires sailors to be able to understand and articulate their own business clearly, to identify their particular contribution to the exercise and to understand the distinctive approaches and requirements of the other services. For this reason, formulations of naval doctrine need to be in concert with a hierarchical family of associated doctrines for all the services and levels of war.
- There is likewise an increasing need to participate in multinational operations with foreign navies. This calls for the development of a common doctrine about the conduct of multinational naval operations. The development of a doctrine for such operations should help 'reconcile different national security and force structures, allow for differences in force capabilities, and resolve a range of equipment and procedural interoperability issues'.[20]
- Navies are increasingly used for tasks such as humanitarian or peace support operations in which traditional notions such as the defeat of an adversary may be a dangerous irrelevance. Those conducting them need doctrinal guidance derived from reflections on the lessons of experience so far.

Inevitably this all sounds sensible enough but rather abstract. In fact, an inability to identify and agree a clear doctrinal approach to severely practical matters of large-scale life and death can have quite disastrous consequences. A recent study of the American landing on Omaha Beach during the Normandy campaign of 1944

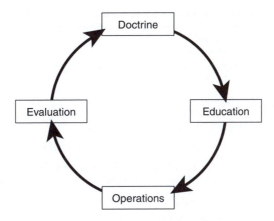

Figure 3.2 The doctrine cycle.

attributes much of the disaster to some very basic doctrinal failings on the Allied side. Defective doctrine is quite clearly the high road to defeat. Conversely, as Section 3.7 will show, telling doctrine is a very significant force multiplier.[21]

At the tactical/procedural level (such as NATO's ATP-1 (Allied Tactical Procedures) *Maritime Tactical Signals and Manoeuvring* book) doctrine is largely prescriptive but at higher levels it is intended to be more than that. Doctrine is supposed to be authoritative in that it establishes a starting point and a sense of direction from which commanders should only depart knowingly. It has been likened to a compass bearing: 'it gives us the general direction of our course. We may deviate from that course on occasion, but the heading provides a common purpose to all who travel along the way.'[22]

But most doctrinal formulations contain references to the need for 'judgement in its application'. 'Nothing', Corbett tells us, 'is so dangerous in the study of war as to permit maxims to become a substitute for judgement.' Doctrine is not dogma. Long established principles are there to be questioned, familiar procedures to be adapted to suit particular circumstances. By stressing the difference between principles (which have an element of free play) and rules (which do not) Mahan made essentially the same point.[23]

Moreover the fact that circumstances are always changing means that doctrine needs to be versatile and adaptive and has constantly to be reviewed and developed. The process by which this should take place is often described as a kind of endless circle of formulating doctrine, telling sailors what it is, trying it out operationally and amending it in the light of experience.

3.3 The early development of theory

Table 3.1 shows that maritime strategy is by no means a modern invention. On the contrary, a good deal of thought was devoted to the subject all around the world well before the major surge of interest at the end of the nineteenth century. This list, while by no means comprehensive, makes some things very clear.

First, the most obvious is that no one country has ever had a monopoly in maritime thinking. It is, however, true that Western expositions are the most well

Table 3.1 The origins of naval thought to 1900 [excluding Anglo-Americans]

Author	Title of work	Year	Country
King Alfonso of Castile	*De la guerre que & face por la Mar* (*Of the War that is Made on the Sea*)	1270	Spain
Ahmad Bin Majid	*The Benefits and Principles of Oceanography/ Book of Profitable Things Concerning the First Principles and Rules of Navigation*	1489	UAE
Suleiman al Malin	*Fundamentals for the Mastery of Naval Science*	1511	Oman
Antoine de Conflans	*Les Faisz de la marine et de la navigaie* (*On the Nature of the Fleet and Navigation*)	1516	France
Alonso de Chaves	*Expejode navegantes* (*Seaman's Glass*)	1538	Spain
Pantero Pantera	*L'Armata navale* (*The Navy*)	1614	Italy
Comte de Tourville	*Signals and Constructions*	1691	France
Pere Paul Hoste	*L'Art de armees navales ou traité des evolution navales* (*The Art of Fleets, or a Treatise on Naval Evolution*)	1697	France
Vicomte de Morogues	*Tactiques naval ou traité des evolutions et des signaux* (*Naval Tactics or a Treatise on Evolutions and Signals*)	1763	France
Vicomtede Grenier	*L'Art de la Guerre sur Mer ou Tactique Navale* (*The Art of War at Sea, or Naval Tactics*)	1787	France
Audibert Ramatuelle	*Cours Elementaire de Tactique Navale* (*Elementary Course on Naval Tactics*)	1802	France
Giulio Rocco	*Riflessioni sul potere marittimo* (*Considerations of Maritime Power*)	1814	Italy
Rear Admiral Jean Grivel	*Considerations Navale* (*Naval Considerations*)	1832	France
Rear Admiral Jean Grivel	*De La Marine Militaire* (*On the Fleet*)	1837	France
Lt Capt. V. Berezin	*Morskaya Taktika* (*Naval Tactics*)	1880	Russia
Stepan O. Makarov	*Discussion of Questions in Naval Tactics*	1898	Russia
Domenico Bonamico	*Il Potere Maritime* (*Maritime Power*)	1899	Italy

known. The modern dominance of Mahan and Corbett (American and British respectively) is partly a function of their conceptual insight, partly a consequence of the maritime power their countries exhibited and partly because they wrote in what has become the most accessible of the world's languages. Even so, the apparent paucity of theoretical writing on the subject in the Asia-Pacific is puzzling, especially given the richness of China's general strategic writing and of the impressive nature of its maritime power at least to AD 1500. The impact of the writings of Sun Tzu on Chinese and Japanese maritime thinking almost certainly deserve much more study than they have received. Many of these observations apply to the extent and depth of maritime thinking in the Indian and Islamic worlds as well.

Second, most of these explorations were by no means limited to, or indeed were particularly interested in, narrow naval concerns. In addition to providing a great deal of information on navigation in the Indian Ocean, Ahmad bin Majid, the 'Lion of the Sea', emphasised the financial benefits to be expected from sea trade, and provided much advice to mariners to help them set about it. As the title of their books suggest, Giulio Rocco and Domenico Bonamico were also both concerned about the much broader aspects of maritime power and on what it could do for Italy.

Third, where the focus of maritime theory did apply to the employment of naval forces, it widened and deepened as time went on, from the narrowly tactical and technical to the comprehensively strategic. The starting point was often a concern to provide guidance on how to improve chances for victory in battle. Chaves, for example, offered advice on the advantages of taking the weather gauge, on forming naval units in squadrons, on ways of manoeuvring in order to maximise combat potential. This was also the basic message of de Tourville, de Morogues, John Clerk of Eldin and of the long string of 'Fighting Instructions' issued by the British Admiralty from 1653. Through the eighteenth century there was a growing tendency to focus on ways of improving the coherence of fleet formations and the effectiveness of command and control arrangements by recommending improvements in naval signalling. These books were full of diagrams describing patterns of advance and analysing the respective merits of various fleet formations and angles of attack.[24]

The overriding preoccupation in such works was how to manoeuvre the fleet in order to maximise its firepower. The aspiration was to be able to put the whole of your force against part of the enemy's, and to prevent his doing that to you. These sources of advice were constantly adapted in light of evolving experience, focused largely on the conduct of battle and the tactical level of war and were offered as authoritative doctrinal guides. They were often prescriptive, even directive, in tone and focused on battle tactics.

The eighteenth century was an era in which naval officers were court-martialled, and sometimes shot, through combat failure brought about by not appearing to adhere to the rules laid down in the 'Fighting Instructions'. Ever since, this has given doctrine a bad name, because it was seen to lead to commanders 'sticking to the book', in the hope that this was their best guarantee of not failing. John Clerk was very concerned about the consequences of this, and concerned to rectify matters. For him, the last straw was the 'feeble and undecisive' attack launched in 1781 by Admiral Graves at the Chesapeake on the French Fleet, the failure of which led to him abandoning Lord Cornwallis and his 'fine army' at Yorktown to their fate, and for that matter much of British America too.

This was just the latest instance of the British being 'baffled' by the French, and unable to achieve their battle aims. Clearly this could not possibly be explained by any 'want of spirit in our seamen' so it must be due to the fact

> that our enemy, the French, having acquired a superior knowledge, have adopted some new system of managing great fleets, not known, or not sufficiently attended to by us ... or that, on the other hand, we have persisted in following some old method, or instructions, which from later improvement, ought to have been rejected.

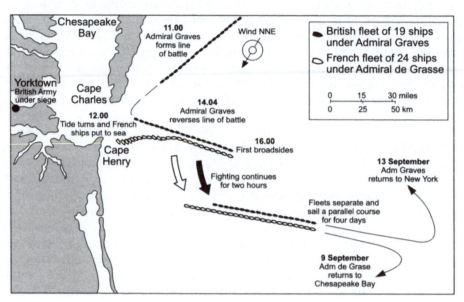

Figure 3.3 The Yorktown/Chesapeake campaign, 1781.

Specifically, Clerk thought that the Royal Navy had become fixated on only attacking from windward, and this had led to it ignoring many other productive possibilities. The problem was caused, Clerk concluded, by the Royal Navy's 'total neglect of Naval tactics': 'Though a superior degree of knowledge in naval affairs be evidently of the utmost consequence to the inhabitants of this island, yet the subject of Naval tactics had long remained among us in a very rude and uncultivated state.'[25] Clerk was determined to change this. Like many other writers on maritime strategy, his intention was not merely to engage in idle pen pushing, but actually to have a practical effect. His was intended to be a practical guide for naval professionals. The Royal Navy certainly took a more innovative and risk-taking approach to the conduct of battle by the end of the eighteenth century – but it is difficult to establish causal links between this and Clerk's efforts, as we have seen.

Fourth, the incentive for abstract thinking was often an attempt to assess the implications of technological and other change. When the industrial revolution began to revolutionise the size and shape of the fleet, maritime writers began to address its possible consequences for the conduct of naval warfare. General Henri Paixhans in the 1820s was amongst the first. He advocated the rapid building of a fleet of modern iron-clads, with a few large guns, that would blow the British out of the water. In this, he ushered in an era in which rapidly changing naval technology resulted in a huge diversity of opinion on the issue of how navies would perform their tasks. Some foresaw a shift from one role to another. Admiral Jean Grivel, for example, wanted France to concentrate on producing a machine-age fleet maximised for a war on commerce. In his book, *Discussion of Questions in Naval Tactics*, Russia's remarkable and versatile Admiral Stepan Makarov dealt with the torpedo-boat tactics for which he is famous but ranged widely over the whole field of new technology and its impact on the conduct of maritime operations. His emphasis was deliberately on the tactical/technical level of war. To him the precise technical details of the best cable grapnel were a subject worthy of detailed analysis, alongside command, leadership and the operational significance of innumerable British naval campaigns.

But all of this was merely a prelude for the dramatic explosion of naval ideas that occurred at the end of the nineteenth century and the beginning of the twentieth.

3.4 Mahan and the bluewater tendency

'It's a tremendously interesting subject,' said Davies, pulling down (in two pieces) a volume of Mahan's *Influence of Sea Power*. Dinner flagged (and froze) while he illustrated a point by reference to the much-thumbed pages. He was very keen, and not very articulate...

'They've [the Germans] got no colonies to speak of, and *must* have them, like us. They can't get them and keep them, and they can't protect their huge commerce without naval strength. The command of the sea is *the* thing nowadays, isn't it? I say, don't think these are my ideas,' he added naively. 'It's all out of Mahan and those fellows.'

...I knew just enough to be an intelligent listener and though hungry was delighted to hear him talk.

'I'm not boring you, am I?' he said suddenly.

'I should think not,' I protested. 'But you might just have a look at the chops.'

Erskine Childers, *The Riddle of the Sands*, pp. 41, 72

These heroes of Erskine Childers' famous novel of 1903 were typical of the sailors of the early twentieth century in their awed admiration for the work and views of the American naval officer, Alfred Thayer Mahan. But like most others then and since, they had doubtless read and understood but few of the great man's works.

Mahan was born in 1840, the son of a professor at West Point Military Academy. He joined the US Navy and developed a strong interest in history. Inspired by reading Mommsen's *History of Rome* in the library of Lima's English Club he began to think about seapower, its role and importance, and eventually joined the staff of the new US War College at Newport, Rhode Island, as lecturer. *The Influence of Sea Power on History 1660–1783*, his most famous book, was published in 1890, to enormous acclaim. Many others followed. He died in 1914.[26]

Mahan and his generation benefitted from a rise in interest in naval history as a repository of experience to process. This owed much to the pioneering work of Professor Sir John Knox Laughton, both for establishing the validity of naval history as a subject and for starting the process of dealing with it professionally. With this kind of help, Mahan went on to produce something like 5000 pages of text in his writing career from 1883 to 1913. Over this long period, his opinions changed, or drifted into self-contradiction. In the manner of his time, his English was mellifluous, his sentences long and complicated, his approach to the study of naval history chronological rather than thematic, with discussion and analysis sprinkled throughout in a way that made summary of his views difficult. The one book in which he sought to bring his ideas together, *Naval Strategy*, was one of his least satisfactory both to him and to his readers. For all these reasons, Mahan is very easy to misinterpret and oversimplify and has become the butt of much unjustified abuse.[27]

Essentially, Mahan built strategically on existing ideas about maritime operations, which were as we have seen largely tactical in their approach, and made some attempt to situate naval thinking in the broader context of the strategic thinking represented by the likes of Clausewitz and Jomini. To a much greater degree than is generally recognised, Mahan addressed the theory and practice of international politics.[28]

His ideas are not easy to summarise accurately, but there is little doubt that his main concern was to correct the widespread ignorance he found around him about the role and importance of seapower even amongst seafaring peoples. In peacetime, national power, security and prosperity depended on the sea as a means of transportation. In wartime, seapower resulted from naval supremacy and provided the means of attacking the enemy's trade and threatening his interests ashore whilst protecting your own. These advantages were so great that as the history of Britain in the period he studied clearly demonstrated, the sea powers would prosper in peace, prevail in war and dominate world events. He concluded: 'Control of the sea by maritime commerce and naval supremacy means predominant influence in the world ... [and] is the chief among the merely material elements in the power and prosperity of nations.'[29] Mahan was careful to say, however, that the importance of seapower can be exaggerated: it was 'but one factor in that general advance and decay of nations which is called their history'.[30]

Seapower revolved around a simple connection. Trade produces wealth that leads to maritime strength. Naval strength protects trade, and in turn depended on:

- geography (access to sea routes etc.)
- physical conformation (ports etc.)
- extent of territory
- population
- character of the people
- character of government.

Naval strength was most obviously expressed by the number of battleships you had and how effectively they were deployed against an opponent's:

> a navy which wishes to affect decisively the issues of a maritime war must be composed of heavy ships – 'battleships' – possessing a maximum of fighting power, and so similar in type as to facilitate that uniformity of movement and of evolution upon which concentration ... must depend.[31]

There was, in many of Mahan's books, a strong focus on battle between concentrations of heavy warships as the ultimate decider of naval power. The outcome of battle depended not merely on the quality of the ships present, however, but on training, morale, the effectiveness of command, tactical disposition (in particular skill in pitting all of your force against a portion of the opponent's) and above all on an offensive spirit – the desire to close and destroy. It is because of Mahan's emphasis on the destruction of the adversary's main battle force, that he is sometimes likened to Clausewitz who said much the same about the conduct of battle on land.

Before moving on to other parts of Mahan's philosophy, it is worth entering a few caveats at this stage:

- Mahan was perfectly willing to concede that battle was not always necessary. The opponent could well be so strategically cowed by superior forces that battles would be few and far between. It might well be that naval supremacy 'appears only in the background ... striking open blows at rare intervals'.[32]
- Mahan's emphasis on naval supremacy did not mean that smaller fleets were powerless:

    [I]t is not necessary to have a navy equal to the greatest, in order to insure that sense of fear which deters a rival from war, or handicaps a rival from war ... A much smaller force, favourably placed, produces an effect far beyond its proportionate numbers.[33]

- Simply relying on brute force was not enough. War is a business:

    to which actual fighting is incidental. As in all businesses, the true aim is the best results at the least cost; or, as the great French admiral, Tourville, said two centuries ago, 'The best victories are those which expend least of blood, of hemp and of iron.' Such results ... are more often granted to intelligent daring than to excessive caution.[34]

Naval supremacy conferred by such means made the commercial blockade possible; this was the only real way by which the enemy's trade could be choked off and decisive strategic effects achieved. It was one of the truest expressions of seapower and was much more likely to be effective than the alternative concepts of the *guerre de course*. A full-grown maritime trading system was much too strong to suffer vital harm through such isolated and localised attacks: 'A strong man cannot be made to quit his work by sticking pins in him.'[35]

Contrary to the claims of some of his critics, Mahan *did* deal with the effects of naval warfare on the strategic situation ashore, although it was a relationship more implied than described. In the book that more than any other made his name, the Yorktown campaign was addressed at some length. By failing to prevent the arrival of French and American reinforcements and supplies to the forces besieging a small British army at Yorktown, and by failing vigorously to contest the French Navy's control of the waters around it, the Royal Navy consigned British America to defeat; correspondingly, the French Navy exerted a decisive impact on events ashore, and maybe even changed their outcome. But apart from quoting generalised comments from both Washington and Clinton there is little real explanation of how this all worked. In large measure, it is a consequence of Mahan's failure to address the operational level of war to be discussed in section 3.7.[36]

The criticism that Mahan failed to deal with the other things that navies do, has also to be much moderated. In fact, his first book, *The Gulf and Inland Waters* (published in 1883) was about what would now be called riverine and littoral operations in the American Civil War, with something of a stress on small-ship warfare and joint operations. Mahan was clear that the north's success by a series of such campaigns in seizing New Orleans, Mobile and the Mississippi split the south and drained its war economy and generally facilitated the victory of the north. Moreover he was certainly aware of the importance of effective coastal defence. But Mahan's point was that naval supremacy was a prerequisite to all this and naval forces should not be drawn away from the central struggle for sea control in order to participate in these lesser activities. 'Seaports', he concluded, 'should defend themselves: the sphere of the fleet is on the open sea, its object offence rather than defence, its objective the enemy's shipping whenever it can be found.'[37]

The influence of Mahan on seapower

The kind of ideas that Mahan expressed caused the United States to discard its nineteenth-century emphasis on coastal defence and commerce raiding, and instead to embark on the acquisition of a first rate battlefleet eventually able to take on all comers in what the French called 'La Grande Guerre'. The extent to which thinkers like Mahan can be considered directly *responsible* for such policy shifts remains problematic but they certainly heavily affected the atmosphere of assumptions in which policy makers actually made their decisions.

Around the world other Mahans appeared, sometimes operating independently (such as Admiral Philip Colomb (1831–1899) in Britain) or consciously applying Mahanian ideas to the context of their own countries (such as Russia's Admiral Nikolai Klado). The Japanese provide a good example of the way this worked. Akilyama Saneyuki and Sato Tetsutaro were nationalists who took Mahan's ideas on board but who also looked for inspiration to other authorities in their own strategic literature and to the recent experience of their own navy in recent wars against China and Russia. France's Admiral Raoul Castex (1878–1968) in many ways followed the earlier example of compatriots Gabriel Darrieus (1859–1931) and Rene Daveluy (1863–1939) in giving Mahan a French spin, and putting his views into a wider intellectual context. His five volume series *Theories Strategiques* (1927–1935) is a comprehensive review of classical maritime theory, with more than a dash of Corbett thrown in and some quite distinctive ideas on *manoeuvre* (for which see Section 3.7).[38]

As in all intellectual movements, it is hard to discern who exactly was responsible for saying what. Differences in outlook, personality, background or national circumstance also inevitably led to differences in emphasis, but the broad thrust of a maritime strategy that focused on the struggle for naval supremacy by offensive action on the open ocean was widely accepted.

These ideas seemed confirmed by the experience of the great powers in the two world wars (although the success of the German U-boat campaign in the First World war caused some wobbles, as we shall see). Not surprisingly, therefore, the US and the British navies went into the Cold War era with a set of very 'Mahanian' attitudes and assumptions, despite the simultaneous advent of nuclear weapons. Hence the stress on the 'offensive spirit' and of moving forward in Europe's northern waters in order to contain a Soviet submarine threat that might otherwise prove fatal for NATO's plans to reinforce and resupply Western Europe across the Atlantic. In the late 1940s and much of the 1950s, these ideas resulted in the 'attack at source' posture of carrier air strikes against Soviet naval bases in northern Europe.[39]

Interestingly, their main adversary of the time, the Soviet Navy, increasingly demonstrated similar views, particularly the requirement to move its naval forces forward and to engage with the opponent aggressively. Indeed, in his 1976 book *The*

Seapower of the State, Admiral Sergei Gorshkov claimed his Tsarist predecessors had to all intents and purposes invented the concept of command of the sea. Some 20 years before Mahan, Colomb and other Western prophets of the faith, Lieu-tenant-Captain Berezin had written: 'it is necessary to gain this dominance by inflict-ing defeats ... on the hostile fleet and only then establish a blockade seeking to destroy the sea trade of the enemy and all his transport by sea'. Mahan would have had no problem in agreeing with such sentiments. Nor apparently did Gorshkov when the Soviet Navy in its prime was able to think about seriously contesting for sea control with Western navies. In the second version of his book (1979) Gorshkov devoted some 4000 words to 'Sea Dominance'. 'History', he concluded, 'does not know of a more ancient and hardier concept.' When he was charged by an American admiral with sounding very Mahanian, Admiral Gorshkov replied 'And why not? The man was eminently sensible.'[40]

The US Navy's 'The Maritime Strategy', the public version of which appeared in 1986, was an even more dramatic demonstration of the fact that the Mahanian tradi-tion was alive and well in the late twentieth century. Whether those who produced it were conscious of the details of Mahan's legacy remains problematic, but the extent to which he contributed to the atmosphere in which the strategy was put together remains beyond dispute. The purpose of 'The Maritime Strategy', as described by George Baer 'was to establish an internal consensus on the offensive value of the forward-deployed, big fleet triphibious Navy and, with Mahan's admonitions ever present, to engage public as well as professional support'.[41]

'The Maritime Strategy' (soon in effect to be accepted as NATO's Concept of Maritime Operations (CONMAROPS)) was an unashamedly offensive plan to seize the initiative by taking on the Soviet Fleet in Europe's northern waters and the North West Pacific, thereby providing the conditions for the most effective defence of NATO's sea lines of communication (SLOCs) across the Atlantic, strikes on the opponent's home territory and the support of forward allies like Norway, South Korea and Japan.

Amongst the many criticisms levelled against 'The Maritime Strategy' (also dis-cussed in Section 6.5) was that it envisaged an independent maritime campaign that had precious little to do with the grim air/land war realities of the European Central Front and that it would jeopardise the humdrum business of the direct defence of NATO's SLOCs. In this it was held by its critics to echo Mahan's obsessive concen-tration on the offensive pursuit of battle at the cost of everything else.[42]

But this was unfair. One of the principal justifications for 'The Maritime Strategy' was to improve the 'correlation of forces' on the central front, by posing an out-flanking threat to the north and threatening the Soviet Union's all-important ballis-tic missile submarines. It might not have worked, but that was certainly the intent. In similar manner, the US Navy's leaders held that maritime forces of the sort needed for a campaign of this sort would also be able to protect a wide range of American interests around the world, in rather more peaceful times.

In this too, the US Navy was echoing an element in Mahan's original philosophy that is often overlooked by his detractors, who generally tend to focus their atten-tion on his thoughts on battle and naval supremacy, almost to the exclusion of everything else. As Jon Sumida has recently shown, however, Mahan was also con-cerned with wider and broader aspects of maritime power in which its function was to defend the international trading system on which the world's peace and prosperity

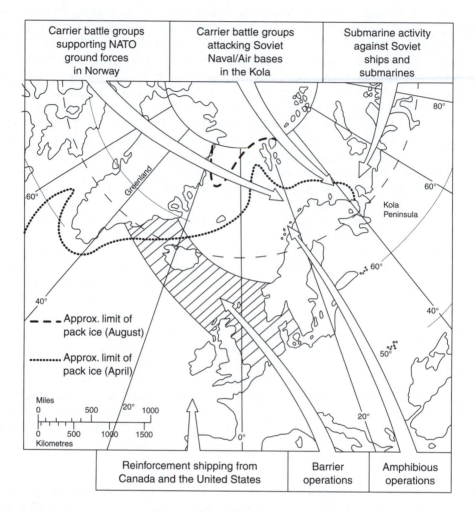

Figure 3.4 The Maritime Strategy.

seemed to depend. Arguably, and as we shall see in Chapter 11, he even anticipated a situation in which this protective function would need to be exercised by a trans-national coalition, because the peoples of democratic countries like Britain and the United States would never be willing to provide their navies with enough resources to perform the task on their own.[43]

In this way too, it would seem that despite its obvious bluewater preoccupations, the Mahanian tradition, fully understood, retains a good deal of contemporary relevance for the twenty-first century.

3.5 Corbett and the maritime tradition

Sir Julian Corbett (1854–1922) came late to maritime affairs and associated with the great men ushering the Royal Navy painfully into the twentieth century. Deeply concerned about the poverty of contemporary naval thought, he sought to improve it, partly through lectures at the Naval War Colleges at Greenwich and Portsmouth. Evidently he did not enjoy the experience, complaining in one letter, 'My strategy lectures are very uphill work. I had no idea when I undertook it how difficult it was to present theory to the unused organs of naval officers.'[44] His teaching was supported by an impressive list of naval histories, including several on the Tudor and post-Tudor Royal Navy, a masterpiece on the Seven Years War, a two-volume work on maritime warfare in the Mediterranean, a staff history of the Russo-Japanese War, *Some Principles of Maritime Strategy* in 1911 and the first three volumes of the official naval history of the First World War.

Paradoxically, Corbett did most of his writing in that particularly interesting period just before the First World War, when Britain was actually moving away from the kind of strategy that he advocated.

Corbett on the value of theory

From the start, Corbett was interested in uncovering the principles that lay beneath the conduct of maritime operations. One of his earliest works was a study of the evolution of the Royal Navy's 'Fighting Instructions'. At Greenwich, and elsewhere, he successfully challenged the all too common preconception that lessons deduced from the age of sail were irrelevant to the concerns of the naval officers of the machine age. As Eric Grove has justly observed, Corbett's defence rested on the way in which he defined such lessons and principles.

> Corbett did not claim that historical study would produce detailed rules for the future conduct of battles and campaigns. Its value lay in bringing to light the permanent characteristics of sea power and the specific nature of its contribution to national strategy; what it could achieve and what were its limitations. Equipped with these insights, the contemporary naval commander would have a pattern of past experience, what had succeeded, what had failed, against which to assess his present situation and desirable course of action.[45]

Corbett's approach to this problem can be seen in his treatment of Drake. On the one hand he lamented the fact that 'in the Elizabethan age, the principles of naval warfare were as little understood as its limitations', and applauded the efforts of such as John Montgomery to produce a set of ideas in 1570 'so sound and so strikingly modern in its ring'. On the other hand, he admired Drake for his readiness, when applying such principles constructively 'to break rules'. Corbett clearly took the principles of war to be a guide to thought rather than directives for action.[46]

Corbett on seapower and policy

As a lawyer, Corbett had a more judicious sense than Mahan of the limitations of sea power, and quite crucially therefore, of its place in the wider scheme of things. What is special about Corbett is his emphasis on the importance of putting naval operations in that broader context which does so much to explain their form and purpose, and which, in his view, was affected so much by their result.

Corbett emphasised that strategy needs to be consciously related to foreign policy. Having digested his Clausewitz, Corbett was well aware of the fact that war was a political act and that the first function of the fleet was 'to support or obstruct diplomatic effort'. He took an overtly *political* approach to seapower; maritime strategy should serve the interests of the state, and in war and peace the type of strategy a navy adopted should reflect national objectives. Corbett was particularly interested in *limited* maritime wars, which were more political than most, but allowed a country's rulers carefully to weigh the costs of war in order to compare them with the benefits. Because maritime operations were more controllable in the sense of being less prone to ruinous escalation they were often particularly cost-effective when compared to ordinary, messy land operations.[47]

Nonetheless, and perhaps not unnaturally given his more adversarial age, the focus of most of his writing was on the directly military characteristics of seapower. His preoccupation was with war, not peace – although he was always anxious to demonstrate the connections between the objectives of war and its form. Chapter 9 shows that it was left to analysts of a much later generation to explore the characteristics of what has since become known as naval diplomacy.

Corbett on the maritime approach

Naval strategy has to be related to land strategy:

> Of late years the world has become so deeply impressed with the efficacy of sea power that we are inclined to forget how impotent it is of itself to decide a war against great Continental states, how tedious is the pressure of naval action unless it be nicely coordinated with military and diplomatic pressure.[48]

Naval strategy has to be seen not as a separate entity but simply as part of the art of war. Landpower and seapower are *not* in opposition, but their relationship with one another will be different for 'world wide imperial states, where the sea becomes a direct and vital factor' from those for whom geography makes the 'German or Continental School of strategy' more appropriate. Britain of course was pre-eminently just such a maritime state and had derived enormous benefit from developing a set of principles governing the conduct of war 'in which the sea is a substantial factor'. But this certainly should not mean the British neglecting the use of armies:

> Since men live upon the land and not upon the sea, great issues between nations at war have always been decided – except in the rarest cases – either by what your army can do against your enemy's territory and national life or else by the fear of what the fleet makes it possible for your army to do.[49]

Sea powers could not defeat land powers on their own but, in conjunction with allies on land, they could determine the outcomes of wars and the nature of the peace.

Britain, he thought, had developed a style of maritime war that combined naval and military power in a uniquely beneficial way. It had allowed the British to 'become a controlling force in the European system' and to maintain and extend their interests by manipulating the balance of power in continental Europe. This they had done by the controlled and careful application of maritime power in peace and in war. Because the secret of British success lay in the combination of land and seapower, Corbett used the word 'maritime' when he reviewed the strategy of seapower rather than the much narrower term 'naval' that Mahan tended to use.[50]

This is a significant difference between the two. As far as Corbett was concerned, naval strategy was about the disposition, movement and immediate purposes of the fleet; this cascaded down from maritime strategy that decided the role of the fleet in relation to land forces. Accordingly, the exact balance to be struck between the naval and the land components of a maritime strategy would depend on general national circumstances (for some nations were clearly more maritime than others) and also on the particular strategic exigencies of the moment. Corbett was at his most interesting on this point when dealing with the Russo-Japanese war. This was a struggle involving one very maritime power, Japan, for the possession of a very maritime prize, namely the peninsula of Korea. Not surprisingly, therefore, the naval element of Japan's strategy would in many cases predominate in a situation in which 'everything turned on the sea factor'. He approved of the way in which the Japanese evolved a joint staff, the detailed mechanics of which rested on this conclusion. He also pointed out that operational priorities between naval and military requirements in what was essentially an amphibious war often had to give precedence to the naval dimension even if this caused tensions with the army.[51]

Nonetheless, Corbett did not neglect the legitimate demands of the land war, even in a maritime environment. Given the circumstances, he thought, 'it is obvious that a war framed on these lines demands a very accurate co-ordination of the land and sea forces. This is, indeed, the paramount necessity'. Once the Japanese Fleet had concentrated:

> the movement of the two services goes hand in hand and our standpoint must be one from which the operations both on land and at sea can be kept in view as closely and clearly as possible. The war, in fact becomes essentially amphibious, and so intimately are naval and military operations knit together in a single theatre that the work of the one service is unintelligible apart from that of the other.[52]

Equally obviously, in less maritime conflicts, the land element could be expected to predominate, but in this case, the naval element might need to be defended.

Corbett argued that navies should accommodate themselves to the simple fact that in the last analysis it was upon the land that mankind's destiny was decided. Some have taken this argument further, to raise doubts about whether the whole idea of having a 'naval strategy' actually makes sense in that, by definition, naval objectives can therefore rarely be strategic. This view was espoused by the Soviet general staff in the Cold war era. It also underlies an interesting conclusion reached by the US Navy's Captain Wayne Hughes: 'there is no *naval* strategic warfare … A maritime campaign by a maritime nation aims at sea control as the means not end, because strategy prescribes wartime goals and missions governed by purposes on the land.'[53] Corbett did not go as far as this, for two reasons. First, some naval activities could have strategic consequence for events ashore (the launching of major amphibious operations, a commercial blockade). Second, navies could be at their most strategic in the *limited* wars and expeditions for which they were ideally suited.

Corbett on limiting liability and increasing cost-effectiveness

One of the great advantages of seapower as an arm of national strategy, Corbett thought, was its particular utility in situations of limited conflict. Where the protagonists were not neighbours, where distance made retaliation difficult and where geography helped isolate or at least contain the extent of any fighting, any conflict could be limited. The nation with command of the sea was in the best position to choose how much or how little of the conflict it wanted. Maritime powers could limit their liability in ways that others could not.[54]

Corbett's was a strategic approach that limited liability if things went wrong, for as Sir Francis Bacon remarked:

> this much is certain, that he that commands the sea is at great liberty, and may take as much and as little of the war as he will. Whereas those that be strongest by land are many times nevertheless in great straits.[55]

Power at sea provided opportunities for the British to make limited interventions for limited objectives in unlimited wars. Through this capacity to exert influence on the continent of Europe from outside, the British, unlike many of their more land-bound competitors, had been able to develop a uniquely business-like approach to the otherwise messy and wasteful processes of war. They generally tried to avoid expensive large-scale military commitments to the continent of Europe, and its ferocious wars. Instead, the British had done their best to limit their involvement to the financial support of continental allies and to the exertion of maritime pressure (through blockade, the threat of amphibious landings, attacks and raids on threatened coastlines and through the seizure of their adversaries' far-flung colonies and bases).

Accordingly, the maritime strategy that Corbett advocated required the kind of army that could work with the navy to conquer overseas territories and to outflank land bound adversaries with amphibious operations, 'more or less upon the European seaboard designed, not for permanent conquest, but as a method of disturbing our enemy's plans and strengthening the hands of our allies and our own position'.[56] This was, Corbett thought, as we saw in Section 2.2, an immensely cost-effective approach to the business of war. Command of the sea, and the opportunities it provided, explained how it was after all, 'That a small country [Britain] with a weak army should have been able to gather to herself the most desirable regions of the earth, and to gather them at the expense of the greatest military Powers.'[57]

Corbett on command of the sea and decisive battle

While command of the sea was ideally won or maintained by decisive battle, this was often not easily or quickly achieved against a reluctant enemy; in such cases, a blockade could be imposed either to neutralise that enemy or to force him to battle. High levels of such command greatly facilitated the strategic use of the sea, but were not always possible and sometimes were not necessary.

Command of the sea implied its control as a medium of communication; the enemy's commercial and military shipping could be attacked, and yours protected. Your military forces could be moved about in safety and his attacked.

The obvious method of achieving command of the sea was to *force* a battle on the enemy's naval forces, destroy them and decide the matter once and for all. The Royal Navy was always attracted by the notion of the decisive battle as the optimum means of winning command of the sea. Their view just before the First World War was usefully summarised for the benefit of the 1902 Colonial Conference:

> The primary object of the British navy is not to defend anything, but to attack the fleets of the enemy, and by defeating them to afford protection to British Dominions, supplies and commerce. This is the ultimate aim ... The traditional role of the Royal Navy is not to act on the defensive, but to prepare to attack the force which threatens – in other words to assume the offensive.[58]

But Corbett warned that this 'old British creed', although generally admirable and effective, could be taken to excess. In some circumstances, it could lead to a distraction from the real aim of the war. He also pointed out that Britain's adversaries, whose naval forces were normally weaker, often sensibly sought to avoid battle with the Royal Navy. This being so, the British needed to be on their guard against the danger of trying too hard in this direction, lest such purist aspirations undermine their practical capacity to use the sea as fully as they often needed to in the meantime.[59]

Although in order to avoid the men with blue pencils, Corbett's account of the Battle of Jutland was a subtle matter of nuance, some members of the Board who read the draft, did not like it, even if they did not quite know why and had inserted in the final volume a note to the effect that, 'Their Lordships find that some of the principles advocated in the book, especially the tendency to minimise the importance of seeking battle and of forcing it to a conclusion, are directly in conflict with their views.'[60] Afterwards, this 'sea heresy' continued to be attacked. An anonymous contributor to the *Naval Review* of 1931 said of Corbett that:

> He had a legal training and mind, which was shown in his preference for getting the better of the enemy in some other way than coming to blows ... his teaching did not preach that to destroy or to neutralise the enemy's armed force was the primary military aim leading to a military decision. As an example one may look at his 'Principles of Maritime Strategy' and see, out of 310 pages, how many are devoted to 'Battle.' ... Is it too much to say that Lord Fisher's Baltic Scheme, Mr Churchill's naval Brigade, even the Dardanelles Expedition, were instances of 'ill digested Julian Corbett's "Seven Years War" '?[61]

This shows that it was where Corbett most irritated his naval audiences that he should have done them the greatest good. Over and over again, Corbett sought to remind sailors that command of the sea should not be seen as an end in itself, and that it was a relative concept. Absolute command of the sea was little more than an ideal; high levels of command of the sea were extremely difficult to achieve – and to a surprising extent unnecessary. Even in a profoundly maritime war, all sorts of useful military manoeuvres could be conducted without it. In 1903, the Russians decided 'they could succeed without getting the command. By merely keeping it in dispute they would gain time enough to bring their vastly superior military strength to bear.' It was equally proper for the Japanese to conclude that in such circumstances they could conduct amphibious operations without securing command of the sea first.[62]

It is important, however, not to exaggerate the extent of Corbett's scepticism about 'command of the sea' and 'decisive battle'. He acknowledged that the concerted pursuit of these two central objectives of 'Mahanian' maritime strategy was usually valid. It was only his willingness to say that sometimes it might not be that got him into trouble with the Admiralty.[63]

Corbett was concerned about the unremitting pursuit of command-through-battle for four reasons. First, it might well prove nugatory in those all-too-common situations where a weaker adversary declined the invitation to his own execution. Second, it might not work for good operational reasons. Third, concentrating on the rigorous requirements of securing command could easily damage a navy's capacity to exploit that command (or the lack of it), particularly through amphibious operations, but also through campaigns against, or in defence of, shipping. Command of the sea in itself did not win wars or decide political outcomes, but being able to exploit (or sometimes deny) that command very well might.[64]

Fourth, and perhaps most importantly, the pursuit of the decisive battle could so easily make it difficult for sailors and others to see what seapower was really about. Thus:

> We require for the guidance of our naval policy and naval action something of wider vision than the current conception of naval strategy, something that will keep before our eyes not merely the enemy's fleets or the great routes of commerce, or the command of the sea, but also the relations of naval policy and action to the whole area of diplomatic and military effort.[65]

All too often, he thought, the simple-minded (in uniform and out of it) confused the incidence of dramatic battle with the role and importance of seapower. They were not the same thing at all.

Corbett on amphibious operations

With command of the sea you could use the sea as a means of transportation, both commercial (to supply the war economy) and military (to facilitate the projection of power ashore).

Based on evidence such as the capture of Havana in 1762, Wolfe's Canadian operations in the Seven Years War, Wellington's Peninsula Campaign – surely the quintessential Combined Operation – and the Crimean War, Corbett agued that properly conducted amphibious operations could indeed be the means by which sea powers could help decide the outcome of wars. Maritime supremacy allowed them to strike at their enemies' weakest points.

Critics responded at two levels, then and since. First, amphibious operations rarely proved as strategically decisive as Corbett claimed. Second, modern technology was making them too difficult anyway.

On the first point, Corbett stuck to his guns. His basic proposition about the disastrous Gallipoli campaign of 1915 for instance, but more generally too, was that 'the continental method' of striking decisively 'where the enemy's military concentration was highest' only made sense where there was 'sufficient preponderance of force to ensure a decision'. In his view this was not the situation on the Western Front, and it was therefore best to 'postpone offence in the main theatre and devote our combined energies' to improving the strategic balance by striking elsewhere.[66]

On the second point, Corbett responded that even the Gallipoli campaign showed such operational challenges could be overcome. The Suvla landings of August were a distinct improvement on the Helles and Anzac landings of April. Moreover, the withdrawal in December 1915 and the following January of 120,000 troops from under the noses of the Turks, was a splendid indication of the level of improvement achieved in all aspects of amphibious warfare:

> In that marvellous evacuation we see the national genius for amphibious warfare raised to its highest manifestation. In hard experience and successive disappointments, the weapon had been brought to a perfect temper, and when the hour of fruition came to show of what great things it was capable, it was used only to effect a retreat.[67]

Disciples and fellow travellers

Corbett no more wrote in a vacuum than did Mahan.[68] Many commentators have pointed out where he was being Clausewitzian (keeping naval strategy alongside its political purposes) and where he was not (doubts about the centrality of battle). Others have likened Corbett's approach to the clever manoeuvrism of Sun Tzu with his emphasis on winning most at least cost, and on the notion of deceptive concentration that will be looked at later.

More immediately, there were others writing on related topics at much the same time, most obviously Major General Sir Charles Callwell (1859–1928). Callwell went on eventually to become Director of Military Operations at the British War Office, but was also a prolific author. Amongst the most significant of his works are: *Small Wars: Their Principles and Practice* (1896), *The Effect of Maritime Command on Land Campaigns since Waterloo* (1897), *Military Operations and Maritime Preponderance* (1905) and *The Dardanelles* (1924). Of these the first is by far the most original but its main thrust is different from the other three and is discussed later in Section 8.1. The central tenets of Callwell's approach can be found in the second and third of these works, and an analysis of their practical application in the last. The most superficial skim through these works shows that Callwell provides an exact fit with Corbett over the core issue of the way in which sea and landpower should be mutually supportive in a properly constructed maritime strategy. Like Corbett, Callwell pointed to the American War of Independence, the Crimean Campaign of 1856 and the Russo-Japanese war of 1905 as demonstrating the extent to which land campaigns may depend on command of the sea. In the many cases where the military balance ashore depended on reinforcements and supplies coming across the sea, maritime preponderance was essential. But, rather more explicitly than did Corbett, Callwell paid equal attention to the help that land forces could offer navies, especially by conducting territorial operations against coaling-station bases where an inferior and blockaded fleet had taken refuge. Over and over again, Callwell emphasised how important it was for sea and land forces to cooperate effectively, and if air forces had existed at the time, he like Corbett would undoubtedly have included them too:

It has been the purpose of this volume to show how naval preponderance and warfare on land are mutually dependent, if the one is to assert itself conclusively and if the other is to be carried out with vigour and effect. There is an intimate connection between command of the sea and control of the shore. But if the strategical principles involved in this connection are to be put in force to their full extent, if the whole of the machinery is to be set in motion, there must be co-ordination of authority and there must be harmony in the council chambers and in the theatre of operations ... 'United we stand, divided we fall', is a motto singularly applicable to the navy and army of a maritime nation and of a world-wide empire.[69]

As an army man, Callwell paid more attention to the *conduct* of amphibious operations than did Corbett. This was not, of course, entirely new. Back in 1759, at the height of the Seven Years War, which seemed so clearly to demonstrate the advantages of the amphibious approach, Thomas More Molyneux an officer of the Royal Navy wrote the pioneering *Conjunct Expeditions or Expeditions That Have Been Carried on Jointly by the Fleet and Army, with a Commentary on a Littoral War.* While Molyneux's bottom line – 'The Fleet and Army, acting in consort, seem to be the natural Bulwark of these Kingdoms' – is very familiar and often quoted (nearly always, wrongly), the rest of this book with its exploration of optimum command arrangements, the advantages of tactical if not strategic surprise, the value of deceptions and feints, the conduct of the landing operation, is largely forgotten these days.[70]

The same fate awaited a number of other books on amphibious operations written in Callwell's time, most obviously Colonel George Furse's *Military Expeditions Beyond the Seas* (1897) and *Letters on Amphibious Wars* (1911) by the Royal Marine, George Aston (1861–1938). Aston also wrote *Sea, Land and Air Strategy* (1914), which was certainly amongst the first to seek to fold airpower into the equation.

This sudden explosion of interest in the conduct of amphibious operations reflected the current strategic debate in Britain as to whether its armed forces should prepare for a continental-style strategy of large-scale involvement in land war on the European mainland or an eighteenth-century type of maritime war of limited continental engagement but an unremitting global sea-based offensive against the enemy's outlying possessions and vulnerabilities.

Admiral Sir Jacky Fisher was in no doubt as to where the balance should be struck and in his *Memories* recalled pacing the sands of Scheveningen with Germany's General Gross von Schwartshoff in June 1899, the latter complaining about the way in which

the absolute supremacy of the British navy gave it such inordinate power far beyond its numerical strength, because 200,000 men embarked in transports, and God only knowing where they might be put ashore, was a weapon of enormous influence and capable of deadly blows.

Animated by such observations, Fisher was quite clear that the army should indeed remain a projectile to be fired by the navy, optimised for coastal military expeditions, and so was always on his guard against the insidious incrementalism of the continentalists – ineffectually as things turned out.[71]

To many, the gruesome experience on the Western Front during the First World War merely confirmed the advantages of a maritime power avoiding this approach to war if it possibly could. Admiral Sir Herbert Richmond (1871–1946), practitioner and naval historian, was certainly so persuaded. Like Corbett, Richmond wanted the Royal Navy to move on from its obsession with battle, to concentrate on securing its sea lines of communication, to prepare for expeditions against the exposed interests of any adversary and to integrate the navy's contribution to national strategy effectively with that of the other two services. Such was also the aspiration of Sir Basil Liddell Hart, another of Richmond's colleagues.[72]

Based on his understanding of 400 years of British history, Liddell Hart produced the concept of 'The British Way in Warfare', which synthesised the work of Corbett, Callwell, Aston and Richmond in an approach to strategy that emphasised:

- the importance of securing command of the sea;
- the effectiveness of sea-based economic pressure;
- the need to avoid continental commitments while securing the aid of allied land-powers;
- generous expenditure on the navy;
- focusing on maritime areas of operation;
- developing synergy between the army and the navy;
- the value of expeditionary operations;
- limited and modest objectives;
- the need to project power ashore.

Although the British had not always followed their own rules in this matter (particularly in spending money on the navy) Liddell Hart concluded that by such means a maritime power like Britain could defeat a continental adversary while avoiding a direct confrontation on the European mainland. It was an example of the 'Indirect Approach' for which he has become famous.

Questions of validity and applicability

Not everyone has been impressed by 'the British Way in Warfare', however. Some doubt the strategic effectiveness of maritime pressure through blockade on a continental power with access to the resources of extensive territory. Others point to the difficulties of amphibious operations on the periphery and wonder about their real impact on the correlation of forces in the centre. And there is also the obvious point that the approach's manifest deficiencies have several times led to Britain taking a leading role in warfare *on* the continent of Europe as well as around it.

A second line of criticism is the 'Britishness' of this school of strategy and the perfectly valid question of how applicable all this is to any other country, (apart that is from Japan and one or two other such island nations) – even if it is true.[73]

Admiral Raoul Castex (1878–1968), was given to making constant references to Mahan, and was sometimes quite rude about Corbett and Richmond, but, for all that, his biographer concludes that he was a secret follower of the Corbett line, perhaps without realising it. One of the most telling illustrations of this coincidence of view is Castex's very French and almost untranslateable notion of 'manoeuvre' – the capacity to move (or act) intelligently in order to create a favourable situation.

This was the thinking behind the 'ulterior objectives' of the French Navy in the eight-eenth century of which Mahan was so dismissive. It was a clever 'approach' to strategy making where the emphasis was not on direct confrontation with the enemy's main forces. Instead, Castex advocated an approach that made the most cost-effective use of forces and was especially useful when those forces could not dominate by sheer weight of number, and indeed might be inferior to those of the adversary.[74]

The British engaged in their maritime strategy because they knew themselves to be weaker than their adversary in continental landpower. Similarly, any weaker power should surely be attracted by at least some aspect of a strategic approach that seeks to maximise the effectiveness of inferior forces, in the presence of stronger ones. Abstract theories of seapower have to be put into effect in the real world of national strategy to the extent and in the manner that the security environment in which that country operates will allow. The precise mix between the Mahanian line and the Corbettian line (to the extent that they can be separated) therefore depends on strategic circumstances, but to some degree or other, all such approaches will be 'relevant' to most countries with navies.

* * *

During the 1990s, the Royal Navy busied itself with writing up and rewriting its thinking about what navies do, why they do it and how they do it. This thinking appeared as *The Fundamentals of British Maritime Doctrine BR 1806* (1995) and more simply in a revised version as *British Maritime Doctrine BR 1806* (1999) with a third edition appear-ing in 2004.[75] These very successful, compact but well-rounded doctrinal statements were a confident restatement of the importance of navies in the post Cold War era:

> The potential and relevance of maritime power in today's world is as great as ever. Maritime forces operate in an environment that allows them access to most potential crisis areas of concern to the UK and our allies. Maritime forces are mobile, versatile and resilient, and can contribute sustained reach and lift capacity to a joint campaign or operation. Their ability to poise makes them powerful tools of diplomacy, and a capacity for leverage particularly in the context of expeditionary operations is of greater importance than ever in today's world of risks and uncertainties.[76]

Although these doctrinal formulations rehearsed the classic 'concepts governing the use of maritime power' in ways that would have been perfectly acceptable to Mahan, the emphasis was essentially Corbettian in the

- stress on manoeuvre not attrition;
- focus on the conduct of expeditionary operations;
- joint approach;
- insistence that doctrine should not degenerate into dogma: 'This book … should be treated with respect as an authoritative publication but not worshipped as holy writ … Nelson would not have done so and neither should those who follow in his footsteps.'[77]

Both publications, however, moved on from Corbett in the attention they paid to maritime operations other than war (MOOTW) particularly peace support operations, naval diplomacy and constabulary functions. They also reflect the focus on the operational level of war and on the tools of campaign planning to be discussed next (Section 3.6). Nonetheless, their intellectual core remains Corbettian. There is quite a strong 'definitional' streak to both publications in which the emphasis is on the 'what is' of maritime strategy rather than the 'how to'. Since then the Royal Navy has moved into a series of papers exploring in more detail how these concepts should be implemented.

More generally, the British set a standard in doctrinal formulation that others have responded to. One of the most interesting such responses is *Australian Maritime Doctrine*, which appeared in 2000. Similar in approach to, and obviously influenced by, British doctrinal formulations it covers much the same ground, but of course gives it an Australian spin reflecting their own particular national context. There is rather more emphasis on sea control, MOOTW (including more than a nod towards environmental concerns), rather less on expeditionary operations. The following passage, however, nicely illustrates the point made earlier about the need for nations to strike their own balance between Mahanian and Corbettian lines of thought:

> Our region includes a large number of nations with significant maritime and air capability and it would be extremely unwise to make the assumption that the preconditions for sea control will exist whatever the strategic situation. Thus, while we may adopt and benefit from much of the work being done in the United States and Europe, it will be necessary for Australia to maintain in the immediate future a greater focus on fundamental issues such as sea control – including control of the air – at the same time as we seek to increase our ability to directly influence events on land.[78]

Interestingly, the US Navy has been much less ambitious in its approach to doctrinal formulation, while being much more ambitious, of course, in the size and power of its forces.[79] The 'Forward From the Sea' family of concepts developed by the US Navy through the 1990s are more 'position papers' than statements of doctrine but, in their modest way, they too reflect the same kind of aspirations and concerns. With the end of the rivalry between the navies of NATO and the Warsaw Pact in the struggle to command and use the sea:

> There was no point in continuing to express sea power in terms of the Mahanian dicta of autonomy and decisive fleet engagement, no point in refusing to let go of the doctrine that navies existed to fight navies ... In 1992, the US Navy after one hundred years, closed its book on sea power doctrine in the image of Mahan. For how long remained to be seen.[80]

With the publication of 'From the Sea' (1992) and 'Forward ... From the Sea' (1994) the navy's preoccupation shifted from sea control to land control. 'Naval Strategy', declared Jan Breemer dramatically, 'is dead.' This did not mean that sea control ceased to matter; it meant only that the US Navy and its allies would now be able to switch their attention to its reward, the capacity to project power ashore, especially in the world's troubled littorals. In fact many of these ideas had been prefigured in 1954 by Samuel Huntington in a famous article likewise produced at a time when

Westerners assumed that sea control was almost a given, and could immediately proceed to its exploitation.[81]

'Forward ... From the Sea' described that exploitation like this:

> Naval forces maneuver from the sea using their dominance of littoral areas to mass forces rapidly and generate high-intensity, precise offensive power at the time and location of their choosing, under any weather conditions, day or night. Power projection requires mobility, flexibility and technology to mass strength against weakness.[82]

The words may not be Corbett's, but the concepts are.

3.6 Alternative visions in maritime strategy

Writers and sailors in particular countries at particular times have naturally tended as we have seen to give their own 'spin' on ideas on the roles of navies and on how they might be used. Generally, they accept and operate within the broad conceptual parameters of maritime strategy. Sometimes, though, there emerge more radical alternatives to the mainstream focus on sea control, defence of trade and the projection of power ashore.

War on commerce/guerre de course *theory*

One such school was the French *Jeune Ecole* of the nineteenth century. The immediate intellectual origin of this movement was Baron Richard Grivel's *De La Guerre Maritime* (1869). Grivel contended that the classical approaches of maritime strategy were inappropriate measures for France to take against Britain. Instead: 'Commercial war, the most economical for the poorest fleet, is at the same time the one most proper to restore peace, since it strikes directly at the very source of the prosperity of the enemy.' These ideals were expanded and publicised from 1874 onwards by Admiral Theophile Aube and the journalist Gabriel Charmes, amongst others. Their infuence peaked in 1886 when Admiral Aube became Minister of Marine. He immediately suspended France's battleship construction programme, built a naval base at Bizerta, boosted France's research and development efforts in submarines and began building cruisers and torpedo boats at a high rate. For a short space of a year and a half, the dream came true – the philosopher was king; ideas could really be put into practice.[83]

These ideas were, however, by no means wholly new, especially in France. In 1706 Marshal Vauban, for example, concluded:

> If we were to be quit of the vanity of great fleets which can never suit our needs and to employ the ships of the navy partly on commerce warfare and partly in squadrons to support it, we should bring about the downfall of the English and the Dutch within about two or three years, in consequence of their great trade to all parts of the world.[84]

Moreover, practice seemed to suggest that there was substance in such theories. The French campaign against British commerce in the wars of Louis XIV, and the Revolutionary and Napoleonic wars showed that this was an effective means of attacking the adversary's vital interest – especially for a weaker fleet. The more recent American Civil War did the same on a smaller scale.

Moreover, in the last quarter of the nineteenth century, technology appeared finally to confirm the promise of this approach. Torpedoes, mines, submarines, all seemed to make the major surface warship more vulnerable, and so to herald the end of the kind of maritime strategy that was based on big ships.

If battleships really were this vulnerable, would the whole concept of command of the sea not need to be rethought? The British Navy would no longer be able to blockade the French into their harbours. Strong enemy naval forces would be so concerned with their own security that their offensive potentiality would be much reduced, while that of the smaller ships would be correspondingly increased. Admiral Aube planned to use torpedo boats against British ports, anchored merchant shipping and blockading squadrons in local waters. Cruisers would prey upon commerce on the great trade routes. A few coastal defence ships would protect the homeland.

Admiral Aube brushed aside the problem that the 1856 Declaration of Paris had made attacking merchant ships illegal, and so politically hazardous. He expected his torpedo boats to 'send to the bottom, cargo, crew, and passengers not only without remorse but proud of the achievement. In every part of the ocean similar atrocities will be seen.' The ends justified the means, and the advantage of such barbarous proceedings would outweigh all scruples.[85]

It is important to note, however, that the *Jeune Ecole* did not expect to achieve its aim by starving Britain into submission. Instead such a campaign would aim to cause panic, a crisis in marine insurance and generally disturb the intricate patterns of British trade. It would strike directly at the shipping interests, the trades people and manufacturers who were the real masters of Britain. Their sufferings would force the government into peace. What the *Jeune Ecole* in fact advocated was a kind of asymmetric warfare.

The parade of such views caused considerable controversy in France for nearly 20 years. Naval policy oscillated wildly as Ministers of Marine came and went (there were 31 between 1871 and 1902) and the whole era was one of much confusion. Other countries were affected too, and people with similar ideas appeared elsewhere, especially in Germany, Austria and Russia, and, at the height of the craze, it damaged battleship construction programmes around Europe. The British, the chief targets of such thinking, were more worried about these ideas than they cared to admit.

Gradually, however, the influence of the *Jeune Ecole* began to wane, and the idea of a war on commerce slowly dropped out of favour, even in France. Amongst the reasons for this were:

- Enmity with Britain was the initial stimulus for the *Jeune Ecole* major incentive in the French Navy, but circumstances changed and the British and French became allies.
- The technological assumptions on which the case rested looked increasingly suspect. In particular the extreme threat of torpedo boat attack on a blockading fleet at night was considered more containable than had been thought. Wireless telegraphy made fleets more controllable and so less vulnerable. A class of small

fast vessels was developed, whose task was to defend the fleet against such attacks – torpedo boat destroyers (increasingly only the latter word was used) and modern ship design made large ships somewhat less vulnerable to torpedo attack.

- A war on commerce was better conducted by a superior conventional fleet. Was it not true, asked one ex-Minister of Marine, J.L. de Lanessan, that a successful war on commerce required at least a degree of command of the sea, and so needed the ships and doctrines best suited to contesting it? 'The only times when it [corsair warfare] was really effective against our own enemies', he wrote, 'was when our fleets were sufficiently strong to be able to dispute with our foes the mastery of the Channel or Mediterranean.' The success of Confederate commerce raiders in the American Civil War was often used as evidence for the *Jeune Ecole*, but had not the northern commercial blockade, based on naval mastery, strangled trade while southern corsairs like the *Alabama* merely harassed it?[86]

- Because of its possible effects on neutral opinion, a campaign against merchant shipping needed to be conducted with considerable restraint and this would limit its operational effectiveness.

- The kind of navy proposed by the *Jeune Ecole* would not be suited for any other type of naval operation. It would not help France extend or defend its empire, protect its coast against invasion or prosecute an offensive war against powers less dependent on overseas trade than the British. For that, more orthodox conceptions of maritime strategy seemed to be needed.

The proposals offered by the *Jeune Ecole* were obviously not the solution to all problems but were nonetheless a bold and novel attempt to solve the historic problem of how best to use a self-evidently inferior navy against a predominant maritime power. Because many countries have found themselves in a similar situation, these ideas have had considerable appeal at various times. They were indeed revived 40 years or so later after the great success of the German U-boat campaign against British commerce during the First World War. Some German writers concluded afterwards that their attempt to construct a conventional fleet for what the French called 'La Grande Guerre' had been a pointless waste of time and resources.

Instead, why not abandon pursuit of command of the sea altogether – especially as this was a contest that Germany with all her territorial preoccupations could not hope to win? Why not rebuild the German Navy for a new war on commerce, rather than on the traditional lines that had so signally failed her in the past? In future, wrote one German admiral, the less one has to reckon with the clash of large battle-fleets, as at Jutland in 1916, 'the more trade warfare is going to become the main operative task of the strategy of naval war'. Writers like Captain von Waldeyer-Hartz and Ernst Wilhelm Rinse argued that trade warfare should no longer be a subsidiary operation, but the main area of activity. The enemy's command of the sea should be accepted, his surface units avoided and his merchant shipping whole-heartedly attacked, by heavy surface ships, cruisers, submarines and aircraft. 'Trade warfare', wrote Waldeyer-Hartz, 'will be the dominant form of the naval warfare of tomorrow.'[87]

These ideas did not win wide currency within the German Navy until the very eve of the Second World War, partly because the Germans were not generally anticipating another war against the British, partly through an acute sense of the politico-strategic implications of a war on commerce (which had, after all, brought the Americans into the war against them in 1917) and partly through a sense that traditional procedures such as convoy-and-escort and new technology in the shape of ASDIC (an early form of sonar) had shown the war on commerce, even by submarine, to be containable.

Nonetheless, as we shall see in Chapter 7, the notion of maritime operations with a focus on attacking trade continues to be of interest.

Coastal defence theory

Coastal defence has been another rather different emphasis in the development of thinking about maritime operations. Again, it has tended to be of particular interest to weaker and smaller navies. In the United States of the nineteenth century, for example, it found expression in the construction of a chain of coastal fortifications along their eastern seaboard, in the development of minefields and the construction of small warships maximised for coastal operation.

Mahan was perfectly content that the static coastal defence element of sea warfare complemented its mobile and offensive element, 'one possessing what the other has not; and that the difference is fundamental, essential, unchangeable – not accidental or temporary'. If anything, with the impact of the new technology of the industrial age, this interest grew in the United States and elsewhere.[88]

It even found expression in Britain, at the time the arch exponent of classical maritime thinking, in the sparkling words of its eccentric but brilliant First Sea Lord, Admiral Sir Jacky Fisher. Paradoxically famous for his invention of the dreadnought battleship in 1904 (which apparently made all other battleships obsolete overnight) and even more for his preoccupation with the battlecruiser/fast battleship, Fisher was at times much more concerned with the future prospects of 'flotilla defence'. He was convinced that new technology, in the shape of the submarine would make it impossible for hostile fleets to operate in comparatively narrow waters like the North Sea. Accordingly it would not be possible for anyone to blockade Britain, or invade it once such a flotilla defence was in place. In 1904, and again in 1914 he wrote:

> *The submarine is the coming type of war vessel for sea fighting.* And what is it that the coming of the submarine really means? It means that the whole foundation of our traditional naval strategy ... has broken down! The foundation of that strategy was blockade. The Fleet did not exist merely to win battles – that was the means not the end. The ultimate purpose of the Fleet was to make blockade possible for us and impossible for the enemy ... Surface ships can no longer maintain or prevent blockade ... All our old ideas of strategy are simmering in the melting pot![89]

On the basis of such ideas, Fisher sought to switch resources from the battlefleet to flotilla defence largely through submarines and aircraft, but with only mixed success against the weight of orthodox opinion.

Fisher had many strengths, but the detailed and articulate enunciation of clear ideas was not one of them. For that, believers in coastal defence had to wait another 20 years until the advent of what has become generally known as the Soviet New

School of the late 1920s and early 1930s. The Soviet New School was stimulated into innovation by a variety of developments. First was the sense that during the so-called War of Intervention, Russia's coasts had been subjected to attack and invasion, especially in areas where little resistance was offered given the virtual disappearance of Russia's naval forces in the Black Sea, and Northern and Pacific waters. The Baltic Fleet was in parlous state too, but its existence required at least a degree of restraint from the Western allies. The lesson seemed clear, and was enunciated by Frunze in February 1925: 'we cannot conceivably safeguard our maritime borders without a strong navy'.[90]

But this seemed impossible. The main threats to Russia came, as ever, from overland and required priority treatment. Surviving naval forces were in a dreadful state and Russia's shipbuilding and repair capacity had virtually collapsed. Further, there were many who thought that the thinking of the 'Navy of Red Workers and Peasants' should be folded into an emerging Proletarian Military Doctrine that would befit an entirely different, revolutionary state.

Given all this, the continuing dominance of the so-called Old School, particularly Professors Gervaise and Petrov at the Naval War College (who followed the example of Nikolai Klado in adapting Mahanian concepts of maritime strategy to Russian's semi-oceanic circumstances) seemed quite bizarre. They argued for a significant navy including battleships and heavy cruisers intended for the forward defence of local waters by 'keeping command of the sea in dispute' just as the Baltic Fleet had tried, with some success, to do in 1919. But in the circumstances, this was completely unrealistic.

In some exasperation, Admiral Zof, the Navy's Chief, complained that the Old School seemed completely to ignore economic and technical reality, and the fact that 'perhaps tomorrow, or the day after, we will be called upon to fight. And with what shall we fight? We will fight with those ships and personnel that we have already.'[91]

Finally, there were many analysts around the world who argued that new technology especially in the shape of aircraft and submarines were in any case fatally undermining traditional naval ways of doing things by exposing the new vulnerability of large surface ships, particularly battleships and aircraft carriers. Command of the sea as a doctrine was not merely irrelevant for Soviet Russia; technology, it was claimed by the likes of A.P. Aleksandrov (Head of Department at the Naval War College) had made it obsolete.[92]

For all these reasons, slavish adherence to foreign concepts of maritime warfare was increasingly questioned by those who argued that the new Soviet Russia needed an entirely different approach to maritime strategy:

> We often … identify with the classical sea powers and try to operate like they do. The battle of Jutland is our model which we study and attempt to imitate. Admirals Beatty and Spee – they are our role models. That which we learn from foreigners is good … But to try to transplant all that directly into our conditions is not correct. We have other forces, other means, and we operate under different conditions. Consequently, it is necessary to work out the tactics for a small navy which acts together with the Army according to a single strategic plan.[93]

Indeed, Aleksandrov observed, the whole notion of the command of the sea was much less a valid strategic concept than 'the operational expression of imperialist policy in the struggle of the imperialist states among themselves for raw materials, markets, spheres for capital investment and for redistribution of the already distributed [colonized] world'. The old theories were no longer valid for anyone, assuming indeed they ever were.[94]

Instead, the New School argued for a much more localised defence of Soviet coasts against serious maritime attack using an integrated system of minefields, coastal artillery, submarines and motor torpedo-boats (MTBs). This called for a joint approach amongst the services and an overall command system that made use of the latest communications technology. It was seen as a means of realising the Leninist aspiration for the Unity of the Forces.

But what was presented by its advocates as a viable alternative approach to classical maritime warfare, as portrayed by the likes of Mahan and Corbett, was gradually discredited as circumstances changed through the late 1930s and the Soviet Navy gradually reverted to orthodoxy. If the Soviet Union was to defend its national and revolutionary needs outside the confines of the Black Sea and the Baltic, the Northern and Pacific fleets would need to be created (1933 and 1932 respectively) and a substantial new construction programme would be necessary, especially of battleships and heavy cruisers. Opponents were accordingly purged (indeed not infrequently shot), and the right-thinking Admiral N.G. Kuznetsov took over as Commander-in-Chief.

Something of the same thing occurred in China in the 1940s and 1950s when circumstances again encouraged the development of a school of maritime thought that put all the emphasis on a large mosquito fleet (with army and air support) whose essential task was coastal defence. Rather than apologise for it, some Chinese naval thinkers argued that their approach was not merely a temporary expedient brought about by resource shortages but a conscious and deliberate alternative conception of maritime strategy, entirely justified by the political and technological conditions of the time. Again, when conditions changed, Chinese leaders (and especially Admiral Liu Huaqing) came to the conclusion that such modest forces would not satisfy their broader strategic aims and in any case would probably not be successful in defending their countries against attack by large naval forces.

Nonetheless, the increase in the number of countries with significant maritime interests and the huge extension in the area of that responsibility brought about for many of them by the UN Convention on the Law of the Sea (UNCLOS), together with certain developments in weapons technology has if anything increased interest in this relatively more limited approach to maritime strategy. According to one recent Norwegian formulation of an accompanying theory, the coastal state's approach to seapower will be characterised by a tendency to make the most of joint action and coastal topography. It will aim at the deterrence of large-scale naval action through the infliction of punishment, rather than crudely attempting to defeat it. A coastal defence navy should be as 'balanced' as resources permit, and should aim to be more than a mere client of any major naval power whose support it needs. The conclusion is straightforward:

> Coastal navies should not be modelled on the navies of the naval powers. Instead they should be tailor-made to fit the local environment. This is because their tasks are different from that of the bluewater navies, their operating conditions are different, and their force structure is different.[95]

There are yet more modest variants in coastal defence theory. The Israeli Navy, for example, was divided for many years between the proponents of a small-scale but balanced fleet of surface ships, fast attack craft and amphibious units (the so-called Big Flotilla school), and the advocates of the Palyam tradition of marine sabotage who thought that small groups of offensive frogmen were all that Israel could afford and needed.[96]

Coastal defence theory clearly comes in many variations and, provided it has an effective concept of operations and the technology to go with it, remains appropriate for many countries.

3.7 Operational art and modern maritime theory

Early thinking about the conduct of maritime warfare tended to concentrate on the tactical level of war. Indeed the word 'tactics' often appeared in the works of the maritime pioneers of the eighteenth century. Here the focus was on how the fleet should be managed in the presence of the enemy – most obviously in order to secure the best chances of success in battle. This was a preoccupation of the later strategists of the nineteenth century too, of course, but they were equally concerned with grand strategy – the contribution that navies could make to the achievement of national aims in peace and war. Historically, not much has been written about anything between these two levels of war.

Perhaps unexpectedly, the last major contribution to modern maritime theory comes from twentieth-century concepts of land warfare. Less unexpectedly, given the land focus of their thinking, Russian thinkers have set the pace in this regard. The failure of the Red Army before Warsaw in 1920, together with a strong sense that nothing should be taken for granted in a revolutionary state, led to an outburst of innovative thinking about the way in which military operations should be conducted, most obviously on land. This led to considerable thinking about what constituted the 'operational art', the creation of a fighting style optimised for large spaces, the operational level of war, a manoeuvrist approach and the 'deep-battle'. In the Oder-Vistula campaign against Germany and the 'August Storm' operation of 1945 against Japan, the Red Army showed that it could put theory into impressive, indeed decisive, practice. After the chastening influence of their failure in the Vietnam War, the United States military likewise developed a strong interest in operational art and other Western military establishments have since followed their example.[97]

The centrepiece of this 'new' way of thinking about the conduct of military operations was the so-called operational level of warfare and the very closely associated concept of 'operational manoeuvre'. In essence, a new level of war was identified that lay between the tactical (the art of battle) and the strategic (the art of war). The 'operational' level of war was said to be about campaigns – hence, operational art is the art of campaigning.

A campaign can be either cumulative (the aggregated consequence of a range of separated even independent military actions – such as a *guerre de course*) or sequential (in which one stage is a prerequisite for the rest – such as securing sea control before launching an amphibious assault).[98] For convenience, the campaign is often thought of in terms of the numbers of military personnel engaged, or the area over which it takes place, or the time it takes, or maybe all three. The campaign involves more of any of these than does a battle, but less than a war. But these are relative not absolute terms. There was, for example, plainly an operational level in the Falklands campaign even though in numerical terms the forces engaged amounted to less than a corps.

The essential point, though, is that the operational level of war *links* the other two. In the familiar words of the Soviet theorist A.A. Svechin:

> Strategy decides questions concerning both the use of the armed force and all the resources of the state for the achievement of ultimate military aims … Operational art, arising from the aim of the operation, generates a series of tactical missions and establishes a series of tasks … Tactics makes the steps from which operational leaps are assembled. Strategy points out the path.[99]

It follows that 'operational art' is the skilled use of military forces to secure strategic objectives through successful campaigning and the winning of battles. The resultant hierarchy of levels of war is shown in Table 3.2.

At the same time Soviet military thinkers realised that the enemy was best thought of as a hostile system, not just an accumulation of menacing forces in an opposing line of battle. Behind their deployed forces lay a complex network of supporting resources, command and control systems, reinforcements, political will and so forth. If these could be attacked directly, rather than indirectly, through the attritional destruction of the enemy forces deployed to defend them, a much more cost-effective style of war became possible. Thinking 'deep' and going for the weaknesses behind the front line was increasingly emphasised. This led to the Russian concept of the 'deep battle'. To some extent this was a misnomer, since the whole point of the approach is that the decision would be sought not at the tactical level of battle, but above it at the operational or 'campaign' level to which, of course, battles contributed. In the Russian August Storm operation of 1945, for example, the Japanese military system in Manchuria was taken apart, chunk by chunk, not in a series of decisive battles but in a decisive campaign characterised by fragmenting, simultaneous strikes and the generation of momentum. Given the scale of forces likely to be involved in many campaigns, decisions will seldom be attained through single engagements.

Achieving this result required what has become known as a manoeuvrist approach, a deliberate and conscious attempt to shape the campaign and to attack the enemy's cohesion (whilst protecting one's own). This could take various forms. It could be, literally, a geographic manoeuvre – an unexpected angle, or combination of angles of attack. Nelson getting between the French battle line and the shore was manoeuvrist at the tactical level in the Battle of the Nile in 1801; the Japanese plan to strike at the US Fleet in Pearl Harbor *from the north* 140 years later was an example of the same kind of thing at the operational level.

But the manoeuvrist approach can be conceptual too. It is better understood as a matter of out-thinking the enemy. The enemy's plan rather than his forces is the main object of attack. It means manoeuvring the enemy by the skilful use of your forces into a situation in which all his options appear unattractive. At this stage, many modern commentators and doctrine writers nod towards Sun Tzu: 'To subdue the enemy without fighting – that is the acme of skill.' Finally, the manoeuvrist approach can be expressed through the configuration of military forces. In the 1970s

Table 3.2 The levels of war

		Description	Example
Strategic	Grand Strategic	Decisions taken by governments or coalitions to achieve political objectives.	British decision to try to re-establish control of the Falklands in 1982 after their seizure by Argentina.
	Military Strategic	Military decision about the resources that need to be allocated for the grand strategic objectives to be met.	Decision to construct and despatch the RN Task Force.
Operational		Command and planning at the campaign level so as to achieve strategic aims.	When and how to deploy the RN carrier battle group and to conduct the amphibious assault.
Tactical		The effective use of military forces, especially in the presence of the enemy, to help achieve aims of the operation.	Disposition and use of the escorts to the carrier battle group or the amphibious landing force.
Procedural/ Technical		Some authorities acknowledge a level below the tactical at which actions are primarily determined by the technical characteristics of the equipment being used.	When and how to fire chaff.

and 1980s, for example, the Russians developed the concept of the operational manoeuvre group (OMG) – in effect a small, hard-hitting, mobile, self-contained army optimised to spread the maximum of dismay and disruption behind NATO lines by attacking its key points, communications, supplies and sources of fire support. At sea, the equivalent of this might be a task force with a range of capabilities packaged for a particular operation. More generally, a US Navy Carrier Battle Group would appear to have most of the historic attributes of the OMG.

This comparatively modern focus on operational art and the manoeuvrist approach has considerable consequence for the use of maritime forces:

1   It has certainly been a means by which campaign planning has been sharpened up. It seems to help in determining force allocation, the provision of fire support, intelligence and command arrangements. The following 'campaign planning tools' have come into use as a means of increasing planning efficiency:

- the end state (the desired result);
- the commander's intent (identifying and communicating the commander's view of the end state and, broadly, how it is to be achieved to everyone who needs to know it);
- The centre of gravity (the source of a force's freedom of action, physical strength or will to fight);
- branches and sequels (alternates to the planned line of operation, introduced as necessary);
- decisive point(s) (prerequisite(s) to the successful attack of an enemy's centre of gravity);
- culminating point (the point where the defender's military capacity begins to outweigh the attacker's; an attack needs to achieve its objective before this point);

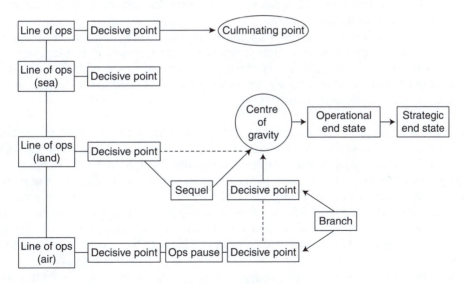

Figure 3.5 Campaign planning tools.

- lines of operation (links between decision points in time and space; may be service specific);
- operational pause (time to reconfigure for the next stage).

Employing these campaign planning tools is not of course a guarantee of operational success, but helps make catastrophic failure somewhat less likely.

2   The focus on operational art also offers a means of re-aggregating forces that have become geographically, or maybe functionally, dispersed so that they recover a sense of cohesion even when engaged in wide-ranging operations against the enemy's military system. With the need to 'go deep' rather than advance in a simple linear manner, this requirement has become increasingly important.

3   It becomes a 'force multiplier' through facilitating better coordination between the forces of different services operating jointly or between the forces of different nations engaged in combined operations. This is important since operations will nearly always be joint and usually combined.

4   It encourages maritime planners not only to conduct their own campaigns more efficiently but also to reflect on the contribution they can make to the outcome of joint operations ashore.

The US Marine Corps were amongst the first to go on to develop the concept of operational manoeuvre from the sea (OMFTS). Their idea was to take the notions expressed in 'From the Sea' and 'Forward … From the Sea' one stage further still and to create conditions for successful manoeuvre ashore by making use of the unimpeded access offered by the sea. Maritime forces, moreover, have a special contribution to make in their mobility (400 miles a day compared to the 30 odd usually achieved by land forces), firepower and flexibility. This seemed an attractive way of applying force intelligently in order to seize the operational initiative:

> Naval forces maneuver from the sea using their dominance of littoral areas to mass forces rapidly and generate high-intensity, precise offensive power at the time and location of their choosing, under any weather conditions, day or night. Power projection requires mobility, flexibility and technology to mass strength against weakness. The Navy and Marine Corps team supports the decisive sea-air-land battle by providing the sea-based support to enable the application of the complete range of US combat power.[100]

The famous landings of UN forces at Inchon, a few miles south of Seoul, in September 1950 during the Korean War revealed the full advantages of maritime manoeuvre of this kind. This surprise amphibious assault by US Marines, deep in the enemy's rear, unhinged their whole plan, threatened their lines of supply and forced a pell-mell retreat from their siege of UN forces in the Pusan area far away to the south west. This landing and the subsequent advance completely transformed the operational scene ashore, and helped create a fluid and dangerous situation for the North Koreans until the intervention of the Chinese in November restabilised the situation for them. But even after that, the continued prospect of amphibious operations against hostile forces in this peninsular war was one of the major ways in which the United Nations avoided having to fight the war on the enemy's terms.

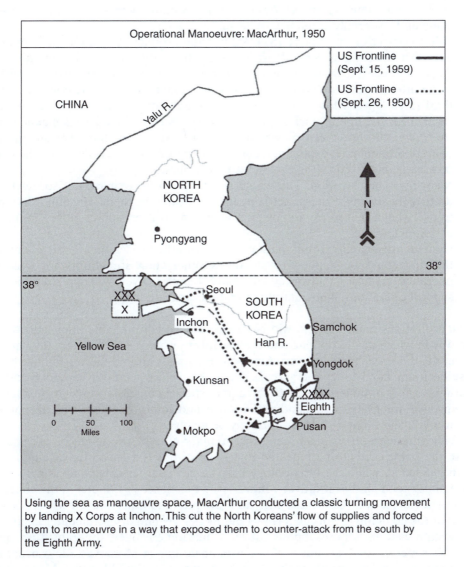

Figure 3.6 Korea: operational manoeuvre from the sea.

OMFTS drew heavily on traditional amphibious thinking as well as on the newer concepts of manoeuvre, deep battle and operational art. It was developed in parallel with a tremendous growth of interest in littoral and expeditionary operations during the 1990s. The result was a synthesis of ideas with some new emphases, including:

• A focus on the littoral, the area of land susceptible to military influence from the sea and the sea area susceptible to influence from the land. This encouraged the notion of 'battle space dominance' rather than sea control, the associations of which were thought to be too exclusively naval.

- A stress on jointery in all respects. This would increasingly require joint command, especially at the theatre level.
- Ship to objective manoeuvre (STOM) was the product of operational level and deep battle thinking. STOM moved away from the idea of the amphibious assault intended to secure a lodgement from which subsequent moves could be made after the traditionally necessary 'operational pause' (as demonstrated by the British San Carlos Water landings of 1982). Instead the assault should go straight for the operational objective in a one-step combined arms manoeuvre, from over the horizon, that was designed to overwhelm the adversary in an operation to enlarge, exploit and control the battle space. STOM rested heavily on greatly improved methods of delivery, of course.
- Manoeuvre not attrition. The whole point was to fight smart, not so much to destroy the enemy's forces, as to disrupt and dismantle them. The aim would be to overwhelm by precise firepower, a high tempo succession of moves, surprise and simultaneity.
- General applicability. From the start, there was the expectation that this kind of thinking could be applied to situations other than straightforward combat operations against an advanced adversary. Increasingly, it was applied to peace support operations, humanitarian operations and so forth.

Such aspirations have had and will continue to have considerable implications for the way in which navies operate and the platforms, weapons and sensors they need. Similarly, the size, shape and purpose of marine forces around the world have likewise been amended to meet emerging needs. As will be seen in Chapters 8 and 9, maritime forces optimised for OMFTS require special emphasis on reach, flexibility, intelligence, integrated command and control and interoperability with the other services and allies that will almost certainly be involved.

Radical though this may all seem, a cautionary note or two might be necessary. First, the point needs to be repeated that none of this is a guarantee of automatic victory. Second, while the terminology may be new, earlier commanders may well have understood all this intuitively. Indeed as we shall see in Chapter 7, the concept of 'ulterior objectives' associated with de Morogues and other French writers of his time, or the common use of the term 'grand tactics' by military commentators in the nineteenth century, all presuppose a level of maritime actively different from, and possibly superior to, the conduct of decisive, linear battle. Moreover, the concept of 'manoeuvre' was first substantially explored long ago by Raoul Castex: 'Manoeuvre is quintessentially a creative activity. 'To create a favourable situation' is the proposed definition. *Manoeuvre* attempts to alter or control the course of events, to dominate fate rather than yield to it, to conceive and bring forth action.'[101] Third, the operational level of war is *a* not *the* critical level of war. The Japanese in the Pacific War of 1941–1945, showed that it possible to be brilliantly successful at the operational level, but still lose. Further, the crucial importance of the *tactical* level has been convincingly reaffirmed by the US Navy's Captain Wayne Hughes.[102] Nonetheless, the recent impact of the operational level of war has clearly had a major effect on maritime thinking.

3.8 Present and future challenges

Even so, there may well be perfectly legitimate doubts about the extent to which all this past and even recent theorising about the conduct of maritime operations still applies today. In the first place, most classical maritime theorists (the likes of Mahan and Corbett, and their entourage) were, as we have seen, largely concerned with operations at sea between the developed fleets of traditional nation states. They were essentially concerned with winning sea control and then its exploitation either to attack or defend shipping, to project military power ashore or to defend oneself against it. Of course, these ideas were redefined and amended, especially under the stimulus provided through the twentieth century by a whole range of technological, social and political developments.

Nonetheless, and however advanced this modified traditional thinking might be, it does not deal directly with a lot of the problems that the world's navies are actually having to deal with on a day-by-day basis – such as piracy, counterterrorism, patrols against illegal immigrants, fishery protection and so forth. Nor does it necessarily seem to help navies cope with the messy political situations in which they often find themselves. Nowadays, the political dimension of conflict, which used largely to be confined to the strategic and higher operational levels of war, reaches down all the way to the tactical, and increasingly seems almost to determine military responses. Peace support operations are often conducted in coalitions; this tends to slow up and complicate decision-making processes in a way that makes all aspects of operational art both different and much more difficult.

The Russians, after all, originally developed the notion of operational art against a background of what might be termed 'heavy metal warfare', but the extent to which the results of their intellectual effort helps guide activities in situations such as Sierra Leone, East Timor or even Afghanistan seems problematic. The less related the activity is to standard combat, in which an 'enemy' is to be 'defeated' the greater the level of strain in massaging the concepts, say of OMFTS, to fit it.

Watering war-fighting concepts like this down in an attempt to make them go farther could all too easily make them banal, ambiguous and unlikely to offer the kind of guidance for force and campaign planners that is the main justification for all the intellectual effort that produces them in the first place. In effect, trying to relate the concept to too many different and competing situations may result in its being too adulterated to say anything useful about any of them. In such a situation, the danger is that military forces engaged in messy situations might be tempted to fall back on to 'heavy metal thinking' even in peace support situations where this was would not be appropriate.

To offset this danger, the world's navies have indeed, as we shall see later, bent their minds to producing doctrine for peace support operations and the conduct of humanitarian activities (often in a joint and combined context) that seem characteristic of a post Cold War, post-modern world. As will be discussed at greater length in Chapter 12, the US Navy and, significantly, the US Marine Corps and Coast Guard came up with a new strategy, 'A Cooperative Strategy for 21st Century Seapower', a 4000-word document issued in October 2007.

This starts with some general discussion of the overall security scene facing the United States and everyone else. It makes the point that rapid change, residual national competition over resources and globalisation itself can cause problems, that 'proliferation of weapons technology and information has increased the capacity of nation-states and transnational actors to challenge maritime access, evade account-ability for attacks, and manipulate public perception'. It is clear about the need to 'sustain the global inter-connected system through which we prosper' and that 'Our Nation's interests are best served by fostering a peaceful global system comprised of interdependent networks of trade, finance, information, law, people and gover-nance.'[103] This post-modern allusion to the need to defend the global system calls for integrated action by the 'maritime services', defined as those responsible for produc-ing the document.

This will require an ability to 'win the long struggle against terrorist networks, positively influence events, and ease the impact of disasters'. It will be necessary to strengthen international partnerships and to 'establish favourable security con-ditions'. 'Additionally, maritime forces will be employed to build confidence and trust among nations through collective security efforts that focus on common threats and mutual interests in an open, multi-polar world.' All this is justified by the central concept that 'preventing wars is as important as winning wars'.[104]

As we shall see later, some much more familiar, 'modern', Mahanian thinking needs to be set against all this quite innovative post-modern thinking. 'Seapower has to be applied in a manner that protects U.S. vital interests even as it promotes greater collective security, stability and trust.' Accordingly 'defending our homeland and defeating adversaries in war remain the indisputable ends of seapower'. This means conducting military operations that 'secure the United States from direct attack; secure strategic access and retain global freedom of action'.

The document is frank about the difficulties of reconciling the demands of these modern and post-modern preoccupations. 'There is a tension, however, between the requirements for continued peacetime engagement and maintaining proficiency in the critical skills necessary to fighting and winning in combat.' The answer appears to be 'an unprecedented level of integration among our maritime forces and enhanced cooperation with the other instruments of national power, as well as the capabilities of our international partners'.[105] The inference would seem to be that the range of requirements is such that not the US Navy, nor the other two maritime services, nor indeed the United States itself, can 'go it alone'.

Because it is both short and necessarily a compromise between two approaches to maritime strategy and the three different maritime services producing it, this docu-ment has not been greeted with universal acclaim even in the United States. Some say it is no more than a bureaucratic cover for the expansion of the US Navy – others that it doesn't illuminate mission priorities or provide much practical guid-ance to force planners. Certainly the inherent difficulties of drafting a maritime strategy for the difficult, complex and unpredictable world of the later twenty-first century are all too clear both in the document and in people's reactions to it.[106] The conclusion is inescapable. We need to go on thinking about the conduct of maritime operations; but knowing what *has* been said about them in the past is surely the first step in the process.

4   The constituents of seapower

Britain's seapower ... lay not just in the navy or the battlefleet, but in the effective integration of her administration, political system, army, colonies and maritime economy towards the ends of the state.[1]

4.1 Introduction

Seapower is the product of an amalgam of interconnected constituents that are difficult to tease apart. These constituents are attributes of countries that make it easier or harder for them to be strong at sea. If seapower is indeed to be defined as the capacity to influence the behaviour of other people by what you do at or from sea, then these attributes must be accepted as part of the mix. The broader conceptions of strategy outlined in Section 3.2 implies that what a national government does to nurture these constituents of seapower should indeed be regarded as part of a well-rounded maritime strategy.

The fact that these constituents are constantly on the move, shifting and changing in accordance with a variety of social, economic, technological and political developments, however, raises the question of the extent to which governments can, or even should, seek to direct this process as a means of increasing their maritime potential. Answers to this question may reflect assumptions about the power of governments in general, especially in the social and economic realm.

Historians have drawn clear distinctions between organic seapower, which develops naturally (Britain, the Netherlands), from the artificial variety that is the product of governmental *fiat* (the Russian Navy of Peter the Great). The latter is often said to be shallow-rooted and unlikely to last; the former is seen as preferable. Even so, most seem to think that governments can, and indeed should want to, develop their seapower and so need to work out a strategy for doing so.

This may not be easy since the significance of these constituents may depend very much on a strategic context over which national governments have little control. For example, the value of a country's merchant shipping industry and its capacity both to influence other people's behaviour and/or provide maritime resources that can be devoted to the navy, must depend in large measure on international tranquillity and the state of the world economy. The strategic context helps determine the value and effect of the constituents, in other words.

The contribution of particular constituents to seapower can be of two kinds:

- It can be a *direct* constituent in its own right. Other people's behaviour is influenced by the fact, for example, that you maintain a large commercial fleet.
- It may have an *indirect* influence through contributing to the effectiveness of one or more of the other constituents of your seapower, most obviously your navy.

Navalists, of course, would argue that naval strength contributes to all the other constituents, directly and indirectly.

4.2 Identifying the constituents of seapower

Richard Harding has argued that naval capability in the age of sail depended on

> a number of related factors, both inside and outside the navy. The actual strength of a navy was heavily dependent upon finance, the capability of central administration, the quality and quantity of real maritime resources, the ships seamen and officer corps, the maritime infrastructure and the quality of political and naval decision-making.[2]

These constituents link together and help determine the development of a country's naval and maritime power, rather in the manner shown in Figure 4.1.

Most of the major constituents of seapower and the specific contribution they make to the development of naval power will be discussed here. Navies and the impact of technology are especially closely connected and will be held over until the next chapter.

4.3 Maritime people, society and government

Traditional writers on seapower tend to extol the virtues of the kind of community produced by a maritime economy. They claim that it creates the conditions in which countries can be influential and in which navies will prosper. Specifically a maritime community:

- Encourages an awareness of the importance of maritime trade in society and government, helping thereby to produce the conditions in which that trade will flourish.

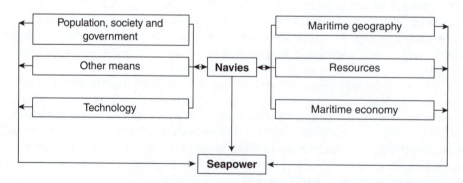

Figure 4.1 The constituents of seapower.

- Elevates the merchant class socially and politically, encouraging thereby the development of a value system and a style of government that fosters trade.[3]
- Facilitates the development of naval power partly because it is simply more efficient at raising the resources navies need and partly because the merchant classes naturally see navies as a means of protecting maritime trade, both directly and indirectly. Nicholas Rodger brilliantly and concisely summarises the argument like this:

> absolutist monarchy was essentially a system of government for mobilizing manpower rather than money. More efficient in its way than the medieval constitutions it replaced, it was poorly adapted to meet the much greater strains imposed on state and society by a modern navy. For that, it may be suggested, what was needed was a system of government which involved the participation by those interest groups whose money and skills were indispensable to sea power – not just the nobility and peasantry whom absolutism set to work, but the shipowners and seafarers, the urban merchants and financiers, the industrial investors and managers, the skilled craftsmen; all the classes in short, which absolutist government least represented and least favoured ... A military regime could sustain itself by force, but a navy had to earn public support. Autocracy was adequate for an army, but navies needed consensus.[4]

For this reason, Spain failed the naval test in the sixteenth century, France in the seventeenth and Germany and Russia in the twentieth.

- Provides direct support for the navy in that most essential of its needs – people. Thus the famous quote by Lord Haversham:

> Your Fleet and your trade have so near a relation and such mutual influence on each other, they cannot well be separated; your trade is the mother and nurse of your seamen: your seamen are the life of your fleet: and your fleet is the security and protection of your trade: and both together are the wealth, strength, security and glory of Britain.[5]

Two caveats need to be entered against this description, perhaps especially today. First, it seems not so much to be a question of whether government and society are democratic and libertarian, as to whether they are efficient. Mahan himself, no great democrat, was worried that government by the people for the people would rather spend its money on things other than defence. In Britain, Laughton concluded much the same:

> One of the doubtful advantages of that system of party government which its admirers acclaim as the palladium of our political liberties, is that – whatever party may be in office – the treasury is unwilling to spend money on our armaments, knowing that, at the next election, it will be denounced as a flock of vultures who have been battening on the very vitals of the poor.[6]

Moreover, some of the most effective navies in history have emerged from countries and regimes hardly noted for their adherence to democratic principles (the sixteenth-century galley fleets of the Ottomans, the Barbary pirates, the Soviet Navy of the Cold war years). The German *Kriegsmarine* of the Second World War, moreover, was highly committed and, given its circumstances, very effective even though it operated in perhaps the most barbarous of all modern dictatorships.

A strong navy seems to depend on a strong state. Thus it was the effective, centralising states of seventeenth-century Europe that first developed the capacity to set up *and maintain* permanent navies. Conversely, when a country is afflicted by domestic political discord its navy, however strong, will tend to fall to pieces. Oman provides but one of countless examples of this. Oman's seapower and its strategic and commercial links with areas and regimes as far apart at East Africa and the coast of China depended absolutely on domestic stability and order at both ends of this chain of maritime communication. Periodic convulsions in China disrupted one of Oman's most lucrative markets, while domestic upheavals within Oman itself damaged the country's ability to defend and extend its maritime interests.[7]

In the worst of cases this political discord can even enter the navy itself, setting one clique against the other or making an effective working relationship between officers and crew impossible. This afflicted the Royal Navy at the height of its powers during the eighteenth century when the officer corps was riven by political factionalism such that it was said that if one naval officer were to be roasted, another could be found to turn the spit. Turning the officer corps and the crew into a 'band of brothers [and sisters]', while crucial, can be very difficult in such circumstances.

Governmental (and therefore naval) effectiveness can also be undermined by the scourge of corruption so prevalent today. The particular fear here is that key political or naval decision makers are suborned by arms manufacturers into acquiring platforms, weapons or sensors that do not really suit national requirements, or that cost too much. A German watchdog group called Transparency International has even produced a system of rating countries for the prevalence of corruption and, as its name significantly suggests, regards the transparency that goes with democratic styles of government as being the best defence against it. Transparency and accountability is also an effective counter to sheer administrative incompetence. Navies are complex and sophisticated organisations that need efficient decision making to match.[8]

Autocracies do seem to have problems that militate against the effective and sustained development of many aspects of seapower. Mahan was aware that despots could sometimes produce great navies and sea commerce, sometimes faster than democracies could. But, as he pointed out, despots come and go and these achievements have often died with them.[9] In countries such as China or Russia, seapower has typically waxed or waned according to the whim of the ruler then in place. The Russian Navy of the tsarist era was the product of an imperial *ukase* usually issued for a particular dynastic or strategic need, and so lacked permanence when circumstances changed. The Stalinist purges of the 1930s and their operational consequences in the early days of the Great Patriotic War were a grisly reminder of the way in which the regime can adversely affect the size, equipment and conduct of the navy. Under Stalin, the lethal effects of political incorrectness (when more than half the navy's senior personnel were shot in the late 1930s) and the depressing impact of the political officers (the *zampolits*) encouraged Soviet naval personnel to 'go by the book'. Tactical and operational initiative was limited and performance uninspired. Only towards the end of the Great Patriotic War were there signs of recovery.

To summarise, it is not liberalism and democratic principles in themselves that were, and are, decisive in the long-term development of seapower, but rather administrative efficiency in raising money and other resources, and in spending it wisely. But, as a very general rule, these qualities do seem to have been particularly associated with freer, stable, more mercantile styles of society and government.

Maritime people

> No man will be a sailor who has contrivance enough to get himself into a jail; for being in a ship is being in a jail, with the chance of being drowned ... A man in a jail has more room, better food, and commonly better company.
>
> Boswell, *Life of Johnson*, April 1755

A country's population, society and government help determine the availability of maritime people. Several of the passages included above make the point that the seafarers of a maritime community can provide navies with the manpower they need, but there are potential problems with this.

Historically, as we saw in Chapter 1, many societies have had an adverse image of the sea. Samuel Johnson's famous comparison illustrates a common public perception of the Royal Navy, even when it was perhaps at the peak of its power. Going to sea, moreover, has often been considered morally as well as physically dangerous because it brought people into contact with exotic and hazardous ideas. This attitude was shared by social groups as diverse as India's Brahmin caste, China's ruling elite in the fifteenth/sixteenth centuries and Russian conservatives of the nineteenth century. But if for such reasons, society or governments foster such perceptions, or even fail to challenge them, all aspects of their seapower suffer.

In the nineteenth century, after the Opium Wars, the Chinese government tried to compensate for several centuries of deliberate neglect of its seapower with a rapid marinisation of its armed forces. But the lack of a wide maritime sector, corruption and a culture that scorned Western ways as much as it feared them combined to prevent the assimilation of the dynamic command and leadership styles required of operations at sea and so doomed this attempt to failure. As a result, China remained stuck in a 'yellow culture' of continentalism that has only recently begun to turn towards the 'blue'. This is illustrative of that 'sea-blindness' mourned by naval traditionalists around the world. Societies particularly beset with such images of the sea are likely to encounter real difficulty in developing their seapower.[10]

This problem and the adverse impact it is likely to have on the availability of people for the navy seems likely to get worse, unless corrective measures are taken, because:

- Seafarers themselves in many parts of the world are becoming a rather scarce commodity, partly for the commercial reasons to be discussed later in this chapter. This reduces the pool of seafarers available for all aspects of maritime activity and who could perhaps challenge popular misconceptions about life at sea. While it may be argued that seafaring experience is now much less relevant than it was, and that a 'landsman' can punch buttons on a console as well as someone with maritime experience, people still need persuading of the virtues of doing it at sea. Nor should the requirements for seamanship even in the twenty-first century be underestimated.
- Sadly some seafarers might in fact rather share the views of life at sea taken by

people ashore since they are often quite poorly paid, have to be away from home for long periods and may not be nurtured by their employers. The social revolution in expectations that is affecting people all around the world, and increasing concerns for health and safety could all make a seafaring life seem relatively less attractive than employment ashore.

- The crews of navy ships are often smaller, but it can be argued that the lives of the survivors are more stressful than they were because they face greatly enhanced technological challenges and a wider range of tasks (everything from high-intensity war to dealing with the desperate victims of the people-smuggling trade).
- Nor should it be forgotten that some countries have severe manpower limits in any case. Kuwait and other Gulf states, for example, need recourse to expatriates in their navies simply because they cannot supply sufficient trained people from their own population. When it was formed, the Indian Navy faced the same problem since it had, for example, only two Indians of commander rank, but subsequently proved able to grow, and more importantly sustain, a sufficient pool, if with some difficulty.[11]

For all these reasons, the appeal of a safe, well-paid ordinary job at home is increasingly difficult for many to resist. In consequence, the recruitment and, in particular, the retention of high-quality personnel is becoming a serious problem for navies around the world. This is aggravated by the fact that it is precisely those skills demanded by navies (technological affinities, analytical ability, commitment, discipline and so on) that are most sought and, significantly, rewarded by industry ashore.

Around the world, navies are devising strategies to cope with this varied, demanding and complicated matter. A general push to reduce crew sizes, and therefore naval manpower, results in fewer people that have to be recruited and makes their retention easier since enhanced terms and conditions of service become more affordable. The attention paid to the size and quality of living and sleeping accommodation in the Royal Navy's new Type 45 destroyer shows that crew comfort is properly regarded as an increasingly important element in warship and submarine design.[12] While old timers might look askance at the mirrors, hairdryer plugs and coffee machines now regarded as essential in modern warships, this is the new reality. Navies that arbitrarily reduce the size of the population pool from which they can fish by adopting recruitment and retention policies that exclude, or unnecessarily limit, the role of women and ethnic minorities are obviously storing up trouble for themselves.

Opinion surveys around the world continually show that job satisfaction (rather than simple considerations of money) is by far the most important element in the retention of skilled personnel. To keep its people, a navy evidently needs to be able to persuade them (and indeed the society from which they come) that what it is doing is worthwhile, necessary and possible. As far as its people are concerned, this is a navy's most important task.

4.4 Maritime geography

> Remember, sir, my liege...
> The natural bravery of your isle, which stands
> As Neptune's park, ribbed and paled in

With rocks unscaleable and roaring waters;
With sands that will not bear your enemies' boats
But suck them up to the topmast.

Shakespeare, *Cymbeline*, III/2

Shakespeare reminds us of the centrality of geographical and topographical considerations to seapower and naval effectiveness. Geography has always been crucial to
a country's strategic situation. As we saw in Section 3.4, Mahan thought this largely
a matter of the conformation of coasts, the availability of harbours, the importance
of rivers, soil fertility and the wealth of the interior, proximity to important sea
lines of communication, ease of access to the open ocean and so forth. It might be
imagined that in a thoroughly globalised world, physical barriers such as mountain
ranges and oceans matter much less than they did; but while in theory this ought to
be true, in practice considerations of maritime geography are just as important as
they were.[13]

Geographic considerations of this sort still shape a country's approach to the sea
and help determine its strategic agenda. The Dutch example shows how this may
work. Geographically, they were positioned to dominate some of Europe's most
important trade routes through the English Channel, and they had easy access to
such important economic centres as Flanders, Brabant and the Rhineland, and the
Baltic coast was not too far away either. The internal economy, which rested heavily
on the Zuider Zee and inland waterways, provided the wherewithal for a financial,
social and governmental system that provided an excellent basis for the development of international trade. Nature favoured the Dutch in other ways too, when
changes in the Gulf stream shifted herring spawning grounds to the south of the
North Sea where Dutch fishermen could easily take advantage. Off-season fishermen used their boats to transport cargoes, thereby easing the Dutch into the lucrative international carrying trade. The imbalance between the size of the Dutch
population and the productive capacity of their limited land area further stimulated
the impulse to seek their fortune at sea – and so did their dependence on supplies
from abroad. Against this background, it is hardly surprising that the Netherlands
should become, and has ever since remained a profoundly maritime country.

Much the same can be said of the United States. Its location means that most of
its major trading partners, allies and enemies are overseas. Indeed the whole nation
was conceived from the sea. American ports are crucial to the survival and identity
of the United States. Even when the country expanded from its original coastal settlements to the land beyond the Appalachian Mountains, its largest cities developed
harbours on major rivers and the great lakes. Of the 20 largest and most important
American cities, all but four have major harbours. Some of America's rivers themselves came to sustain commercial fleets equivalent to those of smaller countries.
The Mississippi with its tributaries the Ohio, the Illinois and the Missouri, provides
2000 miles of navigable river. Every year 400 million tons of cargo is shipped from
Minneapolis to Cairo. Given its geographic setting, the maritime nature of the
United States is hardly surprising.

But despite it all, Mahan worried that the riches of the American interior might
seduce the people and the government away from a proper appreciation of the
importance to them of the sea. Something of the sort, after all, has sometimes happened to the Canadians who have occasionally rejected 'the fading commercial glory

of the maritime provinces and their archaic ocean-based economy and whole heartedly joined the central Canadian business empire'. Canada turned its back on the sea in this way after the First World War, and recovery was slow. If to this we add the sea-blindness of countries whose geographic circumstances are as ostentatiously maritime as, for example, New Zealand, it is clear that maritime geography is *not* an independent variable in the seapower equation. Instead, its effect, whether for good or ill, is determined by a country's perception, quite literally of its place in the world.[14]

This can, moreover, change. When it was the capital of Yugoslavia, Belgrade had access to a long coastline with several good harbours; as the capital of Serbia, it is much less well placed. In 1993, after a 25-year war, Ethiopia was forced to cede independence to Eritrea, and with that lost all access to the sea. Three years later, Ethiopia sold its 16-ship navy (then moored in Djibouti) to the highest bidder and entirely withdrew from the maritime scene. In contrast, the redefinition of the territorial sea from three miles to 12, and the creation of exclusive economic zones (EEZs) through the UN Convention on the Law of the Sea has completely transformed most countries' maritime circumstances. In particular, many small countries find themselves with huge new swathes of marine territory that they now need to protect, often without the resources or the people they need for the job.

Because it is evidently so important to a country's security and prosperity, maritime geography has a major role in setting its strategic agenda. The strategic imperatives it sets can take a variety of forms. Amongst them are:

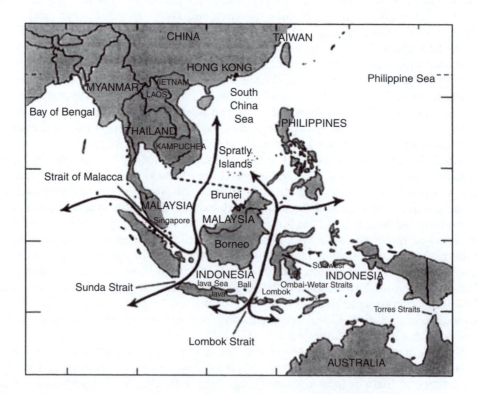

Figure 4.2 The geographic conformation of South East Asia.

- *The need to preserve national unity.* In archipelagic countries, like the Philippines and Indonesia, the coherence of the country depends on the sea communications that either bind it together or allow it to drift apart. Indonesia comprises some 17,000 islands; its very existence depends on the sea between the islands being seen as something that joins its inhabitants rather than divides them. This in turn depends heavily on the nature and success of maritime endeavour on those seas, both military and commercial. Less dramatically the same applies to large countries with large rivers like Brazil or China where riverine maritime activity may serve exactly the same purposes. Countries with overseas possessions or far-flung islands also need seapower simply to stay together. The European colonial empires come into this category, as did Oman with its East African dependencies and as does India with its island possessions around the Indian Ocean.
- *Maintaining balances with land borders.* Island states like Britain, Japan and Singapore are in a (fortunate?) minority. There are far more countries with considerable maritime interests like France, Germany, Russia, China, India and Bangladesh where the fact of having land borders means balances have to be struck between protecting them on the one hand and exploiting maritime opportunities on the other. China has suffered from having to defend long land frontiers against the peoples of Central Asia and for long periods this prevented the Chinese from building navies consonant with its general status or the spread of its maritime trading interests. Exactly the same is true of India. Its land border is about 9900 miles, its sea frontier at 3500 miles is about one-third of that – but so far at least the Indian Navy has received nothing like the share of India's defence resources that this proportion at first sight might suggest.
- *Enforced hostilities.* Geography sometimes makes enemies of countries through sheer proximity. Before the First World War both Britain and Germany felt they needed to be able to control the North Sea to prevent attack on their trade and their homelands. Their strategic imperatives overlapped in the same waters. Rear-Admiral Wolfgang Wegener subsequently criticised the German Navy for paying insufficient regard to such geographic considerations and for trying to solve their problems by tactical means only. 'Strategy', he reminded them, '…is the doctrine of strategic-geographical positions, their changes, and their deterioration.' He recommended an offensive strategy to improve the geographic position. This advice was taken seriously and the next time round, in 1940, Germany transformed the maritime geography of the North Sea by invading Norway.[15]

The maritime experience of Spain and Russia provide two separate examples of how this can all come together. The existence of Portugal and Gibraltar means that Spain has the difficult task of defending three separated coasts with one fleet. Moreover, it has two cities in Africa, Ceuta and Melilla (with some associated islets and rocks), to defend, plus the Canary and Balearic Islands. The security of this sea area is essential for the integrity of Spain. Moreover, Spain sits astride and depends on some of the world's most important shipping routes, with about 70,000 ships passing through the Straits of Gibraltar every year. To the south, the turbulent Maghreb poses a variety of social and strategic challenges to Spanish and West European security. All this helps explain the steady growth of the Armada and its interest in developing a modest expeditionary capability; but common borders with Portugal

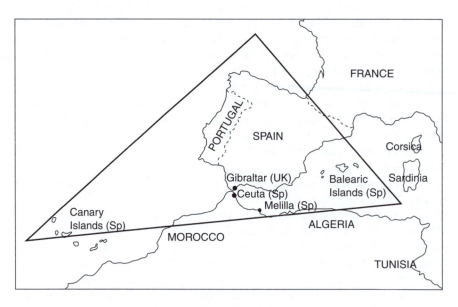

Figure 4.3 Spain and the sea.

and France and the geographic extent and variety of the Spanish mainland, has always posed major distractions from such maritime preoccupations.

Maritime geography has been particularly unkind to Russia. It has four major coastal areas to defend, the North, the Baltic, the Black Sea and the Far East. This makes it extremely difficult for its naval force to be wielded as a coherent whole in a strategic sense or to be operated cost-effectively. Admiral Gorshkov put it this way: 'The considerable difficulty for Russian seapower stemmed from her geographical position, which required having an independent fleet capable of ensuring the performance of missions confronting it in each of [four] far-flung theatres.'

Moreover, Russian access to the open ocean is through four areas that are constrained by the climate or by the close proximity of strong hostile powers – or both. While never a great sea trading power, sea communications are important to it commercially and strategically (for instance the Arctic convoys of the Second World War). The failings of Russian agriculture, particularly in the twentieth century, increased the country's dependence on sea fishing. The connected absence of a large merchant class pushing for maritime endeavour and the imminence of far more serious strategic threats from Russia's menaced borders often combined to undermine the perceived importance of the navy still further.

Russia, observed Mahan in 1900, 'can never be satisfied with the imperfect and politically dependent access to the sea afforded her by the Baltic and Black Sea'[16] and, indeed, successive leaders of Russia from Peter the Great to Stalin have realised the huge problems that maritime geography has set their country – and have been determined to do something about it.

Sometimes improvement came about through the success of the Russian Army (a point discussed later in this chapter) and though diplomatic pressure that sought to capitalise on it. In a deliberate and conscious manner that perfectly illustrates the way in which seapower can become an objective rather than an instrument of foreign policy, Stalin sought to consolidate the success of the Second World War and to do his best to ensure that the bad old days would not return. In 1944, Molotov the Foreign Minister told Trygve Lie, his Norwegian counterpart:

> The Dardanelles, here we are locked in ... Oresund ... here we are locked in. Only in the north is there an opening, but this war has shown that the supply line to northern Russia can be cut or interfered with. This shall not be repeated in the future.[17]

Pressure was put on the Norwegians over Bear Island and Spitsbergen, on the Danes over Bornholm, on the Turks over the Dardanelles and the Causcasus border; through links with Yugoslavia, and more reliably with Albania, Russia became an Adriatic power for the first time since the eighteenth century; there was even talk (mainly in Moscow!) of Stalin being rewarded with Libya for his contribution to the defeat of the Axis powers. And far away to the East, Russia took over Sakhalin and the South Kurile Islands from Japan. Under the Soviet regime, the state did everything it could to develop these areas commercially, maintain rights in the Arctic area and integrate all these far-flung areas into central political authority and, finally, to develop a navy and maritime industries to match the challenge. It was one of the clearest and most ambitious efforts to develop seapower seen for very many years.

Its maritime geography determined the tasks of the Russian Navy through the ages and explains why 'the battle for access' has been so central to Russian naval concerns (whereas it is almost taken for granted by the more fortunate Japanese and British). Sadly for the Russians, their efforts to improve Russia's maritime situation ultimately fell far short of expectations, partly because of the inherent contradictions of the communist system in Russia, and partly because the Soviet Union's adversaries were able to target its continuing maritime and strategic vulnerabilities. Since the end of the Cold War, of course, Russia's maritime geography has got much worse.

However, global warming may well come to Russia's rescue as far as maritime geography is concerned. The melting of the Arctic ice may be a disaster environmentally, but for the Russians it has opened up exciting new sea routes and opportunities to exploit the mineral resources thought to be there and the Russian Navy shows every sign of gearing up to take advantage of all this, even though this has caused tension with its neighbours, with Canada and the United States.[18]

The varied experience of Spain and Russia show the way in which maritime geography helps set a navy's character and composition, its tasks and even the manner in which they may have to be performed.[19]

Coping with geography

The general importance of such geographic concerns suggests a need to develop a strategy to cope with their naval implications. First, navies need to find out as much as possible about the ocean and what it has to offer. Sophisticated submarine operations for instance depend on high levels of knowledge of water currents, seabed topography, seasonal variations and so on, in just the same way that ancient

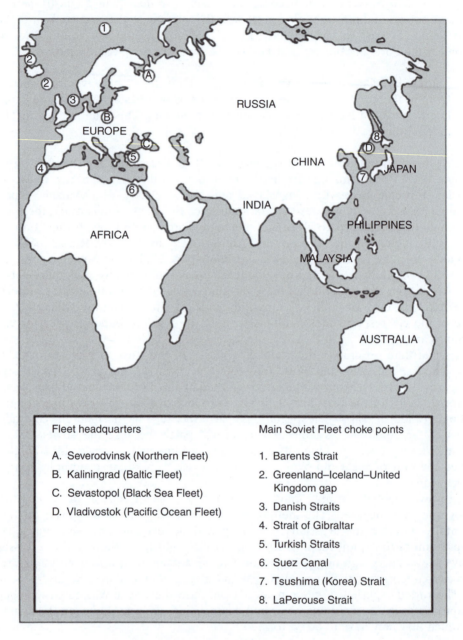

Fleet headquarters

A. Severodvinsk (Northern Fleet)
B. Kaliningrad (Baltic Fleet)
C. Sevastopol (Black Sea Fleet)
D. Vladivostok (Pacific Ocean Fleet)

Main Soviet Fleet choke points

1. Barents Strait
2. Greenland–Iceland–United Kingdom gap
3. Danish Straits
4. Strait of Gibraltar
5. Turkish Straits
6. Suez Canal
7. Tsushima (Korea) Strait
8. LaPerouse Strait

Figure 4.4a Russia and the sea in Cold War days.

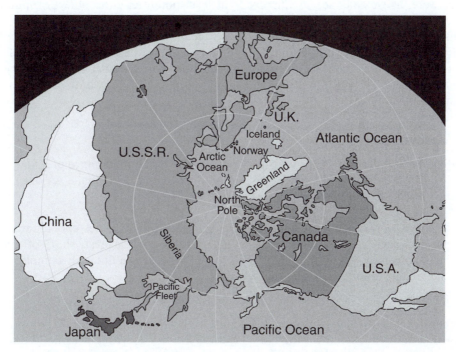

Figure 4.4b Russia and the sea in Cold War days: this Arctic orientation illustrates the crucial importance of Northern waters to the Soviet Navy at the time.

mariners needed to understand the patterns of the monsoon winds. Seriously investing in oceanographic research pays dividends – not least in that it has major commercial spin-offs as well, in terms of fishing, oil exploration and the like.

Second, maritime geography is not an independent variable. It can be altered, or got round:

- It can be improved by legal, political or military action. Working towards the beneficial application of UNCLOS and, most importantly, developing the sometimes quite specialised naval forces required to administer the new sea areas that UNCLOS can provide, is one way of achieving this aim.
- Constructing or widening canals improves the world's transportation system and makes navies more mobile strategically. The strategic advantage of the Corinth, Suez or Panama canals was one reason for building them, and defending and exploiting them became a key feature of maritime strategy afterwards.[20]
- Securing, exploiting and defending bases has also always been an important part of maritime strategy because they provided fleets with a secure and unharried refuge, the easy supply of stores and necessities, somewhere for the repair and refit of ships and the recuperation of personnel. They give navies extra reach and endurance.

While much of this is still true, the range of modern weaponry tends to increase the vulnerability of bases. In Desert Shield/Storm, for instance, the US Navy derived enormous benefit from its access to ports in Saudi Arabia and Bahrain but those bases were, as we shall see in Chapter 9, at least potentially the object of military attack. Equally, they may become unavailable for political reasons.

In some cases, imaginative responses and technological sophistication can compensate for geographic shortcomings. The vulnerability of bases can be dealt with by the creation of fleet trains, or even 'mobile offshore bases'. However, the ability to make the most of your maritime geography often boils down to a matter of resources.

4.5 Resources

Finding the resources necessary for the construction and maintenance of a navy is a particularly demanding challenge for all countries, great and small. As one Australian naval officer put it:

> The experience of the present day, particularly the difficulties encountered by projects such as the *Collins* class submarines, would suggest, short of major incursions into space, that navies continue to represent a uniquely complex and challenging manifestation of state effort.[21]

This has always been the case. When Nelson's favourite warship HMS *Agamemnon* was constructed at Buckler's Hard in Hampshire between 1779 and 1781, it used up the wood of 2000 trees from the New Forest, 100 tons of wrought iron, 20 tons of nails and copper rivets, 4000 blocks and perhaps 30 miles of rope, much of which required regular renewal. *Agamemnon* carried 26×24 lb, 26×18 lb, 10×9 lb and 2×9 lb cannon and was a fighting weapons system produced by industrial processes that were at the cutting edge of the technology of the time. The supporting infrastructure that kept the Royal Navy going in the eighteenth century was probably the world's biggest and most sophisticated industrial concern.[22]

Nor is there any sign that advances in technology since that time have made the creation of a navy any less demanding. This is particularly the case for smaller less powerful countries. As the same Australian naval officer has observed, navies

> place heavy demands on the domestic resources of their nations and on the hard currency reserves of their governments. Navies require substantial industrial and technological infrastructure to support their activities, infrastructure which in the case of the smaller services, may seem disproportionate in relation to the combat capability which it generates.[23]

For smaller navies the issues will be sharper because in dealing with new and unknown technology, for example, they can afford to back fewer horses in the race than can richer countries. For them, playing with unproven technology is particularly hazardous; it is safer to wait for someone else to take the risks. In addition, Australia's experience with aircraft carriers shows that with single ships and tiny classes few economies of scale can be expected. The Royal Australian Navy's original cheap and cheerful carrier programme soon faced real problems with increased aircraft weights and landing speeds; in the end the Australians needed to acquire two carriers (HMAS *Sydney* and *Melbourne*) rather than one from the British.[24]

For a small navy like the Royal New Zealand Navy the cost of even a new frigate is quite daunting, especially at times when the local currency is doing badly. The same applies to the Gulf states where fluctuations in the price of oil make long-term financial planning in, and for, navies very difficult. Eighty per cent of the these countries' governmental revenue comes from oil; when market variations cause the yield to drop by half as it did from 1996 to 1998, long-term naval costings become a nightmare.

Summarising such problems, one British naval officer argued in 1906 that small navies were bound to be inefficient and cost-ineffective:

> There can be no adequate flow of promotion, no large system of training [the cost of naval training establishments will necessarily prohibit this], no opportunities can exist for giving wide sea-going experience with big fleets, and, unless great expense is incurred, the material cannot be kept up to date.[25]

Larger countries have such problems too of course, because the issue is not a simple matter of how much naval force can be afforded. Instead the real issue is how this compares with the size of the commitments that that naval force has to meet – and larger countries tend to have larger commitments to go with their larger navies. Even the Royal Navy of the eighteenth century, the world leader in its time, faced a severe resource problem of this sort during the War of American Independence. This had profound consequences at the tactical/operational level. It was acute shortages in manpower and resources that led Vice Admiral Thomas Graves in 1781 to fall back on New York rather than go immediately to the relief of Cornwallis at Yorktown. Exactly 200 years later, the unviable extent of British defence commitments when compared to their resources forced the government painfully to choose between maritime and continental defence in the notorious Nott Defence Review of 1981.[26]

All concerned with the Nott Defence Review acknowledged that Britain really needed to maintain a strong land/air presence on the continent of Europe and a considerable maritime role in the Atlantic. It was felt that the parlous British economy of the time could not sustain both. Countries like Oman, which with UNCLOS have suddenly been faced with a huge increase in the extent of their maritime responsibilities, face a similar resources–commitments gap.

To some extent, this is a matter of choice, however. Commitments can be acknowledged and accepted but simply not met. Always the constraint is the fear of the harm that excessive defence spending might do the economy maybe turning the virtuous circle referred to in Chapter 2 vicious, as it almost certainly did for the Soviet Union in the 1980s.

How much money a country chooses to spend on its navy is to a large extent, a matter of choice. In the Russian case, extending over several hundred years, studies have shown that there is no particular connection between the amount of money spent on the navy and the extent and health of the Russian economy. When times were hard, the navy did not always suffer proportionately; when they were good the navy did not always benefit. So the extent to which countries can narrow the resources–commitments gap by spending more money on their navy remains a matter of striking a balance between competing risks. On the one hand, there are the strategic risks of not meeting the commitment; on the other there is the risk of damaging the economy if you try to. In the last analysis, deciding such matters is a political issue.[27]

If a governmental really wants to, it can often solve a problem by throwing money at it. For instance, Spanish naval power virtually disappeared in 1700 but the government decided to devote major resources to its rescue and was able to produce some very good ships indeed. In April 1740, British newspapers were full of concern that it took three British 70-gun ships to subdue one Spanish equivalent. Despite its modest economy, Spain managed to build some of the biggest and the best warships of the time, such as the 2879 ton *Santissima Trinidad*.[28]

All this suggests that amongst the strategies by which the resources–commitments gap can be successfully managed are the following:

1   *Effective marketing.* Because there are many other things that governments and populations need to spend their money on, they need to be be persuaded of the prospective role of their navy and of its value in assuring their prosperity and security. According to some, this has sometimes been the problem for the Royal Canadian Navy:

> Unfortunately, no one seems to be addressing the fundamental question, 'What do we want the Canadian Navy to be able to do?' And until that question is answered, and the answer accepted politically, the Canadian Navy will remain at a crossroads.[29]

This will be more difficult for a country that has lost, or perhaps never had, much awareness of the importance of the sea. Surprisingly, given its geographic setting, this is often said to apply to New Zealand. In responding to such challenges, it is particularly important that the navy at least knows what it is for.

2   *Effective resource management.* Effective resource management helps a good deal in every stage of the process from production of the resource at the beginning, to the employment of naval resources at the end. In the eighteenth century, Britain developed a thriving industry, but it was the creation of a financial structure that allowed the country to build and maintain a large navy on credit that was crucial. The fact that governmental income rose and fell and was often dwarfed by the national debt did not matter because the latter could be serviced and managed by the kind of sophisticated financial infrastructure that a strong maritime economy helped develop.

Investment in governments (and in navies) was inevitably related to their reputation for probity and respectable resource management, at least in comparison with the standards of the time. This is why corruption and administrative incompetence were, and are, so fatal to naval endeavour. Accordingly, naval officers should not get over-irritated by accountants and their never-ending search for value for money, intrusive financial discipline and cost efficiencies; they too have their contribution to make to naval power.

The problem for many navies, perhaps especially amongst developing countries, is the lack of institutional machinery and a level of administrative efficiency that properly translates a mission structure (even if they agreed what it should be) into an appropriate and sustainable mix of platforms, weapons and people.

3   *The cultivation of effective friends*. The standard response of a country with an unsustainable gap between resources and commitments is to join forces, in some way, with like-minded countries. This might simply be a question of teaming up with some stronger power, although this can lead to the government scaling down its expectations for its own navy still further. This would increase levels of strategic dependence on allies who might not in the end turn out to be wholly trustworthy. Australia, Canada and New Zealand all signed up, perforce, to the concept of imperial defence led by Britain at the beginning of the twentieth century, but they all had anxieties that their local maritime concerns might not be wholly met by the imperial navy that resulted.[30]

In some ways the United States has assumed this role, and its allies face the perennial choice of wondering which will give them more influence over their patron – supportive action that is separated and independent (Australia assuming responsibility for running the Gulf sanctions operation during the Afghanistan campaign) or totally integrated into the patron's naval effort (Canadian ships being regarded as part and parcel of US Navy carrier battlegroups).

These general choices are particularly acute when it comes to the acquisition of military equipment that cannot be produced at home. India, for example, depends for about 70 per cent of its military equipment on Russia and has frequently expressed its frustration at the lack of transparency in the acquisition process and the poor quality of the spares that sometimes result. The fact that so many of its current inventory of platforms, weapons and sensors are of Russian origin, means that in many cases, India is trapped into dependence on Russia. On the other hand, in the wake of its nuclear tests, India found itself the victim of an embargo, which denied essential spares for a variety of US supplied equipment, including Sea King helicopters. In such circumstances, it is not surprising that India should seek more independence of foreign suppliers through 'indigenisation' of its arms supply, using a variety of devices such as partnership deals in co-research, co-production and local assembly. How far this strategy can go in view of the increasing globalisation of the world's defence industries, however, remains to be seen.[31]

4   *Linking resources and strategy*. Resource management is unlikely to be resolved satisfactorily if the acquisition and expenditure of navy-related resources itself is not accepted as a crucial component of an effective and indeed overall maritime strategy. It is worth emphasising that resource management can be not merely a constituent of naval power but a means by which strategy is conducted. For instance in the nineteenth century, the deterrent effect of British naval power partly rested on its demonstrated capacity to outspend any possible adversary.[32]

Also, the search for resources could set the objectives and define the strategy of seapower. In the age of wooden ships, naval supplies (timber for the hull and masts, hemp for rigging and so on) governed attitudes towards areas such as the Baltic or North America. In 1745, Admiral Sir Peter Warren reminded his colleagues that the conquest of Canada, 'would give us the whole fishery, a valuable branch of trade and a flourishing nursery for seamen, upon whom the welfare and safety of our country so much depend'. For much of the twentieth century, access to oil has performed the same role being both a requirement for an effective maritime strategy and an important determinant of its performance.[33]

4.6 A maritime economy

As we saw in Chapter 3, the sea is, and always has been, a means of transport. Consequently in most maritime countries there have usually been the closest of links between naval power and merchant shipping. Merchant shipping was both a source of maritime power and something that navies naturally needed to defend. So important was this latter function of navies that Mahan came close to suggesting it was the main reason for having a navy in the first place:

> The necessity of a navy springs from the existence of peaceful shipping and disappears with it, except in the case of a nation which has aggressive tendencies, and keeps up a navy merely as a branch of the military establishment.[34]

Accordingly, the attack and defence of seaborne trade were major features of the great maritime wars. This included the imposition of blockades, raiding and a variety of *guerre de course* tactics on the one hand, and classic convoy-and-escort operations plus other forms of trade defence on the other. As we shall see in later chapters, the defence of maritime communications remains a major preoccupation since they are still militarily vital and central to the health of economies forced by largely geographic circumstances to be maritime.

In the eighteenth century, English country squires used to while away their idle hours by reading the monthly *Gentlemen's Magazine*. Whenever England was at war with France (which was all too common) there was a section at the back that listed British merchant ships lost and French and Spanish ones taken, complete with valuations of their cargoes. Its readers could tot up the totals and work out who had won that month. It was, for all the world, like scoring a cricket match.

Nor was there anything reprehensible about this very commercial approach to maritime strategy since mercantile prosperity was what Britain stood for. Thus Robert Earl Nugent in a debate in the Lords in September 1745:

> Let us remember that we are superior to other nations, principally by our riches; that those riches are the gifts of commerce, and that commerce can subsist only while we maintain a naval force superior to that of other princes. A naval power, and an extended trade reciprocally produce each other; without trade we shall want sailors for our ships of war, and without ships of war we shall soon discover that the oppressive ambition of our neighbours will not suffice us to trade.
>
> [If] our trade be lost, who can inform us how long we shall be suffered to enjoy our laws our liberties, or our religion? Without trade, what wealth shall we possess? [A]nd without wealth, what alliances can be formed?[35]

His point was that maritime trade depended on but also sustained a financial infrastructure that in turn provided the wherewithal to finance the war effort, keep the economy going and to subsidise allies. As recent studies have made crystal clear, it was this whole system that financed Britain's industrial revolution, and underpinned Britain's strategy.[36]

The merchant fleet was important for more immediate reasons too. It was an arm of defence. Its centrality to strategic success seems perfectly obvious. The magisterial British Official History of British Merchant Shipping in the Second World War quotes one Director General as saying:

> In the end with the assistance of our American and other allies, we were able to assemble the necessary quantity of shipping for every major operation, but every major operation was, notwithstanding, either curtailed in scope or delayed in time as a result of the limitations imposed by a shortage of the suitable shipping.[37]

In fact, the official historian goes on to cast some doubt on this proposition, but makes the point that it took major efforts and a recognition of the absolute strategic importance of merchant shipping, and everything that went with it, to ensure that this was much less the case than it might have been.

Preoccupations with merchant shipping and its protection continue. In Kevin Falk's measured words: 'Without a strong merchant marine a trading nation like Japan becomes dependent upon other nations for its economic existence. Such a high degree of economic dependency becomes a strategic issue, and thus translates directly into political dependency.' In the United States, many are worried that the US merchant marine has shrunk considerably since 1945 and that only a tiny fraction of its ocean trade is carried in US-flagged ships, and that this share is likely to diminish still further. This matters because relying on the availability of foreign-flagged ships may prove strategically dangerous and commercially harmful. This could seriously compromise the United States' sealift capacity with implications for its expeditionary aspirations. Moreover it is proving difficult to move ordnance and ammunition through commercial ports. In the first phase of Desert Storm, only one layberth was available in Savannah, Georgia, for the load-out of Military SeaLift Command's fast sealift ships. The conclusion seemed inescapable: '*Desert Shield* confirmed what every study ... had concluded, and that was the United States had insufficient sea-lift to deliver the required weapons, supporting equipment and ammunition in an acceptable time frame.'[38] Instead, critics of current policies say the United States must ensure it has the hulls, the transportation system and the loading and storage capacity to meet US national security needs. To do this it must assure the conditions in which the American merchant marine can improve its current performance, through intelligent and targeted support.[39]

These sentiments are echoed in maritime countries around the world, globalisation notwithstanding.[40] In India, for example, relations between the navy and the merchant marine are close (in fact, a bit too close with a lot of certificated naval officers being seduced over into the rather more lucrative command of merchant vessels), but maritime specialists worry that neither get the attention they deserve. In consequence, the overall position of the Indian merchant marine and the share of Indian trade it carries are losing out to the Philippines, China and Eastern Europe, largely it is said through excessive regulation by previous interventionist administrations. Moreover the security of India's oil routes to the Gulf are a constant preoccupation of the Indian navy.[41]

* * *

However, it is also important to remember that there has always been far more to a maritime economy than merchant ships. These are merely the outward sign of a vast maritime system that also includes shipbuilding and repair, the fisheries, ports and land communications, marine insurance and a capitalist infrastructure to underpin the whole. The eighteenth-century Royal Navy may have been the biggest industrial enterprise in the world but it depended absolutely on the health of the maritime economy in general and on the skilled seamen, navigators, shipwrights and artisans, shipyards and materials supplies associated with the merchant shipping industry in particular. Coppering a ship's bottom made it much faster (at least until electrolysis weakened the iron rivets attaching the plates) but only Britain had the coke-fired smelting and steam-powered machinery to roll the copper plates in sufficient quantity.[42]

The advantages of a more advanced shipbuilding industry were equally obvious in the nineteenth century when in the race between the British and the French to produce central battery ships it took the latter twice as long to build them – over seven years as opposed to three and the product was usually inferior in performance.

It was the same in the twentieth century. Naval leaders became very concerned when, for example, they saw the warship-building industry atrophying through lack of orders. The British Admiralty of the interwar period, for example, became deeply alarmed at the malign effect of naval disarmament treaties on British warship-building capacities – with justification, as subsequent events were to show. Building 'holidays' would make it more difficult for shipbuilders to retain the skilled workers they needed.[43]

The conclusion to be drawn from this great store of hard-won experience seems obvious. Merchant shipping and its concomitants are crucial to the prosperity of nations, and to their safety. Naval power depends on it; protecting it is arguably second only in importance as a naval imperative to protect the homeland against invasion. Navies that forget this do so to their nation's peril because a healthy merchant marine and secure sea lines of communication are essential for national security in peace and war.

Challenges to traditional thinking?

If this is the traditional view of the importance of the marine economy to the development of seapower in general and naval power in particular, many of the assumptions on which it rests are under severe challenge in a rapidly globalising world for a whole variety of economic, technological, political or strategic reasons. Let us consider some of the more common modern propositions in turn.

Warship building is becoming increasingly globalised

The notion that any country, perhaps even a superpower, can sustain a purely national capacity to build all the platforms, weapons and sensors it wants is becoming increasingly unrealistic. Western defence industries are in a world of rationalisation and mergers, often across national borders. Many developing countries on the other hand are setting up or encouraging their own maritime defence industries and eagerly looking for foreign partners to help them. For all these reasons, large projects now usually require industrial consortia, often spanning interests in many countries, to come together in cooperative enterprise. For example, the tender that went out from Australia for what became the Collins class of submarine attracted interest from two main consortia put together for the bid; interestingly, many firms had elements in both consortia, the difference in the bids lay largely in the way such elements were put together by the prime contractor – and in what was offered to the customer. Each element in these transnational industrial alliances has its own area of specialisation within a particular project (propulsion systems, anti-air sensors, gunnery systems and so forth) and will expect due reward in accordance with the conventions of the *just retour*. In such a complex world, the old-fashioned glow of pride that a country's leaders got when watching 'their' latest warship, the product of so much national skill and effort, slide down the slipways seems increasingly anachronistic.

Perhaps, instead, it is now much less a matter of having the constructional skills that derive from a maritime economy, as the money and the determination to buy them from the people who have. The real issue confronting the world's leaders therefore boils down to the best way of getting the necessary money!

Merchant shipping is also a global phenomenon

The merchant shipping industry indeed can be seen both as much as a cause of globalisation as its contemporary form is a consequence of it. Shipping connections and information technology have done much to create the phenomenon of globalisation. The fact that an average container goes around the world 8.5 times a year shows just how global the maritime economy has become. As a result, it is now common for beneficial ownership of merchant hulls to be vested in shifting multinational shipping alliances, the finance extended by one country, the cargo owned by another set of companies, the ship in transit from one state to another and crewed by people from a range of other countries. So when a ship is attacked, it is often hard to tell who is being hurt, apart from the immediate victims. Shipping is best thought of as a global rather than a national phenomenon, needing to be treated as such.[44]

Merchant shipping matters less, financially

According to most prognostications, the volume of world trade is set to rise enormously over the next decade or two. The UK Chamber of Shipping anticipates that world seaborne trade measured in ton-miles will nearly double during this period, barring further recession. But this does not make it more important. Despite these increases, it is the electronic web, which now joins the world's markets, that dominates the transfer and accumulation of capital. This does not mean that merchant shipping does not matter, it merely suggests that it matters relatively less.[45]

The continuing overcapacity of the world's merchant fleet and the great reduction of the transport element in the cost of products mean that shippers are operating to tighter and tighter margins. This means they must pay increasing attention to the costs of insurance, crews, fuel charges, mortgage rates, all of which are themselves critically dependent on exchange rates, which are themselves determined by a range of influences that may have little to do with the terms of maritime trade.[46]

The actual operation of conventional merchant shipping is also a less important part even of the maritime economy, not least because of the increasing sophistication

and diversification of its financial infrastructure and the increasing relative importance of marine resource industries. This explains why London with all its support
services is still the centre of the world's maritime economy even though Britain's
merchant fleet has considerably diminished.[47]

But all this is unseen and, in Britain, maritime activists worry that the *image* of
seafaring is declining too, and remain concerned about a kind of creeping sea-
blindness as people travel by air, as the size of the seafaring community and its
social attractiveness diminishes. In a way, the merchant shipping industry is a victim
of its own success; the more shipping costs reduce (and they have gone down tenfold
since the 1980s) the less important shipping seems to be!

Strategically, merchant shipping matters less as well

Commercial pressures and the irresistible rise of the container and huge container
ships like the *Sovereign Maersk* are leading to the disappearance of the smaller ro-ro
and general freighters so useful to navies for purposes of sealift. Light though most
expeditionary forces are, much of their equipment is really basically unsuitable for
containerisation. Nor, often, are there the kinds of sophisticated port infrastructures
needed to load and unload containerised expeditionary forces in the parts of the
world in which they are likely to be operating.

Another consequence of globalisation is the decline of the national flag fleets so
often lamented by traditionalists. The United States, to some extent the UK and
some others have consequently decided that it is only wise to reduce strategic
dependence on ordinary commercial shipping, especially in time of crisis. It is true
that in the Gulf War 14 of the 15 ships that transported the British 7th Armoured
Brigade to Saudi Arabia were foreign and that this did not seem to pose a
problem.[48]

Nonetheless, the confidence that this problem can be solved by throwing enough
money at it, as easily as it was in Desert Shield/Storm, may well prove unfounded. In
a suppliers' market when the required ships are scarce, prices will rise. Even so,
shippers may prove increasingly reluctant to risk long-term market share by breaking existing charters and contracts, whatever the short-term incentive. Merchant
seamen themselves are becoming a rarer commodity, and in the future it may not
prove quite as easy as it used to be to replace one crew by another if political conditions demand it.[49]

Moreover, chronic and expanding overcapacity in the world shipping fleet has
encouraged tighter and tighter margins and the development of a just-enough just-
in-time approach to shipping that tends to increase the tension between liberalised
commercial operation on the one hand and the kind of restriction and regulation
inevitably associated with military use and even military protection on the other. In
the old days, this was simply a question of merchant shippers being reluctant to form
up into convoys because of the delays involved in assembly and the port congestion
so often encountered on arrival. While these tensions may now take different forms,
they are at least as acute now, especially in conditions short of war.

Accordingly, navies feel the need to reduce the risks at least to some extent by
setting up their own specialised if quite modest military sealift fleets and by developing a particular interest in certain identified vessels, especially fast ships, such as the
Royal Australian Navy's HMAS *Jervis Bay*.

A strategic approach to the maritime economy

A recent report issued by US congressmen arguing for the restitution of a shipbuilding loan plan summarised the advantages of supporting such capacities like this:

> Commercial shipbuilding helps to lower the cost of naval ships and it facilitates the incorporation of commercial best practices, technology, and innovation into new naval ships, while maintaining stable employment for hundreds of thousands of high-skilled domestic shipbuilders and vendors.[50]

Acknowledgement of the mutual interest of commerce, the country and the navy in the health of key sectors of the maritime economy warrants a strategic and holistic approach to all aspects of the maritime economy.

On the one hand government needs to avoid the excessive bureaucratic regulation of the shipping industry that characterised India for many years after independence; on the other, they need to steer well clear of the hands-off approach of the more wild-eyed monetarists of the late twentieth century to whom any form of state intervention was a mortal sin. Governmental support needs to be intelligently targeted, for example by tax regimes of merchant shipping aimed at stability (predictable 'tonnage taxes' not taxes on profitability) and on encouraging commitment to future training. Such approaches have improved the outlook for European shippers for the next century. Governments may well also need to foster local defence industrial capacity by encouraging responsible exports through, for example, export credit guarantees. Finally, governments have an important role in mediating between competing interests (fishermen versus oil extractors and submariners for example) but need to be clear on the limits of what they can do, without distorting local access to the global market. Governments need to be realistic, not least in shifting their emphasis from the maintenance of national and independent maritime capability towards the preservation or the increase of a local share in an increasingly globalised maritime economy.

In recent years, the Chinese government has shown extraordinary determination in building up all aspects of its maritime economy and has helped create one of the world's largest merchant fleets with a port, transport and shipbuilding infrastructure to match. The Chinese authorities appear to have a very clear vision of the future importance of the sea and a sense of the strategic leadership needed to develop maritime interests. As so often, Mahan provides a useful summary:

> [T]he government by its policy can favour the natural growth of a people's industries and its tendencies to seek adventure and gain by way of the sea; or it can try to develop such industries and such sea-going bent, when they do not naturally exist; or, on the other hand, the government may by mistaken action check and fetter the progress which the people left to themselves would make.[51]

The notion of a partnership between industry, government and the navy seems a useful one. Industry, disciplined by market competition, brings 'best practice' in all aspects of the maritime economy. Only industry can produce sustainable linkages with other industrial or shipping concerns across the world. Industry provides the maritime skills, artefacts and in many cases the people that navies need. Industry has things to teach both its partners. For example the technology and operating procedures that produced the *Sovereign Maersk* already mentioned, longer than the Eiffel Tower, sails at 25 knots (fast enough for water-skiing), carries 6600 20-foot containers but operates with a crew of just 15 certainly has ideas to offer naval architects. Specialist firms like Federal Express (Fedex) have much to offer military logisticians. In the right conditions maritime defence firms can use commercial linkages (including agreements for local assembly, co-design and co-production) to develop real indigenous industrial capacity. For struggling developing countries, the example of the twentieth-century experience of Japan must be inspirational. First, in the construction of surface combatants, and then in naval aviation, the Japanese (despite a critical shortage of resources) were able to profit from and then outstrip foreign assistance.[52]

For their part, navies need to stay alongside maritime industry in a spirit of partnership, tempered by the requirements of financial probity insisted on by government. Regarding industry as an adversary to be beaten into the ground through the hardest of bargaining is a recipe for long-term failure. Navies need to be clear about what kind of merchant ships they might require in a crisis, and need to stay in touch with likely shipowners to track the ships in question in order to build up the advanced and detailed knowledge of their characteristics that so facilitate speedy adaptation or loading.

Where the market is plainly not going to produce the capability they need (for example in the necessary number of ro-ro ships, or deep research in non-commercial areas) navies will need to resign themselves to the necessity of paying for it themselves (through organisations such as the United States' Military Sealift Command) even if it does mean they can deploy fewer frigates and submarines.

4.7 Seapower by other means

Finally we need to turn to one other source of seapower, one that has been frequently neglected by strategists (with the notable exception of Charles Callwell, as discussed earlier) – the role that the other services can play in developing it.

Landpower

It is a commonplace that armies must be especially configured and equipped if they are to be able to take full advantage of the opportunities provided by seapower. Most obviously, they need to be comparatively 'light' for fast and easy transport by sea and reasonably familiar with the disciplines and demands for them of sea transportation and sea-basing. Many contemporary armies are developing the concepts and equipment that will better suit them to operations of this sort, especially given the stress of expeditionary operations at the moment. For this reason, armies are tending to move closer to classic US Marine Corps thinking (somewhat to the alarm of the US Marine corps it would seem!).

Somewhat less obvious, though, is the reverse of all this – the contribution that armies can make to seapower and naval effectiveness. As we have seen, Charles Callwell is one of the few major strategists really to have studied this issue. Given the frequency with which armies have performed this service, this neglect is quite surprising.

There is certainly nothing new about it. Alexander the Great, for example, had a strong army but only quite modest naval forces. Success against the Persians, however, demanded control of the Mediterranean. Since this was clearly beyond the capacity of his naval forces, he concentrated instead on a series of army operations that knocked out one Persian naval base after another, until control of the Mediterranean was wrested from them – and without a single naval battle. Less dramatically and in much more modern times, the Japanese Army advancing overland on Russian bases like Port Arthur in the Russo-Japanese war of 1904–1905 did much to alert Corbett to the complementarities of sea- and landpower and to weaken Russian naval power in the east irrespective of events at sea. Forty years later, the Russian Army did likewise, although this time against the Germans.

The initial advances of the Wehrmacht in 1941–1942 still further increased Russia's disadvantages in maritime geography, by seizing ports such as Riga in the Baltic, and Odessa and Sebastopol in the Black Sea. But from 1943, the tide turned the other way as the victorious Red Army surged westwards, retaking all the territory it had previously lost. By advancing almost to the Danish border, by cutting Finland off from the north and moving into northern Norway, by occupying Romania and Bulgaria, by moving into northern Korea and taking Sakhalin and the Kurile Islands, the Red Army transformed Russia's maritime geography and put the navy into its best geographic position ever.

This suggests that the usual Mahanian model by which power at sea is the means by which decisive influence can be exerted on events ashore, sometimes works in reverse. The whole of Russia's turbulent naval history in fact bears eloquent testimony to the extent that a country's seapower can be conditioned and determined by the success, or failure, of its armies.

Airpower

Before discussing the contribution that airpower can make to naval effectiveness, an exercise in the 'naming of parts' needs to be undertaken. Here, the term 'airpower' excludes both the air component of a fleet and land-based aviation that is wholly dedicated to maritime purposes. Both of these are discussed in the next chapter. Space, the new 'high ground', now militarised if not weaponised, is likewise held over. But even the airpower that is left may make a very considerable contribution to naval effectiveness, but may also be seen more as a rival than an ally.

It is a rival in the sense of being able to perform some of the functions that were once the exclusive responsibility of navies. Thus in the Second World War the air forces of both sides conducted major operations against the adversary's maritime forces. In European waters both sides conducted air campaigns against the other's shipping and, when they came into range, their main naval forces. Norway, Dunkirk, Crete all saw very significant sea–air battles in which the naval forces suffered losses equivalent to a major surface engagement. By denying the enemy the freedom to operate at will at sea, and by significantly enhancing the battle prospects of friendly naval forces, the Luftwaffe in these campaigns was, in effect, performing naval functions and so could be regarded as a constituent of (German) seapower. Many examples can be found in the Pacific War. In the Battle of the Bismarck Sea of March 1943, to give just one example, a Japanese invasion fleet heading for New Guinea was completely overwhelmed by the efforts of allied airpower, usurping, in a sense, the navy's historic anti-invasion responsibility.

Airpower could also be an ally, helping the navy fight its war. RAF Bomber Command of the Royal Air Force played a significant role in helping the Allies win the Atlantic campaign, for example. Its aircraft attacked U-boat construction yards at Bremen and Hamburg, specialist parts of the U-boat infrastructure such as the Zeiss plant in Dresden that made periscopes, and submarine pens at St Nazaire and La Pallice. An extensive mining campaign was also carried out. More generally Bomber Command conducted innumerable raids against the German surface fleet starting with some extremely costly daylight operations in the autumn of 1939 and ending with the final demolition of Germany's surviving heavy units in the Baltic in the last weeks of the war. If there is controversy about the aerial contribution that Bomber Command made to the maritime war it is only that more could possibly have been done had its strategic priorities been different. Few would dispute that it made a significant contribution to the maritime campaign, and fewer still that capable, modern, land-based aircraft are now at least as capable of doing so.

Joint operations

The distinctions between sea, air, land and indeed spacepower are getting increasingly blurred. Disputes between the services over who should own what platform are becoming steadily more futile. This, together with a growing strategic imperative to cooperate more closely together in the conduct of expeditionary operations, has led to a marked growth of interest in the conduct of joint operations, jointery (or, in American, 'jointness').

There is, of course, nothing new in the concept. The emphasis on the 'combined arms approach' was a leading characteristic of the armed forces of the Soviet Union during the Cold War. This partly reflected the geographic circumstances in Russia which have already been discussed: 'Co-operation between the army and navy in the struggle for access became the hallmark of Russian naval history and gave that history a distinctly un-Mahanian cast.'[53] A pragmatic approach combined with strictly limited resources, introduced healthy realism into much of Russia's naval planning. Most Russian admirals were unpersuaded by the notion that they should be guided exclusively by a naval strategy that was a universal science with rules identified for all time by the likes of Mahan and Corbett and from which inevitably flowed an idealised notion of what a navy should be. We saw, in Section 2.2, what Admiral Chernavin, Gorshkov's successor as the Navy's Commander-in-Chief thought about this. As a result, the contrast between their behaviour and, say, the furious internecine warfare of the late 1940s in the United States or the 1950s and 1960s in Britain when the services (and especially the navy and the air force) were at each other's throats, could hardly be more stark.

It is, however, unsurprising that there should be tensions between the services, because they operate in different environments and, resources being finite, their needs often compete. Moreover, the historical experience of the services differ and this contributes to them having a distinctive strategic culture that may even find expression in different semantics:

We all speak different languages. For instance if you asked the Navy to 'secure a building' they would turn off the lights and lock the doors. The Army would occupy it and let nobody in. The Marines would assault, capture it and lay down suppressed fire to hold it. The RAF on the other hand would lease it for three years with an option to buy.[54]

Indeed, some would argue that constructive tension between the services is a good thing because it ensures that all options are considered and identifies alternatives for policy makers to choose between. The compulsion to 'beat army' is good for team spirit not only at football matches but more generally, especially when there is not a common adversary out there on which such energies can be focused. For all such reasons there is a good deal of 'tokenism' in joint operations, and indeed some very real resistance to the whole idea. Thus the US Navy's Chief of Naval Operations (Admiral James Watkins) on the Goldwater-Nichols Act of 1986: 'You know, this piece of legislation is so bad, it's, it's … in some respects it's just un-American.'[55] This kind of principled resistance in the drive towards more of a focus on joint operations slows a process that is already difficult. The particular reasons for this vary from country to country. In India, for example, the right words are said, an integrated defence staff under a single chief has been established, they do have joint theatre commands, and both a Permanent Joint Force Headquarters (PJHQ) and the concept of joint doctrine are emerging. On the other hand, both the navy and the air force remain worried about the prospect of army domination under these arrangements. Moreover to ensure democratic control of the armed forces, the Indian Ministry of Defence is dominated by civil servants and politicians, and the notion that there should be a powerful and centralised military figure operating there raises constitutional anxieties.

Nonetheless the drive towards joint operations continues – for two main reasons. The first is a generalised sense that the resources–commitments gap that all countries face is unlikely to be bridged if interservice competition produces wasteful duplication. This is true, irrespective of the size of the forces involved. The particular problem many face, however, is the lack of a 'purple centre' to drive it through against the opposition. What may make the difference is experience of the second of the two incentives for change, an acute operational imperative. In India's case, the incentive was the very evident and dangerous failure of its military intelligence services to detect mass intrusions into the Kargil sector of Kashmir in 1999.[56]

The same incentive applies to the United States too, where joint thinking is nowhere near as advanced as it is, say, in Britain, perhaps because in America the individual services *can* achieve so much on their own. But there was nonetheless general acceptance that even in the very successful Desert Storm operation, grave operational deficiencies were revealed that could be traced back to poor interservice coordination. This was particularly evident in two areas:

- *The conduct of the air war.* There were severe differences of opinion and approach between the US Air Force and the US Navy. The latter felt its opinions and needs were being neglected (for example in air tanker support and in the approach to Iraqi air defence, where the navy wanted them destroyed but the air force were content for them to be merely suppressed). The air force insisted on a single Air Tasking Order (ATO) and a Joint Force Air Component

Commander (JFACC) who actually commanded rather than coordinated. The navy resisted this because, 'They feared that an Air Force General, not understanding naval warfare and ordering naval air sorties somewhere at a crucial time, would deprive the fleet of its air and surface defence.' As a result of all this, securing a naval contribution to the ATO was a ponderous and inefficient process that made the air campaign less efficient than it could have been.[57]

• *Operations at sea.* Admiral Mauz the local three-star naval commander (NAVCENT) felt that his place was at sea and was reluctant to provide sufficient high-level representation at General Schwarzkopf's (USCINCCENT) Joint Force Headquarters in Riyadh. This played a part in reducing the effectiveness of some naval operations. This particularly applied to the navy's inability to deal with the Iraqi mine-laying operation that was to produce so much trouble later on: 'Frustrated by USCINCENT's repeated refusal to allow NAVCENT to prevent minelaying activity, Vice Admiral Arthur vowed that if he caught the Iraqis doing it, he would blow them out of the water without asking anyone.'[58]

Through the rest of the 1990s and into the twenty-first century the United States has been seeking to improve its capacity to conduct joint operations by developing the following *instruments for jointness*:

• interoperable systems, procedures and communications;
• people who are experienced and knowledgeable;
• mutual trust and respect;
• joint doctrine;
• command and control structures that do not hinder joint operations.

If used properly, these 'instruments of jointness' should ensure close cooperation without 'dabbling in component business'. It is plainly important that the concerns of all the services involved are recognised and addressed. Moreover the 'slice of the action syndrome' in which all the services insist on representation should be avoided; instead the aim must be to select, and if necessary tailor, the force most appropriate for the particular task in hand.

Clearly joint operations come in a hierarchy. Pokrant identifies them as:

• *Deconfliction* where the aim merely is to avoid mutual interference. This can be dealt with comparatively easily – for example, by geographic line drawing.
• *Harmony of action* where effective coordination ensures that all targets are dealt with and all contingencies covered.
• *Combined arms* where there is an inspired integration of effort: 'In modern warfare, any single system is easy to overcome; combination of systems, with each protecting weak points in others and exposing enemy weak points to be exploited by other systems, make for an effective fighting force.'[59]

There is little doubt that the complicated business of developing the capacity to conduct joint operations more effectively will be high on the agenda of service chiefs in the twenty-first century. Success will depend on each service continuing to be expert and proud of its performance in its own particular domain. A degree of creative tension amongst the services should be accepted as a means of guarding against the tendency to 'level down' to the lowest common denominator between them, since the measure of the success of true joint operations is that each service operates more successfully with the others than it could on its own. This needs to be true at all levels of war, strategic, operational and sometimes even the tactical. During Desert Storm, for example, British and American shipboard helicopters were able to dispose of all the Iraqi fast attack craft they encountered partly because the air superiority provided mainly by land-based air gave them complete freedom to operate. The ability to conduct joint operations has therefore become a particularly important constituent of seapower and naval effectiveness.

Coalition operations

Much of this applies equally well to the conduct of combined or coalition operations with the navies (and indeed the other services) of allies as partners in a particular campaign. Here too one of the aims is to increase the effectiveness of individual navies in helping secure their country's strategic objectives. Here too the same hierarchy of levels and methods of cooperation can be discerned. The big, and perhaps the only real, difference between the two is that in coalition operations there is also the crucial requirement to find sufficient *political* cooperation for the coalition operation to work. Nearly always this is indeed the biggest problem. It tends to find its chief expression in the nature of the rules of engagement issued to participating forces. Harmonising these politically and operationally is very often one of the force commander's biggest problems. The political dimension of this is further discussed in Chapter 8.

More immediately, his task is to make his composite force as effective as its platforms, weapons and sensors should allow it to be. One tactical episode during Desert Storm makes the requirement, the complexity and maybe the rewards quite clear. On 25 February 1991, the Iraqis fired a Silkworm missile at the Anglo-American naval force centred on the battleship *Missouri* that was in the northern Gulf acting in support of a group of Royal Navy minesweepers operating off the Kuwait coast. The Silkworm was detected by HMS *Gloucester* who warned all other ships in the area. The two American ships USS *Missouri* and *Jarrett* both immediately fired flares and chaff to decoy the missile away. The two British ships did not. After their experience in the Falklands campaign when a similarly seduced Exocet missile flew through a chaff cloud, reacquired and then fatally attacked the merchant ship *Atlantic Conveyor*, the Royal Navy has regarded such missiles as something to shoot down not simply decoy, and firing chaff makes this more difficult. In fact HMS *Gloucester* did indeed manage to shoot down the Silkworm but the episode graphically illustrates the problems that may occur in forces with different sets of equipment, assumptions and procedures who are not totally used to working together. Similar problems in coordination occur *within* national navies too, of course, but reduced familiarity tends to make the problem worse in multinational naval operations.[60]

In theory the solutions are simple to describe, being very similar to the requirements of joint operations that have already been noted, but they are often very difficult to implement. They are easiest at the lowest 'deconfliction' level of cooperation where national component commanders exercise command authority in specified and separated geographic areas and operate in parallel with allied operations else-where, and where there is no designated overall maritime force commander. Complete integration, at the other end of the scale, offers advantageous prospects of real synergy but is far more difficult to implement.

The means of maritime cooperation between national forces are many and various. Some are overtly political and include: a common perception of threats; an equitable sharing or burden and risk; an agreed agenda for action that identifies the mission, the criteria needed for its accomplishment and what happens afterwards. Some are more narrowly operational: effective means of command and control at the tactical and operational levels; shared doctrine and publications such as NATO 'Exercise Tactics' (Extacs); information and intelligence exchange; a unified tactical picture; common perception of threats; harmonised rules of engagement; agreed allocation of forces to tasks and so forth.

Most of all, perhaps, coalition operations require familiarity through previous exercises and operational experience and a coincident set of political perceptions and objectives. This is plainly not easy, for as Winston Churchill once remarked, 'In war it is not always possible to have everything go exactly as one likes. In working with allies it sometimes happens that they develop opinions of their own.' It may well be that 'creative tension' of this sort has as much to offer in coalition operations as it does in joint ones, producing a dialectic that in turn progresses the operation. On the other hand it may produce muddle and confusion. The more successfully these and other issues in cooperation are tackled, the greater the contribution that coalition operations will make to naval effectiveness.[61]

Seapower (the ability to influence behaviour by what is done at or from the sea) can be built on activities that are joint *and* combined of course. In Enduring Freedom, an RAF tanker aircraft refuelled US Navy F14 Tomcats en route to Afghanistan from their carriers in the Indian Ocean. Once there, they were directed to their targets by special forces on the ground, targets that perhaps might have first been identified by a Predator unmanned aerial vehicle.

4.8 Doctrine

The British break down the fighting power of a military force into three components. One is the physical component that focuses on platforms, weapons and sensors and on the capacity to supply and use them effectively. Another is the moral component, the ability to get people to fight, which is a function of their motivation, leadership and management. The last two chapters have discussed various aspects of both the physical and the moral component of fighting power.

But there is also the third, conceptual component; this helps determine how well the rest of a military force's fighting power is used. It is the thought process that lies behind the conduct of maritime operations. The importance of this conceptual element in fighting power was the theme of the last chapter.

Doctrine is an important element in the conceptual component of fighting power. It is a great 'force multiplier', enabling the best use to be made of limited means, since it helps develop force coherence, uniformity, reliability and predictability. The trick, as we saw in Section 3.2, is for it to do this without stifling originality and initiative. In the same way, doctrinal understanding facilitates cooperation with armies and air forces and with the military services of allies and coalition partners at all

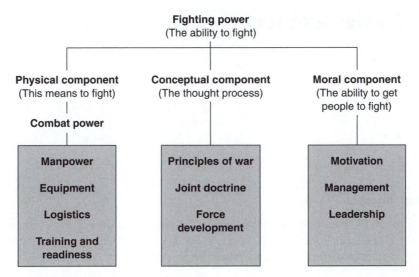

Figure 4.5 The components of fighting power (source: based on MoD (UK) British Defence Doctrine).

levels of war. Last, an interest in doctrinal development encourages the notion that thinking about maritime purposes and procedures in times of turmoil is a front-line task, not merely something to be conducted by consenting adults in private when there is nothing more important to do. All of these consequences are likely to make maritime forces more professional, more useful, more cost-effective and therefore will contribute quite significantly to the development of a country's seapower.

5 Navies and technology

5.1 Introduction

This chapter will review the nature of navies, the most obvious of the constituents of seapower considered in this book, and will focus on the likely impact of technology on their composition, functions and future importance.

5.2 Classifying navies

The first issue, of course, is what do we mean by 'navies'? Not books but whole libraries have been written on this deceptively simple question. There is a widespread notion that there are small, medium and great navies and many have tried to describe and analyse these categories more precisely. Perhaps the most sophisticated of these various attempts at classifying navies was by Eric Grove, who produced the following ninefold hierarchy on the basis of previous work by Michael Morris:

1   major global force projection navy – complete;
2   major global force projection navy – partial;
3   medium global force projection navy;
4   medium regional force projection navy;
5   adjacent force projection navies;
6   offshore territorial defence navies;
7   inshore territorial defence navies;
8   constabulary navies;
9   token navies.

Illustrations of these categories would include the US Navy (Rank 1), the Soviet Navy of 1990 (Rank 2), the French and British navies (Rank 3), the Indian, Chinese and Japanese navies (Rank 4), Portugal, Israel, South Africa (Rank 5), Norway, Egypt (Rank 6), Oman, Singapore (Rank 7), Mexico, Sri Lanka (Rank 8), no examples as it sounds too insulting (Rank 9).[1]

These are evidently difficult and dangerous waters, but it is worth briefly looking at the criteria such scholars use for their classification systems. These include the following.

Size and nature of the fleet

Classification should not be based on mere 'bean-counting exercises', which disregard such issues as technical quality, professional skill and maintenance efficiency. But to some extent the possession of given numbers of large surface combatants is often regarded as a rough indication of relative strength. It is certainly true that maintaining large ships is especially demanding in terms of money and manpower for smaller navies. While there is a rough correlation between the ambitions of a navy and the size and individual fighting capacity of its main units, it is difficult to push the observation much further than this.

Geographic reach

This is another commonly used characteristic. While it can relate to a navy's capacity to cope with the sea states to be encountered in coastal waters at one end of the scale and in the open ocean at the other, this criterion usually relates to a navy's capacity to operate away from home. The problem here is the issue of degree. The fact that Israel managed to sail its fast attack craft (FAC) direct from France, or South African units sail across the South Atlantic to participate in exercises with South American navies, does not make either of them 'regional' in the sense that the Indian Navy is. Clearly this characteristic has to be qualified with considerations of what such navies can do when they get 'there', and for how long? Nonetheless the capacity to operate and maintain naval forces at a distance is a useful partial indicator of the relative strength of a navy.

Function and capability

Here the relevant questions are about what the navy might be used for – ranging from such constabulary duties as fishery protection at one end of the scale to the conduct of expeditionary operations in a high-intensity environment at the other. Some tasks are deemed more ambitious than others, so navies that aspire to the more demanding ones are regarded as propelling themselves into a higher category. As Nicholas Rodger explains, the Royal Navy moved into a higher league when it graduated from sea denial in local waters to sea control in distant ones. Peter Haydon has an attractively simple function-based naval hierarchy, as shown in Table 5.1. Here the problem is that the functions of navies of very different size and ambition are often the same, being distinguished merely by questions of scale. Capability is a very subjective and relative indicator moreover, often only finally demonstrable in war.[2]

Access to high-grade technology

In the past, this might be indicated by the possession of capital ships, such as the gilded, three-decked *Sovereign of the Seas* of 1637. Probably the most powerful individual warship in the world at the time, its mere existence put the Royal Navy into the first division of the world's navies, and it was built for that purpose. Likewise, the nineteenth century saw a race between various European navies in the production of major warships incorporating the latest technology in the shape of armour

Table 5.1 A function-based naval hierarchy

'Power group'	Naval mission capabilities					
	Strategic deterrence and compellence	Power projection	Sea control	Naval diplomacy	National security and constabulary	Humanitarian assistance
Major naval powers	Yes	Yes	Yes	Yes	Yes	Yes
Medium naval powers	No	Mainly cooperative	Limited	Yes	Yes	Yes
Small and coastal state navies	No	No	Over own waters	No waters	Yes	Within own

plating, gunners or means of propulsion. Countries were prepared to spend money on this race because they concluded that being ahead mattered internationally. The relative order of the navies of South America in the early twentieth century was likewise determined by their battleship holdings. The association of a strong battle-fleet of such vessels with seapower has been so close, historically, that many have taken them to mean much the same thing.[3] Having the latest information technology (IT) might be the modern equivalent.

However, to be operationally significant, high-grade technology needs to be maintained and operated effectively and often is not; simply having it is not enough. Through the eighteenth century, for instance, the French Navy and its allies often had better individual ships, and occasionally more of them, than did their usual adversary, the Royal Navy, but always considered themselves second best.[4] The US Navy lost the Battle of Santa Cruz in 1942 when it had radar and the Japanese did not, largely because it was misused on the carrier *Hornet*. High-grade technology is a factor in the relative power of navies but not necessarily one that determines it.

Reputation

Just as the power of countries seems partly to reside in the perceptions of it by others, the reputation of a navy established over the years, may be a considerable factor in its strength relative to others. This was plainly at the back of Admiral Cunningham's mind, in his determination to rescue the British Army from Crete, against all the odds of modern airpower in 1941. In both world wars, the reputation of the Royal Navy made the German Navy more wary of tangling with it than the operational realities necessarily required. The same was true of the French in the eighteenth century.

Sometimes, moreover, the reputation of a navy in fact derives from the reputation of the country from which it comes. A little British gunboat puttering along a Chinese river in the nineteenth century was powerful because it was the symbol of a mighty world empire, not because of the popgun on its prow or its tiny crew. The status of the navy of a powerful state can be quite disproportionate to its own inherent strength. A Chinese frigate nowadays needs to be encountered with respect not merely in recognition of the weapons it carries, but also of the simple fact that it is Chinese.

Naval reputations do not, however, appear from nowhere. There has to be a degree of substance to them. They are established on the basis of previous success that largely derives from factors of the sort listed here.

5.3 Classifying navies: estimating relative effectiveness

There is, it would seem, no single criteria by which the relative status of a navy can be estimated. Instead the power of a fleet is a complicated amalgam of many, or indeed all, of the characteristics reviewed above. In isolation, none of them mean very much.

For instance, the navy hierarchy described above rests largely on the proposition that some functions are more demanding than others, and that navies that aspire to perform them are in a different category from those that do not. In this case, Grove comes to the sensible and pragmatic conclusion that power projection is more demanding than the defence of maritime territory, and that performing both functions becomes more difficult as the area involved increases in size. This verdict rests on a combination of the characteristics of function, reach and professional skill.

Several other conclusions fall out of this analysis:

- Navies of very different sizes often have the same functions, although the area over, or the extent to, which they perform them may differ. Small/medium navies may engage in bitter struggles for sea control just as big ones do; like their smaller counterparts, large navies may engage in very localised riverine and estuary operations (as did the US Navy in the Vietnam war).[5]
- Navies face many of the same challenges and difficulties. They all have to deal with the problems and opportunities posed by new technology, personnel recruitment and retention, the media and changing legal situations. For example, the debate between navies and air forces over the control of maritime aviation seems often to take the same form irrespective of the size of the navy or the air force in question! Most obviously, all navies have to deal with the sea itself and this too tends to enforce commonality. All these factors contribute to the fraternity amongst sailors so often remarked upon by analysts and sailors themselves.[6]
- The power of one navy is a relative thing, which can only be assessed in comparison with that of another navy, given the commitments they both face. A large navy faced with huge commitments may in fact prove surprisingly vulnerable to a much smaller navy with very limited commitments. It was always the hope, for example, of the Royal Norwegian Navy that, during the Cold War (and despite its relative fighting disadvantage on paper) it would be disproportionately effective against the Soviet Northern Fleet. The Norwegians hoped this would follow, partly because they would be fighting in their own fjords and partly because the Russians would have a lot of other things to worry about as well. The need to set the power of a navy against the size of its commitments is often overlooked, especially by bean counters.

Explaining relative effectiveness

In Chapter 2, the point was made that power is both an output and an input. So far, in this chapter, we have been considering the power of navies as an output, in other words on the relative effect that some navies have on other navies, states and people.

In the course of this, however, it became clear that all those characteristics of navies that were 'outputs' in the sense that they helped define their relative status were, confusingly, 'inputs' in that they were constituents of naval capacity as well. Access to high-grade IT, for example, not only provides a useful means of comparing one navy with another, it is also a key constituent in the fighting capacity of that navy. This means that all of the characteristics discussed above need to be thought of as both inputs and outputs.

But they are far from being the only constituents of naval capability. Amongst the others that ought briefly to be identified are the following. The first three should illustrate the vital point that there is much more to naval capability than platforms, weapons and sensors.

The professional skill of a navy's people

In its struggles with the Spanish Navy, especially when dealing with the Armada, the English Fleet derived huge advantage from the fact that its seamen could deliver a rate of fire of one to one-and-a-half rounds per gun per hour, while the Spanish could only manage the same *per day*. This was largely a matter of superior training. As a general rule, the ship-handling skills of the Royal Navy during the French Revolutionary and Napoleonic era were better than their French adversaries, partly because they had more opportunity and space in which to practise them. Sometimes it was also a question of quantity as well as quality. The first generation of Japanese naval flyers in 1941–1942, were very highly skilled (probably better than anyone else) but the Imperial Japanese Navy's inattention to the need for reserves, coupled with wartime attrition produced a situation in which, a couple of years later, ill-trained if immensely courageous pilots could only realistically attack ships by flying into them.[7]

For many years, the small Israeli Navy was superior to its adversaries, despite being much smaller and more constrained geographically, by virtue of its offensive outlook, better training, sufficient technology and operational initiative. The professional skill of its people is often demonstrated by a navy's operational flexibility and capacity to innovate. There is much debate about whether Nelson's famous doubling of the French line at the Battle of the Nile in 1801 was the product of a previously arranged plan or of Captain Foley of HMS *Goliath* seeing a tactical opportunity, and going for it, knowing that Nelson would approve. Either way, it showed what a highly motivated, skilled and confident band of brothers can achieve against the odds.[8]

Readiness

It was in acknowledgement of the huge operational advantages that derived from readiness that navies became permanent or 'standing'. As Nicholas Rodger has argued of the permanent galley squadrons of France, Castile, Genoa, Monaco and Portugal:

> Such a standing force was ready to take the initiative or respond to threats with a speed which no requisitioned fleet could possibly match. With the sea effectively open to all, the side which could mount its raid or expedition before the other, had excellent opportunities of forestalling or disrupting the enemy's projects. For this reason even a small squadron of the king's own ships was of immense value for they could be made available when he wanted them, long before the ponderous fleets of requisitioned merchantmen could be assembled.[9]

The next expensive and demanding step in this evolutionary development was to be able to maintain such standing forces at a distance from the home base. By the sixteenth century, European navies were developing the capacity to do this, most obviously perhaps the Portuguese in the Indian Ocean. The advantages of readiness are equally obvious now.

Supply and infrastructure

Readiness often boils down to questions of supply and administrative efficiency. Here again a historical commentary makes the essential point:

> Warships were and still are the most complex and advanced of all artefacts. To build and operate them requires a mass of technical, industrial and professional skills, ashore and afloat, and a sophisticated system of management to mould them into an effective whole. Above all it requires long-term commitment for seapower which cannot be improvised. Ships can be constructed relatively quickly, but the skills and capabilities which make up an effective navy can only be built up with long years of investment.[10]

During the eighteenth century, the French discovered that building a first class navy was not the problem. The difficulty lay in maintaining it. As a rule, in fact, French ships were better designed than British ones – a French 75-gun line of battleship was the equivalent of British 90; the fatal weakness in the French Fleet was the supply system that lay behind it.[11]

The crucial importance of logistics and supply in all military operations is increasingly recognised. Given the slowly shifting ratio of modern forces from 'teeth' to 'tail' this is just as well, but there will probably always be a tendency to invest in the showier aspects of seapower (glitzy platforms) at the expense of boring things like ammunition stocks. All experience warns of the dangers of allowing navies to be 'hollowed-out' in this way.[12]

Balance

The sailor's traditional preference for a 'balanced fleet' is often ridiculed by those who believe it to be the consequence of a failure to tell what is important from what isn't. It is likened to trying to back all the horses in a race, a tactic that is rarely affordable. Better to be master in some trades rather than mediocre at many. But on the contrary, a navy that maintains a wide range of skills is best placed to cope with a variety of expected and perhaps unexpected operational contingencies. Developing a 'niche specialisation' in which particularly high standards are aspired to in one area tends to make for national irrelevance in all others. Moreover, a rehearsed capacity to operate with other navies and other services is the obvious way of making up for areas of deficiency.

Navies seeking to preserve a reasonable spread of capacities often resort to the device of forming small task groups that may be defined as 'a group of naval and air units optimally suited to the full range of tasks associated with an operational mission'. These have the incidental benefit of being useful building blocks in the construction of multinational coalitions. This has certainly been the approach of the Royal Canadian Navy, which is a medium navy in that it 'invariably participates with responsibility and effectiveness in world events within a partnership of like-minded states'. Canada has made much of the task group approach over the years. When budgetary constraints meant that Canada's one task group was not available, the assumption was that someone else would fill the gap in the coalition. Task groups seem to offer small and medium navies the capacity to maintain a spread of capabilities, opportunities for independent command and sustainment, the ability to operate with others and provide their governments with a wider range of options that would otherwise have been available to them.[13]

While the focus of this chapter has been on the *military* functions of navies, it is worth making the point that 'balance' also relates to the capacity of navies to operate as, or with, coast guard forces in the constabulary functions that will be considered in Chapter 10. This kind of balance makes them effective across the whole range of maritime requirement.

One of the most striking characteristics of the hierarchy of navy types identified at the beginning of this chapter is the obvious one that the lower the position of a navy on the scale, the narrower the range of opportunities it offers. A first rank navy can do everything to some extent; a Rank 9 navy merely exists. The conclusion is unmistakable – the capacity to operate across as wide an operational a spectrum as resources will allow is one of the most important constituents of naval effectiveness.

Moreover, the capacity to enlist new technology effectively in the process is often indispensable to success.

5.4 Navies and technology: an introduction

Navies are material services; where generals command men, the old saying goes, admirals command ships. Certainly, the composition, functions and strategic importance of navies are heavily influenced by technological change. This part of the chapter briefly introduces some of the current debates about the impact that current and contemplated technology may have on naval operations in the twenty-first century, in three main areas:

- platforms
- systems, weapons and sensors
- information.

What general trends are discernible? Will they reduce the importance of navies or increase it? How will they affect the performance of the major naval functions? More generally, does technology determine naval roles, or is it the other way about? These are obviously huge issues. This chapter has no pretensions to answer these questions, aiming merely to explore them. Many will recur later in this book.

5.5 Platforms

Future surface ships?

The 'great ship' has always been the supreme expression of naval power. In the days of sail it could take the form of the famous 'Turtle Ship' of the Korean Navy, Scotland's *Great Michael*, England's *Sovereign of the Seas* or Spain's *Santissima Trinidad*. These were the 'capital' or most important ships of their time; expensive, individually powerful and therefore immensely prestigious. So much did they seem to determine the perceptions of others, that their fighting performance was always the subject of considerable interest and controversy. When wood gave way to iron, and sail to steam, and the modern 'battleship' appeared, this also applied.

The technology that made them so powerful, and at the same time so expensive, also made them vulnerable, really for the first time, to other minor and apparently much less expensive types of naval power. Just as the great ships of the Spanish Armada had been disordered by the fear of 'Antwerp Hellburners' and English fire-ships, many in the nineteenth century believed that submarines, torpedo boats and mines would undermine the whole idea of the capital ship. In the twentieth century, this tension was exemplified by the challenge that airpower was thought to raise not merely to the survival of the battleship in such epic encounters as the sinking of the *Prince of Wales* and *Repulse* by Japanese bombers and torpedo aircraft in 1941, but also to the future strategic importance of seapower. This accounted for the corrosive and in the end mutually destructive relationship that sometimes arose between navies and air forces around the world, touched on in Section 4.7.

The argument continues, however. In the immediate aftermath of the Second World War, there were furious debates about the continued utility of the large surface ship, especially in the United States, the Soviet Union and Britain, in the face of developing airpower, the arrival of anti-ship missiles and, indeed, of nuclear weapons. Criticism was reinforced by the perception that large surface ships were not only excessively vulnerable but also were seen as very expensive. The Soviet leader, Mr Khruschev, famously described the aircraft carrier and indeed all large surface ships as 'metal-eaters' and 'floating coffins'. The real criticism, though, was not that they were vulnerable (because all weapons systems are) but that they were so vulnerable that they could not do their job, or if they could, that their performance would not be worth the price that had to be paid. Despite all this, and despite its historical predilection for maritime forces based on aircraft and submarines, the Soviet Navy came to invest very heavily in large surface ships such as the Kirov nuclear battle cruisers and its Kiev and Kuznestov class carriers.

This was a tribute not to the negotiating skill of Admiral Sergei Gorshkov and his colleagues (although they were evidently considerable!) as to the continued techno-logical validity of the concept of the large surface warship – despite all the techno-logical challenges that have been posed it. Around the world, indeed, there is a marked tendency for all classes of warships to get larger, more expensive and fewer in number. Smaller navies such as Singapore are turning their fast attack craft (FAC) into corvettes or light frigates, and the tonnages of frigates and destroyers are generally going up. Frigates can be 3000 to 4000 tons, Corvettes often exceeding 2000 and both types are likely to increase still further.[14]

Among the reasons for this are the fact that since steel is cheap and air is free, larger size does not necessarily mean a huge increase in relative expense; moreover greater size allows for greater resilience (this could be particularly important for forces that might have to 'take the first shot' for political reasons), a greatly enhanced means of offence and defence at any one time (both in variety and depth) and, provided that ship architecture has been kept open, considerable scope for development through the ship's life. Large multipurpose ships allow the commander greater flexibility across the whole range of operational activity involved in high- or low-intensity conflict and also increases the range of facilities that can be offered in peace support and humanitarian operations. As far as surface combatants are concerned, big is increasingly beautiful.

Against this trend, however, the American 'Streetfighter' concept is based on a return to the *Jeune Ecole* notion that the naval power represented by 'the fleet' should be disaggregated amongst a much larger number of individually smaller units but, this time, to be networked together so that they can act as a cohesive whole. One of the principal incentives for this proposal is the sense that large ships have become prohibitively vulnerable in littoral and narrow waters, especially to FAC and small diesel submarines armed with the latest ship-killing torpedoes or missiles.[15]

But with this possible qualification, there seems little reason as yet to foresee a significant reduction in the future importance of the major surface unit. All the same, the very concept of the surface combatant is subject to a variety of technological changes, including:

- The success of HMAS *Jervis Bay* in the East Timor operation has reinforced a growth of interest in unconventional hull forms (SWATH (small waterplane area twin hull) ships, air cushion vehicles and trimarans such as the British *Triton*.[16])
- Increased stress on ship 'stealth' and survivability. In a littoral environment, the increased range of its weapons and sensors reduces a ship's vulnerability to attack from the shore. The ship itself moreover is conceived of as a distributed system of systems, so that damage in one area need not necessarily lead to a breakdown in the whole.[17]
- Electric drive of the sort being developed for the American DDG-1000 programme may also well lead to a much more powerful weapons load per displacement ton over the next decade or two.[18]
- Continuing interest in modularised systems that can be swapped around existing hulls as occasion demands. The Danish STANFLEX approach has perhaps taken this furthest. By this means, HDMS *Svaerdfisken*, built in 1991, operated initially as a surveillance unit, converted into an ASW unit and then from 1998 became a minehunter. Moreover, since it allowed 16 vessels to do the work of 22 (of three different types) this approach is very cost-effective.[19]
- Reduced manning. Britain's Type 23 Duke frigate class with its modest crew of 180 was considered a major advance, but hardly compares with the 95 anticipated for the original DD-21 concept. Reducing manpower costs like this can be a major saving.
- Surface ship survival and development can also be required by new emphases in naval roles, such as ballistic missile defence, sea-based command, expeditionary logistics and the protection of the offshore estate.[20]

The variety of possible developments facing the surface ship do not suggest it to be an obsolescent species

Future submarines?

> It's astounding to me, *perfectly astounding*, how the very best amongst us absolutely fail to realise the vast impending revolution in naval warfare and naval strategy that the submarine will accomplish!
>
> Admiral Sir Jacky Fisher, 20 April 1904[21]

Curiously, this is a much less controversial area, for few deny the major role that submarines are likely to play in future operations, at and from the sea. Traditionally submarines have operated alone, relying on individual stealth for both their protection and operational effectiveness. Sea denial and the attack on trade has tended to be their main focus, although from their inception they have been used for a much wider range of functions than this. As early as the Gallipoli campaign of 1915, for example, British submarines penetrated the sea of Marmora, attacked Turkish shipping in the normal way, but also landed small parties ashore and shelled railway lines and other targets inland.

From the 1920s, there have been continual aspirations to integrate submarines with the fleet but communications problems (or in modern jargon 'lack of connectivity') led to the effective abandonment of this idea. The appearance of German U-boat packs in the Atlantic campaign of the Second World War revived the idea of individual submarines operating in concert with other units, and this notion has been steadily gaining ground since that time. Improved communications allow closer operational (though not necessarily geographic) integration of submarines with surface and air units. Moreover, the range and power of submarine-based weapons and sensors has increased their potential utility.

For all these reasons, the range of submarine activity has widened appreciably since the Second World War. During the Cold War, anti-submarine warfare tended to become the major preoccupation of both sides' submarine forces although both also developed submarines as the most survivable means of operating their strategic nuclear deterrents. Since then, better communications mean that submarines can now be used more easily for close submarine escort (for example of carrier battle-groups), for intelligence, surveillance and reconnaissance missions, for the support of special forces and for shore attack by means of cruise missiles. Their capacity to approach an enemy shore without being detected facilitates the delivery/extraction of special forces while the shorter flight time of cruise missiles fired just offshore speeds up the target-identification-and-attack cycle. Not surprisingly, more navies around the world are acquiring submarines for all these reasons.[22]

The chief of the South African Navy recently summed up the advantages of the submarine for smaller navies like this:

> Submarines and corvettes are two sides of the same coin, performing complementary tasks as a deterrent and defensive measure ... Submarines make small navies credible and allow us to keep our force relatively unsophisticated. If I were to lose my submarine capability, I would be looking at a complete redesign of the force.[23]

Mostly these submarines are relatively small coastal diesel-powered submarines (SSKs) of the German Type 209 variety. Some nations, North Korea being the most noted example, have a particular interest in very small or midget diesel submarines useful for local inshore operations. As the recent decisions of the French and British to move out of SSKs and the Indian policy to acquire nuclear-powered submarines (SSNs) all show, larger navies are evidently attracted by the 'seven deadly virtues' to be derived from nuclear propulsion, namely flexibility, mobility, stealth, endurance, reach, autonomy and punch. Canadian experience suggests these attributes are very difficult for smaller navies to acquire for a mixture of resource and geographic reasons.[24]

Submarines, too, may be subject to significant technological change. There is, for example, a revival of interest (especially in Sweden, Germany and France) in the idea and potential of the air independent propulsion submarine, which by reducing the need to 'snort' (or take in oxygen from the atmosphere) in some ways provides the SSK with some of the stealth advantages of the SSN. Finally, electric drive would confer the same advantages for submarines as it would for surface ships.

Submarines nonetheless face considerable technological and operational challenges as well as opportunities. The fact that they need to carry virtually all their machinery inside the hull, rather than bolted on its outside, severely reduces space, and means there is room for far less weaponry than can be carried by a surface ship of equivalent tonnage. Making submarines bigger in order to get round this is expensive and may increase vulnerability especially in the shallow seas where they are increasingly expected to operate. Although some systems can now be carried on the outside the hull, the basic problem remains – at the moment it seems fundamental to the very nature of the submarine.

With the increasing global interest in submarines comes a corresponding interest in their weaponry (torpedoes and anti-ship missiles) and a compensating recovery of interest in anti-submarine sensors and weapons.[25] Accordingly, there is continual pressure to increase the stealthiness of submarines (for example by developing optronic masts). The fact that they are expensive to develop and maintain accounts for the fact that the world figure of submarines deployed has actually reduced since the end of the Cold War. Affordability is a major concern. Moreover the failure of Argentina's Type 209 submarines to launch a successful attack on the British task force in the Falklands campaign shows how very demanding the sustained operation of modern submarines can be.

Future aircraft and aircraft carriers?

One of the most significant changes in the composition of the major navies of the twentieth century was the battleship's replacement by the aircraft carrier as the capital ship. This did not in any way diminish the strategic importance of navies, but it did greatly affect the way in which the struggle for sea control was conducted. Aircraft carriers became essential for the protection of the fleet against land-based air attack and, through their developing roles in independent strike and in support of amphibious operations, provided a means by which increased military power could be brought to bear on the shore. The Pacific campaign of 1944–1945 was a triumphant vindication of the aircraft carrier as the new capital ship.

However, the aircraft carrier has been subjected to many of the same criticisms of the sort levelled against all large surface ships – that they are expensive and excessively vulnerable to air and submarine attack. The caution with which India deployed the *Vikrant* in the 1971 Indo-Pakistan war and with which both sides employed their carriers in the 1982 Falklands campaign of 1982 seems to illustrate this. Costs, again, can be very considerable with a Nimitz class requiring some $5 billion and France's new *Charles de Gaullle* not far behind it at $3.4 billion. Despite such concerns, however, more navies seem to be acquiring carriers/air-capable ships of one sort or another.

Partly this is through confidence that air and subsurface threats to the carrier can be contained. Carriers have all the advantages of large ships both in resilience and in the capacity to mount effective defensive weaponry and sensors. Moreover, unlike land airbases, they are mobile. Typically, carriers will have their own escorts that together form a battlegroup with a balanced range of capabilities against all manner of threats. Thus, when the *Charles de Gaulle* set out for the Afghanistan campaign, it was accompanied by one support ship (*La Meuse*), an attack submarine (the SSN *Rubis*), an air-defence frigate (*Jean Bart*) and two general purpose frigates (*La Motte Piquet* and *Jean de Vienne*). This practice complicates costings of course; on the one hand such escorts ought to be included in the total package cost – but on the other they have other independent roles to fulfil as well. With the end of the Cold War, the escort component of US Navy carrier battlegroups is reducing from about 12 units to around half that – and this will certainly reduce production and operating costs quite significantly.[26]

The effectiveness of the carrier in the face of a variety of air and subsurface threats is a function of its own intrinsic defensive and offensive capabilities and of the extent to which it can delegate anti-air and anti-submarine defence to its escorts. The carrier battlegroup, in fact, needs to be regarded as a system capable of providing layered defence for itself and, in British words, 'a floating airfield able to project and deliver decisive joint airpower wherever and whenever required by UK defence policy'.[27]

To judge by the notable recovery of interest in the aircraft carrier, particularly in Europe and the Asia-Pacific, the argument about the continued validity of this species has been won.[28] Costs can be reduced by a whole variety of adulteration measures. Currently, no one but the US Navy can realistically aspire to first class fleet carriers of the Nimitz type – and many Americans wonder whether they can either. Hence the interest in cheaper V-STOL carriers like Spain's *Principe de Asturia* or Thailand's *Chakri Nareubet* (whose relative cost was about $0.29 billion), or even the British LPH HMS *Ocean*, which being based on a commercial hull, cost little more than a frigate but has been able to perform many of the functions of a carrier to the necessary extent. More modestly, the provision of helicopters on frigates and destroyers has enormously increased the offensive and defensive capacities of surface warships

The real point, though, is that costs of performing functions have to be compared either with the cost of *not* performing the function or with that of other ways of doing so. For instance, some have advocated more extensive use of sea-launched missiles or long-range naval artillery as an alternative to expensive carriers. This was the thinking behind the so-called American 'arsenal ship' and led indirectly to the concept of the DD-21 land-attack destroyer. As it turned out, the arsenal ship was cancelled because the US Navy concluded that carriers in fact offered a better deal in the cost-effectiveness and variety of their means of attack. Nimitz carriers carry a payload equivalent to 4000 cruise missiles, for example.

Land-based aircraft may be an alternative. The relative value of sea- and land-based air is complex, and when they are owned by different and competing services, controversial. On the one hand, land-based air can deliver the same or more powerful payloads rather more cost-effectively, and there are levels and types of air attack for which carrier aircraft are simply unsuitable. The massed carrier air strike on Tokyo in January 1945 organised by Admiral Halsey, for example, is generally regarded as a failure. A B-29 Superfortress of the time could carry up to ten times the bomb load of each carrier aircraft, and hundreds of them could attack every night.[29]

On the other hand, land-based airpower may prove critically dependent on the geographic or political availability of bases from which it operates. For NATO's Operation Safeguard in June 1992, for instance, carrier aircraft were available within ten days of the decision to deploy forces, whereas it took nearly three months for NATO Jaguar airbases to become operational in Italy. Furthermore carrier aircraft could sometimes conduct operations when weather conditions grounded the Jaguars. Fixed landbases may become excessively vulnerable to local attack. Some observers conclude, moreover, that 'base access' is likely to prove an increasing problem in the future.[30]

Another angle on the whole question is the survivability of the manned aircraft itself as a future weapons platform. Some argue that the current Joint Strike Fighter programme may be the last exercise in manned sea-based fixed-wing aircraft for such reasons as these:

- During the 1990s, aircraft costs rose at a rate of about 7 per cent per year, compared to 2–3 per cent for hulls.[31]
- Sensitivity to loss when operating against unsuppressed air defences such as in the Kosovo campaign may limit operational effectiveness.
- The potential of unmanned aerial vehicles (UAVs) such as Predator and Global Hawk became clear in the Afghanistan operation. UAVs will surely develop attack potential and greater operational sustainability too.
- Improved IT will reduce the need for a human in the cockpit of an attack aircraft to (re)program the weapon after departure and before delivery.

Whatever the long-term future for manned aircraft, in the shorter time frame future aircraft will be expected to have a long service life (perhaps 25 years) and so must be capable of significant development and improvement. Large aircraft like large ships are probably better placed to cope and evolve throughout their careers.

Many of these arguments apply to ship-borne helicopters too. Because they have enormously increased the defensive and offensive power of the surface ship, helicopters are proving increasingly attractive to the world's navies. They also provide smaller navies with many of the advantages of organic airpower but at more affordable prices. They are developing a huge range of tasks, but at the moment their main focus is on anti-submarine and anti-surface warfare.[32]

Last, there is land-based airpower for wide area surveillance, intelligence gathering and the attack of hostile air, surface and subsurface units. Historically the main issue here has been who controls these aircraft, the navy or the air force. On the whole, experience suggests that the natural imperatives of metropolitan air forces will tend to lead to the comparative neglect of the special requirements of the maritime campaign, unless interservice arrangements are specifically designed to avoid it. In such circumstances, a naval preference for control of all aspects of maritime airpower is certainly understandable. The best solution would be one in which it does not matter who runs maritime airpower, however!

5.6 Systems, weapons and sensors

Many would argue that platforms will be less and less the real issue when it comes to defining the leading characteristics of maritime operations. Instead the focus should be on systems, weapons and sensors. The Danish STANFLEX concept, discussed earlier, is significant in that it divorces the platform from the systems, but these determine its role and nature.

The weapons themselves can be grouped by function. Those connected with the littoral are likely to be particularly important. Mines (even old ones), for example, pose a real problem for naval forces engaged in expeditionary operations. Something of a race is developing between the increasing intelligence of mines on the one hand and the effectiveness of mine countermeasures (MCM) on the other. Current MCM approaches include research into mine reconnaissance using infrared sensors and lasers and various breaching/clearing systems to destroy or neutralise mines in specific areas.

Certainly, navies in general and expeditionary forces in particular will have to pay increasing attention to this obvious means of denying access. Mines inflicted damage on the frigate USS *Samuel B Roberts* (1988), the Aegis cruiser USS *Princeton* and the amphibious assault ship USS *Tripoli* during the Gulf War of 1991 that was out of all proportion to their cost, and certainly complicated US naval operations in the Gulf. Mine clearance after the Gulf War was also a major preoccupation.[33]

Unsurprisingly, mine warfare has moved up the naval agenda. Something like 50 navies deploy mines, 32 countries produce and 24 countries export them. MCM has just about kept track but remains a slow and painstaking business. Harking back to the point about systems, an emerging issue is whether MCM should be the responsibility of dedicated forces (always bound to be in the wrong place at the wrong time!) or more of a modularised package fitted into a general purpose naval formation, for use as and when necessary.

A similar race is underway between means of defence and torpedoes (plus other such underwater weapons) – another type of threat likely to be particularly difficult to deal with in the congested, shallow waters of the littoral. Torpedoes are getting more intelligent, faster and powerful. The Russian Shkval rocket torpedo that travels at 200 knots is a particular challenge. Among the many responses to such underwater threats are:

- The use of friendly submarines against the launching platform, especially hostile submarines. The increasing quietness of submarines has increased interest in active rather than passive sonars, and more exotic means of detection such as bioluminescence, measuring water height and temperature differences, laser observation and so on. Nonetheless, there is little near-term prospect of the littoral being rendered transparent in the way that some visionaries were predicting several decades ago.[34]
- Aggressive reductions in the underwater signatures of surface ships.
- Increasing the effectiveness of decoy systems.
- Area detection, tracking and clearance systems such as the US Navy's 'Distant Thunder' programme.

Missiles directed against maritime platforms and aircraft are also becoming more intelligent, faster, longer-range and with heavier payloads. Their potential victims require increasingly sophisticated means of hard- and soft-kill defence designed to deal with the hostile platform before it can launch the missiles and/or to render them ineffective or shoot them down afterwards. Most agree that missiles are at their most dangerous when fired from modern aircraft; most also agree that maintaining air superiority is the best defence against them.

To the extent that they can be operated from small sea-going platforms, anti-ship missiles may seem to be closing the capability gap between small ships and large ones and between the types of navies that operate them. Concern that large ships might be prohibitively vulnerable against this kind of threat in narrow and congested waters such as the Gulf, led to restrictions and concerns in their employment before and during the 1991 Gulf War. In the event, however, general air superiority allowed the Coalition maritime forces to use helicopters against the Iraqi Navy's fleet of FAC with devastating effect. So far, indeed, technological advance has always failed to substantiate the more extravagant claims of the exponents of 'flotilla defence'.

In 1982, during the Falklands campaign, HMS *Glamorgan* and other warships engaged in shore bombardment, treated the Argentine Exocets known to be near Port Stanley with a level of respect that turned out to be well justified. In such operations the battle space is compressed and the threat axis ill defined. Since then, moreover, long-range land-based anti-ship missiles have increased in effectiveness although they still depend on sophisticated means of targeting possessed by rather few counties.[35]

Nonetheless, the defence of maritime forces against shore-based cruise and ballistic missiles is a growing contemporary preoccupation, especially in countries likely to be involved in the conduct of expeditionary operations. The prospect of situations in which the destruction of potentially hostile platforms capable of launching missile or torpedo attack against surface combatants might be thought politically unacceptable, have led to increased interest in 'soft-kill' systems in which the weapon is either deceived or destroyed, while the launching platform is unharmed. These soft-kill systems might be 'the weapon of least regret' but remain a demanding undertaking in a cluttered and politically sensitive environment. Hence the increasing interest in decoy systems, such as chaff, floating systems, jammers suspended beneath parawings and so forth.

Land-attack missiles, especially in the shape of the Tomahawk missile, have proved an operational success through the 1990s. They are especially valuable in suppressing hostile air defences and means of command and control in the early stages of an expeditionary operation. The military and political effectiveness of unsupported Tomahawks in so-called 'drive-by shootings' is more problematic.

Stimulated no doubt by the growth of interest in all forms of land attack, an energetic debate has also developed over the future importance of modern naval gunfire support (NGS) in the missile age. Some years ago, it became very fashionable to argue that missiles with their increasing range and accuracy would render naval artillery obsolete. More recently, however, gunnery systems have staged a significant comeback, with an impressive potential for extreme accuracy, much extended range and sophisticated submunitions. Their capacity to engage in land attack or the projection of maritime power from the sea as opposed to sea-control anti-submarine or anti-air warfare operations (ASW or AAW respectively) has become 'the great divide' in surface combatants.[36]

5.7 An information revolution?

But while this general survey of platforms, weapons and sensors suggests that change in all these areas is more likely to be gradually evolutionary than revolutionary, this is often specifically claimed not to be the case when it comes to developments in IT. Here, on the contrary, radical advance is widely expected as we plunge deeper into the twenty-first century.

Military experience in the Gulf War and the various coalition operations in the former Yugoslavia much reinforced this proposition. In these conflicts, allied forces seemed able to deliver pinpoint air and missile attacks on enemy targets that included both fixed and hardened sites, and mobile forces. In the Kosovo campaign of 1999 in particular, enormous advances in computers and sensors enabled NATO to launch a variety of precision attacks through stealth aircraft, Tomahawk cruise missiles and joint direct attack munitions that were guided to their targets by the use of the satellite-based Global Positioning System (GPS) – and all at practically no cost to NATO in terms of lives lost. The whole process of locating targets, orchestrating and delivering the various means of attack, were made possible only by enormous advances in computer-based information gathering and processing systems, such as the joint surveillance target attack radar system (JSTARS).

The rate of exponential advance in computer power, which 'Moore's law'[37] claims has so far doubled every 18 months, makes revolutionary change in military operations virtually inevitable. It seems to have had several consequences:

- There has been an extraordinary increase in operational information about the adversary's forces and movements. Such knowledge will be available much faster (even in 'real' time) and more accurate. The fog of war may not have disappeared but it has certainly thinned. Future engagements seem likely to be more related to chess (where the position and value of all the pieces are known) than to poker (where they are not).

- Since knowledge is power, the more you know, the more you will win. Information superiority (or better 'situational awareness' than the adversary) has become even more important as a source of operational success. Defending your information and attacking the adversary's becomes a new dimension of war. Information superiority has been defined as 'The capability to collect, process and disseminate an uninterrupted flow of information while exploiting or denying an adversary's ability to do the same.'[38] This raises the prospect of information as warfare rather than information in warfare. Maybe we need a theory of information supremacy, just as we do one for air or sea supremacy.

- IT offers a means of linking friendly forces up much more systemically. Indeed these linkages tie the individual components of the system together so closely that it hardly makes sense to think of platforms (aircraft, ships, tanks) on their own. Instead they need to be thought of as part of a greater whole, or as a 'system of systems' in fact.

- IT makes this system of command, 'sensors' and 'shooters', much more responsive operationally. Commands will be faster and more precise. Reaction times between the identification of a target and the delivery of an attack will reduce from days (in the case of cruise missile attacks in 1991) to hours, and even minutes. This time reduction will come about partly in consequence of the faster data processing resulting from enhanced computer power, and partly through the advent of more rapid means of attack (such as supersonic missiles). The commander will also have a greater variety of means of attack at his disposal.

- All of these systems of systems involved challenges to the traditional and independent initiative of the local commander since, to make sense of it all, final authority for the disposition and use of the individual units had to be vested in some central authority, probably ashore. Increasingly it will be higher authority

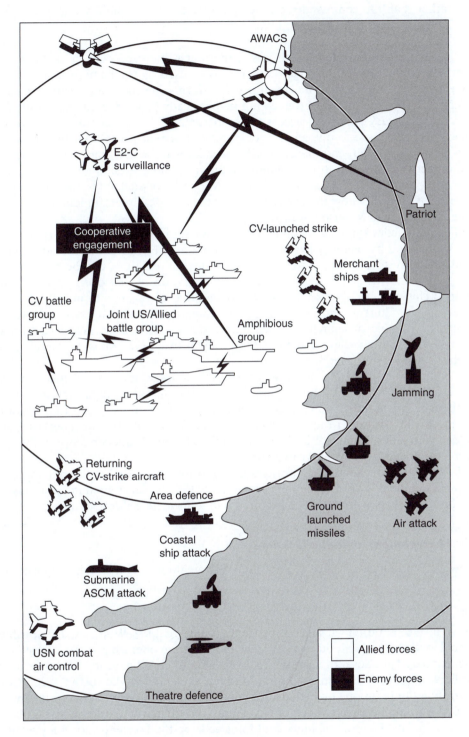

Figure 5.1 Network-centric warfare.

rather than the commander on the spot who has responsibility for locating the adversary, and responding to him.

The maritime equivalent of all this is the much-discussed concept of 'network-centric warfare' (NCW), in which attention is focused on the combined action of a collective fleet, rather than its constituent platforms (be they ships, submarines or aircraft).[39] The fleet, moreover, need not be physically concentrated; indeed the fact that the adversary may have access to comparable IT is an incentive for maritime platforms to be close to one another only in an electronic sense. Maritime power is now best 'distributed' and maritime effectiveness is to be seen more as function of the capacity of the overall information system and the precision-guided munitions that it supports than it is of the fighting power of individual ships, aircraft or submarines. NCW will allow the commander to attack more targets, in less time, over a greater space, with fewer platforms.[40]

The NCW concept is based on a data-link system in which the sensor (perhaps a UAV operated by one ship) gathers operational intelligence about the adversary's land, sea or air forces, and shares it round the fleet in real time. On the basis of this, the commander can use any platform, or combination of platforms, to launch his attack. This has become known as a 'cooperative engagement capability'. This, together with longer and longer-range weaponry, means that sea-based forces should be capable of launching much more effective attacks on land-based forces than before; but at the same time they may prove more open to attack from sophisticated forces onshore.

The maritime prophets of NCW generally emphasise that for all this to work, there will need to be substantial changes to existing maritime organisations, habits of thought, procedures and doctrine. Much more attention will need to be paid to the mechanics (or rather the electronics) of cooperation with the other services, and indeed with allies. The traditional operational and tactical independence of the sea-based commander seems likely to atrophy.

For all these reasons, the information explosion associated with contemporary advances in the power of computers seems likely to have substantial implications for the future of seapower and indeed is often said to have 'transformed' it.

The IT revolution: some qualifications

However, certain caveats need to be entered straight away against this proposition.

How new?

NCW in fact is rather an ancient concept. A line of First World War battleships should really be understood as a single weapons system operating at the behest of its commander. The secret of success was to be able to coordinate its collective heavy artillery effectively. Britain's Admiral Madden explained it like this in 1920: 'Concentration of fire on one objective after another is the all important factor in a naval battle.' But the increasing range of naval guns and the particular lethality of 'plunging fire' meant that commanders could not achieve the concentration they wanted merely by positioning several ships against one, 'as was done for instance, in Nelson's time'. Instead it was a matter of fire control. Now the gunnery of the fleet had to be treated as a whole and often directed from the 'master ship' at targets invisible to the firing ship. For this system of systems (to coin a phrase!) to work properly, the commander needed accurate information on the exact position of the enemy during the battle.[41] He needed to be able to connect sensor to shooter and to ensure that appropriate information was passed around the fleet in a timely manner. In days of sail, when the angle of approach was considered critical to the outcome of battle, the intimate relationship of tactics, signals and communications was the chief preoccupation of fleet commanders. As Brian Tunstall reminded us, 'Success in war depended on an admiral's ability to organise a body of ships into a disciplined fleet, capable of obeying his instructions and signals.'[42] At Jutland, a combination of lost aerials, vibration, gun and funnel smoke, defective message writing and poor visibility undermined signal efficiency at the very time that service culture centred on it. In consequence of the disappointment of Jutland, new divisional tactics came into play by which emphasis was switched to some degree from the single line of battle to smaller, shifting and decentralised units of the fleet engaging in more independent manoeuvre. This increased the need for more diverse approaches to fire control – master ship, independent, sequence and massed firing.[43]

The coastal defence system introduced by the Soviet Union in the 1920s is another example of NCW. Itself a refinement of a similar system put in place by the Germans to defend the coast of Flanders in 1914, it was a radio-linked system by which a shore-based commander could coordinate a large number of active small mosquito craft (coastal submarines, fast attack craft) with land-based aircraft and artillery and passive sea defences (minefields) to repel an assault by superior naval forces. Norman Friedman shows us that the same kind of thinking lay behind Soviet efforts to coordinate their forces to deal with Western carrier and surface forces during the Cold War, and were indeed rehearsed by their large-scale OKEAN exercises of 1970 and 1975. There were similar Western efforts to maintain global surveillance and targeting particularly against Soviet submarines and land-based air forces, most famously through the SOSUS system. In its way, the successful Coalition embargo operation against Iraq in the 1990s also rested on a global information system able to track merchant ship movements all over the world, and to provide the operational information needed for appropriate responses at every level.

The persistence of fog

Expecting IT to lift Clausewitz's 'fog of war' completely seems permanently unrealistic, for two basic reasons. First, in the Cold War examples given above, the speed, efficiency and security of space/satellite-based information flows and of the many links in the system was less than people wanted.[44] Moreover, IT systems can sometimes fall apart of their own volition if the information they pass is wrong, or even if there is too much of it for commanders to handle. Information gridlock remains a real possibility. IT can, finally, complicate rather than facilitate the decision-making process, if too many cooks stick their fingers into the pie, simply because technology means they now can.

Second, there is a huge difference between having a lot of information about the enemy and understanding him. Underestimating the enemy, for example through cultural unfamiliarity and/or lack of attention, seems depressingly easy. The widespread Western failure to appreciate the efficiency of Japanese naval aviation in

1941 is but one example of this. The width of the cultural divide between watcher and watched is an important part of the explanation for this. Without these cultural insights, 'situational awareness' cannot possibly be total, however good the means of surveillance and communication.

The ability to profit from IT

The success of an IT-based network-centric style of war depends on the efficiency with which information is used as a basis for appropriate operational responses. These depend not just on having information about the enemy's position and strength, but having the circumstances and weaponry to do something useful about it. Information is obviously crucial in war, but it isn't all there is to it. The Vietnam war shows that technological superiority in IT does not necessarily lead to operational or strategic success. Despite the unprecedented access to operational information enjoyed by Coalition forces, the success of the so-called 'Scud hunt' in Desert Storm and later the ability to interfere with Serbian Army and police forces engaging in ethnic cleansing in Kosovo, was in fact quite restricted.

Offensive and defensive countermeasures

Moreover, the more IT confers operational advantages to one side, the more it provides incentives for the other to seek tactical or technical countermeasures. These may be offensive, aimed at exploiting vulnerabilities in the system. Most obviously, the growing dependence on IT leads to vulnerability to some kind of 'electronic Pearl Harbor' in which the IT system itself becomes the object of attack. Commercial-off-the-shelf (COTS) technology largely produced the IT revolution, but commercial IT may not prove to have the resilience expected of military equipment and so may be a continuing source of vulnerability. Since the military occupies only a relatively small part of the market, commercial firms may not have sufficient incentive to cater for the most extravagant of their needs.

Moreover, the ready availability of COTS IT means that weaker adversaries may well be able to narrow the gap by buying into the technology and adapting it to their own needs. Insurgents with cell-phones and satellite dishes are now commonplace.

Finally, the weaker adversary's responses may be 'asymmetric' in the sense of exploiting operational, political or even cultural factors in the situation in a way that compensates for their technological disadvantages in the manner discussed in Sections 9.3 and 9.5.[45]

5.8 The challenge of transformational technology

The evident need for caution about the extent and impact of the IT revolution on seapower raises the issue of whether we are in fact in the midst of a general 'revolution in military affairs' (RMA). The phrase has been borrowed from the old Soviet General Military Staff. Soviet General Nikolai Ogarkov, in the late 1970s and early 1980s, was amongst the first to argue that future war was likely to be fought according to 'new physical principles' in accordance with the whole spectrum of emerging technology. His consequent recommendation that the Soviet Union invest even more heavily in new military technology played a significant part in his dismissal and, eventually, in the downfall of a communist system that was hard-pressed to cope with existing levels of defence expenditure, let alone the increases he was suggesting.

Nonetheless, to many Americans the 1991 Gulf War, with its impressive integration of precision-guided weapons, C⁴I (command, control, communications, computers and information) and RSTA (reconnaissance, surveillance, targeting and acquisition), showed Ogarkov was right. New developments seemed to be making previous styles of warfare obsolete.[46] The Americans variously defined the RMA but the following produced by the US Department of Defense's Office of Net Assessment, has won wide acceptance: 'A major change in the nature of warfare brought about by the innovative application of technologies which, combined with dramatic changes in military doctrine, and operational concepts, fundamentally alters the character and conduct of operations.'[47] Some naval writers have cleverly adapted the basic idea behind this concept and talk about a revolution in naval, or maritime affairs, instead.[48]

The sophistication in this formulation is worth noting, and is often overlooked. Plainly it is not just a question of new technology per se (that is, just a Soviet-style 'military technological revolution' (MTR)), but its innovative application that counts. It is not therefore simply a question of 'silver bullets', of merely inventing new technology – the real issue is about how to apply it. For it to work, military technology has to be accompanied by a host of doctrinal and organisational changes as well. Some go further still, pointing to the need for associated, wholesale political, social, economic and cultural changes if the 'military revolution' that affected Europe between say 1750 and 1850 is properly to be comprehended.[49] Here the ancient debate about the balance in war to be struck between unscientific, unquantifiable, human factors on the one hand and hard, 'scientific' quantifiable ones on the other is very relevant.

There is also, frankly, a degree of 'weasel-wording' in the definition of the RMA identified here: what do phrases like 'major change' or 'fundamentally alters' actually mean? Moreover, how does an RMA take place? Is it directed by someone (the military themselves? the state? commercial interests?), or does it just happen? Most important of all, this definition talks about change in the character and conduct of military operations *but not necessarily about change in its overall consequences*. The more, in fact, one looks at the concept of the RMA the looser and the more susceptible to differing interpretation it seems to be.

This, perhaps necessary, ambiguity raises the danger of what is sometimes called 'techno-phoria' – the tendency to exaggerate the importance of technological superiority even if it can be achieved.[50] The sixteenth-century Japanese strategist Migamto Musashi, who deduced his observations on warfare from the principles of swordplay, had some stern words for those who pin their faith on superior technology:

> In this world it is said 'one inch gives the hand advantage' but these are the idle words of one who does not know strategy. It shows the inferior strategy of a weak spirit that men should be dependent on the length of their sword, fighting from a distance without the benefit of strategy.[51]

From this, and a consciousness of the importance of the political context, it is no very great jump to conclude that unless strategic thinking keeps up with technological progress, the field may become dangerously dominated by technocrats.[52]

Navies evidently need to develop a strategy for dealing with technological transformation.

5.9 A strategy for innovation

There is, in fact, a widespread myth, even amongst otherwise respectable scholars, that the military is habitually against new technology, generally preferring to prepare for the last war rather than the next. This myth has two related but separate origins. First, it is often based on an uncritical acceptance of the remarks and memoires of military radicals frustrated at the slow acceptance of their ideas. Second, and more importantly, it often proceeds from a simplistic idea of how innovation usually works. The image is of the instantaneous, totally transforming revolution in military affairs. In 1921, General Billy Mitchell drops bombs on a stationary, leaking, unmanned German warship (the *Ostfriesland*), which unsurprisingly sinks. Were it not for the 'scelerotic conservatism' of battleship admirals, everything in naval warfare would immediately be different.[53]

But, of course, things were not like this. Around the world, admirals took a close interest in the potentialities of airpower and introduced it into their fleets to the extent and as fast as technology and resources would sensibly allow and they had to do so usually incrementally over surprisingly long periods. The normal way in which new technology is incorporated into existing military structures is through a process of continuous revolution rather than through some 'big bang' that the clever recognised and immediately responded to and the stupid didn't.[54]

The arrival of the Portuguese in the Indian Ocean at the end of the fifteenth century, however, would seem to be an example of an instantaneous RMA at least for the local fleets they encountered. Portuguese caravels were nailed and carried naval artillery. Local dhows were constructed from wood bound by coconut fibre; as a result they were more fragile, less able to cope with monsoon weather on the open ocean or to take significant gunnery to sea. As a result, small Portuguese fleets were able to stand off at a distance and batter their adversaries to pieces with complete impunity. The Portuguese Navy's competitive advantage lasted for perhaps 100 years, until other European navies appeared on the scene. Some of the locals indeed were able to adopt and use Western naval technology. The navy of the Sultanate of Oman from the late seventeenth century developed a small Western-style navy that was instrumental in expelling the Portuguese from Muscat.[55] A little later, the famous Bombay Marine even built ships for the Royal Navy.

But discrete and discernible 'jumps' of the sort that occurred when the Portuguese arrived in the Indian Ocean are rare. Usually innovation is not so much a jump or revolution, more a process of evolutionary slither.

For one example, the equally transforming transition from wood to iron to steel, and from sail to steam in the nineteenth century, was for the best of reasons quite a halting process. Wooden merchant sailing ships continued to operate throughout the century because they were cheaper to build and operate and often carried more cargo per ton than their more advanced competitors. Steamships were expensive to build and operate, but were faster and so especially suitable for the carriage of perishable or time-urgent cargoes like people or mail. Until high-pressure boilers and more efficient marine engines appeared, merchant ships were often hybrids – steamships that carried sail. People were inspired into innovation

...Ministry of National Heritage and Culture).

...were often disappointed. The appear-
...xample, seemed an RMA in itself with
...er produced, but the commercial bene-
...f expectation because performance was
...er countries and companies responded

...l impact of maritime airpower on naval
...ously, it took a long time. The first aerial
...major impetus provided by two world
...eful career at least until 1945, although
...carrier by then. Moreover, most of the
...n became clear with the appearance of
HMS *Argus* in 1918 – but took another generation to answer.

The process of 'slither' does, however, appear to be accelerating at an exponential rate. Indeed, the sheer pace of technological change could well mean that the problem changes faster than the solution arrives; as a result, military customers will always be desperately trying to keep up.

Equally, some admirals and some navies are more receptive to change and are better able to innovate over a period than others. Many of the reasons for this may well be outside their control; the capacity to innovate technologically will, for example, tend to reflect the constituents of seapower discussed in the last chapter – the general level of technological sophistication in the country at large, the level of resources devoted to the navy, its strategic circumstances and so forth. Technological change is not an independent variable, but instead is affected by things like the resources devoted to it, attitudes and strategic circumstances

This last point is perhaps worth emphasising. A country's strategic circumstances often seem decisive for the manner in which its navy innovates technologically. As Andrew Krepenevich has sensibly remarked, 'More than anything else, it is perceptions of future contingencies and likely enemies that determine whether and when there is full exploration of the advantages offered by the military revolution.'[56] The development of maritime airpower in the interwar period demonstrates this well. For both the Japanese and Americans, the vast distances involved in any Pacific campaign and the near complete preoccupation that each navy had with the other, both mandated the allocation of high priority to the development of maritime aviation. The absence of friendly landbases quite simply meant that both navies would need to take their airpower with them, or establish it quickly in conquered territory. It was different for the British who faced not only the Germans and Italians, as well as the Japanese, but who were as likely to operate within the confined waters of the Mediterranean as they were the Indian and Pacific oceans. Moreover, the British faced additional strategic challenges, particularly the threat of metropolitan air attack from the European mainland; dealing with this commanded an increasing share of scarce defence resources. All this does much to explain the relative decline of British maritime aviation during the interwar period when compared to the advances made by the Americans and the Japanese. Future contingencies determined attitudes towards transformational technology to a very considerable extent.

And so, of course, does the actual availability of the new technology. To a considerable extent, attitudes are determined by technology, as well as the other way around. Maritime airpower was transformed at the very end of the interwar period by a host of aeronautical advances that came about quite independently of the interest of navies. By the mid 1920s, aircraft tended to be made of steel rather than wood, and being fabric, wood or metal covered. The changing shape of their wings led to big improvements in their aerodynamic qualities. The largest aircraft engines in 1918 developed about 250 horsepower while the typical military aero-engine of 1935 ranged from 500–900 horsepower. Engines were lighter in relation to their power output and much more reliable. Fuel injection, variable pitch propellers, flush riveting, retractable landing gear were all coming into play by that time. All these technological developments made possible the huge advances in maritime airpower that occurred at the very end of the interwar period.[57]

Ten approaches that have worked

But if some of the major stimuli to innovation were coming from outside naval circles, many were, and are, intrinsic to navies themselves, however. Recent history suggests the following ten interrelated approaches to be amongst the characteristics that should be part of a strategy for technological innovation.

Having educated people

An institutional culture in which the professional military education system (courses, staff training, reading material) helps develop naval personnel (both officers and ratings) interested in issues of innovation, skilled enough to analyse them effectively and ready to challenge defective ideas, irrespective of their origin. As a rule, an educated navy, in which ideas are freely distributed and discussed, performs better.

Keeping in touch, technologically

Since technology seems most likely to be in a state of continuous revolution, innovative navies are distinguished by their development and maintenance of close and productive links with industry, often directly involving scientists in their deliberations. This was particularly crucial in the rise of the German Navy at the beginning of the twentieth century and later in the success of the British campaign against the U-boat in the Second World War. The Royal Navy's enforced loss of contact with the otherwise impressive British aeronautical industry in the interwar period, greatly weakened British naval aviation and shows what happens when close touch is lost.[58]

Admittedly, keeping in touch may be expensive and can lead to the creation of what has sometimes variously been called 'a fleet of samples' or, in Admiral Tirpitz's phrase, a 'museum of experiments'. Navies in the late nineteenth century tended to accumulate everything going, producing a heterogeneous mixture of citadel ships, broadside ships and ships of varying speeds and endurance that were almost impossible to operate as a cohesive unit. To some degree this is inevitable in a period of rapid technological change. Better that, than falling so far behind that catching up in time becomes impossible.[59]

Technological innovation often takes place in response to a variety of private, civilian and commercial imperatives. In the nineteenth century, governments, and to a marked extent their military forces, were much more in command of technological and scientific progress than they now seem to be. This change is particularly marked with the arrival of the 'info-RMA' discussed earlier, where so many of the advances in IT have come about in consequence of the demands of commerce. Tracking technology requires navies to stay closely alongside and responsive to civilian industry.

Maintaining options

In a situation of technological uncertainty, there is much to be said for a policy of gradualistic incrementalism that keeps as many options open as possible. From a recent study of British naval procurement in the first half of the twentieth century, Jon Sumida has concluded:

> Even the most promising devices require years – if not decades – of improvement before their full potential can be assessed accurately and appropriate forms of application definitively established. During this period, other technical developments, either independently, or in combination with older *materiel* might offer an effective operational alternative to immature new technology.[60]

US naval experience with torpedo and anti-torpedo technology in the 1920s shows that navies that rush into new developments seem often to get their fingers burnt. The reason for this is quite simple and derives from the well-known 'learning S curve' in which a steep period of technological advance is followed by a flatter

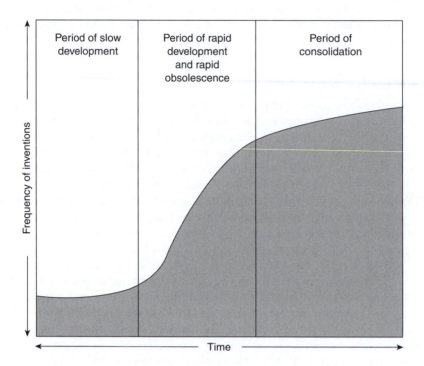

Figure 5.3 The S curve.

period of consolidation. Investing heavily in the early stages of development will produce equipment that is quickly rendered obsolete; better to wait until the dust has settled before plunging into large-scale procurement programmes. Just behind the leading edge is a good place to be.[61]

Navies need a conscious strategy for investment in new platforms, sensors and weapons, and knowing where you are on the S curve in the case of particular technologies is an important part of it. Excessive enthusiasm for new technology can be as damaging as excessive resistance to it. Both are examples of what the German military of the interwar period characterised as *Einseitigkeit* – one sidedness, the inability to take the balanced view of new technology that is so indispensable for effective innovation.

Strong, sustained leadership

The success of such varied innovators as the US Navy's Admiral William J. Moffett (Chief of the Bureau of Aeronautics 1921–1933) and Admiral Hyman D. Rickover (responsible for the US Navy's nuclear propulsion throughout the Cold War), Japan's reforming Admiral Yamamoto Gombei or, perhaps most outstandingly, the Soviet Navy's Commander-in-Chief from 1956–1985, Admiral Sergei Gorshkov, all attest to the value of a long-term vision of the navy's technological future, and the administrative authority to push it through. The more a navy's technological programme is chopped around by regime changes, the less successful it is likely to be. To cope, navies need an institutional and cultural predisposition to adopt, adapt and exploit technological change proactively.[62]

Adaptive institutions

The success of the Polaris procurement programme in both the United States and Britain shows the huge benefits to be derived from institutions adapting to accommodate new technology rather than the other way around. Famously, the Royal Navy's Vice Admiral Sir Hugh Mackenzie was able to set up a unique, special-to-purpose organisation, the Polaris executive, which drove this crucial but highly complex programme through despite political anxieties, widespread ignorance of the technological possibilities it presented and bureaucratic resistance from within the institutions normally charged with submarine development.[63] Had those institutions been sufficiently adaptive, this would have been unnecessary.

The capacity to profit from experience

The ability to make effective use of the experience of others, and indeed to develop a corporate memory in the lessons of previous technological innovation is often crucial. The Japanese maritime airpower programme of the interwar period, for example, benefitted enormously from the help extended it by the British and by the lessons provided from conflict in China from 1931 onwards. The result was a shift from the acquisition of other people's technology to the indigenous production of their own – and very high quality it was too. As one recent and authoritative study concludes:

> By the end of the decade of the 1930s, the Japanese navy had acquired some of the finest combat aircraft in the world and was a leading participant in the world transformation of naval aircraft that moved them from the margins of naval power to its very centre.[64]

Good interservice relations?

Competition between the services, and indeed between different interest groups within the naval service, seems to cut both ways as far as technological innovation is concerned. On the one hand, it can produce wasteful duplication, institutional resistance and dangerous gaps in provision. On the other, such tensions can sometimes be creative in sparking off a host of stimulating ideas. For example, some analysts of the Polaris programme in both the United States and the United Kingdom argue that naval officers rallied behind the project partly because success would be 'one in the eye for the Air Force'. However, British experience with maritime airpower through most of the twentieth century suggests that this kind of competition generally does much more harm than good and has helped determine the move towards more 'jointery' described in the last chapter. Because the functional differences between the services have become more blurred anyway, the habit of cooperation is likely to be steadily more important for effective innovation.

Keeping assumptions under review

Naval staffs clearly need to develop notions of how they will proceed in future conflicts. This process of concept formulation takes time and effort, and human beings being what they are, people may be reluctant to change their ideas as much as they should. Other than developing the proper attitude towards doctrine already discussed and making sure that there is a general spirit of enquiry, there is no easy answer to this problem.

One of the clearest needs here is *not* to think that any technological innovation is completely revolutionary, offering permanent, enduring and radical change in the overall nature of military operations. One of the reasons for this is because, as Clausewitz reminds us, war is a dynamic process between two living and responsive forces. Thus, in most cases, the adversary will respond to some technical or tactical innovation either with countermeasures inspired by the same science that produced the threat or with parallel technical, tactical and even political developments of his own – or, most likely, with both.

Effective marketing

Innovative technology not only has to be invented; it needs to paid for and applied. This often requires effective marketing amongst the press, domestic public opinion and amongst naval personnel themselves. To an extent this may require emphasising the future potentiality of a new weapon system rather than its present limitations. As we have already seen, transforming technology is often much more incremental in its effect than people realise. For instance the battle of Sinope in 1856 when Russia's Admiral Nakhimov overwhelmed a wooden Turkish/Egyptian fleet with modern shell guns has often been portrayed as a turning point in naval history. And so it was – in some ways. However, Nakhimov took over six hours to have this effect; he vastly outnumbered and outgunned his adversary (he had six ships of the line amassing some 600 major guns, while the biggest ship in the opposing fleet was a humble frigate). With these odds, old-fashioned solid shot would have had precisely the same effect![65]

Nonetheless, it was the impression that counted, rather than the reality. Hence Mitchell's bombing of the *Ostfriesland* in 1921 – this was a military performance as theatre. The media may have a crucial role here. Contemporary attitudes towards the appearance of revolutionary warships like the *Monitor* and the *Virginia* during the American Civil War were greatly influenced by the media 'hype' that accompanied them. The *Virginia*, for example, was represented as omnipotent, entirely new and wholly sinister: 'The water hisses and boils with indignation as, like some huge slimy reptile, she slowly emerges from her loathsome lair.'[66] While being properly mindful of the large gap between impression and performance that invariably attends new technology, successful innovators need political as well as technological skills if their proposals are to be accepted.

Coping with the unexpected

Things often do not turn out the way that innovators expect, and successful innovation requires continuous adaptation of even the most basic of their ideas. For instance, modern scholarship shows that the most famous naval transformation of all, the appearance of Admiral Jack Fisher's *Dreadnought* in 1906, was a good deal more complicated than is often realised. Fisher seems to have regarded it as no more than an experimental testbed, but instead it turned itself into a transforming event almost of its own volition. Arguably this even went to the extent of blowing the major innovator's real transforming intention (to introduce 'flotilla defence' as the mainstay of British naval policy in home waters) out of the water. If this argument is right, Fisher's own brainchild was indirectly responsible for the failure of his main expectations and desires. Innovative technology evidently can take on a life of its own, and successful navies need to be able to accommodate that fact.[67]

5.10 Navies and technology: summary and conclusions

Historically, good men with poor ships are better than poor men with good ships, which our own age, with its rage for the last new thing in material improvement, has largely dropped out of memory.[68]

It would seem from all this that navies are likely to be challenged through the twenty-first century by the prospect of a continuous technological revolution, the dynamics of which will usually often not be under their control. But they need to develop a strategic approach towards this process that will help them pick their way through such uncertainties because it has so great an impact on all aspects of their capacity to perform their tasks.

Technology affects all navies, great and small, but may pose them different problems. How it affects their capacity to operate with allied navies of different rank, for example, remains controversial. Observers impressed with IT developments tend to argue that with gateway technologies of various kinds, modern technology can link up the C^4I surveillance and reconnaissance systems of different navies much more easily than was possible before. Sceptics are not so sure and tend to believe that IT widens rather than narrows the gap between the great, the medium and the small. Americans tend to predominate in the first group, their allies in the second. Since technology affects everyone (helping great navies that want to project military power ashore, small navies that might need to resist such efforts and medium navies trying to maintain as many options as they can) navies cannot safely opt out of the process.

But one thing does seem to be clear. Despite its advocates, and despite those who point to the analogy of pocket calculators and computers, which have become much cheaper in real terms, the sensors, weapons, platforms and systems of modern navies, their personnel and all aspects of their infrastructure have become progressively more expensive. Over the past half century, the unit cost of most types of military equipment has risen between about 7 and 10 per cent per year.[69] In consequence, since the financial resources available to navies are finite, most of the world's navies have fewer platforms than they did, although each is a good deal more capable individually, and usually larger, than they were. This shrinkage has been particularly noticeable amongst the erstwhile antagonists of the Cold War era, and is much less marked in the Asia-Pacific and elsewhere. Against such a background the economic need to avoid mistakes in technological investment is considerable.

For all these reasons, navies need to take technology as least as seriously in the future as in fact they have in the past. They need, in short, to develop a strategy for technological innovation. But this does not mean simply having a 'rage for the last new thing in material development'. Here, as elsewhere, in order to avoid *Einseitigikeit*, a sense of balance is necessary. Perhaps the most important aspect of this is the need to avoid being seduced by the excitements of 'techno-babble' into thinking that when it comes to understanding naval capability, technology is really the only thing that matters.[70]

6 Command of the sea and sea control

ANTHONY: Pompey is strong at sea ... No
Vessel can peep forth but 'tis as soon
Taken as seen.

POMPEY: ... I shall do well
The people love me, and the sea is mine.

Shakespeare, *Anthony and Cleopatra*, I/4 and II/1

6.1 Evolution of a traditional concept

As Shakespeare shows, the notion of command of the sea is an ancient one, but to paraphrase Corbett, it is one of those ringing phrases that dominates the imagination but confuses the intellect. It conjures up the spectacular imagery of naval battle, heroism and mastery that adorn the walls of naval establishments around the world. It seems to be what navies are all about.

But in fact most traditional maritime strategists are much more pragmatic about what command of the sea is and what it provides. Broadly, it is no more than a means to an end. Corbett put it like this:

> It never has been and never can be, the end in itself. Yet, obvious as this is, it is constantly lost sight of in naval policy. We forget what really happened in the old wars: we blind ourselves by looking only on the dramatic moments of naval history; we come unconsciously to assume that the defeat of the enemy's fleets solves all problems.[1]

And, of course, it does not. The same point was also made by Admiral Colomb, when discussing the Anglo-Dutch wars of the seventeenth century. 'It is incomprehensible', he wrote, 'that the whole naval force of each side should have gathered against the other again and again and simply fought for the mastery [of the sea], unless something was to follow when it was gained.' Both sides had enormous maritime interests to protect or expand and the ferociousness of their wars reflected, in true Clausewitzian style, the importance of the ends they served.[2]

In essence, the value of commanding the sea lay not in its physical conquest or possession – an idea that only makes sense in land warfare – but in the use to which commanding the sea could be put. If maritime strategy is about the use of the sea, then commanding it means you can use it for your purposes and prevent the enemy from using it for his. Those uses depended on circumstances.

At one level, it could serve as the basis for the creation of a colonial empire, as it did for the Portuguese in the sixteenth century and the Dutch and English there-after. In the twentieth century, the Japanese followed suit, again illustrating what command of the sea could mean. As Richmond put it, the Japanese,

> with an unopposed command of the sea owing to the absence of British sea forces, the disablement of the United States Fleet at Pearl Harbour, and the allied losses of Malaya and in the Java Sea, could move her military forces freely ... against the British, Dutch and American possessions in the Pacific.

But then in a series of battles the Allies broke and destroyed much of the basis of Japanese seapower, wresting command of the sea away from the Imperial Japanese Navy. This transformed the situation. The Allies could now threaten Japan with three measures: invasion of the home islands, bombardment from the air and the sea of her factories and cities, and blockade, cutting off food supplies she could draw both from the mainland and the fisheries around her coasts. 'With our sea power making possible the use of all our other resources', said Admiral Nimitz, 'we gave Japan the choice of surrender or slow but certain death.'[3]

The advantages of command of the sea were conveniently summarised by Admiral Sir Cyprian Bridge like this:

> It enables the nation which possess it to attack its foes where it pleases and where they seem most vulnerable. At the same time its gives its possessor secur-ity against serious counter-attacks, and affords to his maritime commerce the most efficient protection that can be devised. It is, in fact, the main object of naval warfare.[4]

Because these strategic advantages are so great, there is a natural tendency to use the phrase 'command of the sea' as though it were a synonym for maritime great-ness, ruling the waves or even seapower. As we saw in Section 3.4, Mahan himself got close to saying that.

6.2 Limits and qualifications

This seems unwise, for a variety of reasons. First, it encourages the notion that command of the sea is an absolute rather than relative concept, and one that, more-over, suggests that it is unrealistic for smaller navies to have pretensions in this area. Some think of command as being of all the sea for all purposes. 'There is no such thing as partial or incomplete command of the sea', declared Clarke and Thursfield roundly in 1897. 'It is either absolute, or it does not exist.' Mahan has also been accused of thinking that 'Command of the sea... was an exclusive thing: it could not be shared, and was applicable to one nation at a time.'[5]

Mahan sometimes suffers from having written more than most people are pre-pared to read but he often tried to make it clear that he believed that command of the sea, a phrase incidentally that he hardly used, was essentially a relative not an absolute thing. And so did most other maritime strategists. Corbett often used the useful phrase 'a working command', which makes the point exactly. Castex was clearest of all on the matter. 'The mastery of the sea', he argued, 'is not absolute but relative, incomplete and imperfect.'[6]

Amongst the relativities of command are: time, place, extent of use, strategic consequence and necessity.

Time

Command can be a matter of degree, in terms of time. Command of the seas could often prove a fleeting thing, no sooner won, than gone. Mahan declared:

> It is evident that the sea in the past has not been so exclusively dominated, even by Great Britain at her greatest, that a contest for control may not take the form of a succession of campaigns marked by ups and downs.[7]

Sometimes, though, it could last 'for the duration' – as it did for the British and the French in the Crimean War of 1853–1856.

Place

Command is invariably relative in geographic terms. It can be local, general or somewhere between the two. Brodie wrote:

> The absence of overall command is especially likely to be the rule where the areas in dispute are vast and the bases of the opposing forces widely removed from each other. Such a situation is almost inevitable in the broad reaches of the Pacific.[8]

That ocean was so huge that no one could expect to be in command of all of it at one time until the very end of the conflict. The French Navy is often said to have practised a strategy aiming at combining the relativities of time and place in a particularly ingenious way. They hoped to lure away the British Fleet for long enough to sneak an invasion over to England. In 1804, Napoleon wrote. 'Let us be masters of the Straits for six hours and we shall be masters of the World.' In such circumstances, command of the sea that was limited like this might be all that was necessary.

Extent of use

Command of the sea may facilitate the use of the sea, and/or the denial of that use to the adversary, *only to a degree*. Mahan was quite clear that 'however great the inequality of naval strength' the weaker party always had at least some opportunities to sail about the sea, make harassing descents upon unprotected points, enter blockaded harbours. Command could relate merely to the conduct of operations within particular dimensions of maritime war: air, surface and subsurface. Very possibly a different balance of command might apply in one dimension from in another. The German Navy of both world wars illustrates this point rather well, since it was so much more successful in contesting command by its underwater activities than it was on the surface. Similarly, command might apply mainly to particular types of ship and the kind of tasks they performed. During the First World War, Admiral Bacon observed, 'even in the North Sea we had command of the sea only so far as battleships were concerned: the enemy still had the power of using battle cruisers, fleet light cruisers, destroyers and submarines offensively'. As a result and even though the German battlefleet was successfully bottled up during the First World War, the British still needed directly to defend their shipping and coastline.[9]

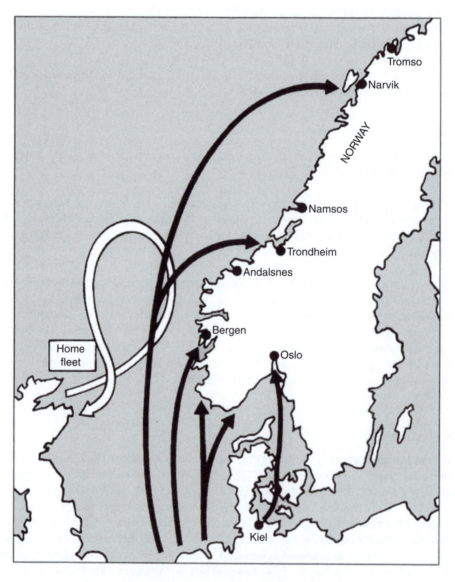

Figure 6.1 The Norway campaign, 1940.

Strategic consequence

Command of the sea could be limited in strategic effect, or sufficiently outflanked through superiority in the other dimensions of war. During the 1940 Norway campaign, the northwards push of German land forces and the spreading influence of their air force drove the British into the sea and harried them even there, the surface supremacy of the Royal Navy notwithstanding. As we saw in Sections 3.7 and 4.7, the ability to command the sea may often depend on supremacy on land, rather than the other way about.

Necessity

The Norwegian campaign also reveals a degree of doubt about the extent to which command of the sea is a prerequisite for significant action at sea. As Admiral Raeder openly admitted, the German invasion was hazardous in the extreme and 'contrary to all principles in the theory of naval warfare', since it would be carried out in the teeth of British naval supremacy.[10] The admiral pinned his faith on the achievement of complete surprise and on being able to counter any subsequent Allied reaction with German airpower. Although the plan worked in the end, according to most traditional strategists, it shouldn't have done! But as the Allied disaster at Dieppe showed in 1942, even a brief amphibious raid could go badly wrong if it turns out that the raiders had less command than they need.[12]

Mahan was clear that 'As a rule a major operation of war across sea should not be attempted unless naval superiority for an adequate period is probable.'[11] But it is worth emphasising that Mahan is not here talking of 'absolute' command, but of 'working' command, possibly limited in time, space and extent. The point was reinforced by Corbett. The notion 'that you cannot move a battalion overseas, till you have entirely overthrown your enemy's fleet', he declared was a ridiculous one that 'deserves gibbeting', but the more ambitious the amphibious enterprise, the more command you needed.

The link between command and the attack or defence of shipping is even more complex than it is with the conduct of amphibious operations. Two points need to be made at this stage. First, as we shall see in Chapter 8, command is not merely a prerequisite to, but actually an intrinsic *part of*, a campaign to attack/defend maritime communications. Second, the possible tension between the requirements of command on the one hand and of the attack/defence of maritime communications on the other is a particularly striking example of the way in which forces and operational priorities designed to contest command could differ quite radically from those intended to exercise it. As Admiral Colomb pointed out 'the forces proper for gaining command of the sea might be quite useless for protecting commerce'.[13]

Corbett rammed the point home: 'No principle of naval warfare', he said, 'is so much ignored in ordinary discussion, as that you cannot command the sea with a battlefleet.' The battlefleet could never be numerous or ubiquitous enough to exercise command and control of the lines of passage: that was the job of 'the flotilla and its supporting cruisers and intermediate ships'. By destroying or neutralising its opposite number, the battlefleet won the command that only these other naval forces could actually exercise.[14] With the benefit of the experience of the First World War, Commander Russell Grenfell made all clear by labelling the small ships exercising command, patrolling focal and terminal trade areas, escorting convoys and military transports, patrolling to intercept enemy commerce and so forth, the 'control fleet'. The gaining and maintenance of command was the work of the 'bat-tlefleet', under whose cover the control fleet operated. The point of emphasising the difference between these two functions was that they had different requirements in warships, tactical procedure and so on. Only with a properly balanced fleet could a navy hope to perform both functions.[15]

* * *

For all these reasons, even 'permanent and general' command of the sea could never be absolute in practice. The adversary would always have at least some mar-itime possibilities, but perhaps not of the kind that would necessarily have a sub-stantial impact on the outcome of the war.

But there is also a second set of reasons why the natural tendency to associate 'command of the sea' with maritime greatness can be misleading, namely that it obscures the fact that the concept is as relevant to small navies as it is to big ones. Small navies have often struggled amongst themselves for command of the sea, and large ones have been known to use flotillas of small ships to do the same on rivers, lakes, inland waters and coastal seas.

- If the famous encounter between the Northerner's USS *Monitor* and the Con-federate CSS *Virginia* during the American Civil War was not a battle for sea control, it is hard to imagine what is.
- And so for that matter were the small-ship struggles between the British and the Americans in the lakes in both the War of Independence and the War of 1812.
- The October 1879 battle north of Antofagasta between the tiny navies of Peru and Chile in the War of the Pacific served the same purpose. The capture of the most important enemy unit resulted in Chile's supremacy of the sea. Having control of the sea, the Fleet then began the transport of the expeditionary Army with an amphibious operation into the heart of enemy territory.[16]
- Likewise the struggles of the Israeli, Syrian and Egyptian navies in 1967 and 1973, when *Komar* and *Sa'ar* FACs armed with anti-ship missiles performed exactly the same functions as the battlefleets of the First World War.[17]

6.3 Pursuing command in moderation

For all these reasons, Corbett warned his readers against the idea of reducing mar-itime strategy to the simple bull-headed pursuit of absolute command of the sea at all costs. While in pure logic it might make sense for a navy first to concentrate in order by battle or blockade to achieve command before dispersing in order to exer-cise it, things are rarely so neat and tidy. 'Extraneous necessities intrude themselves which make it inevitable that operations for exercising command should accompany as well as follow operations for securing command.'[18] It was a 'difficult and disputed' matter, declared Mahan, whether in combined operations 'the fleet and the convoy should sail together, or the convoy held till control of the sea is decided.' It was unwise to make 'sweeping dogmatic assertions': far better to weigh up the particu-lars of the individual case. How much risk was permissible; how near and mighty the enemy fleet; how important the objective? Any decision on precedence must depend on such things as these. Three-quarters of a century later, the Soviet Navy's Admiral Gorshkov agreed: 'Combat actions the aim of which is to secure dominance at sea in selected areas or in particular directions, may either precede the solution by the fleet of the main tasks or be conducted simultaneously.'[19] Most of the major fleet encounters actions of the Second World War, Gorshkov pointed out, were associated with, and a part of, some larger enterprise against sea communications or the enemy's coastline: thus, the Battle of Cape Matapan, the sinking of the *Bismarck*, the battles in the Coral Sea, Midway, the Philippine Sea, Leyte Gulf and so on. He also believed this to be a growing trend.

The point of all this, of course, is that it poses navies with a fundamental dilemma. How should they split their resources and their efforts between the demands of the battlefleet and the control fleet? It used to be said that the Royal Navy concentrated far more on the former than the latter in the period between the First and Second World Wars because of its fixation on the decisive battle (and on avoiding another Jutland), thereby being caught at a dangerous disadvantage by the German U-boat offensive of 1940–1943. Nowadays, this charge is generally dismissed as simplistic, but the strategic choice it identifies remains valid for all that.[20]

The same dilemma can be seen at the tactical and operational levels of war too. Should a convoy escort leave its station, where it directly protects a group of merchantmen, to try to destroy a threatening submarine? Was not Admiral Nagumo's fatal mistake at the Battle of Midway in 1942 his basic uncertainty as to whether he was supposed to be attacking the island with his aircraft or dealing with any American carriers that might be in the area? The pursuit of such divided aims seems to be a violation of the master principle of war (Section 2.2) but circumstances may make it hard to avoid.

Since the notion of command of the sea is evidently such a minefield of potential misconception and general hazard, perhaps we should not use such a grandiose term? The alternatives have their own imprecisions, however, and seem to mean much the same anyway. Accordingly, as Bernard Brodie sensibly concluded:

> So long as one bears in mind that 'command' is always relative and means simply a marked ascendancy in the contest for control, one might as well continue to use a phrase which has so ancient and honourable a tradition.[21]

6.4 Command of the sea yields to sea control

However, a few years later during the Cold War, many analysts concluded that recent developments were making it more difficult to secure high degrees of command of the sea. Admiral Gorshkov, for example, argued that, 'It will be seen that the period of keeping the dominance gained at sea tends to shorten and the struggle for gaining it becomes even tougher.'[22] This partly reflected perceptions of the impact of the new technology on surface naval power. Missiles, torpedoes, mines, land-based aircraft, even in the hands of non-industrial states seemed likely to make it noticeably more hazardous for bluewater navies to pass through, or operate in, sea areas within reach of land. In peacetime, it seemed, there were growing politico-legal restrictions on the freedom of the maritime powers to use the sea as they wished.

Table 6.1 Types of control of the sea by area and by time

1	Absolute control (command of the sea) Complete freedom to operate without interruption. Enemy cannot operate at all.
2	Working control General ability to operate with high degree of freedom, Enemy can only operate with high risk.
3	Control in dispute Each side operates with considerable risk. This then involves the need to establish working control for limited portions for limited times to conduct specific operations.
4	Enemy working control Position 2 reversed.
5	Enemy absolute control (command of the sea) Position 1 reversed.

For such reasons as these, many modern maritime strategists were increasingly uncomfortable about the continued use of the phrase the 'command of the sea', which they thought too absolutist in tone. So they started to dissect the concept coming up with breakdowns such as those produced by the US Navy's Admiral Eccles in 1972, as shown in Table 6.1.[23]

For much of the Cold War the Soviet Navy could hardly aspire to 'absolute control' even though Admiral Gorshkov (see pages 24–25), continued to think that 'sea dominance' was still a thoroughly valid concept. Accordingly, he and his colleagues adapted the notion to fit the Soviet Union's initially rather constrained industrial, geographic and strategic circumstances. Nonetheless, Soviet interpretations of the concept of sea dominance grew increasingly 'orthodox'. By 1976, Gorshkov regarded it as 'A vehicle for creating the definite preconditions that will allow fleet forces and means successfully to accomplish particular tasks in definite regions of the theatre in a concrete time period.'[24] Inevitably, as Soviet aspirations grew, the conceptions of the US Navy grew more modest. The phrase 'command of the sea' dropped out of fashion and was replaced by 'sea control'. According to Admiral Stansfield Turner:

> This change in terminology may seem minor but it is a deliberate attempt to acknowledge the limitations on ocean control brought about by the development of the submarine and the airplane.... The new term 'Sea Control' is intended to connote more realistic control in limited areas and for limited periods of time ... it is no longer conceivable, except in the most limited sense, to totally control the seas for one's own use or to totally deny them to an enemy.[25]

Stansfield Turner argued that sea control comprised two complementary dimensions: 'sea assertion' or 'sea use' and 'sea denial'. The first was to do with the ability to use the sea for traditional purposes. With NATO and the US Navy in mind, the admiral listed four such purposes:

- to ensure industrial supplies;
- to reinforce/resupply military forces engaged overseas;
- to provide wartime economic/military supplies to allies;
- to provide safety for naval forces in the 'projection of power ashore' role.

This makes the essential point that sea control should no more be regarded as an end in itself than command of the sea. Corbett chose his words carefully: 'The object of naval warfare must always be directly or indirectly to secure the command of the sea, or to prevent the enemy from securing it.'[26] Corbett's use of the word *naval* here was quite deliberate; navies must strive for sea control because that facilitated the achievement of naval objectives that would in turn help secure national objectives in a *maritime* campaign or war. He was trying to clarify the relationship between ends and means. He would probably have been worried about the American tendency in the 1970s to conflate the many functions of maritime power into four 'missions' (strategic deterrence, sea control, projection and presence) or even simply to two (sea control and projection) since it stood in danger of running together the two logically discrete procedures of securing command and exercising it, the means and ends of maritime strategy respectively.

This could be a very dangerous form of intellectual shorthand if it leads people to suppose that sea control was an end in itself. From the start of the Cold War period, voices were raised against this practice. In 1948, for instance, Vice Admiral R.L. Conolly commented: 'I believe we err in advancing the proposition that "Control of the Sea" is an end in itself. It is the exploitation of this control that is important.'[27] He was, however, by no means the first American to make the point.

Of course, much of this was merely giving old concepts a new twist. The use of the phrase 'sea control' merely gives greater emphasis to the relativities noted earlier. During the Cold War the practice followed the theory too. The adverse military balance on Europe's Central Front worked against the classic notion that sea control should be gained before reinforcement shipping set off across the Atlantic. In some circumstances, moreover, aspiring for even limited sea control might not be necessary anyway. According to Gorshkov, 'since combat activities had become swift and productive ... the forces waging a struggle at sea did not need the creation of favourable conditions'.[28] Certainly even in the past it was no means unknown for two sides to use the sea and studiously avoid encountering each other's main forces (such as in the Black Sea during the Second World War). It is not inconceivable that the same might happen again.

6.5 Sea denial

The emphasis on sea control was also useful in that it threw up the corollary of 'sea denial', although that too can often prove to be quite a confusing concept. The British definition is: 'The condition short of full sea control that exists when an opponent is prevented from using an area of sea for his purposes.'[29] Here the objective is not to use the sea oneself, but to prevent the enemy from doing so. Stansfield Turner thought of it essentially as:

> guerrilla warfare at sea. The denying naval commander strikes at a time and place of his choosing to achieve maximum surprise; he does not have to stand his ground toe to toe with the enemy but instead hits and runs. In this way a markedly inferior force can successfully thwart a superior force.[30]

Technological developments such as smart mines, FACs, anti-ship missiles even the famous fighting frogmen of Israel and Bangladesh, indicated that through the capacity to inflict asymmetrical harm on powerful forces, sea denial capabilities were rising.[31]

Sea denial works in two ways. First, it may be an *alternative* to sea control. For some countries, the ability to prevent an enemy from using the sea to do them harm is all that is required, rather in the manner of the coastal defence theorists discussed in Section 2.6. Moshe Tzalel argues that Israel comes into this category: 'One may state categorically that Israel had never needed to command the sea in order to prevail in wartime, and an attempt to secure such a position at this day and age is a luxury she cannot afford.'[32] Many smaller, defensively oriented navies may feel this applies to them too, especially when up against far stronger forces.

Second, sea denial may act as a *complement* to sea control, or even a contribution to it. Robert Herrick explained how sea control and sea denial worked together as far as the Soviet Union was concerned:

> Soviet writers for many years have talked about zones of defense. The Soviets hope to command the sea within a couple of hundred miles of their coasts. In these zones, they could use all their small fast craft, surface ships and PT boats, and even their expensive missile artillery. Beyond these zones – which would include their peripheral seas – the Barents, the Baltic, the Black, and the Sea of Japan – they have an area in which they hope to contest us in command of the seas. And beyond that, there is what they call the open-ocean zone, where they have to practise sea denial, because they cannot support their submarines with surface forces until they have more carrier-based air craft.[33]

Even strong navies may need to resort to strategies of sea denial in some areas against one adversary while sticking to sea control elsewhere. The British and the Americans both did this against the Japanese Navy in the Indian Ocean and the Western Pacific, respectively, during the early part of 1942.[34]

This latter version of sea denial can be very confusing, however, because it blurs the difference between it and sea control. It might be safer, indeed, to regard it as an indirect strategy of sea control if the aim of the exercise is in fact to facilitate *your* eventual use of the sea somewhere. This recent comment on the ambitions of the South Korean Navy illustrates the point:

> With limited financial resources, it is true that we can not build a strong navy that could fight and win a naval battle against China or Japan. But we can build a navy, which could deny others' attempts to block the SLOCs of Korea.[35]

'Denying' their enemy's capacity to prevent them using their sea lanes of communication is *not* a form of sea denial; it is, instead, better described as a struggle for sea control as far as the South Koreans are concerned, certainly at the strategic and operational levels. But it might be a campaign of sea denial for their adversary, if that adversary had no serious pretensions for sea use himself.

The balance that navies strike between sea denial and sea control is mainly a function of their strength relative to the putative opposition and the geo-strategic conditions that apply in particular areas of concern. Broadly, the further away from the main source of their maritime power and the weaker they are compared to the threat, the more likely they are to veer towards sea denial.

6.6 Contemporary angles

[I]f our control of the sea had been contested just a little bit ... Korea would have been lost very fast.

Admiral Arleigh Burke[36]

Towards the end of the twentieth century, and especially with the appearance of 'The Maritime Strategy' and the associated quest for a 600-ship navy, American conceptions of sea control, became noticeably less modest and their aspirations for ways of achieving it more ambitious. There was little doubting the importance of sea control, because of what it could lead to. The following is typical of this approach:

Sea control is therefore the fundamental capability of the navy. There is no forward presence on the sea without control of the sea. There is no power projection from the sea without control of the sea. There is no initiation or support of littoral warfare from the sea without control of the seas between the United States and the engaged littoral. Sea control is absolutely necessary, the thing without which all other naval missions, and most national missions, precariously risk catastrophic failure. It is impossible to over-emphasize this point.

...if we cannot command the seas and the airspace above them, we cannot project power to command or influence events ashore; we cannot deter, we cannot shape the security environment.[37]

Many other nations of the Asia-Pacific have demonstrated, in their preparations and deployments, the importance they attach to sea control even if it is rather more limited in geographic and operational extent than the American version. With the growth of their maritime dependence on the resources that can be derived from the ocean and on the shipping that crosses it, such nations have shown an increasing tendency to want to control their own areas of sea more rigorously and to push their capacity to defend their interest outwards. The Chinese Navy shows this regional tendency rather more clearly than most through its acquisition of more capable, longer-range warships, better submarines and maritime air forces and by deploying and exercising these assets as task forces. If there is a global trend in sea control, it is towards applying it to larger areas of sea.

But while this may seem all very traditional, the US Navy has grappled with a rather different problem – that is what to do in a world in which no one seems seriously able to contest American sea control. Admiral William Owens summed up the 'problem' in the aftermath of Desert Storm:

We left knowing that the world had changed dramatically but that our doctrine had failed to keep pace. Little in Desert Storm supported the maritime strategy's assumptions and implications. No opposing naval forces challenged us. No waves of enemy aircraft ever attacked the carriers. No submarines threatened the flow of men and material across the oceans. The fleet was never forced to fight the open-ocean battles the navy had been preparing for during the preceding twenty years. Instead the deadly skirmishing of littoral warfare dominated.[38]

In some ways, this was a return to the point famously made by Samuel Huntington back in 1954. What was a powerful navy to do when it had no effective rivals for mastery of the open ocean? Most analysts have come up with three answers:

- In general it allows a shift in focus from the struggle to secure sea control towards its exploitation. Now, as in the 1950s, the major Western navies are devoting relatively more attention, for example, to the projection of power ashore. As we saw in pages 29–31, it can be argued that 'naval' strategy (as represented by a Mahanian struggle for sea control) has been replaced by a Corbettian 'maritime strategy' in which the emphasis is on influencing events ashore. For many Western navies, sea control has lost the prominence it once had – at least for the time being until another possible peer competitor appears on the scene.

- This does not, however, mean that sea control is any less important, merely that at the moment it does not have to be fought for. One day, great navies might have to fight for it again. Moreover, the capacity to protect oneself against all manner of threats on the open ocean remains the 'gold standard' of naval capability that assures navies of so much else. For both these reasons, navies will certainly seek to avoid the vulnerabilities that could easily come about through the neglect of the demands of sea control.

- The special topographical and operational circumstances that prevail in littoral waters require attention to a special form of sea control needed for the conduct of operations closer to shore. The more future antagonists engage in sea denial/coastal defence measures of the sort to be discussed shortly, the more outsiders will need to address the general issue of the 'battle for access', which should be regarded as a special variant of sea control.

For all these reasons, therefore, it would be quite wrong to argue that sea control has lost its traditional centrality in maritime strategy.

7 Securing command of the sea

7.1 Securing command of the sea: the operational approach

Because it confers the capacity to use the sea while denying that use to the adversary, command of the sea is often important and sometimes crucial at the strategic level of war. Unsurprisingly, the possible ways of achieving or maintaining this advantageous state have dominated the theory and practice of naval warfare. Conversely, ways of limiting or outflanking a stronger adversary's capacity to command the sea or to exploit that command has been a constant preoccupation of weaker fleets.

This chapter will look at the three possible ways in which this can be done:

- by the pursuit of what Nelson called 'a close and decisive battle' in which the enemy's main naval forces are physically destroyed in Clausewitzian style;
- by a naval defensive of some form, often called a 'fleet-in-being strategy' in which strategic advantage is sought by a fleet unwilling to engage in battle against a probably superior adversary;
- by a fleet blockade through which a stronger fleet seeks either to neutralise an adversary reluctant to fight or to force battle on him.

Although they may seem very different, all three methods have one thing in common – they are principally conducted at the tactical and especially the operational levels of war. When discussing the first, Castex put it like this: 'the elimination of the fleet is then the first objective and the search for battle its necessary corollary'.[1] Although we tend to focus on Nelson's tactical conduct *at* the battles of the Nile or Trafalgar, his ultimate operational skill lay less in that than in the successful campaigns he had conducted *beforehand* to ensure that those battles were indeed fought and conducted under favourable conditions. Partly, of course, this was 'merely' a matter of training his forces, tactically and technically, so that they would fight effectively when the time came – but Nelson's operational capacity to read and manipulate the general naval situation so that he could give 'battle with advantage' was at least as important. Exactly the same can be said about the other two methods by which command of the sea may be sought, maintained or attacked.

7.2 Decisive battle

What makes a battle decisive?

> We see the great effect of battles by sea. The battle of Actium decided the empire of the world. The battle of Lepanto arrested the greatness of the Turk. There be many examples where sea-fights have been final to the war.
>
> Francis Bacon, True Greatness of Kingdoms (1618)

In 1921, the British government held an enquiry into the fixture of naval warfare in general and of battleships in particular. In his testimony to the committee, Admiral Richmond summarised the advantages of a decisive battle:

> Much has been done by the destruction of the enemy's capital ships. Concentration of our own units is no longer necessary: in the past, battleships were set free to act as escorts; today it is the cruisers and destroyers. Your defending force is multiplied, your powers of exercising pressure by blockade are increased. If the enemy possesses overseas bases, your powers of affording escorts to expeditions sent to capture them are increased instead. The dangers of invasion are removed and ships and men and material are set free for protection of trade, or attack upon trade. The whole experience of war tells the same tale – a great victory is followed by a dispersion of the ships that had been concentrated ... [for it].[2]

A battle was decisive then, not just for the immediate damage and loss the victor inflicted on the vanquished, but much more importantly for what happened at sea afterwards. A battle decisively won could effectively confer upon the victor command of the sea, the ability to use the sea decisively for his own purposes and to prevent his enemy from doing the same.

Mahan maintained that the total destruction of the enemy's fleet was the best means of achieving control 'cutting off his communications with the rest of his possessions, drying up the sources of his wealth in commerce, and making possible a closure of his ports'.[3]

Nonetheless, Mahan differentiated carefully (and this is a point that is sometimes lost sight of) between battles with decisive results, and sterile battles of no consequence, fought merely for the sake of winning them – such as the frigate actions of the war of 1812. Tactically glorious though they might be, they were, he said, scattered efforts without relation to one another, incapable of affecting seriously the issues of war or, indeed, to any plan of operations worthy of the name.[4]

Nelson's victory in the 1798 Battle of the Nile, on the other hand, *was* a decisive battle worthy of the name, for not only were many ships sunk and casualties inflicted but also much of strategic consequence flowed from it. To illustrate its importance, Mahan quoted Jurien de la Graviere:

> The consequences of this battle were incalculable. Our navy never recovered from this terrible blow to its consideration and power. This was the combat which for two years delivered the Mediterranean to the English, and called thither the squadrons of Russia; which shut up our army in the midst of a

rebellious population, and decided the Porte to declare against us; which put India out of the reach of our enterprise, and brought France within a hair's breadth of her ruin; for it rekindled the scarcely extinct war with Austria, and brought Suwarrow and the Austro-Russians to our very frontiers.[5]

This showed that battle at sea could be decisive at two levels: first for its influence on subsequent events at sea, and second for its consequences on land. Trafalgar (1805), for another example, seems decisive in that it permanently set the conditions for warfare at sea under which the Royal Navy would subsequently prevail, although this did not mean that nothing that mattered happened at sea afterwards. The argument for its decisive effect on land is weaker. Arguably, it finally made an invasion of Britain impossible, and required France to impose the 'continental system', that in turn led to a war against the whole of Europe that even Napoleon could not win.[6]

Mahan thought that these two battles were decisive because:

- at the operational level they decided the nature of future events at sea;
- at the much more important strategic level they indirectly determined events on shore.

The English defeat of the Spanish Armada in 1588 or the Japanese defeat of Mongol seaborne assaults in the thirteenth century are other examples of battles decisive at both levels.

These two encounters also show that battles can also be decisive for *preventing* opponents from changing the geo-strategic situation to their advantage. As at Tsushima (1905), Jutland (1916) or Midway (1942) things would have been very different at both levels of war had the battle gone the other way. At Jutland, moreover, the British actually lost more ships and men than the Germans; but set against its operational and strategic consequence, the tactical aspect of this battle was, in effect, irrelevant. Admiral Gorshkov understood the point. He argued that the Germans fought the battle so they could seize the initiative, destroy the British commercial blockade and impose their own. The British fought to stop them, succeeded and so ensured that Germany would eventually lose the war.[7]

Nonetheless, many Britons were convinced that unambiguous victory at the tactical level as well would have made Jutland even more decisive than it was. They tended to attribute this less than perfect performance to a failure in the Royal Navy of the time fully to appreciate the potentiality of decisive victory at sea. The pursuit of secondary aims (the *maintenance* of command of the sea) had taken over from the primary aim (the destruction of the enemy's forces). Moreover, thought Creswell, this cold, calculating, rational, scientific approach to the conduct of war had been allowed to overshadow the sphere of morale, human nature and the psychological consequences of achieving victory.[8] Some critics attributed this 'failing' to a decline in the Nelsonic belief in the centrality of battle that could be found in some of Mahan's work but more especially in the malign influence of Corbett.

The conclusion seemed clear. Strong fleets should take chances and aim at victory, making it as total as they can, for:

the assumption of a simple defensive in war is ruin. War, once declared, must be waged offensively, aggressively. The enemy must not be fended off, but smitten down. You may then spare him every exaction, relinquish every gain: but, till down, he must be struck incessantly and remorselessly.[9]

Hence the strong criticism for over-clever concepts of avoidance and 'manoeuvre' especially when there was a realistic chance of doing so much more. After his victory at Beachy Head (1690), for example, de Tourville was told:

> it would be more important to capture this [the Smyrna merchant] fleet … than to gain a second victory over the fleet of the enemy. His Majesty's intention is not that M. de Tourville should seek the enemy in the Channel … In the event of their putting to sea, and in superior force, his Majesty does not wish him to attack; on the contrary, he wishes to evade them.

Although such ideas may be associated with Castex's concept of 'manoeuvre', they have been very widely condemned in the orthodox naval literature. 'Deadly instructions these', commented Richmond, for instance. 'They did more to destroy the French Navy than the English guns ever did.'[10] According to their critics, this conscious relegation of the pursuit of command of the sea through decisive battle condemned the French to permanent inferiority. Even when they had the opportunity of inflicting heavy defeat on the British (such as off Minorca in 1756, Grenada 1779 and the Saints in 1782) they passed it up lest they compromise what they thought was their main mission.

The difference between the two approaches to the centrality of battle is best summed up by looking at French and British accounts of the 1794 battle of the Glorious First of June: the former focus on the safe arrival of a 117-ship grain convoy from the United States – the latter on the sinking of one French ship of the line and the capture of six others.

Decisive battle: the need for moderation

> CLEOPATRA: He goes forth gallantly. That he and Caesar might Determine this great war in single fight.
>
> Shakespeare, *Anthony and Cleopatra*, IV/4

To judge by Shakespeare, the attractions of determining all by a single fight has a long tradition and Corbett was attacked (see pages 60–62), for seeming to go against it, but he stuck to his guns:

> The idea that naval strategy necessarily consists in gladiatorial combats between fleets is absurd … By a strange misreading of history an idea had grown up that its [the battlefleet's] primary function is to seek out and destroy the enemy's main fleet. This view, being literary rather than historical, was nowhere adopted with more unction than in Germany, where there was no naval tradition to test its accuracy.[11]

He argued that a bull-headed pursuit of decisive encounters was unwise for two different sets of reasons – the first to do with the practical problems in having them and the second with their perceived importance, relative to other things that the fleet could be doing.

Corbett was clear that single decisive battles are difficult to arrange. Even though they were the 'supreme function of a fleet … it must not be forgotten that convenient opportunities of winning a battle do not always occur when they are wanted'.[12] Decisive victories seem usually to depend on some kind of significant superiority, whether it be in maritime geography, weaponry, operating skill or the number and quality of men and ships. Often the inferior side will have some inkling of this in advance and so will not cooperate in its own destruction. Instead, an encounter between the main fleets may be as strenuously avoided by the weaker side as it is pursued by the stronger. At sea, unlike on land, a weaker force could effectively be removed from the board (by putting it in an inviolable harbour for example); at sea, also, there was much more freedom to manoeuvre and it could often prove difficult actually to find the victim.

Generally, it is almost impossible for both sides to concentrate all, or even most, of their resources in one spot at one time for one grand encounter, even if they wanted to. There will always be ships under construction or repair, in transit from one place to another, or away doing other things in other places. As Tunstall observed:

> Superficially, at any rate, the Battle of Trafalgar appears to have been one of the less important events of the war. Only a small part of Bonaparte's naval forces were destroyed and only one-sixth of the total British ships of the line were actually engaged.[13]

For these two reasons, decisive victory at sea more usually comes about cumulatively, at the operational/campaign level, rather than at the tactical level through single engagements. The normal pattern then, is a sequence of battles that only become decisive when their results are added together. As the commander of the English forces confronting the Spanish Armada in 1588 remarked: 'Their force is wonderfully great and strong; and yet we pluck their feathers by little and little.'[14] This could even apply when both sides actively sought a decision, such as in, for instance, the Dutch Wars of the seventeenth century and the Pacific campaign of the Second World War.

Leaving aside their strategic consequence for operations ashore, battles often proved less decisive for their consequences at sea than appeared the case at the time. Uncommitted forces would help the loser recover after a defeat. This was particularly true of the sailing era, when the disease that was associated with prolonged sea-keeping and the rapidity with which timber warships could be repaired, made even such victories as Beachy Head (1690) surprisingly transient. In any case, it was sometimes difficult to tell who had actually won such battles as Ushant (1778). Admiral German concluded, as a rule of thumb: 'whoever is first at sea may fairly claim the advantage in the late engagement'. Not surprisingly given all these limitations, the naval war just seemed to carry on even after the great Battle of Trafalgar.[15]

Indeed, it is possible to argue that their victory at Jutland actually made things *worse* for the British, since the Germans afterwards chose to concentrate their efforts instead on the U-boat campaign, which initially proved much more difficult for the Royal Navy to handle. Given all the difficulties, it was therefore important to ensure that the strategic consequence was worth the effort. But in many cases this was debateable. On the Battle of Jutland, for example, what difference would a tactically more decisive victory at Jutland have made to British fortunes anyway? If the extra gains were strategically insignificant, what would have been the point of Jellicoe risking all in order merely to sink a few more German ships?

The linkage between victory or defeat in battle and the capacity to use the sea for strategic purposes (successfully defending trade, for example) is evidently more complicated than might be deduced from a simplistic reading of Mahan.

For all these reasons, both Corbett and Castex warned against the unrelenting pursuit of decisive victory at sea. In this, Castex was following the rather different philosophy of naval warfare adopted by the French in the eighteenth century:

> The French Navy has always preferred the glory of assuring or preserving a conquest to that more brilliant perhaps, but actually less real, of taking some ships, and therefore has approached more nearly the true end that has been proposed in war.[16]

The French approach to battle found expression in their famous 'ulterior objects', a mission to accomplish, such as the protection of a convoy, or the support of a land operation, which took precedence over seeking out the enemy and destroying him in a decisive battle. The notion was based on the view that decisive battle, and even the command of the sea that might follow from it, was but one means to an end and there were viable alternatives.

This strategic and operational approach to the business of war at sea was exemplified at the tactical level too. When they were, despite everything, caught at sea by the Royal Navy, the French generally adopted a particular style of battle tactics most appropriate to their conceptions of war. Generally, they preferred to stay to leeward of the British from where they could disengage more easily. They tended to fire at their enemy's masts and rigging to slow him down, making their escape easier.

This, plus high levels of tactical proficiency, partly derived from close attention to the works of Pere Hoste and Bigot de Morogues, made the French very hard to fix and destroy even when located. The difficulty was compounded by the excessive British adherence to the sanctity of 'the line': hence, the continual frustration of the Royal Navy noted by John Clerk of Eldin (see Section 3.3).

For his part, Corbett argued that decisive victory at sea should be pursued, but only in a clear-sighted and moderated way. It should certainly not be allowed to blind the navy to everything else that could, or needed to, be done at sea. Japanese experience provides a good example of the operational and strategic dangers of doing this. Nostalgic memories of the Battle of Tsushima had, by the time of the Second World War, seduced the Japanese into a fixation on the 'one decisive battle' idea. This led them to neglect the defensive aspects of naval war, to misuse the submarine, to pay too little regard to the necessities of protecting their own trade and supply lines and to neglect the possibilities of attacking their enemy's.

Instead, it was a question of striking a balance between the urgency and advantage of the destruction of the enemy's forces, set against its difficulties, risks and requirements – when compared with those of other naval necessities and possibilities. Sometimes, perhaps even most times, the unrelenting pursuit of battle made strategic and operational sense, but sometimes it would not. Corbett made the essential point, this time in his description of Nelson's Mediterranean strategy in the Trafalgar campaign:

No great captain ever grasped more fully the strategical importance of dealing with the enemy's main force, yet no one ever less suffered it to become an obsession; no one saw more clearly when it ceased to be the key of a situation, and fell to a position of secondary moment.[17]

7.3 Forms and styles of decisive battle

As will be seen, decisive battle can take many forms depending on a wide variety of technological and geo-strategical circumstances.

The changing technology of battle

In the days of the galley, battle was a complex affair that mixed the techniques of land and sea warfare. Thus a contemporary report of the battle between Demetrius and Ptolemy in 306 BC off Salamis:

> The two fleets being then about 600 yards apart, Demetrius gave the signal to engage by hoisting a golden shield which was seen by all [and doubtless repeated by light craft in rear of the line]. Ptolemy did the same and the two fleets closed quickly with each other, as the trumpets sounded the charge and the crews cheered. The engagement opened with archery and stones and darts from the catapults, and many were wounded during the approach. The contact was made, the rowers being incited by the boatswains to make their greatest exertions, and the men on deck fell on the enemy with spears. The first shock was violent, some ships had their oars swept from their sides and remained motionless with their soldiers out of action. Others, after striking, rowed astern to ram again and in the meantime the soldiers attacked each other hand to hand. Some captains struck their opponents broadside to broadside, and the ships being held in contact became so many fields of battle with the boarders leaping to the enemy's deck. In some cases these missed their footing and falling overboard were drowned, while others making good their foothold killed the enemy or drove them overboard. Many and varied were the fortunes of the ships. In one case a weaker crew was victorious owing to its higher deck and in another case the better crew lost because its decks were low. For luck has much to do in naval actions. On shore valour is pre-eminent, whereas at sea many accidents occur which bring ruin to those whose valour deserves success.[18]

The Chinese also developed technologies that turned battle more into stand-off affairs, although ramming and close action still usually marked their closing stages. In AD 1161 the large navy of the Song dynasty destroyed an invading Jin armada in two battles in coastal waters and on the Yangtse River at the Chenjia peninsula and Caishi respectively. These battles were won by armoured warships (some equipped with paddlewheels) equipped with stand-off weaponry including fire arrows and bombs and explosives fast-fired from trebuchets on deck. There is no doubt that these two battles were decisive for the future of Song China[19]

In the Indian Ocean of the late fifteenth century, the Portuguese took this one stage further with the marine nail and naval artillery, as we saw in Section 5.9. The result was a series of technology-determined encounters in which small Portuguese squadrons smashed much more numerous fleets and dominated the area for decades. The next stage in the development of naval battle was marked by the attention paid to securing the levels of physical control required to wield the battlefleet as a cohesive whole in order to make the most of the naval artillery that it could provide. As the British discovered, this could, however, lead to a reliance on the sanctity of the line that often stifled tactical initiative and limited battle outcomes.

At the end of the eighteenth century, a Nelsonian stress on 'mission command' in which responsibility for making tactical decisions in the light of the commander's intent (see Section 3.7) was delegated downwards, restored the situation and helped to produce more such decisive encounters as the battles of the Nile and Trafalgar. Nelson conceived an Admiral's task to be 'to bring an enemy's fleet to battle on the most advantageous terms to himself'. No further order should be necessary, 'Being assured that the admirals and captains of the fleet that I have the honour to command will, knowing my precise object, that of a close and decisive battle, supply any deficiency in my not making signals.' The problem was that Nelson's brilliant success produced a set of expectations for future battles that proved impossible for his successors to realise.[20]

Naval technology advanced only incrementally during most of the sailing ship era, but in the nineteenth and twentieth centuries, the world's navies were engulfed in a rising flood of new technology. Propulsion, weaponry and protection were all revolutionised, and there were many who supposed that the principles of maritime strategy and concepts of battle would change too.

Some believed that the sureness and independence of movement that steam power afforded allowed the science of evolutions to be exact and geometric, making possible pretty manoeuvres in triangles, squares and parallel lines. Others thought steam would plunge the naval battle immediately into a ferocious and swirling confusion. Views were equally divided about the ram (the idea of which fleetingly and perversely reappeared after the Battle of Lissa in 1866), the breech-loading gun, the torpedo, the mine, the submarine and, eventually, the aircraft. These developments had a profound influence on the philosophy of ship design: they revolutionised the size and shape of the fleet, completely altering the way in which ships were classified and organised. Instead of the traditional threefold division of ships-of-the-line, cruisers and frigates, there grew up an endless variety of specialised ships and also the almost metaphysical notion of 'the balanced fleet' – a formation in which all the diversity of modern naval warfare was adequately represented and efficiently coordinated. These technological developments transformed the tactics of battle, and therefore the form and style of naval operations and strategy.

This process gathered momentum through the twentieth century. As that century closed, there were many who thought, and who continue to think, that the arrival of a new information age will have equally far-reaching consequences of every aspect of naval activity in the twenty-first century. Even so, as we saw in Section 5.7, access to and use of the latest naval technology is only one of the determinants of the nature and consequence of naval operations.

Battle and the strategic context

The geo-strategic environment, the size of navies, the strength of their maritime preoccupations can be equally or more important.

Analysis of the character of naval battle has tended, perhaps naturally, to focus on the large set-piece encounters such as Trafalgar, the Battle of the Nile, Tsushima, Jutland, Midway and so forth. This might give the false impression that decisive battle is the exclusive domain of the great ships of the great navies.

In fact, the fate of nations may often depend on almost forgotten small-ship encounters. A good example occurred in 1776. As Figure 7.1 shows, at this early stage in the War of American Independence, the British planned to come south from Canada through the Richelieu River and Lake Champlain to take Fort Ticonderoga and then New York, splitting the rebels into two. Sir Guy Carleton amassed a specialist armada of small riverine boats, took them up and over the rapids of St Teresa and St Johns (a considerable achievement in itself). On the way to Fort Ticonderoga, they encountered Benedict Arnold who had likewise constructed a defensive armada at Shenesborough. Arnold's aim and 'the one use of the Navy, was to contest the control of the water, to impose delay, even if it could not secure ultimate victory'. His force comprised five two-masted galleys, eight gunboats (known as 'gondolas') and one sloop. One of the gondolas survives, the *Philadelphia*, which was raised in 1935. With a crew of 44, the *Philadelphia* mounted a 12 lb cannon in the bow, two smaller 9 lb cannon on the side, and several swivel guns intended to fire 1 lb shot specifically at the enemy's rigging and/or personnel. The artillery was an interesting mix of seventeenth-century Dutch and Swedish guns and contemporary British weaponry, illicitly obtained.

The first encounter between the two sides off the island of Vacour was inconclusive with contrary winds and the onset of darkness preventing the British from really getting to grips with the Americans. But on 11 October 1776 there occurred the decisive battle in which the American schooner *Royal Savage* was burnt and the *Philadelphia* sunk by a 12 lb ball (with the British War Office broad arrow still showing after 159 years underwater) below the waterline. In the aftermath, the entire American squadron was captured, driven aground or burnt.

But the delay and the damage inflicted on the British persuaded Carleton to call off his projected assault on Fort Ticonderoga. The campaign against New York was put back a year, and this provided an opportunity for what turned out to be the decisive intervention of the French in the American war. The Americans benefited enormously from 'the invaluable year of delay, secured to them by their little navy on lake Champlain'. The British won the battle at the tactical level but lost the associated campaign, with, eventually, dire strategic consequences. Mahan reasonably called this 'a strife of pigmies for the prize of a continent'.[21]

Mahan also shows how important small-ship activity on rivers could be in his book, *The Gulf and Inland Waters*. Here, too, small ships operated to exactly the same principles as did great ships on the open ocean. The extraordinary campaign between the Germans and the Russians on Lake Ladoga between 1941 and 1944 supports the same conclusion. Supplies shipped across the lake were essential to the survival of Leningrad, then under German siege. Control of the lake was therefore crucial, and was the objective a long campaign in which the Russians lost 124 small ships totalling some 50,000 tons. The main set-piece battle (in fact the biggest of the whole war between the two navies) took place on the night of 25–26 August and saw the destruction of 38 German *siebel* ferries and two Italian MAS (torpedo) boats. Success in the Russian campaign to maintain control of the waters of Lake Ladoga made a material difference to Leningrad's capacity to survive the siege, and so helped shape the strategic conduct of the war on the Eastern Front.[22]

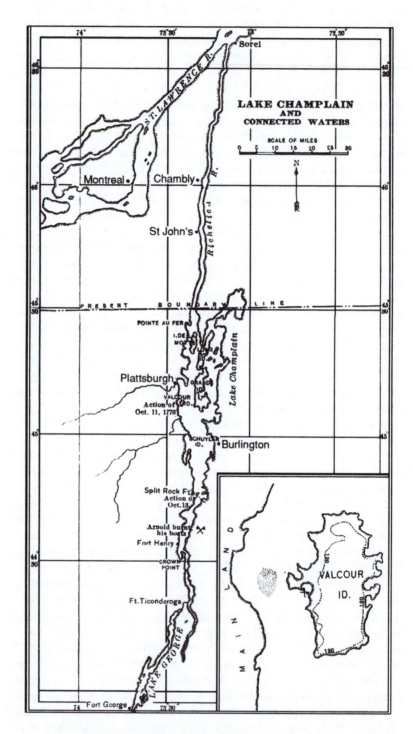

Figure 7.1 The River Richelieu campaign, 1776 (source: Mahan, 1913).

Such encounters show that the characteristics of decisive battle and sea control, usually explained through reference to the activities of the great ships of great navies, apply just as much to those of tiny ships from navies both great and small, and also that their operational and strategic consequence may be as great.

7.4 How to achieve a decisive victory

Diverse though the technological and geo-strategic conditions in which they operated might be, most fleet commanders were mainly interested in how they should seek to win the battles that most analysts thought central to successful naval campaigns and wars. This explains why maritime theory started at the tactical level. Could the principles of war be applied to the conduct of naval battle in a way that applied to all situations? If so, what did history and calm reflection show the results to be? Countless surveys and battle histories suggest that the following characteristics have often been critical, whether or not they be elevated to the status of principles.

Operational level concentration

Commanders at the operational level need to provide the conditions in which subordinates can win battles at the tactical level, if that is indeed the valid priority in the conditions of the time. In the seventeenth century, the Dutch, for example, were plagued throughout by having divided aims: to seek decisive battle and, at the same time, to protect their trade: the British immediately compounded Tromp's difficulty by launching attacks on the Dutch merchant and fishing fleets. 'I could wish to be so fortunate', Tromp wrote, 'as to have only one of the two duties – to seek out the enemy or to give convoy; for to do both is attended by great difficulties.' But the pressure of the mercantile community for direct protection forced Tromp to try to live with his problem. Whenever the Dutch did concentrate on seeking a decision, they were beset with complaints from the 'murmuring community' of merchants upset about delays and losses to their ships. Such difficulties were the reason why Mahan, Colomb and Richmond put so much stress on concentrating forces on the destruction of the enemy's main force and the gaining of sea control before dispersing them to exercise that control.[23]

Having an accurate tactical picture

In medieval times battle usually took place in coastal waters, as the chance of discovering an enemy on the high seas was so slight. At Trafalgar, the two fleets were in each other's sight at the break of day and they slowly approached each other at a rate of two knots until noon. 'The weather was clear and the sun shone on the sails of the enemy and their well-formed line. The British sailors admired the beauty and the splendour of the spectacle.' Nelson had hours in which to make his preparations and for much of the time, even when battle was joined, knew exactly what was happening. At Jutland, on the other hand, the sailors saw their enemy, if at all, as smudges on a distant and murky horizon. The fleets approached each other at 40 knots, and operated for the most part in considerable confusion. 'I wish someone would tell me who is firing', complained Admiral Jellicoe, 'and what they are firing at.' At the battle of the Philippine Sea (1944), Admiral Raymond A. Spruance had a copy of the Japanese battle plan, battle doctrine, order of battle and readiness figures and received decoded intercepts of the Japanese as they executed it. Spruance was able to make a free choice to fight on the defensive and secured his place in history as the commander of one of the most decisive engagements ever fought by the US Navy. The importance of accurate information about the adversary and his movements is obvious.[24]

Effective command and control

More than anything else, it is effective command and control than turns a collection of warships into a cohesive fighting fleet. There seem to be three components to this. First, there is the physical means by which the fleet is commanded, whether this be by trumpet calls, flags, radio or e-mail. Because communications were so central to command and control and therefore to tactical efficiency the Royal Navy's successive Fighting Instructions were strongly linked with its Signal Books. Second, there is the curiously under-studied phenomenon of naval combat leadership. Studies of great leaders, such as Nelson, abound but it is far from clear whether such qualities are transferable, apply to all circumstances at all times, are innate or can be learned. Nearly everyone though would agree that good leadership (in whatever form that takes) is essential. Third, there is the balance to be struck between centralised control and that form of delegated authority that has become known as 'mission command' of the sort associated with Nelson. One of the reasons for the disappointing tactical performance of the British at the Battle of Jutland was Admiral Jellicoe's adoption of a very centralised concept of command at a time when the physical communication system was not capable of passing orders and information up and down the command chain with sufficient speed and accuracy. This shows how the various aspects of command and control interact. Arguably it would have been better for Jellicoe to have adopted the Nelsonic device of telling his subordinates broadly what he wanted them to do and then standing back and letting them get on with it.

Tactical concentration

Custance wrote, 'It is a first principle in strategy to be as strong as possible at the decisive point.' This did not mean necessarily having all your forces in one place, but deployed with the same object in view, carefully coordinated and mutually supported. Even a divided fleet must be a cohesive whole. As Mahan put it, 'Such is concentration reasonably understood, not huddled together like a drove of sheep, but distributed with a regard to a common purpose, and linked together by the effectual energy of a single will.' Intelligent division, indeed, was central to the whole idea of concentration – a point developed by Corbett. 'Without division', he declared, 'no strategical combinations are possible.' The whole of the Trafalgar campaign was a splendid example, he thought, of such elastic concentration. Best of all was the form of divided deployment that lured the enemy to destruction by its appearance of weakness. Nelson aimed always at bringing the whole of his forces against a portion of the enemy's, particularly by means of an assault on the van or the rear of the enemy fleet. Generally the rear was better targeted, as it would take the van longer to turn round to come to the rescue. At the Nile, Nelson even managed the celebrated 'double envelopment': but always what Mahan called 'the essential maxim of all intelligent warfare, which is so to engage as markedly to out-number the enemy at a point of main collision'.[25]

Tactical manoeuvre

To use Mahan's phrase, 'intelligent warfare' requires an effective balance to be struck between the aggressive pursuit of the tactical initiative on the one hand and considered insight on the other. Unadulterated aggressiveness of the sort espoused by Admiral Cochrane: 'Never mind manoeuvres, always go at them', clearly has its place but so does the *considered* pursuit of tactical advantage. Castex puts it well: 'One must mistrust the mystique of the offensive, the sentiment that would lead one to adopt it regardless of circumstances without considering its appropriateness to the situation or its consistency with a rational plan of *manoeuvre*.'[26]

Logistical efficiency

Logistical support may be easier for navies than armies but the vital role of the 'fleet train' in the Pacific war 1941–1945 is but one example of the crucial importance of an efficient supply of all war essentials (ammunition, food etc.). The shape and form of amphibious operations moreover are often dominated by such considerations, as the Falklands campaign showed.[27]

Use of the environment

The capacity to exploit the physical characteristics of the particular battle area (in terms of the wind and weather, the form of the coastline, underwater conditions) is especially important, especially when the sea is actively hostile.

Superior weaponry

The number and power of the guns was often a deciding factor in the battles of the sailing ship era, together with such things as the number, seaworthiness and speed of the ships. Even methods of attaching cannons firmly to the deck, or the fire control systems in the British Fleet at Jutland could apparently make all the difference.

Resilience

The capacity of warships to take damage without unduly impairing their capacity to perform their tasks has often proved crucial. In both world wars, German warships had a significant advantage over their British counterparts in this respect. During the Falklands campaign, the British expensively relearned the dangers of cutting costs (especially in fire retardation) when fitting out their ships. The crew needs to resilient too, especially at times when a desire to avoid casualties could come to dominate tactics, rather than the urgent requirement to defeat the enemy. A sense of being excessively vulnerable to damage or loss might, more generally, lead to a decline in the readiness to take risks that has often proved to be an essential compo-nent of successful tactics.

Fighting spirit

Since the morale and commitment of the officers and crew is often absolutely crucial to the outcome of battle, a navy's personnel tends often to be regarded as the main factor in its success or failure. Battle is chaotic, shambolic and terrifying for both sides; the capacity to survive the chaos in a better state than the opponent is a function of crew training, skills and general commitment. Talking about the Falklands experience, Admiral Woodward points out that there is little new in this:

> I reflected as I looked at the signals now coming from Carlos water that little had changed since the eighteenth century, except of course for the hardware and the speed of the conflict: the people were just the same, the spirit in the ships was just the same, the courage of the men was just the same ... What difference between *Ardent*, crippled and burning, still fighting and Sir Richard Grenville's *Revenge* all those centuries ago?[28]

Fighting spirit is a form of capital, something that needs to be continuously built up and nurtured in peacetime, husbanded and expended only with care in war.

7.5 Modern forms and concepts of battle

In the Cold War era, most analysts assumed that any shooting war would be short either because nuclear weapons would be used, or through fear that they would be used unless conflict was kept short. That being so, the pursuit of battle for its own sake seemed improbable since navies would probably need to move immediately to the multifarious tasks of exercising command, instead of seeking out their opposite numbers for some preliminary encounter. For such reasons, it was easy to see why 'Most analysts would agree that except for possible conflict along the sea lines of communication, the days of battles on the high seas are gone for ever.'[29]

Nonetheless, both the superpower navies clearly prepared for it. Admiral Gorshkov continued to argue that, 'The battle always was and remains the main means of solving tactical tasks.' This view was exemplified by the nature of Soviet naval construction, which clearly aimed at producing ships, submarines and aircraft with considerable battle-winning firepower.

The Americans likewise remained faithful to the Mahanian emphasis on the destruction of the enemy's naval forces. One US Chief of Naval Operations, Admiral Thomas B. Hayward put it like this:

> In a war at sea the most rapid, efficient and sure way to establish the control of essential sea areas is to destroy the opposing forces capable of challenging your control of those seas ... [It is necessary to] ... impose maximum attrition early in the war, on the heart of Soviet offensive capability, the ships, aircraft and submarines capable of attacking our own forces and shipping.[30]

This very traditional thinking lay behind the US Navy's adoption of 'The Maritime Strategy' and explains their aspirations for a balanced fleet of carriers, surface ships and submarines capable of taking on and destroying the Soviet Navy in an offensive campaign well forward of the Greenland–Iceland–UK gap.

Any such battle would have been a particularly diverse affair of subsurface, air and surface engagements. In the far north, the battle between Western carrier battlegroups and Soviet land-based air, and the underwater battle between the submarines of both sides would have been especially important. The campaign would have covered a much wider area of sea than before. Competing fleets would not line up to have a shoot-out but would engage in carefully orchestrated activities involving widely dispersed, complementary and supportive forces.[31] Probably each individual encounter would have been more fleeting too, with much more stress on the first salvo and the first strike, great intensity, rapid expenditure of weapon stocks and high casualty rates, especially on the losing side. The range and precision of the new weaponry and contemporary command and control procedures would have been crucial for the outcome of such a dispersed and diffuse operation. NCW and the other technological developments since the end of the Cold War would probably confirm, indeed exacerbate, these trends.

A brief review of four very different naval encounters over the past generation illustrate the variety of forms that the struggle for sea control through the pursuit of battle can now take.

The Indo-Pakistan War, 1971

There was no doubt that the Indian Navy was animated by the most Mahanian of principles. As Indian Admirals Khrishnan and Kohli put it:

> All our discussions stemmed from one overriding thought, a firm conviction, bordering on an obsession, that should war come, the navy should throw every-thing it had into battle and our entire strategy from the very onset of hostilities should be one of bold offensive. We must scrap, erase and wipe off from our minds any ideas of a defensive posture, we must seek action, taking any risks that were necessary and destroy the enemy in his ports and at sea.
>
> The main thrust of the Western Naval Command Plan was to engage and destroy as many Pakistani main naval units as possible. Their destruction would deny the Pakistani Navy any chance to interfere with our trade or to mount any bombardment attacks on our homeland.

This led to several successful missile attacks on the Pakistan Fleet in and off Karachi, together with operations against Pakistani shipping and shore positions. In response, Pakistani submarines sought out major Indian warships. The PNS *Hangor* sank the Indian frigate INS *Khukri* but PNS *Ghazi*, sent round into the Bay of Bengal to attack the carrier INS *Vikrant* itself sank en route under somewhat myste-rious circumstances.[32]

The Arab–Israeli War of 1973

This was a short, small-ship campaign between territorial neighbours in a war domi-nated by events on land. Israeli fast attack craft quickly established their tactical superiority at sea, and in the second stage of the conflict, the Israelis found it neces-sary to attack the Syrian and Egyptian navies in their harbours with a variety of exotic craft (explosive boats, frogmen dinghies and submersibles) rather in the style of the *Mukti Bahini* in the Indo-Pakistan war two years earlier.[33]

The Falklands Campaign, 1982

The British were aware, that in the Argentine Air Force and Navy (largely trained and equipped by the British and French), they faced potentially serious opposition and would have preferred to have established clear naval and air superiority before having to engage in the hazards of a contested amphibious operation. Not unnaturally, the Argentines refused to cooperate. Instead, after the failure of a pre-emptive Argentine air strike, a suspected pincer movement on the British Task force by major surface units was thwarted by the sinking of the old heavy cruiser *General Belgrano* on 2 May 1982. Argentine submarine efforts proved equally unavailing. Politics played a role too. Permission to attack the Argentine Carrier *Veinticinco de Mayo* in Argentine territorial waters was explicitly turned down by the British War Cabinet for its likely effect on public opinion. As a result the two sides were locked into a long, tiring, cumulative battle between the Task force and Argentine Air Force and naval aircraft, that had to be conducted alongside the amphibious operation.[34]

The Gulf War, 1991

Widespread notions that large surface ships, especially carriers, would be too vulnerable in narrow waters when confronted by swarms of missile-armed fast attack craft were comprehensively disproved in this conflict. British and American ship-borne helicopters took on the Iraqi Navy when it fleetingly appeared and decisively defeated it, especially in the so-called 'Bubiyan Turkey Shoot' of 29 January 1991. But this was critically dependent on the Coalition having established the degree of air superiority that allowed the helicopters to operate so freely in the first place. Moreover this sea control operation took some time, partly for political reasons (there was a reluctance to risk Kuwaiti personnel and installations through attacks on harbours in Kuwait) but mainly because the Iraqi Navy was so very elusive.[35]

Two things emerge from this review. First, that the considerations discussed here do indeed apply to all navies great and small, and second, that even when one side is set on forcing battle on the other, the realities of the short war, the operational elusiveness of the weaker side and political considerations, are major constraints on decisive action. Nonetheless, these considerations quite evidently do not make it impossible. For this reason, most navies continue to take battle-winning capacity as the main criterion by which to judge their development, preparations and performance.

7.6 Operational alternatives to battle

There are two alternative approaches to the pursuit of battle as a means of securing, maintaining or contesting command of the sea. The first is to adopt some kind of fleet-in-being/naval defensive concept of operations. The second is to impose a fleet blockade. Both of these operational approaches are aimed not so much at the enemy's forces but at reducing his capacity to use the sea strategically, while increasing your own. The adoption of a fleet-in-being strategy is intended to reduce the strategic value of the other side's ability to command the sea; the second aims at denying/reducing the enemy's access to the sea. Both approaches proceed from the assumption that the command of the sea is a relative not absolute thing.

7.7 The fleet-in-being approach

This approach is of particular value for a fleet that knows it is inferior to its adversary (in number or quality) and cannot realistically hope to gain or contest command of the sea by the normal method. Countries in conflict with the great maritime powers have faced the problem but, as Castex pointed out, it is by no means restricted to them. The strongest navy may also be forced into a limited defensive in certain circumstances perhaps while pursuing a vigorous offensive elsewhere. At some stage or other, in short, all navies have had to deal with the problem of making the best use of resources too limited to risk in a straightforward pursuit of battle with a superior adversary.[36]

The solution has usually been to adopt one of a number of related naval options often loosely bundled together under the not very accurate title of a 'fleet-in-being strategy'. They range from a moderated offensive at one end of the spectrum to passive defence at the other. They have been attempted on the high seas and in coastal waters, for long periods of time and for short. They appear in many forms:

- Some actually aim eventually to achieve a useful degree of command of the sea, but by a roundabout route avoiding a decision by battle, at least for the time being.
- Others are an attempt by an inferior navy to derive positive strategic benefit from its forces by doing something useful at sea (such as attacking the enemy's trade or his coasts) without aspiring to the defeat of the other side's main forces. Indeed the latter will be avoided as much as possible. Hence the French Navy of the eighteenth century with its doctrine of 'ulterior objects' discussed earlier.
- Others have the essentially negative aim of denying, perhaps by continuous harassment and evasion, a stronger enemy the capacity fully to enjoy the fruits of his superiority.
- Some approaches aim merely to ensure the continued survival of a weaker fleet, rather in the manner of the Russian Navy during the Crimean War.

The widespread use of the phrase itself can be traced back to a study conducted by Admiral Philip Colomb of a controversial event in the summer of 1690. Briefly, the situation was that the Royal Navy had been dispersed in several detachments, each of which was inferior to a large French force under the command of Admiral de Tourville, hovering menacingly off the Isle of Wight. The largest British force in the area was an Anglo-Dutch Fleet commanded by Admiral Lord Torrington. On 26 June, Torrington reported that the French were in

> a strength that puts me beside the hopes of success, if we should fight, and really may not only endanger the losing of the fleet, but at least the quiet of our country too: for if we are beaten, they being absolute masters of the sea, will beat great liberty of doing many things they dare not attempt whilst we observe them.

For this reason, Torrington proposed to avoid the enemy fleet, until reinforcements eventually arrived from elsewhere, In the meantime,

> whilst we observe the French, they can make no attempt either on sea or shore, but with great disadvantage.... Most men were in fear that the French would

invade; but I was always in another opinion: for I always said, that whilst we had a fleet in being, they would not dare to make an attempt.[37]

The government, however, was not persuaded by this line of argument and Torrington was ordered into battle anyway. Possibly it misunderstood his intentions, thinking he meant to do no more than preserve his fleet from danger. At all events, the result was defeat at the Battle of Beachy Head on 30 June 1690. Court-martialled after this affair, Torrington was honourably acquitted but not employed at sea again. The government accepted that Torrington's sensible actions before and after the battle had dissuaded the French from invading, but basically the British preferred their enemies to be safely sunk rather than merely outwitted. Indeed Torrington's critics pointed out his approach largely succeeded because of de Tourville's mistakes. De Tourville should have followed up his victory at Beachy Head: instead he allowed himself to be diverted into a pointless raid on Teignmouth where he destroyed several harmless coastal vessels and carried off a few sheep. As Richmond pointed out, 'if Tourville had observed the great principle that tactical victory should always be followed up and consummated in relentless pursuit', the outcome might well have been fatal for the English.[38]

But Corbett thought that the Torrington affair and British experience at the hands of the French in the Seven Years War (1756–1763) showed the full potentiality of the naval defensive, especially in military or political circumstances where there was benefit in playing for time.

> In the long run and by itself the defensive cannot, of course, lead to a final attainment of the command of the sea. But it can prevent its attainment by the other side … The real lesson of the war is … that we should note the supreme necessity and difficulty of crushing it down before it has time to operate its normal effect.[39]

He warned, however, that for such campaigns to be fully effective, they should be conducted with verve and imagination; their full potential could only be realised through 'a naval defensive, keeping the fleet actively in being – not merely in existence, but in active and vigorous life'. The defensive, he thought, was not the antithesis of the offensive, but its complement. A defensive in one place could make possible an offensive in another. Too many British admirals, he thought, failed to realise that there was something between attack and retreat. This was partly because some navies gave the naval defensive a bad name by carrying it to extremes and being too passive.[40]

In some ways there is an analogy between the fleet-in-being approach and the principles of guerrilla warfare. Even Mahan thought an active fleet-in-being strategy could yield considerably more useful results than either accepting battle with a superior enemy and losing, on the one hand, or letting the fleet rot at anchor, on the other.

> Therefore the aim of the weaker party should be to keep the sea as much as possible; on no account to separate his battleships, but to hold them together, seeking by mobility, by infrequent appearances, which unaided rumour always multiplies, to arouse the enemy's anxieties in many directions, so as to induce

him to send off detachments; in brief, to occasion what Daveluy calls a 'displacement of forces' unfavourable to the opponent. If he made this mistake, either the individual detachments will be attacked one by one, or the main body, if unduly weakened.[41]

Castex linked the naval defensive to his concept of *manoeuvre*, 'in essence, of avoiding a decisive battle while unceasingly harassing the enemy by limited offensives wherever and whenever one finds a favourable opportunity'.[42]

The activities of the German Navy through the first half of the twentieth century, illustrates what an intelligent fleet-in-being/naval defensive can achieve strategically. The superiority of the British Grand Fleet to the German High Seas Fleet in the First World War was such that even the most aggressive German commanders were loath to accept battle except in the most favourable circumstances. The gap between the two was even greater in the Second World War, and the German naval command was correspondingly yet more cautious. Even so, an inferior fleet was found to confer important strategic benefits in both conflicts.

- In peacetime, the mere existence of a powerful, if necessarily second-best, battlefleet constrained Britain's freedom to act as it might otherwise have done *in peacetime*. This was the idea behind the celebrated 'Risk Theory', first openly stated in Admiral Tirpitz's Naval Law of 1900. The notion was that the German Fleet should be strong enough to threaten the superior British Fleet with such damage that Britain would feel dangerously exposed to further threats from elsewhere. Knowing their long-term strategic consequences, Britain would therefore be deterred from using her naval superiority to pursue policies inimical to German interests. Germany wanted 'a sea force which will compel a sea power of the first rank to think twice before attacking our coasts'. In fact, the policy did not work; the British were so alarmed by the German (naval) threat that they took steps to settle their differences with the Russians and French, and the 'other threats' Tirpitz relied on consequently disappeared. Even so, the Risk Theory was an interesting attempt to use an inferior fleet as an indirect political defence of what apparently could not be safeguarded by direct military means.[43]
- In the First World War, the German Fleet was too strong for the British to impose a close blockade. Their more distant variety allowed the Germans to make limited use of the North Sea, thereby providing German surface raiders, and U-boats with some access to the open ocean. The latter's attack on British merchant shipping could have been a war-winner.
- In the First World War, the Germans' concept of operations was to avoid a main fleet encounter but actively to whittle away at British naval superiority until the odds made acceptance of a central battle more sensible. According to Scheer (1920) the policy was that:

> The Fleet must strike when the circumstances are favourable; it must, therefore, seek battle with the English Fleet only when a state of equality has been achieved by the methods of guerrilla warfare ... The Fleet must therefore hold back and avoid actions which might lead to heavy losses. This does not, however, prevent favourable opportunities being made use of to damage the enemy.

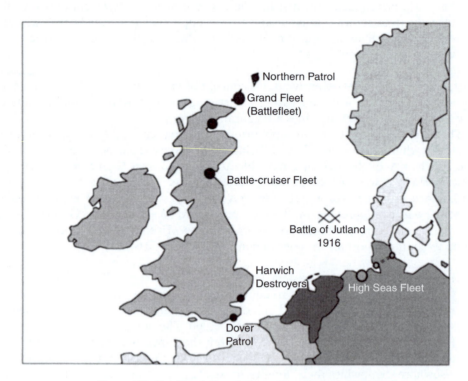

Figure 7.2 The North Sea theatre of operations, 1916.

The climactic Battle of Jutland was an attempt to do this. As things turned out neither it, nor the concept of operations it served, worked in the end – but it might have done.

- In the meantime, the German strategy made it difficult for the British to concentrate their forces. They had to maintain their blockading forces in constant readiness, as they would never have much warning of when the Germans would come out. This meant those assets could not be elsewhere doing things that might be more strategically useful. Much of Britain's destroyer force had to be kept with the Grand Fleet rather than devoted to the defence of its hard-pressed shipping. According to Admiral Scheer, the active existence of the High Sea Fleet, meant 'the English Fleet stayed far north and did not dare to attack our coast and stamp out the U-boat danger at its source'.[44]

- In the Second World War the odds for the German Fleet were worse still. Instead, Admiral Raeder tried to make the most of his limited assets by a more passive version of the fleet-in-being approach:

> Enemy naval forces, even if inferior in strength, are only to be attacked if this should be necessary to achieve the main objective. Frequent changes in the operational area will provide uncertainty and delays in the sailing of the enemy's shipping, even if no material success is achieved. The temporary

disappearance of German warships in remote areas will add to the enemy's confusion.[45]

- The first class battleship *Tirpitz*, in its Norwegian fjord, forced the British to protect each convoy to Russia in strength and exerted a nuisance value out of all proportion to its actual capacity. Churchill summed it up well: 'It exercises a vague general fear and menaces all points at once. It appears and disappears causing immediate reactions and perturbations on the other side.'[46] These reactions and perturbations meant that considerable naval forces were anchored to northern waters that could otherwise have been serving useful purposes elsewhere.

Not everyone was persuaded by all this, however, especially after the First World War. One British commentator, Captain Bernard Acworth was scathing about the whole concept, in terms strongly reminiscent of those who thought that England's safety in 1690 owed more to de Tourville's ineptitutude than to Torrington's insight. The British had been contaminated by the defensive heresy, despite their superiority:

A fleet-in-being, a fleet of great material superiority, was to be regarded as an acceptable substitute for a decisive victory at sea ... safety first became, perhaps for the first time in England's maritime history, a naval doctrine of war.[47]

Instead of following their own traditions, the British skulked about and overreacted to the menace of torpedoes and mines. For this reason, the German Navy's defensive campaign was more successful than it should have been. By extension, the conclusion was that naval defensives would only work when the stronger side allowed them to.

Nonetheless they have often been resorted to and not merely by small navies with little alternative, but by great navies too. Indeed Admiral King's concept of operations for his fast fleet carrier force in the Pacific campaign of 1942 is an excellent example of an active fleet-in-being approach leading eventually to an increasing capacity to control the sea. At the approach to the Battle of Midway, for example, Admiral King instructed Admiral Nimitz: 'Chiefly to employ strong attrition tactics and not, repeat *not*, allow our forces to accept such decisive action as would be likely to incur heavy losses in our carriers and cruisers.'[48] Nimitz accordingly engaged in a campaign of 'offensive hit-and-run tactics to keep the Japanese off balance while the United States remained on the strategic defensive, building up its fleet strength to the point when it could assume the offensive'. The ultimate success of this campaign suggests that an active fleet-in-being strategy would seem to offer the outnumbered fleet better prospects than either complete passivity or the kind of naval death ride against a superior foe that the High Seas Fleet was rumoured to have been contemplating in 1918.

7.8 The fleet blockade

Fleet blockade: purposes

Historically, the fleet blockade has often proved an effective response by a stronger navy to a weaker opponent that has adopted a fleet-in-being approach. The objectives of the fleet blockade were military and so it ought not to be confused with an economic blockade, the intention of which was to cut off the enemy's trade, or deny him essential supplies. The distinction remained, even though the same ships could be executing both types of blockade at the same place and the same time – as, for instance, in the war of 1812 when a British blockade was intended to choke off all American trade *and* to stop US commerce raiders from reaching the open ocean.

The general military object of the fleet blockade was to prevent the enemy interfering in a substantial way with the blockading navy's capacity to use the sea as it wished. If the enemy was thus neutralised, the blockading navy would effectively be in command of the sea behind the blockade line; and surplus ships not actually involved in the blockading operation would be able to exercise that command.

As far as Mahan was concerned, the true station of the British Fleet in the French Revolutionary Wars 'was before the hostile ports and as close to them as may be'. This was the first and main line of defence of Britain's maritime interests, and the most direct route to the attack of the enemy's. Mahan went on:

> As in all military campaigns, the front of operations of a powerful fleet should be pushed as far towards the enemy as is consistent with the mutual support of the various detachments, and with secure communication with their base. By so doing, not only are the great national interests placed more remote from the alarms of war, but the use of the region behind the front of operations, in this case the sea, is secured to the power that can afford to maintain its fighting line close to the enemy's positions.

Since this one fleet disposition would offer an effective indirect defence of all the blockading navy's maritime interests, Mahan argued, it was much more effective than trying to defend those interests directly, as he and many others thought the Royal Navy had mistakenly tried to during the War of American Independence. Instead, the British should have concentrated their resources at the decisive point – off the enemy's main fleet bases. Mahan therefore approved of the way the British Admiralty seemed to be approaching the coming war with Germany. 'The British fleet is concentrated in the North Sea', he wrote. 'There it defends all British Interests, the British islands, British commerce and the colonies; and, offensively, commands Germany's commercial sea routes.' Moreover, a blockade conferred one overwhelming advantage – knowing where the enemy was. It is hard to exaggerate the importance of this in naval warfare.[49]

Another fundamental advantage of the fleet blockade is that it may well prevent a dispersed adversary from concentrating his forces. Mahan made the point that the Royal Navy had often found itself in conflict with an enemy or an alliance whose naval assets were split between several bases or countries – and sometimes the sum total of those assets was equal or superior to Britain's. There was, therefore, an urgent need to prevent the enemy concentrating his forces and so being able to mount significant operations against British colonies or Britain itself.

> The strength of the British strategy lay not in hermetically sealing any one port, but in effectually preventing a great combination from all the ports. It was essential to Bonaparte not merely that his scattered squadrons should, one at a time and another at another, escape to sea, but that they should do so at periods

so ordered, and by routes so determined, as to ensure a rapid concentration at a particular point. Against this the British provided by the old and sound usage of interior positions and lines.

In a justly famous passage, Mahan celebrated the effectiveness of this policy:

> Never in the history of blockades has there been excelled, if ever equalled, the close locking of Brest by Admiral Cornwallis, both winter and summer, between the outbreak of war and the Battle of Trafalgar.... They were dull, weary, eventless months, those months of watching and waiting of the big ships before the French arsenals. Purposeless they surely seemed to many, but they saved England. The world has never seen a more impressive demonstration of the influence of sea power upon its history. Those far distant, storm-beaten ships; upon which the Grand Army never looked, stood between it and the dominion of the world.[50]

Close and distant blockade

The reference to 'close locking' in this last quotation is significant in that maritime strategists usually distinguished between the 'close' blockade and the 'open' or 'distant' blockade. Captain Stephen Roskill put it this way:

> If we keep the fleet more or less permanently off the enemy base, the blockade is said to be of the 'close' type: but if it watches enemy activities from a distance, cruising periodically off the base and exerting only a general control over the local waters, it is said to be of the 'open' type.[51]

The difference between the two was a matter of degree and indicated by a number of things in addition to the blockading squadron's proximity to the enemy base: one indication was often thought to be whether these squadrons replenished on station; another, pointed out by Corbett, was the degree of 'certainty of immediate contact' when the enemy came out. Both kinds, though, had their advantages and disadvantages.

The special advantages of a *close blockade* were as follows:

- There were greater levels of certainty in knowing where the enemy was and what he was doing. The more distant the blockade the less security and control it afforded. Accordingly, if some really important maritime enterprise was about to be attempted (such as an amphibious invasion), it might make real sense to impose a close blockade *temporarily*, reverting to a distant blockade when it was over.
- The experience of the Soviet Baltic Fleet in the Great Patriotic War showed that a fleet confined to harbour in this way tended to deteriorate rapidly. Opportunities for sea training greatly reduced, morale declined and fleet assets got stripped away for other military purposes.
- If the object of the blockade was to seal the enemy into his ports, then a distant blockade was a risky enterprise since it inevitably gave a determined enemy more chances to slip out. A close blockade on the other hand could mean, as

Napoleon complained, that the French, as the blockaded party, could not put a cockle boat to sea without it being pounced on by English men-of-war. Admiral Hawke instituted such a blockade off Brest in 1758–1759. The U-boat campaigns of both world wars would have been profoundly different had it been possible for their bases to have been blockaded like this.

On the other hand:

- An *open* or *distant blockade* avoided the extreme wear and tear of a close blockade. It was less demanding in that ships could return to base to replenish. There was less likelihood of the fleet's fighting power declining (for example by crews becoming less healthy or their ships collecting so much marine growth that they became slower). Sometimes close blockades collapsed under the strain. The weather was often a major factor in this.
- Because close blockades could absorb so many resources in this way, distant blockades reduced the ability of the weaker blockaded fleet, simply by pursuing a policy of masterly inactivity in its own harbours, to inflict steady damage on, and occupy the attention of, more ships (ships-of-line and 'cruisers', the latter always in short supply anyway) than it could hope to incapacitate otherwise. By this means, an outnumbered fleet could 'contain' a superior opponent and enforce upon him 'a disproportionate expenditure of force, to the detriment of his power to take offensive action and to defend his trade'. Trying to impose a close blockade, in other words, might make an enemy's passive fleet-in-being strategy more effective than it deserved to be. A distant blockade, on the other hand meant there was less chance of this.[52]
- If the object of the exercise was not so much to stop the enemy coming out but to encourage him to do so that he could be beaten in battle, then a distant blockade was probably better than a close one. Richmond made the point that close blockades rarely forced an enemy to sea.

    In no case in all the many wars at sea in which an enemy has been forced to keep under the shelter of the defences of his ports has a blockade forced him to sea to fight. Neither Spain, Holland, France or Germany, suffer though they did from pressure at sea, sent their fleets to sea to fight the superior forces which were the cause of that pressure.[53]

- Distant blockades made sections of the blockading fleet less vulnerable to sudden ambush and other forms of attrition because they were further away from the enemy's main bases. The advent of submarines, mines and torpedo boats (together with the extra difficulty of sustaining coal- or oil-fired ships on station when compared to sailing ships), led the Royal Navy to abandon the close blockade just before the First World War – to the disappointment of the Germans who had hoped to exploit it as a means of 'equalising' the British.

Fleet blockades in practice

For all these reasons, the British in the First World War, blockaded the North Sea. The southern half of the North Sea became a kind of naval no man's land.

If the Germans chose to cruise about in this area, they took the chance of being cut off and engaged by the British forces, whose policy it was to leave their bases from time to time for what Sir John Jellicoe in the Jutland Despatch described as 'periodic sweeps through the North Sea'.... Thus for the old policy of close blockade was substituted a new one, that of leaving the enemy a large field in which he might be tempted to manoeuvre: and it had this value, that should he yield to the temptation, an opportunity must sooner or later be afforded to the British Fleet of cutting him off and bringing him to action. Meantime, he was cut off from any large adventure far afield. He would have to fight for freedom.... Thus no naval battle could be expected unless ... the weaker wished to fight, or was cornered or surprised.[54]

If, as in most other distant blockades, the British Fleet blockade of the First World War was partly intended to lure its adversary out to destruction on the high seas, it failed. But it substantially succeeded in its other great purpose, the protection of maritime interests 'behind the line'. The German surface fleet was effectively neutralised. It could not operate outside the North Sea, and so British interests in the oceans beyond were substantially secured from significant surface attack. But, all the same, neutralisation by distant blockade did not provide total protection. The enemy surface fleet could still operate, however gingerly, inside the North Sea, sometimes with embarrassing effects for the British. Probably more to the point, German submarines could still slip out in sufficient numbers to attack British shipping behind the blockade with near devastating consequences. It was because they were conscious of the imperfections of the type of blockade then in operation that so many senior British naval officers of the period strove so hard to achieve a central decisive victory over the German Fleet at sea. And it was because they knew that, bad as it was, the naval situation could be so much worse, that the German Navy strove to avoid it.

Many of these trends continued into the Second World War. Blockading operations became even more closely integrated into and indistinguishable from, the rest of the fleet's activities. They became more multidimensional too, with maritime airpower in particular playing an increasingly important role in the potential or actual detection and destruction of blockading and blockaded forces. Finally, technology and strategic circumstances conspired to give blockaded navies (mainly the German and Italian fleets) more freedom and more sea room than they had before. But even though the practice may have had such difficulties as these, the purpose of blockade remained essentially the same. In this war, as in many of its predecessors, blockade provided the dominant navy with the best means of containing an inferior, though potentially dangerous, enemy, and so improved its chances of being able to use the sea in relative security. But, as always, it offered a degree of protection less complete than the wholesale destruction of the enemy's main forces would have done.

Fleet blockade: modern theory and practice

During the Cold War, blockade appeared in the guise of determined Western attempts largely to contain Soviet naval forces north of the northern gaps between Greenland–Iceland–United Kingdom and Svalbad, Norway, by what became known as 'barrier operations'. The idea was that Soviet naval forces, ships and especially submarines and long-range aircraft would either be stopped or severely 'attrited' in their presumed intention to break out into the North Atlantic by means of underwater detection systems, submarines, mines surface ships, carriers and aircraft concentrated in the gaps. This was a form of distant blockade in all but name. Admiral Stansfield Turner supplied some of these other names:

- *Sortie control* meant:

  > bottling up an opponent in his ports or on his bases ... today's blockade seeks destruction of individual units as they sortie. If we assume an opponent will be in control of the air near his ports, sortie control tactics must primarily depend on submarines and mines ... a most economical means of cutting off a nation's use of the seas or ability to interfere.

- *Choke point control* was an alternative technique: 'Sometimes, the best place to engage the enemy is in a geographical bottleneck through which he must pass.' The advantage of choke point control is that it can use units that would not survive for long in sortie control operations nearer the enemy's bases.[55]

Soviet naval theory focused on the mirror image of this approach – how to get through a blockade. The need for Russia to make 'her break through to the sea' so as to defeat encirclement and wield her scattered fleets as a cohesive whole was a constant if implicit theme of Admiral Gorshkov's writings. This concern echoed Russia's historic difficulty in gaining access to the open ocean. Western navies aimed to ensure this remained a problem.[56]

From time to time, though, dissatisfaction was expressed in Western maritime circles about the necessary limitations of this distant blockade. It seemed to leave the strategic initiative to the Soviet Union, and might make the Soviet general staff think that the waters off Northern Europe or the North West Pacific were a Soviet lake. Worse still, forward allies such as Norway, Iceland, South Korea and Japan might come to this conclusion too and gradually adopt different security policies in response. This lay behind the occasional initiatives to move the blockade forward through the gaps, especially in the late 1940s, and the 1980s, the era of 'The Maritime Strategy'. The idea of Western maritime forces taking up positions off northern Norway to attack the Soviet Northern Fleet in and off its lair in the Kola peninsula, attracted much agitated discussion about the operational pros and cons that was distinctly reminiscent of the historic debate about the balance to be struck between close and distant blockade described earlier.[57]

These issues appeared again, if on a much smaller scale, in the Falklands campaign of 1982. During the diplomatic negotiations that preceded the second stage of the war, there was much discussion about both sides 'withdrawing' their forces 300–400 miles from the disputed islands. Not unnaturally, the British rejected the Argentine contention that they should thus deploy their forces for an indefinite period in some of the world's worst weather conditions, maintaining a kind of (very) distant watching brief over the Falklands while the diplomats sorted things out and the Argentine Fleet stayed in the comfort of its own ports. When the conflict restarted, the sinking of *General Belgrano* 'turned out to be one of the most decisive military actions of the war' because 'the Argentine Navy – above all the carrier – went back to port and stayed there. Thereafter it posed no serious threat to the success of the task force.' The British decided against taking the war into Argentine waters, 'so our submarine commanders were left prowling up and down the Argentine 12 mile limit'.[58] The islands themselves could be less closely blockaded and a number of small vessels and aircraft from the Argentine continued to get through for a time. Despite such limitations, this was close blockade in all but name – and so were coalition operations against the Iraqi Navy in 1991. The use of new labels for blockade and counter-blockade operations should not conceal the fact that these are traditional naval activities with familiar aims, problems and prospects.

8   Exploiting command of the sea

The real reward for having command, or control, of the sea is the capacity to use it for your strategic purposes and to deny its use to any adversary. Broadly, there are two sets of strategic uses; the capacity to project military power ashore and to use the sea as a means of transportation. Each has its mirror image – preventing someone else from using the sea against you for either purpose.

8.1 Maritime power projection: definitions

The ability to project military power ashore suffers from the absence of a consistent vocabulary in maritime strategy. Competing words and definitions jostle to attract support: amphibious warfare, combined operations, land–sea operations, the projection of power ashore, overseas raids and invasions, attacks on territory from the sea. These all have strengths and weaknesses but none have won universal acclaim. 'Power projection' now tends to be the most widely used term, with a qualifying 'maritime' sometimes used.[1]

Maritime power projection involves the use of seaborne military forces directly to influence events on land. It ranges from substantial invasions to conquer territory, at one end of the spectrum, to minor nuisance raids and naval bombardments, at the other. Indeed this less ambitious end of the spectrum merges almost imperceptibly with the more coercive forms of naval diplomacy to be discussed in Chapter 9. Maritime power projection varies considerably in purpose, effort and strategic impact.

For Corbett, maritime power projection is the ultimate justification for having navies, as we saw in pages 58–59.[2]

Gorshkov took the argument one step further. He pointed out that in the Great Patriotic War, as in so many others, 'the goals of a war were achieved mostly by taking over the territory of the enemy'. Accordingly, the ability to influence campaigns ashore was for him the general culmination of the naval art, and by far the most productive way of using naval power:

> Successful operations of a fleet against the shore brought a better result than the operations of fleet against fleet. In the first case the fleet solved a direct 'territorial' task, whereas in the second, victory over the enemy's fleet merely created the pre-requisites for the later solution of territorial tasks.[3]

The use of the word 'direct' is important too. This elevated 'operations against the shore' above the attack/defence of sea lines of communication because in the latter case the operational and strategic impact of seapower was only *indirect*.

In his 1947 Report to the Secretary of the Navy Fleet, Admiral Chester Nimitz, US Navy, put the whole thing very forcefully:

> The final objective in war is the destruction of the enemy's capacity and will to fight, and thereby force him to accept the imposition of the victor's will. This submission has been accomplished in the past by pressure in and from each of the elements of the land and sea, and during World War I and II, in and from the air as well. The optimum of pressure is exerted through that absolute control obtained by actual physical occupation. This optimum is obtainable only on land where physical occupation can be consolidated and maintained. Experience proves that while invasion in some form – of adjacent sea areas, covering air spaces, or enemy territory itself – is essential to obtain decisions in war, it is sometimes unnecessary to prosecute invasion to the extent of occupying a nation's capital or other vital centres. Sufficient of his land, sea, or air territory must be invaded, however, to establish the destructive potential of the victor and to engender in the enemy that hopelessness that precedes submission. The reduction of Japan is a case in point.[4]

The *extent* to which maritime power projection can be decisive tactically, operationally or strategically depends on the circumstances. Sometimes it is merely a strategic 'enabler' – something that provides the conditions in which land and air forces can go on to win the war. The Allied ability to land, sustain and support the invasion of Normandy in June 1944 comes into this category. The Allies were able to force their way ashore by means of the world's biggest amphibious operation, establish themselves, break out and then begin the long advance to Paris and, ultimately, to the heartland of Germany. The farther they got from the sea, the more indirect became their maritime support. Sometimes, on the other hand, maritime power projection can be decisive, even executive, in its own right. If we make the uncontroversial assumption that Japan eventually would have been defeated in due course through the cutting of its crucial maritime communications, even without the dropping of atomic bombs on Hiroshima and Nagasaki, then this would apply to the Pacific War. Significantly, the more maritime the orientation of a country, the more decisive or executive maritime power projection against it can be.[5]

The early evolution of thinking about maritime power projection was largely covered in Section 3.5 through discussion of the views of Callwell and Corbett. It was also a major preoccupation of both American and Soviet naval thinkers during the Cold War era, when it was labelled 'operations of the fleet against the shore', in the Soviet lexicon, or 'the projection of power ashore', in the American. Both categories are notably comprehensive. Stansfield Turner produced a spectrum of projection that ranged from nuclear strike at one extreme to preventative presence at the other. Intermediate stages were: tactical air, naval bombardment, amphibious assault and reactive presence. Although Gorshkov's version of this is the same in many respects, he largely left out 'presence' roles but instead specifically included operations against or in support of military shipping, which the Americans tended to include in their sea control mission instead. The following, though, is common ground:

power projection in conventional warfare connotes the Navy's ability to launch sea-based air and ground attacks against enemy targets onshore. It also involves naval gun bombardment of enemy naval forces at port and installations. It is meant to enhance the efforts of US and Allied land-based forces in achieving their objectives.[6]

Despite occasional and so far unfounded periods of doubt, the navies of the world have continued to stress the importance of maritime power projection. Especially in the days before the Soviet Navy became a sea control competitor, the US Navy tended to regard projection as its main mission. Gorshkov was well aware of the advantages the Americans gained from this in the Korean and Vietnam wars, and somewhat wistfully catalogued their efforts in bombing, naval gunfire support and the attack of enemy supply lines. No doubt this helps explain the later development of his own navy's amphibious capabilities, although these never approached the levels achieved by the United States.[7]

8.2 Maritime power projection: aims

Maritime power projection can take many different forms, and these will usually be determined by their purpose. The same exercise in maritime power projection can, moreover, serve several different purposes simultaneously, although this can prove dangerous. The following outlines the most common aims of maritime power projection.

Determining the outcome of a conflict

The Pacific War comes into this category. A sequence of maritime battles and campaigns took the United States and its allies across the Central and South Western Pacific threatening Japan itself with mass invasion. The Falklands campaign of 1982 is another example. British maritime power effectively isolated the disputed islands from the mainland and projected amphibious power ashore, thereby producing a correlation of forces (in quality if not quantity) that made the Argentine defeat inevitable. The defining characteristics of this type of maritime power projection are the direct impact of sea-based support, even after the conclusion of the amphibious phase of the operation, and the determining effect of victory on the conclusion of the war.

Opening new operational fronts

The Gallipoli campaign of 1915 is an example of a campaign intended to improve the strategic situation by opening a new, more advantageous area of operations. The navy, supported by the army, by-passing the bulk of Turkey's forces to storm through the narrows, reduce Constantinople and paralyse Turkey in one fell swoop, was arguably the best idea of the First World War.[8] Practice fell far short of the concept, however, and the modern use of maritime power projection really only came into its own in the Second World War. As Bernard Brodie observed, 'The Second World War has seen a succession of sea-borne invasions on such a scale as the world has never before witnessed'. They included the Norwegian campaign

(1940), the Japanese operations in the Philippines and the East Indies (1941–1942), the landings in the Mediterranean area (1942–1944), Normandy (1944), the sequence of Australian–American landings in the South West Pacific and the US Navy's amphibious advance across the Central Pacific. These were all large-scale operations intended to have strategic effect.[9]

Direct support of the land forces

According to Admiral Gorshkov, there were some 600 landing operations in the Second World War. They were mostly successful and mostly in direct support of the land forces. On the Eastern Front, this was the essential task of both the German and the Russian navies. As Gorshkov put it, 'our naval science came to the conclusion that the outcome of the war would be decided on land, and therefore the Navy would have to carry out missions in the war stemming from the missions of the ground forces'.[10] Naval forces were expected to provide fire support, put ashore landing parties, defeat the opposition's sea and river forces, get troops across water barriers, transport military supplies and interfere with the enemy's communications. These tasks were by no means new. They were a classic part of every land campaign that either depended on a seaborne assault or which had a maritime front. The Russians developed the concept of the 'desant' landing. Mostly at the tactical level, these were small-scale, often improvised, localised operations (such as those along the north Russian coast and in the Black Sea) in which Russian forces were continually able to outflank German defensive positions from the sea. These operations

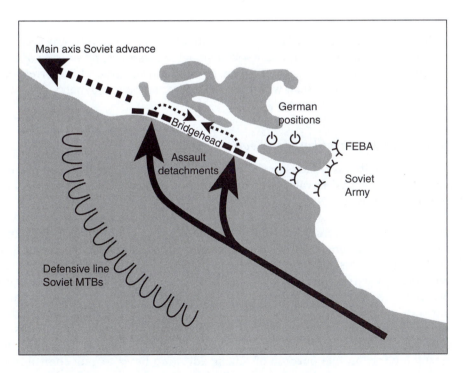

Figure 8.1 A Soviet desant operation.

kept up the momentum of friendly land forces or slowed an advancing enemy. Direct support operations could also sometimes take the form of combat extractions – such as Dunkirk (1940) or Crete (1941).

Force displacement

Corbett was particularly interested in the idea that landings, or threatened landings, from the sea could have a strategic effect out of all proportion to their size through 'the containing power that lies in combined expeditions, and of the disturbing influence which a fleet properly used can exercise upon Continental strategy'.[11] A sequence of such raids later caused Napoleon, then heavily engaged in his Austrian campaign, much aggravation: 'With 30,000 men in transports at the Downs, the English can paralyse 300,000 of my army, and that will reduce us to the rank of a second-class power.' There were distinct echoes of this in the Gallipoli campaign of 1915, the Norway campaign of 1940, the thinking behind 'The Maritime Strategy' in the 1980s and the Gulf War of 1991.

The eighteenth-century British considered force displacement a way of indirectly helping develop their strength at sea. Said the Duke of Newcastle:

> France will outdo us at sea when they have nothing to fear on land. I have always maintained that our marine should protect our alliances on the Continent, and so, by diverting the expense of France, enable us to maintain our superiority at sea.[12]

Economic warfare

Up to the end of the Second World War, maritime power projection was seen as a way of seizing or attacking other countries' colonial possessions and sources of overseas revenue, thereby damaging their prosperity and war revenue while correspondingly improving one's own. Such was the clear aspiration behind Japan's 1941–1942 campaigns through South East Asia.

Seizing or attacking naval bases and ports

By means of amphibious assaults or sea bombardments, countries have often sought to reduce their enemies' naval power by seizing or attacking their bases. In 1976, Admiral J. Holloway, US Navy, put it like this:

> the use of carrier aircraft and Marines in the projection of military force can be an absolute requirement in insuring our control, or continued safe use of areas of the high sea essential to our national needs.... Marine amphibious forces, supported by carrier air, can seize and hold land areas either to deny them to the enemy for their use in indicting our sea lines of communication, or to permit our own forces to exploit these areas as advance bases to attack enemy forces which would interdict our own ... It is interesting to remember that the island hopping campaigns in the Pacific in World War II were not to acquire real estate, but for the sole purpose of seizing advanced bases to gain control of the sea approaches to the recovery of the Philippines and the invasion of Japan.[13]

Forcing an inferior adversary to fight

Threatening something that was so strategically important to an adversary that he was bound to fight to defend it has often seemed an effective means of luring a reluctant adversary, otherwise content with a naval defensive of some sort, into battle. The British had such hopes in various of their schemes for the attacks on the German coast in the early part of the First World War, and so in a modified way, did the Germans with their east-coast raids.

Political coercion

Attacks from the sea, most often sea bombardments but occasionally amphibious assaults, have often to be seen essentially as a form of naval diplomacy – a means of influencing the behaviour of people ashore. The deterrent posture of the Royal Navy through the nineteenth century, based in large measure on its capacity to bombard ports such as Brest, comes into this category, as does the US Marine Corps' operation in the Lebanon in 1958 and the US Navy's attacks on Libya in the 1980s. This form of maritime power projection is discussed further in Section 9.6.

8.3 Amphibious operations

> We have landed in ill time: the skies look grimly,
> And threaten present blusters.
>
> Shakespeare, *A Winter's Tale*, III/3

Types of amphibious operation

Amphibious operations are the main subset of maritime power projection. They come in four varieties:

- *The amphibious assault*, where the aim is to get on to a hostile shore, stay there, build up combat power and establish a new front, maybe materially to alter the course of a war.
- *The amphibious raid*, where the intention is to establish a temporary lodgement to achieve a tactical or operational aim before making a planned withdrawal.
- *The amphibious withdrawal.* The ability to conduct a fighting extraction is the ultimate means of boosting the confidence of an expeditionary force ashore. As we saw in pages 29–31, Corbett praised the success of the evacuation from Gallipoli in glittering terms, pointing out how much it had shown that the necessary lessons had been learned.[14] Withdrawals can, moreover, lead to reinsertions elsewhere and may be seen as a means of exploiting the strategic mobility offered by command of the sea.
- *Amphibious feints and demonstrations*, are intended primarily to deceive an adversary and to tie down his forces in order to improve the correlation of forces elsewhere.

All four types of amphibious operation may be contested to some degree; ones that are not are often known as 'administrative landings'. Clearly then, the difficulty of amphibious operations depends on its form and aspiration – especially in relation to the objective and the quality of the opposition. A brief review of the Gallipoli and Normandy landings of 1915 and 1944 suggest there to be some 'norms' in these most ambitious instances of maritime power projection that would apply to many of its lesser forms too. Although many of the 'lessons' that can be extracted from these landings are of the sort that can be derived from any military operation to which the normal principles of war apply, the focus here will instead only be on those that relate to the special, maritime characteristics of amphibious operations.

Indeed, these characteristic requirements are so special and demanding that failure to give them insufficient attention usually makes defeat inevitable. This was certainly the conclusion of Charles Callwell, especially in regard to the failure at Gallipoli:

> There was no precedent to point to and no example to quote. The subject had been studied tentatively and as a matter of theory, and certain conclusions may have been arrived at, but few works treating of the art of war concerned themselves with the matter at all, and the problem involved had hardly received the consideration to which it was entitled either from the point of view of the attacking or the defending side. Still, all soldiers who had devoted attention to the subject were in agreement on one point. They realised that an opposed landing represented one of the most hazardous and most difficult enterprises that a military force could be called upon to undertake.[15]

In 1897, Colonel Furse did make use of previous experience to try to open the subject up through the exploration of issues such as command and control arrangements, the selection of landing sites, the provision of sufficient transports, the build up of a base ashore and the likely impact of modern technology. He touched on the special problem of 'contested' landings but despite his pioneering efforts, there was much justice in Aston's verdict of 1914:

> Amphibious strategy, or the combined strategy of fleets and armies treated as a special subject has not yet received the attention which its importance deserves, and the Japanese have so far been the only exponents of the art on a large scale under the conditions of modern warfare.

Many key issues in the conduct of amphibious operations remained unresolved, well into the Second World War. For instance, as late as 1944, there was little in the way of abstract discussion, let alone agreement, of the balance that should be struck between 'surprise' and 'security'. At Normandy, the practical experience of the British led them to emphasise the first, that of the Americans the second and the result was a flawed compromise. Command controversies still bedevilled British operations in the Falklands campaign of 1982. The 'norms' of amphibious warfare, in short, seem unfortunately to have been established more in the hard school of experience, than through prior reflection.[16]

What amphibious operations require

Maritime superiority

At the very least, amphibious operations required what Corbett described as 'reasonable naval preponderance' and Furse 'decided superiority' in the relevant area. Roskill declared, 'It is plain that the establishment of an adequate and effective zone of maritime control in the approaches to and the coastal waters off the disembarkation area is an absolute pre-requisite for success in this type of operation.' The task of navies was to 'cover' the force against hostile interception from the enemy main fleet as it crossed the sea. This cover would be 'full' if protection were the first priority; if not, the cover might be merely 'general'. The 'squadron in charge of transports' would protect the force from more local and minor attack. These two functions should be kept separate; the covering fleet had to be left free for independent naval action, lest the enemy appear in strength.[17]

Assured of basic security, the navy should be able to convey the landing forces to the amphibious operations area, offer close support in getting them ashore, help them consolidate their position and sustain them with supplies and reinforcements until the operation ceased to be amphibious. In some circumstances, the navy also offered a means of extracting or repositioning landed forces if the situation required it.

At Gallipoli, the author Compton Mackenzie (then a staff officer on General Hamilton's Staff) vividly encapsulated the soldier's dependence on the navy at a moment when the pressure of Turkish torpedo boats and German submarines forced the navy temporarily to abandon the forces ashore:

> I saw them in full flight, transports and battleships, the *Agamemnon* seeming to lead the van. The air was heavy that evening and ... the smoke of every ship was driven down astern, which gave the effect of a number of dogs running away with their tails between their legs. The sense of abandonment was acute. There was a sudden lull in the noise on the beach, as if every man had paused to stare at the unfamiliar emptiness of the water and then turned to his neighbour with a question in his eyes about their future here. It is certain that the Royal Navy has never executed a more demoralising manoeuvre in the whole of its history.[18]

Because the forces ashore were never able to break out of their restricted beach heads, the Gallipoli campaign remained amphibious throughout, and the navy was required to maintain such hazardous support not for days but for months on end, and had finally to evacuate the landed forces in what was surely one of the most brilliant operations of the First World War. All of this depended on sufficient command of the sea. In 1944, the potential vulnerability to naval attack of the invasion armada, packed with soldiers, chugging its way across the English Channel explains the huge attention paid to the maintenance of near total sea control throughout the Normandy campaign. In the event, this was so great that the weather caused Allied shipping more losses and disruption than did either the German Air Force or Navy.

The sheer scale of the armada assembled for the Normandy landings amazed many of its participants and serves as a useful reminder of the fact that an important aspect of maritime superiority is simply to have the transportation resources (whether these are amphibious craft, ships taken up from trade or simply landing facilities) to get men and supplies ashore in the number required.

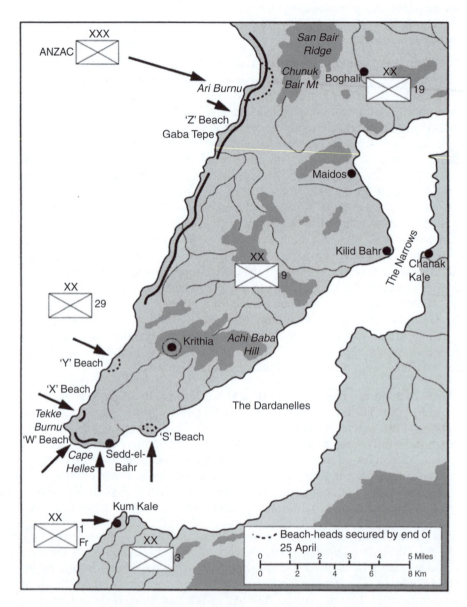

Figure 8.2 The Gallipoli landings, 25 April 1915.

Specialist skills and training

High levels of training and preparation were necessary for the task of shipping the army over, disembarking them, offering military support and keeping them supplied. The lesson appeared to be that neither the skills nor the equipment for this specialised and demanding task could be improvised at the drop of a hat. This, of course, was equally true of the military side of the operation. Forethought was supremely necessary, declared Richmond:

For want of thinking ahead, expeditions have suffered and sometimes failed because the necessary means were lacking – bombarding vessels to assist the landings, adequate shipping to carry the army, properly designed landing craft, maps and charts of the localities, knowledge of the climate.[19]

'Hitting the beach' successfully depended on accurate and extensive knowledge of beach conditions. The Normandy landings followed years of intensive and extremely hazardous beach surveys. Even so, navigational difficulties, the unexpected strength of the currents and the unpredictably high sea state combined to produce real difficulties especially off and near Omaha Beach. The US Rangers heading for the German battery at Point du Hoc were taken to the wrong headland; the leading units of the 1st and 29th Divisions were jumbled up on landing in a way that made cohesive attack impossible. The Duplex Drive tanks struggling to head for their assigned church steeple landmarks against adverse currents took the high waves at the wrong angle, were swamped and mostly sank, depriving the infantry of support as they landed.

At Normandy, the landing forces had months, sometimes years, of intensive specialist training behind them, which generally paid off handsomely. At Gallipoli, on the other hand, the landings of 25 April 1915 were only decided on shortly after the naval failure to force the straits on 18 March; everything was thrown together at the last minute, with few quite realising the scale of the problem they faced in preparing for a contested landing: 'one of the most hazardous and most difficult enterprises that a military force could be called upon to undertake'. In such circumstances, it is little short of amazing that the landing forces did as well as they did on 25 April. The

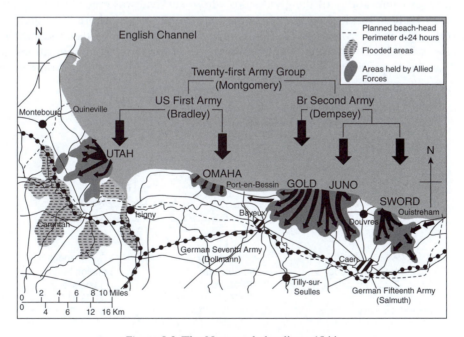

Figure 8.3 The Normandy landings, 1944.

lessons were learned and there were few significant difficulties in getting ashore in the follow-up Suvla Bay landings of 6 August 1915.

The difficulties of getting ashore may indeed so preoccupy both planners and the landing forces that insufficient attention is paid to the business of breaking out and developing success, which is usually the real point of the exercise. This is often said to be true of the Normandy landings.

Joint operations

It is particularly important that a landing be free from 'the corrupting blight' of interservice frictions. The army and navy should operate, thought Corbett, as 'two lobes of one brain, each self-contained and instinct with its own life and law, yet inseparable from the other: neither moving except by joint and unified impulse'. Above all, perhaps, 'the object they desire to obtain shall be clear in the minds both of those who order and those who command the operation'.[20] In the Gallipoli operation, the personal relationships between the naval and land commanders were very good but they rarely consulted and instead operated largely in their own sphere. On both sides there was extreme reluctance to be seen as 'interfering' in the other's business. This contributed to a lack of clarity on the operational aims of the campaign and indeed to its tactical implementation. This was especially true at the beginning of the campaign when there was a distinct lack of clarity about whether this should be a naval operation with army support, or a true amphibious operation.

Inevitably the services have their own operational agendas and procedures at every level of war. The army want total, maximum and permanent support. This sometimes conflicts with the navy's desire to defeat the adversary's naval forces at all levels. The retreat at Gallipoli of 28 May was inspired by an acute awareness of the tactical vulnerability of the great ships whose survival was crucial to the success of the operation, but looked like abandonment to the troops ashore. The shells the British ships chose to take to Gallipoli were better suited to battle at sea than to dealing with Turkish strong points ashore. At Normandy, communications difficulties led to problems in interservice cooperation (for instance in arrangements

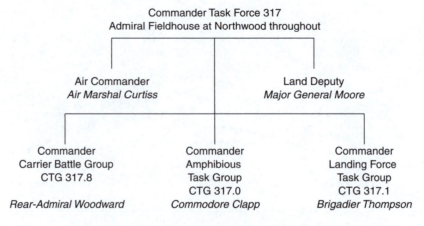

Figure 8.4 Command organisation at the Falklands, 1982.

for naval gunfire support of the troops ashore) but otherwise the operations were indeed effectively joint.

Corbett was quite proud of the fact that the two services retained their own command structure in theatre at Gallipoli. In principle, the British recognised the advantage of a single in-theatre commander but for a variety of reasons (including a lack of appreciation of the operational level of war) did not consistently put one in place until after the Falklands campaign of 1982. Problems in interservice coordination was one of the reasons for the Bluff Cove disaster and contributed to the adoption of an operational-level joint force commander thereafter. Other countries have increasingly adopted this practice too.

Surprise and manoeuvre

Surprise and speed of operation are particularly important as well, because the attacker would inevitably be dangerously exposed if the enemy knew where he meant to come ashore and could rush in reinforcements before the landing forces were able to consolidate. At Gallipoli, the navy helped by providing a demonstration well to the north of the amphibious area and facilitated a temporary landing away to the south. The appalling 'security' of the operation as a whole meant that operational surprise was impossible but at least tactical surprise (as defined by the knowledge of which beaches, when) was in fact brilliantly achieved four times – the landings of 25 April, the follow-up Suvla Bay operation on 6 August and the two-stage withdrawal in December 1915 and January 1916. It was even better at Normandy where operational surprise was achieved as well; for weeks after the landings the Germans thought the main landings could be coming in later in the Pas-de-Calais area and kept crucial reserve forces back, just in case.

The sea also offered a means of enabling the landing forces to avoid strong points, by putting them ashore in unexpected places and by taking advantage of the displacement effect described above. This was generally achieved both in Gallipoli and Normandy, except in some specific locations where the military strength of the strong points was insufficiently appreciated. (V and W Beaches, Omaha) or the topographical difficulties underestimated (Anzac Beach, Omaha).

Compensatory military-technological advantage

Simply because they do not have to be sea-portable, and have the time to prepare static defences, the defenders have a natural advantage over the landing forces. For this reason, many concluded before the First World War that mines, machine guns, the internal combustion engine and improved land communications would make contested amphibious operations much more difficult. The defenders would be able to respond much faster to surprise landings and would be much more effective relative to the landing forces when they did. The official history of the Gallipoli campaign makes the basic point: 'while the defenceless troops scramble out of their boats, and struggle waist-deep in water, they can be shot down as easily, and almost as safely, as bottles at a fair'.[21] This simple truth was cruelly demonstrated at V and W Beaches when tiny numbers of Turkish defenders were able to inflict appalling casualties on the British as they waded ashore. To a large extent this was also true of the first two attacking waves at Omaha.

The requirement to exploit military technology in order to even up the odds between attacker and defender was perfectly well realised, but at Gallipoli most attempts to do this failed. The *River Clyde*, for example, was an imaginative scheme to convert a merchant ship into an early form of amphibious assault ship, with a bow door, armour and forward firing guns, but at V Beach it signally failed to compensate for the intrinsic vulnerability of troops hitting the beach. It was the same at Omaha where the solutions (heavy air and naval bombardment, amphibious 'Duplex Drive' tanks and combat engineers to remove the obstacles) did not work. The first missed, the second sank and the third were largely killed. Fortunately for the Allies, compensatory military technology (in the shape, for example, of 'Hobart's Funnies' – a variety of specialist tanks to deal with mines, strong points, etc.) proved more effective on the other Normandy beaches. However, in all the Normandy landings the initial aerial and naval bombardments proved much less effective than had been hoped for.

Nonetheless military technology frequently *has* been able to deal with the intrinsic odds against landing operations, especially when in combination with the surprise factor and the displacement effects noted above. Of these, sea-based airpower has proved one of the most important levellers of the odds. Admiral Nimitz reported:

> The development between World Wars I and II of naval aviation provided naval forces with a striking weapon of vastly increased flexibility, range and power. It spearheaded our Pacific attack. First, it swept the sea of all naval opposition. Then it became the initial striking weapon in the capture of Guam, Saipan and Iwo Jima.... In all these operations the employment of air–sea forces demonstrated the ability of the Navy to concentrate aircraft strength at any desired point in such numbers as to overwhelm the defence at the point of contact. These operations demonstrate the capability of naval carrier-based aviation to make use of the principles of mobility and concentration to a degree possessed by no other force.[22]

Even so, doubts about the extent to which amphibious technology could keep up with the increasing power of the defender continued – especially with the advent of nuclear weapons. Just after the Second World War, there were those who wished to sweep away the US Marines on the grounds that a small number of atomic bombs could destroy an expeditionary force as now organised, embarked and landed: 'With an enemy in possession of atomic bombs, I cannot visualise another landing such as was executed at Normandy or Okinawa.'[23] Despite the success of the Inchon landings of 1950, large concentrations of ships and men were seen as simply too vulnerable for such operations against the nuclear powers or their immediate allies.

The spread of land-based precision guided munitions and the increasing mechanisation of the world's armies aggravated the problem. For this reason, there was a tendency to focus on the unopposed or 'administrative' landing.

Nonetheless, the major navies of the Cold war era continued to believe in the ultimate feasibility of contested landings – at least when their strategic importance was seen to justify the necessary investment. Thus Admiral K.A. Stalbo, one of the Soviet Navy's leading strategic writers, in 1970:

We would stress that the basic reasons which force the warring sides to resort to amphibious landings [in the Second World War] have not only been maintained under modern conditions, but have been considerably enhanced. Because of this, amphibious landings have not lost their importance to the slightest degree.[24]

The US Marine Corps maintained the faith as well and by the end of the 1980s the concept of 'operational manoeuvre from the sea' had arrived.

8.4 Operational manoeuvre from the sea

The concept of operational manoeuvre from the sea (OMFTS) and its application to the Inchon landings of the Korean War was introduced in Section 2.3. In developing their thinking on OMFTS, the US Marine Corps took as a source of inspiration an early attempted application of such principles in the US Civil War – the Peninsula Campaign of 1862 – and sought to apply its lessons to the 1990s.

In 1862, the main forces of both sides were concentrated in the narrow area between Washington (the Federal capital) and Richmond (the capital of Virginia and of the Confederacy). On the Northern side, General George B. McClellan, young, able, extremely well read in military history, came up with a brilliant idea. Instead of a costly, frontal assault on the Confederate forces (which he mistakenly thought were much stronger than his own) why not make use of the North's maritime supremacy to sweep round the Southern army and launch a direct assault on Richmond. The whole idea 'was to leave the enemy where he was and fight him where he was not'. The Southern army should be outmanoeuvred and fought on better terms. 'I have my mind actively turned towards another plan of campaign that I do not think at all anticipated by the enemy', he said. Attacking Richmond, he thought, was the best way of defending Washington.[25]

In the event, the Confederates fell back a little while McClellan was making his plans and so he shifted the landing point from Urbanna to Fort Monroe on the tip of the Virginia Peninsula. While this increased the distance to Richmond to 75 miles, the change had a huge advantage in that the advance up the peninsula could be supported on both sides by the navy on the York and the James rivers. If McClellan's Army of the Potomac could get to Richmond before the Confederates had time to fall back and build sufficient defences, the war could be won in one glorious campaign.

The idea was certainly bold (and President Lincoln took some persuading to accept it) but McClellan was well aware that the British had used similar strategies in their assaults on Charleston and New York in the War of Independence and on Washington and New Orleans in the War of 1812. Moreover, the Confederates had already taken warning from the Northerners' earlier small-scale assaults on Fort Hatteras, Port Royal and Island No. 10 in the Mississippi, of the dangerous vulnerability of Richmond to amphibious assault up the York and James rivers. To some extent, McClellan was pushing on an open door.

Accordingly a huge army of over 120,000 men, the biggest so far assembled in the Civil War, was embarked in 400 vessels together with all their wagons, guns, pack animals 'and the enormous quantity of equipage etc required for an army of such magnitude'.[26] It was the biggest amphibious operation conducted by the United

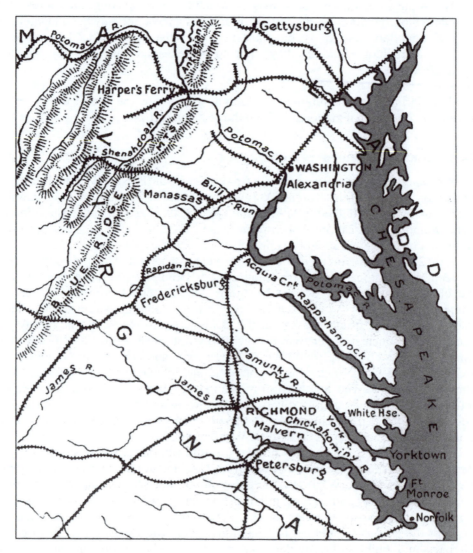

Figure 8.5 The Peninsula Campaign 1862: strategic setting (source: Callwell, 1996a [1903]).

States until the Normandy landings of 1944. The first ships departed on 17 March 1862. They landed, unopposed, at the Northerners' own Fort Monroe two to three days later. Thereafter McClellan did indeed advance up the peninsula supported from both maritime flanks by the navy. He took the Confederate strongholds at Yorktown and Williamsburg and approached Richmond.

On 15 May 1862, a five-ship Northern flotilla headed by the gunboats *Galena* and *Monitor* came up the James River, in what the US Marines would later christen 'ship to objective manoeuvre' (STOM). The idea was 'to reduce all the works of the enemy as they go along ... and then get to Richmond, all with the least possible delay, and shell the city to surrender'.[27] This advance was stopped in a battle at

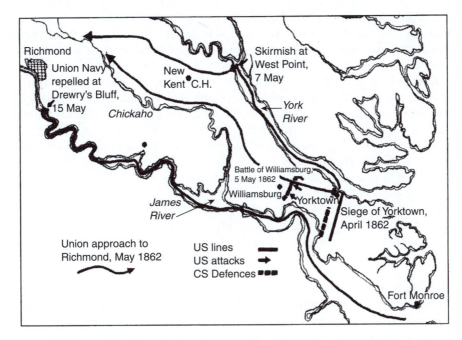

Figure 8.6 Drewry's Bluff: manoeuvre from the sea (source: Martin, 1992).

Drewry's Bluff so decisive for the Confederacy that both President Jefferson Davis and General Robert E. Lee rode out to witness the aftermath, and Richmond rang its bells in victory. Even so, some of McClellan's people remained convinced that a combined attack by the army and navy could still prove irresistible. But, in fact, the moment had passed. The Northern Army of the Potomac slowly fell back on Fort Monroe and by August 1862 began to evacuate. The Peninsula Campaign was over.

So what had gone wrong? Looking back on it, does the failure of this campaign invalidate the concept of OMFTS – or was it merely a matter of faulty implementation that could be corrected by the technology and techniques of a later age? The US Marine Corps seem to have concluded the latter provided some obvious deficiencies were corrected:

- *Insufficient sea control.* The terrifying Southern ironclad CSS *Merrimack/ Virginia*[28] devastated a Northern naval squadron of wooden ships at Hampton Roads on 8 March 1862. Two ships were sunk, and another driven aground. What if the *Merrimack* got into the invasion fleet, or even went up the Potomac to attack Washington? Fortunately for the North, the US Navy's answer was the USS *Monitor* that arrived the following day, when the famous encounter between the two ironclads took place. Tactically the result was a stand-off. Afterwards, both ships warily watched each other and made menacing movements that effectively neutralised the other. The fear and loathing that *Merrimack* inspired can be deduced from the following description: 'She remained there smoking, reflecting and ruminating till nearly sunset, when she slowly crawled off nearly concealed in a huge, murky cloud of her own emission, black and repulsive as the perjured hearts of her traitorous crew.'[29] *Merrimack*'s role as a one-ship 'fleet-in-being' required a large squadron to watch her and this meant that the Northern Navy's support to McClellan on the York River was reduced, and virtually none was available for the James River during the first critical few weeks of the campaign. Only when the Northern Army took Norfolk and its shipyards on 10 May, forcing the destruction of *Merrimack*, was the James effectively opened; the battle of Drewry's Bluff took place five days later. Such experiences help explain the modern stress on total 'battle space dominance' and the assumption of high levels of sea control both on the open ocean and in littoral waters.

- *Loss of momentum*. Lincoln had warned that:

  > going down the [Chesapeake] Bay in search of a field [of battle], instead of fighting at or near Manassas, was only shifting, and not surmounting a difficulty: that we should find the same enemy, and the same or equal entrenchments, at either place.[30]

The solution to this was speed and surprise. The second was achieved but not the first. McClellan became known as the original Virginia Creeper because of the army's very slow rate of advance. This was due to the awful state of the roads, the weather and an exaggerated notion of the size of the forces opposed to him. These combined to make McClellan reluctant to divide his forces for 'desants' further up the peninsula. One such exercise was the unloading of General Franklin's specially trained amphibious division at Eltham's Landing 20 miles up the York River on 6 May, but it was typical of the conduct of this campaign that the Confederates had already slipped past this outflanking movement by the time it was eventually launched.

These days, the argument goes, a clear sense of mission, fast ship to shore movement and great overland/aerial mobility should avoid such problems. Ideally this should be achieved by STOM. The invaders should not need to come ashore at Fort Monroe and then laboriously work their way up the peninsula; instead they should be conveyed straight to the objective, in this case Richmond. Unsurprisingly, US Marine Corps Doctrine concludes: 'Superior mobility – the capability to move from place to place faster than the enemy while retaining the ability to perform the mission – is a key ingredient of maneuver.'[31] In modern times, the use of fixed and especially rotary wing aircraft as a means of developing speed and momentum has been particularly important. The concept of 'vertical envelopment' was employed first by the British in the Suez operation of 1956.

- *STOM technology not up to the job*. Naval gunfire support in this campaign was useful rather than decisive, especially in comparison with the shore-based artillery it had to defeat. At the Battle of Drewry's Bluff, most of the effective gunnery was conducted by *Galena* because the *Monitor*'s guns could not elevate sufficiently to deal with the Confederate's guns 200 feet above them. It demonstrated the need for sea-based craft specifically optimised for littoral operations of this sort.

The Confederates had their problems too. They needed to depress their guns so much they had problems stopping the cannon balls rolling out of the barrels before they were fired. The result of this was a technical/tactical stand-off and a decisive failure in STOM. Nowadays, the theory goes, firepower should 'shape the battle space'. US Marine Corps Doctrine approvingly quotes Russell Weighley on this concept: 'Shaping activities may render the enemy vulnerable to attack, facilitate maneuver of friendly forces and dictate the time and place for decisive battle.'[32] In short, military technology of this sort has to be good, but it has also to be effectively integrated into the other aspects of the operational art. It does not win battles on its own.

- *Insufficient jointery*. In responding to the threat posed by *Merrimack*, the navy clearly had its own agenda. Nonetheless, it played a vital role at the tactical and operational levels in getting the invaders to the operational area in safety, in keeping them supplied, in continuously transporting men and material up and down both rivers, in providing fire support and, finally, in extracting the army back to Washington when the campaign effectively ended. Probably there could have been more. Had, for example, the navy's advance on Drewry's Bluff been supported by an overland assault the outcome might have been very different. The navy's dependence on the land forces in such littoral operations was also exemplified by the fact that, in the end, *Merrimack* was effectively destroyed by the army not by Federal warships.

In sum, advocates of OMFTS tend to conclude that the James was indeed 'the River of Lost Opportunities' and that more modern technology and techniques make the concept behind the Peninsula Campaign finally achievable.

OMFTS: the strategic consequences

Callwell was rather more interested in the grand strategic consequence of the Peninsula Campaign as an example of OMFTS (not, of course, that he used this phrase!). He thought the various campaigns in Virginia vividly depicted 'the influence of sea-power over the course of the conflict on shore'. Later, when Lee invaded Maryland, McClellan 'was hastily brought round by sea from the James to near Washington, and so Lee found himself confronted on the Antietam by an army which was too strong for him and consequently withdrew to Virginia'. In short, even after the failure of the Peninsula Campaign, the Northerners' control of the sea in the Chesapeake Bay and their consequent capacity for operational manoeuvre on the grand scale, saved them from disaster.[33]

The same strategic consequence of a demonstrated capacity for OMFTS can be seen in the Gulf War of 1991, the more dramatically because this was a campaign of opposites. On the Iraqi side it was all attritional and static, a linear confrontation of forces and resources; the Coalition, on the other hand, was manoeuvrist in its approach. The 'amphibious feint' by the US Marines first distracted Iraqi forces to the Kuwait coastline and then, much more importantly, reinforced their impression that the allies were planning to come straight across Kuwait's southern border. This 'maritime contribution to joint operations' was reinforced by the Coalition's air superiority, which blinded the Iraqis to the Coalition's actual focus 200 miles to the west, where they were able to develop a sweeping outflanking move deep into Iraq's

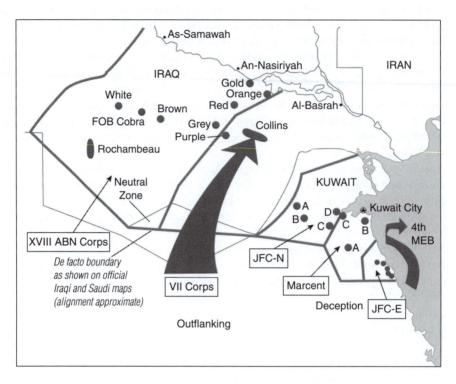

Figure 8.7 The Coalition plan, 1991: operational manoeuvre from the sea.

defensive system. Once allied forces began to move, their operational superiority was evident; the air supremacy enjoyed by the Coalition meant that the Iraqis did not know what was going on, and when they did, it denied them the capacity to respond coherently. OMFTS can evidently play a crucial strategic role even in a war of geographic contiguity.[34]

To achieve all this in contemporary circumstances, a sea-based force (most obviously comprising a combination of naval and marine forces) would need the capacity to assault from over the horizon (to maximise surprise) and a STOM capacity of some sort (to maintain speed and momentum). The landed forces would depend on maritime firepower and sea-based supplies. The commander would need full 'situational awareness' (through effective reconnaissance and command and control). Sea-based forces may also provide a manoeuvre reserve. General McClellan would not have been familiar with the words, but he would certainly have recognised the aspirations! How realistic these aspirations are for forces other than the US Navy and Marine Corps, depends on the resources they devote to it and, as always, on the relative strength of the opposition.

8.5 Sea-based strategic missile attack of the shore

During the Cold War, for the first time some of the world's leading navies acquired, in their capacity to operate ballistic missile firing submarines, a fundamentally new role. Admiral Gorshkov pointed out how revolutionary this was:

Today, a fleet operating against the shore is able not only to solve the tasks connected with territorial changes, but directly to influence the course and even outcome of a war. In this connection the operations of a fleet against the shore have assumed paramount importance in armed conflict at sea.[35]

Practically for the first time, navies were able to have a direct, immediate and decisive impact not just on the tactical and operational levels of war but on its *strategic* conduct and result.

According to Gorshkov, there were, and remain, four basic reasons for putting such strategic nuclear forces to sea:

- It increases reach, since ballistic missile firing nuclear powered submarines (SSBNs) can use the sea to approach their target more closely. The shorter the range of the missile, the more important this advantage.
- It conceals the missiles from pre-emptive attack and reduces the incentive to use them early in a conflict. This may help stabilise a dangerous situation. Moreover, it means that however skilful the aggressor's attack, he will still be subject to devastating retaliation. This was the whole basis of 'mutual assured destruction' – 'a most important factor deterring his nuclear attack'.
- Attacks can be launched from different directions, complicating the enemy's protective task.
- Putting such forces at sea, reduces the enemy's incentives to launch disarming strikes against the homeland with all the horrifying death and destruction that would cause.[36]

Clearly the relative invulnerability of the SSBN was key to all this, and explains why so many resources were devoted to the protection of SSBNs and to investigating ways of detecting and attacking them. During the Cold War, various SSBN operating procedures were adopted. Broadly Western SSBNs were operated in forward positions, and relied on their stealth for protection. Soviet SSBNs, on the other hand, tended increasingly to operate in 'bastions' (in the Norwegian Sea and North West Pacific Europe) where they could be protected partly by the efforts of the fleet (which included land-based aviation) and partly by the environment (most obviously Arctic ice).

In the event, this became a major naval activity during the Cold War. The US Navy conducted some 35,000 SSBN patrols during the twentieth century, taking some 130,000-man years of effort, and through their Blue/Gold teams maintained an astonishing 70 per cent deployment rate. The technological effort was immense too. The first SSBN, the USS *George Washington*, was completed five years early in 1958 and the 41 SSBNs eventually produced in less than eight years testify to the priority given this mission. Estimates vary, but counting in the US Navy's nuclear propelled submarine (SSN) programme, the seaborne deterrent took about one-third of the $2 trillion spent on nuclear forces by the United States.[37] There was a very comparable effort in the Soviet Union too.

The fact that American SSBNs took up some 10 per cent of the US Navy's budget between 1959 and 1964 explains why American admirals were notably cool about accepting this new mission. The resources and technological effort required for this programme could not be devoted to other more conventional naval activities. Their wariness also reflected a strong sense that the thinking behind the *use* of the missiles the SSBNs carried generally had very little to do with maritime strategy. This mission seemed to stand apart from the main maritime effort.

But, increasingly, a process of convergence changed this, not least because the protection or attack of such forces absorbed considerable operational effort. Indeed, in the 1980s under 'The Maritime Strategy' there was much discussion of the putative advantage of Western forces attacking Soviet SSBN bastions as a way of tying down Soviet naval forces that would otherwise be free to attack Western reinforcement shipping coming across the Atlantic. In such ways, the capacity to fire ballistic missiles against the shore for strategic purposes became thoroughly integrated into the mainstream of maritime strategy, and in the same way, sea-launched cruise missiles have become an integral part of the maritime power projection mission at the tactical and operational levels.

8.6 Defence against maritime power projection

[W]ith eight tall ships. Three thousand men of war
Are making hither with all due expedience
And shortly mean to touch our northern shore.

Shakespeare, *Richard II*, II/1

We should now turn to the mirror image of all this – the need to defend yourself against maritime power projection forces hostile to you.

Defence against amphibious assault and raids

As we saw in pages 31–33, many navies, great and small, have been concerned about coastal defence. This comprises four interlinked elements, and most nations have employed some combination of all of them.

Deterrence

The Royal Navy has always emphasised the role of a strong fleet in defending the country against amphibious assault, raids and/or passing bombardments. Such a fleet should so dominate the sea around the country that all but the smallest of raids would be intercepted and destroyed. 'I do not say the French cannot come', declared Lord St Vincent confidently in the Trafalgar era, 'I only say they cannot come by sea.'[38]

The maintenance of command (either by a restless pursuit of decisive victory or by blockade) was the first line of defence against invasion but would normally work indirectly, very possibly as a deterrent. Few would try to send major invasion forces through waters commanded by the defending fleet. In such a case, all the maritime deterrence needs to do is maintain a direct defence against sneak attacks and minor infiltrations. These in turn could be deterred by the known strength of your defences closer to shore and on land.

The less confident an invader was in his capacity to exercise command through projecting power ashore, the more effectively could an imaginative fleet-in-being strategy deter an amphibious assault. This was, arguably, Torrington's objective in 1690, as we saw in Section 6.7. Mahan and Castex both concluded that Colomb exaggerated the *extent* to which an invader needed command of the sea before launching his attack and so overestimated the ability of the fleet-in-being (which sought to limit the degree of that command) to deter such attempts. It is certainly true that there are many examples of invasions being attempted when a significant defending fleet *was* still 'in being' (most recently the German invasion of Norway in 1940, where the British Fleet in fact was more or less present and clearly superior to the amphibious force).

Indirect forward defence

But, as we saw in Chapter 6, command of the sea is rarely absolute and the more the sea is 'uncommanded' (in the sense that neither side has an overwhelming advantage) the more feasible is the prospect of invasion. In such a case, thought Mahan (most of the time), the stronger fleet should resort to offensive action:

> The navy's proper office in offensive action, results as certainly in battleships as the defensive idea does in small vessels. Every proposal to use a navy as an instrument of pure passive defence is found faulty upon particular examination ... the effectual function of the fleet is to take the offensive.[39]

This offensive action could take at least three forms or more likely some combination of them:

* building an accurate picture of the enemy's position, strength and possible moves;
* spoiling attacks of the sort launched in 1587 by Drake against the Spanish Armada at Cadiz;
* interception at sea.

Discovering the enemy's intentions was especially important since an enemy seeking to invade across a relatively uncommanded sea had two choices. He could either put all his forces together, battlefleet and transports, and fight his way through if that was necessary; or he could split the two up and use his battlefleet to lure the defender away and then send his transports over in their absence. Either way, the defender needed to know what was intended.

Corbett thought that the speed of modern intelligence and an increased capacity to catch and overwhelm an invasion of convoy-and-escorts made the chances of successful interception at sea much better, not worse, than they were in days of sail. And yet, in both world wars, the majority of invasions succeeded in reaching their objectives safely: only a few were even partially intercepted at sea (Crete 1941, Coral Sea and Midway 1942, for instance). Arguably, though, the fear that they would be intercepted by substantial forces at sea, especially with the advent of airpower, deterred many other amphibious enterprises from setting out in the first place.

When an incoming invasion fleet *was* detected, Corbett recommended holding back the attack until the enemy was 'hopelessly committed to an [amphibious] operation beyond his strength'. This might produce better results than a precipitate offensive. Certainly, he declared, 'whether the expedition that threatens us be small or of invasion strength, the cardinal rule has always been that the transports and not the escort must be the primary objective of the fleet'.[40] It was just as well for the

British in the Falklands campaign that Argentina's airmen were either unaware of this rule, or were unable to observe it by virtue of the strength of the British air defences.

Direct defence offshore

Some invaders/raiders were likely to leak through the strongest fleet, especially when it was limited in size and/or operational aspiration. For this reason, it was necessary to have a final line of naval defence, just off the coast. Admiral Pellew, in the period before Trafalgar, said:

> I see a triple naval bulwark composed of one fleet acting on the enemy's coast, of another consisting of heavier ships stationed in the Downs ready to act at a moment's notice, and a third close to the beach capable of destroying any part of the enemy's flotilla that should escape the vigilance of the other two branches of our defence.[41]

This was the thinking behind Admiral Fisher's notion of flotilla defence based on small warships, submarines, mines and aircraft, just before the First World War. As we saw in pages 71–73, this idea, a development of the 'fortress fleet strategy', was taken forward by the Soviet New School, when the navy's task was defined thus by Chief Commissar Mucklevitch in 1930:

> In war the fleet would accompany the army during its advance and it would not be guided in its activities by lessons drawn from the study of the Battle of Jutland, because it would not seek to solve its problems by an open sea encounter with the enemy's fleet, but would carry on a small war, relying on minefields, submarines and naval aircraft.[42]

Russian naval strength, in other words, should not be concentrated in a few large units, but diffused amongst a host of minor ones. The resultant 'mosquito fleet' could mount an ever more intensive and ferocious attack on an enemy invasion fleet the closer it approached the shores of Russia. Aided by modern technology, the Soviet New School hoped to conduct its war at sea on lines quite novel in maritime strategy.

Since land forces ashore would have a major role to play as well, this required close cooperation with the army, especially if the enemy did, after all, land and consolidate himself ashore. In this case, by harassing his maritime communications, the navy would hinder his every movement, or even oblige him to withdraw. Richmond noted an example of this: 'Korea, when invaded by Hideyoshi in 1592, was saved by investment of the Japanese army, the Korean navy cutting off its communications and investing it, forcing it thereby to evacuate the country.'[43] The Chinese Navy of the 1950s exemplified this approach. Its first post-Revolution commander, Xiao Jingguang, said the navy, 'should be a light-type navy, capable of inshore defence. Its key mission is to accompany the ground forces in war actions. The basic characteristic of this navy is fast deployment, based on its lightness.'[44] During and after the Second World War, the following were common characteristics of direct defence at sea against amphibious operations:

- Coordinated attack by small submarines, fast attack craft, assault swimmers (as the Germans attempted off Normandy in 1944).
- Air assault on invasion forces. Towards the end of the Pacific War, the Japanese resorted to kamikaze attacks with considerable effect. Smart munitions now pose a significant threat and explain current preoccupations with air and anti-missile defence.
- Extensive minefields such as those deployed by the North Koreans off Wonsan in November 1950, and the Iraqis in 1990–1991.

In contemporary circumstances, the defender has a range of political and techno-logical options to ensure that an expeditionary invader may need to fight for access both in transporting his forces to the operations area and in getting them to their objective, against a range of terminal defences. These will be discussed at greater length in Section 8.7. Such defences may well include theatre ballistic missiles, hence the interest in developing defensive systems against them.

Direct defence onshore

In the course of a long, heated debate about the respective roles of the army and the navy in the defence of nineteenth-century Britain, the army argued that there was a fundamental unreliability about the possibilities of naval defence – which meant that the country needed strong defences behind the shoreline. General Lord Wolseley commented in 1896:

> I know of nothing that is more liable to disaster and danger than anything that floats on the water. We often find in peace and in the calmest weather our best ironclads running into each other. We find great storms dispersing and almost destroying some of the finest fleets that ever sailed. Therefore, it is essentially necessary that it [Britain] should always have a powerful Army, at least suffi-ciently strong to defend our own shores.[45]

In some instances, indeed, orthodox naval power may seem so irrelevant to the defensive task in hand that the only contribution that major warships can make is to be disarmed so that their guns and manpower can reinforce defences on land. This was the fate of the French Navy in the war of 1870–1871, and the Russian Navy in the Crimean War and during the German siege of Leningrad 1941–1943.

But even the strongest naval power may well feel the need to guard against unex-pected descents with a system of coastal fortifications, guns and reserve land forces behind them. This was certainly what Furse expected.[46] Even in the nineteenth century, at the height of *Pax Britannica*, the British spent a fortune on the extensive coastal fortifications that still dominate much of the coast of southern England.

That impulse is still more marked amongst countries that do not themselves maintain large sea-going fleets:

- Humiliated by the British burning the White House, President Madison in 1815 urged 'a liberal provision for the immediate extension and gradual completion of the works of defence of our maritime frontier', but progress was slow and the works around Charleston, the second biggest port on the east coast, were not completed by the time that the Civil War started, actually at Fort Sumter, in 1861.

- In the Australian case, the priority was to defend places like Sydney from local but overland attack and its harbour and installations from sea bombardment. Its formidable Martello tower of 1857 at Fort Denison with two 10-inch guns, one 8-inch gun and 12 32-pounder cannon was one of the last such fortifications to be built anywhere in the world.

- In the Norwegian, Swedish and Finnish cases, a large fleet of small warships was backed up by extensive and sophisticated coastal artillery batteries – both being supported by airpower and a 'total mobilisation' defensive system. In their 1940 invasion, the Germans suffered their biggest single loss, the sinking of the heavy cruiser *Blucher* to a torpedo fired from a coastal fort on the Oslo fjord.

- The Argentine Exocet attack on HMS *Glamorgan* in the Falklands campaign and the Iraqi firing of a Silkworm against coalition forces in the northern Gulf in 1991, are contemporary versions of this.

The defender's main difficulty in dealing with forces hitting the beach derives from the fact that the invader has the initiative in deciding the time and place of his assault. The defender therefore has to spread his defences along the coastline and to keep a reserve back to deal with landed forces that local defences cannot contain and expel. The famous dispute between Rommel and von Runstedt before the Normandy landings was not about defence either on the beaches or further inland; instead it was about the balance that should be struck between the two. Here the critical issue to be decided was the extent to which the invader would be able to slow up the movement of German reserves through superior airpower. The more closely the landing force can be contained, the less able will it be to build up its combat potential for break-out and the more vulnerable to counter-attack by the defender's reserve.

In the Salerno landings of 1942, the mobile defence system adopted by the Germans stressed counter-attack on the landed forces by heavy armour was very nearly successful in driving the Allies back into the sea, but this did not work in the Normandy landings because the reserve Panzer divisions were held back lest the real landing took place in the Pas-de-Calais – and, when they were eventually committed, Allied aircraft and the French resistance greatly slowed their progress. In the Pacific, however, the Japanese faced a different set of problems in defending their gains. The islands were often too small for the safe marshalling of effective reserves, banzai charge counter-attacks were wasteful and it was difficult for them to bring reinforcements across seas largely controlled by the Americans. Accordingly, there was a tendency to focus on beach defences and, when accumulated American naval/air firepower made that unproductive, the Japanese resorted to 'cave tactics' (as at Iwo Jima) or even spoiling counter-landings in or near the American beachhead.

The variety of these responses shows there are there are no simple rules in defending against invasion. The defender has to make up his strategy on a case by case basis. Moreover, defenders should be aware that despite their obvious and much-vaunted difficulties, most amphibious assaults succeed, and most attempts at defence against them fail.[47] Further, an invader's capacity to engage in STOM operations, makes the defender's task even more difficult.

Defence against missile attack

At the end of the twentieth century, a special variant of the historic requirement to defend against maritime power projection came into prominence – namely defence against missile attack. The acquisition of missiles and weapons of mass effect by an increasing number of countries, and the technological blurring of the differences between strategic, operational and tactical actions, highlighted two maritime issues.

First, was a growing recognition of the need for the protection of expeditionary forces from cruise, and increasingly ballistic, missile attack. This concern was not wholly new. If Germany in 1944 had directed its V1 missiles against the Allies' ports of embarkation rather than London, the Normandy operation would have been in jeopardy. General Eisenhower was quite clear about this: 'If he [Hitler] had succeeded in using these weapons over a six-month period, and particularly if he had made the Portsmouth–Southampton area one of his principal targets, *Overlord* [the Normandy invasion] might have been written off.'[48]

The Iraqi Scud missile that landed on the dockside of the port of Al-Jubayl in February 1991 exemplified a concern that has led the US and many other navies to explore means of expanding existing anti-missile and anti-aircraft defences in order to cope with short- to medium-range ballistic missile attack of bases, ports, deployed forces or local allies. Thus an Aegis ship operating off South Korea could protect the port of Pusan and its immediate area. A more ambitious variant of this area defence is the notion that it could be extended to cover whole theatres of operation (theatre ballistic missile defence (TBMD)) under which the same ship could also protect the whole of Japan.

Second, there is the still more ambitious notion that sea-based forces at sea off an adversary's coastline could significantly contribute to national missile defence

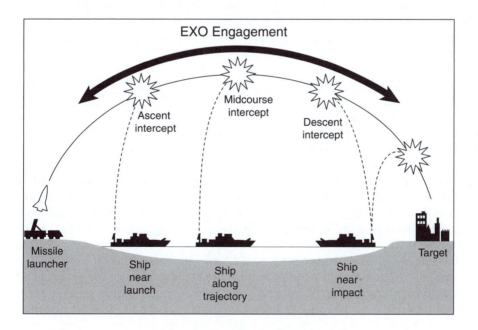

Figure 8.8 Defence against missile attack.

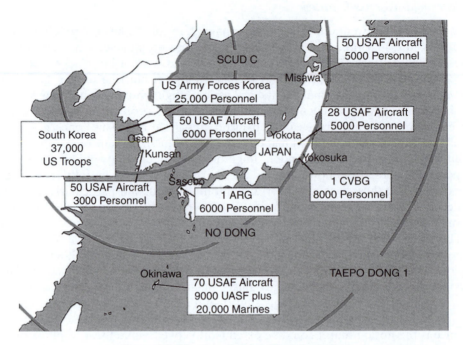

Figure 8.9 The threat of land-based missiles.

(NMD) by intercepting missiles in their ascent phases. This is much more demanding technologically; moreover it challenges the traditional 'mutual assured destruction' conception of strategic nuclear deterrence, together with the treaties that enshrine it. It is accordingly highly controversial.

Naval forces such as Aegis-equipped cruisers and destroyers have much to offer TBMD because:

- they are likely to be faster into theatre than air-lifted alternatives like the Patriot system;
- they require no airlift;
- they do not depend on host nation support;
- the sea allows them to deploy forwards against the threat.

But there are trade-offs here, because forward deployment might reduce their capacity to conduct other maritime operations and certainly provides a new operational commitment to be serviced. Both types of sea-based missile will be very demanding technologically, not least in the requirement for sophisticated battle management technology and an ambitious level of 'cooperative engagement' between different naval and other forces. They will absorb the expenditure of considerable maritime resources and provide another illustration of the extent to which naval activities now need to be integrated with other forms of military activity.[49]

8.7 The attack on maritime communications

The second use of the sea is as a means of transportation. Mahan and others have made the strategic value of this clear. Not surprisingly, therefore, activities against, or in support of, the ability to use the sea as a means of moving people and goods around the world have always been an important aspect of naval conflict. As Figure 8.9 shows, the attack on maritime communications can take a variety of forms, depending on their purpose and the means available.

Attacking military shipping

In the Cold War, expectations of any major war being quite short together with a realistic appreciation of the vulnerability of ports, and the large stocks of fuel and food held by most modern countries, all led to a focus on the attack on maritime communications as a way of interrupting the flow of *military* personnel and equipment to the area of operations. This reflected a long-held view of the *symbolic* importance to the Western alliance of sea lines of communications (SLOCs). In 1953, for instance, the US Chief of Naval Operations pointed out:

> Our entire politico-military philosophy today is based on the concept of collective security, which comprises overseas alliances, overseas bases, and US military forces deployed overseas. The keystone of this entire structure is the confidence felt by our allies that we can and will maintain control of the sea communications in the face of any threat.[50]

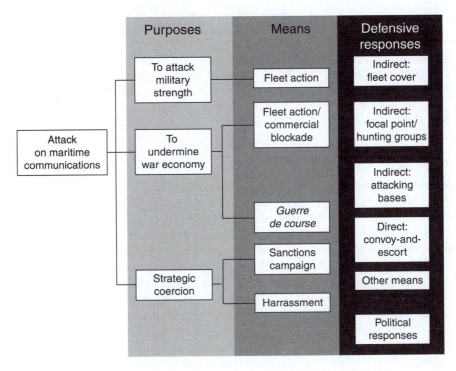

Figure 8.10 The attack on maritime communications.

It was essential that the United States should not allow itself to be 'decoupled' from its allies. Accordingly, and despite doubts that a major East–West war would be over too soon for even this to be very significant in strategic terms, NATO devoted considerable thought and resources to identifying the seriousness of the threat and its means of reply. The safe and timely arrival of military reinforcement and resupply shipping coming to Western Europe from across the Atlantic, therefore, became a major Western preoccupation.

For his part, Gorshkov's discussion of the First and Second World Wars made clear how important it was to sever military communications at sea. During the Great Patriotic War, this had been a major feature of maritime operations, especially in the Black and Norwegian seas. Gorshkov was well aware of the West's particular vulnerabilities in this respect: 'The most zealous advocates of military adventures in the West ought to stop and think of their ... greatly extended communication lines', he warned.[51] While the Soviet Navy probably never thought as much about attacking NATO shipping as NATO did to defending it, the longer and more important the conventional phase of any putative East–West war, the more attention the Russians paid to the issue. One of the reasons for this was an appreciation that attacking such Western vulnerabilities might reduce pressure on Soviet SSBN bastions by sucking more NATO naval assets away from offensive and into defensive activities. If the Soviet Navy had decided to launch such a campaign, its literature and exercises both suggest that the missile and torpedo-firing submarine would have been the main vehicle for attack, supported by large numbers of land-based aircraft. More directly, if Soviet pressure had forced the reinforcement convoys to take a very southerly route (perhaps by way of the Azores) potentially crucial delays in their arrival on the Central Front might have ensued.

In more recent times, the potential vulnerability of military shipping remains an issue. During Desert Shield/Storm, for example, there was much concern about the possibility of a high seas attack on Coalition forces en route to the Gulf. The threat was, in fact, remote but the severe political consequences of a successful attack meant it was taken seriously. Moreover, the Iraqi missile attack on Al-Jubayl in that same conflict revealed the vulnerability of ships and military cargoes in their ports of receipt.

Undermining an opponent's war economy

Undermining an opponent's war economy would reduce his finances, resources and materials and so cut away at every aspect of his capacity to make war. It would also force him to devote relatively more effort to the production of the necessities of life. If the enemy had particular needs and vulnerabilities then it made sense to target them (bullion fleets in the sixteenth and seventeenth centuries, oil tankers in the twentieth). Sometimes attacking the enemy's war economy seemed especially logical when the war was about trade anyway. 'What matter this or that reason?' demanded General-at-Sea, George Monk. 'What we want is more of the trade which the Dutch now have.' In the case of the Dutch wars, therefore, attacking the enemy's merchant shipping seemed to make obvious and practical sense.[52]

Orthodox opinion was clear that the commercial blockade imposed by the side with command of the sea was the preferred method of undermining an opponent's war economy. This aim was best achieved, thought Mahan, by 'the possession of that overbearing power on the sea which drives the enemy's flag from [the sea], or allows it to appear only as a fugitive'.[53] It was Cromwell's main fleet, not his commerce raiders, that destroyed Dutch trade and made grass grow in the streets of Amsterdam. The imposition of a commercial blockade was the supremely effective way of destroying the enemy's maritime commerce. Thus Mahan, in one of his most celebrated passages:

> Amid all the pomp and circumstance of the war which for ten years to come desolated the Continent, amid all the tramping to and fro over Europe of the French armies and their auxiliary legions, there went on unceasingly that noiseless pressure upon the vitals of France, that compulsion, whose silence, when once noted, becomes to the observer the most striking and awful mark of the working of Sea Power.[54]

The British commercial blockade, argued its proponents, could devastate the enemy's war economy because, in Richmond's phrase, it strikes at the root, where sporadic warfare hacks only at the branches.[55]

Some reservations need to be entered against this view, however:

- Attacking the enemy's commerce has always been fraught with moral, legal, political and strategic difficulty, especially when it infringes the rights of powerful neutrals. The unrestricted German U-boat offensive of 1917 was clearly counterproductive for this reason. The need to establish the real intentions of particular ships, on what in their cargoes should be construed as contraband and on the moral legitimacy of the action, makes the whole business difficult, even when the military means are readily available.[56]
- Historically, it is often difficult to assess just how effective such commercial blockades have been in strategic terms, because their effects have usually been entangled with other consequences of war. To what extent, for example, was the chronic shortage of food in Germany, that is so often ascribed to the activities of the Royal Navy, also due to the neglect of agriculture caused by the flow of men to the trenches? To what extent can the effects of blockade be compensated for by methods of substitution? Nonetheless, it is significant that both in the British view and in the view of a succession of their victims – the Dutch (seventeenth century), the Americans (1812–1814) and the Germans (1914–1918) – the strategic impact of the commercial blockade at least *seemed* to be very important strategically.

Commercial blockades were imposed in much the same way as the fleet blockades discussed in Section 6.8, often at the same time and by the same warships. They need to be sensitive to the legitimate concerns of neutral shipping, a requirement usually met by an interception and inspection regime of some sort.

The ideas behind the *guerre de course* were discussed in pages 31–33. Traditionally, it seemed to be a particularly logical course for the weaker naval side to adopt. So much so, in fact, that Corbett argued:

> A plan of war which has the destruction of trade for its primary object implies in the party using it an inferiority at sea. Had he superiority, his object would be to convert that superiority to a working command by battle or blockade.[57]

By accepting conventional operations, the weaker side would be forced into 'inevitable and rapid defeat, whereas by a guerre de course it prolongs operations very considerably and knows that before going under it will do some damage'. A few years later, Germany's Admiral Hipper echoed these sentiments exactly with his notion that 'carrying out of cruiser war with the battle cruisers of the Atlantic remains the one way in which our High Seas fighting ships can damage the enemy and thereby justify their existence'.[58]

This approach was reinforced by the belief that since the offensive, not the defensive, was the stronger form of war at sea, a war on commerce would be disproportionately effective in soaking up the resources of the defending side. For the attacking side the *guerre de course* often seemed cheap to operate (especially when privateers were its main protagonists) and surprisingly effective. Gorshkov made the essential point:

> Therefore the question of the ratio of submarine to antisubmarine forces is of great interest even under present-day conditions, since if ASW forces, which were so numerous and technically up to date [for that time], possessing a vast superiority, turned out to be capable of only partially limiting the operations of diesel submarines, then what must this superiority be today in order to counter nuclear powered submarines, whose combat capabilities cannot be compared with the capabilities of World War Il-era submarines.[59]

In some circumstances, indeed, a *guerre de course* might be the only means of producing a sufficient 'displacement of forces' for a weaker navy ever to have a hope of defeating a stronger one. 'Commerce destroying', thought de Lanessan, could be 'a strategic means to compel our rivals to disperse their ships over the world, so as to lessen the difference in strength which exists between their forces and ours in European waters.' Such ideas inspired President Thomas Jefferson and his successors in the United States during the nineteenth century, and various leaders of the Germany Navy in the twentieth.[60]

Of course, the value of these strategic devices ultimately depended on the success of the other naval activities they led to. But, although they were indirect and conditional, the possible strategic consequences of attack on the enemy's maritime communications could be at least as great as those deriving from any direct tally of ships sunk and cargoes lost. Moreover, the sensitivity to loss of powerful trading classes could make it difficult for governments to resist their complaints, thereby making the *guerre de course* perhaps more strategically effective than, objectively, it was.

Nevertheless, orthodox opinion tended to be sceptical about the long-term strategic effectiveness of a *guerre de course* even when conducted by submarines, partly because the marine resources of a great maritime power were so huge, partly because a truly effective *guerre de course* would have to be conducted in a barbaric way, which could backfire on the perpetrator (*vide* the manner in which 'unrestricted' U-boat warfare precipitated the American entry in the First World War in 1917), but mainly through confidence that the defensive measures possible to a fleet that otherwise commanded the seas would always, in the end, prevail.

Corbett, for example, criticised the notion

> so often proved fatal and so often reborn as a new strategical discovery that a naval war may be conducted on economical principles and a great power be

brought to its knees by preying on its commerce without first getting command of the sea.

Mahan was equally unimpressed by the efforts of the commerce destroyers in the Dutch wars. Unless properly supported, the cruiser 'can only dash out hurriedly, a short distance from home, and its blows, though painful, cannot be fatal'. Interestingly, Raoul Castex was particularly scathing about the ideas of the *Jeune Ecole*, his own countrymen. He believed that the *guerre de course* needed the support of the *guerre militaire* to effect a decision. Employed by itself, an offensive directed against communications and commerce would fail. The submarine warfare on commerce of 1914–1918 failed because the support of a surface force was wanting. The master of the surface would always dominate essential surface communications: an offensive by submarines would not overcome that preponderance unless it was accompanied by surface action to dispute command. Gorshkov made exactly the same point of the German submarine campaign of the Second World War. Nicholas Tracy has sensibly concluded:

> naval action to deny an enemy the use of the sea for his trade is a strategy which only has decisive military and political significance when it is undertaken by the strong against states which are at once weak and economically vulnerable.[61]

Strategic coercion

Interrupting, or disrupting, an adversary's capacity to use the sea as a form of maritime transportation may best be seen as a form of strategic coercion of the sort discussed in Section 9.6, but a brief reference is needed here because of its superficial similarity to the attack on maritime communications in wartime. Strategic coercion may take the form of a sea-based sanctions campaign of the sort imposed on Iraq in the wake of the Gulf War and on Serbia in the 1990s. Here the aim is to force the target nation into a course of political action he is reluctant to accept, and the method is similar to the imposition of a commercial blockade. It may be specifically targeted against the passage of military forces or equipment (as was the US quarantine operation against Warsaw Pact shipping to Cuba in 1962).

Alternately, such strategic coercion may involve harassment of shipping for political purposes. In the case of the 'tanker war' in the 1980s this took an extreme form involving lethal military attacks on neutral shipping entering the Gulf. The US mining of Haiphong harbour as a means of deterring the Soviet Union from resupplying North Vietnam was a milder form of the same sort of thing.

Such similarities, however, should not be pressed very far. They are much more political in inspiration, as are the appropriate responses, and they are intended by the participants to be seen more as forms of naval diplomacy rather than as acts of war.

8.8 The defence of maritime communications

To Mahan and many others, the ability to use the sea as a means of transportation was, 'the very root of a nation's vigour' and was the basis of human development. The conclusion was obvious: 'the necessity of a navy ... springs, therefore, from the existence of a peaceful shipping, and disappears with it'. The attack and defence of maritime communications lay at the heart of maritime strategy.[62]

But exactly how maritime communications should be defended has probably become the most contentious of all issues of maritime strategy, not least because there was, and is, no single solution to the problem, and few simple answers. Time and again, it has been found necessary to adopt a number of complementary defensive strategies and the maritime strategists have all recognised this to be the case. The general validity of their arguments and the various differences between them are essentially matters of degree and emphasis in the mix of responses the task requires. These responses are often not clearly distinguished from each other and include the following:

Indirect and general fleet cover

Mahan's view, in brief, was that command of the sea whether established by decisive battle or blockade was the essential recondition for the successful defence of maritime communications, since it would prevent most raiders getting out in the first place and would also provide essential cover for the flotillas protecting commerce against the relatively few that did. In the view of a later generation (Richmond, Castex and Rosinski) the First World War showed just how true this proposition was. The essential point was made by Richmond to a British committee of enquiry on battleship construction in 1921:

> The small craft acting as escorts, patrols or hunting were able to operate freely ... solely by virtue of the cover afforded by the Grand Fleet. If an earthquake had closed the mouth of Scapa Flow and the fleet had been shut up inside, there would have been nothing to prevent heavy German ships in company with lighter vessels from going out to sea and sweeping away all the small vessels that constituted the defence of trade.

Herbert Rosinski agreed. Since the German Fleet was safely blockaded, convoy escorts had only to deal with the U-boats that wriggled their way through to the open ocean. Had those escorts needed to guard against significant surface attack as well, their task would have been impossible. The difficulties facing the Scandinavian convoys, which had perforce to sail in front of the Grand Fleet blockade line, showed that only too clearly.[63]

There was, however, some danger in pushing this argument so far that it led to a navy to concentrate so much on securing command that it neglected the exercise of command in the direct defence of shipping. In 1917, arguably, the British did this in their reluctance to release destroyers tasked to protect the battlefleet (where their influence of SLOC protection was at best indirect) in order to provide *direct* defence through the escort of the merchant shipping that was proving so vulnerable to U-boat attack. Sir John Colomb put the matter in very uncompromising terms:

> The primary business of our war fleet is to destroy, capture or contain in ports, the enemy's warships. Until the work is done, all thought of applying the navy to the direct protection of commerce must be abandoned. To what extent our shipping and commerce may suffer in the interval between the

outbreak of war and the completion of the Navy's real business, will depend upon previous arrangements made for, and carried out by, our Mercantile Marine itself.[64]

There are those, indeed, who maintain that the US Navy itself lost sight of the mundane necessities of the protection of shipping during the 1980s, with embarrassing consequences in the tanker war of the 1980s.[65]

Indirect general cover at focal points and on patrolled sea lanes

Under this heading comes a cluster of responses under which threatened shipping is afforded indirect support *in particular areas*. Here, the idea is that maritime communications should best be protected by warships patrolling 'the ocean paths which connect one part of an extensive empire with another, which sea-borne commerce must traverse, and along which belligerent expeditions must proceed'. This kind of 'maritime highway patrol' would be supplemented by hunting groups intent on 'the dogging, hunting down, and destruction of every enemy cruiser. The dogging to continue, if necessary, to the world's end.'[66]

Since raiders would find their targets more easily in terminal areas than on the open ocean, this was where they should be sought in their turn. As Corbett said: 'Where the carcase is, there will the eagles be gathered together!' As each focal point was secured, a chain of sanctuaries straddling the world would gradually be constructed.

The track record of this cluster of responses was not in fact very encouraging in the twentieth century, however. In 1916, for example, it led the notorious second Battle of Portland when three U-boats operated in the waters between Beachy Head and the Eddystone Light, an area dominated by the great naval bases at Portsmouth, Portland and Plymouth. Despite the urgent attentions of 49 destroyers, 48 torpedo boats, seven Q-ships, several hundred armed auxiliaries and numerous aircraft, the U-boats sank 30 merchant ships in one week and escaped unscathed. Surprisingly, the hunting group fallacy persisted well into the Second World War, with the Americans only finally abandoning it after less than two dozen U-boats in the Western Atlantic had sunk one million tons of shipping in six months in early 1942.[67]

To many, such failures were a natural consequence of the use of the metaphor of the 'sea lane' or the 'sea lines of communications' (SLOCs). This encouraged the notion of naval forces strategically defending sea highways and focal areas, just as an army did a road. But the comparison was wrong. Unlike the land, the sea had no intrinsic value and did not need possessing or guarding. All that mattered was what passed over it. As Admiral Gretton remarked, 'it is *ships* which must be protected, not lines drawn across charts' and the deployment of flotilla craft should reflect this basic fact. Instead of guarding sea routes, therefore, one should escort merchant ships as they passed along them.[68]

Nonetheless, in some quarters there was a significant resurgence of support for the notions of 'offensive methods' and 'protected sea lanes' during the Cold War when it was argued that submarines were faster, much better armed and, with external help, could find their targets far more easily than they could before. These developments were held to have robbed convoys of several of their traditional advantages: modern surveillance systems robbed convoys of their former capacity to reduce encounter probabilities; the relatively increased lethality and greater speed of submarines (which could now attack and keep up with surface forces) seemed to increase the substance of the old 'all the eggs in one basket' objections to convoy. Perhaps in the new circumstances there ought to be a return to the old 'offensive' strategies, such as mining submarine transit areas, 'forward roving hunter/killer groups and open sea air patrols'.[69]

Attacking bases

Dealing with raiders at sea by attacking their bases has long been a standard naval response around the world. It was, for example, a constant feature of the naval warfare of the Gulf and Indian Ocean areas for many centuries. It was so much more effective than the generally futile mounting of general patrols in open waters. 'Those who advocate the small cruisers on patrol', wrote Fred T. Jane, 'are really no more logical than he who would suggest that instead of destroying the nest, individual hornets should be slain on the wing.' In the First and Second World Wars, this traditional device found expression in amphibious and air raids against German naval bases in France. In the late 1940s and the 1980s, there were thought to be very considerable strategic advantages in dealing with the Soviet submarine threat to NATO shipping 'at source' by forward operations north of the Greenland–Iceland–UK gap.[70]

Direct defence: convoy-and-escort

Here the emphasis is on the direct defence of shipping, not of the routes by which it travels. Gretton argued that the Mediterranean campaign of 1940–1943 showed that high levels of general and permanent sea command were welcome, but difficult to achieve and often unnecessary as a means of protecting shipping. The Mediterranean was a disputed sea, but both sides were able to use it. They squeezed convoys through as needed, their tracks crossing each other at right angles 'fortunately without collision', Gretton added drily. This showed that it was only strictly necessary to maintain temporary control of a moving zone 'of water in which the ships float, as well as the air above and the depths below'.[71]

Convoy made sense for two basic reasons. First, it offered the individual merchantmen the greatest mathematical chance of escaping detection and attack altogether – even if they were totally unescorted. Grenfell explained it thus:

> If we assume a ship to be visible at sea from ten miles away a vessel on the ocean will be represented by a visibility circle of ten miles radius, which visibility circle will move along with the ship as she alters her position. If, say, twenty-five ships are pursuing separate tracks through an area out of sight of each other, they will present twenty-five separate ten-mile visibility circles moving through the area. Those twenty-five ships, if formed in convoy will, however, present a visibility circle of little more than one ship; perhaps one of twelve miles radius … It can … be seen that the chances of a convoy being sighted by hostile warships are very much smaller than of a similar number of ships sailing separately.[72]

Even if a raider did spot a large convoy, most of the ships would be able to escape while it was dealing with an unfortunate one or two of their number. This argument, it was claimed, demonstrated the falsity of the proposition raised from time to time that convoys could not be organised because there were too few escorts to look after them, and challenged the intuitive notion that large convoys placed too many eggs in one basket.

Second, a convoy conversely also offered the best chance of finding, destroying and neutralising commerce raiders. It was, as Mahan pointed out, the best way of 'wisely applying the principle of concentration of effort to the protection of commerce'. 'The convoy system', he went on, 'when properly systematised and applied.. . will have more success as a defensive measure than hunting for individual marauders – a process which, even when most thoroughly planned, still resembles looking for a needle in a haystack.'[73] Convoy-and-escort, in fact, can be seen as a sea control strategy since it offers the prospect of 'a series of battles of annihilation on a small scale' and may indeed even force the enemy to make use of his major forces. Richmond pointed out how enduring the advantages of convoy-and-escort seemed to be. He added: 'Instruments alter, principles remain: a fact which those who so loosely talk of the new weapons – the submarine, the aircraft, and the mine – having "revolutionised" warfare would be wise to bear in mind.'[74] But, however traditional convoy-and-escort might be, it was rarely popular with offensive-minded sailors, who tended to make much of the system's inevitable drawbacks. It was, for instance, true that ship time lost in the assembly of convoys, and the rush at ports when several hundred merchantmen arrived at once was commercially expensive: it often paid for 'runners' to break away early so as to reach port before the rest of the convoy arrived. There were also occasions when the merchantmen had neither the skill nor the discipline to keep their station in convoy. 'They behaved as all convoys that ever I saw', said Nelson, 'shamefully ill; parting company every day.'[75] In the machine age, some argued, would not the collective smoke of large numbers of freighters attract the attention of raiders who might otherwise miss fast single ships?

For such reasons, there was always a temptation to abandon convoy-and-escort when the slightest excuse offered, or to modify its operation and switch more of the effort to the alternatives discussed above. It rarely worked, however.

The debate continued into the Cold War era with some pinning their faith on 'sanitised sea lanes' instead. Others concluded that with faster and more sophisticated merchant ships and the increasing range of ASW measures, now including the use of submarines in a protective function, the balance was shifting the other way. One study concluded, 'Compared to thirty years ago the submarine merchant convoy balance has shifted dramatically in favour of the convoy.'[76] While, fortunately, there was no proof either way, it is hard to believe that military shipping and particularly valuable oil tankers and the like would have been consigned to the open ocean without direct protection.

Other means of defence

Even this wide range of protective devices far from exhausts the list of protective possibilities. The advent of airpower, for example, has not only added an often crucial dimension to all the measures discussed above, but has contributed new ones as well, such as the bombing of submarine pens and factories. Important contributions to the Allied victory in the Atlantic campaign were also made by the shipbuilding and repair industries, by efficiency in the management of merchant shipping at every stage in its journey and so forth.

Political responses

Clearly navies have to take the security of their military sealift seriously but, these days, it is hard to envisage a scenario in which a prolonged assault on commercial shipping within the context of a general war would seem a sufficiently likely contingency for navies seriously to prepare for. Instead, the world's commercial shipping is vulnerable to a range of minor attacks and harassment. In these cases, naval responses will need to be carefully calibrated with a wide variety of political, military and economic responses. The main approach might well be to seek out and deal with the root causes of the problem ashore by means such as those discussed in the next three chapters.

9   Expeditionary operations

Military operations which can be initiated at short notice, consisting of forward deployed or rapidly deployable self-sustaining forces tailored to achieve a clearly stated objective in a foreign country.[1]

9.1 Origins and background

In recent years, there has been a marked increase in the attention paid to the concept of expeditionary operations, particularly but not exclusively by Western navies. Expeditionary operations are not, of course, new. A visitor to St Ann's Church in the Naval Dockyard in Portsmouth, England, will see physical evidence of this in the epitaphs all over the walls to naval officers who fell (often ashore) in the course of the now forgotten minor wars and conflicts of the nineteenth century. Rear-Admiral W. Arthur who served in the Maori war (1845–1847), the Kaffir War (1851–1852), the Baltic Expedition (1854), the Crimean Campaign (1855) and the China war (1857–1860) had a particularly busy but by no means unique career. Perhaps oddly, this preoccupation and the wealth and variety of the experience it generated, attracted little professional interest, even at the time. Thus Sir John Colomb: 'It is reasonable to suppose, and past history shows it to be the case, that for every war we have with a civilised power, we have about ten with savages, yet ... that fact appears to be totally passed over.'[2] In fact, Colomb was exaggerating. The subject was comparatively neglected in favour of professional interest in military developments in Europe, rather than totally passed over. About 25 per cent of the articles in the *Journal* of the Royal United Services Institution were about the conflicts of empire. Much of the reasoning about them was gathered together by Charles Callwell in his remarkable *Small Wars* of 1896. This synthesis of British nineteenth-century experience was added to, and refined, by the US Marine Corps in a deliberate and reflective process that culminated in 1940 with the publication of the *Small Wars Manual*.

Included within the category of the latter's small wars were: the Philippine Insurrection (1898–1902), Philippines Moro Revolt (1903–1906), Cuba (1906–1909), Haiti (1915–1934), Dominican Republic (1916–1924) and Nicaragua (1927–1933). The British, the French and other European colonial powers had their equivalents.

Even so, most military professionals concentrated their thoughts on the nature of conventional warfare with their peers rather than on operations of this sort. There was a brief resurgence of interest in small wars and expeditionary operations, at times, during the Cold War era, for three reasons:

222 Expeditionary operations

- The apparent need to do something about the instabilities associated with the decolonisation process.
- Cold War rivalries leaking into the Third World, requiring action there. Moreover, the necessary response could well be distinctive and specific – thus the American flirtation with counter-insurgency theories in the 1960s.
- The prospective use of nuclear weapons sometimes seemed likely to reduce the need for, or likelihood of, conventional high-intensity operations, but would not have this effect on small wars.

Navies were particularly interested in expeditionary operations, especially in those Cold War periods when strategic thinking made their role in general, nuclear war 'somewhat uncertain'.[3] Since the end of the Cold War, there have been many such operations. As a result, the other services have also had to develop equivalent interests and capabilities.

Critics of expeditionary operations come in two main groups:

- The first, more specialist type of criticism focuses on the apparent woolliness of the whole concept of expeditionary operations, dismissing it as little more than a glittery label for an untidy ragbag of messy but undemanding things that military forces have always had to do.
- The second set of criticisms is often essentially political in origin and involves scepticism about the need for, desirability and likely success of such military activity. These concerns were clearly in evidence in both the United States and Western Europe in regard to both the Afghanistan and Iraq conflicts.

9.2 Definitions

In contrast to the definition of expeditionary operations offered at the start of this chapter, the US Marine Corps *Small Wars Manual* of 1940 considered small wars to be:

> Operations undertaken under executive authority, wherein military force is combined with diplomatic pressure in the internal or external affairs of another state whose government is unstable, inadequate or unsatisfactory for the preservation of life and such interests as are determined by the foreign policy of our nation.[4]

The first definition tends to focus on the nature of the force conducting it, the second on the political aims of the exercise. Both are notably broad in concept but can be separated from conventional amphibious operations even though marines are often its main agents. Amphibious operations are different in that they are primarily military in purpose, usually being related to other operations in the course of a conventional campaign or war. Expeditionary operations on the other hand may grow out of the coercive aspects of naval diplomacy and are usually highly politicised. Normally they involve joint action of a more sustained kind, with key parts being played by ground and air forces.

If expeditionary operations are not simply conventional amphibious operations or examples of naval coercion, what *can* be said positively about them? The following interconnected criteria seem often to apply:

- *Operational*. Expeditionary operations are usually 'interventions' conducted at the 'operational' level.[5] They are best thought of as campaigns, not wars, even small ones. Afghanistan and Iraq 2003 are difficult cases to define. Both could perhaps be regarded as (very quick) wars followed by very long and much more difficult stabilisation campaigns.
- *Western?* The association of this concept with colonial campaigns of the past century reinforces the impression that these are an exclusively Western activity. Certainly this applies to the bulk of the examples normally given. But this should not be exaggerated. Some non-Western states have conducted expeditionary operations of their own. China's Indian war of 1962, its seizure of the Paracels in 1974, its Vietnam campaign of 1979, could all be regarded as expeditionary except in that they were not conducted at great distance. India's Maldives operation of 1988 and activities in Sri Lanka at around the same time also both come into this category. Moreover, in many recent cases there has been extensive non-Western involvement in UN-mandated expeditionary operations led by the United States (most obviously the Afghanistan operation). There are strong expeditionary overtones to most peace support operations.
- *Distant*. They are usually conducted at some distance from the homeland of the participants. Manifestly, such operations are not expeditionary for those against whom they are conducted!
- *Self-contained*. Partly because of the distance normally involved the forces conducting expeditionary operations will tend to be self-sustaining, tailored to the specific tasks. The emphasis is on portable, mobile, self-contained but hopefully decisive force packages.
- *Limited in aim*. Again this tends to apply to the expeditionary forces, rather than to their adversaries. They are campaigns of choice, with limited aims and are usually conducted in the hope of limited costs. Such aims show a disturbing tendency to grow, however.
- *Of short duration*. Normally these operations are (very) short, although in some cases they might involve a sequence of operations over many years (US Marine Corps operations in Haiti mentioned earlier are an example of this). The Korean War of 1950–1953 probably lasted too long to be regarded as an expeditionary operation, although it conforms to the notion in other ways.
- *Against varied opponents*. Although such operations will often be conducted in countries seen as threatened or obviously failing and disorderly (most nineteenth- and twentieth-century colonial campaigns, East Timor, Sierra Leone) they can be conducted against quite advanced states whose purposes are considered hostile (Korean War, Falklands, the Gulf War, Kosovo).
- *Demanding and specialised*. Thinking of expeditionary operations as relatively easy for professional forces trained for full-scale operations has often led to major difficulty (Boer War, Vietnam War). The fact that military technologies and skills useful for first class war are often useful for expeditionary operations too does not mean they always are.
- *Fought in urbanised littorals*. Although often true in the past, this criterion has become much clearer recently. This is an important topic about which much more needs to be said.
- *Highly politicised*. This, too, is increasingly important and deserving of much fuller treatment.

Because so many mixtures of these criteria may apply to particular cases, definitions of expeditionary operations remain highly imprecise, but closer examination of the last two should help define some of the general requirements for force planners.

9.3 Expeditionary operations: the political dimension

Expeditionary operations have come into greater prominence in the post Cold War era, for two major reasons:

- *Increased disorder.* This can be seen as the consequence of the disappearance of the structured and controlled bipolarity of the Cold War era, the uneven impact of globalisation and anti-globalisation resentments.
- *Globalisation* means that events in one area have greater impact in other areas than they used to. Instability in distant areas can have grave impacts on the security/prosperity of others. From this comes the argument that 'If we do not go to the crisis, the crisis will come to us' and a policy of developing policies, and forces, capable of intervention in case of need. The Afghanistan campaign may prove a classic example of this. Post Cold War neglect of the region, led to a failing state hosting an undoubted international threat to the established order; this in turn required an expeditionary operation.

This concern for the course of events elsewhere is manifested in the heightened attention paid by the world community to human rights, partly for its own sake and partly because it is considered the only secure foundation for long-term political stability. This obviously harks back to the association of stable trade and liberal values discussed in Chapter 1. There has developed a strong interest in the defence of values, to ensure that, in Kipling's phrase, 'a court-house stands where the raw blood flowed'.[6] Such concerns have led to a decline in the concept of the sovereign immunity of states and a corresponding rise in the notion of humanitarian intervention. As the UN Secretary General Kofi Annan once remarked, there is a 'developing international norm in favour of intervention to protect civilians'.[7]

The result has been a spate of expeditionary operations including Iraq from 1990, Somalia 1991–1992, Haiti, 1994, IFOR in Bosnia 1995, Albania 1997, Sierra Leone from 1997, East Timor 1999, Kosovo 2000 and Afghanistan 2001–2002.

This is highly contentious stuff. Some would dispute the whole assumption that global disorder is on the rise.[8] Others are wary of the implication that some values are morally superior and need to be imposed on others. Still others dispute the effectiveness of remedies based on intervention, especially of a military sort. Another group worry about the costs of intervention and seek to limit them by pragmatic policies that focus not on ideals but on practicalities and degrees of risk. To the latter, the protection of the force and the defence of a guaranteed exit may easily become the principal focus of the activity!

Such controversies have three consequences for the military forces conducting expeditionary operations.

First, because of the very differing views such operations often elicit, they are usually politicised in origin, style and consequence. Every military move at every level bears tremendous potential political and strategic significance. The levels of war become extraordinarily compressed, in that the action of an individual marine patrolling a city street may have major consequences at the level of grand strategy.

Second, these are campaigns of choice. Expeditionary forces do not *have* to get involved; they can sail away. This makes politicians and the media acutely conscious of the costs, especially the human costs, of intervention. This fact greatly reinforces aversion towards casualties, even amongst prospective adversaries. It offers adversaries an obvious means of compensating for military inferiority.

Third, expeditionary operations are often conducted under UN auspices of some sort, as peace support operations (PSOs). PSOs are intrinsically difficult because of the centrality of the notion of 'consent'.

In a so-called 'Chapter 6 peacekeeping operation', such as that carried out in Cyprus, the consent of all sides is assumed. All parties want the UN force there to hold the ring and so fully cooperate in its operations. At the other extreme of peace enforcement, 'a Chapter 7 operation', consent is something that has to be enforced by military coercion, as was the case in the 1991 Gulf War. The interesting and difficult area is the area in the middle where consent is partial – some parties consent, others do not – or the consent itself is limited in some way. In such cases the peace support forces, therefore, have to 'manage' consent by delicate mixtures of persuasion and coercion. This characterised most PSOs in the former Republic of Yugoslavia.

Naval forces engaged in these three kinds of PSOs may find themselves doing very different things. Peace enforcement such as the Kuwait operation of 1990/1991 required sanctions and the conduct of conventional high-intensity operations. Peacekeeping could involve the collection of weapons, monitoring and observation, provision of coast guard services, mine clearance and the provision of safe havens. In the middle case, it could be the delicate business of enforcing safe havens, separating forces, disarming opposing forces, the guarantee/denial of movement.[9]

Few would dispute Callwell's point, 'The advantage of having a well-defined objective even for a time can ... scarcely be over-rated.' But there is always a danger of 'mission creep' especially when boots hit the ground. Britain's commitment in Sierra Leone, after all, developed out of what was originally intended to be a non-combatant evacuation operation (NEO) for about 800 people. Imperceptibly it turned into a major and sustained stabilisation operation. The political complexity

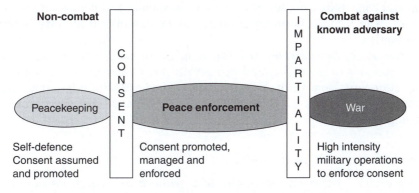

Figure 9.1 The consent hierarchy (source: loosely based on MoD (UK) Peace Support
Operations JWP 3–50).

of expeditionary operations makes coherent politico-strategic direction essential but difficult.[10]

9.4 Expeditionary operations: the urban dimension

Three-quarters of the world's population live in the littorals, less than 200 miles from the sea; 80 per cent of its capital cities and nearly all major centres of international trade and military power can also be found there. The littorals are where the major trade routes intersect. They also contain sources of offshore energy and mineral resources that will prove of increasing strategic and economic importance in the twenty-first century.

Two things flow from all this. First, this is where the world's most important problems are likely to be encountered. Second, they will increasingly need to be dealt with in the kind of urbanised environment that traditional military thinking has preferred to avoid in favour of open country and the wide oceans. The urban environment poses particular problems for the conduct of expeditionary operations.

Urban operations are distinctive in that they represent a special kind of terrain (like mountains, jungle, desert) that has to be catered for. But the requirement is even more challenging than having to prepare for another battle of Stalingrad, bad enough though that might seem. The really distinctive thing about urban operations is that they have to be conducted amongst large numbers of people, in a politically complicated situation. The US Marine Corps has vividly described this as 'three block war':

> Our enemies will not allow us to fight the 'Son of Desert Storm' but will try and draw us into a fight on their own terms, more resembling the 'Stepchild of Chechnya.' In one moment in time, our Marines will be feeding and clothing displaced refugees and providing humanitarian assistance. In the next moment, they will be holding two warring tribes apart, conducting peacekeeping operations and, finally, they will be fighting a highly lethal mid-intensity battle, all on the same day, all within three city blocks. We call this the three block war … It is an environment born of change and adaptability.[11]

Worse, as Figure 9.2 shows, these activities may differ from one area to another, overlap and change in a matter of moments, improving and deteriorating all at the same time. The balance between political, humanitarian and military imperatives will constantly shift.

Such operations can easily absorb large numbers of military forces, have a considerable propensity to go wrong and bring with them an increased requirement to clear up afterwards. Few of the characteristics associated with urban operations are actually new in themselves, it is the combination of them all that makes the concept so challenging.

9.5 General demands on the military

Together with the other characteristics of expeditionary operations noted earlier, their political and urban dimensions produce some general requirements for the military forces conducting them. These include the following:

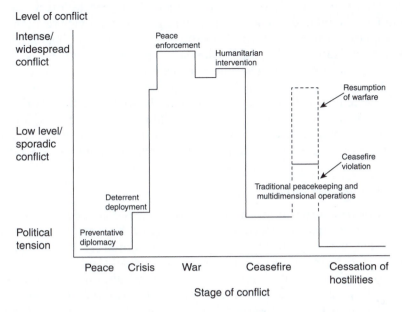

Figure 9.2 Peace operations and the stages of conflict (source: Henry L. Stimson Center).

A good picture

Superiority in knowledge – or what the Americans call 'situational awareness'. This should aim at telling everyone from the individual commander to the soldiers, sailors or marines on the ground what they need to know in order to do their jobs properly. This is a question of first collecting the information and then disseminating it appropriately. The means of processing information are undoubtedly expanding exponentially as we saw in Section 4.7 but so, unfortunately, is what expeditionary forces need to know about. In novel, politically confused and changing circumstances gathering information is not easy, especially in large shanty towns where much basic data is simply not available. The physical conditions will often make dissemination difficult too. Many current communication systems are not especially good at reaching people inside large buildings for example. Nonetheless, sophisticated, secure sea-based systems could have much to offer here.

Precise effect

The need to avoid unwanted casualties amongst the military forces themselves, innocent by-standers and even in some cases the adversary, reinforces the need for precise weaponry, and maybe for non- or less-lethal means of coercion.

Force protection

The attack on the USS *Cole* in 2001 reminded observers that like all weapons systems, warships are vulnerable when unable to set up all their defensive systems.

While the USS *Cole* could have made itself much less open to attack, these measures would have militated against the political signal of improving relations that the visit was supposed to have furthered. In this way, the political imperative behind expeditionary operations can pose commanders particular problems even in the basic area of force protection. The same problem applies, usually in a more acute form, to the landed forces as well. The requirement to avoid casualties in the Kosovo air campaign obliged allied air forces to fly above the heights that Serbian air defences could reach, but this sometimes militated against the required precise effect in the bombing, and carried political consequences. In such circumstances, there is a danger that force protection almost becomes the aim of the operation.

The dangers of decisive force

Decisive action from concentrated force is a common and understandable aspiration amongst military people, and encouraged by many of the great masters of strategic thought – Clausewitz in particular. The gradualistic approach to the air campaign in both the Vietnam War and the Kosovo operation is widely considered to have dissipated the strategic effect that airpower provides by allowing the adversaries to become accustomed to its consequences and to find ways of exploiting its limitations. But this all-or-nothing approach has its dangers too. It may be disproportionate or inappropriate to the political aims of the operation. Because it takes time to concentrate forces, it may, moreover, come at the cost of the 'rapid effect' that politicians and military planers also usually want. The aspiration for this kind of decisive action may deprive expeditionary forces of their capacity to nip troubles in the bud.

'We're here to help, but don't mess with us'

There is much to be said for the conventional wisdom that in most situations expeditionary forces should retain real war-fighting capacity. In the East Timor operation, Major General Cosgrove wanted overwhelming force ashore on Day 1, followed within a week by the bulk of the force, robust rules of engagement and substantial naval and air combat power.[12] This deterred resistance. In contrast, 'Task Force Smith' (whose task had been to re-establish the civilian infrastructure in occupied Japan), was overwhelmed by the North Koreans when sent suddenly to the Pusan perimeter in the early days of the Korean War. Striking a balance between the two imperatives of being nice and being potentially nasty is far from easy, however. It may require compromises in force protection and decisive effect that military people will not like, but these may avoid the dangers of the so-called 'turtle mentality' when military forces are so weighed down by their military strength that they are unable to relate to the people they are supposed to be helping.

Outmanoeuvring clever adversaries

Expeditionary forces should, it seems, expect an adversary clever enough to avoid the temptation to ape their methods. Instead, a resourceful and adaptive adversary can be expected to have identified the vulnerabilities of the expeditionary force and to have focused on them. This may be a question of exploiting their unfamiliarity with the terrain (jungle, mountains, city, their aversion to taking or inflicting casualties, their manifest desire for the minimum of force levels, a quick decision and early departure, their multinational composition and so forth). The expeditionary force will, therefore, face a situation that is confused, dispersed, fragmented and episodic: just the kind of battle space that military people most dislike. This plainly requires the expeditionary force (which will often be smaller in number than the adversary) to be 'manoeuvrist' in the sense of avoiding attritional encounters at the tactical level but going instead for the adversary's decisive points and centre(s) of gravity, whatever these may be.

Agility

The requirement to conduct expeditionary operations in unexpected places at very short notice and their tendency to change character once embarked upon demands high levels of all-round adaptability.

* * *

All these characteristics could well be dismissed as blinding glimpses of the obvious were it not for the fact that they so often are either hard to discern in particular situations or else prove to be unattainable. It is the sheer complexity of this mix of ingredients that makes expeditionary operations seem substantively different from conventional military operations, although the difference is still only a matter of degree. They are, moreover, sufficiently different from conventional operations to require examination in their own right. Expeditionary operations are manifestly not an easy option but, on the contrary, have to be prepared for and thought about very rigorously.

9.6 Expeditionary operations: the maritime dimension

What naval forces can offer

Navies clearly have a good deal to offer in the conduct of expeditionary operations, not least because the physical location of the operation will require transportation by, and support from, the sea. In some circumstances, they can play a key role in their own right:

> Finally, maritime forces provide the quickest means of deploying a logistically self-sustaining and tactically coherent force over long distances, providing an invaluable capacity for timely presence and thus the ability to nip trouble in the bud. If this fails, they have recourse to demonstration, coercion and warfighting; they can shape the joint operational environment in advance of heavier forces and play a role in support of them once they are established in theatre.[13]

The advantage that naval forces have in being able to operate without the need for host nation support is also highly valued. However, experience shows that navies have to prepare for this kind of thing. Packages of maritime force tailored for particular situations cannot, or at least should not, just be thrown together at the last moment. This would be a recipe for incoherence, gaps and vulnerabilities.

The mobility, flexibility and adaptability characteristic of naval task forces can also be manifested in individual platforms. Thus a nuclear powered submarine can get to a troubled area rapidly (either covertly or not), can gather information, launch cruise missiles from up to 1000 miles away, insert special forces, threaten or attack enemy forces, thereby being able simultaneously to 'provide presence, a capacity for coercion and the preparatory moves for warfighting'. The same individual flexibility, if of a more benign sort, was demonstrated by a single New Zealand supply ship, HMNZS *Endeavour*, off East Timor in 2000.[14]

And what they can't ... and therefore need

Although naval forces can offer a wide range of services both at and from the sea, experience shows they are rarely decisive on their own. As a general rule their efforts will need to be integrated with others in joint, combined and multi-agency action.

Joint operations

Because the major focus of most expeditionary operations is on events ashore (or at least the consequence ashore of events at sea), air and ground forces will normally play a crucial role and navies will rarely find themselves in the lead. This calls for high degrees of jointery – but jointery of the right sort in which the complementarities of the individual services are built upon so that the total is more than a sum of the parts.

After the successful British operation against the island of Elba in 1796 Nelson reported: 'The harmony and good understanding between the Army and the navy employed on this occasion will, I trust, be a further proof of what may be effected by the hearty co-operation of the two services.'[15] To achieve this, navies may well have to compromise on their traditional (and much valued) independence of operation at sea in order to ensure that the maritime element of the force mix is properly represented and exploited. In the Gulf campaign of 1991, both the US and Royal Navies were criticised for failing to provide joint headquarters with officers of sufficient rank for this reason.[16]

In the UK, Gulf experience and memories of the frictions caused in the Falklands campaign by the absence of an in-theatre commander, made people aware of the need for thinking, planning, preparation and command arrangements for expeditionary operations to be sorted out on a joint basis. This led, in 1994, to the creation of the Permanent Joint Force Headquarters (PJHQ). When situations arise, PJHQ staffs should have contingency preparations and forces to hand and the capacity to deliver a trained-up Joint Force Headquarters to command them. This system proved itself in Sierra Leone, but does denote a historic shift away from the traditional emphasis on centralised naval operational command. This appears to be a universal process.

While recognition of the need for effective cooperation between the services is obviously not new, the increased attention paid to expeditionary operations has greatly reinforced it. In sum, engagement in expeditionary operations will tend to diminish the independence of navies whilst at the same time enhancing their utility.

Combined operations

In the same way, expeditionary operations will usually be acts of coalition, multinational and conducted in the company of others. This is partly to spread the risks and costs and partly to increase and demonstrate legitimacy. As we saw in Section 4.7, multinationality is a force-multiplier but it does add a level of complexity to every aspect of an expeditionary operation. The real problem is usually *not* technological but divergence in what the French call the 'interoperability of the mind' that is attributable to different *political* perceptions of the situation and what needs to be done about it.[17]

German naval participation in embargo operations in the Straits of Otranto during the Bosnian crisis, for instance, was complicated by their warships having very restrictive rules of engagement (ROEs); they were not allowed to fire except in extreme self-defence, were precluded from conducting boarding operations or approaching the coast of Montenegro. For all these reasons, the force commander assigned them to picture-building activities on the farthest, somewhat separated, edge of the force.[18]

In the same way, allied warships in the run-up to Desert Storm had to be deployed around the Red Sea and the Gulf in a highly complicated manner, which paid regard to their individual operational capabilities and, more importantly, their ROEs. Keeping control of this coordinated rather than integrated force was a complex undertaking; given the political delicacy of the situation it was also very

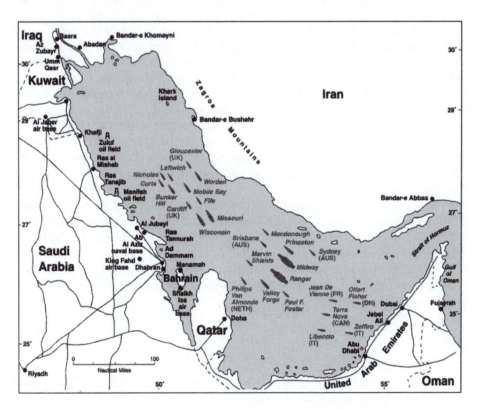

Figure 9.3 Allied ship positions in the Gulf (source: Marolda, 1998).

important to get it right. While they obviously add to the difficulties facing the force commander (if there is one), such arrangements do bolster the perceived political legitimacy of the operation. They also nicely illustrate the intrinsic flexibility of naval force, since the fact that governments can so finely tune their naval contributions (in terms of number, capability, accepted position and ROEs) actually means that more of them can find ways in which to participate on terms they can be happy with.

Experience in the Gulf and the Adriatic in the 1990s showed that these political distinctions *can* be accommodated at acceptable cost in operational performance. However that the 22 navies engaged in Desert Shield/Storm worked as well together as they did owed much to common acceptance of NATO procedures and to shared experience in such NATO formations as STANAVFORLANT, the Standing Naval Force Atlantic.

Providing the political conditions for this is an important aspect of the coalition-building activities discussed in Section 9.7. NATO experience and the growing adoption of NATO procedures is obviously helpful in providing the means by which navies can work efficiently with each other around the world. Developing familiarity with such procedures on an international basis provides one of the main operational incentives for the plethora of international exercises that currently take place.

Multi-agency operations

The obvious need to deal with some of the commonest causes of the problem (failures in governance, poverty, disease, resource shortage) as well as with its symptoms (conflict, disorder, the collapse of services) means that expeditionary operations also increasingly require the military to cooperate with non-governmental organisations (NGOs) and with other government departments (OGD). This may not be easy. The avowedly impartial approach usually adopted by NGOs is not always the same as that of military forces and OGDs (which obviously act in support of national policies). Moreover, NGOs will often follow different, less formal procedures and are usually organised on very different lines. Even so, effective coordination between them and the military forces engaged in expeditionary forces remains essential.

The novelty of this requirement for sea-based forces to get heavily involved in civil affairs ashore is more apparent than real, however. At the beginning of the twentieth century, for example, US Marine Corps small wars doctrine reflected their experience and developed expertise in many civilian tasks such as public works, road building, medical support and education. On the basis of this, the US Marines became expert in these aspects of expeditionary operations along with the more conventional military ones.[19]

Implications for navies

There is nothing new about the conduct of expeditionary operations but, with the end of the Cold War, there is a shift towards them and away from conflict at sea and preparation for decisive bluewater engagement against other main fleets. Nor is this shift a characteristic merely of the larger navies. A different kind of process, though with the same result, has been affecting the world's smaller navies as well. In Europe, for example, there has been a conscious shift in emphasis towards participation in expeditionary operations. Maintaining such capacities has long been characteristic of the British, French, Spanish, Dutch and Italian navies, but has become more noticeable. In some ways, similar movements within such navies as those of Belgium, Denmark and Germany has been more remarkable. In their case, the cultural shift has been away from their erstwhile coastal preoccupations and towards quite different projects in distant waters. The Danish Navy, for example, participated in Desert Shield and Desert Storm and sent HDMS *Tordenskold* to participate in Operation Sharpguard in the Adriatic. The extending reach of the Chinese, South Korean, Japanese and Singaporean navies suggests that the same kind of process is at work around the Asia-Pacific as well.

As we have seen though, expeditionary operations are no easy option for navies. They are specialised activities that need to be taken seriously. Along with all the operational requirements to be discussed next, navies will need a sense of humility – for there is much that they cannot do. They should remember that little French gunboat puffing around the coast of Africa in Joseph Conrad's *Heart of Darkness*, firing its popgun into a continent:

> In the empty immensity of earth, sky and water, there she was, incomprehensible, firing into a continent. Pop, would go one of the six-inch guns; a small flame would dart and vanish, a little white smoke would disappear, a tiny projectile would give a feeble screech – and nothing happened. Nothing could happen … The steamer toiled along slowly on the edge of a black and incomprehensible frenzy … We were cut off from the comprehension of our surroundings; we glided past like phantoms, wondering and secretly appalled, as sane men would be before an enthusiastic outbreak in a madhouse.[20]

Conrad's bleak pessimism is a useful reminder that there are many awful situations ashore that military forces cannot do much about however willing and well prepared they may be.

9.7 Staging a sea-based expedition: the maritime requirements

> Expeditions beyond the seas are all those enterprises in which large bodies of troops are conveyed in ships to a distant country, there to be landed to undertake military operations.[21]

As we saw in Section 3.5, two of the most interesting books for the conduct of expeditionary operations were written at the end of the nineteenth century; namely, Furse's *Military Expeditions Beyond the Seas* (1897) and Callwell's *Small Wars* (1996b). Neither, in fact, wrote about expeditionary operations as currently understood. Furse focuses on the conduct of amphibious operations at a distance, Callwell on 'savage' conflicts. But putting the two together shows that while expeditionary operations are quite distinctive in many ways they are not particularly new in concept. Moreover, recourse to their work conveniently identifies the main phases of an expeditionary campaign and the contribution that maritime forces can make to their prosecution.

Expeditionary picture building

> But it is a very important feature in the preparation for, and the carrying out of, small wars that the regular forces are often working very much in the dark from the outset.[22]

Stories of officers of the British Task force having to raid the charts of the Geography department of Portsmouth University before setting out for the Falklands in 1982 and basing their operational planning on an informal guide written by a Royal Marine sailing enthusiast some years before, shows that ignorance of the operational area can be overcome, but is hardly a good basis for sound planning.

The more military planners know about the political and military situation ashore, and the earlier they know it, the better. 'Situational awareness' should include monitoring of political developments ashore, military activity and relevant geographic and oceanographic conditions. It reduces the prospect of unpleasant surprises and facilitates timely and effective planning. It is even better to be able to supplement this by 'knowledge superiority' over any adversary through 'keeping our intentions thoroughly concealed from our adversary and from his allies'.[23]

Navies capable of sustaining 'forward presence' can be expected to maintain a capacity to monitor areas of concern to them on a routine basis as we shall see in Section 9.5, but this will need to be amplified as the expeditionary situation develops. Crucially, sea-based intelligence needs to be effectively integrated with all other forms of picture building, especially with the strategic intelligence to be derived from satellites and UAVs.

Maritime picture building is based on a variety of sources:

* Submarines can intercept communications and locate surface-to-air missile (SAM) sites, command and control centres, troop concentrations and so forth. They can detect mines and map the sea bottom. Although they are capable of covert and sustained operations, their ability to communicate the information they gather is sometimes limited by satellite accessibility.
* Aircraft, both manned and unmanned, sea and land based, are another source of essential information and were much in evidence during the 2001 Afghanistan campaign, when the US Navy's P-3C Orion maritime patrol aircraft (MPA) were integrated with Predator UAVs to produce a coherent information system for the US Marine Corps and other forces. Orions first impressively appeared in this capacity during the Kosovo campaign. Their 're-roling' from a previous focus on ASW is a neat illustration of the transition that many navies have made from conventional peer conflict at sea to expeditionary operations in the littoral.[24]
* Surface ships have the advantage of almost unlimited endurance, the capacity to operate for almost unlimited periods from international waters and, above all, have the space for ambitious ranges of sensors and supporting services. For this reason also, they are the obvious means of providing for at-sea operational command of the expeditionary force and/or of any of its components should conditions ashore suggest that to be wise. During the course of the Afghanistan campaign, the French Navy announced the ordering of a new 'eavesdropping' ship to replace the intelligence-gathering AGI *Bougainville*, thereby providing a

timely reminder of the role that surface ships of this sort can play in this activity.[25]

The advantages offered by maritime picture building were graphically demonstrated during the INTERFET operation in East Timor. The situation ashore was potentially very confusing, and those conducting the operation needed to know two things: were elements of the Indonesian armed forces collaborating with those committing the atrocities; what, actually, was likely to be the response of Indonesian aircraft and submarines to the arrival of foreign ships in East Timor waters? Clearly the force commander's concept of operations depended absolutely on the answers to these two questions.

Amongst many other means of picture building, the Australian and US navies deployed SIGINT specialists on the RAN's frigates and patrol boats and a variety of Orion aircraft. These, together with other means of picture building, confirmed that some elements of the Indonesian armed forces were indeed in collusion with criminal elements ashore. Moreover, there was clear evidence that Indonesian aircraft and submarines were actively tracking the ships of the expeditionary force. By a variety of means, the force commander was able to let the Indonesians know that he knew, and had evidence, of what was happening, and this appears to have played a significant part in persuading them to pull back their forces ashore and at sea. A potentially dangerous encounter between Indonesian and INTERFET forces was thereby avoided to the great benefit of all concerned.[26]

Of course sea-based systems need to be thoroughly and effectively integrated with other sources of operational intelligence. Even the Americans found in the 2001–2002 Afghanistan operation that many of their systems could not 'plug and play' very easily. Perhaps because they are expensive, and less visible and intelligible to politicians than, say, ships or aircraft, information-gathering systems seem particularly vulnerable to cost-cutting exercises.[27]

Strategic transportation

An expedition across the seas differs from other military operations, inasmuch as an army does not step over a frontier or advance from a selected base of operations, but is thrown into a hostile country, and all the combatants, materials and stores have to be conveyed thereto from a distance in ships. Operations of this nature demand very thorough preparations.[28]

By definition, expeditionary operations take place at a distance from the countries undertaking them. Accordingly, maritime forces usually have a major enabling role to play in transporting the troops needed, their equipment and supplies, into theatre. There are two aspects to strategic transportation. The first is a matter of timely conveyance, the second, of providing protection at every stage of the process.

In the case of small-scale operations, a moderate maritime task force, for example an amphibious task group, may be able to conduct the early and decisive phases of both aspects of strategic transportation on its own. Such a task group could move quickly into the area (at the rate of 400 nautical miles per day) with effective, coherent, mobile and sustainable forces, supplied from the sea. Such a force might nip a situation in the bud and/or create the conditions in which larger, heavier, slower follow-on forces can finish the job. Something of this sort occurred during Operation Palliser (off and in Sierra Leone) when the carrier HMS *Illustrious* and an amphibious ready group (ARG) centred on the new LPH HMS *Ocean* with 42 Cdo Royal Marines aboard, just happened to be in the area after an inspired example of the 'contingent positioning' discussed in Section 10.4.

There is always the danger, of course, that such relatively small-scale operations will expand unexpectedly, bringing further unwanted complications and requirements with it. Moreover some operations are from the start just too big to resolve in this expeditious way. The Gulf War of 1990–1991, for example, was an entirely different kind of exercise for the British; strategic transportation by sea was not simply a capacity intrinsic to the nature of naval forces, but a discrete and demanding task that they had to perform. A few statistics make the essential points. For the British, while their troops arrived, in the main, by air,

> *Operation Granby* entailed the sea movement of 260,000 tons of general cargo, plus 102,000 tons of ammunition, plus 5200 A vehicles (fighting, tracked), plus 11,700 B and C vehicles (wheeled and specialist). Air movement was much quicker of course, but could only contribute another 53,000 tons over the whole period. Finally, some 19,000 tons of cargo a week was required once the land battle started.[29]

This example is also a useful reminder of the *extent* to which the conduct of expeditionary operations depends on strategic transportation by sea.

The requirements of conveyance

> In an undertaking of this nature, the large number of transports required of itself imposes a limit to the number of troops employed.

> The military staff have not only to deliver at the port of embarkation the troops and all that the troops will need on shore, but must also see that all parts go together, and that the sequence in which everything is embarked is in strict keeping with the order of its necessity at the place of disembarkation.[30]

These two quotations show conveyance is a matter of hulls and other means of handling cargoes, on the one hand, and of logistic skills, on the other.

New Zealand's difficulty in locating two merchant ships capable of transporting its forces to East Timor was a salutary reminder of the unavoidable need for the necessary means of conveyance that was discussed in Section 4.6.[31] A little less obviously, the capacity to move large numbers of people and their equipment also include effective loading/unloading and transportation arrangements to and from the ports of despatch and receipt, and an effective information management system to track the movement of supplies from store to consumer. It is important to remember that such considerations must include unloading requirements in the operational area. The fact that sophisticated facilities were available for expeditionary forces in the Gulf in 1990–1991 (although in fact only three ports were available) should not conceal the fact that they are often not – especially in the large swathes of the Third World where expeditionary operations are most likely to take place. In this case they will need to be improvised.

Furse is clear that success depends on skill as much as hulls and facilities. While commercial firms like Fedex or the United Parcel Service have general experience to offer here, many of the issues involved are distinctive. For example, informed choices requiring military judgment are needed over such questions as whether equipment should be combat-loaded for instant use in the area of operation or more economically and according only to the size and nature of the cargo.

Although this all sounds painfully obvious it is worth remembering the many instances in which this kind of thing has gone wrong, from the Crimean War of 1853–1856 when, famously, the horses arrived (by steam) long before their forage (by sail) or the tragic inadequacies of strategic transportation during the Gallipoli campaign of 1915. Strategic conveyance is a complicated matter and the success of the operation will often depend on getting it right.

The protective function

For that same reason, any adversary is likely to try to disrupt its every stage. Accordingly, a crucial *protective* function is intrinsic to this transportation task. The heterogeneous and possibly cumulative effects of an adversary's campaign of resistance can be seen by following through the three stages of the strategic transportation process:

- *Assembly.* A resourceful adversary might be able to disrupt the gathering together of the expeditionary forces by a media campaign designed to increase domestic opposition against the expedition. There could be acts of selective terrorism, or sabotage in the docks and on the domestic transportation system. The fact that only one lay-berth was available for the transportation of ammunition through the major port of Savannah in 2000–2001 suggests surprising vulnerabilities in this area and helps explain the current growth of interest in port security in the United States and elsewhere. Disruption of the assembly of expeditionary forces could also include cyber attack on military logistic information systems.[32]

- *Passage.* Recent expeditions such as the Falklands campaign or Desert Shield/Storm faced little or no opposition on the high seas and at the moment this situation seems likely to continue, although the 2002 attack on the *Limburg* confirms that it would be dangerous to assume that this will always be the case. The attention paid by the allies to the possible disruptive effect on supply shipping in the Mediterranean in 1990–1991 by Libya's two obsolescent Foxtrot submarines shows how seriously such an attack could be, not least for its possible political consequences. Greater danger might be expected in the narrow seas through which an expeditionary force may have to pass – from sea mines, Boghammer-like fast attack craft such as those operating out of Iran during the 1980s, modern diesel submarines, aircraft, anti-ship missiles, such as the Russian SS-N-22 and its derivatives, and, of course, land-based aircraft.

- *Arrival.* In January 1991, an Iraqi Scud missile landed in the Saudi port of Al-Jubayl, close to a huge stack of anti-tank ammunition and to a jetty where a number of allied ships were tied up, including a Polish hospital ship. Sea mines and sabotage against the ships and facilities of the ports of receipt may also need dealing with. In 1971, Bangladesh's *Mukti Bahini* frogmen were very successful in just such a campaign against Pakistani ships in the port of Chittagong.

All of this has reinforced concern for the security of expeditionary forces in and off the ports of receipt.[33]

The variety of present and future threats to strategic transportation needs is clearly to be taken seriously. In the East Timor operation it certainly was:

> *Interfet* warships escorted both naval replenishment ships and chartered merchant ships carrying supplies to East Timor; without the protection provided by the warships it is highly likely that many of the chartered merchant ships would not have agreed to sail to East Timor.[34]

Inevitably, these activities merge with those of force protection.

Force protection

> Of all the conditions necessary for effecting a landing on a hostile coast, the most essential one is to possess a decided superiority over the adversary at sea.[35]

By definition, expeditionary operations take place in the littoral, which British maritime doctrine defines as: 'The area from the open ocean to the shore which must be controlled to support operations ashore, and the area inland from the shore which must be supported and defended from the sea.'[36] The actual extent of the area is largely a function of the reach of the weaponry involved. The Afghanistan operation of 2000–2001 showed that for the United States the littoral could extend hundreds of miles inland. Other navies take a more modest view of its extent, but all are agreed that the littoral environment is a highly complex one.

It is a congested place, full of neutral and allied shipping, oil-rigs, buoys, coastline clutter, islands, reefs and shallows and complicated underwater profiles. Expeditionary forces operating there will be well within reach of hostile aircraft, shore-based anti-ship missiles and coastal artillery. Fast attack craft may be expected, along with coastal submarines and minefields. Because of the short distances involved, attacks will be sudden, unexpected, coming from unpredictable axes of threat and requiring instantaneous responses. The narrowness and shallowness of the waters will often make it difficult for large surface ships or submarines to manoeuvre freely. Less obviously, airspace limitations might often pose equivalent challenges for expeditionary aircraft too.

This litany of possible evils shows how challenging the littoral can be, and experience in the Gulf in the last 20 years of the twentieth century provides many examples of the range of threats that expeditionary forces could find themselves facing. But their real challenge is to overcome such threats and to protect every aspect of the operation with sufficient margin in capability to be able to project effective military power ashore. If they cannot do this, if their whole effort is absorbed by self-defence, then there will be little point in their being there in the first place.

What they have to win, in fact, is a 'battle for access' in which

> twenty-first century enemies might use sophisticated, low-cost weapons to gain an asymmetric advantage in the contest for local control of the sea. Such an

opponent will not seek to win a battle with a major naval power, but rather to make the cost of its defeat prohibitive.[37]

The main challenges to expeditionary forces have already been identified in Section 6.6. They include:

Mine warfare

The North Korean mine threat famously impeded allied operations during the Korean war of 1950–1953. Forty years later the mine threat was equally potent in the Gulf where some 300 bottom mines and 744 moored mines were recovered by Coalition forces and another 233 were found floating or beached. Many of these mines had been laid incorrectly and would not have gone off anyway; moreover they were laid much further out than the allies had expected, probably too far out for the Iraqis to have any real prospect of defending them. Even so, they were a real constraint on Coalition planning and, had large-scale amphibious operations been necessary, the preliminary MCM effort required would have been very considerable. Minefields rarely defeat maritime forces (the Turkish success in defending the Dardanelles against the British and French navies in 1915 being one striking exception) but they do impose delays and costs, especially when adequately defended, and so can act as a significant limit to an expeditionary force's freedom to manoeuvre.[38]

The effectiveness of the sea mine lies in the fact that the adversary has the advantage of knowing the waters through which the expeditionary forces need to pass in order to achieve their objectives. Mines are cheap and come in a huge variety. In 1991, Coalition forces had to cope with a bewildering range of mines from veterans of the First World War to the latest and most sophisticated Italian types. Moreover the sea bottom in the littorals is notorious for being covered in a remarkable diversity of old iron (wrecks, oil drums, old washing machines, the list is endless) and this makes mine detection extremely difficult. New unmanned underwater vehicles (UUVs) may, however, help.

Littoral anti-submarine warfare (ASW)

The difficulties encountered by the British Falklands Task force in dealing with Argentine Type 209 coastal diesel submarines (SSKs) serves as a useful reminder of the complexity of conducting ASW in the littoral. Here, the SSK can simply lurk in familiar waters and, acting as a weapon of position, wait for its targets to approach. The high ambient noise of coastal waters, their shallowness and complicated salinity and temperature levels make coastal ASW difficult even for the most proficient, as the Swedish Navy's problem in tracking down suspected submarines in their own waters in the 1980s indicates.[39] Modern SSKs can reduce their traditional vulnerability by operating in battery mode for up to 72 hours, and air independent propulsion is coming of age. There will be responses to all this of course, such as multistatic active radar, but the current technical ASW challenge in littoral waters is unlikely to diminish significantly in the next few years. On the other hand, the number of countries able to mount and maintain such a sophisticated challenge is not great. Nor are most of them likely to be the venue for expeditionary operations.

Area air and anti-missile defence

The Scud attack on Al-Jubayl already referred to and the proliferation of anti-ship missiles of increasing range, stealthiness, speed and homing capacity explain the current interest in theatre ballistic missile defence and the attention paid to a variety of soft and hard kill systems, discussed in Section 8.6.

British surface ship losses to Argentine aircraft in 1982 and the surprise Iraqi air attack on the USS *Stark* in 1987 are potent reminders of the potential vulnerability of surface warships in narrow waters if sufficient air defences are not in place. These defences should include counter-air activity against hostile airbases, airborne early warning (AEW), protective combat air patrols (CAPs) and sufficient sensors, anti-aircraft missiles and guns and damage control facilities on the ships themselves. Sophisticated expeditionary forces have so far been able to deal with this range of problems without too much difficulty so far, but the more relatively advanced the opponent, the greater the challenge.

Gulf experience reveals the particular problem faced by expeditionary forces when the air threat is combined with something else. The tragic USS *Vincennes* affair, when an innocent Iranian airbus was mistakenly shot down, shows the 'overload' problem that can arise when a task force operating in congested waters is having to deal with harassment by Iranian Boghammer fast attack craft and possible air threats *at the same time*. Combinations of threats are the real problem. But, so congested are littoral waters, that this kind of thing could often happen unless effective countermeasures are taken.

Moreover, political constraints may make the commander's task much more difficult. The Iraqis were allowed to lay their mines, and indeed were not closely monitored in doing so, because of political constraints on Coalition naval movements north of the Saudi–Kuwait border. As it turned out, this was a serious mistake that greatly complicated Coalition operations afterwards. In the East Timor operation, the force commander was extremely anxious to avoid engaging Indonesian submarines and aircraft. Detecting them, and warning them off before they could launch attacks was a demanding aspiration, but a politically necessary one.[40]

Force protection: overall maritime responses

While these are the main challenges in force protection facing expeditionary forces it is difficult to generalise about their extent, and about the requirement to respond. In the Gulf War, force protection had to be taken very seriously; in the case of the British operation off Sierra Leone and the allied operations against Afghanistan it was not a serious operational priority, although in both cases routine precautions had, of course, to be taken. In the case of allied operations in the Adriatic and the East Timor operation the situation was somewhere between these two extremes.

Nonetheless, these threats, especially in combination, require serious and sophisticated response. Even in a relatively benign environment, the conduct of expeditionary operations demands high levels of skill and technologically advanced sensors and weaponry and require, especially for the major Western navies, a paradigm shift away from the open-ocean preoccupations of the Cold War years. The fact that expeditionary operations are almost invariably wars of choice for the expeditionary forces, in which there are high levels of casualty aversion, moreover, increases the need to take the least possible chances.

For the future, two schools of thought seem to be emerging and typically they focus on the question of the future shape of the fleet and the continued role of the large surface ship in the conduct of expeditionary operations.

The first school focuses on the unavoidably large size of the ships carrying the military personnel and supplies and of the air support that they will need. Large conventional platforms of this sort are basically unavoidable, they conclude. More-over, each of the threats discussed above can be countered individually or in concert. For instance, there were doubts about the wisdom of putting large ships, especially aircraft carriers, into such narrow waters as the Gulf in 1990–1991. In the event, of course, the risk was taken, and the Iraqi FAC threat proved a chimera partly because they were so ineptly used by the Iraqis but mainly because the Coali-tion's air supremacy provided the conditions in which British and American heli-copters could destroy them all before they became a threat. Throughout history, in short, every new weapon has spawned its counter, and this will continue. Moreover, the advantages of size show that while FACs continue to proliferate amongst the world's smaller navies, they are tending to get bigger and more powerful, mimicking the capabilities of the larger warships they are supposed by some to be replacing!

But against this conventional view of the future for force protection should be set a more radical view that argues:

It is better to fight fire with fire using expendable, missile carrying aircraft or small surface craft ... In fact, ever since the introduction of numerous torpedo boats, coastal submarines, and minefields early in the ... twentieth ... century, contested coastal waters have been taboo for capital ships and the nearly exclu-sive province of flotillas of small, swift, lethal fast-attack craft.[41]

This approach is linked to Admiral Cebrowski's so-called 'Streetfighter' concept. Here, the offensive and defensive power of the fleet is disaggregated amongst a large number of small, and individually less valuable platforms that are networked through an information and control system to provide the same combat power as a conventional fleet. Indeed with new directed energy weapons, fleet defence might be revolutionised in the years to come with a decided move away from the concentra-tion of assets and towards dispersed tactics, designed to deceive and confuse the adversary. Although compromise between the two positions is the most likely outcome, this argument about the future of force protection and fleet defence is set to run for many years yet.

Force insertion and extraction

Almost by definition, expeditionary operations will require 'boots on the ground' because it is ashore that most of the problems that will have sparked the expedi-tionary operation in the first place will be found, and must be dealt with. Accord-ingly, the capacity to insert forces ashore is central to the whole concept of expeditionary operations. Everything else facilitates it. The aim is to take maximum advantage of the flexibility offered by the sea in order to engage in a campaign of lit-toral manoeuvre.[42]

Generally, two types of ground forces will be required – special forces and light infantry, especially in the robust shape of marines and airborne/para forces. The Gulf operation of 1990–1991 was exceptional in the prominence it gave heavy metal in main battle tanks and artillery. Generally such forces will not be required in such large numbers. The distinctive nature of these special forces and light infantry determines the nature and conduct of the force insertion and extraction task, thereby raising the issue of *why* special forces and light infantry are so central to the conduct of expeditionary operations.

Why special forces?

Special forces vary around the world. They have a particularly important picture-building role. They conduct reconnaissance missions, locate key military targets (in Iraq, looking above all for mobile Scud launchers), link up with local forces where appropriate and generally prepare the way for larger forces later. It is not their function to engage in sustained combat.

Tending to operate in small teams, they can be inserted by a great variety of covert means – by parachute, helicopter, submarine, swimmer-delivery vehicles of various sorts or by a variety of stealthy surface craft. The US Navy is seriously considering the conversion of old ballistic missile firing submarines for this purpose (evidently at the rate of 120 soldiers per missile tube!). The North Koreans are specialists in the use of Sang and Yugo midget submarines and two-man swimmer-delivery vehicles. The British see the delivery of special forces as being one of the main roles of their SSNs. Other nations play their own variations of the tune.

Why marines?

> History suggests God is on the side of the bigger battalions – unless the smaller battalions have a better idea.[43]

Although some of the points that follow apply equally well to airborne and parachute forces, marines have particular advantages for the conduct of expeditionary operations. Liddell Hart made many of the essential points: 'A self contained and sea based force is the best kind of fire extinguisher because of its flexibility, reliability, logistic simplicity and relative economy.'[44]

Sea portability

But he misses one of the key ingredients that marines can provide, because they are sea portable and sea based – the need for speed. As Kofi Annan remarked in the last year of the old century, 'One of the problems with Peacekeeping has been the speed of deployment. With each delay the problems get worse.'[45] Being sea portable, marines can be moved into most operating areas with little political constraint. For the same reason, their limited logistic 'footprint' ashore requires much less in the way of depots and bases and so presents fewer targets and a reduced need for host nation support. The 1992 attack on the Khobar Towers in Saudi Arabia shows that land bases can be vulnerable. Sea-basing reduces such vulnerabilities.

Reach

The contemporary emphasis on STOM means that modern well-equipped marine forces can have very considerable reach. In the case of the Afghanistan campaign, 600 US Marines from the USS *Peleliu* and *Bataan* were flown 400 miles to Bibi Tera airfield in four hours, probably the longest fastest operational deployment in US Marine corps history. This contrasts strongly with the 'operational pause' endured by the British in 1982 resulting from the difficult business of getting the forces ashore at San Carlos, sorting them out and equipping them before they advanced inland towards their objective. This delay provided the Argentines with potential targets and caused the British government some political difficulty. Nowadays, the idea would be to get the marines to their objective much faster and by more direct means. For this reason, US Marines have generally been redesignated from 'amphibious' to 'expeditionary' although 'hitting the beach' is likely to remain one of their many accomplishments. Given their previous veneration for such famous battles as Iwo Jima and Okinawa, this is a major paradigm shift.

Interestingly, the French have required no such shift in emphasis. Their accent has always been expeditionary rather than amphibious. French marines are part of the army not the navy, continue to be regarded as an elite light infantry, and have been extensively used in France's overseas departments and colonies (Reunion, New Caledonia, Tahiti) with a substantial training role in francophone Africa.[46] This versatility is, however, something of a hallmark for all marines.

Light and self-contained

One consequence of this emphasis on sea portability, speed, manoeuvre and, increasingly, small-team-based operations, is that marine forces will tend to be self-contained, with delegated command and 'light' in terms of armour and firepower. The contrast between marines and the army was exemplified in the Vietnam War. In contrast to the army with its preference for the big firepower intensive battle, the US Marines were good at counter-insurgency and had an appropriate small wars doctrine derived from long 'Banana Wars' experience.[47]

Very often outnumbered and sometimes outgunned, marines have had to develop the approach of out-thinking an opponent they were unable to overpower through brute strength. Their innovative proclivities have recently produced the concepts, skills and capabilities of OMFTS, discussed in Sections 3.7 and 8.4, which are so appropriate to expeditionary operations.[48]

The US Marines therefore depend on networked command and fire and logistic support from the fleet or from land-based air. They are not intended in the main to engage in sustained, attritional operations against heavy enemy forces. Should heavy enemy forces need to be dealt with, marines will be, in their own favourite phrase, 'the tip of the spear' while the army provides the shaft that follows it. They are light enough to get there fast, but heavy enough to remain until help arrives. Nonetheless such things are relative. Western marines have far more firepower than most of the forces they are likely to encounter in expeditionary operations around the Third World.

Withdrawability and poise

Because marine forces are not supposed to get enmeshed with enemy forces but are, on the contrary, to be always ready to disengage so they can be poised offshore or reinserted elsewhere, they are especially trained for the 'fighting withdrawal'. Given its potential confusions, morale problems, reducing battle space and so forth, this is one of the most difficult of all military manoeuvres, but crucial for the conduct of expeditionary operations.

Experience

Quite simply, marines are used to expeditionary operations. They tend to have a particularly global outlook and a wide and varied set of operational interests. As we saw in Section 3.5, they have long been specialised in the business of small wars, and have developed the habits of thought that go with them. The diversity of skills this has required suits them for counter-insurgency tasks, humanitarian relief, PSOs, NEOs and service protected evacuations (SPEs). It was no coincidence that marines were chosen to lead in the relief operation of the Kurdish parts of Iraq in the immediate aftermath of the Gulf War.

The conceptual gap between the army and the marines is likely to narrow, however, partly because in the light of experience in the Gulf, there has been something of a tendency in the marines to make themselves somewhat heavier in response to the challenge of operating against heavier adversaries in the open, or in a difficult urban environment. Moreover, under the leadership of people like US General Shinsecki, many of the world's armies are going 'lighter' in preparation for a more expeditionary future.[49]

Support for landed forces

Either way, landed forces will require transport and usually being quite light will need sea-based fire support. Accordingly, around the world, navies are building up their amphibious warfare capabilities. This may be a question of enhancing it (in the case of the United States, Britain, France, the Netherlands, Spain and Italy) or of developing it (Australia, Japan, Singapore) or of beginning to get interested (Malaysia, South Korea). A new type of multi-role amphibious warfare ship is appearing that will offer the ARG, or its equivalent, all round and dedicated support in addition to that provided by other non-specialist naval forces in the Task Group. The rationale for this is that the first duty of these other maritime forces may need to be force protection, rather than the support of landed forces.

The same ships and services will also be a means of extracting the force, either when difficulties arise or when the mission is accomplished, for as Furse reminds us, 'An operation for which it is necessary to provide, in all expeditions beyond the seas, is the re-embarkation of the army.' The ultimate means of boosting the confidence of an expeditionary force ashore is the traditional ability of the navy to pull them out safely if things go wrong. During the difficult allied operations in the former republic of Yugoslavia, the knowledge that there was a secure line of retreat should things go awry gave peacekeeping forces the confidence to continue with their difficult work.[50]

Maritime firepower

> In all conjoint expeditions of the army and navy, the landing and transporting of
> cannon is performed by the seamen, after which the artillery officers mount the
> guns and complete the batteries.[51]

Because, in expeditionary operations, light sea-portable forces cannot take much in
the way of artillery with them, fire support needs to be supplied by the fleet, especially in circumstances where land-based air support is either unavailable (the Falklands, Sierra Leone) or insufficient (Desert Storm, Yugoslavia, Afghanistan). These
expeditionary operations show that such support comes in three main forms: sea-
launched cruise missiles, carrier-based aviation and naval gunfire support (NGS).
Experience over the past 20 years shows that such fire support needs to be timely,
discriminating and accurate, and capable of unexpectedly sustained operation. It
now comes in the following varieties:

Sea-launched cruise missiles

The Afghanistan campaign was the tenth operational occasion in which Tomahawk
TLAM cruise missiles have been used. Technical improvements have much
increased their accuracy and reliability over this period. Fired from a submarine or
surface ship, they have shown themselves to be relatively affordable, accurate and
reliable. With a range in excess of 1000 nautical miles and access to the Global Positioning System (GPS), they present few risks to the attacker.

Although regarded by some as weapons of coercion and strategic punishment,
they have also shown themselves to be particularly useful as force enablers. In
Desert Storm and Afghanistan they were used especially in the early stages of an
integrated and properly de-conflicted air campaign, essentially to degrade the
enemy's immediate capacity to resist subsequent air attacks. While they could be
used for more general fire support, this would require much larger inventories and it
might be more cost-effective to invest in more aircraft or modern NGS systems
instead. Nonetheless, an increasing number of navies are considering the acquisition
of sea-launched cruise missiles, including the Australians, Canadians, Dutch,
French, Israelis, Japanese, Spanish and Italians.[52]

Carrier aviation

The operational effectiveness of all types of airpower in the conduct of expeditionary operations has increased hugely over the last few years. In Desert Storm
only some 10 per cent of the bombs dropped were 'smart'; in Afghanistan only 10
per cent were not. It was claimed that American airpower now had the capacity to
deal with targets as they emerged. Thus, a reconnaissance aircraft identifies a spike
in satellite phone communications in a known Taliban office, a Predator goes in to
have a look, and the consequent real-time video picture of bodyguards lounging
around outside is transmitted to targetting teams in Saudi Arabia and USCENT-
COM at Tampa, Florida. GPS coordinates are worked out, sent, punched into the
cockpit of a Navy F-14 Tomcat, which completes the cycle by dropping a precision
bomb on target, before going off to wait for the next order.[53] It is indeed now a

question of distributing targets to aircraft not aircraft to targets. This is not to say that things always work out with this clockwork precision – because they manifestly do not; it is merely to establish that air support of expeditionary operations is usually indispensable and is now potentially of very high quality indeed.

As we saw in Section 4.5, the question of *how* that airpower is to be delivered is a complicated one. With the extraordinary range of modern, and specifically American, bombers it is hard to imagine an expeditionary operation anywhere that is not within range of secure land bases somewhere or other. In recognition of the strategic benefits this may produce, the US Air Force has recently reconfigured itself into an 'Air Expeditionary Force'. But this capacity is available to very few countries, can be subject to political air transit problems and the Afghanistan operation showed that it can be very expensive in terms of tanker aircraft.

Shorter-range land-based aircraft have much to offer too, if available. Typically, they manage higher sortie generation rates and a higher proportion of attack to defensive aircraft than can carriers. But bases may not be available, or there may be political, operational or climatic limitations on the performance of aircraft operating from them. Carrier aircraft, surprisingly, tended to be closer to the action in both the Gulf and Adriatic operations of the 1990s and are, of course, largely independent of host nation support.

Nonetheless all this airpower comes at considerable cost and effort not just in terms of the aircraft and the weaponry but also of the huge support infrastructure that keeps it going. The fact that so many countries are looking at the procurement of aircraft carriers, despite their apparent cost, amply testifies to their demonstrated utility in support of expeditionary operations as a crucial part of the general airpower package. However, the fact that even in the benign air environment prevailing over Afghanistan, aircraft crashed and their crews were either killed or had to be located and rescued both on land and at sea, points to a continuing disadvantage that manned aircraft have in comparison with cruise missiles, naval artillery and fast developing UAVs.

Naval gunfire support (NGS)

Navies are well suited to provide this kind of support because, for centuries, concentrated firepower has been their principal preoccupation in the struggle for command of the sea. The relative power of sea-based artillery over its land-based equivalent is graphically illustrated by a comparison between the guns of Napoleon's *Grand Armée* and Nelson's battlefleet. The French Army had 366 6–12 lb cannon, needing 9000 artillerymen, together with enormous horse and fodder *matériel* to move it. The fleet, on the other hand, had no less than 2232 cannon of 12 lbs and more, requiring only 14,000 men and much less in the way of *matériel*. In brief, six times as many guns, of much heavier calibre, could be transported daily by Nelson's fleet as by Napoleon's army, at one-fifth of the logistic costs and at five times the speed.[54]

Occasionally the prospect of naval bombardment has been effective in its own right. In 1840, the Royal Navy delivered a devastatingly successful bombardment of Acre in one of the cheapest major victories it has ever secured purely by the power of its artillery.

More commonly, NGS supports landed forces. Its nineteenth-century success was replicated in the very different conditions of the twentieth, for example during the

Second World War, the Falklands campaign and Desert Storm. Furthermore, with the arrival of extended range gun munitions (ERGM) surface ships will be able to fire smarter, guided projectiles over far greater distances.

Historically, naval artillery could be turned to other purposes as well. It could be taken ashore and used in direct support of the army ashore. Initially, the notion was that the navy would provide the guns but the army should man them as we saw at the start of this part of the chapter.

This was not sensible and it was soon realised that seamen had better fire their guns rather than simply hand them over to the army. In the Boer War, naval guns were unshipped and taken far inland complete with naval crews to offer direct support for the army. Often, naval guns (12 pounders and 4.7 inch) were the biggest and most accurate guns available to the British. During that conflict, Captain Percy Scott even came up with the idea of an armoured train, which for some time was very effective against the Boers. Even more remarkably during the course of the 1918–1920 War of Intervention between Soviet Russia and the Western allies, the crew of the cruiser HMS *Suffolk* built and manned a heavily armed and armoured train that fought the Bolsheviks thousands of miles from sea in the middle of Siberia – arguably the longest-range naval battle ever fought! This was a matter of brilliant improvisation with forces essentially intended for, and justified by, the performance of other tasks.[55]

The purpose-built river gunboats that assisted Lord Kitchener in the Sudan Campaign of 1896–1899, on the other hand, represented an entirely different approach. These vessels were a crucial part of Kitchener's overall firepower. His force of 25,000 British, Egyptian and Sudanese troops had 44 guns and 20 maxim guns on land and 36 guns and 24 maxims on the gunboats. Gunboats provided extra mobility and enhanced Kitchener's capacity to manoeuvre.[56] The riverine forces developed by the US Navy in the Vietnam War is a more recent example. Neither Kitchener's nor Westmorland's gunboats had any utility whatsoever in the standard naval conflict of the time and so nicely illustrate the way in which the naval requirements of expeditionary operations and of sea control can differ widely.

The fact that navies seem often able to adapt systems to land operations that were actually designed for something else, raises the issue of divided aims, explains why marines generally want dedicated fire support expressly designed to help them achieve their aims and are wary of relying on systems that may be switched off if maritime forces unexpectedly encounter shifting priorities.

Sea-based logistics

> In fact, war is not fighting and patrolling and bullets and knocks; it is one constant worry about transport and food and forage and ammunition.
>
> Colonel A. Hunter

> I don't know what the hell 'logistics' is, but I need a lot of it.
>
> Admiral Ernest J. King[57]

These two quotations make all the essential points. The success of all military operations depends heavily on the success of the system by which supplies and equipment are provided for the forces engaged. As Callwell remarks, 'the administration of supply' and the 'strategy of the campaign' are interdependent in small wars.[58]

The dependence of modern military forces on their supplies has, moreover, greatly increased since the Second World War. In Desert Storm, the UK First Armoured Division, when preparing to attack, needed 1200 tons of ammunition, 450 tons of fuel, 350 tons of water and 30,000 individual rations per day, the equivalent of the requirements of an entire army group in the 1944 Normandy landings.[59] Getting all the supplies needed for the Coalition for Desert Storm was probably the largest and fastest movement of material to a single operating area in the history of warfare, with the exception of the Normandy campaign itself, and that took two years to prepare.

If anything, the logistic demands of expeditionary operations are even worse, since the physical distance involved between the theatre of operation and the home base imposes particular challenges. The transportation infrastructure in the areas of concern will often be primitive or under attack, or both, thereby throwing the expeditionary forces very much back on their own resources. And, as we have seen, the current emphasis in expeditionary operations on STOM and the avoidance of large vulnerable stockpiles on the beach or the jetty or anywhere else where they could be attacked, poses yet more challenges for today's sea-based logisticians.

The aspiration is for 'focused' logistics such that the logistics plan should be entirely responsive to each phase of the campaign and on what might happen afterwards (in current military jargon on the 'branches and sequels'). The plan has to be able to sustain teeth arms in whatever they happen to be doing and, ideally to be able to react rapidly to unplanned contingencies. In the Afghanistan operation, according to Admiral David C. Brewer, Commander of Military Sealift Command, 'We found that we've had to anticipate possible changes in strategy and operational level focus in order to ensure that we were ready for changes in sealift tasking.'[60] Current discussion of ways and means of achieving these ends include the acquisition of modern auxiliary supply ships (AORs), the establishment of small-scale versions of the United States' Military Sealift Command and a developing interest in fast ships, including, after the success of the Australian HMAS *Jervis Bay* in the East Timor operation, catamarans and large floating mobile offshore basing systems. Some argue that the latter may prove the only way of meeting the expanding logistics needs of expeditionary forces; others conclude that the idea merely expensively transfers depot vulnerability from shore to sea, and worry about the practicality of the idea when sea states are less than totally benign.

9.8 Sea-basing

The developing concept of sea-basing, encouraged by worry about the logistic deficiencies revealed by the 2003 Iraq operation[61] is a further development of much of this. The idea, again, is to make use of the ocean as the world's biggest manoeuvre space to influence events ashore. Provided they have the right aircraft vessels and aircraft, naval forces can reach an operational area quickly and project power, both of the hard and soft varieties, ashore for as long as it takes and with greater flexibility and relative impunity when compared to forces and supplies deployed ashore. They are much less liable to attack, and much less likely to ruffle the sensitivities of the locals than conventional forces based ashore.

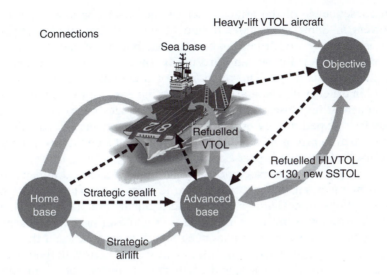

Connections

Heavy-lift VTOL aircraft

Sea base

Objective

Refuelled
VTOL

Refuelled HLVTOL
C-130, new SSTOL

Home
base

Strategic sealift

Advanced
base

Strategic
airlift

Figure 9.4 Sea-basing. (Sea and air 'connectors' producing a sea-based system projecting power and supporting landing forces ashore.)

Sea-basing can, of course, be in support of conventional military operations, as it was, for example, in 2003, when political difficulties in Turkey required the Coalition preparing for operations in Iraq suddenly to swing its forces from the Eastern Mediterranean to the Gulf. It can likewise assist in alleviating humanitarian distress when the collapse of governance ashore rules out an effective and timely response to the destruction of utilities such as electricity and water supplies. Navies around the world, but especially in the US, Canada and Europe are responding to this with determined and innovative construction programmes of large all-purpose amphibious vessels and supply ships that will serve both purposes.[62] There are, of course, diplomatic advantages to be had through sea-basing too.

9.9 Conclusions

Four tentative conclusions emerge from this review of modern expeditionary operations. First, they are by no means new. Navies around the world have conducted them for centuries. They were indeed the main activity of the British and other European navies during the nineteenth century. They continued throughout the twentieth century, overshadowed perhaps by the greater attention that had to be paid to classic peer conflict on the open ocean resulting from the urgent demands of the First and Second World Wars and the Cold War. With the conclusion of the latter, the attention of many navies has reverted to the conduct of expeditionary operations.

Second, some have wondered how permanent a shift this will prove to be in the twenty-first century. On the one hand, the emergence of new maritime powers, such as Japan and China, or the recovery of Russia, might lead to a resurgence of old-fashioned maritime rivalry on the high seas. Others speculate about the long-term consequence of the attacks such as the Al-Qaeda assault on the World Trade Towers in September 2001. If one of the justifications for expeditionary operations is the space – or distance – between the homeland and the political insta-bilities threatening world peace and prosperity, that attack really closed such gaps and brought the crisis home. The reluctance of potential expeditionary powers to get involved in other people's quarrels might be increased if this is the kind of thing that can happen in response. Additionally, such outrages might lead to a switch of effort away from expeditionary operations towards all aspects of homeland defence. It is possible to argue from such points that we might at some future time unexpect-edly find ourselves entering a 'post expeditionary' era.[63]

Third, the realisation that expeditionary operations are indeed difficult, expensive and demanding might encourage a reluctance to participate. They are not easy, job-preservation options for navies deprived by international developments of their normal adversaries. The lesson seems to be repeated over and over again. To engage success-fully in expeditionary operations, navies need first class capabilities of the sort equiva-lent to those normally associated with high-intensity operations with their peers. This is partly because of casualty aversion, and partly in consequence of the proliferation of serious maritime capabilities. To illustrate the point, the forces engaged in the East Timor operation found themselves being shadowed by Indonesian Type 209 SSKs with much greater tactical flare than had been anticipated. This required complex counter-measures and 'illustrates the importance of sophisticated force protection to a contemporary peace making operation in a maritime littoral environment'.[64] If expedi-tionary operations are to be conducted, they need to be conducted very seriously.

Finally, expeditionary operations *are* different. As Callwell remarked, 'The conduct of small wars is in fact in certain respects an art by itself, diverging widely from what is adapted to the conditions of regular warfare.'[65] In particular, they are highly politicised to an extent that 'normal' conflicts are not. For evidence of this we may need to look no further than the political restraints on MCM, or even monitor-ing, activity north of the Saudi–Kuwait border that hugely complicated subsequent maritime operations in Desert Storm. The fact that these operations take place in a littoral environment, moreover, also make for substantial differences in the conduct of the various maritime disciplines – for example, ASW (because of the complexity of the underwater environment in shallow, narrow seas) and AAW (because of the background clutter caused by nearby land masses). As a result, expeditionary forces require high-grade equipment and skills that are specific to their particular task.

9.10 A humanitarian postscript

> We have heard your miseries as far as Tyre
> And seen the desolation of your streets
>
> ...And then our ships happily you may think
> ...Are stor'd with corn, to make your needy bread
> And give them life, whom hunger starv'd half dead.
>
> Shakespeare, *Pericles*, I/4

Those engaging in expeditionary operations usually do so in the expectation that it will contribute to international stability, and their activities are typically directed against governments or other forces that seem to threaten it. But physical and human disasters such as cyclones, earthquakes and civil wars can threaten good order too. Humanitarian operations to restore good order from the sea by preventing or alleviating distress have become very common. They include:

- Sea-based attacks on the forces of disorder. Operations against pirate or slave-trading centres used once to be a commonplace naval activity. In 1998, US Marines helicoptered into an inaccessible part of St Vincent to burn cannabis plants.[66]
- Humanitarian relief operations in the aftermath of natural disasters, such as the massive multinational Asian Tsunami relief operation of 2004.[67] Many would argue that with the advent of global warming such activities are likely to be even more common in the future than they have been in the past. Already there are about 70 operations of this sort every year
- Non-combatant evacuation operations, where the object is to move people from areas where deteriorating security situations are putting lives at risk. The Royal Navy conducted such operations from Cyprus in 1974, Aden in 1986, Sierra Leone in 2000. There are dozens of other examples of expeditionary forces being used in this way.
- Proactive humanitarian missions in which naval forces get to needy places *before* disaster strikes, hoping thereby to alleviate its potential consequences. Thus, in 2007, the hospital ship USS *Comfort* and the amphibious warfare ship USS *Peleliu* sailed around Africa and South America, visiting 20 countries, treated more than 130,000 medical patients, 29,000 dental patients and 20,000 animals, conducted 1400 surgeries and expended 3000 man-days in well over 60 community relations and engineering projects.[68]

Their intrinsic characteristics make navies good at this sort of thing. The 1992 activities of Canada's naval auxiliary HMCS *Preserver* off Somalia illustrates the point. Its three helicopters and boats, including three small landing craft were invaluable at transporting people and materials from ship to shore. It had extensive medical facilities and was able to produce much drinking water in conditions in which this was a scarce commodity. Its workshops provided much technical and engineering assistance. Its galleys could feed over 300 people, and it provided rest and recuperation for people engaged in the arduous business of relief. Its communications suite enabled it to link in with all other aspects of the relief operation and enabled Canada to make a vital contribution to the successful conduct of a relief operation a long way from home.[69]

Naval forces have a mobility that means they are often the first to arrive in a crisis area in strength and thus often deliver the military capacity needed to provide the secure environment in which humanitarian relief operations (including those of the relief agencies) can progress. Much of the capacity to perform these functions derive naturally from the skills, hulls and equipment needed to conduct 'normal' military operations – and it is generally true that the more militarily capable the force is (and therefore the more expensive!), the more help it can offer. The justly famous Royal Navy Disaster School[70] illustrates the difference that sheer military professionalism makes to the conduct of such relief operations.

There are, however, costs and tensions. While modern military forces are expected to deliver everything from bombs to babies, the more they focus on one end of the spectrum, the less time, energy and effort will be available at the other. Navies have to strike their own future balances in this area. Their individual answers will reflect judgments on how important and frequent such operations are thought to be in comparison with the other functions they are required to perform, and on the particular contribution they can make as compared to non-military relief agencies.

10   Naval diplomacy

They [the fleet] would then pass along the coast before the eyes of the other cities and display the visible power of Athens.[1]

10.1 Coverage of naval diplomacy in the literature: who said what?

Despite the fact that naval diplomacy is as old as civilisation, the great masters of maritime thought only partially dealt with its complexities. Of course, they nearly all made, even laboured, the point that maritime strategy and the use of naval forces should be appropriate to the overall national strategy and the political purposes the country's leaders hoped to achieve. '[T]he means', said Mahan, 'are less than the end, and must be subjected to it.' He, like Corbett, Richmond and the rest of them had obviously read their Clausewitz![2]

They all accepted that, to quote John Stuart Mill, 'our diplomacy stands for nothing when we have not a fleet to back it'.[3] As far as Corbett was concerned, the first function of the fleet was 'to support or obstruct diplomatic effort'. Mahan argued, too, that the possession of seapower increased a country's prestige, security and influence: it was necessary for great powers to be strong at sea. With some reservations, he quoted Nelson: 'I hate your pen-and-ink men; a fleet of British ships of war are the best negotiators in Europe.'[4] The reverse was equally true. Being weak at sea put you in political and strategic danger both at home and abroad.

Nonetheless, the bulk of their attention was directed at the wartime, high-intensity uses of navies. Mahan hardly mentions the contemporary day-to-day activities of the US Navy's 'forward squadrons' or the manifold lessons of its 'Banana Wars'. Corbett likewise pays scant regard to the political functions of the Royal Navy and its involvement in countless small wars and operational deployments through the nineteenth century. Apart from recommending that navies should prepare efficiently and visibly for war in the expectation that this would shape the perceptions of other countries, the classic maritime strategists in fact had little advice to offer about naval activities in peacetime.

The gap they left has, however, now largely been filled by their modern-day successors. The greater costs and risks of applying force in the nuclear age concentrated naval minds on the issue of what could be, and should be, the role of navies in situations (well) short of outright and major war. Here the pioneer was the US Navy's Admiral Stansfield Turner who encouraged thought about what he called the 'Naval

Presence mission … the use of naval forces, short of war, to achieve political objectives'. Turner discussed 'preventive deployments' (where the appearance of naval forces prevents a problem from becoming a crisis) and 'reactive deployments' (where naval forces respond to a crisis). Deployments, threatened or actual, need to be appropriate to the situation, pose a credible threat to the opposition and must suggest the capacity to engage in any of five basic actions; amphibious assault, air attack, bombardment, blockade, or exposure through reconnaissance.[5] When Turner took over the US Naval War College at Newport, he put such ideas into practice by completely revamping its educational syllabus so that his students studied the demands of presence alongside those of war-fighting.

Likewise, Admiral Gorshkov had a good deal to say on the matter and was, of course, in an excellent position to put his ideas into global effect. Especially from the late 1960s, Soviet fleets and squadrons appeared on all the world's oceans, considerably complicating Western assumptions and reminding everyone that the Soviet Union was now a global player to be reckoned with. Gorshkov was clear that navies could

> demonstrate graphically the real fighting power of one's state. Demonstrative actions by the navy in many cases have made it possible to achieve political ends without resorting to armed struggle, merely by putting on pressure with one's own potential might and threatening to start military operations. Thus, the navy has always been an instrument of the policy of states, an important aid to diplomacy in peacetime.[6]

This interest has been taken still further by naval professionals in the post Cold War era. 'Naval Force in Support of Diplomacy' features significantly in British maritime doctrine, much encouraged by the governmental emphasis given to the whole concept of defence diplomacy. In the United States, 'Forward … From the Sea' likewise claimed:

> Naval forces are an indispensable and exceptional instrument of American foreign policy. From conducting routine port visits to nations and regions that are of special interest, to sustaining larger demonstrations of support to long-standing regional security interests, our naval forces advance US diplomatic initiatives overseas.[7]

While the cynic may reasonably dismiss all this as the sort of thing you might expect admirals to say, their conclusions have largely been backed up by a substantial body of academic opinion. Throughout the Cold War period and beyond, academics have added a level of helpful detail on how naval diplomacy works and on the political purposes it can serve. Their work has been in many ways an outgrowth of the burgeoning literature on the diplomacy of force associated with such writers as Thomas Schelling, Oran Young and Alexander George.[8]

Laurence Martin's *The Sea in Modern Strategy* dealt extensively with less-than-absolute types of maritime conflict and the seminal *Gunboat Diplomacy* produced by James Cable has become a minor classic. Edward Luttwak's *The Political Uses of Sea Power* and Ken Booth's very thorough *Navies and Foreign Policy* took these ideas further. Surveys of this kind are inevitably quite general and so were complemented by more specialised works focusing on particular crises and navies.[9]

These academic analysts produced their own varying taxonomies of the purposes and methods of naval diplomacy. James Cable distinguished between four kinds of naval force: the definitive (where it is used to produce a fait accompli, as in the case of the seizure of the US spy-ship USS *Pueblo* by the North Koreans); the purposeful (to persuade other nations to change their policy – the object of the British naval deployment to Kuwait in 1961); the catalytic (such as the sending of the *Enterprise* to the Bay of Bengal in 1971 merely to influence events); the expressive (just to emphasise attitudes, with no other object necessarily in view). Edward Luttwak, on the other hand, discussed what he called 'naval suasion', which was either 'latent' (routine and undirected deployments) or 'active' (by conscious design). Such actions could support allies, deter adversaries or compel them to change their policy. Like Luttwak, Ken Booth argued that the tools and tactics of naval diplomacy included the manipulation of the size, composition, locality, readiness and activity of deployed naval forces, naval aid (help in training and arms supply), operational calls and specific goodwill visits.

Naval diplomacy is clearly a serious activity in its own right. It is not simply something that navies do when they haven't got a decent war to fight. It matters, internationally. For all these reasons, it needs to be understood.

10.2 The diplomatic value of naval power

Navies are of diplomatic value for two reasons. First, they are military services, perform at least some of the strategic functions that armies and air forces do and so, like them, have instrumental value as a part of the diplomat's toolkit. There is a vast literature on the role of military force in international politics, both in peace and in war, and much of it applies to navies.

In some strategic circumstances, however, the leverage of naval power could seem quite slight, even irrelevant, when compared to land- or airpower. When contemplating with satisfaction the strategic outcome of the British bombardment of Acre in 1840, Lord Palmerston considered it:

> an event of immense political importance as regards the interests of England, not only in connection with the Turkish Question, but in relation to every other question which we may have to discuss with other powers. Every country that has towns within cannon shot of deep water will remember the operations of the British Fleet ... whenever such country has any differences with us.[10]

But the point was that many countries and interests were not in fact within cannon shot of the British Fleet. Thus, when the British wished to dissuade Bismarck from unsettling the European status quo by taking on Denmark in 1864, they found their naval power to be practically useless in political terms. This kind of example led Paul Kennedy to argue that naval power was of declining utility, compared to other forms of military power.[11]

Of course, sometimes, the strategic consequences of victory or defeat in battle at sea can be very considerable. When, in 1798, Nelson took what would now be called a Task force (since it was a detached squadron rather than a full-scale fleet) into the

Mediterranean to deal with its French equivalent at Toulon, the First Lord of the time described it as 'a condition on which the fate of Europe may at the moment be stated to depend'. The result was the Battle of the Nile when 'amid the shoals of Aboukir Bay, the result of a contest between two modestly-sized sailing squadrons changed the balance of world power, literally overnight'. And many other examples of this claimed degree of consequence can be found. As we saw in Chapter 1, the strategic 'leverage' of seapower in war has been and continues to be very considerable. Both James Cable and Colin Gray conclude that elegant though Kennedy's argument seemed in 1976, it was, in the last analysis, substantially wrong.[12]

While they both followed the example of the traditional strategists in focusing on the effect of navies *in wartime*, their analysis of the Cold War and, in Cable's case from his study of the 'violent peace' that accompanied and succeeded it, led them to conclude that naval power was an important aspect of peacetime diplomacy too.

Far from becoming more common, the peacetime situations in which navies have nothing to contribute politically are actually becoming rarer. This is partly a consequence of the growth of strategic interest in the littoral and the increasing value of the ocean (as discussed in Chapters 8 and 10 respectively) and partly through a growing acceptance of the need in today's globalised world to manage crises, and to prevent, limit or resolve conflict.

But, second, the growing diplomatic utilty of navies is also a consequence of the fundamental characteristics of naval forces themselves. China's Vice Admiral Chen Mingshen made the obvious point like this:

> [T]he navy ... whether [in] peace or war ... is also a means of pursuing national foreign policy. Navies possess many specific characteristics that differ from those of the [other] armed forces. The navy has international capabilities of free navigation on the high seas, and in peacetime it can cruise the world's seas, even conducting limited operations, outside the territorial waters of hostile countries.[13]

Gorshkov was also fond of pointing to the particular advantages that navies have in the more benign, coalition-building aspects of naval diplomacy. It is not simply that sailors are a nicer set of people; the other services find it difficult to replicate parts of the spectrum of possibilities offered by warships, in which something that is potentially quite menacing can easily be made to seem warm and cuddly while alongside in a foreign harbour. It certainly quite hard to conceive of an equivalent courtesy visit by a division of main battle tanks.

Nor are these advantages the exclusive property of the larger naval powers. Ken Booth argued that 'it is only the greatest navies which have important foreign policy implications'.[14] The rest of this chapter will establish, however, that naval diplomacy is a role in which all navies can and do engage, whatever their size and whatever the political persuasion of their governments.

Several points about the complicated relationship between naval power and politics should be made. First, maritime operations in peace and war can develop their own momentum, producing their own imperatives and unintended political consequences. The evolution of the German U-boat war between 1914 and 1918 and its disastrous impact on American opinion is a case in point. Navies sometimes *make* foreign policy rather than simply serve it.[15]

Second, the influence arrows between a navy and its environment go both ways; navies do have a political impact on their environment, but they are affected by it too. Navies themselves, their size and use, are often a consequence (rather than a cause) of political processes either on the domestic or the international scene. In all these ways, as Mahan observed: 'Diplomatic conditions affect military action, and military considerations diplomatic measures. They are inseparable parts of a whole; and as such those responsible for military measures should understand the diplomatic factors, and vice versa.'[16]

For all these reasons, naval diplomacy for the first time has become a significant preoccupation of maritime strategists, an important declared function of navies and justification for having them. No longer is it merely a kind of bonus, something one does with navies when there are no wars to fight.

10.3 The range and extent of naval diplomacy

So, what does naval diplomacy involve? How can we break it down into manageable components? Naval presence facilitates, but is not necessarily a condition for, picture building, acts of coercion and coalition-building activities. Naval coercion can be further broken down into deterrence and compellence operations.

Several points need to be made about the various functions on the naval diplomacy spectrum.

- The distinctions between these functions are based on their purpose, not their format.
- Naval diplomacy *is* a spectrum, a continuum, in which the boundaries between the functions are inherently fuzzy. The activities they lead to may differ not in type, but merely in degree.
- Moreover, the same maritime force may find itself engaged in more than one sort of activity simultaneously. A naval force intercepting illicit coastal steamers full of arms may be deterring, compelling and coalition building all at the same time.

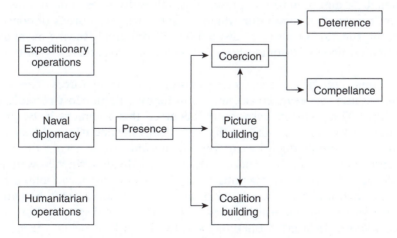

Figure 10.1 Naval diplomacy: the components.

- The relative importance and intensity of these three sorts of activity may constantly change day by day, and not necessarily in a straightforwardly linear way with each generally getting better or generally getting worse. The constant shifts and varying roles of external navies in the Gulf tanker war of the 1980s illustrates the point exactly and show just how demanding this requirement for this level of operational flexibility can be.
- As though this were not enough, naval diplomacy merges at either end of the spectrum with related activities, most particularly with expeditionary operations at one end and humanitarian ones at the other.

As we saw in Section 9.3, the US Marine Corps sought to capture this complexity with their analogy of the 'three block war', in which a force can find itself involved in a humanitarian relief operation on one city block, mediating between two fighting groups on another and enforcing peace against a hostile adversary on a third. Worse, the same marines may have to do all three in sequence or even simultaneously – a challenge because the demands of each in terms of deployment, demeanour and weaponry will probably be very different.

Clearly, naval diplomacy can be difficult and demanding for those who practise it, for those simply trying to understand the phenomenon – especially, perhaps, if they are the people ultimately paying for it. What follows then, is an explanatory analysis intended to make the range of possibilities clearer and more discrete than they actually are.

10.4 Naval presence

> And, most opportune to our need, I have
> A vessel rides fast by, but not prepar'd
> For this design.
>
> Shakespeare, *A Winter's Tale*, IV/iii

Naval presence: definitions

If the immediate aim of maritime presence is indeed to be present, to have a vessel 'riding fast nearby' and handy for whatever may turn up in areas of concern, it is clear that this function needs to be distinguished from simply having naval forces. In other words, we need to distinguish the 'presence' of naval forces from their 'existence'.

This is important because the mere existence of naval forces may well have worthwhile politico-strategic consequences in its own right. Most recently Indonesia's President Megawati Soekarnoputri rehearsed this argument in Beijing, when she reminded her Chinese hosts (not that they really needed it) that 'A strong naval force reflects a nation's dignity, thus [by having one] we can gain the respect of other countries in the world.'[17] This can be true of individual ships as well as navies as a whole. As one recent scholar observed: 'Ships have long symbolised technical achievement, national pride, maritime power, and a host of other human accomplishments (witness the enduring appeal of the *Victory* on display in Portsmouth or the *Constitution* in Boston).'[18] Back in 1637, the English launched the significantly named 100-gun line-of-battleship the *Sovereign of the Seas* 'to the great Glory of the

English Nation, and not to be paralleled in the whole of the Christian World'. The princely sum of £868 6s 8d was spent on decorating the ship, especially the stern. Phineas Pett, the shipbuilder, was appalled by this, confiding in his diary that 'she was so gorgeously ornamented with carving and gilding, that she seemed to have been designed rather for a vain display of magnificence than for the services of the state'. But, of course, poor Phineas was missing the point – the display of magnificence *was* serving the state, because then as now so much of international politics is about perception, of how strong and resolute you seem in the eyes of others. Moreover, behind all the carving and gilding, the *Sovereign of the Seas* (or the 'Golden Devil' as the Dutch called her) was easily the most powerful ship in the world.[19]

The construction of navies can have more specific purposes in mind than simply 'for general purposes of greatness'. Thus, in the nineteenth century, Napoleon III thought that the construction of a first class fleet would help persuade the British to accept his scheme for reorganising Europe in accordance with French interests. Forty years later, Tirpitz's so-called 'risk fleet' was his response to Germany's 'most dangerous enemy … against whom we most urgently require a certain amount of naval force as a political power factor'.[20]

Drawing attention to one's naval power was also the point behind Oman's Sayyid Said, first in having built and then sailing an impressive modern warship, the *Sultanah*, first to New York in 1840, where she delivered Oman's ambassador with due pomp and circumstance, and then to London in 1842. Almost overnight, Oman became noticed by the world's great powers.[21]

Sayyid Said realised, however, that there was little point in having the ship unless it was drawn to the attention of the people whose opinions he sought to influence. It is only when you do something with your naval forces that you switch from the merely 'existential' dimension of seapower to something more focused and purposeful. And with this we move towards maritime presence as currently understood.

This is how the Royal Navy currently describes the concept: 'The exercise of *naval diplomacy* in a general way involving deployments, port visits, exercising and routine operating in areas of interest to declare interest, reassure friends and to *deter.*'[22] Three things emerge immediately from this definition:

- Maritime presence is seen as valuable for what it makes possible.
- Maritime presence can be the first step to a very wide range of ways in which maritime force can be used in order to achieve foreign policy objectives.
- Because of this huge range of consequential possibilities, it is very difficult (and in fact not very helpful) to seek to define the characteristics of forces apparently engaged in 'maritime presence' solely in terms of that purely enabling activity. Instead platform/force characteristics have to be derived largely from the activities that maritime presence may lead to. But the word 'solely' is important, for presence does have some specific requirements as we will see later.

Naval presence: varying forms

Naval presence, moreover, comes in many different forms. First, there is the aspect of time. Presence can be routine and continuous, particularly in important areas where a country wishes to demonstrate a permanent interest. It can, on the other hand, be periodic and in accordance with some regular deployment rhythm, once a year, once a month or 'whenever we can'. This will usually reflect a less acute sense of interest in an area, or a shortage of resources.

Finally there is 'contingency positioning' – when a government orders a naval force to an area in a way that diverts ships from existing schedules but without quite knowing what it wants that force actually to do. James Cable was quite rude about some types of this stand-by presence: 'Warships are moved or deployed as a political gesture, as an alternative to effective action or an outlet for emotion' but often it will be precautionary 'just-in-case' insurance against the unforeseeable. The covert British despatch of SSNs to the Falklands in the crisis of 1977 is an excellent example of contingency positioning; in the event, the crisis blew over without their presence needing to be revealed. But Cable is nonetheless right to warn against the unconsidered, automatic creation (or reinforcement) of presence forces, lest it gets nations involved in issues unnecessarily and, more generally, devalues the currency of naval presence.[23]

Then there is the actual *composition* of the presence force. What kind of mix of capabilities does the force (or the single ship) possess and project? What is its state of readiness? Where exactly is it? Is the presence real or 'virtual' (say in the form of the rumours that SSN was on its way to the Falklands very early in the 1982 crisis)?

Naval presence: advantages

Not least because of its flexibility of form, naval presence offers diplomats a wide range of policy options that they may choose to exploit in order to defend national interests around the world. It facilitates picture building, coercion and coalition building. It offers a cost-effective means of exploiting advantages special to the sea and navies.

Its specific advantages are:

- *Independence* of host nation support and the political limitations and complications that this often entails. The sea is a neutral medium, and the presence of naval forces in international waters is much less provocative to wary populations than the presence of ground or air forces might be. The United States, and some European forces, have considerable strategic interests in the Gulf region, for example, but local sensitivities to ground force deployments mean that military means of defending those interests often have largely to be sea based.
- *Reach*. In the age of the ballistic and cruise missile, much improved NGS, modern sea-based aircraft and STOM, navies now have much extended strategic reach, although plainly not as much as airforces.
- *Flexibility*. There are many different types of warship, and many of them, being multipurpose, are individually very versatile. Because of this, a ship can be used to convey entirely different messages to adversaries or friends by the way it is used. Lights and canvas can transform the dourest man-of-war into a floating discotheque for visiting dignitaries in a matter of hours; a ship's geographical position is often used as a political signal and can easily be altered to suit the circumstances; the range of its weaponry provides a whole variety of diplomatic instruments. For all these reasons, it is hard to imagine a squadron of either aircraft or main battle tanks having the same diplomatic versatility as a modern warship.

- *Controllability*. Because warships can so easily be inserted into an area or grace- fully withdrawn from it if events take an unpleasant turn, naval power limits the liability of those using it. In any case, there are fewer civilians at sea than on land, no cities and fewer state resources may be involved. A confrontation at sea is less sensitive, and less prone to accidental escalation, than one on land. The use of naval forces is, therefore, usually regarded as less provocative, less dangerous and more controllable than that of their equivalents in the other ser- vices in the thick of events ashore.
- *Strategic mobility*. The slowness of ground formations, and the logistic difficulty of shifting them from one place to another, is well known. Aircraft, on the other hand, tend to be less mobile than they appear because they will often depend on routes over other people's countries and bases in them – neither of which may be available when needed. Formations of warships, however, can, with support- ing auxiliaries, loiter in likely areas for weeks and sometimes months at a time, being on hand and on call. Naval forces are moreover surprisingly fast. Steam- ing at 25 knots they travel at 600 miles a day and often arrive in theatre first, immediately ready for action, provided the individual units have the necessary range, endurance and reliability. These advantages in strategic mobility over the alternatives offered by the other services, means that naval forces are often the best way of giving a country global reach.

But an obvious question arises. Is naval presence, with all its advantages, an actual prerequisite for the coercive and coalition-building operations it may lead to? Obvi- ously, the quick answer to this question is no. It is possible to imagine an expedi- tionary war of intervention, for example, that boils up from nowhere and for which no preparations have been made, by way of preliminary naval deployments, to prevent the crisis from happening and to gain initial military, political and environ- mental intelligence.

But this is manifestly undesirable in that the response is purely reactive, aban- dons all prospects of using maritime force to manage or shape the strategic environ- ment and tends to militate against the speed and effectiveness of the operation.

It follows from this that maintaining a maritime presence in an area increases national readiness, contributes to the capacity to signal strategic interest, offers a means by which the strategic environment may be shaped to national advantage and facilitates the activities that may follow.

Naval presence: tailoring and sustaining the package

Governments have to think very carefully about how they craft their naval presence packages. The starting point will presumably be an attempt to identify the impor- tance of national interests in particular regions and some kind of assessment of the likelihood that those interests might be jeopardised. The next stage in the process will be some consideration of the extent to which naval forces are relevant to identi- fied threats and risks. If so, what naval capabilities would be required to respond effectively to those risks and threats? Do those capabilities need to be deployed permanently, periodically or only on a contingent basis?

Western navies and for that matter, the Soviet Navy too, seem to have followed this procedure when considering the worsening situation in the Gulf in the 1980s when Iraq and Iran were at war. It was thought important to keep the oil flowing. From a derived military objective to protect shipping, could be determined a list of consequential military tasks, like dealing with mines, defending against attack by aircraft and small attack craft, maintaining air superiority and so on, because these capabilities would simultaneously deter the unrighteous, reassure friends and by-standers and offer a means of limiting the damage if deterrence failed. From these necessary tasks a naval force package could be got together that was consistent with available resources, the likely actions of other navies and the perceived imminence of the threats and risks.

Finally, a host of technical factors need to be entered into the equation – and these are ones that *are* derived purely from presence and not from the activities it might lead to:

- How many ships are needed to support one on a particular station?
- What are reliable transit speeds?
- What assumptions are to be made about maintenance schedules, and the rotation of personnel?

From this, it is easy to see how the requirements for presence may determine the size and structure of the fleet.[24]

While it would be nice to think that decision makers followed such a tidy and logical estimate process in their deliberations on the matter, this kind of scientific exactitude has its limits. International politics is a chancy, unpredictable business. The sums may go wrong. For this reason, there is a natural tendency to err on the side of safety, even to over insure. The US Navy, for example, has long been noted for its emphasis on *combat-credible* forward presence. Thus 'Forward ... From the Sea':

> Forces deployed forward for routine exercises and activities are also the forces most likely to be called upon to respond to an emerging crisis. The potential for escalation dictates that presence forces must be shaped for missions they *may* encounter. This provides theater commanders with credible crisis-response cap-abilities in the event *normal* conditions or outcomes do not turn out as we expect.[25]

Forces that cannot act decisively, even to the extent of looking after themselves, cannot be said to be 'poised'; instead, they are a kind of helpless jetsam like HMS *Amethyst* the British frigate caught up the Yangtse by the Chinese Communists in 1949.[26] Naval presence packages that are weaker than the situation requires are little more than a hostage to fortune, and may become a liability for foreign policy makers rather than a way of helping them to resolve problems.

For their part, naval professionals have often pointed to the tension between the demands of naval presence operations and war-fighting. Admiral Jacky Fisher elimi-nated the Royal Navy's detached squadrons before the First World War so that he could redeploy their men into a battlefleet that would deal with the new German Navy across the North Sea:

> Showing the flag ... was the cry of the baying hounds in 1905 when we brought home some 160 vessels of war that could neither fight nor run away – and whose

Officers were shooting pheasants up Chinese rivers and giving tea parties to British consuls. How those Consuls did write! And how agitated was the Foreign Office![27]

The Royal Navy of the 1920s continued to regard 'showing the flag' activities as a distraction from their main task of preparing for war, although they warmed to it in the 1930s. There were similar concerns in the US Navy too.[28]

The main worry was and is the kind of 'skill fade' that may so easily set in when ships are unaccompanied on distant stations for long periods of time. The commander of the British Invincible carrier group pointed out that when they were strategically 'poised' in the Eastern Mediterranean in 1990 there were no aircraft to practise against and this 'did give rise to the potential for erosion of the operational capability of my Joint Air Group'.[29] Historians point out that war-fighting experimentation and innovations tend to come from concentrated forces at home (such as the US Atlantic and Pacific fleets of the interwar years that, for example, greatly advanced the cause of naval aviation rather than dispersed squadrons operating forward).[30]

The US Navy has for the last 50 years or so solved this dilemma by concentrating its forces into two powerful forward deployed fleets and has been wary of either of the two alternative devices of:

- Keeping one fleet back at home and 'surging' units forward to reinforce weak forward squadrons when the occasion demands. While that may facilitate experimentation and is less demanding in personnel terms, the forward squadrons may not be strong enough to deter or reassure.
- Devoting all the fleet to widely dispersed forward squadrons.

But there are problems with this approach, understandable though it might be. The presence of large naval forces offshore, while perfectly legal, might seem inappropriate to the locals, especially if those forces are used or presented in an insensitive way. In this, the demands of coercion and coalition building might well conflict. We will return to this issue later.

And then there is the issue of how these dilemmas affect all the world's other navies. It may seem at first glance that forward naval presence of this sort is the province only of a superpower fleet, but that is not the case. Indeed, when the US Fleet was perhaps tenth to twelfth in the world's naval pecking order during the late eighteenth and early nineteenth centuries, it still managed to deploy a surprising number of small detached squadrons around the world, specifically six between 1815 and 1840 in the East Indies, the Pacific, West Indies, Brazil, the Mediterranean and Africa.

In fact, lesser naval powers have simply to adjust their approach to naval presence to suit their circumstances. This may require them to limit the regions they frequent, the time spent on station and the capability of their presence packages, and also means that they must, of course, expect less of the advantage offered by superpower-style naval presence. But, even so, the advantages may still be considerable.

The increasing opportunity costs of highly capable war-fighting vessels aggravate the problem by generally reducing the numerical size of the fleet. As a rule, navies have fewer general purpose frigates than they used to for this reason and this reduces their ability to cover their areas of interest; it tends to mean fewer ship visits and standard routine deployments, and possibly less capacity to interact constructively with other navies. But since the opinion and behaviour of friends, bystanders and possible adversaries can be influenced by the presence of frigates, their absence matters. Paradoxically, in these post-modern days, a navy's natural fixation on preparing for high intensity operations may therefore actually *reduce* its diplomatic ability to secure the kind of maritime situation regime it would like to see – in peacetime at least.[31]

10.5 Naval picture building

As we saw in Section 9.7, collecting, processing and disseminating data about the actions and policies of allies and potential adversaries is essential in order to anticipate emerging risks and threats and to be in a better situation to do something about them if that seems necessary. This activity is the province of foreign offices, ambassadors and the intelligence services.

It is hard to exaggerate the importance of this activity. The failure of British deterrence and compellence in the 1982 Falklands crisis was largely due to the mistaken assumptions that both sides made about each other's intentions and capacities. Britain underestimated Argentina's military intentions; Argentina likewise underestimated Britain's resolve before the landings on South Georgia and then subsequently overestimated it. The result was a war that no one wanted. This failure may be compared with success in handling tricky parts of the sanctions campaign against Iraq. At one point, the Iraqis provocatively sailed the 'Baby Milk Peace Ship', the *Ibn Khaldoon*, through the Coalition blockade hoping to spark a confrontation with media-worthy pictures of tough US marines attacking the many stroppy women on board. Forewarned by an excellent global surveillance system, the allies knew all about this, handled the matter sensitively and still managed to locate the contraband hidden under the baby milk.[32] Knowledge is, indeed, power.

Although these shadowy activities do not generally attract much publicity, naval forces have an important role to play in picture building. It is conducted by naval attaches and liaison officers, satellites and naval intelligence and policy staffs – but here the focus is on its sea-based forms, and these will be both part of, and a contribution to, the coercive and coalition-building operations to be described shortly. These are aimed at accumulating data on the geographic characteristics of littoral areas of interest, on monitoring the political situation and on assessing the strengths and weaknesses of other military forces in such regions. To a surprising extent, it is a one-way process in which navies gain much more information than they give away. Naval forces over the horizon are very hard to detect, even in the age of satellites and for the foreseeable future will remain so. With increasing access to UAVs, naval picture building is likely to become even more effective.[33]

Successful picture building means that those 'playing away' have some of the advantages of those 'playing at home'. It facilitates subsequent actions of coercion and coalition building, and is therefore seen by the US and other navies as a persuasive rationale for forward presence and fleet deployments 'out-of-area'.

The advantages of naval picture building are indirectly suggested by the strong exception that many countries take to such activities in their areas of concern, and to the dangerous situations that often seem to develop from their attempts to eliminate or reduce them. During the Cold War, underwater confrontations between the intelligence-collecting submarines of both sides were quite common, and indeed the recent concern about the activities of Russian merchant ships in the vicinity of US naval bases suggests that this phenomenon has not entirely disappeared. The loss of the USS *Liberty* to an Israeli air attack in 1967 and the USS *Pueblo* incident of 1968 in which North Korean forces captured a US spy ship just outside their territorial waters, show both the importance and the hazards of this activity. The USS *Pueblo* was ill prepared for her mission, and unsupported by friendly naval/air forces. The US Navy seems to have made the unwise assumption that she would be safe since she was operating in international waters. The whole lamentable incident shows how seriously this picture-building role needs to be taken.[34]

The recent sinking of a North Korean spy ship disguised as a trawler after action by Japanese maritime forces in December 2001 demonstrates that the task of naval picture building is as important as ever it was and suggests that navies engaging in this kind of activity should be prepared for trouble, and that there are strong practical as well as political incentives for conducting it in an unobtrusive and non-provocative way as possible.[35]

10.6 Naval coercion

To subdue the enemy without fighting, that is the acme of skill.

Sun Tzu[36]

The whole business of using coercive force to influence the behaviour of other people and to get them to do what you want them to do by means (well) short of full-scale war has produced an enormous literature, no doubt because the costs and uncertainties of war are now so potentially horrendous. Accordingly, diplomats prefer to get their way by much less risky and costly means and, these days, take Sun Tzu's adage with great seriousness.

Naval coercion has always had an important role in this. It has a very long historical track record and, as Malcolm Murfett has justly remarked: 'Despite the vast changes that have taken place in the world since the mid-Victorian era, the coercive role that a navy – whether great or small – can perform in peacetime against a littoral state has survived virtually intact.'[37] All naval activity is, or should be, in support of political policy, but coercion operations are particularly politicised. British maritime doctrine describes coercion as the: 'Threat or use of limited action . . . to deter a possible aggressor or to compel him to comply with a diplomatic *demarche* or resolution.'[38] Coercion, or as it is sometimes called 'coercive inducement', thus comprises two very closely related dimensions: deterrence and compellence. Acts of deterrence are aimed at preventing someone from doing something by creating an expectation that the likely costs of the act would exceed the likely benefits. Deterrence is a matter of intentions and perceptions, tends to be passive rather than active, general rather than specific and in itself will not have lethal consequences even for the deterred party. Compellence, on the other hand, may (or may not) have lethal consequences; it is specific, active and is intended to *oblige* an adversary to do something, or maybe to stop doing something.

A single act may have both compellent and deterrent purposes. Thus the US Navy's 'Operation El Dorado Canyon' of 1986 was intended to force Libya's Colonel Qaddafi to stop supporting international terrorism, and to deter him from restarting his support at some later date. That controversial operation does, more-over, raise a number of interesting issues about naval coercion:

- The fact that more or less the same Sixth Fleet forces were used for this opera-tion as were used for earlier deterrent 'freedom of navigation' exercises in the Gulf of Sidra in 1981 and in the first three months of 1986 illustrates the flexibil-ity of seapower.
- But, in Washington's view, those earlier acts of deterrence failed to have the desired effect on the Libyan leader, and may even have inspired further support for international terrorism, specifically the bombing of the *La Belle* discothèque in Berlin. From this perspective, the 1986 raid in fact can be seen as just one round in a gradually escalating conflict over which neither side had full control.
- The limited alternative of a sea-based coercive campaign of economic sanctions being ruled out by the prospect of only half-hearted European support, the Americans felt they had to resort to force. They did try to reduce the risk of casualties, even amongst the Libyan military. Some might regard this gradual-ism as likely to prove operationally ineffective. John Lehman, for example, bemoaned the personnel losses and military ineffectiveness of a campaign framed by the 'academic game theory approach of "sending messages" with "surgical strikes" and "measured responses" '.[39]
- The conduct of the air strike was marred by equipment malfunctions and some of the bombs missed their targets, damaging foreign embassies in the Bin Ghasir area of Tripoli. A total of 37 Libyans were killed and a further 93 injured, including members of the Libyan leader's family. Nor was the raid cost free for the Americans; they lost one F111 and both its crew, and attracted political criti-cism from various bystanders. But the raid did result in serious damage to facili-ties valued by the Libyan regime.
- Subsequent events show how hard it is to measure the success of naval coercion. According to some estimates, the Lockerbie bombing of 1988 was an indirect consequence, together with the downing of a French airliner in Chad. Others, however, point to a declining level of Libyan support for international terrorism after this attack. Sooner or later analysts move into the murky waters of coun-terfactual speculation; what would Libya have done if the attacks had not taken place? On the basis of this experience it may be unwise to expect clear-cut answers to the quite fundamental issue of whether this was indeed 'clear and effective retribution' and, more generally, whether such acts should be regarded as worth the risks and dangers.
- The issue of the extent to which the Libyan regime was engaged in the support of international terrorism and was, therefore, an appropriate target for attacks in support of defeating it, shows the centrality of accurate picture building in the success of naval coercion.
- The perceived requirement to extend the action to land targets illustrates the political limitations of acts of naval coercion that are restricted to the sea.[40]

This case study shows that, for all the literature, coercion remains an imprecise art that is depressingly easy to get wrong. Its definitions, purposes and mechanics remain vague and often the coercive effectiveness of an action only becomes clear afterwards – and often not even then. Naval practitioners and their political masters anxious for a doctrinal handbook on naval coercion that will give them the kind of detailed advice on what to do, which is in any way equivalent to the guidance they can derive from tactical/technical rule books on mine clearance, for example, will have quite some time to wait. Nonetheless the questions remain as far as force developers and foreign policy makers are concerned: what does naval coercion require of naval forces? What sort of naval forces are most suited to such activities and how should they best be used? A look at both components of naval coercion in a little more detail may help.

Naval compellence operations

> Most mighty sovereign, on the western coast
> Rideth a puissant navy.
>
> Shakespeare, *Richard III*, IV/4

These are maritime operations intended to compel an adversary to do something he does not want to do, through the coercive use of sea-based forces. Such operations come in a wide variety of forms. Typically, they will avoid the sustained engagement of ground forces, and will be limited in extent and duration. Because they require the adversary to do something measurable, there is some hope of assessing their effectiveness.

Recent naval operations against Iraq, such as Desert Fox in 1998, and others of the sort, which were intended to compel the Baghdad regime to accept UN arms control inspectors through sea- and land-based air strikes, come into this category. Before the advent of airpower, such coercion was chiefly conducted by offshore bombardment – and the British attack on Acre of 1840 that has already been looked at is a good example of this. James Cable describes such operations as the use of 'definitive force' – the short, sharp exercises of naval power intended immediately to resolve an unsatisfactory situation. But while Acre was a clear-cut victory, the results of naval compellence on Iraq in the 1990s were more ambiguous.

The demarcation between naval compellence operations and the conduct of a small war may admittedly be a muddy one. The Falklands campaign of 1982 and naval support for the Kosovo operation of 1999 could be regarded as small, expeditionary wars rather than as distinct acts of compellence. But the original Argentine invasion of the Falklands – Operation Rosario – can be regarded as a definitive act of naval compellence that went seriously wrong. If the consequent despatch of the British Task force was indeed intended to be an act of non-lethal compellence, by which the Argentines would feel obliged to vacate the islands before the British arrived, then that also failed.[41]

Often, there seem to be more lessons in failure than in success so it might be worth looking at these two aspects of the Falklands campaign in a little more detail. Why, as a definitive act of naval compellence, did Operation Rosario fail to end the matter? No doubt because the British found the outcome unacceptable and, crucially, felt they had the diplomatic and military wherewithal to have a reasonable prospect of doing something that would make the outcome more acceptable. Since that proved in the end to be the case, the operation was obviously a serious Argentine military and political misjudgment of the strategic capacity of their opponent. Argentina's compellent strategy was ruined by what was essentially, a monumental failure in picture building, although as we shall see next, this was partly explained by the woolliness of earlier British acts of deterrence.

Britain's subsequent despatch of the Task force raises more complicated issues but also failed in that the Argentines were not persuaded to leave the islands peacefully or to come to some diplomatic resolution acceptable to the British. There seem to be two reasons for this. First, the Argentines continued to overestimate their own military strength relative to the British, putting excessive faith in the air bridge to the Falklands, in the bombing capacity of their air force and in the strategic effectiveness of their small Exocet armoury. Much of this is perhaps understandable given the inexperience of an armed force that had not seen significant action for over a century. Moreover, others shared their view, including some military professionals in the United States.

Second, if the primary aim of the task force at the beginning *was* to persuade the Argentines to leave peacefully (and that is still open to debate), the Argentines may well have misinterpreted British motivation, and instead concluded from this and the general ratcheting up of the seriousness of the British response (through their apparent disinclination to explore ways of handing over sovereignty diplomatically, through the largely symbolic seizure of South Georgia and the declaration and implementation of the various 'exclusion zones') that, in effect, hostilities had already begun and that it was now too late in political terms for them to withdraw with honour. If this was indeed the case and if the British did think of the despatch of the task force primarily in terms of non-lethal compellence, then it had precisely the reverse effect to that intended, kicked off a general action it was intended to avoid and graphically illustrates the dangers and deficiencies of using naval force in this way.

From this perspective, naval compellence as the use or promised use of violence in direct pursuit of specific political objectives is plainly an imprecise art. The opponent may misinterpret the motivation behind the act, and may not react as intended.

Alternatively, the despatch of the task force can be seen, and was indeed seen by many, quite simply as a large-scale act of 'contingent positioning' that soon turned into preparation for a straightforward and ultimately highly successful act of lethal compellence on a scale approximating a small war.

The efforts of Coalition navies against Serbia over Kosovo in 1999 and Afghanistan's Taliban regime in 2001/2002 can be seen in exactly the same light. On a smaller scale, the US Navy's Operation Praying Mantis against Iranian minelaying in the Gulf in April 1988 effectively knocked the Iranian Navy out of the campaign and, even though it was restricted to the maritime environment, arguably played a significant part in persuading the Iranian government to seek an overall accommodation with Iraq. The 'lessons' of these 'successful' examples of naval compellence must surely include:

- Having naval forces with a range of capabilities sufficient for the task. The greater the safety margin, the better. The sooner the adversary is made aware of this margin the better.
- Basing compellent action on an accurate picture of the adversary's character, level of attachment to the objective and his capability, intentions and capacity to react in the desired manner.
- Using naval force with rules of engagement militarily appropriate to the desired effect.

- Ensuring that military actions do not make it impossible to keep necessary allies on board.

But all this tends to be much clearer in retrospect than it is at the time. Things that can go wrong, frequently will, especially in such crowded and complicated waters as the Gulf. Even the world's most capable navy can make horrendous mistakes. Famously, in the course of Praying Mantis the USS *Merrill* was on the point of firing a Harpoon missile at an Iranian frigate when the target turned out to be a Soviet Sovremenny-class guided missile destroyer whose captain evidently wanting 'pictures for history' got so close as nearly to be part of it. That was a disaster averted, but the tragic shooting down by the USS *Vincennes* of Airflight 655, an Iranian airbus full of pilgrims bound for Mecca serves as a terrible example of the potential hazards involved in naval compellence, for all concerned.[42]

Military professionals also often express their concern about the possible tension between 'graduated response' and 'rapid effect' *both* of which foreign policy makers seem to want as guiding principles in the conduct of compellence operations. Those with a preference for decisive and overwhelming force are wary of the pinprick attacks characteristic of a graduated response. They may be politically advantageous in reducing casualties and winning political support around the world, but they may harden the resolve of the opponent and prove counterproductive in the long run. Deducing how much force is necessary for effective compellence is clearly very difficult.

Maritime interception operations (MIOPS)

These difficulties explain the natural preference for non-lethal forms of compellance, particularly for international sanctions campaigns through MIOPS, intended to oblige one or more states to change their policy by attacking parts of their (war) economy. Associated tasks include the stopping, searching, seizing and diverting of suspect ships and aircraft. Again, MIOPS has a long track record. Previous examples include sanctions against Italy in the 1930s, the British Beira and Armilla patrols and recent operations against Iraq and Serbia. In all there have been over 100 sanctions campaigns since 1945. Their advantage is that being non-lethal (at least in direct terms) they tend to attract more support than lethal forms of compellence.[43]

But they are not an easy option. They often require sophisticated multinational coordination of air and sea forces across a wide area. Either the forces engaged need compatible rules of engagement, or the operation has to be conducted such that ROE differences do not matter. Where the target of the sanctions campaign chooses to resist, they can be very difficult to implement in practical terms. This is especially so in cases where the seas concerned are narrow (the Gulf and the Adriatic), where the adversaries resist boarding and where the targets are potentially explosive and in many cases poorly maintained and operated oil tankers. The Iraqi practice of fortifying the bridges of their ships with metal barriers and dodging in and out of territorial waters is particularly difficult to deal with without hazarding life and limb. The British solution of the direct insertion of inspection teams by helicopter proved to be the secret of success in dealing with steadily increasing but still passive resistance on the part of the Iraqi ships, without having to resort to disabling fire.

But the real problem is less than total compliance with the implementation of the blockade even by those who in principle support it, either because they cannot control the entrepreneurial instincts of their citizens, or because they dislike some of the detail or because they are tempted by the economic incentives of cheating.

For this reason, however well the MIOPS are conducted, sanctions campaigns usually fail – at least in the sense of forcing the adversary to change policy. One recent estimate puts their success rate at about 20 per cent.[44] Nonetheless they may succeed in other ways. The Beira patrol, for instance, may have been worth the effort in that it showed black Africa that Britain's resistance to Rhodesia's bid for unilateral independence on terms the rest of the continent found unacceptable, was in fact serious. The sanctions campaign during Desert Shield may have failed to persuade Iraq to vacate Kuwait but it did demonstrate that all means short of lethal force had been tried and so developed the necessary domestic and international support for the much more coercive Desert Storm. Unsurprisingly, therefore, MIOPS are a particularly politicised aspect of naval compellence and the record during Desert Shield shows them to have been minutely controlled by the political authorities involved. Moreover, the manner in which the participating forces informally came together, without adhering to a common command structure, in order to make the operation successful, was in itself a usefully political activity. From this perspective, sanctions campaigns of this sort are less acts of compellence than of coalition building.

The same might be said for the cunning sanctions campaign launched by the Iraqis themselves in the 1980s. This took the form of a sustained campaign against Iran's oil industry, by means of a series of land-based air attacks on tankers in the Gulf. But while this might have been the ostensible purpose of the attacks, and so should be seen simply as an operation of war, most analysts are agreed that the Iraqis' real intent was to change the strategic balance between them and the Iranians by sucking the Americans and others into the conflict. The Iranians made this much easier by extending their retaliation not just to Iraqi oil/tankers but to vessels from Arab countries that they suspected were tacitly supporting Baghdad. This had precisely the effect that Saddam Hussein would have wished.

It brought the Americans and others into the conflict and directed most of their effort against Iran, and so played a role in forcing Iran to accept terms in the subsequent peace less generous than they might otherwise have hoped for. Iraq's conduct of the tanker war was both an act of naval compellence and a coalition-building exercise. From both points of view it was successful and deserves study as an example of how very limited and inefficiently conducted acts of force (which in the case of their attack on the USS *Stark* went badly wrong) could have beneficial strategic consequences out of all proportion to the effort.

Naval deterrence

Some definitions

Since the advent of nuclear weapons, much thought has been devoted to the concept of deterrence because actually using force seemed to have become suddenly so much more costly. The focus of this thinking was on *nuclear* deterrence. A capacity to influence other people's behaviour by the implicit or explicit threat of nuclear weapons at sea is obviously the most extreme variant of naval deterrence. This is an ongoing concern for a handful of advanced navies and indeed has recently generated arcane discussions about its 'pre-' and 'sub-strategic' configurations.

Of much wider interest, however, is the notion of deterrence by conventional means and applying it to the maritime environment. Here, the aim is to use naval forces to persuade an adversary *not* to do something through showing that the likely costs may well outweigh the hoped for benefits. It is based on the potential rather than the actual use of force. It is essentially preventative and so, if successful, will probably be a more cost-effective way of using force than attempting to remedy a bad situation after it has already developed.[45]

Broadly, naval deterrence comes in two forms. The first is general, passive and implicit. The mere existence in an area of a capable naval force loitering with intent in international waters near an area of concern, may be all that is required. This may often represent an unarticulated threat to possible malefactors of the consequences of wrongdoing. Thus, the US Secretary of State in 1801: 'Such a squadron cruizing [*sic*] in view of the Barbary Powers will have a tendency to prevent them from seizing on our commerce, whenever passion of a desire for plunder might intice [*sic*] them thereto.'[46] Later in the nineteenth century, the Royal Navy adopted a deterrent posture consciously aimed at putting at risk an adversary's coastal forts, dockyards and ports. Indeed, the threat to St Petersburg of the Anglo-French 'Great Armament', a powerful fleet dedicated to large-scale shore bombardment, played an important role in concluding the Crimean War of 1853–1856, although no such policy was ever announced.[47]

The second type of naval deterrence on the other hand is specific, active and explicit. A possible situation has arisen in which an adversary might be tempted to do something that the deterring party does not want. There is an identifiable adversary and a course of action that it is to be deterred. Naval forces may be ostentatiously surged into the area to bring the prospective adversary to realise the error of his ways. Here the naval advantage most of value for purposes of deterrence is their speed and strategic mobility.

Both types of deterrence have their effect through either the promise of denial (the forces present will prevent him gaining his objective) or the promise of punishment (the adversary may gain his objectives, but the political/military costs will be prohibitive). This latter explains how small navies can sometimes deter large ones.

Finally, deterrence may extend into war. Thus the presence of the Royal Navy's 'Western Squadron' deterred the French from exploiting the periodic absence of the bulk of the British Fleet in order to support Jacobite rebellion in eighteenth-century Britain.[48] Thus, according to 'The Maritime Strategy', Western hunter-killer submarines threatening Soviet SSBNs would not only deter Soviet aggression in peace but would prevent them attacking NATO reinforcement shipping in the Atlantic in the event of war.

It is often difficult to tell if deterrence has worked, and if so, how.

Some examples

The deterrent effectiveness of 'The Maritime Strategy' was backed up by candid and articulated statements and by demonstration deployments. It was explicit and highly active. Western submarines were always present in northern waters but covert; the presence of large-scale surface forces was intermittent but highly publicised. In peacetime the aim was general (to deter the Soviet Union from aggression): in war it would have been quite specific, as a means of defending NATO's Atlantic shipping.

It was at the same time a strategy of deterrence and of coalition building, in that it was clearly intended to reassure the United States' forward allies with the promise of effective support. At the time, this policy had many critics – some of whom were deeply sceptical of its likely effectiveness. Since the end of the Cold War, however, its impact on Soviet behaviour and its contribution to the ending of that conflict has become much clearer.[49]

Operation Vanguard was a British combined arms reinforcement of Kuwait in 1961 when it seemed as though Iraq was about to attack the country 11 days after it came into existence. It was specific and explicit and, again, very active. When the crisis passed, British maritime forces remained in the area for a while in passive and general mode. After the famous withdrawal from East-of-Suez was rescinded, the British maintained a small naval presence in the area, the Armilla Patrol, the function of which was to signal continuing interest and to deter actions against British interests, but in a low-key, generalised and passive way. The French did much the same. The Americans maintained a fleet in the area, even after the conclusion of the Iran–Iraq war. None of these forces deterred the Iraqi assault on Kuwait but neither were they intended to.

In Desert Shield, in 1990, there was some concern that Iraq might be tempted to move on from its apparent success in Kuwait to attack Saudi Arabia. The speedy arrival of US naval forces reassured local allies of American support and made it possible for them to receive elements of the US Marine Corps, the 82nd Airborne Division and, in due course, US land-based air forces. The level of Arab resistance to any further Iraqi advance, backed up by American forces in Saudi Arabia with the prospect of sea-based American air and possibly amphibious attack on the flank and rear of Iraqi forces entering Saudi, should certainly have deterred Saddam Hussein, had he any such intention. This was another attempt at specific, active and explicit deterrence, built on surged deployments. While it may (or may not, depending on whether Iraq actually intended invading Saudi Arabia) have succeeded, as an act of compellence (to oblige Iraq to leave Kuwait) it clearly failed.

The US Seventh Fleet is forward based (not merely forward deployed) and is intended to act in the general deterrence of anything that might threaten local stability and US interests in the area. Most of the time its deterrent function is general, passive and largely implicit. Only when a situation arises (such as the apparent Chinese threat to Taiwan in 1996 when two carrier battlegroups ostentatiously moved into the area) does the deterrence become explicit. The Seventh Fleet is expected to be able to deal with most crises without surged reinforcement from elsewhere, although in this instance the arrival of a second carrier battlegroup from the Indian Ocean probably concentrated minds.[50] Generally, the Western Pacific has avoided major crises, but the extent to which the Seventh Fleet can take the credit for this remains problematic. Certainly, the prospect of a substantial US naval reduction caused many anxieties in the area, even, if in muted fashion, from the Chinese.

An example of failure

If it is sometimes hard to see when an act or a policy of deterrence has succeeded, it is much easier to tell when it has not. One of the most spectacular examples of this was the British failure to deter the Argentine invasion of the Falklands in 1982. This failure, indeed, was so comprehensive as to invite the suspicion that the British had no deterrent policy at all – a factor that must go some way to explaining and perhaps even justifying the Argentine conclusion that the British would in the end accept their takeover of the islands as a fait accompli (or a definitive act of maritime com-pellance).

What might usefully be learned from this episode? First, since the dispute between Britain and Argentina over the Falklands has a long history, there was a requirement for sustained deterrence and the nature of the dispute meant that deterrence would need to be maritime. The problem with sustained deterrence, however, is that its success appears always to reduce the need for the force levels that produced it. Accordingly there is always the temptation to reduce the deterrent force to dangerously low levels. Some recent US naval analysts conclude that the Thatcher government's announced deactivation of nearly a quarter of the Royal Navy's surface combatants, its offer of the carrier, HMS *Invincible* to Australia and, specifically, the decision to withdraw HMS *Endurance* from the area combined to undermine the effectiveness of the deterrent: 'the British government's reduction in spending for force projection and sustainment in the months prior to the Argentine invasion played its part in the failure of deterrence that brought about the conflict in the first place'.[51] Interestingly, this reduction in Britain's capacity to defend the Falklands had not in fact yet taken place by April 1982 when the Argentines invaded. Indeed HMS *Endurance* was still on station sending back despairing warnings to London. The real point was that the Argentine government concluded that Britain lacked not just the means but, more importantly, the *will* to defend the islands. Again, it is not difficult to see why the Argentines may have come to this conclusion for the British had been famously obscure on the matter for years. Worse, in the previous crisis, they had given the impression that they would not respond to quite remarkable provocation.

In February 1976, the Argentine destroyer ARA *Storni* opened fire on a British survey ship, HMS *Shackleton*, 78 miles from Port Stanley. In response the British despatched a secret task force towards the area – a nuclear powered hunter-killer submarine with some supporting surface ships, HMS *Alacrity* and *Phoebe*, which were decently kept 1000 miles away from the scene. But this was an act of 'contingent positioning', which the British did not tell the Argentines about. This approach

> spoke well for British restraint … but argued poorly as a demonstration of British will to the Argentines … Since Argentina was not informed of the submarine's presence in the area, it was neither militarily deterred nor made aware of the potential cost of an invasion. [Thus] the attack on a British vessel and the other hostile measures [that is the seizure and retention of South Sandwich island] were not met with any known British response other than a return to the negotiation table.[52]

Perhaps the main reason for the British failure was an exaggerated view of what naval deterrence in this situation would require. Their foreign secretary took the maximalist line that deterrence required 'demonstrably making an attack unlikely to achieve even initial success'. Maintaining this level of deterrence was naturally considered too onerous and expensive. Argentina was actually extremely anxious to avoid the spilling of blood (lest it antagonise world opinion) and a much lower and more affordable level of deterrence would probably have done the trick.[53]

Against this lamentable background, it was not surprising that British deterrence failed and that events transpired as they did.

The requirements of naval deterrence

Difficult though it is to summarise the requirements of naval deterrence in very varied situations, some broad generalisations drawn from the experience considered earlier, seem possible.

The first principle of successful naval deterrence has to be the criticality of political will and clarity and consistency of aim. Since deterrence is a psychological phenomenon, this often seems to be more important than the actual characteristics of the naval force involved. Clearly, an accurate 'picture' is absolutely essential, but even so one might be up against an adversary who seems either irrational, and so not deterrable, or who is convinced that asymmetric strategies will see him through despite the military odds. And sometimes such an adversary might be right.

The second principle must be to have naval forces with the necessary capacity to poise, strategic mobility and flexibility. Naval forces that could have significant impact on land through air/missile attack or through amphibious assault of some sort seem particularly effective as deterrents. Naval power can sometimes seem out of sight, and so out of mind. The evident capacity to bring that power to the attention of the land-bound adversary therefore helps.

More generally, big, powerful ships do seem to deter better. One example may illustrate this. In the Spanish Civil War, the British sought to prevent interference with British shipping, but their destroyers were not having the desired effect on the Nationalist 8-inch cruiser *Canarias*, until the battlecruiser HMS *Hood* with its 15-inch guns turned up on the scene and transformed perceptions.[54] Radicals urging the distribution of fighting power around more, smaller, cheaper ships will come up against this problem in perception for some time yet. Only when it can be shown that the actual fighting power of such a 'transformed' fleet has delivered on its promises may the large surface ship lose its deterrent glitter.[55]

The issue of the deterrent power of the modern submarine is related to this. The Argentine Navy appears to have been driven back into its ports by the successful attack on ARA *Belgrano* by the nuclear hunter killer submarine HMS *Conqueror*. This shows that the hidden menace of a modern submarine may, in some circumstances, be a very effective 'virtual' deterrent, especially now that submarines may be armed with land-attack missiles. But they still seem more appropriate to the more coercive end of the deterrent spectrum, even though they can these days participate in fleet reviews and it is just about possible to hold cocktail parties aboard them.[56]

The suitability of particular naval forces for deterrence operations is not, however, just a question of their offensive power to deter though punishment. They must also have the defensive power that allows deterrence through denial. The US Navy's 1987 Operation Earnest Will was an example of the way in which deficiencies in this area can undermine deterrent effectiveness. This operation was an attempt to convoy Kuwaiti-bound tankers into the Gulf as a means of deterring Iranian attacks. Security leaks from the US Congress about the convoy's departure time, route coordinates and speed of advance helped the Iranians lay a minefield in the convoy's path. The US Navy's well-known weaknesses in mine clearance led to the unedifying spectacle of the convoy's escorts huddling behind the VLCC

Bridgeton for protection as it went through the minefield. The resultant mine damage to *Bridgeton* (which would probably have been fatal for the escorts) and an escalating conflict with the Iranians, was the inevitable result of this classic failure of deterrence. The situation has been summarised by Nadia El-Shazly like this:

> Four months of preparations, followed by three drill exercises, starting in early July [1987] ended in chaos and embarrassment. The 600 ship navy – the world's most formidable naval power, which amassed a staggering array of potent fire-power and with the most sophisticated equipment in the region – was humiliated by an ancient pre-World War One [1908] mine. This was an example, *par excellence*, of cost-effectiveness on the part of the Iranians.[57]

What this example mainly illustrates is the importance of defensive fighting power on the part of would-be naval deterrent forces. But it also shows that naval deterrence does not necessarily require an armada, provided the deterring party is willing to accept a degree of risk and loss in the pursuit of his aims.

By exploiting such political realities, a weaker party may deter not through denial but through the prospect of inflicting punishment of a political sort. In the so-called Cod Wars between Britain and Iceland, for example, the Icelanders emerged as the winners despite the fact that in every engagement British ships could have blasted their adversaries out of the water with total operational impunity. But in the circumstances prevailing, such action would have been wildly inappropriate. What mattered in this jostling match was, first, the physical strength of the hulls banging into each other in the North Atlantic (and here the tough little Icelandic boats had all the advantages) and, second, the international spectacle of a powerful country seemingly intent on bullying a weak one. By forcing the more powerful to take on the international opprobrium associated with the use of force against the weak, a grossly inferior naval power, can sometimes make use of political possibilities to even the odds against much more powerful forces. An effective naval force of some sort is, however, a prerequisite for this kind of existential deterrence.

10.7 Coalition building

Coalition building is a range of activities expressly intended to secure foreign policy objectives not by threatening potential adversaries but by influencing the behaviour of allies and potentially friendly bystanders. This is just as much a matter of strategy, as defined in Section 2.2, as the more traditional business of coercing adversaries.

In many cases, countries may advance their interests more through influencing the behaviour of their friends, especially if those friends are powerful, than through more menacing activity aimed at adversaries.

An Australian minister recently summarised this aspect of maritime strategy like this:

> As the most mobile of Australia's services, the RAN is well placed to enact a policy of regional engagement. It exercises with most other Asia-Pacific navies and it encourages regional navies to develop capabilities for national defence. In effect, it builds relationships which, in turn, contribute to regional stability and security.[58]

Navies are particularly involved in this kind of thing not just because of their mobility but for a variety of other reasons as well. One of the most obvious is that the sea is a truly international medium that unites, as much as it divides, separated countries and regions. The sheer scale of naval activity around the world means that there are countless navy-to-navy interactions on a daily basis that can be devoted to the improvement of relations with other naval colleagues. The desirability of the maritime consensus building outlined in Section 1.2, and discussed more fully in Section 12.3, was the inspiration for the widely supported American initiative of the 'Global Maritime Partnership', or 'Thousand Ship Navy' concept, as it used to be known.[59]

There is, indeed, a kind of spiritual bond between sailors that perhaps derives from the fact that the medium on which they operate, the sea, is dangerous and poses them all the same risks. Over the centuries, this has resulted in a well-established and relatively universal tradition of rules of the road, behaviour, custom and courtesy. It is a unique operational environment with a developed body of long-established and universal precedent. Whether in chance passing encounters, in informally gathering to watch someone else's exercises or in conscious coming together in response to some humanitarian crisis, there is a spontaneous camaraderie of the sea that can easily be turned to constructive political purpose.[60]

This extends ashore as well, of course. Most sea-going navies devote considerable effort to port visits and interactions with the peoples of other countries. They host thousands of visitors every year, participate in enormous numbers of routine public service projects such as refurbishing schools, digging wells, running medical clinics and so forth. The American notion of 'global fleet stations' discussed later is only a development of a type of naval activity so familiar it hardly attracts comment.

Perhaps because all these activities are so routine, they may not be given the attention they deserve either by sailors or by scholars. The complete academic neglect of the extensive activities of the US Navy around the waters of Latin America for the last 50 years perfectly illustrates this.[61] There may be another reason too, and that is that war-fighting sailors sometimes find this kind of activity an irksome intrusion into their normal professional routines, which they would rather not encourage. It is certainly true that involving other navies, largely for the political sake of it, in one's exercises, and still more in one's equipment procurement projects, complicates operations as we saw in Section 9.3

Aims and types of naval coalition building

Coalitional activities range across a spectrum of intensity. Navy–navy personal contacts in professional gatherings, such as the Western Pacific Naval Symposium (WPNS) or the Organisation for Indian Ocean Marine Affairs Cooperation (IOMARC), are usually the first step in improving relations, followed by simple port visits. These can be tiring yet politically very important. Following on from this, there are exercises with varying degrees of operational aspiration ranging from casual, opportunistic, passing bilateral exercises (PASSEX), to highly organised multinational exercises such as the annual RIMPAC exercises in the Pacific. At the most demanding end of the scale, there are endeavours at institutional integration. These have gone furthest in the NATO area where national units are devoted for long periods of time to standing multilateral naval forces, and come under the direct operational command and control of the officers of other navies. Here, the national identity of the unit should become subsumed by its international mission, and the coalition, theoretically, is all.

The motivation behind such coalitional activity is hugely varied but some of the more common are as follows.

Sending messages

This can be particularly important in circumstances where those relationships have become strained for some reason. In November 1999, the British Type-23 frigate, HMS *Somerset*, joined with an Argentine MEKO corvette, a support vessel, an Orion P3 maritime patrol aircraft and a Hercules aircraft in an exercise near Cape Horn. This imaginative fence-mending initiative was centred on the very common interest of coordinating search and rescue (SAR) skills.

Ship visits can be a useful form of diplomatic exchange, help maintain or secure good relations and win popular favour, provided the sailors ashore spend their money constructively and do not get too drunk, too often. The complex signalling that went on between the Chinese and the Americans in the immediate aftermath of the collision between their aircraft off Hainan in April 2001 shows how non-lethal messages of approval and disapproval can be communicated by subtle requests and responses over which ships were allowed to visit which ports. In the immediate aftermath of the crisis, contacts and pre-arranged ship visits were first of all cancelled or greatly curtailed, then partially revived when, for example, China allowed two small US MCM vessels to visit Hong Kong but refused permission to a larger one, or when Secretary Rumsfeld cut off navy-to-navy personal contacts except for participation in a multilateral symposium on relief operations. The visit of the battlegroup led by USS *Constellation* to Hong Kong in August 2001 showed that relations were getting back to normal.[62]

Reducing the risks of inadvertent conflict

The continual proximity of foreign warships, submarines and planes in the same waterspace can often seem potentially dangerous, leading to accidents and unfortunate incidents. In a more general way, naval arms programmes can lead to unintended tensions. Maritime arms control and confidence building are important aspects of naval diplomacy and coalition building. It is a well-studied phenomenon that need not be deeply analysed here, save from making the point that it *is* a form of strategy in the sense defined in Section 2.2, and that while it is now of little concern between the erstwhile opponents of the Cold War, it is alive and well in the Indian Ocean and the Pacific. Here, despite local cultural inhibitions about discussing such matters in public, sailors are beginning to explain their preparations to others in the hope of showing that they are not intended to be threatening. Both regions are seeing the extension of the 'incidents at sea' network to more pairings of countries.[63]

Naval reassurance

In less happy times, ships' visits and exercises may be intended to reassure threatened countries of support from others. The visit of the US battleship, *Missouri*, to

Turkey in 1946 was a seminal event of this sort, followed by countless visits of reas-surance by the United States to countries that were forward and thereby felt exposed to Soviet pressure, including Norway, Denmark, Turkey, Greece, Japan and South Korea. Nor is this kind of thing in any way new. Thus one British Foreign Office official of 1919:

> I have been credibly informed ... that the arrival of HMS battlecruiser *New Zealand* in the middle of December to convey the Queen of Norway and crown prince Olaf to England created a profound impression in Bergen, especially amongst the working classes and the socialists. This visit ... brought home to every Norwegian the fact that Great Britain continued to take the warmest interest in Norway. I venture to state the considered opinion that the dispatch of this fine cruiser to fetch her Majesty was entirely justifiable and advisable not only from the dynastic point of view, but more especially from that of British interests.[64]

Improving future coordination efficiency

Mahan pointed out the particular problems of allied fleets in dealing with unitary ones[65] but sailors increasingly accept that for resource reasons and in order to share risk, their activities are increasingly likely to be multilateral. For this reason, it behoves them to find out how others do things. Improving interoperability is there-fore a major incentive for many bilateral and multilateral exercises. It is certainly the guiding principle behind, for example, the US Navy's cooperative afloat readi-ness and training (CARAT) bilateral exercises with Brunei, Indonesia, Malaysia, Singapore and Thailand.

NATO provides the most sophisticated examples of maritime coalition opera-tions with standing forces, such as those in the Atlantic and Mediterranean and with specialist minewarfare and amphibious groupings. These are regarded as 'an essen-tial element of NATO's maritime defence diplomacy effort, highlighting force unity and developing friendships between ships and bonds between nations'.[66] This level of integrated collaboration is exemplified in mixed command structure and doctrine, innumerable exercises and has been buttressed and refined in operational experience especially in the Adriatic. The attachment of individual ships or foreign formations for long operations are increasingly common, being much aided by the widespread adoption of NATO Extac procedures, now available on the internet. Cross training at staff colleges and so forth obviously increases mutual understand-ing and the capacity to work together, and to build coalitions between NATO members and others.

Even so, difficulties will remain. Some are technological; many observers worry about differing levels of equipment creating real problems of coordination in a 'netted' environment. Others argue that it is often possible to find compensating ways 'to plug and play'. Instead, the real problem lies in what the French call the 'interoperability of the mind', where cultural/political differences make for different approaches in:

- readiness to accept command from officers of foreign navies;
- propensity to call home, whatever the command arrangements, when something

unexpected comes up on the plot and commanders fear they might need to deal with something that their political masters find sensitive;

- willingness to delegate command authority downwards.

For both reasons the requirement to improve interoperability is likely to remain constant:

> We must, collectively, continue to believe that there are always new ways to operate and exercise together; that there are always new forms of dialogue, and that there are always new tools and solutions that the largest *and* the smallest navies bring to the table.[67]

That the Americans and the Europeans continue to find such close levels of integrated collaboration challenging suggests that NATO-style arrangements cannot simply be imported into other areas and applied. In the Gulf, Indian Ocean and Pacific regions, nations are on their own in a security sense, to a degree that the Europeans have almost forgotten about. In this, as in other areas, naval diplomacy has to conform to political realities as well as influence them.

Common acts against common threats

Kicking off Exercise Malphi-Laut 4/2001, Admiral Ruben Domingo of the Philippines Navy, remarked 'We need to maintain and enhance our existing defense cooperation specially in the face of existing threats from terrorists, pirates and other lawless elements in our common border', and so it was necessary for the Malay and Philippine navies to become familiar with each other's equipment, organisational procedures and operational approach in order to respond more quickly and efficiently to emergencies, ship accidents and acts of cross-border crime.[68] As a bonus, such activity can hardly fail to improve general relationships between countries cooperating for these specific purposes.

In defence of arms sales

Not all navies can or chose to do this. The US Navy does not engage in it but many European navies do and have governmental organisations specifically designed to foster this activity. Warships, being relatively sophisticated systems, have always been regarded as a means of displaying technological prowess to others.

Requirements and conclusions

Because coalition operations cover such a wide spectrum, it is hard to come to conclusions about their effectiveness, especially in the long term. They certainly seem to work best when they are part of an overall package of other diplomatic, military and economic measures. That hard-pressed treasuries and navies around the world have so extensively paid for and participated in such activities, presumably suggests a widespread conclusion that they are worthwhile.

But it is equally difficult to make many generalisations about ships or approaches that may be good for coalitional operations. Big powerful ships offer commanders a wide range of capabilities and give them operational flexibility in planning and con-ducting exercises. Small ships, on the other hand, may be better suited for opera-tions with small and modest navies. Manifestly, operational efficiency makes for effective coalition building. Mistakes happen and can be politically costly. The inad-vertent sinking of a Japanese fishing boat by a US submarine, or the shooting down of an American A6-E Intruder aircraft by a Japanese destroyer in a RIMPAC exer-cise or the embarrassment caused by the suspected pipe fracture in the British sub-marine HMS *Tireless* in Gibraltar, are all examples of the way in which naval activity can hinder diplomacy rather than help it.[69]

One thing at least is clear, and that is that coalition building is by no means restricted to large bluewater navies, indeed the problems that some of these have had with visits by nuclear propelled or nuclear armed vessels suggests that in this type of naval diplomacy at least, one can be too powerful.[70]

10.8 Naval diplomacy: implications for strategy makers

On the need to think

Naval diplomacy is thus a relatively new phrase covering maritime activity on a spectrum without discontinuities, which ranges from limited compellent military attack at one extreme, through deterrence, to thoroughly amicable cooperation at the other. The aim is to influence the behaviour of other people. Although, in naval diplomacy, power is exploited rather than force expended, particular occasions may be thought to warrant physical, even lethal action. Naval diplomacy can have as wide a range of purposes and effects as any other instrument of diplomacy. Naval diplomacy, like the alternatives, will sometimes succeed and sometimes fail.

It can be used in many ways to convey messages and influence events. The sending of a dominant force, likely to prevail, will whittle away the adversary's options, demonstrate commitment and may make the desired outcome more likely. A weak force, on the other hand, may be interposed between two competing parties to cool a situation. Forces can be left uncommitted or even sent in the opposite direction to indicate a determination not to get involved. The fact that the more dra-matic and coercive manifestations of naval diplomacy command the attention should not conceal its many other roles.

These qualities are in increasing demand because the prevention of war and con-flict remains the prime task of navies and the costs of failure could be horrendous. These have discouraged the tendency to resort to wars (or at least full-scale ones) as a means of settling international disputes. This does not, of course, mean that the disputes themselves have gone away, but merely that countries prefer other ways of sorting them out.

By providing a means by which diplomats can respond to the burgeoning chal-lenges of the post Cold War world, navies seem to offer states a wide range of diplo-matic instruments to use in normal peacetime, in times of strain and in times of crisis.

So, to revert to the Shakespearean quotation used at the start of this chapter, how should navies 'prepare for this design' of diplomatic activity?

Naval diplomacy: some initial observations

The following tentative observations need to be borne in mind by those who wish to practice naval diplomacy.

Success is hard to prove

One of the main difficulties is in the business of measuring success and, if some exercise in naval diplomacy *has* been deemed a success, what has made it so? This problem has been widely recognised. James Cable has talked about the need to 'produce reasonably reliable evidence that the naval force achieved the political objectives of the government employing it. The results must also last long enough to seem worth the cost of achieving them.'[71] But how are these answers to be agreed? His is the classic method of objective historical enquiry long enough after the event for the dust to have settled. Another recent attempt at 'operationalising' success, in the Gulf region at least, has been to plot its consequences for oil or stock market prices (on the assumption that stable prices are best for everyone). The assumption is that successful naval diplomacy will contribute to price stability. The big attraction of this approach is that it offers navalists the ultimate hope of actually proving to Treasury sceptics that naval diplomacy may be a paying proposition – with financial benefits outweighing the costs of the operation. But for the time being, this approach seems to beg more questions than it answers.[72] More thought is still needed.

Naval diplomacy is only part of the package

Naval diplomacy is rarely decisive on its own. Naval force may, in many cases, be an indispensable part of the overall diplomatic package but often other parts of the package will prove more important in the long run. This was why Admiral Beatty, that great exponent of the Royal Navy, was so sceptical of the use of naval diplomacy against the Soviets in the 1920s:

> We have now presented Soviet Russia with an ultimatum ... We have now no men and no money. We have ships, but what can they do against a Power that is without Sea Forces. Blockade, yes, but that amounts to nothing. We can send ships, big ships, into the Baltic to obtain moral effect – but will that accomplish anything?[73]

Too much should not be expected of navies in the diplomatic mode, however good at it they might be.

Naval diplomacy is no better than the policy it serves

The effectiveness of naval diplomacy can be undermined by deficiencies in political aim. According to John Lehman, for example, a confused political aim and inappropriate ROEs contributed much to the tribulations of the US Navy and Marine Corps off the Lebanon in the 1980s. It felt its defences against asymmetric attack were inadequate, especially in the aftermath of the bombing of the US Marines ashore, and its responses to threats ashore were counterproductively weak.[74] However efficient the naval force may be in operational terms, its efforts can be rendered ineffective by policy failures higher up.

There are naval costs to manage

Inherent contradictions between the requirements of naval diplomacy and warfighting often appear; however policy makers reluctant to make choices would wish them not to. Thus, in 1973, the US Sixth Fleet was torn between the political attractions of dividing the fleet for a programme of port visits around the Mediterranean on the one hand, and keeping it concentrated for war readiness on the other.[75] Thus, coalition building may require a warship to engage in a series of single-ship port visits, which imply skill fade in those higher intensity disciplines that are best rehearsed in company. Such tensions may need to be recognised and managed, by something of a shift in emphasis away from a preoccupation with the requirements of general war towards a greater emphasis on the requirements of lower-order missions.

What naval diplomacy needs

Naval diplomacy is invariably conducted by ships designed for something else. This is because the wide range of the activities it incorporates means that ships cannot be constructed for this function in the same way that they can for something specific like mine or anti-submarine warfare. Ships expressly designed for coalition building (with provision made for large cocktail lounges, for example) would not necessarily be suited for the rest of the range of tasks this mission comprises. Nonetheless, the force planner should be able to plot a matrix of task, fleet and platform requirements at least in general terms. The overall needs of the task should influence the size and structure of the fleet and its platform constituents.

In generic terms, the naval diplomacy task requires:

- *An accurate picture*. Hence, again, the urgency of the need for effective maritime domain awareness.
- *Offensive and defensive power* both sufficient for and appropriate to the task. These two qualities are more complex than they might seem. On the one hand, the force has to avoid having inappropriate strength: if shots may need to be fired either across bows or in salute, platforms armed only with missiles or torpedoes obviously will not do. On the other hand, the force must conjure up the right perceptions. Since the cruiser HMS *Mauritius* was airily dismissed by Persia's Hussain Makki in the 1951 Abadan crisis with the wounding comment that 'The British cannot frighten us with that matchbox',[76] it clearly failed in this respect. In some circumstances, sending in forces too weak for the job, or too weakly used, could make the situation even worse.
- *Force tailored to the circumstance*. Thus naval diplomacy in the waters of nineteenth-century China required not 'Line of Battle ships [which] are not adapted to the Chinese coasts', but light-draught gunboats that could carry, support, supply and withdraw troops, take on forts and impress with a generally imposing air, '32 pounders … [being] … more efficacious than other arguments'. They

needed to be commanded by men who knew the political realities of their station, who could navigate skilfully and cope with severe winters, 'muddy and shallow waters, full of unseen dangers, violent tides, eddies and ripplings'.[77]

- *A speedy response.* Preventing problems is usually more effective than curing them, and speedy responses may help nip troubles in the bud. This is the principle behind the French *aviso* concept. Investing in an additional class of cheaper combatants might provide the greater number that facilitates a speedy response. Were it not for the increased maintenance and crew costs involved, keeping old first-line ships for longer periods would serve the same purpose.

- *Controllability.* Naval forces can slip out of the tight control needed to ensure they accomplish political aims either if they are too vulnerable (the attack on the USS *Stark*) or, perhaps because of this, they are too aggressively defensive (the USS *Vincennes*'s shooting down of an Iranian airbus). Failures of either kind limit the controllability and therefore the diplomatic utility of naval forces.

- *A conformable media.* Because naval diplomacy is so much a matter of perception, the media are peculiarly important to its success. Unsympathetic or insensitive reporting increases the prospects of failure. Because of the effect of the media this is a world in which the weak can often bully the strong. To guard against this, media requirements (accommodation, briefings, access sometimes to communications, protection) may therefore need to be factored into the naval force equation. Managing the media is a crucial operational skill.

A few implications for the size and nature of the fleet emerge from this broad list of generic task requirements. The US Navy's Admiral Jay Johnson drew one clear conclusion:

> One thing that the past few years has taught us is that we must pay greater attention to a wide range of 'peacetime' operations. To be effective in keeping the peace, deterring aggression, and maintaining stability, we must sustain the capability to act decisively across that entire spectrum – and not just in hi-tec … operations.[78]

This means that the fleet needs to provide a wide variety of force packages tailored for specific missions. If the mission is to exercise in coalition with small navies, small units may be more acceptable than large, over-capable ones. If there is an expectation of escalation, those same large, capable forces may, however, be exactly what is required. If the mission, on the other hand, is likely to turn humanitarian, ships with extensive room for stores, medical facilities, large-scale electricity generation or water production facilities may be at a premium. Moreover the same activity may require very different forces when dealing with different adversaries and different areas. Maritime deterrence against the Chinese over Taiwan obviously requires different forces from those required for the deterrence of the West Side Boys in Sierra Leone.

It may well be that for most navies, and in fact arguably all, this bewildering range of requirements is simply too much for single national naval budgets to cope with, especially up the coercive end of the scale and dealing with serious adversaries. Here, navies are increasingly likely to operate with others in multinational forces. These are a way of sharing risk and multiplying resources, but they bring with them extra demands in terms of interoperability, effective command and control facilities and so forth.

And, last, what of the individual platform itself? Although naval diplomacy is not something for which ships can be specifically designed, balances will surely need to be struck between the following:

- *Versatility in the individual platform.* The greater the flexibility of the unit, the more contingencies it will be able to cope with.
- *Defence and offence.* All units and formations must be able to look after themselves, but in a way that does not undermine the mission. Vulnerability sometimes drives naval commanders to ask for permissive rules of engagement based on the notion of 'anticipatory self-defence' (i.e. attacking someone else is justified if he is believed to be on the point of attacking you). However understandable this may be, it reduces the controllability, and therefore the diplomatic value, of naval forces, especially in the kind of crisis when a delicacy of touch is most needed. Sinking all possible threats on sight in order to avoid the fate of the USS *Pueblo*, *Stark* or *Cole* often leads to diplomatic failure. On the other hand, the capacity to handle possible escalating threats (such as the deterrence of possible interference by Indonesian submarines during the East Timor operation) is clearly necessary.
- *Cost and capability.* A similar balance needs to be struck over platform cost. To be effective against a wide range of possible threats, individual units need to be capable, and this means they will be expensive. But to be reliably present they also need to be affordable.
- *Single and group deployments.* Skill fade in those disciplines that are best rehearsed in company is a problem for ships on single deployments. While increasing the means of simulation on board may be a palliative, ships in company seem better able to prepare for the range of activities required of them under the naval diplomacy mission.
- *Prepared personnel.* Platforms and formations will require educated and prepared personnel who understand the mission, can robustly identify its military needs to the political authorities, can secure workable and appropriate ROEs and can then be trusted to operate effectively within their political constraints.

All of this seems to support the widespread conclusion reached by navies around the world that the naval diplomacy mission works best through navies endowed with as much general war-fighting excellence as can be afforded. While there may need to be a shift of emphasis from the higher to the lower intensity missions, where there are significant differences between the two, the capacity to operate effectively in the most hazardous situation usually increases prospects for success in the most probable. The simple fact that the reverse is not true should guard against the danger of going too far down the reductionist road.

Nonetheless, this should not be an excuse for not taking the naval diplomacy mission seriously. Naval diplomacy does not come naturally. The range of activities contained within this function and their often very demanding nature, makes it unwise to rely on improvisation. As with any other naval mission, naval diplomacy needs thinking about and preparing for. Nonetheless, there was much in Stansfield Turner's comment:

I think that we who exercise naval presence do not know enough about how to fit the action to the situation: how to be sure that the force we bring to bear, when told to help in some situation, is in fact the one most appropriate to the circumstances.[79]

Twenty years later, it is still possible to encounter the complaint that 'the profession as a whole does not value presence as an important military task, demanding the same expertise and careful study as strike warfare or anti-air warfare'.[80] In today's world, naval diplomacy has a crucial role to play because as a means of 'engagement' it can materially help shape the international environment, and contain, resolve or prevent conflict. But to make the most of this, navies and foreign ministries need to develop a strategic approach to naval diplomacy, designed to integrate it effectively with all other relevant aspects of a country's security policy. An engagement policy in a particular theatre might seek to establish a conscious ship-visit programme, for example, that would identify who should be visited (allies, wary bystanders or the frankly hostile?), why, to do what and with what. For their part, navies need to develop a rigorous way of thinking about naval diplomacy (perhaps even a doctrine?) and reflect the importance of the mission in their budgetary and force structure decisions.[81]

11 Maintaining good order at sea

11.1 Introduction: good order and maritime security

Back in Chapter 1, it was argued that the sea's past and continuing contribution to human development could be boiled down to the four main attributes, or ways in which it has been used, namely:

- for the resources it contained;
- for its utility as a means of transportation and trade;
- for its importance as a means of exchanging information;
- as a source of power and dominion.

These attributes are obviously interlinked and interdependent.

The focus of much of this book has been on the last of the four values, on the traditional way in which the sea has been used to foster, maintain or contest political power, in the interests of what is, these days, sometimes called 'hard' security.

This chapter, however, will try to restore the balance by looking more at the area of 'soft' security and focusing mainly, but not exclusively, on the other three historic values of the sea. It will argue that each is at least as important as ever it was, and that each faces a range of risks and threats that threaten the good order on which their continued contribution to human development depends and which navies can help manage.

The importance of this 'good order', and the corresponding threats of disorder, are such that navies around the world are focusing much more on their role in helping to preserve it. So much so, in fact, that a new phrase 'maritime security operations' has become fashionable. The Royal Navy defines these as: 'Actions performed by military units in partnership with other government departments, agencies and international partners in the maritime environment to counter illegal activity and support freedom of the seas, in order to protect national and international interests.'[1] Many navies implicitly divide maritime security into a 'home' game and an 'away' game. This recognises the global indivisibility of good order at sea. The 'away' game is seen as a matter of extending homeland defences forwards in order to intercept problems before they arrive home and to gain time for adequate responses and counters, and to do so as part of an integrated global strategy with other navies and coast guards.

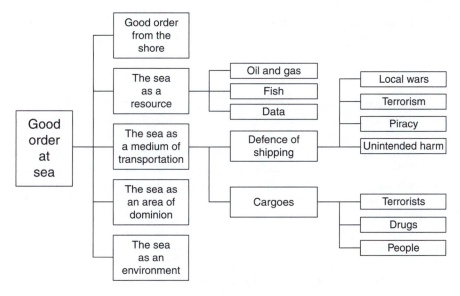

Figure 11.1 The attributes of the sea.

11.2 The sea as a resource

For thousands of years, the sea has been a bounteous source of all manner of resources, living and non-living, and a major contributor to human development. Navies and other maritime forces have been increasingly involved in defence of this activity, and everything suggests that these responsibilities will expand in the future.

Oil and gas

One-third of the world's petroleum reserves are at sea, and these are likely to be of increasing commercial interest as land sources become depleted. Moreover, exploitation of these resources is steadily being conducted in deeper and deeper waters, currently reaching 10,000 feet in some cases. Oil and gas resources also need to be defended against all manner of intentional and unintentional harm. Here, too, the focus of concern is on such disputed areas as the Caspian and South China Seas where there have been small-scale clashes and confrontations at sea between the navies of the disputing parties.

With the growth of the offshore oil and gas industry, there has arisen an interest in its military utility and its defence. Mainly this is regarded as a matter of controlling the area in which the rigs and platforms are situated. The possibility of terrorist attack, however, has led some countries to develop special forces of one sort or another for the task of getting to trouble spots quickly and dealing with such threats. In both the Gulf wars of the 1980s and 1991 there were naval clashes on and around oil rigs. More recently, defending Iraq's crucial oil revenues from the depredations of oil smugglers and from insurgent attacks on its two main oil rigs, has been a major preoccupation of allied navies operating in the Gulf.

Fish and other living marine resources

> Ha, come and bring away the nets...
> Nay then, thou will starve sure: for here's nothing to be got nowadays, unless
> thou canst fish for it.
>
> Shakespeare, *Pericles*, II/1

The world commercial fishing catch has more than quadrupled since 1950. The demand for edible fish produce is likely to rise from 80 million tons now to 115 million tons by 2015 as the population grows. But, in 1990, the world's fish catch actually fell and, in 1994, a World Bank study warned that 'the current harvesting capacity of the world's fleet far exceeds the estimated biological sustainability of most commercial species'.[2] Already, most world fishing grounds are under severe pressure, and many local fishing communities around the world are further threatened by the advent of highly mechanised distant-water fishing fleets from elsewhere, which have moved into new fishing grounds, because they have exhausted their own. European Union fishing boats operating off the coast of Senegal, Mauretania and other parts of West Africa are a typical example. Here, as elsewhere, licences are often granted by struggling Third World governments desperate for immediate capital with inadequate means of supervising the activities they have allowed offshore. In effect, they feel they have to mortgage their future for the sake of the present.[3]

The basic reason for the crisis in fish supply is not pollution, as is often said, but a simple matter of taking fish at a faster rate than can be naturally replaced. Partly, this is a matter of a refusal to lower fish-takes to sustainable levels, and partly of irresponsible methods (taking fish before they reach the age of reproduction, violating agreed limits by landing illegal 'black' fish, unwillingness to switch to alternate and less vulnerable species). Pollution, of course, aggravates the problem. In the Gulf of Thailand, climate change, the destruction of spawning grounds and habitats through coastal development and land- and sea-based pollution have all increased the extreme vulnerability of local fishing stocks.

Even in areas (such as the European Union) where there are high degrees of political consensus, agreeing a way out of the crisis is extremely difficult, but when political enmity is added to the mixture, resolution of the fishing problem becomes highly problematic. Examples of this include the regular fishing clashes between India and Pakistan, the two Koreas, and the uneasy triangle of Japan, Russia and the two Koreas. In the civilised days of the so-called 'Cod Wars' between Britain and Iceland, rivalry was limited to some aggressive seamanship, and of British fishermen broadcasting spirited renditions of 'Rule Britannia' and throwing potatoes at the Icelandic vessels seeking to drive them off. Nowadays, all too often, such disputes are a matter of rocket propelled grenades and heavy machine guns.

This is particularly evident in the Asia-Pacific where the imbalance between supply and demand is severe, since one billion of its people depend on fish as the main source of their protein. In such circumstances, competition for dwindling resources may easily spill over into conflict. During the 1990s, lethal force was used and people were killed in at least ten fishing disputes. Although there remain tricky differences of national opinion virtually everywhere, the really serious contentions are in the Gulf of Thailand, the South China Sea and the Sea of Okhotsk.

In theory, the solution to the problem is easy enough, being a matter of:

- Accepting that a crisis exists before it is too late to do anything about it. The total collapse of the fish population of the Grand Banks and its ominous failure to recover, despite a complete cessation of fishing, has made people realise how serious the general situation is.
- Agreeing sustainable fish-takes, sensible measures of conservation and regulation, together with a general reduction in the future size of fishing fleets.

In practice, of course, this is extremely difficult politically and means that before such agreements can be reached, navies and/or coast guards have to protect both 'their' fish populations and their local fishermen.

In many situations, naval forces become involved in the supervision of national fishing grounds, protecting them against both irresponsible locals and intruding foreign poachers. Even this can be difficult and dangerous, frequently involving the risk of collision and potentially lethal force, especially in the waters around South East Asia.[4] Less dramatically, it can involve some very long chases indeed. Perhaps the record is the epic pursuit of the Togo-registered fishing boat *South Tomi* detected illegally fishing for Patagonian toothfish in Australian waters and followed all the way across the Indian Ocean to South Africa where it was finally apprehended by Royal Australian Naval personnel with the cooperation of the South Africans. It was indeed the 'one that didn't get away'.[5] But, of course, few protecting navies or coast guards have the equipment, time, resources, professionalism and maybe inclination to do this kind of thing.

Less often, fishing quarrels lead to navies becoming involved in shooting matches against each other. The famed blue crab, together with disputed jurisdictions in the Yellow Sea, led to bloody clashes between the North and South Korean Navies in the June of both 1999 and 2002 in which warships were sunk and sailors killed and wounded.[6] On the one hand, clashes such as these and those that have occurred in the South China Sea enormously complicate the regulation of fishing and so threaten the long-term viability of the whole area. On the other hand, intense local competition for the fish exacerbates such political disputes and sometimes even seems to set their pace.

Although in most cases, the supervision of the fisheries is largely a constabulary matter for navies and coast guards, it may sometimes nonetheless escalate to limited war-fighting. Fishing interacts with other forms of sea use and demands, for many navies, a major effort in terms of the proportion of their ships and sailors needing to be deployed on the task.

Less obviously, the crisis in world fishing is tending to encourage the extension of jurisdiction even over the high seas because fish so often straddle national jurisdictions. The so-called 'Turbot War' of 1995 between Spain and Canada on the Grand Banks off Newfoundland is an example. Even though this was beyond Canada's EEZ, the Canadian Navy felt that marine conservation justified it seizing a Spanish trawler, the *Estai*, fishing there in defiance of a local agreement that the area should be allowed to recover from former depredations. This was an interesting indication of the extent to which jurisdiction is slowly being extended to the high seas.[7]

11.3 The sea as a means of transportation

The sea's value as a means of transportation is a particularly complicated and wide-ranging topic. Because all countries benefit to a greater or lesser extent from the free flow of world trade, global security and prosperity remain absolutely dependent on maritime transportation. Indeed, sea-based trade is likely to expand considerably over the next 30 years, possibly tripling in fact.

Sea-based trade faces many risks, and these also threaten the international order of which it is so important a part. Naval forces, customs and coast guards seek, in peacetime, to control those threats to good order at sea that might put it at risk. In some cases what ships carry may pose a threat to good order. But before considering that, this chapter will look first at the safety of the ships themselves.

Some of the threats that ships face are intentional, some are not. Intentional threats may include cyber attacks on the electronic communication systems that increasingly lubricate the shipping system, and land-bound disruption of ports of despatch and receipt. Restrictive legislation (for environmental or jurisdictional reasons) on rights of passage through straits and narrow seas could also be represented as a worrying constraint on the freedom of navigation. Moreover, the prevalence today of a 'just-enough-just-in-time' operating philosophy makes the modern shipping system much more fragile and less resilient than once it was. Higher value cargoes are now concentrated in fewer hulls. But, so far, the main intended threats to international shipping have been its inadvertent involvement in other people's quarrels and the effects of modern-day piracy.

Deliberate threats to shipping

The effects of local wars

Neutral merchant shipping has always been at risk in war zones. In the so-called tanker war of 1981–1988, both Iraq and Iran chose to attack and harass international shipping as a means of influencing the policies of the great powers. Some 450 merchant ships belonging to 32 countries were attacked and 471 merchant seamen were killed. Iraq relied on air attacks and Iran on mines and shelling.[8]

Although the tanker war of the 1980s is the most obvious example of this type of intended threat, it is far from being the only one. Merchant ships in the vicinity of the Arab–Israeli, Indo-Pakistan and Vietnam wars were vulnerable to attack. More recently, the United States has made it clear that while it takes no stand on jurisdictional quarrels over the South China Sea, it will not tolerate any consequential disruption of the sea traffic passing through the area. It is possible to imagine smaller-scale contingencies of the sort elsewhere in the Asia-Pacific too, in the troubled waters around Indonesia or through some confrontation between hostile neighbours (the two Koreas, the PRC and Taiwan).

The protection of shipping in this kind of situation against this kind of intended harm is a familiar and apparently continuing requirement.

Moreover, shipping is now but a part of a complex intermodal goods distribution shipping, involving ports, railways and roads in which the essential unit is increasingly the container being transported by a variety of means. It may well turn out to be much easier to disrupt this system by threatening the port or its approaches, or launching a cyber attack on the computerised logistics system that keeps the process going, rather than seeking to threaten the container ship on passage. Responses to this would seem more a matter of port security and modern shore-side policing.

Terrorism

Protecting shipping against terrorists, on the other hand, is a relatively new requirement, brought into high relief by the attack on the French tanker, the *Limburg*, off Aden in October 2002.[9] Ships passing through the Indonesian and Philippine archipelagos in recent years have likewise been harassed and attacked by terrorists from Aceh separatists and the Abu Sayef terrorist group, respectively. ETA terrorists have sought to blow up ferries in Spanish ports and Indian shipping has been attacked by the naval wing of the TTE, the Tamil Tigers organisation. For all that, these attacks have been relatively few. In 2004, for instance, of the 651 terrorist actions worldwide plotted by the (US) National Counterterrorism Center, only two took place at sea. Instead attention is increasingly being paid to the security of ports, their approaches and facilities against terrorist attack. Hence, the widespread international effort that led to important amendments to the Safety of Life at Sea (SOLAS) and Suppression of Unlawful Acts (SUA) conventions and the introduction of the International Ship and Port Facility Security Code (ISPS Code) in 2004.[10]

Piracy

> ... and I must
> Rid all the sea of pirates.
>
> Shakespeare, *Anthony and Cleopatra*, II/6

Modern-day piracy threatens the security of some of the world's most important sea lines of communication, restricts the free and orderly passage of the maritime commerce that underpins the current world order, raises insurance rates, increases local tensions and puts people's lives at risk. Although most authorities consider piracy (however tragic for the victims) more as a nuisance than a systemic threat to world trade, it both reflects and increases local instabilities. In addition to the economic consequences of piracy, the potential for environmental catastrophe is immense. In 1991, for instance, the tanker *Eastern Power* was boarded and taken over by pirates in the Philip Channel off Singapore. The crew were robbed, tied up and the pirates departed. For 20 minutes this 275,000-ton tanker, fully loaded with oil, steamed through these narrow and congested waters completely unmanned, until some of the crew managed to free themselves. There have been other instances of this sort of thing. Moreover, criminal attacks on shipping have grown both in number and in the level of violence employed. The ungoverned waters off Somalia are a major current focus of concern.[11]

Strictly, piracy only relates to such acts in waters outside the jurisdiction of any state. Attacks within territorial seas are more properly described as 'sea robberies' – and in fact the great majority of such attacks take place in or near ports. This means that there are immense jurisdictional problems in dealing with them, because different countries have different regulations and approaches towards the problem. Effective responses become especially difficult when people in powerful states, sensitive about their jurisdictions, are suspected of implication in the attacks themselves. In the 1990s, many believed this applied to some Chinese authorities, a matter that came to a head in April 1998 with the infamous *Petro-Ranger* affair when a large tanker was seized by pirates, but later turned up in a Chinese port with a new name, a new crew and no cargo. To the dismay of the Australians and the Malaysians, the Chinese refused to prosecute, and for a long time kept the ship. Moreover, the fact that shipping is now a completely globalised business much affected by small countries in no position to protect the ships flying their flags, makes a coordinated response necessary, but very difficult.[12]

Naval responses to attacks on shipping

While piracy and maritime terrorism can often be attacked by normal onshore police work, naval responses to these threats to shipping are important.

Because so much of the world's oil came through the Gulf in the 1980s, President Reagan spoke for many when he concluded that 'Neither we nor the Western world as such would stand by and see the straits of the Persian gulf closed to international traffic.'[13] The result was the biggest exercise in shipping protection since the end of the Second World War involving at its height some 60 Western warships and 29 Soviet ones.

There were some obvious operational difficulties that were responsible for the mistakes described in Section 10.6. The protecting powers were not belligerents and so were always *reacting* to events. The operational environment was difficult. The Gulf was narrow and confined, with ships surrounded by a host of land-based threats. The water was shallow, ideal for mining; sandstorms, humidity and hot temperatures were a continuing problem, and the waterways were thick with air and sea traffic in all directions. The protective powers, the Americans, Russians and Europeans, were far from agreed on aims and methods. The most that could be achieved, even for the Europeans, was 'concertation' – namely, that protecting naval forces would be doing much the same thing in much the same area and with a degree of consultation. Finally, they were facing, especially from Iran, a variety of asymmetric threats:

> The scourge of America's high-tech Navy is a weapon system stunning in its simplicity: high explosive mines so rudimentary they could be made in a garage, planted from teak-hulled boats of a design so ancient that Marco Polo marvelled they could sail at all. Meanwhile the Americans are geared for Star Wars.[14]

Many of the methods adopted were similar to those adopted in the conventional defence of shipping campaigns discussed in Chapter 8, qualified only by the essential fact that these navies were not at war. Through the ages, the fundamental principle has been that assured sea control is the best means of protecting shipping (or indeed of attacking it). But, since the protecting navies were not belligerents, this took the form of maintaining a strong and effective naval force capable of defending the freedom of navigation in the area through general deterrence. Since only between 1 and 2 per cent of the shipping using the Gulf was actually attacked, this seems to have been reasonably successful.

But this general policy did sometimes require quite robust rules of engagement allowing, for example, the US Navy to attack the *Iran Ijr* in September 1987 for laying mines. American and other warships escorted tankers that were sometimes especially flagged for the purpose. The Royal Navy's Armilla patrol conducted by far the most extensive operation of this sort, 'acompanying' 1026 British-owned ships through the Straits up to November 1988.[15] The French were prepared to extend their protection to any merchant ship in danger. All warships, of course, stood by to offer humanitarian assistance to any ship that was attacked, whatever its flag.

Different navies and coast guards have different procedures for dealing with pirates. Naval vessels have a right, and, some would argue, duty to arrest and punish pirates on the high seas – but many don't. By national law, a US warship is only entitled to intercept pirated ships if they have cause to believe life is at risk; Australians warships can intercept and may feel able to do so in the territorial seas of other countries if, under the SOLAS convention, they believe safety is at risk; they may not, however, arrest the pirates or protect property. The expectation that prosecution of pirates caught at sea becomes the responsibility of the warship that seized them is a major disincentive to decisive action, since this could ruin an exercise or visits programme. The fact that protocols vary so widely much complicates international responses to piracy.

Even so, there is a need for:

- Coordinated and enhanced picture building. Information needs either to be gained by technological means, such as the use of UAVs,[16] or by the fitting of transponders to merchant ships, thereby continuously providing details of their position, course, cargo and general state – and then, critically, shared. Often owners only hear of a piratical attack four or five days after the event. Singapore's introduction of a 'vessel traffic information system' demonstrates acceptance of the fact that shipping needs to be more closely monitored. One modern suggestion is that merchant ships should be treated like airliners, and so are handed from one 'sea traffic controller' to another. This explains the considerable increase in the importance now attached by most navies to improving maritime domain awareness, with an emphasis on the information-sharing procedures characteristic, for example, of NATO's Operation Active Endeavour in the Mediterranean.[17]
- Jurisdictional accommodations and harmonised regulations and procedures obviously help.
- Combined action. In the 1990s, the Japanese repeatedly urged that the coast guards of South Eastern Asian countries join with others to maintain patrols. The idea of Japanese warships of whatever sort operating in this area is but one example of the political sensitivity of such proposals.[18] The Indonesian–Singaporean model of coordinated anti-piracy patrols in which warships keep in touch and hand over responsibility when the merchant ship crosses lines of jurisdiction, is a more modest example of what can be achieved by such means
- Naval capabilities. Chinese/Japanese coast guard cooperation in the East China Sea was much reinforced by the independent patrols of Russian Navy warships in 1993. The deterrent effect of this system significantly reduced the incidence of piratical acts in the area. But, such patrols require support from helicopter and maritime patrol aircraft, sustainability and, if the warships are coming from elsewhere, sufficient *roulement* to provide the necessary numbers. The ships

themselves need to be fast and sufficiently armed, guns generally being more useful than missiles. Armed soldiers or sailors skilled in rapid-roping and other boarding techniques will often also be needed. Warships on such duties also need appropriately ROEs.

Unintended threats to shipping: the naval response

The mundane need to protect shipping against accident and other forms of unintended disruption is important too. The world's seas and straits are ever busier, often with much larger and more valuable ships. In European waters, as elsewhere, there is a continuing trend towards increasing regulation of sea traffic for safety and environmental reasons, with the adoption of traffic separation schemes, more intrusive inspection regimes for seaworthiness, collision avoidance regulations and so forth. While such arrangements have gone farthest in Europe, the tendency towards them is global.

But all this costs money and requires effort. For this reason, while countries have generally been eager to secure their rights under UNCLOS, they have sometimes been less keen to assume the responsibilities that go with them.[19] Progress has been slower than many would wish. The notion, in particular, that market forces can be relied on to produce the necessary improvements and thus make decisive political action less necessary, bears some of the blame for this.

Protecting shipping against accidental harm is not a principal focus for warships but they are likely to become increasingly involved in the process, especially if/when shipping regulations are applied to them. At the moment, warships:

- regularly engage in search and rescue missions and contribute towards the coordination of international effort at the tactical, operational and strategic levels;
- are the main means of dealing with the physical consequences of past wars – especially in the detection and elimination of sea mines in the Mediterranean and the Gulf. Similarly, NATO navies came together to clear up the ordnance dropped in the Adriatic by aircraft returning from Bosnia. The exercise in which 16 Asia-Pacific navies came together in 2001 for large-scale mine clearance exercises off Singapore, is another example.

One additional benefit of such arrangements is that not only do they contribute to safety at sea, they also improve international relations, since they encourage cooperation against common threats and risks.[20]

Threatening cargoes

What ships carry may itself threaten national, regional or global security, in a variety of ways. Governments view with hostility cargoes that threaten the values they represent. In 2001, the passage of the Dutch 'abortion ship', the *Aurora*, for example, was seen in just this way by governments in countries like Ireland, Malta and Spain because what it offered was seen as a direct challenge to the fabric of their societies. US Coast Guard cutters operating against 'rum-runners' in the Prohibition era came into the same category. The interception of tankers illicitly carrying oil from Iraq can be seen as an indirect defence of international society as represented by the United Nations and its resolutions.

The passage of hazardous cargoes, such as spent nuclear fuel, is thought by many to be a threat to local safety, and has led to the arming (for the first time since the Second World War) of British merchantships engaged in the business.[21] Less dramatically, 'ordinary' smuggling can be seen as an attack on state revenue. Finally, green activists have been known to take great exception to passage of oil rigs and to the arrival of ships loaded with genetically modified soya, fearing that they represent a threat to the environment.[22] But for all that, most attention has been paid to three types of cargo dangerous to good order in their various ways – terrorists, drugs and illegal migrants.

Terrorist cargoes

The events of 11 September 2001 in New York and Washington are a reminder of the threat posed to good order by terrorism. Navies need to respond to three aspects of this threat:

- The interceptions of the MV *Nisha* by the Royal Navy in December 2001 and of the *Karine-A* by the Israeli Navy in January 2002 in the wake of 11 September, show that terrorists may like anyone else use merchant vessels to transport people and weaponry from place to place. Through 2002 Coalition warships operating off the coast of Pakistan and into the Arabian Sea monitored passing shipping to ensure that Al-Qaeda/Taliban forces were not escaping from Afghanistan by this means. The practical problems this task involved were considerable. The MV *Nisha* took weeks to search (nothing was found in the end) and illustrated the potential tensions between optimal trading conditions on the one hand, and the requirements of security on the other. Moreover, tracking trans-shipments and the passage of particular ships in the murky world of containers and flags of convenience, calls for a complex and integrated global effort from all states interested in the maintenance of good order. It also exemplifies the death of distance – and the way in which far-off threats can unexpectedly appear in one's own waters.[23]
- At the same time, there was a good deal of concern that terrorists might use merchant ships as weapons of war, perhaps attacking key bridges or port facilities. In Japan, the coast guard service was enlisted to help defend the country's 51 nuclear reactors from sea-based attack.[24] In the United States, the US Coast Guard exercises the main responsibility for dealing with this, and has become part of the country's Homeland Defence arrangements. Around the world, there is increased focus on all aspects of port security. Even the out-going US Navy has found itself returning to the role of defending the country's sea frontiers from potential attacks of this sort, in a set of duties that merges with the coastal defence tasks discussed earlier.[25]
- Sometimes this threat may extend to warships themselves, and to their bases. While the attack on the USS *Cole* in Aden is, so far, the most notorious example of this, there have been several other instances off Sri Lanka and, in June 2002, there was much talk of Al-Qaeda terrorists targeting US and British warships passing through the Straits of Gibraltar. There is, of course, nothing

new in this. British warships, and their crews, maintaining the Palestine patrol in the 1940s were in constant peril of ambush and sabotage from Jewish terrorists when in harbour in Haifa and had to take active measures against, for example, frogmen attack.[26] While constant vigilance was the answer it was tiring and sometimes demoralising. Since the attack on the USS *Cole*, and the earlier failed attempt against the USS *Sullivan* (when the terrorist boat sank under the weight of its own explosives), the US Navy has been actively exploring technical means of defending its ships against such attacks, which would provide sufficient security for their ships without having to resort to desperate pre-emptive measures (such as automatically blowing any suspect vessel out of the water) that would hardly be conducive to effective naval diplomacy. As always, a balance needs to be struck between security and operational effectiveness.

The drugs trade

The drugs trade is certainly a threat to good order, nationally and internationally. It kills about five times as many Americans every year as did Al-Qaeda on 11 September. At about $500 billion a year, it is larger than the global oil trade.[27] It often operates alongside other forms of organised crime and damages social prosperity and stability at every level.

There is a significant but varying maritime dimension to the supply of drugs. Across the Indian Ocean, conventional merchant ships bring heroin and opium to Europe from the so-called 'Golden Triangle' by way of major ports such as Karachi, Mumbai, Dubai and Istanbul. In the Caribbean, specialist 'go-fast' boats, semi-submersibles and large cruise ships take drugs to the United States. The International Maritime Organisation (IMO) takes a leading part in establishing guidelines in dealing with the trade, which it encourages all agencies of its member countries to follow. Almost invariably, international collaboration is required to deal with what is in effect a global crime, in which national borders are no more than a minor inconvenience.

Sometimes naval forces are required merely to monitor traffic, sometimes they may engage in dramatic raids and chàses. In February 2006, HMS *Southampton* in the Caribbean surprised the MV *Rampage* and, with the aid of the RFA Grey Rover and its Lynx helicopter using radar and infra-red detection equipment, seized cocaine worth £350 million. In the four years from 1998–2002, Royal Navy warships seized drugs worth an estimated £1.25 billion and this rate has continued since, although it is still reckoned only to be a small proportion of the drugs that get through.[28] To play their part in combating the drugs trade, navies and coast guards need access to the intelligence provided by global tracking arrangements, extensive, integrated air and radar surveillance, fast, agile and specialist craft, a host of special skills and the ability to interoperate with other forces of law and order, including those of other countries. While many of these characteristics typify standard naval equipment and operations, some of the most important are special to task and require dedicated training and sustained effort.

About half the Caribbean cocaine seizures in 2000 were made with naval help, but the fact that the USCG, arguably the best coast guard in the world, *aspires* to a seizure rate of just 15 per cent of the drugs passing through this transit zone, indicates the scale of the problem.

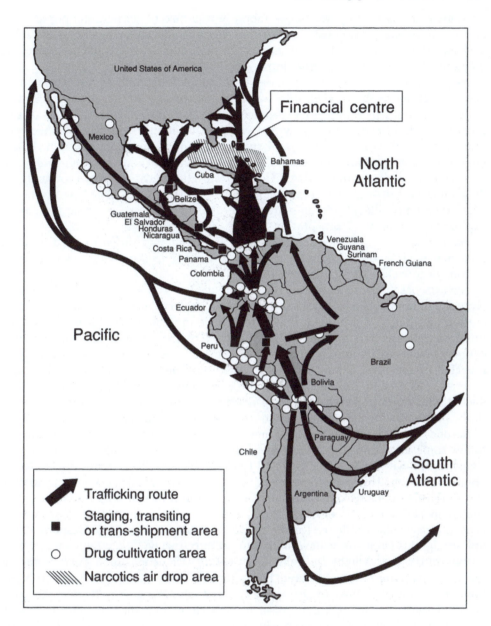

Figure 11.2 South American drug routes.

Illegal migrants

The large-scale movements of people from one area to another have always been a part of human development and appears inevitable for the foreseeable future. It has an important part to play in the economic stabilisation of ageing populations in places such as Western Europe; it can also be seen as a means of increasing social equity around the world. However, the increase in the *rate* of migration, especially from areas devastated by war, social failure in the face of accelerating populations or natural disaster, has reached levels that many in the receiving countries feel is unsustainable. Limits and qualifications for acceptance of people as economic migrants or refugees are therefore imposed.

Nonetheless, their desperation makes such people impatient of regulation and a prey, therefore, to the 'snakeheads', the criminal gangs who illegally ship them to their destinations in return for exorbitant fees. The adverse consequences of this dreadful trade in people are many and various. It enriches criminals who are also often associated with other forms of smuggling, and sometimes terrorism. Illegal migrants are shipped around often in appalling conditions and substandard ships in total contravention of the SOLAS Convention. Hundreds, perhaps thousands, of illegal migrants drown every year when their boats sink. Even once inserted in the host community, illegal migrants are vulnerable to ruthless economic and social exploitation, a prey to prostitution and working conditions akin to slavery. In extreme cases, they can themselves become an involuntary threat to good order in their new environment. Taken together, all this can indeed be regarded as a threat to good order at sea and stability onshore.

Navies, coast guards and marine police only deal, of course, with the symptoms of the trade in human beings, not its causes. Although surveillance, international coop-eration and patrol will be as useful here as it is in dealing with drugs smugglers, three special considerations also apply. First, there are real legal difficulties. Some countries (such as Indonesia) do not regard people smuggling as a crime and, as was revealed by the Australians' experience with the *Tampa* incident in August 2001, there are no precise and agreed regulations on how such matters should be con-ducted. The absence of such common ground rules makes the international coopera-tion so necessary for the containment of this trade very difficult.[29]

Second, there are the sudden and unexpected surges in attempted migration that follow some unpredicted disaster, which can simply overwhelm the maritime forces trying to deal with it. Between 1992 and 1994 neither the US Navy nor the US Coast Guard could on their own have coped with the flood of illegal migrants coming across the Caribbean from Haiti and Cuba. Around 60,000 migrants were inter-cepted in seven months in 1994 alone. In recent years, the Mediterranean has proved a particular challenge for the navies of Southern Europe as desperate eco-nomic migrants from Africa have sought to get into Europe.[30]

The third problem is the tactical task of dealing with people, innocent civilians for the most part, desperate to avoid being turned back. This is no new problem, however. From 1945–1948, the Royal Navy maintained the highly effective Palestine patrol, designed to stem the flood of illegal Jewish migrants flooding into Palestine. The fact that of the 50,000 migrants who sought to come ashore, less than 3000 made it, was remarkable enough in the adverse conditions prevailing; what was more remarkable still was the very low rate of loss of life for either side – even in the face of desperate provocation and in the full glare of an international media largely on the side of the migrants.[31]

Migrant ships, which were sometimes desperately unseaworthy, weaved about to make boarding by smaller naval vessels very difficult. Once on the ship, the small boarding parties were abused and assaulted often by women, children and old people, attacked with iron bars, hatpins, boiling oil and steam hoses. Bridgehouses were often effectively fortified and steerage systems sabotaged. Initial attempts to deal with all this had but mixed success but hard, realistic and specialist training by Royal Marines based in Malta made later boarding parties much more proficient in seizing the initiative and in controlling the situation with the minimum of injury to either side. This largely neglected campaign deserves much study, since it provides a model of how such distasteful duties should be performed.[32] Nonetheless, they will always be very difficult and will require high standards of seamanship and specialist training, not least in the use of non-lethal force. The widespread and growing incidence of this trade in human beings suggests that most navies will need to prepare for it, whether they like it or not.

11.4 The sea as a means of gaining and exchanging information

In some ways, of course, the historic function of the sea as a means of acquiring and exchanging information and ideas has been lost to the internet, although the use of the phrase 'surfing the internet' perhaps harks back to it! All the same, the sea remains a hugely important source of knowledge about the planet we live on and about human history.

Understanding our future

The sea perfectly illustrates the paradox that we do not know what we do not know, and the more we know the more we realise how true that is. Most obviously, as the Australians have pointed out, marine biotechnology is a developing field and since marine biological diversity is so much greater than its terrestrial equivalent it 'represents a vast, relatively untapped source of potential new materials, compounds and organisms'.[33] The need to protect this invaluable storehouse of future knowledge from present, unknowing damage reinforces the drive towards more regulation and environmental protection of the sort to be discussed in the next chapter.

The more we know about the sea the better able we are to exploit its benefits sustainably. This is an obvious explanation for the burgeoning growth of interest in oceanographic research, since it could easily prove crucial to our future. The ocean floor, for example, is covered with the results of volcanic activity, much of it violent and continuous. This is associated with earthquake activity, the movement of the tectonic plates forming the continents and produces huge molten lava lakes under a thin mobile canopy of frozen solidified volcanic rock. Harnessing the tremendous energy to be found in these volcanic magma chambers and exploiting the unimaginably rich minerals they produce through undersea vents could be the key to global survival in the generations to come.

Understanding our past

> Methought I saw a thousand fearful wrecks;
> Ten thousand men that fishes gnaw'd upon;
> Wedges of gold, great anchors, heaps of pearls,
> Inestimable stones, unvalued jewels,
> All scattered in the bottom of the sea.

Shakespeare, *Richard III*, I/4

While the sea may prove crucial to our future, it helps us understand our past as well. Indeed, current research indicates the ocean may have provided the real origins of life on this planet – perhaps in the bacteria colonising volcanic rock of the ocean depths in a process of chemosynthesis quite independent of the sun.

More familiarly, there is growing acceptance that the sea should be seen as a repository of mankind's maritime heritage. While legal ownership of the actual arte-facts that can be found on the bottom of the sea may be a complicated matter, the heritage it represents belongs both to particular peoples and to mankind in general. Extraordinary advances in underwater technology in the hands of undersea explor-ers such as Dr Robert Ballard have produced amazing discoveries of Roman mer-chant ships lost on their way to Carthage through the Tyrrhenian Sea, of the RMS *Titanic*, of the USS *Yorktown* 17,000 feet down in the Pacific. Even more excitingly, the absence of oxygen in the dark saline depths of the Black Sea may well have pre-served wooden ships of the ancient world and an ancient civilisation lost in a disas-ter 7000 years ago that may have originated biblical traditions of Noah's flood. These discoveries all show that the sea preserves human history in a way the land doesn't.[34]

In recent years, UNESCO has taken the lead in pushing for legislation and arrangements that will protect mankind's maritime heritage from the plundering and destructive activities of treasure hunters operating on the ancient but irresponsi-ble principle of 'finders keepers'. Dealing with this is a function of resources and priorities. It is still lamentably true that many governments either do not have, or do not choose to devote, sufficient resources to the protection of their own underwater heritage, preferring to license exploration and salvage rights out to private, foreign (usually Western) commercial concerns. These concerns have demonstrated a particular interest in finding bullion ships, and so are active in the waters of the old Spanish Main, off Cuba, Venezuela, Panama and so on. They are often more trea-sure hunters than marine archaeologists.[35]

In some countries, the naval interest here arises from their responsibility for the supervision of wrecks and underwater historic sites. More substantially, it derives from the fact that it is their direct forebears who so often are the object of concern. An American history professor exploring the underwater wreckage of the 1944 Nor-mandy landings made most of the main points in 2000:

> The site is being taken apart. Charter boats are going over from Southampton, and there are divers from France and elsewhere who are going down there and getting things out – helmets, flame guns, and so on. These are the war graves of the largest naval action and probably the most significant, in the history of the world, yet they have no protection. A lot of men are in tanks and landing ships that never made it to shore, and these sites should be every bit as hallowed as the grounds of the military cemeteries on the cliffs above.[36]

Moreover, these sites help navies and others to understand the evolution of ship design, the course of particular maritime events and their own historic experience and current culture. For that reason, quite rightly, navies themselves are usually keenly interested in underwater exploration, because of its implications for their own identity and values. This is exemplified by the recent and remarkable recovery of the CSS *Hunley*, in effect the world's first operational submarine that sank in action off Charleston in 1864 during the American Civil war. The CSS *Hunley*:

- is a war cemetery;
- may help explain a mysterious event not fully understood before;
- represents a crucial stage in the evolution of a particular form of naval warfare.

For all these reasons, it is a matter of great interest for the US Navy, and to all naval historians.[37]

Nautical archaeology can reveal much bigger issues too. In 2001, Britain's 'Ferriby boats' from the estuary of the River Humber were re-examined. The boats themselves were large, melon-slice shaped, elegant, sturdy ships made of thick oak planks tied together with twisted yew. They show there to have been a flourishing trade between Britain and the continent of Europe 4000 years ago and thus illustrate the ancient and continuing linkages of the sea and mankind's development discussed at the beginning of this book.[38]

Navies clearly have an interest in ensuring, directly or indirectly, that their underwater maritime heritage is not damaged or destroyed by governmental neglect or irresponsible treasure hunters.

11.5 The sea as an area of dominion

This review of the benefits the sea has to offer shows just how important jurisdictional issues can be to their full enjoyment. Because those benefits are seen to be of increasing importance (not least as a contribution to a country's political, economic and military power), more and more attention is being paid to the sea as an area over which jurisdiction is claimed and exercised. The notion that parts of the sea 'belong' to certain parts of the land mass is not in itself a new one. In 1494, at the Treaty of Tordesillas, the Pope, after all, divided the whole world between Spain and Portugal. The idea that the sea could be 'owned' in the same way as land lay behind the tradition of the 'closed sea' advocated by the English seventeenth-century jurist John Selden.

Sovereignty usually means having absolute and independent authority over a stretch of territory, and maritime sovereignty simply extends this concept to the sea. In effect, an area of sea is regarded as part of the territory of a state.

Maritime sovereignty comes in two complementary varieties:

- *Instrumental*, in that it is something countries need in order to enjoy the benefits of the sea. In the case of archipelagic countries (like Indonesia or the Philippines), or countries with poor internal land communications (like nineteenth-century Norway or Brazil),[39] maritime sovereignty may also be fundamental to national integrity.
- *Expressive*, in that it is a symbolic representation of the power and values of a country. This is particularly evident in the ownership of islands. At times of national weakness, a country's capacity to maintain jurisdiction over its islands may often become quite tenuous. Its capacity to hold on to its islands becomes a kind of performance indicator of national pride and effectiveness. This helps explain the deep feelings Argentina exhibits towards the Falkland Islands,

China towards Taiwan, Greece and Turkey towards the Imia/Kardak rocks and so on.

To be accepted by others, both types of sovereignty need to be asserted, exercised and, if necessary, defended. It is because the protection of its (in this case, marine) territory and its citizens from 'all enemies domestic and foreign' is the basic duty of, and justification for, the state, that these matters are taken so seriously and, indeed, need to be. Accordingly, countries are increasingly concerned to exert and, in many cases, to extend their jurisdiction over the sea. The adoption of UNCLOS provides the framework within which this is being done. A total of 151 coastal states have sovereign rights over adjacent seas and their continental shelf. Of them, 54 may be able to claim extensions to their sea area beyond 200 nautical miles from the coast. The result is that jurisdiction may well be extended over a total area of some 75 million square kilometres of sea, equal to more than half of the Earth's land surface.[40]

Unsurprisingly, this has led to many problems. First, there are a great many areas of maritime dispute as a result. This is especially the case in the Asia Pacific where a chain of islands, stretching from just off Singapore to the South Kuriles to the north of Japan, is the subject of often ferocious dispute between various countries. The ongoing dispute in the South China Sea is perhaps the most complicated, important and potentially dangerous dispute of this nature in the world. To this must be added a plethora of simpler and more technical disputes over the drawing of lines of maritime jurisdiction between neighbouring countries. UNCLOS does not in itself end these disputes; it provides a set of parameters by which such disputes should be resolved with the agreement of all parties concerned.

Second, since it is a fundamental principle of international law that for sovereignty to be recognised it needs to be asserted and exercised, many countries have now been faced with a real challenge on how they can possibly do it. Amongst the worst placed are the Pacific mini-states of Kiribati, with 690 square kilometres of land but 3.5 million square kilometres of sea and the Marshall Islands with 181 and 2.1 million square kilometres, respectively. These are extreme examples of a common problem.

In an instructive analogy, Harold Kearsley has likened the task to looking after a big ranch – checking the fences, keeping out predators, constantly looking round and being seen, ensuring that its assets are always used to the best benefit of the owners.[41] It is difficult to specify what countries need in order to exercise their maritime sovereignty, since this is a function of the extent of their sea area, its weather and the strength of the civilian and naval forces that might challenge it. But the first requirement is for a country to know what is going on in its sovereign area. In cases where the size of the area makes it impossible to maintain a continuous presence, sufficient surveillance of the area has to be conducted by other means. Where that reveals actual or potential infractions of national laws and territorial rights, the sovereign state must have a demonstrable capacity to respond with graduated force,[42] but it does not follow that such forces must be all-powerful, since their main function may be symbolic. Even weak forces can make a difference in maintaining sovereignty through the existential deterrence discussed in Section 9.6. The mere existence of low-level forces, which the more powerful may physically need to brush aside, can impose severe *political* limits on their freedom of action.

Nonetheless, experience provides many examples of the damage that inadequate levels of maritime strength can do a country's capacity to maintain its maritime sovereignty. The evident difficulties of the Philippines in responding effectively to the Chinese 'occupation' of Mischief Reef show the risks run by states unable or unwilling to demonstrate a capacity to defend their sovereignty claims. The reinvigoration of the Japanese Coast Guard (JCG) and the issue of more robust rules of engagement to the Japanese Navy in the wake of apparent Chinese and North Korean 'intrusions' into their area of concern and the willingness of both Koreas to take extreme measures in defence of their views of the line of demarcation between them in the Yellow Sea, both suggest this lesson has been well taken in the Asia-Pacific.[43]

11.6 The sea as an environment

I'll throw't into the creek
Behind our rock; and let it to the sea.

Shakespeare, *Cymbeline*, IV/2

The marine environment: critical, unknown, threatened

To these four traditional values of the sea must now be added a fifth, the marine environment. For centuries taken for granted if thought about at all, its perceived importance grew dramatically through the twentieth century, roughly in line with increasing levels of threat. This, too, is likely to have significant implications for navies.

Although human beings are air-breathing, sun-loving bipeds, and not aquatic creatures at all, life started in the oceans and is still hugely determined by them. Ocean currents help regulate our climate. The sea slows and masks the effects of global warming because of its immense thermal inertia and its ability to absorb carbon from the atmosphere. Its water level, coral reefs, fish stocks act as a barometer of the physiological health of the planet as a whole. The deep ocean, in particular, may prove crucial to understanding our past and assuring our future. And yet much is still mysterious about the way in which the ocean system actually works.

But one thing we do know is that it is under increasing threat. In 1995, the United Nations set up the Independent Commission on the World Oceans (IWCO) to investigate threats to marine resources and possible ways of protecting them. Forty international scientists and political figures worked to produce a report that was released by Mario Soares, Portugal's leading elder statesman at Expo '98. It made sombre reading. It argued that there was a 'crisis of the oceans' caused by pollution, jurisdictional disputes, over-exploitation and widespread ignorance. What takes hundreds, even thousands of years, to develop can be unknowingly destroyed in days, and all too often is. Already two-thirds of the world's population lives within 100 kilometres of the coast, and the pressure this puts on the fragile environment of the ocean is tremendous and bound to get worse, when the total population doubles over the next few generations.[44]

For an illustration of what mankind's use, and misuse of the ocean has done to the ocean, and the long-term risk it might pose to our own future, we need look no further than the poisoned sea off Mumbai. A thick pollution haze hangs over the scene. The slick from offshore oil refineries, dead fish, litter, untreated sewage lie on the surface of the water. No one swims from its beaches. To catch surviving fish, local fishermen must now venture much further from shore.

The general results of marine pollution loom over all aspects of sea use. In the seventeenth century, the seas were crystal clear, cleaned by trillions of shell fish, and so abundant in fish that early seafarers talked of simply lowering baskets into the water to catch cod in areas such as the Grand Banks of the North Atlantic. But these days the ocean here and elsewhere has darkened and emptied and threatens all aspects of sea use and indeed of human life in a way that makes the arguments of states about who owns particular stretches of water look utterly trivial in comparison. In many ways, the collapse of the marine environment would be the ultimate disorder, fatally weakening prospects for the stability and security of settled society ashore.

And yet everywhere in Mumbai, there are signboards urging more concern for the environment, a hopeful indication that at last the problem is being addressed. Indeed, around the world, environmentalism has come in from the margins of debate and is fast becoming a part of the mainstream of politics. UNCLOS, indeed, provides a comprehensive set of principles for the protection of the marine environment, and in Article 92 specifically obligates states to follow them. Similar commitments on the protection of the oceans are contained in Chapter 17 of the UN's Agenda 21.

Broadly, there is agreement about the causes of the problem – the sheer extent of mankind's appetite for the resources of the sea, land-source pollution of every kind and the clash of competing sea uses. The IWCO report and Expo '98 were not content merely to delineate the problems. They went on to suggest very many practical solutions. In fact, in some areas there have been substantial improvements already. For example, vessel source pollution is now much reduced on previous levels with the outlawing of such sloppy practices as washing out fuel tanks at sea, and so forth.

Much of this may be regarded as 'soft security' (distinct from the 'hard' security of alliances and wars) but it is 'security' all the same because it concerns an indirect attack on the prosperity and stability of international society and its constituents. Indeed, in the case of small island countries like the Maldives, Kiribati and Tuvalu facing the prospect of extinction or massive damage through rising sea levels, it is hard to imagine a security issue that deserves to be taken more seriously.[45]

Navies and the marine environment

Although civilian agencies bear most responsibility for the protection of the marine environment, navies also have a role to play. In January 1998, the Advisory Committee on the Protection of the Šeas meeting in Stockholm sought to 'encourage states to use the capacity of their military and intelligence organisations towards environmental security in partnership with their civilian counterparts'.[46] The committee recognised that simply by being navies they had skills and technical qualities to offer both in terms of research and of environmental protection.

It makes sense for navies to become involved for less prosaic reasons also, not least because there is a security dimension to environmental stress. For many of the tiny island states of the South Pacific, together with the Maldives in the Indian Ocean, their very existence is at stake. Many other low-level areas like Bangladesh, coastal China, even Florida are at increasing risk. Moreover, experience suggests that political quarrels and instability may accompany disasters that undermine the authority of government. In helping deal with humanitarian disasters such as Hurricane Mitch, navies were not only responding to the indirect consequences of global warming, but also helping avert worse things that might otherwise follow.

Navies and coast guards may also have a mediation role in dealing with the frequent disputes between different kinds of sea users, where there is often a need to keep the peace, for example between Japanese whalers and Greenpeace/Sea Shepherd boats in the Southern Ocean.[47] Lastly, the concept of 'environmental crime' is fast developing and navies may well have a role in suppressing it.

But what can navies do to protect the marine environment directly? They do frequently help clear up or avert pollution risks that result from other types of sea use, most obviously from shipping accidents, such as the grounding of the *Exxon Valdez*, by contributing to the disposal of oil wastes. Navies can be first to the site ready to conduct the first survey, to take emergency measures (such as early spraying of oil slicks) and to provide command and control arrangements.[48] Usually, other agencies are better suited and more cost-effective for longer term responses to pollution incidents.

Sometimes other specialist naval skills can help as well. The US Navy's eventual torpedoing off the coast of Oregon of the paper-carrying freighter the *New Carissa* is a recent illustration, for example, of the capacity to sink the wrecked ships that might otherwise produce pollution. Illustrating the same point Thai Navy SEALS are, as part of their normal training, given courses in marine conservation so they can help protect the country's coral reefs.[49]

A yet more important contribution that navies make is not to be a cause of pollution themselves. This may involve helping clear up the dangerous and noxious detritus of war and military operations (dealing with mines and bombs dropped in the sea, disposing of dangerous or polluting wrecks such as the USS *Mississinewa* sunk during the Second World War and now leaking oil on to Ulithi atoll in Yap state in Micronesia).[50] Perhaps the most serious environmental threat of this sort is the requirement safely to dispose of unwanted reactors from nuclear submarines and contaminated hull parts of the former Soviet Navy.[51] It may mean navies doing their best to make sure that the environmental impact of training activity and research is properly understood and weighed in the balance before decisions are taken.[52]

Self-interest is tending to push things this way, since unless navies conform to such environmental concerns their own utility could be affected. Some countries, for example, want to reduce the sovereign state immunity of warships so that they become susceptible to the safety and environmental regulations that bound civilian shipping. This encourages increased interest in 'environmentally friendly' warship design. The onboard disposal of ship wastes (especially oil, plastics, hazardous material, medical wastes, etc.), for example, allows navies to demonstrate leadership in the stewardship of the oceans. But it may also facilitate naval operations in that there is less chance of floating plastic debris being confused with mines as sometimes happened in the aftermath of the Gulf war.

Moreover this would reduce the prospect of naval operations being one day constrained by regulations of the International Convention for the Prevention of Pollution by Ships (1973 MARPOL Treaty, and 1978 Protocol) designating special areas such as the Mediterranean and Black Seas, the North and Baltic Seas, the Red Sea and the Gulf and the Gulf of Mexico and the wider Caribbean, in a manner that would be uncomfortable for warships.

And, perhaps above all, through their research effort navies can help mankind know and understand more about the marine environment.

11.7 The need for good order at sea

In the year 2001, the International Maritime Bureau (IMB) issued a report lamenting the increase in piracy in Indonesian waters, and attributing this to a general breakdown in law and order in the area, and to the activities of separatist guerrillas in Aceh and elsewhere. This was creating a vicious downwards spiral; it disrupted passing shipping and local fishing activities, and damaged local and national economies, thereby reducing the revenues and authority of local governments and weakening their capacity to maintain good order at sea and, more to the point from the terrorist's angle, ashore.

Because the sea is increasingly important, in relative terms, to local economies, disorder at sea only makes things worse ashore. The success of transnational crime such as drugs smuggling elevates the power of the kind of people who challenge civilised states and everything they stand for; it undermines their prosperity, security and ability to connect with other countries. Countries that fail for such reasons tend, moreover, to become the security concerns of others.

This example demonstrates both the intimate, two-way linkages between good order at sea and good order on land and the simple fact that without it, mankind's ability fully to exploit its potential value will be severely constrained. The director of the IMB's conclusion was unambiguous: 'Security along the coast has to be tightened.' To a greater or lesser extent, this recommendation should be extended to all the world's seas.[53]

The maintenance of good order at sea requires an improved level of awareness, effective policy and integrated governance. Only a 'holistic' all-round maritime approach does justice to the complexity and importance of the linkages between the different values of the sea and its manifold connections with events ashore.

Navies, coast guards and other maritime agencies have an increasingly vital contribution to make in support of good order at sea. Until very recently, however, such activities have been almost totally ignored by the main maritime thinkers. They were regarded as something that navies could do when nothing more important was occupying their attention; usually other maritime agencies bore the main burden. Nonetheless, the need for navies to address such issues more seriously grew steadily through the last century and seems likely to develop even faster in this one.

As Figure 11.3 shows, the remainder of this chapter will review the role of navies in helping to resolve present and future difficulties in the maintenance of good order at or from the sea under five main headings. It will show that such activities only make sense when seen in the context of the many other uses of the sea.

11.8 Increasing maritime awareness

The ocean may well prove the key to our future as well as to our understanding of the past. And yet, despite all this there is much that we do not know. We are still only speculating about the physical, chemical and biological processes at work in the

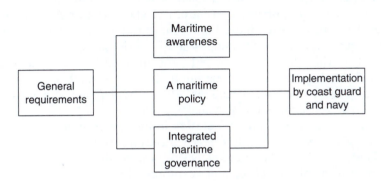

Figure 11.3 Good order at sea: general requirements.

ocean–earth–atmosphere system. Exploration of the deep ocean only began 25 years ago and much of it, especially in the southern hemisphere, is virtually unexplored. We know far less about the deep ocean than we do about the surface of the moon, and barely 5 per cent of it has been properly 'imaged'. Discoveries in the huge mid-ocean ridge (which comprises some 23 per cent of the world's surface and contains the highest mountain ranges we have) are recent and often accidental, or incidental. One new marine species is discovered every two weeks. The more we discover about the deep ocean, the more we realise what we don't know.[54]

In fact, many would argue that this applies more generally. The real conclusion here may be that we do not really understand how important the ocean is to the world's climate and environmental health; still less how important it will be in the future. We need to understand what we are doing in, and to, the ocean as a basis for future policy.

Navies and scientific exploration

Navies have always had a stake in ocean exploration. In the early days, as we saw in Chapter 2, this was largely in pursuit of improved navigational capability and an overwhelming desire to get to profitable places faster and safer than anyone else. In the eighteenth and early nineteenth centuries, naval expeditions usually involved scientists anxious to know more about distant lands for what they might reveal about the mysteries of life. Charles Darwin's epic voyage in the warship HMS *Beagle* showed that scientific exploration was part and parcel of seapower.

But interest in the ocean itself (rather than in places on the other side of it) is traditionally traced back only to 21 December 1872 when HMS *Challenger* departed on a three-and-a-half year of exploration under Edinburgh University's Professor Charles Wyville Thomson. This formulated the goals, systematic methods and careful analysis that became the standard of oceanographic research around the world.

In the twentieth century, naval interest in oceanography was hugely stimulated by the advent of the submarine, since information on the depth, temperature, salinity, colour and currents of seawater and the contours of the ocean floor could be hugely important for obvious operational reasons. If you were skulking about off an enemy

coast in a submarine and seeking to avoid sonar detection, it could be really important whether you were in the presence of hard, reflecting rock or soft and yielding
mud and ooze. This became even more important during the high-technology Cold
War era.[55] With such developing techniques and incentives, the sailor's attitude to
the environment in which he operates may be transformed. The deep-sea bed, for
example, instead of being dark, mysterious and frightening, something to be avoided
at all costs, may need to become a familiar area to be exploited for its scientific
interest and its commercial and strategic value.

The Arctic and the secrets of polar operation in the presence of ice masses have
become increasingly important too. For nearly a century, the Russians led the way
in this area. Under Stalin in the interwar period, the Soviet Navy and Air Force
were keenly involved in all aspects of polar exploration partly reflecting and partly
moulding a social dream of a pure Northern world where physical bravery, ideological fervour, scientific expertise and party support would establish an exciting
new soviet society, becoming folk heroes in the manner of the astronauts of the
1960s.[56] More mundanely, the observations of nuclear submarines on ice thickness
provides invaluable data for scientists struggling to understand the possible impact
of global warming. Sadly, certainly in the Arctic and possibly later in the Antarctic,
this seems likely to arouse controversy and competition between national claimants
to the resources and opportunities it offers.[57]

The same kind of operational incentives inspired naval interest in the conduct of
amphibious operations, especially of the Second World War. Extensive surveys
were conducted before major landings such as the Torch landings (1942) and the
Overlord operation (1944), because the predictability of sea swell, surf and beach
conditions could make all the difference. As has been recently pointed out: 'By
1943, oceanography had clearly demonstrated to the frontline officer that knowledge of the environment could mean the difference between victory and defeat, life
and death.' Hence the growing interest in naval hydrography.[58]

The need for more knowledge is more apparent than in the littoral – currently the
primary area of maritime interest. The Rapid Environment Assessment (REA) programme sponsored by SACLANT arose from the fact that the littoral is an extraordinarily complex environment in which 30 key factors (currents, reefs, salinity levels
and gradients, etc.) could decisively affect the outcome of operations have been
identified. Near instantaneous access to modelled sets of data on the world's littorals, almost at the touch of a button, could easily prove of enormous military
benefit. It also helps establish the basis for jurisdictional claims.

For all these reasons, navies need to keep abreast of, and contribute to, the accumulation all types of marine data through such means as the Global Ocean Observation system. The IWCO report was clear that this kind of research could be of
benefit for non-military purposes too, in a host of ways. 'Navies', it says 'should also
play a growing role in sharing the information and capabilities required to safeguard
environmental security.' They do, already, in fact. The unmanned deep-water vehicles used to explore the *Titanic*, for example, developed from systems originally
intended by the US Navy to monitor two sunken SSNs, the *Thresher* and the *Scor-
pion*. Because the resources (money, scientists, research platforms, facilities) they
devote to ocean science can be so huge, navies can make an enormous difference to
our knowledge of the sea and the protection of the marine environment. This could
be increased still further, if old data of scientific interest was more fully released,

and if, to quote Captain Cook's Admiralty, in the 'same enlarged and benevolent spirit' environmental data collection was added to warship missions as a matter of course.[59]

Navies could also be instrumental in selling the importance of the sea to governments and public opinion around the world who would seem to be increasingly afflicted by what has been called 'sea-blindedness' – or at least is how it is frequently seen by seafarers around the world. In some ways, therefore, the biggest threat to the maritime future is an insidious one of ignorance and neglect amongst the general population and some parts of government. All too often the image of the sea is associated with images of decline, reducing fisheries, environmental catastrophes, shipwrecks. Even the common phrase 'all at sea' betokens chaos and confusion.

Maritime analysts and naval historians constantly bemoan the fact that the sea is given such scant intellectual regard in the study of international politics and history at university from which future generations of decision makers will come.[60] It is to correct this tendency that so many maritime forums and foundations have been set up around the world.

Navies are in a good position proactively to help sell the sea in all its aspects, strategic, commercial and environmental, because they are often in the public eye, they are inevitably involved in scientific and oceanographic exploration, institutionally they are integrated into government at the national level and operationally they are multinational at the regional, if not global, levels.

But, of course, in many cases this would go against the grain of services preoccupied with more urgent operational matters, and culturally averse to engagement in politically contentious matters. In the Royal Navy of the interwar period, for example, there was thought to be 'something very sordid' about the use of 'propaganda' to win public favour in this way. Officers owned to 'an intense feeling of repulsion at this blazoning forth of the deeds and acts of what they have always been proud to think was a "silent service" '.[56] Nonetheless, the requirement for more knowledge, and for more public awareness of the importance and the characteristics of the ocean may now have become so important to the future of life on this planet, that furthering it by every means possible, should probably be regarded as a subsidiary function, even a duty, of the world's naval and coast guard forces.

11.9 Developing maritime policy

Maritime good order is most often threatened when sea uses clash. The interests of oil extractors may compete with those of fishermen. When the old oil tanker *Erika* went aground on the coast of Brittany in December 2001 as a result of sloppy operational practices, it released oil that polluted beaches, hurt the tourist industry, threatened nearby oyster beds and killed thousands of guillemots and other seabirds. Likewise, it would be easy to imagine an incident in the Straits of Malacca in which a hijacked oil tanker founders on a distant reef, causes pollution, requires naval forces to break off from important multinational exercises, puts up marine insurance rates, bankrupts a P & I club in London, rescues a struggling Dutch salvage firm, devastates local fisheries, sets local countries at odds with each other and ruins a nearby resort catering for Japanese and European tourists.

This shows that the ocean needs to be thought of as a global system characterised by countless interconnections in which a disturbance in any one component may well affect all the others. It means the ocean system has to be thought of and treated *as a whole*, while at the same time properly integrating elements of it into land-based systems. For instance, the British government's desire to shift freight off the roads should clearly consider ro-ro ferries as well as railways, but for that to make sense, shore-side port unloading, storage and transport facilities need to be linked into a thoroughly inter-modal transportation system. Maritime interests do not stop at the shoreline.

Australia can justifiably boast that it has established itself 'as a world leader in implementing integrated oceans planning and management' through the establishment in 1998 of a comprehensive oceans policy of the sort that has long been advocated by analysts. Australia has one of the world's largest EEZs and intends to:

> provide a strategic framework for the planning, management and ecologically sustainable development of Australia's fisheries, shipping, tourism, petroleum, gas and seabed resources while ensuring the conservation of the marine environment.

> ...If we were to continue without integrating our oceans planning and management, we could not be confident that Australia would avoid following so much of the rest of the world in a spiral of marine resource degradation.[62]

There is much to be said for the view that this should become something of a model for other countries to adapt to their own circumstances and follow.

11.10 Developing integrated maritime governance

The naval and civilian agencies that seek to maintain good order at sea need to develop an increasingly integrated approach to oceans management; they must think, talk, plan and operate together.

This applies at the international level as well as the domestic. The IWCO report urged that the high seas, the area outside any form of national jurisdiction, should be treated as a public good 'to be used and managed in the interests of present and future generations' of all peoples of the world, not just the fortunate few whose rights were already recognised and who had the capacity to enforce them. Ocean resources must be distributed efficiently and equitably and that requires good governance at an international as well as national level.

The IWCO report also emphasises the fact that many ocean problems cannot be sorted out at a national level. Fish do not recognise national jurisdiction and the effective management of 'straddling stocks' requires collective agreement. Pollution control, anti-drugs operations, the control of people smuggling and so on also require international agreement and collaboration. In all these cases, an insistence on traditional sovereignty would hamper progress.

The development of regional conservation regimes in the Arctic under the stimulus of scientists, environmentalists and local publics shows what can be done with a 'bottom-up' approach to effective and agreed ocean management. In the Arctic, this is complemented by a top-down approach centred on governmental agreement by the eight countries operating under the umbrella of the Arctic council. This is a common pattern although, as just noted, global warming and the paradoxical opportunities it offers have put this system under real strain.[63] Naval cooperation aids this process of specialised coalition building; conversely this improves security relationships between countries too.

The law of the sea: a framework for action?

On the face of it, the extensive development of the law of the sea should provide a much improved legal framework for the defence of good order at sea. This is largely the result of the UN Convention on the Law of the Sea (UNCLOS), which after many years of tortuous negotiation, finally came into effect in 1994. Its main provisions are:

- coastal states have sovereignty over their territorial sea extending up to 12 nautical miles (nms) from the shoreline;
- they also have certain rights over a 'contiguous zone' for up to another 12 nms;
- coastal states have sovereign rights over the natural resources of an exclusive economic zone (EEZ) extending up to 200 nms;
- coastal states have sovereign rights over their continental shelf, in certain conditions, beyond the EEZ;
- seabed resources outside national jurisdiction are regarded as the common heritage of mankind and any revenues they produce are to be equitably shared amongst the international community;
- traditional freedoms of navigation, overflight, scientific research and fishing are enjoyed by all states on the high seas;
- foreign vessels, including warships, are allowed 'innocent passage' through territorial seas;
- the International Tribunal for the Law of the Sea settles disputes and facilitates and settles disputes between members;
- detailed guidance is provided for the resolution of jurisdictional disputes between members;
- finally, and this is a point often overlooked, with all these rights go equivalent duties of care.

Overall, UNCLOS provides a flexible and comprehensive framework for the maintenance of good order at sea that is likely to be further developed in the years ahead. UNCLOS illustrates the way in which mankind's relationship with the sea is fundamentally changing. UNCLOS was indeed, in the words of the UN secretary-general, 'one of the greatest achievements of this [the twentieth] century'.[64]

Implementation and enforcement remain a problem, however. While some countries, including at the time of writing the United States, have yet to ratify the treaty formally, there is no serious objection to its main provisions. Nonetheless, considerable problems remain in interpreting and applying legal provision to the particular problems in particular areas in which people tend to be more interested. In some ways, UNCLOS by raising so many issues has triggered as many disputes as it has resolved. Moreover, the powers of the tribunal are limited to countries that agree in advance to be bound by its findings.

The problem is as much a matter of enforcement as of jurisdiction, however. This is best exemplified by looking at an activity that nearly everyone thinks a bad

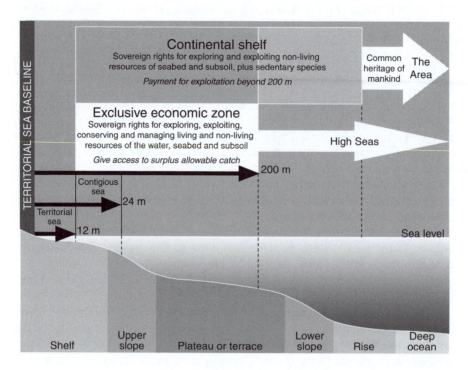

Figure 11.4 Maritime zones.

thing – namely, piracy. When, at the end of a long international pursuit, India took the initiative by arresting and trying the pirates who stole the *Alondra Rainbow*, they found they had no satisfactory modern legislation to deal with it, and eventually had to release all the perpetrators.[65]

The Gulf of Aden and the approaches to the Bab el Mandeb Strait have become a piracy hotspot, partly because it's a natural area of concentration for ships going to and from the Mediterranean and so a 'target rich environment' and partly because Djibouti and Somalia both lack effective law enforcement capabilities. Unusually, Somalia has recognised this and asked for help. Local pirates have become quite sophisticated, being able to locate prospective targets by tuning into the unsecured radio communications of local regional maritime traffic and even employing 'mother ships' several hundreds of miles offshore. Warships operating against pirates off the coast of Somalia, for example, have run into all sorts of legal complications, even so. The Royal Navy, for example, was constrained in its efforts by Foreign Office pressure that warships should not take the perpetrators into custody lest under European legislation they claimed asylum or that their human rights had been violated.[66]

Frustration at the deficiencies and inadequacies of the overall legal regime have in some cases led navies to operate against maritime crime by commercial rather than legal means. They try to change the terms of trade for pirates and drugs smugglers and so deter them in the future by destroying their cargoes and wrecking their equipment. While better than nothing, a long-term answer needs to be sought in radical improvements to the legal regime.

The United Nations and its agencies have a role to play here. The protocols since 2005 attached to the SUA Convention have specifically outlawed the carriage or discharge by ship of biological, chemical or nuclear material if intended to cause harm, and so will authorise navy ships to board suspect vessels, even on the high seas, if the flag state agrees. In the shorter term, a large number of states have come together under the Proliferation Security Initiative to implement broadly similar arrangements. UN rulings have helped navies tackle piracy off Somalia too.[67]

Developing domestic maritime governance

Enforcement problems are frequently mainly attributable to degrees of state failure and difficulties in governance ashore, as in the Indonesian case mentioned above. Often the most serious adversaries are not competing nations but non-state actors of one sort or another, bent on extracting benefit from the sea in total disregard of everyone else. Even for effective countries, differing sea uses overlap, often compete and need supervision.

But this will not be easy, since there remain differences of interest and perception between different types of sea users. Satellite surveillance of the oceans, for example, show how frequently MARPOL restrictions on marine pollution are flouted by merchant ships. Although this is happily declining, far more oil is deliberately released into the ocean through sloppy ship operation than through marine disaster. Most agree the answer to such violations is the extension of coastal and port state controls so that passing merchant ships can be identified and later punished when they dock. This approach is enthusiastically supported by marine conservationists but often viewed with much less favour by certain parts of the shipping industry.

To many of the latter, the tendency towards the expansion of regulation, in this or any other area, is always controversial. Some dispute the need for more regulation arguing instead either that hard-pressed governments cannot afford to take up this extra administrative burden, or that economic rationality will in the end provide the disciplines needed. An integrated oceans policy should provide an effective framework for mediation between such interests and differences of view.

India provides an interesting example of the tensions and disagreements that may arise. Some authorities, citing the 'abysmal neglect' of maritime matters, call for a national maritime security policy, pointing out that as many as 14 ministries of the central government, in addition to the departments and organisations of local and central governments, are currently involved in various aspects of the country's maritime affairs, leading to considerable confusion and overlapping of jurisdiction. But, in other Indian circles, there is fear that an equitable balance between all interests will be distorted by excessive emphasis on the naval/security element (especially given the country's problems with Pakistan in the wake of the events of 11 September 2001). Yet others worry that too much emphasis on regulation in, say, the shipping industry, will stifle the enterprise culture now surging ahead after decades of central control.[68]

Generally, the need to regulate activities at sea, and activities on land that could threaten other people's uses of it, is increasingly accepted. This has resulted in a growing body of national and international regulation that naval and coast guard forces will increasingly need to monitor and enforce. The bigger their EEZ, the greater their responsibility.

Navies and coast guards should clearly be parties to the formulation and development of such an integrated policy of ocean management, partly because their own sectional interests might be affected and partly because they are likely to be involved in its consequent implementation.

11.11 Policy implementation: the navy–coast guard spectrum

Good order at sea requires a range of activities extending from law enforcement at one end of the spectrum to the defence of security at the other. As Figure 11.5 shows, responsibility over this spectrum may be shared between naval forces and a variety of coast guard and civilian agencies, with a degree of overlap in the middle.

With the widening of the concept of security, accelerated perhaps by the events of 11 September, the extent of potential overlap is increasing in ways that raise issues over who should be responsible for what. Because no one can do everything, the main emphasis in ocean management will be on the efficient coordination of the various forces concerned with its implementation.

These forces include navies, coast guards and other governmental agencies. The US Coast Guard, now part of the US Department of Homeland Security, for example, shares responsibility with a whole host of other organisations including:

- National Marine Fisheries service
- Office of Hazardous Material Safety
- Immigration and Naturalisation Service
- US Customs Service
- Drugs Enforcement Agency
- Federal Bureau of Investigation.

Added to this, in countries such as Australia and India there is a need to coordinate policy implementation between a variety of local and regional authorities. Finally, some governments have been attracted by the apparent cost reductions promised by 'outsourcing' activities to private contractors.

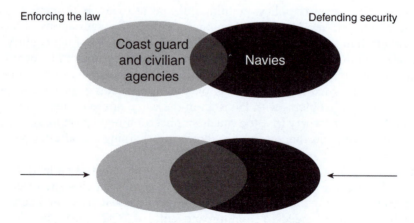

Figure 11.5 Closing circles of jurisdiction.

The result of all this is an infinite variety of models of how countries have decided to coordinate the various agencies involved in oceans management, according to their individual geographic conditions, constitution, political outlook and so on. The British 'solution' to the problem is an extreme example of a system that has just evolved organically over the years, adapting as necessary to changing conditions.[69] Other countries (India, Argentina, Taiwan, much of South East Asia) have taken conscious decisions to set up coast guards to look after their maritime domains, and have picked and mixed from the various possibilities being practised elsewhere.

Broadly, four approaches can be discerned. These involve ascending degrees of naval involvement in ocean management (and see Figure 11.6).

The US Coast Guard (USCG) model

The USCG is a separate military service, the only one with law enforcement powers. It is a specialist force concentrating on a wide variety of ocean management tasks. It contains a force of ships and aircraft stronger than many other navies and in wartime performs a variety of military functions. In peacetime, it can go 'out of area' in the wider defence of American maritime interests and can engage in a variety of activities that could be termed 'coast guard diplomacy'. The USCG, for example, prides itself on the international assistance it can and does offer other countries. The Japanese Coast Guard (or Maritime Safety Agency) has likewise been involved in delicate negotiations with its counterparts in South East Asia to increase cooperation against pirates. Coast guard ships are often more acceptable politically than standard warships.

Although separate from their navies, such coast guards maintain close relations with them in the expectation that this will facilitate economies of scale and efficient coordination. This is the thinking behind the idea in the United States of a 'National Fleet' formed of both the USCG and the US Navy. With the US Navy downsizing to some 300 ships, the USCG's 40-odd 'cutters' begin to look rather important to the navy's capacity to cover all its tasks in time of conflict. This is especially true with

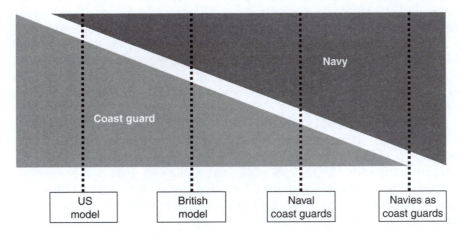

Figure 11.6 The Navy/coast guard spectrum.

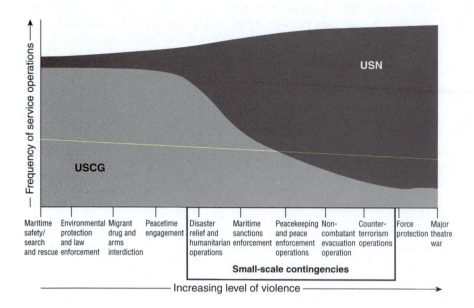

Figure 11.7 The US Coast Guard and the US Navy.

the USCG having embarked in 2002 on its ambitious 'deepwater' re-equipment programme.

Although as Figure 10.7 shows that naval and coast guard roles do still overlap, there is a clear differentiation of function between the two. The navy has no powers of arrest and even to engage in maritime interception operations of merchant ships will normally embark USCG personnel.

Pure coast guards of this sort may sometimes be seen as rivals rather than partners to the navy. Conversely they may not attract sufficient funding. Even the famous USCG has suffered years of underinvestment, partly because its ownership was once shared between two departments (Defense and Transport) neither of which regarded it as their top priority.[70]

Many countries have followed the US example, including Korea and Japan, and more recently India, although most have given it an individual spin. For political reasons, the Japanese Coast Guard not the navy is responsible for sovereignty maintenance; in India, however, the navy very definitely retains responsibility for dealing with anything that might be a threat to the state, such as mines, sabotage, the examination of suspicious merchant ships and so forth.

If, in terms of size and capability, the USCG is clearly up the powerful end of the coast guard spectrum, there are many less ambitious but still effective versions. The Hong Kong Marine Police 1948–1997 was a unique variant on this theme, perfectly suited to Hong Kong's geographic and political circumstances. It was responsible for dealing with illegal immigration, crime, political disorder, sovereignty disputes, typhoon relief, SAR and any crime that just happened to have a maritime connection.[71]

The British model

Most patrol vessels are operated by the navy, SAR helicopters by the Royal Air Force and other assets by various government departments, civilian contractors and even in the splendid Royal National Lifeboat Institution (a charitable organisation run by part-time volunteers). This federated rather than integrated system looks untidy and should not work but, oddly, seems to most of the time. The Royal Navy does have power of arrest, but most law enforcement tasks are carried out by civilian agencies with the navy standing by to provide military assistance as necessary.

Australia has established an inter-agency organisation, led by customs and defence, entitled 'Border Protection Command'. A 'dual hatted' navy rear admiral functions as a Joint Task Force Commander, to control defence units assigned to civil maritime surveillance and response, and as the National Director of a customs division to control customs patrol craft and the contractor operated 'Coastwatch' civil maritime surveillance aircraft. The Command responds to arising events and plans its surveillance programme through a risk assessment process that involves all its 'clients' (including Fisheries, Customs, Immigration, Environment and other agencies). The major client agencies have embedded liaison officers in the national operations centre of the Command to ensure that their needs are met and that onshore responses are coordinated with the effort at sea.[72]

Naval coast guards

Norway and Chile provide a good example of the third model – when the navy runs the coast guard but differentiates it from the rest of the naval service.[73] In some variants of this, personnel remain attached to the coast guard for most of their careers, in others people are rotated through at various stages. Either way relations are close.

Navies as coast guards

Most navies, in fact, are coast guards in all but name. Of the 32 navies in Latin America only those of Argentina, Brazil and Chile really look like conventional navies, with a capacity to operate major units out of area. Indeed, some authorities believe that a preoccupation with good order tasks is what defines a small navy. They are 'primarily designed, planned, prepared, and constructed to protect and enforce the national rights, as conferred by the 1982 United Nations Law of the Sea Convention, within the 200-mile limit of national [economic] waters'.[74] Malaysia decided not to follow the USCG route, thinking it too costly, and the navy is tasked with the maintenance of its maritime domain, in striking distinction to its neighbour Singapore, where such activities are specifically left to coast guard and other maritime agencies.

Naval capabilities and constraints

In this bewildering patchwork of diverse solutions to common problems, certain naval/military capabilities enable ocean management even when exerted by 'coast guard' forces. They include:

- Access to graduated force is useful for dealing with pirates, terrorists, aggressive poachers and vessels disputing sovereignty especially when globalisation is an increasing interest in other people's maritime domains. Although there are exceptions (Japan and Hong Kong) navies seem especially appropriate to sovereignty patrol. In fact, experience suggested that the Japanese Coast Guard needed to be beefed up in order to respond effectively to Chinese and North Korean incursions.[75]

- Naval forces are more likely to be able to provide the network-centric approach so useful in coordinating responses between different agencies.

- The capacity to operate in rough seas for prolonged periods. Having to deal with the sailing challenges of the southern ocean helps explain, for example, heavy naval involvement in ocean management in Chile, New Zealand and Australia.

- Military organisations tend to pride themselves on their discipline and efficiency, usually with some justification. Expertise in campaign planning makes navies good at threat analysis, strategic thinking and planning. In contrast, the events of 11 September showed that even the USCG had no off-the-shelf contingency plans for port security, and had got rid of more or less all its 'contingency planning officers'.[76]

- Navies have a public visibility that coast guard forces do not, and may therefore be especially good at selling the sea to governments and publics.

But there are constraints on the use of naval forces too. Most obviously, many countries have reservations about using the military (even the navy) for constabulary duties, and will insist on high levels of political control and naval subordination to law enforcement agencies. Equally obviously many of these tasks are quite specialist, and it is asking a lot of sailors trained for high-intensity operations to improvise effective responses to challenges as diverse as disposing of oil slicks or handling attacks by desperate female migrants old enough to be their grandmothers. The Palestine patrol experience shows that navy sailors can be trained for this, of course, but at some cost to their primary missions. Warships are usually more sophisticated, capable and expensive than most low-level tasks require and so may not offer particularly cost-effective solutions. Above all, the involvement of grey painted warships is often seen as unhelpfully escalatory.

Satisfying all levels of the ocean management requirement

The following requirements of effective ocean management seem to emerge from this review of the tasks involved and of what their effective performance usually demands, and incidentally illustrates the advantages of applying military planning techniques to this kind of thing.

- *The grand strategic level.* The world community needs to come together to provide integrated, overarching and global responses to the many threats to good order at sea that cannot be dealt with at the national or even the regional level. Such an 'away game' approach may well require significant efforts in building the governance and enforcement capacities of other countries. Australian and New Zealand maritime forces regard the provision of sea-based support to the struggling micro-states of the South Pacific as a means of helping them develop the natural resources of the area, its own economy and thus contribute to the area's stability.

- *The strategic level.* Countries need to think through their requirements in ocean management and arrive at a properly balanced policy that is comprehensive – not captured by any particular sectional interest but represents them all with sense and equity. It will identify the end state and an agenda for consequent implementation. It is likely to require establishing the importance of 'the sea affair' relative to other areas of government activity.
- *The operational level.* The importance and comprehensive nature of the task demands effective coordination between all customers and service providers. The ideal should be to provide a level of coordination that is so effective that it does not matter who is in charge of it. The most important operational level requirement is a capacity for sufficient surveillance and awareness across the area.[77] This will be achieved by means of everything from human intelligence through maritime patrol aircraft to UAVs at one end of the spectrum to oceanographic expertise at the other. Above all, it calls for a culture of information sharing between government agencies and foreign partners. The better this is, the more likely is it that ocean management will succeed.
- *The tactical level.* This requires specialist skills across this diverse field and, of course, the equipment to go with it. Probably no one but the USCG can aspire to the comparative riches of the 'Deepwater' programme, but it is plainly intended (not least by the manufacturers involved!) to set the gold standard for everyone to aspire to.[78] It involves a 30-year contract to deliver up to 91 ships, 35 fixed-wing aircraft, 34 helicopters and 76 UAVs, together with an upgrade of 49 existing cutters and 93 helicopters. Additionally, it will provide sophisticated systems for communications, surveillance and command and control so as to be able to 'integrate [the] operations of the new ships and planes, but also improve coordination of all Coast Guard operations, as well as with other federal agencies and the Department of Defense'. Partly reinforced by the events of 11 September and the requirements of homeland defence, the aspirations are clear:

> As the leader in Maritime Homeland Defense, the Coast Guard must have the most capable ships, aircraft, sensors and communications technology available to protect our nation and carry out our many missions. The Deepwater Program will give us the necessary tools to create an effective, layered defense of our nation's maritime interests.[79]

The ambitious scale of the 30-year Deepwater programme should not obscure the fact that even the USCG has often been critically underfunded in its chequered history, as have been some coast guard navies (such as Ireland's). Effective oceans management in the twenty-first century has required this problem to be addressed.[80]

11.12 Good order at sea: implications for navies

To the extent that they participate in good order tasks, all this is likely to affect naval preoccupations, attitudes, training and equipment. Two months in the life of HMS *Sheffield* illustrates the range of the challenges navies face:

- 1998 – deployed to Caribbean to support Britain's overseas territories and engage in counter-drug operations with the Dutch and US navies and the USCG.
- 22–24 September – conducted disaster relief in the island of St Kitts after Hurricane George. Repaired St Kitts' hospital and reopened the airport.
- 25 September to 23 October – counter-drug operations.
- 24 October – stood by LPG carrier *Arcadia* after an explosion killed three crew, injured four and put engines out of action. Lynx helicopter evacuated the casualties, engineers restarted the engines and *Arcadia* escorted to port.
- 5–13 November – disaster relief in Honduras and Nicaragua in the wake of Hurricane Mitch, providing extensive medical aid, fresh water, repair parties and command and control facilities. The Lynx was especially useful for initial reconnaissance, lift of aid stores and access where roads were blocked. On the first day off Honduras, 15 tonnes of drinking water was pumped ashore.

But the real point is that HMS *Sheffield* was not designed with such operations principally in mind. It is a highly capable Type-22 ASW frigate, originally intended for Cold War operations in the North Atlantic.

This, and the apparently unlikely 1993 deployment of the 2400-ton Canadian diesel submarine *Ojibwa* on fishery protection duties, reveal the versatility of the modern warship but should not conceal the crucial point that low-intensity good order tasks are often intrinsically different, demanding in terms of skill and equipment and most definitely not a soft option that can be exercised by any decent bluewater navy at a moment's notice. They require skills and equipment that are not necessarily very useful in high-intensity operations.

Conversely, trends in preparation for the latter may be at some tensions with the requirements of good order. The whole approach may be very different. To warfighting sailors, C3 means command, control and communication, but in good order tasks it more usually implies collaboration, cooperation and coordination, for example. Again, there are tensions in ship design. Humanitarian operations benefit from the manpower provided by large crews, but the trend in modern warship design is towards greatly reduced crew size. This may improve their cost-effectiveness in modern combat, but it would not help in disaster relief.

On the other hand, some trends in naval development are narrowing some aspects of the gap between good order tasks and conventional war-fighting ones. The current stress on expeditionary operations in the littoral, for example, is increasing interest in vessels well suited for disaster relief and in techniques such as surveillance in 'broken waters' rather than on the open ocean. This should facilitate operations against drug and people smugglers, help in environmental protection and so on.

Nonetheless, there is little doubt that these good order tasks are rising both in relative importance and in scope and difficulty. Moreover, the many good order tasks are notably diverse in themselves and have very different requirements for the forces performing them. A ship optimally suited for fishery protection, for example, would not be particularly well suited to disaster relief.

All this raises obvious choices for navies. Should they diversify in order to accommodate all these functions, or should they seek to hive off responsibility for good order tasks to coast guards, either within or without the naval service?

Their responses to such questions will reflect their own assumptions and approaches to future maritime operations. But these assumptions themselves may be affected by the increased attention being paid to general good order tasks, and it is to this broader question of future priorities and attitudes that we will finally now turn.

12 Theory and practice: the Asia-Pacific region

A case study

12.1 Introduction

The future modern/post-modern balance in the development of the world's navies will tend to reflect the importance of, and attitudes towards, the four attributes of the sea introduced in Chapter 2. While there is likely to be a considerable increase in cooperative naval/maritime endeavour both at and from the sea, traditional Mahanian ideas and naval necessities based on national and alliance competition will act as a constant if, possibly, changing constraint. To explore these issues a little more closely, this chapter will briefly review maritime developments in the Asia-Pacific as a case study of the way in which the ideas discussed in this book are being translated into naval practice. It will take the developing relationship between the navies of China, Japan, India and the United States as a means of doing this, in order to see what general conclusions can be drawn about the nature and future of seapower.

12.2 The maritime context

The Pacific and Indian Oceans certainly demonstrate the rising importance of the sea as a resource, as a means of transportation and as an area for dominion. Demand in oil and other mineral resources in these oceans will increase as the region's population, level of industrialisation, living standards and expectations go up. The local appetite for fish and other living marine resources is likewise expected to grow. These seas will be called upon to deliver new benefits as well; tide and wind energy, and very possibly potable water given existing shortages.[1]

But as we saw in the last chapter, all this is under increasing threat both from the prospect of enhanced competition (for example in the South and East China Seas) and bio-degradation resulting from pollution and climate change. These could lead to drastic falls in future economic activity at sea, and therefore ashore, at just the time when an increased population and environmental challenges require more resources. While many would conclude from this that mankind is facing the prospect of increased conflict over resources,[2] it is also possible to draw the opposite conclusion – namely, that unbridled competition for oil or fish, or for any other of the many resources of the sea, is likely to be increasingly recognised as a disaster for everyone.

The Indian and Pacific Oceans are also crucial to the peace and prosperity of the region as a means of transportation, not least of oil. Aware of its absolute economic dependence on marine transport and animated by one of the world's most coherent long-term maritime plans, China has developed into an all-round maritime player. Of the world's containers, 90 per cent are manufactured in China. It is the world's third largest shipbuilder after Japan and Korea. Chinese ports are expanding at a bewildering rate. Shanghai is now the world's largest cargo port and is putting considerable pressure on both Hong Kong and Singapore as container ports. Uncomfortable with an excessive reliance on foreign shipping, China first set up the China Ocean Shipping Company and then, to provide internal competition and the efficiencies that come with it, China Shipping Container Lines. These have both become major international shipping concerns and operate on a global scale being the sixth and eighth largest shipping companies in the world respectively. At the same time, China is seeking to develop an oceans policy and, in its maritime code, a set of commercial regulations intended to produce a sustainable long-term maritime future for the country. But along with its economic success has come a set of economic vulnerabilities that in turn provide major incentives to fit in with, and help protect, the world trading system from which it so obviously benefits.

Much of this is of economic and strategic benefit to the United States, for without it the general American cost of living would be higher and standards of living lower. In the same way, for all their economic competition and historic antipathies, trade binds China and Japan together. The recovery in the Japanese economy, for example, owed much to an expansion in Chinese demand. The same mutual benefits may be seen in the burgeoning economic links between China and India – countries that by 2040, according to Goldman Sachs, are likely to be the biggest and third biggest world economies. Bilateral trade in 1993 was a meagre $350 million. By 2007, this had risen to $30 billion and by 2015 could reach $50 billion. Joint China–India ventures are all the rage.[3]

Free trade and strong economic interdependencies, the argument goes, may not guarantee international peace, but they do provide real disincentives against reckless policies, and help improve relations between India and all its neighbours. Thus Admiral Mehta, Chief of the Indian Naval Staff in 2007:

> [W]e in India find ourselves in the midst of an unprecedented globalisation of trade, technology, media and a host of other areas of human activity. We are acutely aware that this interdependence is, in fact, the defining characteristic of the modern world. In the wake of this interdependence has come the realisation that there is a pressing need to assure security in all its myriad forms ... We recognise that in the maritime domain, the security of one is intimately connected to the security of all.[4]

Leaders of the other countries in the region are broadly sympathetic to such views, and to the consequent notion that the international community has collectively to address the problems and threats that globalisation faces.

All these countries, moreover, have suffered from, and so have common interests against, terrorism and other forms of transnational crime both on land and at sea. For such reasons they have all gone out of their way, wherever possible, to emphasise the benign nature of their intentions and expectations.

Such comforting expectations of increasing cooperation are, however, countered by those who point out that there is a strong element of competition in these linkages too, not least for foreign investment and in particular for oil and other resources, and this could well have the reverse effect, especially when India's manufacturing industries start seriously to grow. Energy demand in the Asia-Pacific region has been rising at an annual rate of 3–5 per cent for nearly 20 years – faster, some say, than new supplies can be located. Japan is actually more dependent on oil from abroad than is China.[5] China, India and Japan are engaged in acute competition for oil and gas resources in Russia, Kazakhstan, Myanmar, Iran and the Sudan, and this could easily develop geo-political consequences. Moreover both Japan and China show great concern about their reliance on shipping routes across the Indian Ocean and especially through the Straits of Malacca.

The continued survival of national or sectional interests is often associated with old-fashioned mercantilist images of trade, in which competition rather than cooperation is emphasised, and which are consequently different, in tone and expectation, from the arguments advanced by the proponents of globalisation. Indeed, from this perspective, globalisation is seen less as something that is in the interest of all, more as something to exploit in the national or company interest.

The Asia-Pacific provides plenty of evidence of all this. The three cornered relationship between China, Japan and South Korea is heavily influenced by trading rivalries. China's entry into the WTO provides both a gigantic market and a ferocious low-cost competitor. Malaysia's establishment of the container port of Pelars Tanjong in Jahore, which threatens drastically to undercut Singapore's more expensive facilities, is a more localised example of the economics of competition. The survival of such ancient attitudes suggests a need for caution about the extent to which the world has changed through free trade and globalisation:

> There is a fashionable view that geography and geopolitics are no longer relevant in the post-Cold War era. That is demonstrably untrue in Asia, where there is a fierce sense of national sovereignty, enormous variations in culture and civilisation, and a struggle for power and influence among the region's great powers.[6]

All this raises echoes of a more pessimistic view of human possibilities than was held by nineteenth-century free traders. It leads to the conclusion that proclivities towards intense competition will endure, despite economic convergence between different countries through globalisation, and that international peace remains fragile.[7] The survival of the assertive nation state as a unit of concern may combine with sometimes ferocious levels of economic competition to produce an environment in which the sea continues to be seen as a medium for dominion in ways that are all too familiar from previous eras. In consequence, navies can be expected to have much the same set of operational preoccupations as their predecessors.

The Asia-Pacific region is therefore characterised by a complex, shifting sea-based strategic environment in which modern conflictual elements in the relations of states are mixed with post-modern cooperative ones. From this we should expect that in their thinking, their activities and the size and shape of their fleets, all the region's navies will reflect this mixed approach.

12.3 Strategic thinking

There has been a marked tendency on the part of the world's navies to produce doctrinal statements, partly to prepare for a more joint future with the other services, and partly to remind their own governments, publics and media of the expanding importance of seapower. In the case of India and China, this is essentially a matter of *rediscovery* of a maritime past after centuries of extremely harmful neglect. Although their approach to the theoretical exposition of their naval roles and purposes is different, all the navies in this brief survey exhibit a blend of modern and post-modern naval assumptions about the balances to be struck in their current and future roles, and clearly demonstrate an awareness of each other's activities and apparent intentions.

China

The Chinese, for example, are perfectly aware that while their increasing integration into the world system may both reduce the incentive for, and even the possibility of, independent national action, their global exposure in some ways is actually increasing the perceived need for more capable naval forces. Thus, as one Chinese analyst has observed: 'Economic globalization entails globalization of the military means for self-defence ... With these complex and expanding interests, risks to China's well-being have not lessened, but have actually increased.'[8] This would require a move away from traditional People's War type of thinking and towards a substantial accommodation to 'modern conditions'.

As a result, the Chinese People's Liberation Army Navy's (PLA(N)) policy and thinking has come a long way since the early 1980s, when the PLA(N)'s tasks were seen as essentially to offer an immediate defence of the country's coastline and the direct support of the operations of the all-important PLA, particularly against the threat of a major assault from the north. The appointment of Admiral Liu Huaqing as Commander-in-Chief of the PLA(N) in 1982, together with the professional need to learn the lessons of the Falklands campaign of the same year and the Gulf War of 1991, accelerated the need to consider the way in which 'modern conditions' required a rethink of the navy's place in China's defence. The result has been a steady increase in the maritime rather than continental orientation of Chinese thinking, and a forward rather than a rearward defensive approach. This was reflected in a continuing ferment of professional theoretical discussion in China about the way forward, that is surprisingly candid and accessible.

By the end of that decade the *Liberation Army Daily* and a number of senior naval officers were calling for a new 'offshore defence strategy' that would extend China's operational areas into the North and South West Pacific. According to Admiral Lin Zhiye, then Commandant of the Naval Academy, this concept of 'adjacent sea defence' could see the development of fleets able to engage an enemy, sometime in the twenty-first century, with a 'decisive seaward blow' to, and ultimately beyond, the 'first island chain' of Japan, Okinawa, Taiwan and the Philippines.[9] This would require the PLA(N) to move forwards from inshore waters (*Jinan*) to 'green waters (*Jinhai*) with a prospective move later to the bluewaters of the 'second island chain'.

China clearly had all the Mahanian attributes of seapower and all that was needed was a policy directive to move in this direction.[10] The rise to influence of

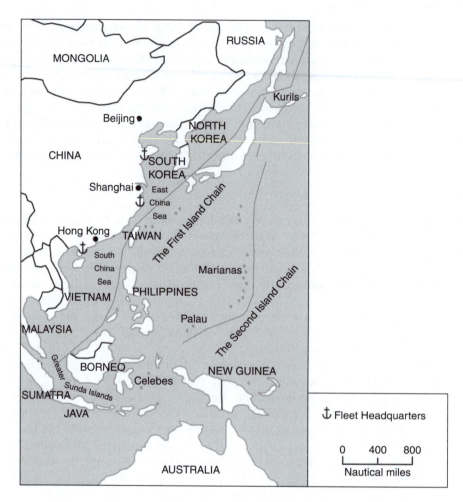

Figure 12.1 The first and second island chains.

Admiral Liu Huaqing as member of the Politburo Standing Committee, a member and then the chairman of the Central Mission Commission, was seen by many as an indication that such a directive had been given and that the navy was increasingly seen as *primus inter pares*. Along with the navy commissar, Li Yaowen, Admiral Liu produced in February 1987 the doctrinal statement 'On the Question of Establishing the Naval Strategy'. Subsequently approved by the Central Military Commission, it has acted as an outline doctrinal guide ever since. Much of the thinking about what 'adjacent sea defence' actually meant remained notably opaque, however. Some light was cast on this by the appearance in 1993 of a book entitled *Can China's Armed Forces Win the Next War?* Evidently written by a number of anonymous naval writers, it seemed to suggest a primary focus on China's needing to advance its interest in the South China Sea (for which it would need a carrier force) while, in the longer term, developing the capacity to take on the United States over Taiwan should the need arise.[11]

Japan

Since the Yoshida doctrine of the 1940s, Japan's navy or, more correctly, the JMSDF has tended to accommodate its thinking to, and so been reliant on, American thinking about maritime security in the Asia-Pacific. But in their emergent independent strategic thinking, the Japanese are plainly aware of the modern/postmodern choices they need to make. 'A rich and powerful Japan in a region as dangerous as East Asia', wrote Vice Admiral Hideaki Kaneda recently, 'cannot go on playing bit parts forever. The question is whether Japan's SDF [Self Defence Forces] work beside America and the world in defence of peace now, or eventually do so alone in defence of Japan.'[12] Assessing how this translates into conceptions of mission is complicated by the fact that, like the Chinese, the Japanese Navy does not make its doctrine publicly available. This has accordingly to be inferred from a variety of sources, most obviously the country's official defence policy, and the statements of retired officers. The country's National Defence Programme Outline (NDPO) of December 2004 and its Defence White Paper of August 2005 identify two major strategic requirements for the country's armed forces. The first is 'to prevent and repel any threat against Japan' – clearly a traditional, modernist perspective. Since Japan comprises some 400 inhabited islands, has the world's sixth largest EEZ and is dependent on sea lines of communication by which come 95 per cent of its raw materials, over 60 per cent of its food and nearly all its trade, a recognised need for significant forces to defend its maritime space and interests is hardly surprising. Japan has very long SLOCS and an enormous sea frontier of some 17,000 miles to defend – and it enjoys little strategic depth. Honshu, for example, is barely 160 miles east-to-west.

These constraints are relevant to two of the Japanese Navy's main preoccupations – with the defence of its SLOCs and increasingly with the need for ballistic missile defence, most obviously against North Korea, but also against China. The resultant stresses on modern anti-air and anti-submarine capabilities are expensive naval disciplines. Investing in them seriously means fewer resources and ships available for such other post-modern purposes, such as collective action against international terrorism. Naturally many of these traditional preoccupations have analogies to those of previous times. In this regard the slow parallel shift in attitude in recent years towards the Imperial Japanese Navy is significant. Unsurprisingly, this has reinforced perceptions in some quarters that Japan is indeed re-embarking on a more assertive course, which could destabilise the security of Asia.

But against all this must be put the other, markedly post-modern focus of official Japanese defence pronouncements. Recent defence policy formulations are clear about the diversity and the unpredictable nature of the threats confronting Japan and the need for proactive measures against them. The NDPO contains much, in any case, that is notably post-modern and collectivist in approach: 'Japan will engage in its own diplomatic activities to prevent the emergence of threat by improving the international security environment, based on the principle of acting closely with the international community and Japan's alliance partner.'[13] In its actions in the Indian Ocean and Iraq, Japan seems to be rethinking its alliance with the United States, considering it as a partnership intended to contribute to global stability rather than merely a traditional exercise in national defence.

India

In its slow development of a concept of the role of maritime power that would guide its programme of acquisition and procurement, and perhaps protect the navy from the vicissitudes and sea-blindness so often lamented in the past, the Indian Navy has increased emphasis on sea-based deterrence, economic and energy security, forwards presence and naval diplomacy. In this, the publication in 2004 of *Indian Maritime Doctrine* (*IMD*) was an important development; although still largely operational in focus, it reflects an interesting blend of broader ideas. This was followed up by the appearance of *Freedom to Use the Seas: India's Maritime Military Strategy* (*MMS*) in 2007.[14] This latter publication was clearly intended to move the debate closer to the business of 'relating ends to means' and of offering 'a foundation for the planning and conduct of operations'. It was also clearly associated with the need to overcome the interservice rivalry that has so bedevilled Indian military affairs in the past.[15]

Both reveal an interesting blend of modern and post-modern preoccupations and both are entirely consistent with the foreign policy approach adopted by Dr Manmohan Singh. Blocked to some extent by Pakistan, Afghanistan and China to the north, Indian policy has taken a markedly maritime turn, particularly in its 'Look East' and 'Look West' policies, reflecting a notable expansion of India's internationalist interests, the expanding role in globalisation, India's concern for its diaspora and its awareness of the impact on its strategic environment of the expanding reach of other key players, such as the United States but, most notably, China.[16]

The Indian Navy's current transformational emphasis is on expanding its reach, in potential general defence of the system, alongside its maritime partners. Consequently there is a good deal of emphasis on constructive engagement with others; on the other hand, the tone of much of its discourse still seems to reflect continuing modernist concerns about Pakistan and possibly China.

The United States

Finally, the challenges of dealing with the conditions of the twenty-first century were explicitly addressed by the US Navy with the production of *Sea Power 21* in 2002. The aim of this was 'to ensure that our nation possesses credible combat capability on scene to promote regional stability, to deter aggression throughout the world, to assure access of joint forces and to fight and win should deterrence fail'. The pillars of *Sea Power 21* were Sea Strike, Sea Shield and Sea Base the whole integrated by FORCEnet, 'the means by which the power of sensors, networks, weapons and platforms are harnessed in a networked combat force'.[17]

The differences and indeed the tensions between modern and post-modern tendencies were later interestingly revealed in the rather contrasting treatments given the challenges posed by 'rising peer competitors' (a modernist preoccupation), on the one hand, and 'a variety of violent extremists, insurgents, pirates, criminals and paramilitary forces who seek to destabilize legitimate governments' (a postmodernist approach), on the other, in both the *Naval Operations Concept*, 2006, and the *Navy Strategic Plan* of May 2006.[18]

'Despite the current focus on fighting the GWOT',[19] says the *Strategic Plan*, 'the United States still faces traditional threats from regional powers with robust conventional [and in some cases, nuclear] capabilities.'[20] Modernists in the US Navy are

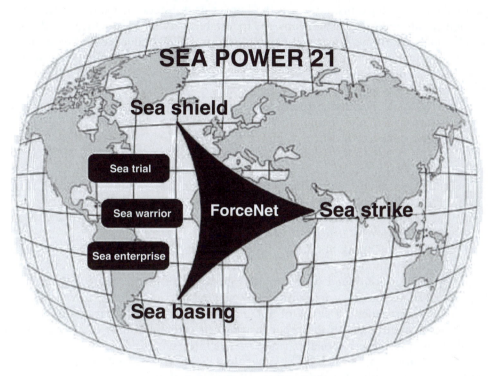

Figure 12.2 Sea Power 21.

clearly substantially concerned about the development of the Chinese Navy and about the future situation in the East and South China seas.[21] '[The] Navy must possess the capabilities, and communicate to other nations that it possesses the will to employ those capabilities, to help the Joint Force deny, deter, dissuade and defeat a future competitor.'[22]

On the other hand, the same document exhibits a good deal of concern about current and future risks to good order at sea and the need to keep:

> the maritime domain free and open to the unimpeded flow of vital resources, goods and commodities … Transnational threats are becoming increasingly problematic because today, more than ever, promoting and maintaining the freedom of the seas is critical to any nation's long-term economic well-being.

These issues were further explored later in 'A Cooperative Strategy for 21st Century Seapower', the 4000 word document issued in October 2007 that was briefly reviewed in Chapter 3. This document is clear about the need to 'sustain the global inter-connected system through which we prosper' and that 'Our Nation's interests are best served by fostering a peaceful global system comprised of interdependent networks of trade, finance, information, law, people and governance.'[23] This post-modern allusion to the need to defend the global system calls for integrated action by the 'maritime services', defined as the US Navy, Marine Corps and Coast

Guard. This will require an ability to 'win the long struggle against terrorist networks, positively influence events, and ease the impact of disasters'. It will be necessary to strengthen international partnerships and to 'establish favourable security conditions'. 'Additionally, maritime forces will be employed to build confidence and trust among nations through collective security efforts that focus on common threats and mutual interests in an open, multi-polar world.' All this is justified by the central concept that 'preventing wars is as important as winning wars'[24] – a concept wholly consistent with the 2005 National Defense Strategy's emphasis on 'the importance of influencing events before challenges become more dangerous and less manageable'.

The same concept, however, applies to the 'modern' preoccupations against which all this needs to be balanced. Seapower has to be applied in a manner that 'protects US vital interests even as it promotes greater collective security, stability and trust'. Accordingly 'defending our homeland and defeating adversaries in war remain the indisputable ends of seapower'. This means conducting military operations that 'secure the United States from direct attack; secure strategic access and retain global freedom of action'.

The document is frank about the difficulties of reconciling the demands of these modern and post-modern preoccupations. 'There is a tension, however, between the requirements for continued peacetime engagement and maintaining proficiency in the critical skills necessary to fighting and winning in combat.' The answer appears to be 'an unprecedented level of integration among our maritime forces and enhanced cooperation with the other instruments of national power, as well as the capabilities of our international partners.'[25] The inference would seem to be that the range of requirements is such that neither the US Navy, nor the other two maritime services, nor indeed the United States itself can 'go it alone'.

A document of merely 4000 words trying to address so large a subject is probably bound to encounter criticism, but the difficulties in striking the modern/post-modern balance are clear both in the document and in people's reactions to it.[26]

12.4 Mission issues arising

Nuclear deterrence/ballistic missile defence

All four of these navies currently direct considerable thought and effort to the nuclear deterrent mission and/or the erection of defences against it. This is perhaps the most quintessentially modern of all the possible functions of seapower since it is about the potential survival or destruction of nations, and generally requires national levels of effort. The Chinese and the Indians have clearly articulated an interest in creating a capacity for Continous At Sea (Nuclear) Deterrence (CASD), India making the modernist case most explicitly:

> India stands out alone as being devoid of a credible nuclear triad. It is one of the tenets of the post Cold War era that the ability of a nation to adopt a truly independent foreign policy/posture is inexorably linked with such a strategic capability either directly or indirectly.[27]

In the United States, too, there remain high levels of agreement about the necessity for a secure nuclear deterrent force at sea and for the navy to be able to defend itself against anti-access strategies based on the use of ballistic missiles and/or weapons of mass destruction.[28] 'Maritime ballistic missile defense', Admiral Roughead told Congress in February 2008, 'directly contributes to the navy's core capability of deterrence, and enables our core capabilities of power projection and sea control.'[29] Accordingly it has very high priority. Arguably ballistic missile defence (BMD), particularly in the shape of its *Kongou* class destroyers, is Japan's top priority, given its proximity to North Korea and the likely growth of Chinese nuclear missile power, and there has been talk in some circumstances of their acquiring more proactive defences against it. As yet, however, neither Japan, China nor India are able to deploy CASD although this does seem the direction of travel, and in current circumstances it seems a very modernist one.

Sea control/denial

Because this concept is at the heart of seapower, the local debate about its future direction is particularly significant. Western commentators believe there to be a growing stress on Mahanian thinking in Chinese naval discourse. At a symposium conducted in Beijing in 2004, Chinese analysts pointed out the need for China to 'build up a strong sea power guarding against the threats to our "outward leaning economy" by some strong nations'. Globalisation did *not* mean the end of such traditional conceptions as the command of the sea, bearing in mind that 'Mahan believed that whoever could control the sea is achieved through decisive naval battles on the sea; that the outcome of decisive battles is determined by the strength of fire power on each side of the engagement.' 'One can only guarantee smooth sea traffic and eventually gain sea domination by annihilating the enemy' in large-scale fleet engagements. This is quite different from the language of protracted local defensive resistance that was all that China was once thought to have aspired to.[30]

There are clearly three aspects to Chinese thinking on sea control/denial. The first is to do with the concept's role in the direct defence of China itself. Here the role of the navy is seen to be of an expanded Gorshkovian system of concentric defence of the type aspired to by the Soviet Navy of the Cold War era. Hence Admiral Liu's successor, Admiral Zhang Lianzhong, in 1988:

> The exterior perimeter is conceived as encompassing the seas out to the first chain of islands. This region will be defended by conventional and nuclear submarines [some of which will be armed with anti-ship missiles], by naval medium-range aircraft and by surface warships. The submarines will play a dynamic role to ensure defence in depth, including the laying of mines in the enemy's sea lines of communication. The middle distance perimeter extends 150 miles from the coast and comes within, but in most cases does not reach the first chain of islands. Anti-ship aircraft, destroyers and escort vessels will carry the main burden in this area. The interior defence perimeter extends to 60 miles from the coast. This will be the theatre of operations for the main naval air force, fast-attack boats and land-based anti-ship missile units.[31]

To support this kind of modernist sea denial thinking, the Chinese are building good quality submarines, aircraft and surface combatants armed with an increasing variety of longer-range high speed anti-ship missiles that would put some key American assets at significant risk at least within the first island chain. Such missiles include the new HN3 2500 km range naval cruise missile and the supersonic 2200 km YJ12; together with the SS-N-22 Sunburn missiles of the Sovremennys and the SS-N-27 Sizzlers of the Kilo class of submarine, this would constitute a significant threat that Chinese strategists might feel would help deter the Americans from aggressive action, perhaps in support of some Taiwanese démarche.

Chinese strategists also tend to emphasise the determining effect of their local maritime geography, especially the island of Taiwan and the first island chain. The second aspect of their sea control thinking might come into play were these concerns to be resolved in the wider Pacific. Those concerned that China's seizure of those islands would transform the strategic situation opening the Pacific and Indian Ocean to endless further Chinese advance tend to have the same traditional, geo-strategic perspective.[32] Here, the worry is that later in the century, China will develop, and possibly exploit, sea control capabilities well beyond the first island chain, which seem less about the immediate defence of the homeland and its islands and more about challenging the American dominance of the Pacific. This longer-term aspiration is held to be an important driver in China's military modernisation. Thus, the 2007 report by a task force sponsored by the American Council on Foreign Relations: 'China's military modernization has two main drivers, one with a clear *operational* objective [Taiwan] and the other with a clear *strategic* objective [to be a modern power].[33] The third and final focus is on the defence of Chinese SLOCs, given the country's absolute dependence on trade in general and the transportation of oil in particular. President Hu Jintao has alluded to the country's 'Malacca dilemma', by which China's prosperity and strategic independence rests on secure sea lines of communication over which it can currently exert little or no control. Chinese post-modernists tend to be quite relaxed about this, doubting the likelihood of serious attack on its SLOCs, on the one hand, while offering the prospect of collaborative solutions to such problems should they materialise, on the other. According to one speaker at a conference held in Beijing in 2004:

> China should not act by following traditional sea power theory in pursuing a strong navy, because today's world situation is different from the time of Mahan … that the globalisation of the world's economy has made various countries' interests interconnected, mutually dependent on each other to a great degree, and that if a country wants to preserve its life line at sea, the only way to do so is to go through 'cooperation' rather than the traditional 'solo fight'.[34]

Modernists, however, contend that the potential insecurity of its SLOCs remains a major strategic vulnerability that needs to be corrected in the long run, not least because the continued goodwill of the United States (or for that matter other countries such as Japan or India) in all circumstances should not be assumed. *China's National Defence in 2004* argued that 'struggles for strategic points, strategic resources and strategic dominance [would] crop up from time to time' and that because of this the PLA(N) should build forces capable of 'winning both command of the sea and command of the air', evidently the first such explicit mention of the notion in official documentation.[35] Major General Jiang Shiliang made the same point: 'In modern times, efforts aimed at securing the absolute control of communications are turning with each passing day into an indispensable essential factor in ensuring the realisation of national interests', not least since economic development depended on 'the command of communications on the sea'.[36]

Chinese naval discourse has acknowledged the obvious problems they would encounter in any bid to protect their SLOCs against serious opposition, namely, problems in forwards logistics support, weak anti-submarine capacities and an absence of organic airpower and ocean-going battlegroups.[37] China is clearly now in no position to defend its more distant foreign energy supply and general trade routes but may feel the need to build such a capacity up for the longer term. This kind of thinking has led to China's alleged 'string of pearls' concept for an extension of their areas of concern around South East Asia and across the Indian Ocean to the Gulf and East Africa. 'China has to turn to the international resource supply system, and will seek military force to safeguard its share when necessary', said Zhang Wenmy of the China Institute of Contemporary International Relations in 2005: 'There has never been a case in history where such a pursuit was realised in peace.'[38] The aspiration to defend these interests *individually* and possibly against the United States, India and even Japan would seem markedly modernist in conception, and certain to provoke countervailing reactions.[39]

* * *

A concern for the security of their SLOCs is also manifest in the thinking of the Indian, and especially the Japanese navies, Japan being the most dependent of all on the sea-based importation of such life essentials as oil and food, and having the bitter historical experience needed to drive home the strategic consequences of such dependence. The Japanese share the conception that SLOC security is a systemic problem. Thus Admiral Akimoto: 'the defence of sea lanes is not so much a national interest of individual states as it is … a global interest' that calls for maritime countries like Japan to contribute to the system's defence.[40]

* * *

Perhaps unsurprisingly, Indian naval officers often refer to Mahan's conclusion: 'Whoever controls the Indian Ocean dominates Asia. This ocean is the key to the seven seas. In the Twenty-first Century, the destiny of the world will be decided on its waters.'[41] Their perspective on sea control and SLOC defence is accordingly both national and global. Indian expositions tend to emphasise the extent to which the Indian Ocean is an international waterway crucial to the well being of the world economy, particularly given its absolute dependence on energy security. Accordingly, the 'Indian navy sees itself as a major stabilising force in this great movement of energy across the Indian ocean, not just for India, but for the world at large'.[42] Here, India would act as a responsible post-modern stakeholder in the world trading system against all those who would disrupt it, ensuring 'a measure of stability and tranquillity in the waters around our shores' for '[s]maller nations in our neighbourhood as well as nations that depend on the waters of the Indian ocean for their trade and energy supplies'.[43]

At the same time, India has its own strictly national concerns about the SLOCs too. The need to secure energy supply lines from the Gulf is regarded as 'a primary national maritime interest'.[44] 'The likely shortage of oil and gas supplies in the future could even lead to conflicts over this vital resource, as has happened in the recent past.' Given that India is the sixth highest energy consumer in the world, it is hardly surprising that providing 'maritime security for supply lines and installations will remain a primary responsibility of the Indian navy' against both 'internal sabotage and external attack'.[45]

This is clearly part of a broader, traditional more modernist philosophy of sea control:

> [O]ur primary maritime military interest is to ensure national security, provide insulation from external interference, so that the vital tasks of fostering economic growth and undertaking developmental activities, can take place in a secure environment. Consequently, India's maritime military strategy is underpinned on 'the freedom to use the seas for our national purposes, under all circumstances'.

Accordingly sea control is valued for the independence of action it confers. Because this independence of action is so crucial, 'sea control is the central concept around which the Indian Navy is structured'.[46] *Indian Maritime Doctrine* is quite explicit about what this might mean: 'One school of thought avers that the fleet battles of the past are part of military history and that such exigencies will not occur again. It is only a rash security planner who will be so complacent.'[47] Accordingly, 'The Indian Navy is structured to comprehensively subdue a range of potential adversaries in a conflict.' This emphasis no doubt derives from India's experience of three wars with Pakistan and explains both the devotion in *MMS* of a whole chapter to how the navy would be employed in a conventional state-on-state conflict and India's wary reaction to an ambitious, modernising Chinese Navy's 'attempts to gain [a] strategic toe-hold in the IOR'.[48]

* * *

US thinking on sea control is also interestingly varied. On the one hand there are strong 'modernist' perspectives in 'A Cooperative Strategy'. Sea control is seen as the crucial enabler, and American determination to maintain it is manifest:

> We will not permit conditions under which our maritime forces would be impeded from freedom of maneuver and freedom of access, nor will we permit an adversary to disrupt the global supply chain by attempting to block vital sea-lines of communication and commerce. We will be able to impose local sea control wherever necessary, ideally in concert with friends and allies, but by ourselves if we must.[49]

This involves maintaining the capacity to deal with 'anti-access strategies' based on ballistic missiles as we have seen, or swarming attacks by small attack craft, by aircraft from shore and, most particularly, from submarines. 'Submarines', said Admiral Roughead recently, 'remain an immediate threat and their roles and lethality increasing. More countries are buying submarines; some are building anti-access strategies around them. Maintaining the ability to detect, locate, track and destroy submarines is essential.'[50]

On the other hand, when he was still CNO, Admiral Mullen, as we saw in Section 1.2 has made some very different post-modernist remarks about the essential nature of copntemporary sea control.

But there is a third angle to US thinking and policy on sea control as well, namely, a concern to bridge the gap between bluewater operations and the land. 'A naval force floating off the continental shelf with no impact onshore is not decisive', remarked Admiral Mullen. 'We must go forward to the very reaches of the sea, operating effectively in every part of the littoral and beyond.' Pointing to the fact that nearly one-third of the waters of the north Arabian Gulf are inaccessible for ships with drafts more than 20 feet he urged the need to:

> Think of the vast areas of the world covered by shallow water those connected to the oceans by rivers, and harbours, and rugged shorelines. These are the decisive strips of sea that make all the difference. And we need to be there.

To operate in places where the ground was, in President Lincoln's words 'a little damp' requires the navy to win the inshore battle as well as the offshore one.[51] Hence the notable increase of US interest in riverine warfare, and battle space dominance in littoral waters.

The actions of these four navies are entirely consistent with the broad, largely modernist aspects of their thinking and China once again appears to be the point of common interest, and the naval balance between the US and Chinese navies key to regional reactions. The Chinese have frequently evinced a determination to demonstrate a capacity to contest sea control outside as well as inside their waters. In November 2006, in an incident that could be construed as a part of China's preparations for a campaign of sea denial, a diesel powered Song submarine surfaced within five miles of the USS *Kitty Hawk* battlegroup operating near Okinawa. Denying this was a deliberate part of their developing anti-access strategy against the United States, the Chinese claimed it to be nothing more than an accidental encounter, and that the submarine in question did not have the speed to trail the battlegroup. Perhaps in part because of their embarrassment at having been thus surprised (to the extent they were), and partly in a bid to prevent this incident turning into a crisis, the response of US Fleet commander, Admiral Fallon, was quite muted. He pointed out that the battlegroup had not been exercising its ASW capabilities at the time but if it had been 'and if this Chinese submarine came in the middle of this, then it could have escalated into something that could have been very unforeseen'.[52]

China's more recent and more controversial anti-satellite test of January 2007 was also widely and likewise interpreted as an exercise in the PLA(N)'s developing anti-access capability. Commentators point out that the US Navy, with its emphasis on networking and cooperative engagement, is heavily reliant on satellite communications and that an attack on its satellites would therefore much degrade its performance, unless sufficient counters were found.[53] Some of the more ambitious Chinese operations have also led to difficulties with Japan. The passage of a Han class SSN around Guam while exercises involving the US Pacific Fleet were taking place and then, in November 2004, its return journey through Japanese waters, was taken by both countries as evidence of a need to build up ASW capabilities. The fact that the submarine had left the area of concern before the Japanese Navy was able to intercept it, despite prior notification from the US Navy, brought home to the Japanese their need for greater command flexibility and more sophisticated equipment if they really aimed to control their own seas against such intrusions, especially as the Chinese Navy seemed engaged in a major programme of hydrographic survey and testing throughout the area.[54] The subsequent pursuit of the submarine until it reached Chinese waters and the extraction of a private apology shows how seriously the Japanese took this incident.

Japanese sensitivity about sea control in their immediate area was undoubtedly reinforced by similar less publicised incidents involving Chinese units on previous occasions in the Osumi and Miuyako Straits and, even more, by the dramatic intrusions into Japanese waters by North Korean vessels. After an earlier incident in 1999, which alerted the Japanese to a rising problem, a North Korean spy ship was intercepted by the Japanese Coast Guard (JCG) in Japanese waters in December 2001 and was then chased out into Chinese waters where after an exchange of fire, it sank with the loss of all 15 crew members. Again the Japanese felt so strongly about this challenge to their capacity to control their own seas that they sought an accommodation with the Chinese by which they could salvage the vessel, proving conclusively that it was indeed North Korean, and then put the wreck on to public display as evidence of the need for continued vigilance, better coordination between the navy and the JCG and more heavily armed coast guard patrol boats.[55] In short, this requirement seems to be attracting a steadily more robust response from the Japanese.

* * *

Although during its two wars with Pakistan in 1964 and 1971, the Indian Navy engaged in standard sea control operations, its sea control experience since then has largely been restricted to exercises in the hard disciplines of ASW and anti-air warfare, which have been conducted in a manner entirely consistent with the notion that war-fighting remains its core function. However, the Indian Navy's experience in the messier post-modern situation in the Palk Strait in consequence of its involvement in the Sri Lankan conflict has shown just how difficult it is to identify and deal with irregular adversaries. It has brought home to them just how difficult and how different is the force protection variant of sea control in littoral operations.

Finally, and turning briefly back to the issue of SLOC protection, the JMSDF and JCG have shown themselves more than willing to engage constructively with other forces in South East Asia and indeed with India over this in recent years. Like the other three navies, China and India, Japan has evinced a post-modern desire to contribute to the defence of the SLOCs, over a much wider area than it used to. At the same time the JMSDF's efforts have been backed up by the 'soft power' resources of organisations like the coast guard and the Nippon Foundation in contributing, for example, to SLOC security and navigational safety in the Straits of Malacca.[56] India and the United States have followed the same post-modern path in emphasising the *collaborative* nature of this campaign.

Expeditionary operations/maritime power projection

For different reasons, neither China nor Japan devotes much public discussion to the issue of power projection or its post-modern expeditionary variant, and their capabilities for other than local operations, while growing, remain modest. The Chinese South China Sea Fleet conducted a successful takeover amphibious operation against the Vietnamese in the Paracels in 1974, rehearsed this capability again in 1980 and carried out a similar operation, again against the Vietnamese, on Fiery Cross reef in the Spratleys in 1988. Their East China Sea Fleet has conducted a number of large amphibious operations in a manner and a location plainly intended to convey messages of dissuasion to Taiwan. All of these operations were modern in conception. The same would seem to go for Japan's theoretical capacity to engage in small-scale amphibious operations in any of Japan's disputed island territories, but its actual exercises in power projection, however, have been determined in the main by the post-modernist agenda of supporting stability operations in a wider world. Although it is still constrained by its current constitution, recent reinterpretations of that constitution have allowed the JMSDF to take on an increasingly expeditionary character with its involvement in the multilateral Afghan and Iraq operations, especially through continuing logistical support for coalition forces engaged in Operation Enduring Freedom in the Indian Ocean and, indeed, for its own reconstruction teams in Iraq.

Indian thinking, operations and construction, while demonstrating the same tendency to cater for both modern and post-modern contingencies, has a strongly modern tone. In its extended and business-like discussion of the employment of the navy in a conventional state-on-state conflict, most obviously but by no means exclusively in renewed conflict with Pakistan, *MMS* makes the point that the function of the navy would be to have as early and as significant an impact on the land battle as possible. The phasing of information dominance, sea control/denial, support operations, the all-arms battle leading to the final joint operations phases is given prominence. 'This is a major shift from the earlier strategy which believed that victory in the war at sea would produce its own beneficial effects on the land battle, albeit is a delayed and roundabout way.' Now, by contrast:

> The sea war is a phase that now has to be gone through in a shorter time frame, so that the navy participates in the final phase aimed at the enemy's Centre of Gravity, which invariably will be on land.[57]

Accordingly, influencing events on land is seen as one of the primary roles of the Indian Navy.

This is, perhaps, hardly surprising given India's experience. The Indian Navy has been instrumental in a number of relatively small-scale land attack/expeditionary operations – against Goa in 1961, and in the suppression of an insurrection in the Maldives in November 1988. In the 1971 war with Pakistan, the navy intervened in operations in what was to become Bangladesh and its missile craft attacked Karachi. During the so-called Kargil War of 2002, the Indian Navy deployed into the Arabian Sea stripped for action; its potential capacity to repeat this performance with attacks on the shore was clearly intended as a deterrent.[58]

The navy's developing interest in littoral operations was suggested by a large-scale Tropex (theatre readiness operational exercise) held in February 2007 in the Arabian Sea involving ships of Western and Eastern commands, plus specialist army units, air force fighters and coast guard ships. According to a spokesman:

> The thrust of this year's edition was to validate the concept of 'Maritime Manoeuvre from the Sea' that is designed to ensure that is a short swift and intense conflict, the navy is able to directly address and favourably influence the progress and outcome of the air–land battle.[59]

The Indian Navy has also developed expertise in complex expeditionary operations, thanks largely to their hard-won experience in the long-drawn out and, for India, politically complex conflict in Sri Lanka between the government and the

Tamil Tigers. This has involved the support of forces ashore for long periods, and the protection of Indian fishing boats and merchant ships from Tamil Tiger attack.

This latter is one of those areas where a certain Indian–American convergence is noticeable. For the US Navy, the ability to access, project and sustain power ashore 'is the basis of our combat credibility' and depends heavily on a 'robust strategic sea-lift capability'. 'A Cooperative Strategy' emphasises the advantages conferred by the 'expeditionary character and versatility of maritime forces'. It says:

> U.S. maritime forces will be characterised by regionally concentrated, forward-deployed task forces with the combat power to limit regional conflict, deter major power war, and should deterrence fail, win our nation's wars as part of a joint or combined campaign.

The 'global reach, persistent presence, and operational flexibility inherent in U.S. seapower' will allow it to 'limit regional conflict with forward deployed, decisive maritime power ... [with powerful forces] capable of selectively controlling the seas, projecting power ashore, and protecting friendly forces and civilian populations from attack'.[60] At the same time such forces should be able to win any war that it has been unable to deter.

Surprisingly, there is no specific mention of sea-basing, amphibious assault or strike warfare in 'A Cooperative Strategy' but these concepts have become familiar since the launch of 'From the Sea' in 1992. Thinking here, not unnaturally, was led by the US Marine Corps whose aim was to make the maximum use of the sea as the world's greatest manoeuvre space, together with the traditional mobility, firepower and flexibility of maritime forces to seize and exploit the operational initiative ashore. The result, as noted earlier, was the concept of 'operational manoeuvre from the sea' with its particular emphasis on 'ship to objective manoeuvre', namely, the capacity to go straight to the operational objective without the automatic need for tiresome median steps such as securing an amphibious lodgement area first.[61] This, it is believed, will enable a variety of subsequent operations ranging from large-scale amphibious assault to special forces operations and humanitarian assistance.

As also already noted, the central concept of sea-basing was fleshed out in *Sea Power 21* and was well described by Vice Admiral Brewer in 2003:

> Sea basing will enable this force to use the sea as manoeuvre space to increase the asymmetric advantage of surprise. By keeping the sea base over the horizon far from shore, it will also be less vulnerable to enemy attack. At the same time, many of the military logisticians would be performing their functions from the relative safety of the mobile sea base, resulting in fewer personnel remaining ashore in higher risk environments for long periods of time.[62]

While all this sounds quite conventional, specific mention is made of the more post-modern benefits of forwards deployed expeditionary capabilities, particularly their capacity to contribute to homeland defence in depth, their advantages in fostering and sustaining cooperative relationships with other nations and, most significantly, their ability to 'prevent or contain local disruptions before they impact the global system'. This is a partial reference to what the US Navy calls 'stability operations'.

The US Navy has devoted most of its operational activities since the end of the

Cold War to the conduct of expeditionary operations most obviously against Iraq and the Taliban and Al-Qaeda in Afghanistan. These experiences have refined American thinking, capabilities and have secured a major focus on the construction of expeditionary capabilities in the US Navy's projected building programme, as demonstrated by its new DDG-1000 Zumwalt land attack destroyers, its San Antonio amphibious warfare ships, the LCS programme and its ambitious sea-basing programme.

Stability operations/HADR

The post-modern tendency is perhaps clearest when it comes to that clutch of naval missions variously called 'stability operations' or humanitarian and disaster response (HADR) operations. These are clearly not new, but the doctrinal attention given to them, especially in the United States, is. Although the armed forces of both China and Japan have been used for such purposes, particularly within their own countries, they have not figured prominently in doctrinal debate. HADR operations are, however, regarded by the Indian Navy as one of the most likely contingencies for which it needs prepare. These are treated as one of the many benign roles that navies undertake in time of peace, and one particularly relevant to the India Ocean area, given the incidence of climatic and other disasters in the region, the spread of the Indian diaspora and the particular capacity for sea-based forces (both naval and coast guard) to arrive early and usefully on the scene. The Asian Tsunami relief operation of 2004, however, brought home to the Indian Navy just how demanding this task can be, and catering for it has assumed a greater priority ever since. The same goes for Japan and China, although Chinese experience derives from domestic experience rather than the Asian Tsunami disaster in which they were not involved.

Thinking about this has accordingly gone much further in the United States. HADR or what are increasingly called 'stability operations', or more expansively 'stability, security, transition and reconstruction' (SSTR) operations, are said to be 'a core U.S. military mission' that may 'involve providing humanitarian and civic assistance to the local populace … activities may include the provision of health care, construction of surface transportation systems, well drilling, construction of basic sanitation facilities, and rudimentary construction and repair of public facilities'.[63] As the title suggests, the aim of the exercise is not only to mitigate human suffering at home and abroad, but also to buttress the stability on which the world system depends, and to prevent such crises leading to conflict.

The US Navy's particular angle on this has been the development of the notion of the 'global fleet station' – a sea-based force able to respond to needs and crises in a physically appropriate and culturally sensitive manner. To make this work, 'combatant commanders require tools that are not only instruments of war, but implements for stability, security, and reconstruction in our global neighbourhood'.[64] The emphasis here is very much on the navy working alongside other civilian aid agencies as necessary. Global fleet stations are about massaging the environment, but in a nice way.

The US Navy has often engaged in HADR/stability operations in the past, as have many other navies, but the tempo appears to be picking up, both in terms of delivering humanitarian assistance during or after conflicts, and in response to natural disasters of one sort or another. Examples of the former would include

Yugoslavia (1992–1996), East Timor (2000) and the democratic Republic of the Congo (1996–1997); of the latter, Operation Sea Angel off Bangladesh (1991), responding to the Cuban and Haitian boat people (1994–1996), the Philippines (1992), the Asian Tsunami relief operation (2004) and so forth. The latter was particularly significant, not simply because of the scale of the devastation encountered but because the Abraham Lincoln carrier strike group and the Bonhomme Richard expeditionary strike group delivered more than six million pounds of relief more quickly, efficiently and with much less political hassle than comparable operations based on land or delivered by air would have seen.[65]

Encouraged by the international goodwill this generated, and as part of its expanding interest in stability operations, the US Navy has further developed the notion of 'global fleet stations' by sending hospital ships on cruises around Africa and South America, and in using other warships as means of offering help in the medical and civil engineering fields. An emphasis on stability operations of this kind, together with intensive efforts at naval engagement, has been a hallmark of the new Miami-based, Southern Command. Intended to be a model for Africa Command, this organisation is unique in the weight it attaches to non-military 'soft' approaches to security, as evidenced, for example, in the number of senior positions allocated to civilians.

Nonetheless, suspicions remain – especially as there has been reluctance in some parts of the navy to accept this as a mission equal in practical terms to other more conventional ones, lest it impact badly on the resources available for more conventional operations.[66] To an extent, though, the capacity for HADR/stability operations is a natural byproduct of conventional war-fighting tasks, not least expeditionary operations. It is true that the capacity to engage in such operations is a natural byproduct of expeditionary or standard war-fighting capabilities. Japan's interesting new 13,500-ton Hyuga class of 'helicopter-carrying destroyers', for example, is officially said to be capable of conducting disaster-relief operations. This is a good example of the way in which multifunctionality makes neat and tidy allocation of naval assets to clear cut missions extremely difficult.

Moreover, these operations clearly benefit the benefactor politically and so contribute to the country's diplomatic agenda as well.

Maritime security

In the maintenance of maritime security, or good order at sea, there is, as we saw in Chapter 11, a 'home' and an 'away' dimension. Both China and Japan have a historic tendency to focus on the more modern, home game. This is taken largely as a matter of excluding others from their territorial waters, partly because of their economic potent in terms of oil, fish and gas, partly because of their historical significance in the instinctive protection of their sovereignty and partly because their capacity to maintain such maritime interests are seen as an indicator of government performance. This exclusive approach is reinforced by the contentious and sometimes deadly nature of the local island disputes between China, Japan, South Korea and Russia.[67] This results in rigorous responses to the presence of unwanted foreigners. The US publication, *Military Power of the People's Republic of China 2006*, indeed argued that China was, in effect, waging a legal war to shift opinion 'away from interpretations of maritime law that favour freedom of navigation and toward interpretations of increased sovereign authority and control' over the EEZ.[68]

Alongside this, both countries have developed substantial coast guard forces. The 1999 disaster in which the Yantai–Dalian ferry sank with a loss of 291 passengers was both a tragedy and a national humiliation for China. It inspired them to a major overhaul of the Maritime Safety Agency, the maritime units of the People's Armed Police and the Chinese Coast Guard, producing much more efficient reactions when the passenger ship *Liaohai* caught fire and sank in November 2004.[69]

But both the Chinese and the Japanese have also demonstrated a post-modern willingness to work with neighbours in campaigns against piracy and maritime terrorism in a wider 'away' game.[70] The Chinese have demonstrated a willingness to link up with the USCG, and have joined in with the North Pacific Coast Guard Forum, established by Japan in 2000. The despatch of a small Chinese task force to join the international campaign against piracy off the coast of Somalia in January 2009 confirms the trend. The JCG, while fully prepared in 2002 to sink a fleeing North Korea spy ship, has also been active in contributing to anti-piracy measures off South East Asia, through participation in local exercises, the provision of equipment and general capacity building. The Japanese have been particularly involved in the exploration of ways of improving navigational safety in the Strait of Malacca and the development of maritime domain awareness (MDA) through the ReCaap organisation in Singapore.

This expanding maritime, rather than strictly naval, activity is seen as a natural Japanese contribution to the international community's response to threats to the international system, while helping to secure Japan's own SLOCs against irregular attack. In parallel, such activity is also seen as a means of engaging with other maritime powers (particularly the United States, China, India and the countries of South East Asia). In this respect, Japan was one of the first countries to enter fully into the Proliferation Security Initiative and, in October 2004, hosted *Team Samurai* multilateral training exercises involving nine navies/coast guards – plainly aimed at North Korea – and the first such exercise in East Asia.[71]

The Indian Navy, while equally concerned to preserve its own waters, points out that the whole of the Indian Ocean region is the 'de facto home of global terrorism' and points out that the sea is the means by which much drugs and arms trafficking is conducted. The Golden Crescent on one side of India and the Golden Triangle on the other provide financial support for Al-Qaeda and Jemmiah Islamiah. 'Add to this, the freewheeling piratical activity in locations like the Horn of Africa, the Bay of Bengal and the Malacca Straits, and one gets an idea of the vigil that is necessary to maintain order in these waters.' Accordingly, '[a]s a major maritime power, the Indian Navy is duty-bound to work towards improving the maritime security environment in the region'. Moreover, the practical, professional advantages of performing these very post-modern low-intensity maritime operations (LIMO) in the company of other like-minded maritime powers through a deliberate policy of constructive engagement, produce better coordination, information sharing and the absorption of best practice.[72]

All this chimes closely with American thinking. Maritime security is one of the 'new' core capabilities in the new 'A Cooperative Strategy' and the focus is on mitigating the threats to good order at sea that fall short of war, 'including piracy, terrorism, weapons proliferation, drug trafficking, and other illicit activities'. Dealing with these irregular and transnational threats, the documents says, 'protects our homeland, enhances global stability, and secures freedom of navigation for the benefit of all nations' and will involve joint naval/coast guard action nationally and internationally.

The US Coast Guard has also been active in the North Pacific Coast Guard Forum and its North Atlantic equivalent set up in 2007, and is expected to take the leading role in translating these aspirations into reality both in home waters and more distantly. There is a recognition that the United States needs to develop a strategic approach to the problem of maritime security in the round. This, in turn, requires developing not simply new tactical and operational techniques and technologies (needed to screen containers for example), but also the institutions and procedures that will integrate the efforts of other government agencies at home and abroad.[73] Inspired by the sense that politically and operationally it is best to help the locals deal with maritime security issues as much as they can, much of the coast guard's activity is directed towards capacity building, the provision of equipment, the establishment of an international doctrine for maritime constabulary operations and, perhaps above all, facilitating enhanced global MDA. Thus, the then CNO, Admiral Mike Mullen:

> Technology offers us the opportunity – now – to help thwart [our enemies'] efforts by building and fielding, among other things, Web-enabled global maritime awareness. It will allow maritime forces to share knowledge in real time, without regard to geography, distance, and eventually even language. It will allow people and goods to move rapidly, efficiently and safely. For those within our maritime security network, we will maintain a high degree of confidence and trust, so that mariners won't be stopped and checked at every point along the way. And that will enable all of us to focus more of our resources and our time on those outside the network to find and fix the threats and to close the gaps where we are most vulnerable.[74]

International engagement with other countries in the drive for maritime security is sometimes complicated by the American tendency to focus on counterterrorism where other countries identify piracy, illegal fishing or people smuggling as more immediate threats. Moreover, there remains a degree of resistance within the US Navy to the adoption of these softer post-modern roles, especially if it is seen as conflicting with the requirements of its harder modern disciplines. Finally, the USCG and the navy clearly have urgent largely domestic priorities in the never-ending campaigns against terrorists and drugs and people smugglers in their own waters.

Naval diplomacy

The success of China's 'smiling diplomacy' in winning support in South East Asia, and its apparent efforts to secure more consensual solutions to the problem of managing the dispute in the South China Sea attest to a thoroughly post-modernist appreciation of the value of soft power, in contrast to more traditional earlier concepts that power was simply something to be displayed. Thus Admiral Liu Huaqing, extolling the benefits of sea-based defence diplomacy:

> The Chinese naval visits to other countries have given foreign countries a better idea of the Chinese navy, expanded our military's influence in the world and

exalted our navy's image ... These visits have also tempered the officers and men of the navy, broadened their thinking and contributed to the Navy's modernisation drive.

Thinking about the need for, and the techniques of, naval diplomacy was another novel aspect of the upsurge in professional strategic thinking in the navy from the mid 1980s. It was considered to involve 'altering the deployment of the maritime military force, or developing such force and facilities to express our political and diplomatic intentions'. Ship visits and participation in scientific exploration and survey 'serve to promote mutual understanding, and to propagate China's independent foreign policy and the accomplishments of construction and reform'.[75]

The Indian Navy shows similar appreciation of the value of naval diplomacy as a means of, first, displaying power in order to influence the behaviour of others and, second, reaching out to others in an act of constructive engagement. Naval activity is seen as a means by which the country's 'Look East' and 'Look West' aspirations can be met, and constant reference is made to Indian warships visiting countries as far removed as Japan and South Africa. These visits are seen as a mechanism by which India can influence perceptions abroad to national benefit. There is an element here of old-fashioned rivalry, especially perhaps with China: 'As the geographical competition-space between the two coincides in the Indian Ocean, wisdom and forbearance are going to be needed in generous measure to ensure that competition does not transform into conflict.' The fleshing-out of this 'Look East' policy automatically brings maritime diplomacy to the centre of the international security stage.[76] This policy resulted in activities as varied as the visit of an Indian destroyer, INS *Tabar*, to Tonga in July 2007 (the first such visit since 1960) and the much heralded three-month cruise of a warship squadron to Singapore, Yokosuka, Qingdao, Vladivostok, Manila and Ho Chi Minh City. While fairly described as 'constructive engagement in the maritime domain', these cruises bear more than a passing resemblance to the famous cruise of Theodore Roosevelt's 'Great White Fleet' before the First World War. To some extent they are undifferentiated exercises 'for general purposes of greatness'.[77] Specifically, there was an undoubted element of rivalry with China in all this, something of a riposte for Chinese activities in the Indian Ocean.

But, in addition to these traditional concepts of naval diplomacy, there has more recently appeared in doctrinal exposition considerable interest in the post-modern notion of 'constructive engagement in the maritime domain':

> India advocates the need to evolve a new paradigm of cooperation, relevant to the contemporary world, in which global threats are addressed by global responses, and multilateralism becomes the preferred norm for addressing global challenges.

Building partnerships and enabling all forms of maritime cooperation is therefore seen as an important part of the navy's business in time of peace and the principal weapon against all manner of threats to maritime security. Consolidating the pioneering approach of a former chief of the naval staff, Admiral L. Ramdas, multinational naval cooperation of this sort is seen as an accelerating and necessary development for the twenty-first century.[78]

The US Navy's 'A Cooperative Strategy' sought to develop this line. 'Trust and cooperation', it says, 'cannot be surged.' They have to be built and sustained over time, through the development of increased understanding amongst US maritime forces and the forging of international partnerships. The document's discussion of naval diplomacy accordingly focuses on coalition building, with the 'Global Maritime Partnership' initiative being its most significant expression.[79] This becomes one of the navy's six strategic imperatives and is clearly crucial to two of its six core capabilities, namely maritime security and HADR. Since this concept has grown out of Admiral Mullen's earlier concept of a 'Thousand Ship Navy',[80] this emphasis is not entirely new, of course. But the retitling of the concept is more than merely cosmetic. It suggests a significant move away the traditional 'modern' thinking that probably explains the 'Thousand Ship Navy' label originally given to the concept. Striking though it was, this title was profoundly misleading since it seemed to exclude coast guard forces, had clear hierarchical connotations that inevitably sparked the unwelcome question of 'Who's in charge?' and raised equally unfortunate suspicions that the navy's hidden aspirations were to recreate a grander vision of the '600 ship navy' of the Reagan years. Hence in Admiral Morgan's words, 'we are beginning to distance ourselves from that moniker'.[81]

The US Navy is perhaps at its most post-modernist in the focus of its current operations. It is putting a huge stress on a heavy programme of naval engagement with prospective maritime partners all around the world, but perhaps especially in and around the Gulf and the Asia-Pacific. The United States is well aware of the symbolic importance of its forwards deployed naval forces and its home-porting policy, not least in, and for, Japan.

In this, the US Navy also recognises that the range of requirements also calls for the strongest possible integration of the naval effort with other forces of maritime order, particularly the USCG. Often, indeed, as both the Japanese and the Americans discovered in the Strait of Malacca, coast guard forces will provide a far more appropriate response to developing situations, which may well be able to head off the need for more forceful interventions later on. The USCG is a unique organisation unlikely to be replicated anywhere else; nonetheless, it has much to offer in advice on many aspects of maritime security that can be adopted or adapted by anyone else – and it can make that advice available in a manner that represents little threat to the sovereignty of others.[82] By doing so, it indirectly defends the system, whilst at the same time serving US national interests and contributing to the United States' maritime outreach.

The navy recognises that the positive encouragement of allied participation in all manner of maritime operations calls for a focused, deliberate and intelligent maritime assault on all the things that make this difficult at the moment. Interoperability is key. This is partly a matter of shared technical proficiency, which is ultimately 'fixable', and also of protocols and standard operating procedures,[83] matters in which the American tendency to overclassify everything does not help.[84] Policy divergences with coalition partners may be rather less tractable, especially if the United States is thought to be pursuing a unilateralist and nationalist agenda.

Certainly with its emphasis on building the trust that cannot be surged, 'A Cooperative Strategy' and, indeed, in the public statements of regional commanders around the world, there is at least declaratory acceptance of the need to accommodate such differences of view. As Admiral Mullen said:

> [T]he changed strategic landscape offers new opportunities for maritime forces to work together – sometimes with the U.S. Navy, but oftentimes without. In

fact, a greater number of today's emerging missions won't involve the U.S. Navy. And that's fine with me.[85]

The US Navy recognises that putting the concept of partnership into effect, however, will require practical steps. These include a concerted effort to make 'maritime domain awareness' work, by moving from an information culture based on 'the need to know', to one based on 'the need to share' and by the open-handed provision of skills and equipment in a sophisticated capability-building campaign for those countries that need it. Sophisticated, in this case, means two things. First, a practical appreciation of the need fully to integrate naval efforts with coast guards, both foreign and domestic, in a manner that gives the latter full credit for their particular strengths in this area. Second, it will require particular awareness of the political and cultural sensitivities of the region in question. The current emphasis on language training and cultural awareness, together with the creation of a 'Civil Affairs Command' of foreign area officers is a step in this direction.

Nonetheless the US Navy obviously still retains the potential for independent diplomatic action of a more traditional kind, a potential perhaps best exhibited by its campaign of naval pressure on Iran.[86] What is less traditional, however, is the evident intention to make such presence permanent, proactive and systemic as an intended means of preventing wars and ensuring a better peace.[87]

12.5 Asia-Pacific conclusions

The Asia-Pacific maritime scene suggests that navies here and elsewhere are grappling with three different but inter-related types of balance. The first is the balance to be struck between modern and post-modern priorities. With their emphasis on expeditionary operations, HADR, maritime security and cooperative engagement with each other and with external navies, the navies of Europe are certainly taking on markedly post-modern characteristics at least for the time being. A similar drift is discernible in the thinking, operations and fleet constriction programmes of the Chinese, Japanese, Indian and American navies. The US Navy's 'A Cooperative Strategy', and its focus on expeditionary operations, HADR and the global maritime partnership, is certainly moving in that direction. Both India and Japan exhibit the same characteristics, the first perhaps rather more than the second. The Indian Navy's Indian Ocean Naval Symposium of 2008 démarche and its avowed sense of responsibility for securing maritime security in the Indian Ocean are good examples of this. Constrained by their constitution, experience and circumstances, the Japanese have been somewhat more circumspect, but they did organise the North Pacific Coast Guard Forum, are supporting Operation Enduring Freedom, the Proliferation Security Initiative (PSI) and have been both active and sensitive in helping secure shipping safety in the Straits of Malacca. Encouraged by the success of their 'smiling diplomacy', even the Chinese have shown a greater willingness to participate in cooperative measures of maritime security.

All this reflects recognition of their mutual interest in securing both the globalised economic system on which their peace and prosperity depend, and the shipping that makes the system work. For this reason, they all demonstrate an acute awareness of the dangers of conflict in an era of remarkable naval change and in many cases significant expansion. Hence, the strong declaratory interest in confidence-building measures and greater transparency over force plans in order to ensure that a common arms dynamic does not turn into a peace-threatening arms race. The annual RIMPAC exercise, in 2008 held off Hawaii, is illustrative. It involved ten navies, 20,000 sailors, marines, airmen and coast guards, 35 ships, six submarines and 150 aircraft. For Admiral Locklear of the US Third Fleet, it showed 'a recognition that no one country can maintain the global security environment. It requires us working together.'[88]

All the same, the exercise did involve Singapore firing off a Harpoon missile and an Australian ship torpedoing a (decommissioned!) US warship, showing that Asia-Pacific navies also exhibit and, indeed, rather more strongly, the 'hedging' tendencies characteristic of the traditional 'modern' approach to naval policy. There is a noticeable tendency for the navies of Japan, India and the United States to benchmark their policies against China, and for China, most obviously, to do so against the United States – although all of these navies have other modern distractions as well; Pakistan in the case of India, Iran and North Korea in the case of the United States, North (and to a certain extent, South) Korea and Russia, for Japan and Taiwan and the South China Sea for China. These preoccupations especially manifest themselves in both their declaratory thinking and in their fleet construction programmes, being especially observable in the attention paid to their nuclear and conventional deterrent postures, ASW and fleet air defence. Such approaches sometimes also surface in their actual rather than their declaratory willingness to compromise on operating procedures and jurisdictional propriety in the common pursuit of maritime security.

The particular modern/post-modern mix these navies exhibit varies in ways that are hard to measure or quantify but, of the four, the US Navy exhibits most postmodern tendencies and China the least. None of them, however, demonstrate the degree of change common in Europe.

This is suggested by the attention paid in the area to the strategic implications of the second of the three 'balances' characteristic of the area, namely, the present force balance, most obviously that between China and the United States, which has clearly become central to the naval security architecture of the region.

Although the gap between the US Navy and the rest of the world may be narrowing in platform number terms, it remains considerable in capability. In 2005, according to Robert Work,[89] the US Navy had a 17 navy tonnage standard, operated 12 of the world's 15 aircraft carriers as well as 12 of its 19 light carriers. Its 71 major combatants (thanks to its vertical launch systems) were equal to the total capacity of the 366 combatants of the next 17 navies. Moreover, the American lead in new as well as established naval technologies is at least as great. For instance, in its programme for unmanned naval systems, a development as potentially revolutionary as the introduction of the aircraft carrier, the US Navy is far ahead of any competitor.

For all that, the US Navy faces a number of challenges that impact on its capacity to 'balance' China. First, there is the 'distributed' nature of its commitments, which require a corresponding distribution of its assets. Second, in contrast to the relative stability of the Cold War period, twenty-first-century threats seem much less predictable both in incidence and type and so are more difficult to prepare for.

Even with its new 60/40 force allocation to the Pacific theatre, the US Navy has an emerging problem with numbers. Moreover, the diverse nature of the contingencies for which the United States needs to prepare is such that assets cannot simply be switched from one contingency to another. The forces required for a possible Taiwan-related Chinese contingency are fundamentally different from stabilisation forces or those thought necessary to fight the Global War on Terror in Iraq and Afghanistan. Further, some new technologies such as 'swarming' fast attack craft or modern diesel powered submarines pose particular problems. Designed for local operation and unencumbered with the larger magazine and open-ocean transit requirements of SSNs, SSKs, for example, would be difficult to deal with in shallower waters.

Moreover, the PLA(N) exhibits a tendency to make the most of these difficulties by preparing deterrent and anti-access strategies that include the measured development of a sea-based nuclear deterrent, a marked increase in the ship-killing capacities of increasingly capable submarines, aircraft and surface combatants and significant investment in signals intelligence and in electronic warfare, which are intended to disrupt the networks that bind the US Fleet together.[90] This latter would be entirely consistent with discussions about the importance of 'electromagnetic dominance' and the 'informationalisation' of warfare that were a feature of China's 2000 Defence White Paper and have been much discussed since.

For its part, the US Navy in the Asia-Pacific could deploy a number of obvious counters, not least significant forces in place, together with early reinforcements. Providing the necessary forwards-based *roulement* of ships, submarines and aircraft will clearly be a major determinant of the US Navy's future acquisitions and deployment strategy. Moreover, the same requirement accentuates the value of home-porting units in places like Yokusuka, Guam and Singapore, and may lead to a further reallocation of US naval assets from the Atlantic to the Pacific.

The prospect of an increasing Chinese capacity to maintain a strategic nuclear deterrent force at sea may well inspire the US Navy to develop a seabed-based sensor network to track Chinese SSBNs, like the SOSUS system developed during the Cold War, together with the TAGOS-type ocean-surveillance ships and sufficient high quality SSNs to track and if necessary prosecute Chinese SSBNs. Such a response would clearly carry with it the prospects of increased tension and possible accident characteristic of the Cold War.

Given the PLA(N)'s increasing emphasis on anti-access weapons and platforms such as theatre ballistic missiles, anti-ship cruise missiles, including the advanced SS-N-27 and the SS-N-22, land-based aircraft, sophisticated submarines, ships and mines, the US Navy would clearly need to develop counter-strategies to cope with all these prospective threats. These strategies would most likely continue to rely on carrier-borne aircraft and seem likely to reinforce the perceived need for the 11–12 carrier-based force currently envisaged within the navy's projected 313 ship force, for an attempt to build up the quality of its carrier-based aircraft and for the use of unmanned aerial vehicles of various sorts.

For the same reason, and given the improvement in Chinese ship-killing missiles, there is likely to be pressure to upgrade the anti-air warfare capabilities of US warships, by the development of better radars, networking, decoy systems, standard air defence missiles, close in weapons systems and even potential directed-energy weapons such as solid state or free electron lasers.

In some ways, Chinese submarines represent the most serious threat, perhaps especially around Taiwan where the ASW conditions are reportedly poor. This, plus a deteriorating force ratio (in which even old Ming submarines have a residual value as distracting targets) seems to be reinforcing an American move away from one-on-one ASW techniques towards a more networked system approach to the problem. Admiral Vernon Clark, then CNO, alluded to this in 2005:

> What I believe is going to happen in the future is that when we apply the netted force construct in anti-submarine warfare, it will change the calculus in that area of warfighting for ever. And it will be a courageous commander who decides that he's going to come waltzing into our network.

The network envisaged would comprise a large number of distributed off-board sensors, including unmanned vehicles of various sorts designed to facilitate fast access, enemy force location and attack.[91] The apparent revival of interest in regenerating open ocean ASW capacities allegedly lost through the post-modern focus on fighting the GWOT, the developing preoccupation with BMD and increasing recognition of the need to harden information and communication systems against cyber attack and the consequences of nuclear explosions, are all good examples of a possibly reviving modernist tendency in US naval development because they all postulate a conventional adversary, or at least an asymmetrical adversary with access to equivalent capabilities.

Given this possible range of US responses, the PLA(N) could not hope to overwhelm the US Navy for the foreseeable future provided the US were able to concentrate sufficient assets in the area of concern. But the PLA(N) would nevertheless seem able to hold the US Pacific Fleet at increasing risk. Certainly, China's deliberate and conscious pursuit of such capabilities indicates a very 'modern' approach to force planning. But in declaratory terms, both sides continue to acknowledge that a hedging strategy, if over done, could be counterproductive, precipitating the very situation it was designed to deter. This is likely to be particularly true for China, facing three notional adversaries as it does.

Such a perception is shared by the Japanese and Indian navies too; they feel that China should indeed be contained but as softly as possible. While for them, the force balance between the US and China is key, they nonetheless have their own more local concerns. Not the least of these is a shared problem reminiscent of the fraught naval balance between Britain and Germany before the First World War, namely, a common and entirely legitimate, even defensive, strategic interest in the same area sea as a potential adversary.

The third and final balance being struck in the Asia-Pacific is the one of time, particularly as to how the two balances already discussed will play out in the future, and what the trend lines are. In 2007, the US DoD concluded that 'The Intelligence Community estimates China will take until the end of this decade or later to produce a modern force capable of defeating a moderate-size adversary.'[92] Given the increasingly formidable capabilities of Japan, India and even South Korea and Taiwan, and however unlikely the contingency, the PLA(N) would find this quite a challenge (although, given its advances, possibly less of one than some authoritative observers predicted some years ago)[93] and arguably remains its main preoccupation. In the longer run, though, more ambitious aspirations might be possible. 'China', says the Pentagon's recent report to Congress, 'is investing in maritime surface and subsurface weapons systems that could serve as the basis for a force capable of power projection to secure vital sea lines of communication and/or key geo-strategic terrain.'[94] Such a view would be consistent with the PLA(N)'s apparent ambitions at some future date of extending an effective reach beyond the first and even the second island chain.

The extent to which the PLA(N) will actually seek to put these putative aspirations into effect, and what would be the strategic consequences were they to do so, depends in large measure on the probable reactions of Japan, India and the United States. In all three countries, there are those who argue that current fleet construction plans as a hedge against *future* Chinese maritime power are inadequate. Here they hark back to the first of the balances discussed here. They suggest that, to the extent it exists, the current emphasis on post-modern concerns may decline in a future world calling for an increased capacity to deal with high-level threats. Some, as we have seen, believe that post-modern trends have already gone too far.[95]

> This then ought to remain the cardinal role for US military forces in the years ahead: to serve as the backbone of global deterrence of interstate war and thus to lend continuing momentum to the emerging norm against territorial aggression.

Post-modern developments, in other words, are *contingent* on a prior satisfaction of modern needs.

Inevitably, such views are countered by those who anticipate continuing and strengthening post-modern preoccupations which, in turn, would call for rather different forms of naval power – provided that hedging strategies are closely constrained. The results of this debate, of course, will be a significant determinant of the future maritime security of the Asia-Pacific and, indeed, of the rest of the world as well.

13 Conclusions?

Thou knowest that all my fortunes are at sea.

Shakespeare, *The Merchant of Venice*, I/1

Since the relative economic, political and strategic importance of the Asia-Pacific region discussed in the last chapter is set to rise through the twenty-first century, and since it is plainly such a very maritime region, it seems sensible to conclude that the conclusions derived from this short review will be generally applicable to other areas of the world as well. There are five such conclusions.

13.1 The relative importance of the sea and seapower will tend to rise in the twenty-first century

The historic importance of sea seems more likely to rise than to decline in the immediate future. The value of its resources will grow as the world population increases and as a means of transportation the sea will remain central to the world trading system on which everything depends. As a physical and human environment also, the sea will help shape the world's future.

Inevitably, the role and importance of naval and other maritime forces will reflect all this. Whether their function is to help police and defend a globalised world or to deal with narrower, more traditional national concerns in more restricted waters, navies will have increasingly vital tasks to perform.

This explains why navies seem busier than ever as we move into a new century:

> Our naval forces, in the post-Cold War era are now almost three-times busier than they ever were prior to 1990. I am referring to actual calls to action, from peace-keeping to crisis response to humanitarian efforts ... Our naval forces are, more than ever, the right tools for the job [of dealing with the instabilities of the post Cold War world.[1]

It will have been noticed from this book that sailors are prone to consider themselves as intimately involved in, and responsible for, the grand sweep of human destiny. Either they are persistent victims of *folie de grandeur*, or their claims are true. While this book inclines to the latter conclusion, it should all the same be pointed out that the new wars and disorders of the twenty-first century are actually taking place on land. Moreover, disorder at sea is largely attributable to events ashore. This is the opposite of Mahan's central argument and suggests that sailors should maintain a precautionary note of becoming modesty in their claims for what they can achieve on their own.

13.2 Attitudes to the sea will change

Attitudes towards the sea and its future importance are accordingly likely to change in the long run. Navies too are likely to need to rethink their attitudes not just to themselves and what they do but to the sea itself. Their traditional attitude has two components:

- *the notion of the high seas*, owned by no one and free for all to use without impediment;
- *the notion of the territorial sea*, owned by a particular country and so available for its exclusive benefit.

The notion of the high seas reflects the views of the Dutch jurist Hugo Grotius in his *Mare Liberum* of 1609, although he was by no means the first to do so.[2] Because the sea is seen, first, as a limitless resource and, second, as an essential means of transportation for the purposes of the trade on which the world's prosperity and peace depends, the ability to use the high seas freely has for centuries been regarded as an essential right.

The result has been a great emphasis particularly amongst the more maritime powers on 'free navigation' and a sometimes almost metaphysical insistence on the freedom of the seas. In Admiral Jacky Fisher's words:

> The Admiralty should *never* engage itself to lock up a single vessel even – not even a torpedo-boat or submarines – anywhere *on any consideration whatever. The whole principle of sea fighting is to be free to go anywhere with every d—-d thing the Navy possesses*. The Admiralty should … reserve entire freedom of action.[3]

Obviously, this notion is qualified by the fact that particular areas of the sea *are*, on the contrary, owned by particular countries and available for their exclusive use. This is the alternate but complementary proposition of the 'closed sea' as developed by John Selden, the brilliant British jurist, back in the seventeenth century. Selden challenged Grotius's arguments in principle and pointed out that his later attempt to justify the closing of the East Indies spice trade to all but Dutch merchant ships was hardly consistent with the views on free navigation he had espoused a few years before.

Selden's view was that bits of sea *were* worth owning and therefore were capable of being owned perhaps because of the fish stocks that could be found there, or because they allowed the exertion of decisive power ashore or because control of the transportation routes that passed through them was commercially or strategically valuable. Under UNCLOS, this approach resulted in the extension of the territorial sea and the assertion of ownership of marine resources within and in some cases without the EEZ. The result is that the high seas have shrunk to only about 64 per cent of the world's total sea area.[4]

This enclosure of the high seas is associated with traditional ideas about what 'sovereignty' means: 'To be sovereign at sea, the United States must control what takes place in the waters under its jurisdiction and exercise influence in the waters that it deems of high interest.'[5] As we saw in Section 11.5, maritime sovereignty can be both instrumental and expressive.

Selden's case rested on the idea that countries would control their parts of the sea in proportion to their military/naval strength. In wartime, the capacity to make use of all the sea (within and without the territorial sea) was always conditioned by military strength and, indeed, as we have seen, securing and exploiting that capacity was the main focus of maritime strategy. Nowadays, however, maritime geography rather than military power is seen as the main criterion for deciding who owns what bit of sea.

Traditional attitudes to the sea have, therefore, been determined by the balance struck between the Grotius and Selden approaches to maritime sovereignty. As a result both the rights of free navigation on the high seas and of exclusive ownership of the territorial sea have, in fact, always been subject to a degree of constraint. Free navigation could be limited in certain sea areas and in times of war; maritime sovereignty, on the other hand, was determined by a country's ability to enforce it.

The notion that the open ocean is an unregulated space seems likely to come under increasing pressure in the twenty-first century for a number of reasons. First, pressure will tend to follow increasing concern for diminishing sea resources. The Sealing Convention Treaty of 1911 between Russia, Britain, Japan and the United States is an early example of the need to accept constraint in securing the resources of the sea. The parties to the treaty also accepted the US Revenue Cutter Service as a de facto international maritime police force that would enforce the Convention.[6] In more recent times, the freedom of the open seas has been qualified through agreements that fishing limits may be applied to the high seas (such as the UN Agreement on Straddling Fish Stocks, 1995, and the prohibition on wall-of-death driftnet fishing in the Pacific) and by measures to protect the general marine environment (the London Dumping Convention of 1972).

As we saw in Chapter 11, the resources of the sea need increasingly to be protected from pollution and unsustainable levels of exploitation; this can only properly be done on a collective and global basis. Grotius's argument reflected the then fact that the sea could be used by one country without reducing its value for anyone else and the assumption that the resources of the sea (especially fish) were limitless. Manifestly, centuries of overfishing means that they are not. Accordingly, the main plank of this part of Grotius's argument falls away.

Second, worries about malefactors of one sort or another exploiting any absence of governance for their own malign purposes will likewise provide incentives for rules and regulations to grow even on the open ocean, because such rules and regulations will increasingly be seen as the means of *guaranteeing* (rather than limiting) continued, legitimate use of the sea. UNCLOS articles are increasingly regarded as providing the framework for international maritime cooperation in the suppression of piracy, the drugs trade, international terrorism and the protection of the marine environment. The freedom of navigation depends on the suppression of other people's freedom to misuse or interfere with it. This in turn requires the maritime powers to accept limitations on their freedoms as well.

This is not, of course, completely new. Because pirates have always been seen as the enemy of all mankind (*hostis humanis generis*) it has become widely accepted

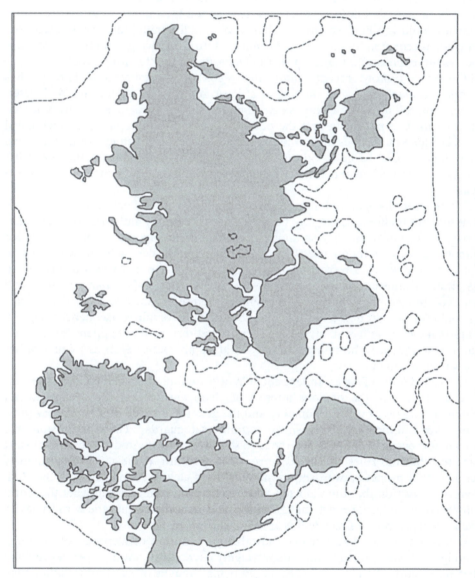

Figure 13.1 The decline of the high seas.

that their suppression warrants interference with ships on the high seas flying the flags of other states. But now such constraints apply more widely as, for example, in the new protocols to the SUA convention and the PSI arrangements noted earlier. For security and environmental reasons, ships are no longer allowed to go anywhere and do anything.

Third, maritime distance seems increasingly less of a driver for the law of the sea than it once was. Technology effectively determined the *extent* of the sea areas that countries could justifiably regard as their own. Traditionally, this was the sea area that could be covered by shore-based cannon. With a following wind this could be as much as three miles, and became the usual measure of the 'territorial sea'.

However, in more recent times, the reach of shore-based technology has extended so much that, to some extent at least, it covers all the ocean. With satellites and patrolling UAVs, the ocean is under surveillance to an unprecedented degree. This does not mean that the ocean has ceased to be a place in which naval forces can hide but it does mean that its surface at least is much less of an unknown desert than it used to be. Modern technology allows the countries that have the necessary technological and military capacity to extend their influence over the open ocean.

The high seas have shrunk not just in a literal way with the extension of the territorial sea, but metaphorically too, because the processes of globalisation mean that geographic distance matters so much less than it did. In the Tampa affair, for example,[7] Australia found itself dealing with migrants fleeing from a conflict in Afghanistan in which a terrorist group led by a Saudi national was attacked by an American-led international coalition involving countries as far apart as Japan and Denmark. Indeed, the events of 11 September themselves showed how distant quarrels could be brought home to the United States with horrific consequences. This all means that everyone has an increasing security interest in what happens 'over there' and, in consequence, the intervening ocean areas are better seen as joining rather than separating them.

All this led Mario Soares' Independent World Commission on the Oceans to conclude that, 'It is in the obvious interest of all to ensure that the oceans do not become a zone of rampant criminality and the general absence of a regulatory presence makes it difficult to establish the required safeguards.'[8] The Commission proposed a new ocean order in which the high seas would be treated as a public trust. It suggested that the roles of navies be reoriented to afford the missing 'regulatory presence' that proper stewardship requires. This is clearly connected with the challenging proposition that the sea itself needs to be protected and that what the world really needs is not just a coast guard, but an 'oceanguard' and that the world's navies have growing responsibilities in this area.[9]

As a result, we are likely to see radical shifts in future conceptions of maritime sovereignty. Instead of thinking of sovereignty as 'control' and independence from other jurisdictions, it is being increasingly being thought of as relative rather than absolute, inclusive rather than exclusive, something that can be and perhaps should be pooled or shared.

This signifies a third and potentially quite profound shift in attitudes to the sea – the idea that the ocean is a global commons. This increasingly seems to mean something quite different from it being outside jurisdiction and so free for everyone to use. Instead, the ocean is regarded as a common domain belonging to everyone, including future generations as yet unborn. Instead of being the object of a free-for-all where those who can have the licence to do what they want, the sea is regarded as a huge area of shared sovereignty and agreed regulation on current and future use, in the common interest of all mankind, present and future.[10] In short, the high seas are increasingly seen as belonging to everyone, rather than to no one.

This could easily lead to an acceleration of a long-established trend that limits the concept of free navigation. A growing concern for safety at sea, for example, led to the 1899 International Maritime Conference in Washington, which established many of the navigational safety rules still in place today; but these conventions implied that anyone who did not do what they said was regarded as 'breaking the rules'.

Nor have navies been immune to this. Despite the emphasis on the freedom of the seas, naval activity, even on the high seas, has in fact long been subjected to constraint. In the nineteenth century, for example, the Declaration of Paris (1856) followed international agreement about the conditions in which trade could or could not be attacked. But it also demonstrated that the usage even of the open ocean could be constrained by legal regulation. Indeed, in such instances as the Battle of the River Plate (1939), both the British and the Germans regarded making use of the laws regulating armed conflict at sea as an important part of their strategy.[11]

Despite the safeguards won for them in UNCLOS, sailors are aware that their ancient freedoms are under threat, because:

> an alarming number of countries have tried to impose prior notification and consent regulations that are nowhere recognised or contemplated in the Law of the Sea Convention, and there are developing threats to the basic principle of the 'sovereign immunity' of warships.[12]

The likely increase in this kind of constraint, of course, dramatically conflicts with the notion that the sea is the 'largest manoeuvre area in the world' and is principally of strategic value for the unimpeded access it affords. On the other hand, arguably, enforcing these new collective responsibilities could give navies even more to do.

Progress in this area is likely to be a complex balancing process. On the one hand, agreement to the SUA conventions advances the collective cause; on the other, the continued preference for flag state approval suggests the need to accommodate traditional concepts of national sovereignty. For all these reasons, working out how they should respond to all these probable developments is likely to become a major feature in strategic thinking for the navies of the twenty-first century.

13.3 There will be a continuing focus on the littoral

Despite common perception, most naval activity has taken place in the littoral. This is likely to continue, even increase, at least for the time being. Part of the reason for this is that many of the world's problems manifest themselves in the littoral regions where access and support from the sea is available. Indeed, the Afghanistan operation of 2001–2002 shows just how far inland such sea-based operations can go.

The characteristics of classical naval power (mobility, assured access, reach, flexibility, controllability) will continue to be well suited to the conduct of wide-ranging and politicised operations in the littoral. Because the requirements of littoral operations are both wide ranging and hard to predict, flexibility is surely key. The ability of the British carrier HMS *Illustrious* to 're-role' itself into a helicopter-carrying amphibious warfare ship in five days at the end of the Saif Sareea II exercise in 2001 so that it could participate in operations in Afghanistan aptly illustrates the immense value of growth and development potential both in fleets and in individual units.

Another key is a navy's capacity to maintain vigilance in every level of their activity. Mahan emphasised that 'accurate intelligence is one of the very first desiderata of war'[13] and, as we saw in Chapter 11 in the discussion on maritime domain awareness, his point extends to peacetime operations as well. Technology increasingly offers the means for sea-based surveillance to be persistent, and navies are doing all they can to take the offer up.

All the same, while the capacity to participate in expeditionary operations is at the moment the key to being a security provider it should not be assumed that this will forever necessarily be the main focus of significant navies. Nor should it be assumed that this focus in any sense reduces either the need for sea control, or the abiding value of the qualities that are required to gain and maintain it.

To judge from the global trend towards the acquisition of more capable coastal submarines, and the tendency to move from inshore patrol craft to offshore and indeed corvettes and ocean-going patrol vessels, many of the world's smaller navies are also taking a more ambitious view of what the littoral means as well, even if their perspective on this tends to focus more on protecting their own littoral rather than conducting operations in other people's. Accordingly, they are disinclined to regard themselves 'merely' as coast guards. The quiet upgrading of the Singapore Navy through the acquisition of Swedish Sjoormen diesel submarines, the French La Fayette Light frigate/Corvette and the locally built Endurance class landing craft, the completion of new base facilities at Changi and Singapore's determined coalition-building activities, provides a good example of this.

13.4 The range and diversity of naval tasks is likely to increase

As a result of all this, maritime forces are facing a new, much more politicised, complex and messy set of situations in which they may be called upon to deliver everything from bombs to babies. In many foreseeable situations, conventional forms of military power have their limits. Navies, therefore, need to diversify, to include in their repertoire an additional range of constabulary and stabilisation functions that call for new attitudes and new skill sets. The future is indeed an unknown country and the apparently increasing sheer unpredictability of the future will not make it easy for naval planners to strike balances between modern and post-modern options, and between present threats and future ones. And this at a time when many of them are also facing budgetary limitations that cut down on their ability to keep their options open.

But one thing, at least, does seem certain and this is likely to be related to probable (certainly necessary) shifts in mankind's attitude to the oceans themselves. By not being pollutants themselves, by making scientific data as accessible as possible, by selling the sea to indifferent publics and by enforcing protective regulations, navies have much to offer in the task of safeguarding the sea itself.

13.5 Navies have some thinking to do

All of this has some obvious implications for how navies should develop and behave in the twenty-first century. As Harlan Ullman points out, their expanding and widening role will require thought. 'What will be needed', he concludes, '...is a new mentality and way of thinking that goes beyond traditional war-fighting and its professional skills.'[14] Navies face a range of choices. Many of the issues discussed in this chapter, and before, mean that navies confront hard choices in force development about where they should put their emphasis – on this capability rather than that, on independent operation rather than interoperability with others, on green or brown waters rather than blue, on a military orientation rather than a constabulary one. The balance they strike in these key areas of choice will reflect their size, strategic circumstance and national priorities and will be demonstrated by their particular concept of what 'a balanced fleet' means to them, by their force development and by their overall policy.

Another issue they will need to confront will be to work out their evolving relationship with new technology. Strategic thinking needs to keep up with technology in order to avoid being taken over by it. Navies need to ponder the probability that the technological transfomation hitting them at the beginnings of the twenty-first century is not a one-off process, but a continuous one that will never stop.

Transformational technology can be mishandled in many ways. One is to focus exclusively on the use navies can make of exciting new technology rather than on the effects they need to have. Strategy needs to centre on objectives, and what is necessary to achieve them rather than on acquiring and exploiting the latest technology simply because it is available. Strategy should be based on effects not technological capability. The current obsession with 'network-centric warfare' rather than 'network enabled capabilities' is a classic example of such dangerous thinking. Another all-too-common danger is the procurement-led approach to strategy. Technology *is* only a means to an end, and constant strategic reflection is needed to help remind us of that enduring fact. Getting the balance between strategy and technology right will continue to be one of the most important determinants of twenty-first-century seapower.

The key question dominating all the others, however, is the balance they choose or need to strike between modern and post-modern alternatives, between preparing for a state-centric strategic future as opposed to a system-centred one. It may be, of course, that they need to cover both contingencies, not least because the situation they confront today may well be utterly different from tomorrow's, but, all the same, they need to prepare for tomorrow's situation today. Moreover, a capacity to focus on post-modern tasks may well depend on a prior ability to manage modern ones. For all these reasons, deliberations in this difficult area are likely to result in a blend of both alternatives. This should be no surprise for, as we saw in the first chapter, the international competition that still dominates international politics is itself a mix of cooperative and conflictual relationships, with the first hopefully prevailing, but both needing to be catered for.

There is plainly a need to rethink all of this – to reconsider old roles and to speculate on new ones. To the extent that navies do get 'denationalised', for example, it might be necessary to question the continued validity of some of the assumptions of classical maritime strategists such as Mahan and Corbett since they were generally based on the old-fashioned nation state as the basic unit of concern, and conflict as the state of nature. These days, developing strategic concepts for the conduct of naval diplomacy or refining their approach to interoperability and soft maritime security issues might prove rather more to the point. But for all that, Mahan, Corbett and the rest of them still do matter because, the trend towards cooperative maritime endeavour and widening interpretations of what is covered by the concept of maritime security notwithstanding, many navies will still need to be primarily interested in developing their independent battle-winning capacity.

Clearly, navies are in a transitional period of historic significance in which they need to rethink, change and expand the useful effects that they can have. It would be wrong to suppose that mankind has in any sense reached the end of the road. The nature of the challenges it has faced has frequently changed before, not least because the 'losers' have every incentive to change the rules they lost by. The current stress, for example, on manoeuvre warfare and expeditionary operations may well not survive the next disaster, and their apparent failure could easily revolutionise the subsequent agenda. Believing that one has the final answer is a certain way of ensuring that one has not. The navies of the twenty-first century, in short, face a grossly uncertain future about which future sailors and those interested in their ways will need constantly to reflect. Given the centrality of seapower to the peace and prosperity in the twenty-first century, it is truly important for them to get the answers to these questions right. It is hoped that this book will help them do so.

Notes

1 Seapower in a globalised world: two tendencies

1 For the background to this convoluted and still developing debate, see Cooper (2004), pp. 37–43; Tangredi (2002b); Baylis and Smith (2001).
2 Tony Blair, 'Reflections on 21st Century Security', Speech on HMS *Albion*, Plymouth, 12 January 2007.
3 Brendan Nelson, interview, *Jane's Defence Weekly*, 14 March 2007.
4 Ferguson (2006), pp. lix–lxii.
5 Mahan (1902), p. 144.
6 'Cod sold in hundreds of chippies linked to Russian black market', *Guardian*, 20 February 2006.
7 Frieden (2006), pp. xvi–xvii.
8 Weatherford (2004).
9 Frieden (2006), p. 16.
10 Ferguson (2006), p. 73.
11 Timothy Garton Ash, 'Global capitalism has no serious rivals. But it could destroy itself', *Guardian*, 22 February 2007.
12 The Black Death, however, played a significant part in the collapse of the Mongol world empire. These are complex matters. Some analysts, for example, argue that today's globalisation is deeper and so more resilient than in earlier periods because manufacturing is not merely relocated; it is *redistributed* amongst a number of countries in ways that increases mutual dependence. Using the computer industry as an example, Friedman calls this the 'Dell effect' (2006, pp. 529–536). Such confidence, however, is partly based on expectations of secure transport. Resource concerns, especially those to do with sea-fish, water and maybe fresh air are depressingly discussed in Easton (2007), pp. 143–150.
13 Ferguson (2005), pp. 176–177; Stiglitz (2007), pp. 245, 278.
14 Friedman (2006), p. 458.
15 Mullen (2006), p. 2.
16 Gray (2005), p. 370.
17 New Zealand Maritime Doctrine, para 1.10.
18 Coulter (1998), p. 167.
19 Thomas Campbell (1777–1844) *Ye Mariners of England* in Jay (2005), p. 45.
20 The level of this attrition is often forgotten these days. But with the exception of such grand disasters as the early days of the Crimean war, the retreat from Kabul or the battle of Isandlwana, such casualties rarely attracted political controversy, even comment. It was accepted as an inevitable part of the burdens of empire.
21 Quoted in 'USN seeks wider seapower definition', *Jane's Navy International*, July–August 2006, p. 11.
22 Conway *et al.*, 'A Cooperative Strategy for 21st Century Seapower', October 2007, pp. 1–2.
23 MoD (UK) (1998), para 6.
24 MoD (UK) (2002), Introduction.
25 Mahan (1890), p. 23.
26 'Gates plans to use Air Force, Navy funds to cover Army costs in Iraq, Afghanistan',

National Journal CongressDaily AM 12 April 2007. George Friedman, 'The limitations and necessity of naval power', *Stratfor*, 10 April 2007.

27 Paul Kennedy, 'The rise and fall of navies', *International Herald Tribune*, 5 April 2007.
28 Corbett (1911/1988), pp. 15–16. See Section 3.5.
29 See Till (2006b) and Section 9.8.
30 *U.S. Coast Guard Strategy* (2007), p. 51.
31 See Section 11.11.
32 Posen (2003), pp. 8–13.
33 MOD (UK) (2004), p. 58. Interestingly earlier editions of this had rather more on this concept. Compare with pp. 33–36, 103 in the first edition of 1995.
34 See Elleman (2007), pp. 101–106, 108–109ff.
35 *New Zealand Military Doctrine* (2004), paras 10.22, 8.11.
36 Singapore MoD (2000), p. 35.
37 Cited in Ritchie (2002), p. 9.
38 Cecil (1954), p. 115.
39 Tom Bower, 'The sale of Liverpool shows how Britain lets its lifeblood drain away', *Guardian*, 9 February 2007.
40 Huxley (2000), p. 33.
41 Deck (1999), pp. 252ff.
42 Jeshurun (1999), p. 227.
43 Huxley (2000), pp. 25, 45.
44 Rear-Admiral Grensted, interview in *The Navy* (NZ) February/March 2008, pp. 20–22. Arguably the Danish Navy with its *Absalon* power projection ships is an even more striking case.

2 Defining seapower

1 Quoted in George (1978), p. 86.
2 Falk (2000), pp. 15ff.
3 Corbett (1911/1988) p. 67.
4 Till (1997).
5 Gray (1999), pp. 217–227, and more extensively in (1992).
6 Sater (1991).
7 Rodger (1986), p. 15.
8 This section relies heavily on Cunliffe (2001) and the work of Professor Michael A. Crawford, Institute of Brain Chemistry and Human Nutrition, London. See also 'Eating fish is good for brain', *Guardian*, 25 October 2002.
9 'Divers surprised by Iron Age port', *Guardian*, 17 September 2002.
10 Gilbert (2008), p. 7.
11 Forage (1991), p. 6. Also Kane (2001), pp. 15–32, esp. pp. 25–26.
12 Cole (2001), pp. 2–3.
13 Deng (1997), pp. 50–51; Menzies (2003).
14 Oliver Burkman, 'The shipping news', *Guardian*, 27 January 2007. See also Levinson (2006), esp. pp. 264–278. '178 flavours of container', *Military Logistics International*, September 2007.
15 UN Conference on Trade and Development (2006), pp. 5, x.
16 Coulter (2003).
17 Facts and arguments of this sort may be found in 'Shipping and world trade' reports online, available at: www.shippingfacts.com (accessed 5 February 2007) and the OECD's report, *The Role of Changing Transport costs and Technology in Industrial Relocation* of May 2005.
18 Mahan (1900), pp. 37–38; Falk (2000), p. 88. Adam Smith, *The Wealth of Nations*, London, 1776.
19 Cable (1998), pp. 22–23.
20 Smith, op. cit. p. 29.
21 See also Chandhury and Morineau (1999).
22 Mahan (1900), p. 99.

23 See Wong (1998); Beeching (1975).
24 Mahan (1900), p. 177.
25 See Chapter 1, note 5.
26 Platt (1989).
27 de Souza (2001), pp. 185ff.
28 Deng (1997), pp. 155–158.
29 de Souza (2001), pp. 131–132ff.
30 Matheson (1964), 137–160.
31 Hough (1994); Padfield (1999), pp. 232–236.
32 Hough (1994), p. 1.
33 Mahan (1900), p. 174.
34 A thesis explored at length in Ingram (2000), pp. 126–127.
35 Quoted in Jane (1906), p. 179.
36 Cited in Livezey (1981), pp. 281–282.
37 Freedman (2000a), pp. 402ff; Tangredi (2002), p. 127.
38 Corbett (1911/1988), p. 49.
39 Alam (1999).
40 Forage (1991), p. 6.
41 Rodger (1986), p. 29.
42 Casey-Vine (1995), p. 323.
43 de Lanessan (1903).
44 Notably Padfield (1999) and Harding (1999).
45 Cited in Padfield (1999), p. 69.
46 Rodger (1997), pp. 432–433.
47 Forage (1991), pp. 8–9.
48 Strausz-Hupe (1942), p. 26.

3 Who said what and why it matters

 1 Mahan (1902), p. 77.
 2 Churchill cited in Lehman (1988), p. 25.
 3 Corbett (1904), p. 154.
 4 This is the burden of Gordon (1996).
 5 Heuser (2002) is a recent and accessible review of Clausewitz, nicely complementing Handel (2001). The classic summary is Howard and Paret (1976); Heuser (2002), p. 578.
 6 Fisher (1919b), p. 82. For a strong counterblast see Lambert (2002).
 7 Musashi (1995), p. 37.
 8 Osgood (1962), p. 5.
 9 Cited in Heuser (2002), p. 34.
10 Liddell Hart (1967), p. 335.
11 Corbett (1905), p. 285; Shulman (1995), pp. 78, 121.
12 Mahan (1911), pp. 2, 299–301; also Corbett Vol. I (1907), pp. 332–333.
13 Gray (1999), p. 364; Reeve (2001), p. 9.
14 Gray (1999), p. 222; Booth (1977), p. 6; Brodie (1965), p. 115.
15 Slade (1993), p. 183.
16 Lavery (1998), p. 168; Mahan (1902), pp. 151–169; Rodger (1999), pp. 178–200. See also Tritten and Barnett (1986).
17 Lavery (1998), p. 77.
18 MoD (UK) (1995), pp. 185–188.
19 Admiral V. Chernavin 'On Naval Theory' (trans.) *Morskoi Sbornik*, No. 1, January 1982.
20 (US) Naval Doctrine Command, *Multinational Maritime Operations*, Norfolk, VA: NDC, 12 October 1995; also Tritten (1996).
21 Lewis (2001).
22 Brigadier General I.B. Holley Jnr, cited in Tritten (1994), p. 18.
23 Corbett (1911/1988), pp. 3–11, 322–325; Mahan (1911), p. 2.
24 Corbett (1905); Tunstall (1990).

25 Clerk (1790), pp. 17–18, 147–148; Clerk (1804), p. 5.
26 Hattendorf (1984, 1991a) discusses the interplay of Mahan and the Naval War College.
27 Hattendorf (1991a), Chapter 2; also N. Lambert (1998) and Sumida (1997).
28 Sumida (1999).
29 Cited in Livezey (1981), p. 42.
30 Mahan (1890), p. 91.
31 Mahan (1899a), p. 264, 38–39.
32 Mahan (1890), p. 209.
33 Mahan (1899a), p. 305.
34 Ibid., p. 203.
35 Ibid., pp. 300–301.
36 Mahan (1890), pp. 383–400.
37 Ibid., p. 32.
38 See Hattendorf (1991a) generally, and Castex (1994), esp. pp. 69–70.
39 Palmer (1988) and Hegmann (1991).
40 Ranft and Till (1989), pp. 163–171; Hattendorf (1991a), p. 4.
41 Watkins (1986); Friedman (2001), pp. 219ff. is a good introduction. For a variety of competing views amongst the various progenitors of 'The Maritime Strategy', see Goldrick and Hattendorf (1993), pp. 185–186, 202, and Miller and Van Evera (1988), pp. 16–170. Also Baer (1994), pp. 429ff. The definitive history of the development of 'The Maritime Strategy' is Peter Swartz's unpublished Centre of Naval Analysis Study 'The Maritime Strategy of the 1980s: Threads, Strands and Line'.
42 Komer (1984).
43 Sumida (1997), pp. 80–98.
44 Cited in Schurman (1981), p. 44.
45 Corbett (1911/1988), pp. 15–16.
46 Corbett (1917), Vol. I, p. 6; cited in Corbett (1911/1988), p. 58; ibid., p. 66.
47 Heuser (2002), pp. 124–133; Handel (2001), pp. 277–295.
48 Corbett (1907), Vol. I, p. 5.
49 Corbett (1911/1988), pp. 15–16.
50 Corbett (1917), Vol. I, p. 6.
51 Corbett (1914), Vol. I, p. 17; ibid., pp. 174–175, 328.
52 Ibid., pp. 68, 187.
53 Hughes (1997), pp. 36–37.
54 Corbett (1911/1988), pp. 53–58.
55 Cited in ibid., p. 58.
56 Ibid., p. 66.
57 Ibid., pp. 57–58.
58 Cited in Kennedy (1989), p. 168.
59 Corbett (1911/1988), p. 167.
60 This was inserted into Vol. III of Corbett (1920–1931). For background see Ranft (1993) and Till (2006b), pp. 80–88, 114–151.
61 See the anonymous 'Sea Heresies' and 'Some Notes on the Early Days of Royal Naval War College' in *Naval Review*, 1931.
62 Corbett (1914), pp. 46, 73; Corbett (1911/1988), pp. 103–104.
63 Ibid,. p. 91.
64 Ibid., p. 164.
65 Corbett (1907), p. 5.
66 Corbett (1920–1931), Vol. II, pp. 41–42.
67 Ibid., pp. 93, 241.
68 For an account of British thinking in the interwar period, see Till (2006b), pp. 103–133.
69 Callwell (1996a), p. 444. Colin Gray's introductory summary is particularly useful.
70 I am grateful to Christian Liles for reminding me of Molyneux's operational focus.
71 Fisher (1919a), p. 212.
72 Hunt (1982, 1993); Baugh (1993); Liddell Hart (1967).
73 For an example of this response, see comment by Schurman in Goldrick and Hattendorff (1993), p. 113.

74 Castex (1994), pp. xxxvi, xx.
75 For an account of the writing of *BR 1806*, see Eric Grove, 'The discovery of doctrine: British Naval thinking at the close of the twentieth century' in Till (2006b), pp. 182–191.
76 MoD (UK) (1995), p. 63. Also Grove (1996) and MoD (UK) (2004).
77 MoD (UK) (1995), p. 184.
78 *Australian Maritime Doctrine* (2000), p. 45.
79 Documents relating on the evolution of US naval thinking at this time are conveniently summarised in Hattendorf (2006b).
80 Baer (1994), p. 451.
81 Copies of these two documents are conveniently found in the *Marine Corps Gazette* for November 1992 and February 1994 produced by successive Secretaries of the Navy, Sean O'Keefe and John H Dalton. Breemer (1994); Huntington (1954).
82 Dalton (1994), p. 21.
83 Grivel (1869), p. 50; Roksund (2003) is a convenient recent summary of the *Jeune Ecole*.
84 Quoted in Richmond (1953), p. 43.
85 Quoted in Marder (1940/1972), p. 87.
86 De Lanessan (1903).
87 Von Waldeyer-Hartz, 'Naval Warfare of Tomorrow', *Wissen and Wehr* (1936), Ernst Kovse, *Neuzeitliche Seekriegsfuhrung* (Berlin, Mittler, 1938); quoted in Rosinski (1977), p. 64.
88 Mahan (1899a), pp. 49–50.
89 Fisher (1919b), pp. 174, 182–183.
90 Quoted in Tyushkevich (1978), USAF English translation, p. 163.
91 Quoted in Herrick (1988), p. 7.
92 Ibid., pp. 79ff.
93 Quoted in ibid., p. 10.
94 Ibid., pp. 71–72.
95 Borressen (1994) and more recently in Hobson and Kristiansen (2003).
96 Tzalel (2000), p. 11.
97 Naveh (1997) provides a stimulating introduction to understanding operational art.
98 MoD (UK) (1999), Chapter 7.
99 Svechin (1926), pp. 15–17.
100 Amongst the USMC's excellent series of publications on this are Krupp (1999) and the Marine Corps Association (1996); O'Keefe (1992), p. 92.
101 Castex (1994), pp. 101ff., esp. pp. 105, 169.
102 Hughes (1991, 2000).
103 Conway *et al.*, 'A Cooperative Strategy', October 2007, pp. 1–2. Curiously this document lacks formal page numbers.
104 Ibid., pp. 2–3.
105 Ibid., pp. 2–3.
106 A number of articles commenting on the strategy are usefully collected in the *Naval War College Review*, Spring 2008.

4 The constituents of seapower

1 Harding (1999), p. 286.
2 Ibid., p. 121.
3 Padfield (1999), p. 3.
4 Rodger (1997), pp. 433–434.
5 Quoted in Richmond (1934), p. 38.
6 Cited in Lambert (1999), p. 168.
7 Harding (1999), p. 60; this is also a constant theme in Casey-Vine (1995), pp. 341, 346, 389, 402ff.
8 For discussion of examples in Taiwan and India see *Defense-aerospace* (France), 10 July 2001, 15 October 2001; *Janes Defence Weekly*, 21 March 2001. *China Times*, 18 May 2001, 3 October 2001.
9 Mahan (1890), pp. 58–88.

10   You Ji (1998), p. 10. For an India example see Mihir K. Roy in ibid., p. 85.
11   See Goldrick (1997), pp. 6–8; Roy (1995), pp. 43–51.
12   *The Times*, 25 July 01.
13   Gray and Sloan (1999) is an excellent introduction to the impact of geography on strategy.
14   Griffiths *et al.* (1998), p. 13; Cozens (1996), esp. pp. 231–233. A book that derived from a conference set up specifically to recommend new attitudes to the sea. Cdr R.J. Jackson, 'Developments in NZ', *Naval Review*, January 2001.
15   Cited in Rahn (2001), p. 117. For an Australian example, see Stevens (2001a), p. 1.
16   Mahan (1900), p. 117; Gorschkov (1979), p. 13.
17   Quoted in Bertram and Holst (1977), p. 37.
18   'Russia plans military build up in the Arctic', *Daily Telegraph*, 12 June 2008; 'Russia deploys to Arctic as relations with Norway cool', *Jane's Defence Weekly*, 23 July 2008.
19   For two comprehensive and detailed reviews of this see Lindberg (1998) and Lindberg and Todd (2002).
20   'Panama hopes to sail into 'first world' by enlarging its waterway', *Guardian*, 13 June 2006.
21   Goldrick (2001), p. 292.
22   Rodger (1986), p. 29.
23   Captain James Goldrick RAN, 'The medium power in the 21st century', *Naval Review*, April 2001, p. 103.
24   Wright (1998), pp. 111–161.
25   Cited in Lambert (1998), p. 125.
26   Dorman (2002).
27   Olkhousky (1992).
28   Harding (1999), p. 25.
29   Peter Haydon 'The Canadian Navy at (another) crossroads', *Naval Review*, January 2001, p. 37.
30   Wright (1998), pp. 14, 69, 93, 122–123, 130–131.
31   *Straits Times*, 4 April 2001; *Times of India*, 6 April 2001. This issue is discussed later in Chapter 12.
32   Lambert (1998), p. 137.
33   Letters of 2 April 1745 and 14 March 1745/6 in Gwyn (1973). pp. 71, 223.
34   Mahan (1890), p. 23.
35   Speech reported in *Gentleman's Magazine*, September 1745, pp. 465–466.
36   Harding (1999).
37   Quoted in Behren (1955), p. 479.
38   Falk (2000), pp. 24, 87 – part of an especially effective discussion of the topic; US Coast Guard (1998), p. 16; Gibson (1992).
39   Gibson (1992).
40   'Rusting and faulty – the decrepit fleet that took Britain to war', *Guardian*, 29 September 2003.
41   Interview with D.T. Joseph, Mumbai and material from Indian Maritime Foundation, Pune (February 2002).
42   Padfield (1999), p. 250.
43   Sondhaus (2001), p. 89; Bell (2000), pp. 182–183.
44   'The box that launched a thousand ships', *New Yorker*, 11 December 2000.
45   Coulter and Goldman (1998).
46   Ibid. and J.H. Parry cited in Cable (1988), p. 22.
47   A point made with some vehemence by Hugh McCoy, Chairman of the Baltic Exchange in 'World trade and the role of the City of London', in Till (2001), p. 179.
48   Cable (1988), p. 168.
49   See Chapter 11 in Till (2001).
50   Quoted in *Defense News*, 27 February 2001.
51   Kane (2001) and Wilson (2001a) are good introductions to this; Mahan (1890), p. 71.
52   Evans (2001); Evans and Peattie (1997).
53   Kipp (1990), p. 188.

54 For example Rosen (2001); some badinage from the UK Joint Services Command and Staff College.
55 Crowe (1993), p. 159.
56 Interview with Rear Admiral Bryce (Chief of Staff Western Command Mumbai) and with the Assistant Chief of the Naval Staff (Delhi). Rear Admiral Venkhat ACNS (Air) February 2002, also *Jane's Defence Weekly*, 7 March 2001.
57 Pokrant (1999a), pp. 61, 64, 67, 72.
58 Ibid. p. 235.
59 Pokrant (1999b), pp. 281–293, esp. p. 291.
60 Ibid., 176–178.
61 Crickard *et al.* (1998) and Haydon (1998). Haydon and Griffiths (1995) take this issue further. Wilson (1998) discusses the need to harmonise rules of engagement in multinational naval operations. The Churchill quote is cited on pp. 1–1/12 of US Naval Doctrine Command (1995).

5 Navies and technology

1 Grove (1990), pp. 236–240. See also Lindberg (1998) and Lindberg and Todd (2002). Also Hill (1986), pp. 14–27.
2 Rodger (1997), 150–152.
3 But see Harding (1999), pp. 143ff., 281–287.
4 Ibid., p. 143.
5 Hill (1986) explains where medium powers such as India, Australia and Canada fit into this.
6 Stevens (1999) shows exactly the same arguments between the RAAF and the RAN as between the RN and RAF, see p. 4ff.
7 Harding (1999), p. 270; Woodman (1998), p. 10; Evans and Peattie, (1997) p. 351.
8 The victories of the Nile, Copenhagen and Trafalgar were all won against superior forces, Lavery (1998).
9 Rodger (1997), p. 105.
10 Ibid., p. 430.
11 Harding (1999), pp. 181, 203.
12 See Creveld (1977) and Thompson (1991).
13 Griffiths *et al.* (1998), pp. 132, 97; ibid., pp. 101, 117, 124.
14 See special review *Armada International*, April 2000.
15 Michael Moran, MSNBC, 'In the navy, size does matter', MSNBC.com, 29 March 2001; 'The supersonic anti-ship missile threat', *Stratfor*, 18 April 2008.
16 'Making waves: multihulls move in on military markets', *Jane's International Defence Review*, January 2002. For another useful summary see David Andrews 'Technology, shipbuilding and future combat beyond 2020', in O'Brien (2001), pp. 248–262.
17 'Survival of the fittest', *Jane's Defence Weekly*, 23 January 2001.
18 Friedman (2001), pp. 245–246.
19 'Flexing a snap to fit fleet', *Jane's Defence Weekly*, 7 November 2001.
20 'Interception at sea: opening a new chapter for BMD', *Jane's Navy International*, January–February 2006; 'Floating command', *Defence Technology International*, January–February 2008; 'Ruling the waves: offshore patrol vessels aim to keep crime at bay.' *Jane's International Defence Review*, February 2007.
21 Fisher (1919b), p. 174.
22 Edmonds (2001) is an excellent introduction to this issue.
23 Reported in *Jane's Defence Weekly*, 18 October 2000.
24 Cdr Nick Harrap, 'The submarine contribution to joint operations', in Edmunds (2001), pp. 83–89, also pp. 154–168, 243.
25 'Back in business', *Defence Technology International March 2008*; 'ASW resurfaces', *Jane's Defence Weekly*, 11 June 2008; 'US Navy in bid to overhaul undersea combat', *Jane's Defence Weekly*, 9 March 2005.
26 Keith Hartley, 'An economic evaluation of the UK government's decision on a future carrier', in Hirschfield and Hore (1999), pp. 77–98.

27 See Friedman 'The future of shipboard aircraft', in Hirschfield and Hore (1999), pp. 117–130. Reported in *Jane's Navy International*, May 1999, and Vice Admiral Dennis McGinn, 'Why the aircraft carrier is still a worthwhile national asset', *Jane's Defence Weekly*, 20 June 2001.

28 Richard Bitzinger 'Aircraft carriers back in fashion', *Straits Times*, 26 June 2008; '£4bn carrier deal will deny funding for troops', *Daily Telegraph*, 4 July 2008. The muted reaction to the British carrier decision attests to the strength of the continuing prejudice against the carrier, in Britain, if nowhere else.

29 Friedman (2001), p. 306.

30 Coté (2001), p. 50.

31 Ken Grause, 'Consideration for 21st century carrier navies', in Hirschfeld and Hore (1999), pp. 177–212.

32 See the survey in *Armada* 4/99.

33 Pokrant (1999a), pp. 231–241, and survey in *Jane's International Defence Review*, Issue 2, 2000.

34 Ullman (2001); Coquinot (1997); Friedman (2001), p. 254.

35 Inskip (2002), pp. 150–185.

36 Friedman (2001), p. 260.

37 Gordon Moore, co-founder of Intel Corporation noted in 1979 that the density of transistors on chips and thus the price to performance ratio of computers doubled every 18 months and that this would continue indefinitely.

38 Lovelace (1997), p. 48.

39 Mitchell (2006) is a useful introduction to this.

40 Owens (1995a); Cebrowski (1998). Gongora and Riekhoff (2000) is a useful introduction, especially Martin Libicki, 'What is information warfare?' pp. 37–60.

41 Cited in Till (1979), p. 145.

42 Tunstall (1990), pp. 202–203.

43 This is the general argument of Gordon (1996).

44 Friedman (2000b), pp. 129ff., 148, 163, 172, 175–179, 227.

45 Hammes (2005) dwells on the contextual challenges to technological superiority.

46 Benbow (2003) remains a useful review, but see also the debate between Colin Gray and Steven Metz in *Journal of Defence Studies*, March 2006.

47 Cited in E.H. Tilford, 'The RMA: prospects and cautions', US Army War College Strategic Studies Institute Paper, Carlisle, PA, 1995, p. 1.

48 For example, Menon (1998), pp. 182–183.

49 See Clifford J. Rogers, 'Military revolutions and revolutions in military affairs: a historian's perspective', in Gongora and Riekhoff (2000), pp. 21–36.

50 Donald Rumsfeld has been much criticised for this. See Thomas P.M. Barnett, 'Donald Rumsfeld: old man in a hurry', *Esquire*, 31 August 2005.

51 Musashi (1995), p. 86.

52 MacGregor (2003) discusses the way in which the concept of Transformation has been assailed.

53 Barnett (1991), p. 11.

54 For competing views see O'Connell (1991) and McBride (2000) on the one hand, and the more historically based views expressed in Moretz (2002), Ranft (1977) and Bell (2000) on the other.

55 Casey-Vine (1995), pp. 345, 409–416.

56 Krepinevich (1994).

57 Evans and Peattie (1997), p. 300; Edgerton (1991), p. 34.

58 O'Brien (2001), pp. 43, 48, 6–8; Till (1979), pp. 102–104.

59 Sondhaus (2001), p. 103.

60 O'Brien (2001), p. 143.

61 Ibid., p. 157: Reason (1998), p. 51.

62 This assumes the strong leader is pursuing a coherent vision. For an alternate view of the Gorskkov era, see Evan Mawdsley, 'The Russia Navy in the Gorskkov era', in O'Brien (2001) esp. pp. 173–179. On Admiral Gombei see Evans and Peattie (1997).

63 Mackenzie (1995), pp. 226, 212–242, also Nailor (1988), pp. 99–105.

64 Evans and Peattie (1997), p. 304.
65 Sondhaus (2001), p. 68.
66 Mindell (2000), p. 71.
67 Sondhaus (2001), pp. 199–2000 is a useful summary of the views expressed in Sumida (1989) and Lambert (1999).
68 Mahan (1892), Vol. I, p. 102.
69 C.V. Bett's 'Development in warship design and engineering', *Proceedings of the Institution of Mechanical Engineers*, Vol. 210 (1996).
70 I am grateful to Major Irvin Lim of the Singapore Navy for his lively and stimulating comments on much of this chapter.

6 Command of the sea and sea control

1 Corbett (1907), Vol. I, p. 6.
2 Colomb (1899), p. 173.
3 Richmond (1946), pp. 326–336.
4 Bridge (1910), p. 84.
5 Clarke and Thursfield (1897), pp. 126–127; comment by G.S. Graham, quoted in Reynolds (1974), p. 211.
6 Castex (1994), p. 53ff.
7 Mahan (1911), pp. 260–261.
8 Brodie (1965), p. 108.
9 Mahan (1890), p. 14; Bacon (1936), p. 192.
10 Raeder, report to the Führer, 9 March 1940, Führer Naval Conferences (London: Greenhill Books, 1990).
11 On their way to Dieppe some of the raiders ran into a strongly escorted German convoy and were badly mauled. This greatly disrupted the effectiveness of their landing operations. Robertson (1963), pp. 194–213.
12 Mahan (1911), p. 218.
13 Colomb (1899), p. 212.
14 Corbett (1907), Vol. II, pp. 20–21.
15 Grenfell (1937), pp. 92–93.
16 *Armada de Chile*, Chile, p. 11.
17 Tzalel (2000), p. 86.
18 Corbett (1911/1988), p. 211.
19 Gorshkov (1979), pp. 122, 217.
20 See Franklin (2003) for a detailed review.
21 Brodie (1965), p. 74.
22 Gorshkov (1979), p. 233.
23 Rear Admiral Henry E. Eccles, US Navy, notes of 20 January 1972. I am grateful to Professor John Hattendorf for bringing this to my attention.
24 Cited and discussed in Ranft and Till (1989), p. 163, and more generally pp. 159–171.
25 Stansfield Turner (1974).
26 Corbett (1911/1998), p. 87.
27 In a comment on the ideas of Admiral Raymond A. Spruance in Eccles Papers, Naval Historical Collection, Naval War College, Newport, RI.
28 Gorshkov (1979), p. 232.
29 MoD (UK) (2004), p. 289
30 Stansfield Turner (1977).
31 Tzalel (2000), pp. 9, 29; Hiranandani (2000), pp. 127–129.
32 Tzalel (2000), p. 160.
33 Robert W. Herrick, in 'Discussion', in George (1978), p. 84.
34 Reynolds (1998), p. 201, and his article 'The US fleet in being strategy of 1942', produced for the Battle of the Coral Sea 1942 Conference proceedings. Australian National Maritime Museum, Sydney, 1993.
35 Lee (1994), p. 177.
36 Cited in Howarth (1991), p. 491.

37 Reason (1998), p. 18.
38 Owens (1995b), p. 4.

7 Securing command of the sea

 1 Castex (1994), p. 72.
 2 Richmond, Evidence to the Cabinet Sub-Committee on Shipbuilding, 5 January 1921, Cab 16/37, Public Record Office, London.
 3 Mahan (1911) quoted in Puleston (1939), p. 294.
 4 Mahan, quoted in Taylor (1920), pp. 234–235.
 5 Quoted in Mahan (1892), Vol. I, p. 284.
 6 Breemer (1993) explores this issue in a most stimulating way.
 7 Gorshkov (1979), pp. 98–99.
 8 Creswell (1944), pp. 54–75 for a balanced discussion of this issue.
 9 Mahan quoted in Westcott (1919), pp. 128–129, and Puleston (1939), p. 294.
10 Richmond, book review, *Naval Review* (1933).
11 Corbett (1920), Vol. I, p. 2.
12 Corbett (1907), Vol. I, pp. 3–4.
13 Tunstall (1936/1990), p. 173.
14 Quoted in Padfield (1999), p. 53.
15 Padfield (1999), p. 139; Syret (1998), p. 46.
16 Ramatuelle, quoted in Rosinski (1977), p. xiii.
17 Corbett (1918), p. 143; ibid., p. 153.
18 Quoted in Rodgers (1937), p. 241.
19 Forage (1991), p. 23.
20 Cited in Tunstall (1990), p. 248; Breemer (1993), pp. 33–37.
21 Mahan (1913), pp. 27, 7, 18; Gorshkov (1979), p. 147.
22 Mitchell (1974), pp. 436–439.
23 Quoted in Wilson (1957), p. 72.
24 Rodger (1997), pp. 105–106; Jellicoe, quoted in Bacon (1936), p. 247; Tritten (1996), p. 24.
25 Mahan, quoted and discussed in Corbett (1911/1988), pp. 128–152; Corbett (1910), p. 250; Mahan, quoted in Westcott (1919), p. 156.
26 Cited in Lambert (1998), pp. 76–77; Castex (1994), p. 322.
27 Thompson (1991), pp. 15–17, 249–288.
28 Woodward (1992), p. 265.
29 George (1978), p. 93.
30 Gorshkov (1979), p. 224; Admiral Thomas B. Hayward, Chief of Naval Operations, Statement Before Seapower Sub-Committee of House Armed Services Committee, 20 December 1979 (HASC Hearings 1979).
31 Junguis (1979); Friedman (2000b), pp. 236ff., has a good discussion of the aerospace dimension of such a campaign.
32 Hiranandani (2000), pp. 120ff, 124, 145–153, provides an excellent account of this conflict.
33 Ibid., p. 127; Tzalel (2000), pp. 53–54.
34 Nott (2002), pp. 294–295.
35 Pokrant (1999b), pp. 55–92.
36 Castex (1994), pp. 111, 228–343.
37 Quoted and discussed in Colomb (1899), pp. 115, 122.
38 Richmond (1953), p. 217.
39 Corbett (1907), Vol. I, pp. 329, 475; ibid., Vol. II, pp. 373–375.
40 Corbett (1911/1988), pp. 212, 226–227.
41 Mahan (1911), pp. 243–244, 295–296.
42 Castex (1994), pp. 345, 338–343.
43 Quoted in Steinberg (1965), p. 165.
44 Scheer (1920), pp. 25, 68.
45 German Naval War Order of 4 August 1939, Führer Naval Conferences.
46 Churchill, August 1941, quoted in Frere-Cook (1973), p. 12.
47 Acworth (1930), p. 12.

48 Reynolds (1993).
49 Mahan (1892), Vol. I, p. 340; Mahan (1911), p. 183.
50 Mahan (1892), Vol. II, p. 126; ibid., Vol. I, p. 339; ibid., Vol. II, pp. 118–119.
51 Roskill (1962), pp. 48–49.
52 Callendar (1924), pp. 253–254.
53 Richmond (1934), p. 163.
54 Pollen (1918), p. 287.
55 Stansfeld Turner (1974).
56 Gorshkov (1974), pp. 13, 14–17.
57 For a sample of the debates see Miller and Van Evera (1988).
58 Thatcher (1993), pp. 215, 228.

8 Exploiting command of the sea

1 The British do use the word 'maritime', MoD (UK) (2004), p. 272. Lovering (2005) is a convenient summary of the history and development of amphibious operations.
2 Corbett (1907), Vol. I, p. 5.
3 Gorshkov (1979), p. 214.
4 Nimitz (1948).
5 Gray (1989), pp. 236–246.
6 'Planning US General Purpose Forces: The Navy', Congressional Budget Office, Washington, DC, December 1976), p. 1.
7 Gorshkov (1979), pp. 240ff.
8 Marder (1974), p. 1.
9 Brodie (1965), p. 157.
10 Gorshkov (1979), p. 3.
11 Corbett (1911/1988), p. 69.
12 Napolean, quoted in Brodie (1965), pp. 155–156; quoted in Richmond (1946), p 117.
13 Quoted in Lt Col. Michael K. Sheridan, 'The power projection of marines is an essential part of sea control', *Marine Corps Gazette*, September 1977.
14 Corbett (1921), Vol. III, p. 7.
15 Callwell (1924), p. 105.
16 Furse (1897), Vol. I, pp. 133ff, 163ff, 198–199, 296; Aston (1914), p. vii; Lewis (2001).
17 Furse (1897), Vol. I, p. 35; Roskill (1954), p. 11; Grenfell (1937), pp. 28–29.
18 Mackenzie (1929), pp. 75–76.
19 Richmond (1941b).
20 Corbett (1907), Vol. I, pp. 218–219.
21 Aspinall-Oglander (1929), Vol. I, p. 222.
22 Nimitz (1948).
23 Lt Gen. Roy S. Geiger, USMC 21 August 1946. Comments after the atomic bomb test at Bikini Atoll. My thanks to Professor J. Hattendorf for this.
24 Article in *Morskoi Sbornik,* March 1970.
25 Sears (2001), pp. 6, 9. I am indebted to Colonel Gary Anderson then of the USMC Warfighting Laboratory for these insights. Furse (1897), pp. 215–219 is an interesting summary.
26 Sears (2001), p. 24.
27 Admiral Louis M. Goldsborough quoted in Bearss (1995), p. 45.
28 The former name is often used, though the latter is more correct.
29 Paymaster William Keeler, quoted in Mindell (2000), p. 94.
30 Greely (1867), Vol. II, p. 131.
31 (US) Marine Corps Doctrinal Publication, MDP1–2, p. 82.
32 Ibid., p. 84.
33 Callwell (1996a), pp. 291–292.
34 Naveh (1997), p. 331.
35 Quoted in Ranft and Till (1989), pp. 190–191, and 187–199 more generally.
36 Gorshkov (1979), pp. 192–195.
37 Much of this material was derived from the excellent 'Fast Attack and Boomers' Exhibit at the Smithsonian Museum of American History, Washington, March 2002.

38 Quoted in Grenfell (1937), p. 43.
39 Mahan (1911), pp. 151, 293.
40 Corbett (1907), Vol. I, pp. 93–94; Corbett (1911/1988), p. 236.
41 Quoted in Richmond (1930), p. 74.
42 Quoted in Woodward (1965), pp. 206–207.
43 Richmond (1930), p. 24.
44 Quoted in Kondapalli (2001), p. 1.
45 Quoted in Marder (1972), p. 65.
46 Furse (1897), Vol. I, pp. 322, 343; Vol. II, pp. 338–372.
47 See Gatchel (1996) for an interesting and trenchant discussion of all these points.
48 Eisenhower (1948), p. 250.
49 C. Taylor, 'The preseason is over: ballistic missile defence: the naval option', *Seapower*, October 2001, and booklet *Navy Theater Ballistic Missile Defence Underway at Sea*.
50 Memo by Chief of Naval Operations for the Joint Chiefs of Staff on Military Strategy and Posture, 7 December 1953, Ser. 0001250P30. I owe this to Professor John Hattendorf.
51 Gorshkov, quoted in Herrick (1968), p. 95.
52 Cited in Wilson (1957), p. 72.
53 Mahan (1890), p. 138.
54 Mahan (1892), Vol. II, p. 184.
55 Richmond (1930), p. 56.
56 Syret (1998), pp. 94–97.
57 Corbett (1911/1988), p. 236.
58 Jane (1906), p. 145; Hipper, quoted in Philbin (1971).
59 Gorshkov (1979), p. 101.
60 De Lanessan (1903); Harding (1999), p. 56.
61 Corbett (1898), pp. 129, 335; Mahan (1890), pp. 132–133; Castex (1939), Vol. IV, pp. 113–114, 285–344; Gorshkov (1979), p. 120; Tracey (1991), p. 235.
62 Westcott (1919), pp. 16, 18. But see also Mahan (1911), pp. 355–356.
63 Richmond, evidence to Bonar Law Enquiry, 5 January 1921, Cab. 16/37, Public Record Office, London; Rosinski (1977), p. 13; Friedman (2001), pp. 89–90.
64 Quoted in Waters (1957).
65 Landersman (1986).
66 Bridge (1907), p. 123; Fisher, quoted in Marder (1940/1972), p. 95.
67 Roskill (1954), pp. 10ff; Roskill (1962), pp. 158, 179.
68 Gretton (1965), p. 22.
69 Letter by Captain W.J. Ruher, US Navy, to *Proceedings* of the US Naval Institute, December 1961.
70 Casey-Vine (1995), pp. 326, 342; Jane (1906), p. 174; Palmer (1988), pp. 24–27.
71 Gretton (1965), p. 22.
72 Grenfell (1937), p. 54.
73 Mahan (1892), Vol. II, p. 217.
74 Richmond (1930), p. 65.
75 Quoted in Mahan (1899b), p. 28.
76 Karber and Lellenberg (1977), p. 50. See also Nitze (1979), pp. 312–318, 337–382; Friedman (2001), pp. 83–88.

9 Expeditionary operations

1 MoD (UK) (1999), p. 208.
2 For example, 'Italy outlines 15-year expeditionary strategy', *Jane's Navy International*, March 2006; Colomb, cited in Paul Adams, 'The military view of the empire 1870–1899: as seen through the *Journal of the Royal United Services Institute*', *Journal* of the Royal United Services Institute, June 1998.
3 A reference to the British Defence White Paper of 1957's view of the role of the navy in a general war.
4 Bickel (2001), p. 1.
5 Arnold (2008) provides a useful review of the bewildering range of interventions.

6 Rudyard Kipling, 'The Widow's Party'.
7 Cited in 'Two concepts of sovereignty', *The Economist*, September 1999.
8 Sadowski (1998) and Timothy Garton Ash, 'Crusading is not the answer, but nor is pulling up the drawbridge', *Guardian*, 3 July 2008, are examples of a long-running debate.
9 Pugh (1994) is an excellent introduction to this subject, fast changing though it is. See also E. Grove, 'Navies play their part: peace support operations', *Jane's Navy International*, March 1999.
10 Callwell (1996b), p. 23; *Guardian*, 'Marines face unknown enemy', 23 May 2000.
11 *Concepts and Issues '98, Building a Corps for the 21st Century* (Headquarters, US Marine Corps Programs and Resources Department: Washington, DC, 1998), p. 14; for a useful review of the general problem see Evans (2007).
12 Dickens (2001); Crawford and Harper (2001), pp. 168–169. I am grateful to Colonel Gary Anderson (USMC) for his views on this.
13 Admiral Sir Jock Slater, 'Maritime contribution to joint operations', *Journal* of the Royal United Services Institute, December 1988.
14 Griffiths *et al.* (2000), p. 215. See useful chapter in ibid. on Canadian PSO. Also Crawford and Harper (2001), pp. 108–109.
15 Cited in Hore (2001), p. 59.
16 de la Billiere (1992), pp. 130, 62, 275, and Pokrant (1999b), pp. 205–218.
17 I am indebted to Drs Daniel Whiteneck and Ken Gause of the Center for Naval Analyses, Washington, DC, for their help on this.
18 Griffiths *et al.* (2000), p. 223.
19 Bickel (2001), p. 74.
20 Conrad (1978), pp. 20, 51.
21 Furse (1897), Vol. I, p. 2.
22 Callwell (1996b), p. 43.
23 Furse (1897), Vol. I, p. 107.
24 *Jane's Defence Weekly*, 16 January 2001.
25 *Jane's Defence Weekly*, 23 January 2002.
26 Ball (2001); Dickens (2001); Crawford and Harper (2001).
27 *Jane's Defence Weekly*, 16 January 2002.
28 Furse (1897), Vol. I, p. 84.
29 Admiral Sir John Woodward 'UK maritime forces: role and structure into the 21st century', *RUSI Brassey's Defence Yearbook 1992* (London: Brassey's, 1992), p. 47.
30 Furse (1897), Vol. I, pp. 208, 227.
31 Crawford and Harper (2001), pp. 48, 55–56.
32 See Section 3.6.
33 Pokrant (1999b), pp. 146–149; Hiranandani (2000), pp. 127–128.
34 Crawford and Harper (2001), p. 63.
35 Furse (1897), Vol. I, p. 35.
36 MoD (UK) (1995), p. 221.
37 McCarthy (2000), p. 15.
38 Pokrant (1999b), pp. 231–257.
39 See Leitenberg (1987) but also Tunander (2003) for an alternative explanation.
40 Dickens (2001).
41 Captain Wayne Hughes, 'How to take the small boat threat seriously', paper in Small Boat Workshop of Office of Naval Intelligence, Washington ONI, May 2000.
42 Richard Scott, 'Exploiting the maritime flank', in MoD (UK) (2008), pp. 52–55.
43 Lind (1985), p. 2.
44 Basil Liddell Hart, 'The value of amphibious flexibility and forces', *Journal* of the Royal United Services Institute, November 1960.
45 Quoted in 'Britain sets limits to show of force', *Guardian*, 9 May 2000.
46 I am grateful to Colonel J. Michel of the French Marines for this.
47 Hennessy (1997), p. 5. Since the Americans were engaging not merely guerrilla forces, but also the North Vietnamese main army, it should not be assumed that the army was 'wrong' and the US Marines were 'right' about this.
48 Lind (1985), pp. 1–3.

49 Peter Boyer, 'A different war', *New Yorker*, 1 July 2002.
50 'British troops face tough winter in Bosnia', *Guardian*, 20 November 1993.
51 Captain Brunton, cited in Hore (2001), p. 41.
52 Lee Willett, 'The Royal Navy, TLAM and British strategic planning', in Till (2001), p. 74; *Navy International* special report September 2001.
53 *Washington Post*, 2 December 2001.
54 Keegan (1988), p. 47.
55 For the background, see Roskill (1968), pp. 131–180, esp. pp. 165–169.
56 E.M. Spiers, *Wars of Intervention: A Case Study – The Reconquest of the Sudan 1896–9* (Camberley, UK: Strategic and Combat Studies Institute Occasional Papers, No. 32, 2007).
57 Colonel A. Hunter, quoted in ibid. p. 15; King cited by Scott Truver, 'Military sealift command', *Jane's Navy International*, January 2002.
58 Callwell (1996b), p. 65. See also Van Creveld (1977) and Thompson (1991).
59 Bin *et al.* (1998), p. 71.
60 Quoted in Scott Trouver, 'Military sealift command', op. cit.
61 'US build-up is fast but "not fast enough"', *Jane's Defence Weekly*, 19 March 2003.
62 Douglas M. King and John C. Berry Jnr, 'Seabasing: expanding access', *Joint Forces Quarterly*, 3rd Quarter 2008, usefully introduces the subject. For a more expanded discussion, see Till (2006a). For examples of European construction of amphibious/expeditionary shipping see reports on the Dutch *Johan de Witt* and the Danish *Absalon* class in *Jane's Defence Weekly*, 21 and 7 November 2007, respectively.
63 I am grateful to Major General Rob Fry, Royal Marines for this thought.
64 Dickens (2001).
65 Callwell (1996b), p. 23.
66 Sondhaus (2001), pp. 7–8. 'Marines sent in to burn world's finest cannabis', *Guardian*, 8 December 1998.
67 Elleman (2007).
68 Statement by Admiral Gary Roughead, Chief Naval Officer before the Senate Armed Services Committee, 28 February 2008.
69 Griffiths *et al.* (2000), pp. 215–218.
70 Now Bull Point near Plymouth, Devon.

10 Naval diplomacy

1 Jowett (1900), Book VI, line 47.
2 Mahan (1902), p. 143.
3 Quoted in Graham (1978), p. 415.
4 Mahan (1899b), p. 463.
5 Stansfeld Turner (1974).
6 Gorshkov (1979), p. 248.
7 Dalton (1994), p. 2.
8 For contemporary treatment of these issues see Freedman (1998), esp. pp. 15–36.
9 Howe (1971) and Dismukes and McConnell (1979) are good examples. Blechman and Kaplan (1978) and Zelikow (1984) usefully review US Navy experiences.
10 Quoted in Hore (2001), p. 92.
11 Kennedy (1976).
12 Lavery (1998), pp. 94, 303; Gray (1992), pp. 289–290; Cable (1998), pp. 163–167.
13 Quoted in Kondipalli (2001), p. 185.
14 Booth (1977), p. 10.
15 Ibid., p. 96 and Yerxa (1991), p. 31.
16 Cited in Puleston (1939), p. 273.
17 *People's Daily* (People's Republic of China), 10 September 2001.
18 Mindell (2000), p. 15.
19 Hough (1969), pp. 120–125.
20 Sondhaus (2001), pp. 73, 179.
21 Oman, Ministry of National Heritage and Culture (1991), pp. 185–188.

22 *British Maritime Doctrine, BR 1806* (2004), p. 284.
23 Cable (1998), p. 62; Friedman (2001), p. 51.
24 I am grateful to Captain Peter Swartz and his colleagues at the Center for Naval Analyses, Washington, DC, for suggestions here.
25 Dalton (1994), p. 3.
26 See Murfett (1991).
27 Fisher (1919a), p. 42.
28 Bell (2000), pp. 160–161; Laning (1999), pp. 145, 189.
29 Captain James Burnell-Nugent, *Journal* of the Royal United Services Institute, August 1998.
30 More valuable points made by Peter Swartz.
31 For a robust if controversial exploration of the quality versus quantity theme, see Vice Admiral Sir Jeremy Blackham and Gwyn Prins, 'Storm warning for the Royal Navy', *Proceedings* of the US Naval Institute, October 2007.
32 Pokrant (1999a), pp. 192–195; Friedman (2000b), pp. 310–311.
33 Friedman (2000b), pp. 310–311.
34 Brooks (1993), p. 24; Tzalel (2000), p. 144; Lerner (2002), pp. 5–98.
35 'Japan defiant over boat sinking', *Guardian*, 24 December 2001.
36 Sun Tzu (1971), p. 77.
37 Murfett (1999), p. 82.
38 MoD (UK) (1995), p. 89. Interestingly, the definition is different on p. 204 and again in MoD (UK) (1999), p. 198.
39 Lehman (1988), p. 64.
40 This passage owes much to Stanik (1996).
41 Freedman and Gamba-Stonehouse (1991), *passim*.
42 Perkins (1989), p. 69.
43 Pokrant (1999a), p. 26.
44 Ibid., pp. 26, 27–37, 185–195 and (1999b), pp. 265ff.
45 Edmonds (2000), pp. 16–17.
46 General Samuel Smith quoted in Hattendorf (2000), p. 11.
47 Lambert (1990), pp. 309–325.
48 Padfield (1999), p. 194.
49 Komer (1984); Miller and Van Evera (1988); Weeks (1994).
50 Barbara Starr, 'USA deploys carriers, but doubts invasion threat against Taiwan', *Jane's Defence Weekly*, 20 March 1996; 'East Asia after the Taiwan crisis', *Strategic Comments* (London: IISS, April 1996).
51 Hooker and Waddell (1992), p. 83.
52 Kinney (1985), p. 85.
53 Carrington (1988), p. 351; Freedman and Gamba-Stonehouse (1991), p. 99.
54 Cable (1979), p. 8.
55 Usefully discussed from a historical perspective in Sondhaus (2001), pp. 225ff.
56 The French submarine FNS *Perle* and others made quite an impression at the magnificent Indian International Fleet Review of 2001.
57 El-Shazly (1998), p. 294.
58 Gary Punch, 'The future of Australian sea power in the new century', in McCaffrie and Hinge (1998), pp. 111–112.
59 Admiral Mike Mullen (then Chief Naval Officer) formally launched this concept at the 17th International Seapower Symposium in September 2005. See Hattendorf (2006a), pp. 3–8. For the generally supportive attitudes of the leaders of other navies, see 'The commanders respond', *Proceedings* of the US Naval Institute, March 2007, and 'Charting the course: world navy chiefs look to the future', special supplement to *Jane's Defence Weekly*, 2 May 2007.
60 For an example see the *Taipeh Times*, 10 July 2001, and the way in which Chinese, Philippine, South Korean and Indian warships just turned up to watch Taiwan firing Patriot missiles!
61 Roth (2001) and discussions with author at the Center for Naval Analyses, Washington, DC, November 2001.

62 Reports in the *New York Times*, 6 April 2001, 9 July 2001; *Herald Tribune*, 17 August 2001; *Washington Post*, 27 July 2001.
63 Hill (1988) is a good introduction. See also Sakhuja (2001) for an Indian perspective.
64 I am grateful to Dr Joe Moretz for bringing this episode to my attention. Confidential Monthly Intelligence Report No. 15, 15 July 1920, Richmond MSS, National Maritime Museum, Greenwich.
65 N. Lambert (1998), p. 116.
66 Captain C.A. Silcock, 'UK operations', *NATO Broadsheet* (London: MoD, 1999/2000).
67 The Hon. John H. Dalton, 'Navies and world events in the 21st century', *Journal* of the Royal United Services Institute, October 1998.
68 *Philippines Star*, 22 October 2001.
69 *Jane's Defence Weekly*, 6 November 1996.
70 Report on 'HMS Tireless', *Guardian*, 8 May 2001; Pugh (1989).
71 Cable (1998), p. 14.
72 See Robert E. Looney and David Shrady, 'Estimating the economics of naval forward presence: a brief summary', in Tangredi (2001b).
73 Letter, 5 August 1920, in Ranft (1993), Vol. II, p. 97.
74 Lehman (1988), p. 363.
75 Admiral Gene La Roque, in George (1978), p. 197.
76 Quoted in Goode (1997), p. 33.
77 Quotation from various officers on the China Station, in Graham (1978), pp. 58, 135ff.
78 Keynote address to Fourteenth International Seapower Symposium, US Naval War College, Newport, RI, 2–5 November 1997, in Hattendorf (1998), p. 29.
79 Stansfeld Turner, quoted in Nathan and Oliver (1979), pp. 72–73.
80 Brooks (1993), p. 2.
81 Ibid.; Tangredi (2001b); Benson (2001).

11 Good order at sea

1 Cited in Simon Mitchell, 'Maritime counter-terrorism', in *Royal Navy: A Global Force* (London: MoD, 2008), p. 71.
2 Dupont (1998), pp. 41–42.
3 'We need to start caring about fish, or there won't be any left to eat', *Guardian*, 31 October 2005; 'EU fishing fleets devastate Third World', *Guardian*, 16 March 2002.
4 For example, see Bernama News (Malaysia), 26 June 2001, Yahoo News (Philippines), 26 September 2001.
5 Gibson (2001).
6 *The Economist*, 19 June 1999; *Guardian Weekly*, 6 July 2002.
7 Tracy (1995), p. 233.
8 Politakis (1998), p. 627.
9 'Al-Qaida suspected in tanker explosion', *Guardian*, 7 October 2002; 'Seafarers want navy escort', *Guardian*, 12 October 2002. Murphy (2007) is a useful study of piracy and sea-based terrorism and the alleged links between them.
10 Cited by James Pelkofski, 'Before the storm: Al Qaida's coming maritime campaign', *Proceedings* of the US Naval Institute, December 2005; the background to the crafting of the ISPS Code is usefully summarised in 'IMO 2004: focus on maritime security', in *IMO News*, No. 3, 2004.
11 'Bloodthirsty and beyond the law: rise of the gun-toting pirates terrorising the seas', *Sunday Telegraph*, 25 May 2008; 'Somali lawlessness spills into sea', *Washington Post*, 2 April 2006.
12 Allen (1997); the quarterly reports of the Recaap Information Sharing Centre nicely complement those of the International Maritime Bureau.
13 Politakis (1998), p. 627; Reagan, quoted in Creighton (1992), p. 32; O'Rourke (1998).
14 *Newsweek* article quoted in El-Shazly (1998), p. 268.
15 Cordesman (1990), p. 544; Politakis (1998), p. 567. 'Maritime surveillance UAVs: shaping up for naval roles', *Jane's Defence Weekly*, 15 June 2005.

16 'Maritime surveillance UAVs: shaping up for naval roles', *Jane's Defence Weekly*, 15 June 2005.

17 Interviews with Rear Admiral Richard Leaman, *Jane's Defence Weekly*, 13 December 2006 and *Jane's Navy International*, June 2006.

18 *South China Morning Post* (PRC), 27 June 2001; *Japan Today* (Japan), 28 September 2001.

19 Simon Saradzhyan, 'Russian ships at the mercy of pirates', *ISN Security Watch*, 10 July 2008.

20 For the political value of SAR, for example, see *Armed Forces Journal International*, February 2001.

21 International Institute for Strategic Studies (IISS) Adelphi Paper No. 319, p. 37. Reports in *Guardian*, 11 June 2002 and 17 September 2002.

22 'Greenpeace climbers board GM soya ship', *Guardian*, 26 February 2001. For *Aurora* see *Guardian*, 16 May 2001.

23 'UK halts ship after intelligence alert', *Guardian*, 22 December 2001; *Daily Telegraph*, 13 December 2001.

24 *Japan Today*, 3 October 2001.

25 US *Union Tribune*, 12 September 2001. I am indebted to Peter Swartz of the Center for Naval Analysis for his views on this.

26 Stewart (2002), pp. 37–38, 74, 171.

27 Krass (1988); 'US anti-narcotics strategy "At war with reality"', *Strategic Comments* (London: IISS, 5 March 2000).

28 'Cocaine with £50 million street value seized by navy in Caribbean raid', *Guardian*, 4 February 2006. Despite such successes the operational emphasis on Iraq and Afghanistan has resulted in budgets cuts leading to a reduction in Royal Navy patrols in the area.

29 *Guardian*, 30 August 2001.

30 For a good review of the European dimension of all this, see Pugh (2000); 'Spain steps up patrols as 1000 migrants died during desperate quest for Europe', *Guardian*, 23 March 2006; 'EU launches marine border squad', *BBC Online Report*, 4 August 2006.

31 Stewart (2002), op. cit.

32 Ibid., pp. 173–175 and Cohen (1994).

33 Australia's Oceans Policy (1998), Vol. II, p. 7.

34 Ballard presentations at Expo '98 Conference, Lisbon. Also, 'Evidence found of Noah's Ark flood victims', *Guardian*, 14 September 2001.

35 'Greece's seas: the looters next destination', *Guardian*, 6 December 2005.

36 Professor Brett Phaneuf of the Institute of Nautical Archaeology at Texas University. Quoted in 'Divers looting sunken D-day war graves', *Independent*, 31 October 2000.

37 *Washington Post*, 10 July 2001.

38 *Guardian*, 22 March 2001.

39 Vidigal (1985).

40 Cook and Carleton (2000), p. 3.

41 Kearsley (1991), p. 76.

42 Crickard *et al.* (1998), p. 338.

43 *Korean Herald*, 15 June 2001, 19 June 2001, 4 January 2002; *South China Morning Post*, 19 June 2001; *Japan Times*, 6 October 2001; *Associated Press Area Network*, 9 July 2001.

44 'Sewage and fertilisers "are killing the seas"', *Guardian*, 30 March 2004; 'Time is running out to curb effects of deep sea pollution', *Guardian*, June 2006. For the background, see Van Dyke *et al.* (1993). For IWCO Report, see Herr (2000), pp. 44–51.

45 'Global warming sinks islands', *Guardian*, 13 June 1999.

46 Griffiths *et al.* (2000), p. 369.

47 'Fishermen cry foul over UK's scramble for gas', *Guardian*, 10 April 2006; 'Military may defend Japanese whalers', *New Zealand Herald*, 11 January 2006.

48 'The Exxon Valdez – stains that remain', *The Economist*, 20 May 1999; MoD (UK) (1999), p. 61.

49 'Sea burial set for Japanese freighter', *Omani Observer*, 20 February 1999; *Straits Times*, 19 September 2001.

50 BBC World News online, 24 August 2001.

51 'Russia says its rusting fleet could poison Arctic', *Guardian*, 18 September 2002.
52 'NATO blamed for dead whales', *Guardian*, 28 September 2002.
53 *Agence France Press*, 27 June 2001; Politi (1997), p. 59.
54 Australia's Oceans Policy (1998), Vol. II, p. 34; *Sydney Morning Herald*, 23 February 2002.
55 Weir (2001), p. 154.
56 For that remarkable story see McCannon (1998).
57 'Scientists fear waste of crucial navy polar data', *Guardian*, 23 August 2000; 'Ocean warming threatens Antarctic wildlife', *Guardian*, 19 October 2005; 'As polar ice turns to water, dreams of treasure abound', *New York Times*, 10 October 2005; 'Arctic declaration denounced as territorial "carve up"', *Guardian*, 29 May 2008; 'Russia plans military build-up in the Arctic', *Daily Telegraph*, 12 June 2008.
58 Weir (2001), p. 144; 'Military hydrography ventures into uncharted waters', *Jane's International Defence Review*, October 2005.
59 Prins and Stamp (1991), pp. 146–151.
60 Falk (2000), pp. ix, 2; Palmer (2000).
61 Bell (2000), p. 164.
62 *Australia's Oceans Policy* (1998), Vol. I, p. 3.
63 'Opportunities to make the Arctic a model', *Arctic Bulletin*, Vol. 2, 1999; 'Russia "unlawfully" annexing the Arctic for control of oil', *Sunday Telegraph*, 18 May 2008.
64 Cook and Carleton (2000), p. 3.
65 Vijay Sakhuja, 'Maritime legal conundrum', Institute of Peace and Conflict Studies, Paper No. 1778, 29 June 2005.
66 'Somalia calls for piracy help', *Jane's Defence Weekly*, 2 November 2005; John S. Burnett, 'Captain Kidd: human rights victim', *New York Times*, 20 April 2008.
67 Allen (2007) is the best guide to this complicated and fast moving area; 'UN grants navies power to tackle Somalia piracy', *Jane's Defence Weekly*, 11 June 2008.
68 Roy-Chaudhury (2000), pp. xviiiff; interview with D.T. Joseph, Director General of Shipping, India, Mumbai, February 2002.
69 'Maritime agency all at sea', *Daily Telegraph*, 4 April 1999.
70 Johnson (1957), p. 368.
71 Ward (1999) is an excellent review of this unique organisation.
72 I am indebted to Rear-Admiral James Goldrick for this insight.
73 I am grateful to Commodore Tor Nikolaisen, RnorNavy, and Captain E. Le May, Chilean Navy, respectively, for their help in this area.
74 Nien-Tsu and Oliver (1988), p. 46.
75 'Japanese navy fires on spy ships', *Guardian*, 25 March 1999; *The Economist*, 21 September 2000; *Japan Times*, 6 October 2001.
76 I am grateful to Captain Bruce Stubbs of the USCG for his continuing advice and help. See his letter to the *Washington Post*, 1 December 2001. Also, Prins and Stamp (1991), p. 32.
77 'Maritime awareness: briefing', *Jane's Defence Weekly*, 4 April 2007.
78 See Press Release from US State Department and Department of Transportation 25/26 June 2002.
79 Admiral Thomas H. Collins quoted in ibid. Although there have been programmatic problems, the intent is unchanged. Gordon I. Peterson and Scott C. Truver, 'The multi-mission U.S. Coast Guard', in *Naval Forces*, No. 4, 2006. See also Admiral Thad W. Allen, in USCG, *The US Coast Guard Strategy for Maritime Safety, Security and Stewardship* (2007).
80 Johnson (1957), pp. 57ff, 368; 'Guarding the green seas', *Jane's Navy International*, May 1996.

12 Theory and practice: the Asia-Pacific region: a case study

1 Bill McKibben, 'A special moment in history', *Atlantic Monthly*, May 1998, p. 60.
2 Klare (2001).
3 Malik (2008).

4 Address to International Institute for Strategic Studies (IISS), 21 June 2007. This passage also owes much to an address by Dr Sanjaya Baru, 12 June 2008.

5 Andrew-Speed *et al.* (2002); IISS Adelphi Paper No. 346, p. 78. This paper contains a valuable and balanced account of this subject.

6 In Taylor (2001), p. 10.

7 Howard (2001).

8 Professor Zhang Wenmu of the Beijing University of Aeronautics and Astronautics, cited in Gordon Fairclough, 'As China grows, so does its long-neglected navy', *Wall Street Journal*, 16 July 2007.

9 Captain E.D. Smith, 'The dragon goes to sea', *Naval War College Review*, Summer 1991.

10 Tun-hwa Ko, 'China as a potential maritime power', in Kim (1988), p. 135.

11 Ross H. Munro, 'Eavesdropping on the Chinese military: where it expects war – where it doesn't', *Orbis*, Summer 1994.

12 Vice Admiral Hideaki Kaneda, 'Japan's national maritime doctrines and capabilities', in Prabhakar *et al.* (2006), p. 123.

13 His Excellency Mr Shohei Naito, Ambassador to Belgium, address at SHAPE, 17 March 2005, p. 7.

14 *Indian Maritime Doctrine* (henceforth *IMD*) (New Delhi: Integrated Headquarters, Ministry of Defence (Navy), 2004); *Freedom to use the Seas: India's Maritime Military Strategy* (henceforth *MMS*) (New Delhi: Integrated Headquarters, Ministry of Defence (Navy), 2007).

15 'India releases joint war doctrine', *Jane's Defence Weekly*, 31 May 2006.

16 Vijay Sakhuja, 'Indian navy: keeping pace with emerging challenges', in Prabhakar *et al.* (2006), p. 191.

17 Testimony of Vice Admiral Joseph A. Sestak, Junior Deputy Chief of Naval Operations, before the Subcommittee of the Senate House Armed Services Committee, 19 April 2005.

18 As their titles suggest, these documents were issued in 2006 by the then CNO Admiral Mullen and General Hagee, Commandant of the USMC. They are both intended to guide the use of resources to achieve the aims of the US Navy's 'Vision' statement – *Sea Power 21*.

19 The Global War on Terror.

20 US Navy, *Navy Strategic Plan* (2006), p. 7.

21 Larry Wortzel, 'The trouble with China's nuclear doctrine', *Jane's Defence Weekly*, 22 February 2006; see also *Navy Times*, 26 February 2007 for an interesting report of the range of views on appropriate responses to the rise of the Chinese Navy.

22 *Navy Strategic Plan*, p. 15.

23 Conway *et al.*, 'A Cooperative Strategy for 21st Century Seapower' (henceforth 'A Cooperative Strategy'), October 2007, pp. 1–2. Curiously this document lacks formal page numbers.

24 Ibid., pp 2–3.

25 Ibid., pp. 2–3.

26 A number of articles commenting on the strategy are usefully collected in the *Naval War College Review*, Spring 2008.

27 *IMD*, op. cit., p. 54.

28 Amy F. Woolf, 'Nuclear weapons in US national security policy: past, present and prospects', Congressional Research Service, 29 October 2007.

29 Statement by Admiral Gary Roughead, Chief of Naval Operations, before the Senate Armed Services Committee, 28 February 2008.

30 Holmes and Yoshihara (2005), pp. 8, 53–71, and their excellent *Chinese Naval Strategy* (2008). You Ji, 'The evolution of China's maritime combat doctrines and models' (Singapore: IDSS, May 2002), Working paper No. 22.

31 Admiral Zhang Lianzhong, cited in J. Downing, 'China's evolving maritime strategy: part II', *Jane's Intelligence Review*, April 1996, p. 187.

32 For example, Ross Munro, Robyn Lym in Holmes and Yoshihara (2008), pp. 59–60.

33 Cited in Ronald O'Rourke, 'China naval modernization: implications for U.S. navy capabilities – background and issue for Congress', Congressional Budget Office Report, 18 October 2007, p. 41.

34 Professor Ni Lexiong (Research Institute of War and Culture), 'Seapower and China's development', *Liberation Daily*, 17 April 2005, cited in Holmes and Yoshihara (2008), p. 42.

35 People's Republic of China, *Chinese National Defence in 2004*, cited in Holmes *et al.* (2009).

36 Jiang Shiliang, 'The command of communications', *China Militray Science* (Beijing), 2 October 2002, pp. 106–114. Cited in Holmes *et al.* (2009).

37 You Ji, op. cit., pp. 27ff.

38 Quoted in Declan Walsh, 'US uneasy as Beijing develops a strategic string of pearls', *Guardian*, 10 November 2005.

39 Ian Storey, 'China as a global maritime power: opportunities and vulnerabilities', unpublished paper.

40 Cited in Graham (2006), pp. 182, 196.

41 Although widely cited, there is some doubt that Mahan ever said this. No matter. He should have done!

42 Admiral Mehta, address to IISS, 21 June 2007.

43 Admiral Mehta, forward to *MMS*, op. cit., p. iv.

44 *IMD*, op. cit., p. 63.

45 *MMS*, op. cit., pp. 46–49.

46 *IMD*, op. cit., p. 75.

47 Ibid., p. 50.

48 Foreword to *MMS*, op. cit., p. iv; *MMS*, p. 41.

49 Conway *et al.* (2007), p. 11.

50 Admiral Roughead to the Senate Armed Services Committee, February 2008, op. cit., p. 7.

51 Peterson (2006).

52 Reports 'Chinese sub got within striking range of US ship', *Gulf Times*, 14 November 2006, *Washington Times/Post*, 11 January 2007. Accounts of this incident vary widely. See O'Rourke (1998), p. 44.

53 'Chinese ASTA test rekindles weapons debate', *Jane's Defence Weekly*, 24 January 2007; G. Friedman, 'To be prepared is to survive', *Straits Times*, 25 January 2007.

54 'Submarine that intruded into Japanese waters likely to be Chinese vessel', *Mainichi Shimbun*, 11 November 2004; 'Eagle eyes: self defense forces keep tabs on nations mapping East Asia's seabed', *Asahi Shimbun*, 16 February 2004.

55 'Japanese navy fires on spy ships', *Guardian*, 25 March 1999; reports in *Japan Times*, 2 and 16 April 2002.

56 Graham (2006), pp. 119, 123–124, 141.

57 *MMS*, op. cit., pp. 111–112.

58 'Indian warships sail away from Pak waters', Reuters, 11 June 2002.

59 NewKerala.com (accessed 26 February 2007).

60 Office of the Secretary of Defense (US) *Military Power of the People's Republic of China* (2008), p. 7.

61 Marine Corps Association, 'Operational manoeuvre from the sea: a concept for the projection of power ashore', *Marine Corps Gazette*, June 1996. See Section 8.4.

62 Vice Admiral David L. Brewer, 'Strategic deployment: a US navy perspective', *World Defence Systems*, April 2003. See also Douglas M. King and John C. Berry Jr, 'Seabasing: expanding access', *Joint Forces Quarterly*, First Quarter 2008.

63 *Military Support to Stabilization, Security, Transition and Reconstruction Operations*, US Department of Defense, Directive 3000.5, 28 November 2005; US Navy, *Naval Operations Concept* (2006), p. 19.

64 Mike Mullen, 'What I believe', *Proceedings* of the US Naval Institute, Vol. 132, No. 1, January 2006.

65 Young testimony, op cit, p. 1.

66 'Global Fleet Stations' may be another term that needs further examination. To some observers it implies something more akin to a floating naval base for possibly offensive action than a means of alleviating local distress. The Myanamar disaster of 2008, furthermore, shows that even sea-based help may not be acceptable to local regimes.

67 'Russian coastguards kill Japanese fisherman in disputed waters', *Guardian*, 17 August 2006.
68 *Military Power of the People's Republic of China* (2008), p. 38.
69 Lyle J. Goldstein, 'China: a new maritime partner', *Proceedings* of the US Naval Institute, August 2007, pp. 26–31.
70 Channel News Asia, 25 October 2005.
71 'No place to hide – maybe', *The Economist*, 30 October 2004.
72 Admiral Arun Prakash (former Chief of the Naval Staff), 'A vision of maritime India: 2020', *Seagull*, August 2007; *MMS*, op. cit., pp. 89–94.
73 Eaglen *et al.* (2008), p. 13 (Index).
74 Admiral Mike Mullen at the Regional Seapower Symposium in Venice, 12 October 2006, quoted in Eaglen *et al.* (2008), p. 16.
75 Liu Jixian, as cited in Nan Li (2002), p. 7.
76 Admiral Mehta, address to IISS, op. cit.
77 'Indian warship visits Tonga', online, available at: www.chinaview.cn (accessed 11 July 2006); Admiral Mehta at the IISS, op. cit.
78 Admiral L. Ramdas, 'Dismantling prejudice: the road to a people based peace strategy', *Seagull*, May 2005. *MMS*, op. cit., p. 29; *IMD*, op. cit., p. 51.
79 Christopher J. Castelli, 'New maritime strategy would emphasize soft and hard power', *Inside the Navy*, 18 June 2007; Vice Admiral John G. Morgan and Rear Admiral Charles W. Martoglio, 'The 1,000-ship navy global maritime network', *Proceedings* of the US Naval Institute, November 2005.
80 Admiral Mike Mullen formally launched this concept at the 17th International Seapower Symposium in September 2005. See John Hattendorf (2006a), pp. 3–8.
81 Vice Admiral John G. Morgan, quoted in 'Maritime strategy to be unveiled next month', *Navy Times*, 26 September 2007.
82 The Model Maritime Service Code issued by the US Coast Guard in 1995 and now being reworked is a good example of this since it is intended to 'assist other nations in developing a Maritime Force to help them meet the changing needs of the twenty-first century'.
83 See Mitchell (2006).
84 This was even a problem in the Asian Tsunami relief operation. Elleman (2007), p. 72.
85 Admiral Mullen at the 17th International Seapower Symposium, op. cit., p. 6.
86 'US considers naval build-up as warning to Iran', *Guardian*, 20 December 2006; 'Bush settling America on the road to war with Iran', *Guardian*, 16 September 2007.
87 Robert C. Rubel, 'The new maritime strategy: the rest of the story', *Naval War College Review*, Spring 2008, p. 77.
88 'Kitty Hawk remains in Hawaii for RIMPAC', *Honolulu Star Bulletin*, 4 July 2008.
89 See online, available at: www.aei.org/docLib/20050620_work.pdf (accessed 5 December 2008) for details of the AEI conference on 'The future of the United States Navy', 20 June 2005.
90 O'Rourke (1998), pp. 5–7.
91 At an American Enterprise Institute conference of 20 June 2005 and cited in CRS Report for Congress, p. 51.
92 O'Rourke (1998), p. 38.
93 Cole (2001), pp. 185–186.
94 *Military Power of the People's Republic of China* (2008), p. 1.
95 Michael J. Mazarr, 'The folly of "asymmetric war"', *Washington Quarterly*, Summer 2008; Kagan (2008).

13 Conclusions?

1 Dalton (1998).
2 See the chapter by Anand, R.P., 'Changing Concepts of freedom of the Seas: A Historical perspective' in Van Dyke et al (1993) pp 72-86.
3 Letter of 8 April, emphasis in original, Fisher (1919a), p. 197.
4 Pugh (1994), p. 218.
5 Johnson (1957), p. 571.

6 Ibid., p. 566.
7 See Chapter 11.
8 Commission Report, p. 39, cited and discussed in Herr (2000), pp. 44–51.
9 Prins and Stamp (1991), p. 144.
10 UNCLOS, Part ix, Section 2, Articles 136, 137.1, 137.2, discussed by Gwyn Prins, in Flanagan (2001), p. 554.
11 O'Connell (1975) and Grove (2000), pp. 94–115.
12 Hattendorf (1998), p. 63; Haydon and Griffiths (1995), pp. 62–63.
13 Mahan (1899a), p. 142.
14 In Flanagan (2001), p. 505.

Bibliography

(Semi) official documents

Australian Maritime Doctrine (Canberra, Australia: Defence Publishing Service, 2000).

Commonwealth of Australia, *Caring, Understanding, Using Wisely, Australia's Oceans Policy* (Vols I and II) (Canberra: Department of the Environment, 1998).

Conway, General James T. (Commandant of the US Marine Corps), Roughead, Admiral Gary (Chief of Naval Operations) and Allen, Admiral Thad W. (Commandant, U.S. Coast Guard), 'A Cooperative Strategy for 21st Century Seapower', October 2007.

Dalton, Hon. J.H., Boorda, Adm. J.M. and Mundy, Gen. C.E., 'Forward ... From the Sea', US Naval Institute Proceedings, *Marine Corps Gazette*, October 1994.

Franks, Rt Hon. the Lord, *Falklands Islands Review Report of a Committee of Privy Counsellors* (London: HMSO, 1983).

Indian Maritime Doctrine (New Delhi: Integrated Headquarters, Ministry of Defence (Navy), 2004). Also *Freedom to Use the Seas: India's Maritime Military Strategy* (New Delhi: Integrated Headquarters, Ministry of Defence (Navy), 2007).

Krupp, Major-General K.T., *Naval Amphibious Warfare Plan. Decisive Power from the Sea* (Washington, DC: Dept of the Navy, 1999).

Marine Corps Association, 'Operational maneuver from the sea: a concept for the projection of naval power ashore', *Marine Corps Gazette*, June 1996.

MoD (UK), *The Fundamentals of British Maritime Doctrine* (BR 1806) (London: HMSO, 1995).

MoD (UK), *Strategic Defence Review* (London: The Stationery Office, 1998).

MoD (UK), *British Maritime Doctrine* (BR 1806) (2nd edn) (London: The Stationery Office, 1999).

MoD (UK), 'Introduction', in *The Strategic Defence Review: A New Chapter* (London: The Stationery Office, 2002).

MoD (UK), *British Maritime Doctrine* (BR 1806) (3rd edn) (London: The Stationery Office, 2004).

MoD (UK), *Royal Navy: A Global Force* (London: MoD, 2008).

Mullen, Adm. Mike, 'CNO guiding principles,' in *CNO Guidance for 2006: Meeting the Challenge of a New Era* (Washington, DC: US Dept of Defense, Dept of the Navy, Office of the CNO, October 2006).

Naval Doctrine Command, *Multinational Maritime Operations* (Norfolk, VA: NDC, 12 October 1995).

New Zealand Defence Forces, *Foundations of New Zealand Military Doctrine* (*NZDDP-D*) (Wellington, NZ: HQ NZDF, 2004). Also *New Zealand: Maritime Doctrine for the Royal New Zealand Navy* (Wellington, NZ: RNZN, 1998).

Nimitz, C.W., *Report to the Secretary of the Navy, 1947* (London and New York: Brassey's Naval Annual, 1948).

O'Keefe, The Hon. Sean C., Kelso, Adm. Frank B. and Mundy, Gen. C.E., 'From the sea: a new direction for the naval services', *Marine Corps Gazette*, November 1992.

O'Rourke, *China Naval Modernization: Implications for U.S. Navy Capabilities – Background and Issue for Congress* (Washington: Congressional Research Service, 18 October 2007).

Office of the Secretary of Defense (US), *Military Power of the People's Republic of China* (Washington, DC: US Government, 2008).

Oman: A Seafaring Nation (Muscat, Sultanate of Oman: Ministry of National Heritage and Culture, 1991).

Ritchie, Vice Admiral C.A. (Chief of Navy), *Australia's Navy for the 21st Century 2002–2003* (Canberra: Defence Publishing Services, 2002).

Rhodes, J.E., *United States Marine Corps Warfighting Concepts for the 21st Century* (Quantico, VA: Marine Corps Combat Development Command, 22134–5021).

Scales, Maj. Gen. Robert H. Jr (Cmdt US Army War College), 'America's army in transition: preparing for war in the precision age', Army Issue Paper No. 3, Fall 1999.

Singapore MoD, *Defending Singapore in the 21st Century* (Singapore: Ministry of Defence, 2000).

UN Conference on Trade and Development, *Review of Maritime Transport* (Geneva, UN, 2006).

US Coast Guard, *21st Century Hemisphere Maritime Security: A USCG Deepwater Vision* (Washington, DC: USCG: 1998).

US Coast Guard, *The U.S. Coast Guard Strategy for Maritime Safety, Security, and Stewardship* (Washington, DC: USCG, 2007).

US Navy, *Naval Operations Concept* (Washington, DC: Department of the Navy, 2006).

US Navy, *Navy Strategic Plan* (Washington, DC: Department of the Navy, 2006).

Watkins, Adm. James, 'The maritime strategy', Special Supplement, *Proceedings* of the US Naval Institute, January 1986.

Books and articles

Abbott, Adm. Sir Peter, 'The maritime component of British and allied military strategy', *Journal* of the Royal United Services Institute, December 1996.

Acworth, Captain B., *The Navies of Today and Tomorrow* (London: Eyre and Spottiswoode, 1930).

Alam, Cdre Mohd Khurshed, 'Maritime strategy of Bangledesh in the new millennium', *Bangladesh Institute of International Studies Journal*, Vol. 20, No. 3, 1999.

Allen, Craig, *Maritime Counterproliferation Operations and the Rule of Law* (Westport, CT: Praeger Security International, 2007).

Anderson, Bern, *By Sea and By River: The Naval History of the Civil War* (New York: Da Capo Press, 1962).

Andrews-Speed, Philip, Xuani, Liao and Dannreuther, Ronald, *The Strategic Implications of China's Energy Needs* (London: IISS, 2002).

Antal, John F., 'Thoughts about maneuver warfare', in Hooker, Richard D. (ed.), *Maneuver Warfare: An Anthology* (New York: Presidio Press, 1993).

Arnold, Michael J., 'Intervention', in Snyder, Craig A. (ed.), *Contemporary Security and Strategy* (Basingstoke: Palgrave Macmillan, 2008).

Aspinall-Oglander, C.F., *Military Operations: Gallipoli* (London: William Heinemann, 1929).

Aston, Sir George, *Letters on Amphibious Wars* (London: John Murray, 1911).

Aston, Sir George, *Sea, Land and Air Strategy: A Comparison* (London: John Murray, 1914).

Aston, Sir George, *Memorial of a Marine: An Autobiography* (London: John Murray, 1919).

Aver, James E. and Lim, Riohy, 'The maritime basis of American security in East Asia', *US Naval War College Review*, Winter 2001.

Bacon, Adm. Sir Reginald, *The Life of John Rushworth Earl Jellicoe* (London: Cassell, 1936).

Baer, G., *One Hundred Years of Sea Power. The US Navy, 1890–1990* (Stanford, CA: Stanford University Press, 1994).

Ball, Desmond, 'Silent witness: Australian intelligence and East Timor', *Pacific Review*, Vol. 14, 2001.

Barnett, Corelli, *Engage The Enemy More Closely: The Royal Navy in The Second World War* (London: Hodder and Stoughton, 1991).

Bateman, Sam, 'Dangerous water ahead', *Jane's Defence Weekly*, 28 March 2001.

Baugh, D., 'Admiral Sir Hubert Richmond and the objects of sea power', in Goldrick, J. and Hattendorf, J. (eds), *Mahan Is Not Enough: The Proceedings of a Conference on the Works of Sir Julian Corbett and Admiral Sir Herbert Richmond* (Newport, RI: Naval War College, 1993).

Bayliss, John and Smith, Steve (eds), *The Globalization of World Politics* (Oxford: Oxford University Press, 2001).

Bearss, Ed, *River of Lost Opportunities: The Civil War on the James River 1861–1862* (Lynchburg, VA: M.E. Howard, 1995).

Beeching, Jack, *The Chinese Opium Wars* (London: Hutchinson, 1975).

Behren, C.B.A., *Merchant Shipping and the Demands of War* (London: HMSO, 1955).

Bell, Christopher M., *The Royal Navy: Seapower and Strategy Between the Wars* (Basingstoke: Macmillan Press Ltd, 2000).

Benbow, T., *The Magic Bullet? Understanding the Revolution in Military Affairs* (London: Brassey's, 2003).

Benson, Stephen, 'Formative and operative engagement', in Flanagan, Stephen J., Frost, Ellen L. and Kugler, Richard L. (eds), *Challenges of the Global Century*, Report of the Project on Globalization and National Security (Washington, DC: National Defense University, 2001).

Bertram, C. and Holst, J.J. (eds), *New Strategic Factors in the North Atlantic* (Oslo: Universitetsforlaget, 1977).

Biass, Eric, 'Missiles on a cruise', *Armada International*, Issue 3, 2001.

Bickel, Keith B., *Mars Learning: The Marine Corps' Development of Small Wars Doctrine 1915–1940* (Oxford: Westview Press, 2001).

Biddle, S., 'Victory misunderstood: what the Gulf War tells us about the future of conflict', *International Security*, Vol. 21, No. 2, 1996.

Billiere, Gen. Sir Peter de la, *Storm Command* (London: Harper Collins, 1992).

Bin, Alberto *et al.*, *Desert Storm: A Forgotten War* (London: Praeger, 1998).

Blechman, B.M. and Kaplan, S., *Force Without War: US Armed Forces as a Political Instrument* (Washington, DC: Brookings Institute, 1978).

Booth, K., *Navies and Foreign Policy* (London: Croom Helm, 1977).

Borresen, Jacob, 'The seapower of the coastal state', in Till, Geoffrey (ed.), *Seapower: Theory and Practice* (London: Frank Cass, 1994).

Borresen, Jacob, 'Coastal power: the sea power of the coastal state and the management of maritime resources', in Hobson, Rolf and Kristiansen, Tom (eds), *Navies in Northern Waters 1721–2000* (London: Frank Cass, 2003).

Bowman, Adm. Frank L. 'Skip' (USN), 'Submarines in the new world order', *Undersea Warfare*, Spring 1999.

Boyer, Pellman G. and Wood, Robert S., *Strategic Transformation and Naval Power in the 21st Century* (Newport, RI: NWC Press, 1998).

Breemer, Jan S., *The Burden of Trafalgar: Decisive Battle and Naval Strategic Expectations on the Eve of the First World War* (Newport, RI: Naval War College, 1993).

Breemer, J., 'Naval strategy is dead', *Proceedings* of the US Naval Institute, Vol. 120, No. 2, February 1994.

Bridge, Adm. Sir Cyprian, *The Art of Naval Warfare* (London: Smith, Elder, 1907).

Bridge, Adm. Sir Cyprian, *Sea Power and Other Studies* (London: Smith, Elder, 1910).

Brodie, B., *A Guide to Naval Strategy* (New York: Praeger, 1965).

Brooks, Linton F., *Peacetime Influence: Through Forward Naval Presence* (Alexandria, VA: Center for Naval Analyses, October 1993).

Cable, J., *The Royal Navy and the Siege of Bilbao* (Cambridge: Cambridge University Press, 1979).

Cable, J., *The Political Influence of Naval Force in History* (Basingstoke: Macmillan Press Ltd, 1998).

Cable, J., *Gunboat Diplomacy 1919–1979: Political Applications of Limited Naval Force* (3rd edn) (Basingstoke: Macmillan Press Ltd, 1999).

Callendar, Geoffrey, *The Naval Side of British History* (London: Christopher, 1924).

Callwell, Charles E., *The Effect of Maritime Command on and Campaigns Since Waterloo* (London: Blackwood, 1897).

Callwell, Charles E., *The Dardanelles* (London: Constable, 1924).

Callwell, Charles E., *Military Operations and Maritime Preponderance: Their Relations and Interdependence* (Annapolis, MD: Naval Institute Press, 1996a).

Callwell, Charles E., *Small Wars: Their Principles and Practice* (reprint) (London: University of Nebraska Press, 1996b).

Carrington, Lord, *Reflect on Things Past* (London: Collins, 1988).

Casey-Vine, Paula (ed.), *Oman in History* (London: Immel Publishing for Ministry of Information, Sultanate of Oman, 1995).

Castex, Adm. R., *Theories Strategiques* (5 vols) (Paris: Societé d'Editions, 1929–1935), reprinted as Kiesling, Eugenia C. (ed.), *Strategic Theories* (Annapolis, MD: Naval Institute Press, 1994).

Cebrowski, Vice Adm. Arthur K. and Gartska, John J., 'Network centric warfare: its origin and future', *Proceedings* of the US Naval Institute, January 1998.

Cecil, David, *Lord M: Or the Later Life of Lord Melbourne* (London: Constable, 1954).

Chandhury, Sushil and Michel Morineau (eds), *Merchants, Companies and Trade: Europe and Asia in the Early Modern Era* (Cambridge: Cambridge University Press, 1999).

Childers, Erskine, *The Riddle of the Sands* (London: Sidgwick and Jackson, 1935).

Clarke, G.S. and Thursfield, J.R., *The Navy and the Nation* (London: John Murray, 1897).

Clemins, Adm. Archie, 'Interview with Cincpacflt', *Undersea Warfare*, Summer 1999.

Clerk, John, *Essay on Naval Tactics* (1782; London: Cadell, 1790; Edinburgh: Constable, 1804).

Cohen, Stuart A., 'Imperial policing against immigration: the Royal Navy and Palestine 1945–8', *Journal of Imperial and Commonwealth History*, May 1994.

Cole, Bernard, *The Great Wall at Sea* (Annapolis, MD: Naval Institute Press, 2001).

Colomb, P., *Naval Warfare* (London: Allen, 1899).

Conrad, Joseph, *Heart of Darkness* (London: Penguin, 1978).

Cook, Peter J. and Carleton, Chris, *Continental Shelf Limits – The Scientific and Legal Interface* (Oxford: Oxford University Press, 2000).

Cooper, Robert, *The Breaking of Nations: Order and Chaos in the Twenty-first Century* (London: Atlantic Books, 2004).

Coquinot, J.P., 'Submarines on loose leash: countermeasures', *Armada International*, Issue 2, 1997.

Corbett, Sir Julian, *Drake and the Tudor Navy* (London: Longmans,Green, 1898).

Corbett, Sir Julian, *England in the Mediterranean* (2 vols) (London: Longmans, Green, 1904).

Corbett, Sir Julian (ed.), *Fighting Instructions, 1530–1816* (London: Navy Records Society, 1905).

Corbett, Sir Julian, *England in the Seven Years War* (2 vols) (London: Longmans, Green, 1907).

Corbett, Sir Julian, *The Campaign of Trafalgar* (London: Longmans, Green, 1910).

Corbett, Sir Julian, *Some Principles of Maritime Strategy* (London: Longmans, Green 2nd edn, 1911; reprinted with 'Introduction' by Eric Grove (Annapolis, MD: Naval Institute Press, 1988)).

Corbett, Sir Julian, *Maritime Operations in the Russo-Japanese War 1904–5* (2 vols) (London: Admiralty War Staff, 1914).

Corbett, Sir Julian, *Drake and the Tudor Navy* (2 vols) (London: Longmans, Green, 1917).

Corbett, Sir Julian, *History of the Great War: Naval Operations* (5 vols, last two by Sir Henry Newbold) (London: Longmans, Green, 1920–1931).

Cordesman, Anthony H., *The Lessons of Modern War: The Iran–Iraq War* (Oxford: Westview Press, 1990).

Coté, Owen R., *Mobile Targets From Under the Sea* (Cambridge, MA: MIT Security Studies Program Conference Report, 2000).

Coté, Owen R., *Assuring Access and Projecting Power: The Navy in the New Security Environment* (Cambridge, MA: MIT Security Studies Program Conference Report, 2001).

Coulter, Daniel and Goldman, A., 'Global shipping trends and implications for navies', in Crickard, Fred W., Deveaux, Fred and Orr, Katherine D. (eds), *Multinational Naval Cooperation and Foreign Policy into the 21st Century* (Aldershot: Ashgate, 1998).

Coulter, Daniel Y., 'Navies and globalization: an estranged couple', in Robert H. Edwards and Ann L. Griffiths (eds), *Intervention and Engagement: A Maritime Perspective* (Halifax, NS: Dalhousie University, Centre for Foreign Policy Studies, 2003).

Cozens, Peter (ed.), *A Maritime Nation: New Zealand's Maritime Environment and Security* (Wellington, New Zealand: Centre for Strategic Studies, Victoria University of Wellington, 1996).

Crawford, John and Harper, Glyn, *Operation East Timor: The New Zealand Defence Force in East Timor, 1999–2001* (Auckland, New Zealand: Reed Publishing, 2001).

Creighton, John, *Oil on Troubled Waters: Gulf War 1980–89* (London: Echors, 1992).

Creswell, Cdr John, *Naval Warfare: An Introductory Study* (London: Sampson, Low, Marston & Co, 1944).

Creveld, Martin van, *Supplying War: Logistics from Wallenstein to Patton* (Cambridge: Cambridge University Press, 1977).

Crickard, Fred W., Deveaux, Fred and Orr, Katherine D., *Multinational Naval Cooperation and Foreign Policy into the 21st Century* (Aldershot: Ashgate, 1998).

Crowe, Adm. William J. with Chanoff, David, *The Line of Fire* (New York: Simon and Shuster, 1993).

CSCAP, Memo No. 5, 'Cooperation for law and order at sea', Council for Security Cooperation in the Asia Pacific, February 2001.

Cunliffe, B., *Facing the Ocean* (Oxford: Oxford University Press, 2001).

Dalpech, Thérèse, 'The perfect war: a view from France', *World Defense Systems*, 2001.

Dalton, The Hon. J.H., 'Navies and world events in the 21st century', *Journal* of the Royal United Services Institute, October 1998.

Daniel, Daniel C.F. *et al.*, *Coercive Inducement and the Containment of International Crises* (Washington, DC: United States Institute of Peace Press, 1999).

Dash, Mike, *Batavia's Graveyard* (New York: Crown Publishing, 2001).

Deck, Richard A., 'Singapore: comprehensive security – total defence', in Booth, Ken and Trood, Russell (eds), *Strategic Cultures in the Asia-Pacific Region* (Basingstoke: Palgrave, 1999).

Deng, Gang, *Chinese Maritime Activities and Socioeconomic Development c 2100 BC – 1900 AD* (Westport, CT: Greenwood Press, 1997).

Dickens, David, 'The United Nations. East Timor: intervention at the military operational level', *Contemporary Southeast Asia*, Vol. 32, No. 2, August 2001.

Dillon, Dana, 'Piracy in Asia: a growing barrier to trade', The Heritage Foundation, Washington, DC, 22 June 2000.

Dismukes, Bradford and McConnell, James M., *Soviet Naval Diplomacy* (New York: Pergamon, 1979).

Dorman, A., *The Nott Review Witness Seminar* (London: Centre for Contemporary British History, 2002).

Dorman, A. *et al.* (eds), *The Changing Face of Maritime Power* (Basingstoke: Macmillan Press Ltd, 1999).

Dupont, Alan, *The Environment and Security in Pacific Asia* (London: IISS, Adelphi Paper No. 319, 1998).

Durch, William J., *UN Peacekeeping, American Policy and the Uncivil Wars of the 1990s* (Basingstoke: Macmillan Press Ltd, 1997).

Eaglen, Mackenzie M., Dolblow, James, Andersen, Martin Edwin and Carafano, James Jay, *Securing the High Seas: America's Global Maritime Constabulary Power* Special Report (Washington, DC: Heritage Foundation, 2008).

East Asian Strategic Review 2001 (Japan: National Institute for Defence Studies, 2001).

Easton, Brian, *Globalisation and the Weatlth of Nations* (Auckland, New Zealand: Auckland University Press, 2007).

Edgerton, David, *England and the Aeroplane: An Essay on a Militant and Technological Nation* (Basingstoke: Macmillan Press Ltd, 1991).

Edmonds, Martin, *Defence Diplomacy and Preventative Diplomacy* (Lancaster: Centre for Defence and International Security Studies, Bailrigg Memo 34, 2000).

Edmonds, Martin, *100 Years in the Trade. Royal Naval Submarines: Past, Present and Future* (Lancaster: Centre for Defence and International Security Studies, 2001).

Eisenhower, Dwight D., *Crusade in Europe* (New York: Doubleday, 1948).

Elleman, Bruce, *Waves of Hope: The US Navy's Response to the Tsunami in Northern Indonesia* (Newport, RI: Naval War College Press, 2007).

Ellen, Eric, 'Bringing piracy to account', *Jane's Navy International*, April 1997.

El-Shazly, Nadia, *Gulf Tanker War: Iran and Iraq's Maritime Swordplay* (Basingstoke: Macmillan Press Ltd, 1998).

Erickson, John, 'The development of soviet military doctrine: the significance of operational art and the emergence of deep battle', in Gooch, J. (ed.), *The Origins of Contemporary Doctrine* (Camberley, UK: Strategic and Combat Studies Institute Occasional Papers, No. 30, 1997).

Evans, David C., 'Japanese naval construction, 1878–1918', in O'Brien, P.P. (ed.), *Technology and Naval Combat in the Twentieth Century and Beyond London* (London: Frank Cass, 2001).

Evans, David C. and Peattie, Mark R., *Kaigun: Strategy, Tactics and Technology in the Imperial Japanese Navy, 1887–1941* (Annapolis, MD: Naval Institute Press, 1997).

Evans, Michael, *From Deakin to Dibb: The Army and the Making of Australian Strategy in the 20th Century* (Duntroon: Land Warfare Studies Centre, Working Paper No. 113, 2001a).

Evans, Michael, *Australia and the Revolution in Military Affairs* (Duntroon: Land Warfare Studies Centre: Working Paper No. 115, 2001b).

Evans, Michael, *City Without Joy: Urban Military Operations into the 21st Century* (Weston, Canberra: Australian Defence College, Occasional Paper No. 2, 2007).

Falk, Kevin L., *Why Nations Put To Sea: Technology and the Changing Character of Sea Power in the Twenty-First Century* (New York: Garland Publishing, 2000).

Ferguson, Niall, *Colossus: The Rise and Fall of the American Empire* (London: Penguin Books, 2005).

Ferguson, Niall, *The War of the World* (London: Allen Lane, 2006).

Fisher, Lord, *Memories* (London: Hodder and Stoughton, 1919a).

Fisher, Lord, *Records By Admiral of the Fleet Lord Fisher* (London: Hodder and Stoughton, 1919b).

Flanagan, Stephen J., Frost, Ellen L. and Kugler, Richard L., *Challenges of the Global Century*, Report of the Project on Globalization and National Security (Washington, DC: National Defense University, 2001).

Forage, Paul C., 'The foundations of Chinese naval supremacy in the twelfth century', in Jack Sweetman *et al.* (eds), *New Interpretations in Naval History 10th Symposium* (Annapolis, MD: Naval Institute Press, 1991).

Franklin, G., *The Development of Britain's Anti-Submarine Capability Between the Wars* (London: Frank Cass, 2003).

Fraser, Stewart, *Littoral Warfare and Joint Maritime Operations: UK Approaches and Capabilities* (Lancaster: Centre for Defence and International Security Studies, Bailrigg Memo 32, 1986).

Freedman, L., *Strategic Coercion: Concepts and Cases* (Oxford: Oxford University Press, 1998).

Freedman, L. and Gamba-Stonehouse, V., *Signals of War: The Falklands Conflict of 1982* (Princeton, NJ: Princeton University Press, 1991).

Freedman, Lawrence, *The Official History of the Falklands Campaign* (vols I and II) (London: Routledge, 2007).

Frere-Cook, G., *The Attacks on the Tirpitz* (London: Ian Allen, 1973).

Frieden, Jeffrey A., *Global Capitalism: Its Fall and Rise in the Twentieth Century* (New York: WW Norton, 2006).

Friedman, Norman, 'Littoral anti-submarine warfare', *Jane's International Defence Review*, Issue 6, 1995.

Friedman, Norman, *Fifty Year War: Conflict and Strategy in the Cold War* (London: Chatham Publishing, 2000a).

Friedman, Norman, *Seapower and Space: From the Dawn of the Missile Age to Net-Centric Warfare* (London: Chatham Publishing, 2000b).

Friedman, Norman, *Seapower as Strategy: Navies and National Interests* (Annapolis, MD: Naval Institute Press, 2001).

Friedman, Thomas L., *The World is Flat: The Globalized World in the Twenty-first Century* (London: Penguin, 2006).

Fry, Brig. Robert, 'Myths of manoeuvre', *Journal* of the Royal United Services Institute, December 1997.

Fukuyuma, Francis, 'The end of history', *National Interest*, Summer 1989.

Furse, *Military Expeditions Beyond the Seas* (2 vols) (London: William Clowes, 1897).

Gaffney, H.H. *et al.*, *US Naval Responses to Situations 1970–1999* (Washington: Center for Naval Analyses, December 2000) (unclassified mini report of a classified original).

Gatchel, Theodore L., *At the Waters Edge: Defending Against the Modern Amphibious Assault* (Annapolis, MD: Naval Institute Press, 1996).

George, J.L. (ed.), *Problems of Sea Power As We Approach the Twenty-first Century* (Washington, DC: American Enterprise Institute, 1978).

Ghosi, J., 'Revising gunboat diplomacy: an instrument of threat or use of limited naval force', *Strategic Analysis* (Delhi), February 2001.

Giambastian, Vice Adm. Edmund (Deputy Chief of Naval Operations, Resources, Requirements and Asessments), 'An investment portfolio for the navy after next', *Seapower*, April 2001.

Gibson, Andrew E., 'After the storm', *Naval War College Review*, 1992.

Gibson, Lt Cdr Trevor, 'The one that didn't get away', *Journal of the Australian Naval Institute*, Autumn/Winter 2001.

Gilbert, Gregory P., *Ancient Egyptian Sea Power and the Origin of Maritime Forces* (Canberra: Australian Sea Power Centre, 2008).

Goldrick, J., *No Easy Answers: The Development of the Navies of India, Pakistan, Bangladesh and Sri Lanka 1945–1996* (New Delhi: Lancer Publishers, 1997).

Goldrick, J., 'A fleet not a navy: some thoughts on the themes', in Stevens, David and Reeve, John (eds), *Southern Trident: Strategy, History and the Rise of Australian Naval Power* (Sydney: Allen and Unwin, 2001).

Goldrick, J. and Hattendorf, J. (eds), *Mahan Is Not Enough: The Proceedings of a Conference on the Works of Sir Julian Corbett and Admiral Sir Herbert Richmond* (Newport, RI: Naval War College, 1993).

Gongora, Thierry and von Riekhoff, Harald (eds), *Toward a Revolution in Military Affairs* (London: Greenwood Press, 2000).

Goode, J.F., *The United States and Iran* (Basingstoke: Macmillan, 1997).

Gordon, Andrew, *The Rules of the Game: Jutland and British Naval Command* (London: John Murray, 1996).

Gorshkov, Sergei, *Navies in War and Peace (Red Star Rising at Sea)* (Annapolis, MD: Naval Institute Press, 1974).

Gorshkov, Sergei, *The Seapower of the State* (London: Pergamon, 1979; first published in Russia, 1976).

Graham, Evan, *Japan's Sea Lane Security, 1940–2004: A Matter of Life and Death?* (London: Routledge, 2006).

Graham, G.S., *The China Station* (Oxford: Clarendon Press, 1978).

Gray, Colin S., *The Leverage of Sea Power: The Strategic Advantage of Navies in War* (New York: The Free Press, 1992).

Gray, Colin S., *Modern Strategy* (Oxford: Oxford University Press, 1999).

Gray, Colin S., *Another Bloody Century: Future Warfare* (London: Phoenix, 2005).

Gray, Colin S. and Barnett, Roger W. (eds), *Seapower and Strategy* (Annapolis, MD: Naval Institute Press, 1989).

Gray, Colin S. and Sloan, Geoffrey (eds), *Geopolitics: Geography and Strategy* (London: Frank Cass, 1999).

Greely, Horace, *The American Conflict: A History of the Great Rebellion* (2 vols) (Hartford, CT: OD Case & Co, 1867).

Grenfell, R., *The Art of the Admiral* (London: Faber, 1937).

Gretton, Adm. Sir Peter, *Maritime Strategy* (London: Cassell, 1965).

Griffiths, Ann L. and Haydon, Peter T., *Maritime Forces in Global Security* (Halifax NS: Dalhousie University, Centre for Foreign Policy Studies, 1995).

Griffiths, Ann L., Haydon, Peter T. and Gimblett, Richard H., *Canadian Gunboat Diplomacy: The Canadian Navy and Foreign Policy* (Halifax, NS: Dalhousie University, Centre for Foreign Policy Studies, 1998).

Grivel, Baron Richard, *De La Guerre Maritime* (Paris, 1869).

Grove, E., *The Future of Seapower* (London: Routledge, 1990).

Grove, E., 'From shackle to springboard: birth of a doctrine', *Jane's Navy International*, March 1996.

Grove, E., *The Price of Disobedience: The Battle of the River Plate Reconsidered* (Stroud: Sutton Publishing, 2000).

Gruber, David J., 'Computer networks and information warfare: implications for military operations', Maxwell Air Force Base, AL: Air University, Center for Strategy and Technology, Occasional Paper No. 17, July 2000.

Gwyn, Julian (ed.), *The Royal Navy and North America* (London: Navy Records Society, 1973).

Haas, Richard N., *The Reluctant Sheriff: The United States After the Cold War* (New York: Council on Foreign Relations, 1997).

Hammes, Col. Thomas X., *The Sling and the Stone* (St Paul, MN: Zenith Press, 2005).

Handel, Michael I., *Masters of War: Classical Strategic Thought* (London: Frank Cass, 2001).

Harding, Richard, *Seapower and Naval Warfare 1650–1830* (London: University College Press, 1999).

Hattendorf, J., 'A review of naval practice', unpublished paper for conference on 'Significance of Seapower in the 21st century', US Naval War College, Newport, RI, November 2000.

Hattendorf, John, (ed.), *Report of the Proceedings 19–23 September 2005* (Newport, RI: US Naval War College, 2006a).

Hattendorf, John (ed.), *US Naval Strategy in the 1990s: Selected Documents* (Newport, RI: US Naval War College, 2006b).

Hattendorf, John B., *The Influence of History on Mahan* (Newport, RI: Naval War College Press, 1991a).

Hattendorf, John B., *Mahan on Naval Strategy* (Annapolis, MD: Naval Institute Press, 1991b).

Hattendorf, John B., *Doing Naval History: Essays Toward Improvement* (Newport, RI: Naval War College Press, 1995).

Hattendorf, John B. (ed.), *Fourteenth International Seapower Symposium: Proceedings, 1997* (Newport, RI: Naval War College Press, 1998).

Hattendorf, John B. and Jordan, Robert S. (eds), *Maritime Strategy and the Balance of Power* (Basingstoke: Macmillan Press Ltd, 1989).

Hattendorf, John B. *et al.*, *Sailors and Scholars: The Centennial History of the US Naval War College* (Newport, RI: Naval War College Press, 1984).

Haydon, Peter T., *Navies in the Post Cold War Era* (Halifax, NS: Dalhousie University, Centre for Foreign Policy Studies, 1998).

Haydon, Peter T., *Sea Power and Maritime Strategy in the 21st Century* (Halifax, NS: Dalhousie University, Centre for Foreign Policy Studies, 2000).

Haydon, Peter T. and Griffiths, Ann L. (eds), *Multinational Naval Forces* (Halifax, NS: Dalhousie University, Centre for Foreign Policy Studies, 1995).

Hegmann, R., 'Reconsidering the evolution of the US maritime strategy 1955–65', *Journal of Strategic Studies*, Vol. 14, No. 3, 1991.

Hennessy, Michael A., *Strategy in Vietnam: The Marines and Revolutionary Warfare in 1 Corps, 1965–1972* (London: Eurospan Group, 1997).

Herr, R.A. (ed.), *Sovereignty at Sea: From Westphalia to Madrid*. Wollongong Papers in Maritime Policy No 11, Centre for Maritime Policy, University of Wollongong, 2000.

Herrick, R.W., *Soviet Naval Strategy* (Annapolis, MD: Naval Institute Press, 1968).

Herrick, R.W., *Soviet Naval Theory and Policy* (Washington, DC: US Government Printing Office, 1988).

Heuser, Beatrice, *Reading Clausewitz* (London: Pimlico, 2002).

Hewish, M., 'Return of the big guns at sea', *Jane's International Defence Review*, Issue 4, 2000.

Hill, Richard, *Maritime Strategy For Medium Powers* (Annapolis, MD: Naval Institute Press, 1986).

Hill, Richard, *Arms Control at Sea* (London: Routledge, 1988).

Hiranandani, Vice Adm. G.M., *Transition to Triumph: Indian Navy 1965–1975* (New Dehli: Lancer Publishers, 2000).

Hirschfeld, Thomas J. and Hore, Peter (eds), *Maritime Aviation: Light and Medium Aircraft Carriers into the Twenty First Century* (Hull: Hull University Press, 1999).

Hobson, Rolf and Kristiansen, Tom, *Navies in Northern Waters 1721–2000* (London: Frank Cass, 2003).

Holmes, James R. and Yoshihara, Toshi, 'The influence of Mahan upon China's maritime strategy', *Comparative Strategy*, January/March 2005.

Holmes, James R. and Yoshihara, Toshi, *Chinese Naval Strategy in the 21st Century: The Turn to Mahan* (London: Routledge, 2008).

Holmes, James R., Winner, Andrew C. and Yoshihara, Toshi, *Indian Maritime Strategy in the Twenty-first Century* (London: Routledge, 2009).

Hooker, Capt. Richard D. and Waddell, Capt. Ricky L., 'The future of conventional deterrence', *Naval War College Review*, Summer 1992.

Hore, P. (ed.), *Seapower Ashore* (London: Chatham Publishing, 2001).

Hough, Richard, *Fighting Ships* (London: Michael Joseph, 1969).

Hough, Richard, *Captain James Cook: A Biography* (London: Hodder and Stoughton, 1994).

Howard, Michael, *The Invention of Peace: Reflections on a War and International Order* (New Haven, CT: Yale University Press, 2001).

Howard, Michael and Paret, Peter, *Carl von Clauzwitz, On War* (Princeton, NJ: Princeton University Press, 1976).

Howarth, Patrick, *Lifeboat: In Danger's Hour* (London: Hamlyn, 1981).

Howarth, Stephen, *To Shining Sea: A History of the United States Navy, 1775–1991* (London: Weidenfeld and Nicholson, 1991).

Howe, J.T., *Multicrises* (Cambridge, MA: MIT Press, 1971).

Hughes, Wayne, 'Mahan, tactics and principles of strategy', in Hattendorf, John B. (ed.), *Mahan on Naval Strategy* (Annapolis, MD: Naval Institute Press, 1991).

Hughes, Wayne, 'Naval maneuver warfare', *Naval War College Review*, Summer 1997.

Hughes, Wayne, *Fleet Tactics and Coastal Combat* (Annapolis, MD: US Naval Institute, 2000).

Hunt, Barry D., *Sailor-Scholar: Admiral Sir Herbert Richmond 1871–1946* (Waterloo, ON: Wilfred Laurier Press, 1982).

Hunt, Barry D., 'Richmond and the education of the Royal Navy' in Goldrick, J. and Hattendorf, J. (eds), *Mahan Is Not Enough: The Proceedings of a Conference on the Works of Sir Julian Corbett and Admiral Sir Herbert Richmond* (Newport, RI: Naval War College, 1993).

Huntington, Samuel, 'National policy and the transoceanic navy', *Proceedings* of the US Naval Institute, May 1954.

Huxley, Tim, *Defending the Lion City: The Armed Forces of Singapore* (London: Allen & Unwin, 2000).

Ingram, Edward, *The British Empire as a World Power* (London: Frank Cass, 2000).

Inskip, Ian, *Ordeal By Exocet:* HMS *Glamorgan and the Falklands War 1982* (London: Chatham Publishing, 2002).

Irwin, Ash, *The Levels of War: Operational Art and Campaign Planning* (Camberley, UK: Strategic and Combat Studies, Occasional Paper No. 5, 1993).

Jane, F.T., *Heresies of Sea Power* (London: Longmans, 1906).

Jay, Peter, *The Sea! The Sea!* (London: Anvil Press Poetry, 2005).

Jeshurun, Chandran, 'Malaysia: the delayed birth of a strategic culture', in Booth, Ken and Trood, Russell (eds), *Strategic Cultures in the Asia-Pacific Region* (Basingstoke: Palgrave, 1999).

Johnson, Robert Erwin, *Guardians of the Sea: History of the United States Coast Guard, 1915 to the Present* (Annapolis, MD: Naval Institute Press, 1957).

Jowett, B., *Thucydides Translated into English* (Oxford: Clarendon Press, 1900).

Jungius, Adm. Sir James, 'The balance of power at sea', *NATO Review*, December 1979.

Kagan, Robert, *The Return of History and the End of Dreams* (London: Atlantic Books, 2008).

Kane, Thomas M., *Chinese Grand Strategy and Maritime Power* (London: Frank Cass, 2001).

Karber, P.A. and Lellenberg, J.L., 'The state and future of US naval forces in the North Atlantic', in Bertram, C. and Holst, J.J. (eds), *New Strategic Factors in the North Atlantic* (Oslo: Universiteitsforlagt, 1977).

Kearsley, Harold J., *Maritime Power and the Twenty-First Century* (Aldershot: Dartmouth, 1991).

Keegan, J., *The Price of Admiralty* (London: Hutchinson, 1988).

Kennedy, P.M., 'The relevance of the prewar British and American maritime strategies to the First World War and its aftermath', in Hattendorf, John B. and Jordan, Robert S. (eds), *Maritime Strategy and the Balance of Power* (Basingstoke: Macmillan Press Ltd, 1989).

Kennedy, Paul M., *The Rise and Fall of British Naval Mastery* (London: Allen Lane, 1976).

Kim, Dal-choong (ed.), *Resources, Maritime Transport and SLOC Security in the Asia-Pacific Region* (Seoul: Institute of East and West Studies, 1988).

Kinney, Douglas, 'Anglo-Argentinean diplomacy and the Falklands crisis', in Coll, Alberto and Arend, Anthony C. (eds), *Lessons for Strategy, Diplomacy and International Law* (London: Allen & Unwin, 1985).

Kipp, Jacob, 'The second arm and the problem of combined operations', in Gillette, P. and Frank, Willard C. (eds), *The Sources of Soviet Naval Conduct* (Lexington, MA: Lexington Books, 1990).

Kirkpatrick, Prof. David, 'Revolutions in military technology and their consequences', *Journal* of the Royal United Services Institute, August 2001.

Klare, Michael T., *Resource Wars: The New Landscape of Global Conflict* (New York: Metropolitan Books, 2001).

Komer, Robert F., *Maritime Strategy or Coalition Defense?* (Cambridge, MA: Abt Books, 1984).

Kondapalli, Srikanth, *China's Naval Power* (Delhi: IDSA, 2001).

Kraas, Louis, 'The drugs trade', *Fortune*, 20 June 1988.

Krepinevich, Andrew F., 'Cavalry to computers: the pattern of military revolution', *National Interest*, No. 37, Fall 1994.

Lambert, Andrew, *The Crimean War: British Grand Strategy Against Russia, 1853–6* (Manchester: Manchester University Press, 1990).

Lambert, Andrew, *The Foundations of Naval History: John Knox Laughton, the Royal Navy and the Historical Profession* (London: Chatham Publishing, 1998).

Lambert, Andrew (ed.), *Letters and Papers of Professor Sir John Knox Laughton, 1830–1915* (Aldershot: Ashgate, Navy Records Society, 2002).

Lambert, N., *Australia's Naval Inheritance: Imperial Maritime Strategy and the Australia Situation 1880–1909* (Canberra: Department of Defence (Navy), Maritime Studies Programme, 1998).

Lambert, N., *Sir John Fisher's Naval Revolution* (Columbia, SC: University of South Carolina Press, 1999).

Landersman, S.D., 'Naval protection of shipping: a lost art?', *Naval War College Review*, June 1986.

Lanessan, J.I. de, *Le Programme Maritime de 1900–1906* (Paris: 1903).

Laning, Adm. Hans, *An Admiral's Yarn*, with an introduction by Shulman, M.R. (Newport, RI: Naval War College Press, 1999).

Larsen, Col. Randall J., 'Homeland defense: state of the union', *Strategic Review*, Spring 2001.

Lavery, Brian, *Nelson and the Nile: The Naval War Against Bonaparte 1798* (London: Chatham Publishing, 1998).

Lee, Choon Kun, 'Korean sea power's contribution towards national security', in Lee, Choon Kun (ed.), *Seapower and Korea in the 21st Century* (Seoul: Sejong Institute, 1994)

Lehman, John F., *Command of the Seas: Building the 600 Ship Navy* (New York: Charles Scribener's Sons, 1988).

Leitenberg, Milton, *Soviet Submarine Operations in Swedish Waters 1980–1986* (New York: Praeger, 1987).

Leopold, Dr Reuven, 'The next naval revolution', *Jane's Navy International*, January/February 1996.

Lerner, Mitchell B., *The Pueblo Incident: A Spy Ship and the Failure of American Foreign Policy* (Lawrence, KS: Kansas University Press, 2002).

Levinson, Marc, *The Box* (Princeton, NJ: Princeton University Press, 2006).

Lewis, Adrian R., *Omaha Beach: A Flawed Victory* (Chapel Hill, NC, and London: University of North Carolina Press, 2001).

Liddell Hart, B.H., *Strategy: The Indirect Approach* (London: Faber and Faber, 1967).

Lind, William S., *Maneuver Warfare Handbook* (Boulder CO: Westview Press, Special Studies, 1985).

Lindberg, Michael, *Geographical Impact on Coastal Defence Navies: The Entwining of Force Structure, Technology and Operational Environment* (Basingstoke: Macmillan Press Ltd, 1998).

Lindberg, Michael and Todd, Daniel, *Brown-, Green- and Blue-Water Fleets: The Influence of Geography on Naval Warfare, 1861 to the Present* (Westpoint, CT: Praeger, 2002).

Link, Charles D., '21st century armed forces: joint vision 2010', *Joint Services Quarterly*, Autumn 1996.

Livezey, William E., *Mahan on Sea Power* (Norman, OK: University of Oklahoma Press, 1981).

Loughran, R-Adm. T., 'Projecting power from the sea: the Royal Navy's contribution to the air battle', *Journal* of the Royal Services Institute, December 1996.

Lovelace, Douglas C., *The Evolution in Military Affairs* (Carlisle, PA: US Army War College Strategic Studies Institute, 1997).

Lovering, Tristam (ed.), *Amphibious Assault: Manooeuvre From the Sea* (Woodbridge, UK: Seafarer Books, 2005).

Luttwak, E., *The Political Uses of Sea Power* (Baltimore, MD: Johns Hopkins University Press, 1975).

Luttwak, Edward N., 'The operational level of war', *International Security*, Winter 1980/1981.

McBride, William M., *Technological Change and the United States Navy* (Baltimore, MD: Johns Hopkins University Press, 2000).

McCaffrie, Jack and Hinge, Alan (eds), *Sea Power in the New Century* (Canberra ACT: Strategic and Defence Studies Centre, 1998).

McCannon, John, *Red Arctic: Polar Exploration and the Myth of the North in the Soviet Union 1932–1939* (New York: Oxford University Press, 1998).

McCarthy, William J., 'Directed energy and fleet defense implications for naval warfare', Maxwell Air Force Base, AL: Air University, Center for Strategy and Technology, Occasional Paper No. 10, 2000.

MacGregor, Douglas A., *Transformation Under Fire: Revolutionizing How America Fights* (Westport, CT: Praeger, 2003).

Mack, Major Alistair, 'Intervention in East Timor: from the ground', *Journal* of the Royal United Services Institute, December 1999.

Mackenzie, Compton, *Gallipoli Memories* (London: Cassell, 1929)

MacKenzie, Vice Adm. Sir Hugh, *The Sword of Damocles* (Gosport, UK: Royal Navy Submarine Museum, 1995).

McKercher, B.J.C. and Hennessy, M., *The Operational Art: Developments in the Themes of War* (London: Praeger, 1996).

Mahan, A.T., *The Gulf and Inland Waters* (New York: Scribners, 1883).

Mahan, Capt. A.T., *The Influence of Sea Power Upon History 1660–1783* (London: Sampson, Low, Marston & Co. Ltd, 1890).

Mahan, Capt. A.T., *The Influence of Sea Power Upon the French Revolution and Empire 1793–1812* (vol 1) (Boston: Little, Brown & Co, 1892).

Mahan, Capt. A.T., *Lessons of the War with Spain* (London: Sampson, Low, Marston & Co. Ltd, 1899a).

Mahan, Capt. A.T., *The Life of Nelson* (London: Sampson, Low, Marston & Co. Ltd, 1899b).

Mahan, Capt. A.T., *The Problem of Asia and its Effect Upon International Policies* (London: Sampson, Low, Marston & Co. Ltd, 1900).

Mahan, Capt. A.T., *Retrospect and Prospect* (London: Sampson, Low, Marston & Co. Ltd, 1902).

Mahan, Capt. A.T., *Naval Strategy: Compared and Contrasted with the Principles and Practise of Military Operations on Land* (Boston: Little, Brown & Co, 1911; reprinted 1919).

Mahan, Capt. A.T., *Major Operations of the Navies in the War of American Independence* (London: Sampson, Low, Marston & Co. Ltd, 1913).

Mahapatra, Chintamani, 'Cooperative efforts in the Indian Ocean region', Paper No 13, Australia Defence Studies Centre, 1996.

Makarov, Vice Adm. Stephen O., trans. Bernadov, J.B., *Discussion of Questions in Naval Tactics* (Annapolis, MD: Naval Institute Press, 1990).

Malik, Mohan J. 'The dragon rises, the elephant stirs', *Guanxi*, Vol. 2, No. 8, 2008.

Marder, Arthur J., *The Anatomy of British Sea Power, 1940* (reprinted London: Frank Cass, 1972).

Marder, Arthur J., *From the Dardanelles to Oran* (London: Oxford University Press, 1974).

Marolda, Edward J. and Schneller, Robert J. Jr, *Shield and Sword: The United States Navy and the Persian Gulf War* (Washington, DC: Naval Historical Center, 1998).

Martin, David G., *The Peninsula Campaign March–July 1862* (Conshohocken, PA: Combined Books, 1992).

Martin, L., *The Sea in Modern Strategy* (London: Chatto and Windus, 1967).

Matheson, P.E. and Matheson, E.F. (eds), *Francis Bacon* (Selections) (Oxford: Clarendon Press, 1964).

Menon, Rear Adm. Raja, *Maritime Strategy and Continental Wars* (London: Frank Cass, 1998).

Menzies, Gavin, *1421: The Year China Discovered The World* (London: Bantam, 2003).

Michaels, G.J., *Tip Of the Spear: US Marine Light Armour in the Gulf War* (Annapolis, MD: Naval Institute Press, 1998).

Mies, Adm. Richard W., 'The SSBN in national security', *Undersea Warfare*, Fall 1999.

Miller, Stephen E. and Van Evera, Stephen, *Naval Strategy and National Security* (Princeton, NJ: Princeton University Press, 1988).

Mindell, David A., *War, Technology and Experience aboard the USS Monitor* (Baltimore, MD: Johns Hopkins University Press, 2000).

Mitchell, Donald W., *A History of Russian and Soviet Sea Power* (London: Andre Deutsch, 1974).

Mitchell, Paul T., *Network Centric Warfare: Coalition Operations in the Age of US Military Primacy* (London: IISS, Adelphi Paper No. 385, 2006)

Molyneux, Thomas M., *Conjunct Expeditions or Expeditions That Have Been Carried on Jointly by the Fleet and Army, with a Commentary on a Littoral War* (London: R& J Dodsley, 1759).

Montgomery, Capt. C.P.R., 'The Royal Navy and future joint operations', *Journal* of the Royal United Services Institute, April 2002.

Moran, Michael, *Sacred Cows in the Cross Hairs*. Online, available at MSNBC.com (accessed 29 March 2001).

Moretz, Joseph, *The Royal Navy and the Capital Ship in the Interwar Period* (London: Frank Cass, 2002).

Morgan, John (Captain US Navy), 'Anti submarine warfare: a phoenix for the future', *Undersea Warfare*, Fall 1998.

Murfett, Malcolm H., *Hostage on the Yangtze: Britain, China and the Amethyst Crisis of 1949* (Annapolis, MD: Naval Institute Press, 1991).

Murfett, Malcolm H., 'Gunboat diplomacy: outmoded or back in vogue', in Dorman, A. *et al.* (eds), *The Changing Face of Maritime Power* (Basingstoke: Macmillan Press Ltd, 1999).

Murphy, Martin, *Contemporary Piracy and Maritime Terrorism* (London: IISS, Adelphi Paper No. 388, 2007).

Musashi, Miyamoto, *A Book of Five Rings* (London: Harper Collins, 1995).

Myers, Gen. Richard B., 'Six months after: the imperatives of Operation Enduring Freedom', *Journal* of the Royal United Services Institute, April 2002.

Nailor, Peter, *The Nassau Connection: The Organisation and Management of the British Polaris Project* (London: HMSO, 1988).

Nan Li, 'Reconceptualising the PLA Navy in post-Mao China: functions, warfare, arms and organisation', Singapore: RSIS Working Paper No. 30, August 2002.

Nathan, J.A. and Oliver, P.L., *The Future of United States Naval Power* (Urbanna, IN: Indiana University Press, 1979).

Naveh, Shimon, *In Pursuit of Military Excellence* (London: Frank Cass, 1997).

Nien-Tsu, Alfred Hu and Oliver, James K., 'A framework for a small navy: the 1892 UN Law of the Sea Conference', *Naval War College Review*, Spring 1988.

Nitze, P.H., *Securing the Seas* (Boulder, CO: Westview Press, 1979).

Noer, John H., 'Southeast Asian chokepoints: keeping the sea lines of communications open', *Strategic Forum*, No. 98, December 1996.

Nott, John, *Here Today, Gone Tomorrow: Recollections of an Errant Politician* (London: Politico's Publishing, 2002).

Nye, Joseph and Owens, William, 'America's information edge', *Foreign Affairs*, March/April 1996.

O'Brien, P.P. (ed.), *Technology and Naval Combat in the Twentieth Century and Beyond London* (London: Frank Cass, 2001).

O'Connell, D.P., *The Influence of Law on Sea Power* (Manchester: Manchester University Press, 1975).

O'Connell, Robert L., *Sacred Vessels: The Cult of the Battleship and the Rise of the US Navy* (Boulder, CO: Westview Press, 1991).

O'Rourke, Ronald, 'The tanker war', *Proceedings* of the US Naval Institute, May 1998.

Olkhousky, Paul, *Russia's Navy from Peter to Stalin: Themes, Trends and Debates* (Washington, DC: Centre for Naval Analyses, Repr. of CRM 92–40, June 1992).

Osgood, R.E., *NATO: The Entangling Alliance* (Chicago, IL: Chicago University Press, 1962).

Owens, Adm. William A., 'The emerging system of systems', *Proceedings* of the US Naval Institute, May 1995a.

Owens, Adm. William A., *High Seas: The Naval Passage to an Uncharted World* (Annapolis, MD: Naval Institute Press, 1995b).

Padfield, Peter, *Maritime Supremacy and the Opening of the Western Mind* (Woodstock and New York: Overlook Press, 1999).

Palmer, Michael A., *Origins of the Maritime Strategy: American Naval Strategy in the First Postwar Decade* (Washington, DC: Naval Historical Center, 1988).

Palmer, Sarah, 'Seeing the sea: the maritime strategy in history', Inaugural Lecture Series, University of Greenwich, 11 May 2000.

Paranjpe, Shrikant, 'India's security policy: an evaluation after fifty years', *International Studies* (New Delhi), Vol. 35, No. 2, 1998.

Parry, Capt. Chris, 'Maritime manoeuvre and joint operations to 2020', in Duffy, M. *et al.* (eds), *European Defence in 2020* (Exeter, UK: University of Exeter, 1998).

Payne, Keith B., *Deterrence in The Second Nuclear Age* (Lexington, KN: University Press of Kentucky, 1996).

Pengelly, Rupert, 'Grappling for submarine supremacy', *Jane's International Defence Review*, Issue 7, 1996.

Perkins, J.B., 'Praying mantis: the surface view', *Proceedings* of the US Naval Institute Vol 114, No 5, 1989.

Peterson, Capt. Gordon I., 'The US navy expeditionary combat command: a new focus on green and and brown water missions', *Naval Forces*, Vol. 4, 2006.

Philbin. T., 'Admiral Franz Hipper on naval warfare', *Naval War College Review*, Fall 1971.

Platt, Suzy (ed.), *Respectfully Quoted: A Dictionary of Quotations* (Washington, DC: Library of Congress, 1989).

Pokrant, Marvin, *Desert Shield at Sea: What the Navy Really Did* (Westpoint, CT: Greenwood Press, 1999a).

Pokrant, Marvin, *Desert Storm at Sea: What the Navy Really Did* (London: Greenwood Press, 1999b).

Politakis, George P., *Modern Aspects of the Laws of Naval Warfare and Maritime Neutrality* (London: Kegan Paul, 1998).

Politi, Alessandro, *European Society: The New Transnational Risks* (Paris: Institute For Security Studies, 1997).

Pollen, A.H., *The Navy in Battle* (London: Chatto & Windus, 1918).

Posen, Barry, 'Command of the commons: the military foundations of US hegemony', *International Security*, Vol. 28, No. 1, Summer 2003, pp. 5–46.

Prabhakar, Lawrence W., Ho, Joshua H. and Bateman, Sam (eds), *The Evolving Maritime Balance of Power in the Asia-Pacific* (Singapore: World Scientific and IDSS, 2006).

Preston, Antony, 'High tech on the high seas', *Armada International*, Issue 5, 1999.

Prins, Gwyn and Stamp, Robbie, *Top Guns and Toxic Whales: The Environment and Global Security* (London: Earthscan Publications, 1991).

Pugh, Michael (ed.), *Maritime Security and Peacekeeping: A Framework for United Nations Operations* (Manchester: Manchester University Press, 1994).

Pugh, Michael, *Europe's Boat People: Maritime Cooperation in the Mediterranean* (Paris: Institute for Security Studies, Chailot Papers 41, 2000).

Pugh, M., 'Nuclear warship visiting: storms in ports', *World Today*, October 1989.

Puleston, W.D., *Mahan: The Life and Works of Alfred Thayer Mahan* (Newhaven, CT: Yale University Press, 1939).

Rahman, Chris, 'Naval cooperation and coalition building in Southeast Asian and the Southwest Pacific: status and prospects', Royal Australian Navy Sea Power Centre, Canberra, October 2001.

Rahn, W., 'German naval strategy and armament 1919–39', in O'Brien, P.P. (ed.), *Technology and Naval Combat in the Twentieth Century and Beyond London* (London: Frank Cass, 2001).

Ranft, B. (ed.), *Technical Change and British Naval Policy 1860–1939* (London: Hodder & Stoughton, 1977).

Ranft, B. and Till, G., *The Sea in Soviet Strategy* (Basingstoke: Macmillan Press Ltd, 1989).

Ranft, B.Mcl., *The Beatty Papers* (Vol. 2) (London: Scolar Press, 1993).

Reason, Adm. J. Paul, *Sailing New Seas* (Newport, RI: Naval War College, 1998).

Record, Jeffrey, 'Failed states and casualty phobia: implications for force structure and technology choices', Maxwell Air Force Base, AL: Air University, Center for Strategy and Technology, Occasional Paper No. 15, October 2000.

Reeve, John, 'The rise of modern naval strategy c 1850–1880', in Stephens, David and Reeve, John (eds), *Southern Trident: Strategy, History and the Rise of Australian Naval Power* (Crows Nest, Australia: Allen & Unwin, 2001).

Reynolds, Clark G., *Command of the Seas* (New York: Morrow, 1974).

Reynolds, Clark G., 'The US fleet-in-being strategy', in the 'Battle of the Coral Sea 1942' Conference, *Proceedings*, Australia National Maritime Museum, Sydney 1993.

Reynolds, Clark G., *Navies in History* (Annapolis, MD: Naval Institute Press, 1998).

Richmond, H.W., *Naval Warfare* (London: Ernest Benn, 1930).

Richmond, H.W., *Seapower in the Modern World* (London: Bell, 1934).

Richmond, H.W., *Amphibious Warfare in British History* (London: Historical Association, 1941).

Richmond, H.W., *Statesmen and Seapower* (Oxford: Clarendon Press, 1946).

Richmond, H.W., *The Navy as an Instrument of Policy 1558–1727* (Cambridge: Cambridge University Press, 1953).

Robertson, T., *Dieppe: The Shame and the Glory* (London: Hutchinson, 1963).

Rodger, N.A.M., *The Wooden World: An Anatomy of the Georgian Navy* (London: Collins, 1986).

Rodger, N.A.M. (ed.), *Naval Power in the Twentieth Century* (Basingstoke: Macmillan Press Ltd, 1996).

Rodger, N.A.M., *The Safeguard of the Sea: A Naval History of Britain. Vol. I 660–1649* (London: Harper Collins, 1997).

Rodger, N.A.M., 'Weather, geography and naval power in the age of sail', in Gray, Colin S. and Sloan, Geoffrey (eds), *Geopolitics: Geography and Strategy* (London: Frank Cass, 1999).

Rodgers, W.L., *Greek and Roman Naval Warfare* (Boston, MA: Harvard University Press, 1937).

Roksund, Arne, 'The jeune ecole: the strategy of the weak', in Hobson, Rolf and Kristiansen, Tom, *Navies in Northern Waters 1721–2000* (London: Frank Cass, 2003).

Rosen, Stephen, 'The strategic traditions of the United States', in Taylor, D. (ed.) *Asia and the Pacific Region* (Newport, RI: Naval War College Press, 2001).

Rosinski, H., 'New thoughts on strategy', in Simpson, B.M. (ed.), *War, Strategy and Maritime Powers* (New Brunswick, NJ: Rutgens University Press, 1977).

Roskill, Capt. S.W., *The War at Sea 1939–1945* (Vol. I) (London: HMSO, 1954).

Roskill, Capt. S.W., *The Strategy of Sea Power* (London: Collins, 1962).

Roskill, Stephen, *Naval Policy Between the Wars* (Vol. I) (London: Collins, 1968).

Roth, Patrick H., 'From the Brazil squadron to US navy forward presence in Latin American waters', Washington Navy Yard, US Navy Forward Presence Bicentennial Symposium, Washington, 21 June 2001.

Roy, VAdm. Mihir K., *War in the Indian Ocean* (New Delhi: Lancer Publishers, 1995).

Roy-Chaudury, Rahul, *India's Maritime Security* (New Delhi: Knowledge World, 2000).

Sadowski, Y. *The Myth of Global Chaos* (Washington, DC: Brookings Institute, 1998).

Sakhuja, Vijay, *Confidence Building From the Sea: An Indian Initiative* (New Delhi: Knowledge World, 2001).

Sater, William F., 'The rise and fall of the Chilean navy 1879–1905', in *New Interpretations: Naval History 10th Symposium* (Annapolis, MD: Naval Institute Press, 1991).

Scales, Maj. Gen. Robert H. Jr, 'America's army in transition: preparing for war in the precision age', Strategic Studies of the US Army War College, Army Issue Paper No. 3, Fall 1999.

Scheer, Adm. R., *Germany's High Sea Fleet in the World War* (London: Cassell, 1920).

Schurman, Donald M., *Julian S. Corbett 1854–1922* (London: Royal Historical Society, 1981).

Scott, Richard, 'Future ambition: charting the course of CVF', *Jane's Navy International*, May 1999.

Scott, Richard, 'Project partners sail diverging courses to new horizons', *Jane's International Defence Review*, Issue 1, 2000.

Sears. Stephen W., *To The Gates of Richmond: The Peninsula Campaign* (Boston, MA: Houghton Mifflin, 2001).

Semmel, Bernard, *Liberalism and Naval Strategy: Ideology, Intent and Sea Power during the Pax Britannica* (Boston, MA: Allen & Unwin, 1986).

Shekawat, Adm. V.S., 'Maritime dimension of India's security: the future Indian maritime foundation', *Seagull* (Pune), August/October 2001.

Shulman, Mark Russel, *Navalism and the Emergance of American Sea Power 1882–1893* (Annapolis, MD: Naval Institute Press, 1995).

Shultz, Richard H. and Pfaltzgraff, Robert L., *The Role of Naval Forces in 21st Century Operations* (Washington, DC: Brassey's, 2000).

Slade, Stuart, 'Naval radars and command systems', in Friedman N. (contrib. ed.), *Navies in the Nuclear Age: Warships Since 1945* (London: Conway Maritime Press, 1993).

Snyder, Craig A., *Contemporary Security and Strategy* (Basingstoke: Palgrave, 2008).

Sondhaus, L., *Naval Warfare 1815–1914* (London: Routledge, 2001).

Souza, Philip de, *Seafaring and Civilisations: Maritime Perspectives on World History* (London: Profile Books, 2001).

Stanik, Joseph T., *Swift and Effective Retribution: The US Sixth Fleet and the Confrontation with Qaddafi*, The US Navy in the Modern World Series, No, 3 (Washington, DC: Naval Historical Center, 1996).

Stansfield Turner, Adm., 'Missions of the US navy', *Naval War College Review*, March/April 1974.

Stansfield Turner, Adm., 'The naval balance: not just a numbers game', *Foreign Affairs*, January 1977.

Steinberg, J., *Yesterday's Deterrent: Tirpitz and the Birth of the German Battle Fleet* (London: Macdonald, 1965).

Stevens, David, *Prospects for Maritime Aviation in the Twenty First Century*. (Canberra: Maritime Studies Program, 1999).

Stevens, David (ed.), *The Royal Australian Navy Vol. III* (Melbourne, Australia: Oxford University Press, 2001a).

Stevens, R-Adm. Robert, 'The British submarine service: past, present and future', *Journal* of the Royal United Services Institute, June 2001b.

Stewart, Cdr Ninian, *The Royal Navy and the Palestinian Patrol* (London: Frank Cass, 2002).

Stiglitz, Joseph, *Making Globalization Work: The Next Steps to Global Justice* (London: Penguin, 2007).

Strausz-Hupe, R., *Geopolities: The Struggle for Space and Power* (New York: Putnam, 1942).

Sumida, Jon Tetsuro, *In Defence of Naval Supremacy: Finance, Technology, and British Naval Policy* (Boston, MA: Unwin, Hyman, 1989).

Sumida, Jon Tetsuro, *Inventing Grand Strategy and Teaching Command: The Classic Works of Alfred Thayer Mahan Reconsidered* (Baltimore, MD: Johns Hopkins University Press, 1997).

Sumida, Jon Tetsuro, 'Alfred Thayer Mahan, geopolitician', in Gray, Colin S. and Sloan, Geoffrey (eds), *Geopolitics: Geography and Strategy* (London: Frank Cass, 1999).

Sumida, Jon Tetsuro, 'Getting new insight from old books: the case of Alfred Thayer Mahan', Conference Paper, Newport, 2000.

Sun Tzu, *The Art of War* (trans. and 'Introduction' by Samuel B. Griffith) (Oxford: Oxford University Press, 1971).

Svechin, A.A., *Strategiia* (Moscow: Voenizdat, 1926).

Swartz, Peter M., *A Deep Legacy: Smaller Scale Contingencies and the Forces That Shape the Navy* (Washington, DC: Center For Naval Analyses, CRM 98–95.10, December 1998).

Synge, Ian, 'Redefining naval doctrines', *Jane's Navy International*, December 1999.

Syret, David, *The Royal Navy in European Waters During the American Revolutionary War* (Columbia, SC: University of Southern Carolina, 1998).

Tahiliani, Adm. R.H., 'Maritime strategy for the nineties', *Indian Defence Review*, July 1989.

Tangredi, Capt. Sam J., 'Globalisation and naval forward presence: issues and insights', Institute for National Strategic Studies, NDU Washington, Global Forum, Vol. 2, No. 1, April 2001.

Tangredi, Capt. Sam J., 'Security from the ocean', in Flanagan, Stephen J., Frost, Ellen L. and Kugler, Richard L., *Challenges of the Global Century*, Report of the Project on Globalization and National Security (Washington, DC: National Defense University, 2001).

Tangredi, Capt. Sam J., 'Sea power: theory and practice', in Baylis *et al.*, *Strategy in the Contemporary World: An Introduction to Strategic Studies* (Oxford: OUP, 2002a).

Tangredi, Sam J. (ed.)., *Globalization and Maritime Power* (Washington, DC: National Defense University Press, 2002b).

Taylor, C.C., *The Life of Admiral Mahan, Naval Philosopher* (London: John Murray, 1920).

Taylor, Paul D. (ed.), *Asia and the Pacific: US Strategic Traditions and Regional Realities* (Newport, RI: Naval War College Press, 2001). (Especially Dibb, Paul, 'Strategic trends in the Asia Pacific region'.)

Thatcher, Margaret, *The Downing Street Years* (London: Harper Collins, 1993).

Thompson, Julian, *The Lifeblood of War: Logistics in Armed Conflict* (London: Brassey's, 1991).

Till, Geoffrey, *Airpower and the Royal Navy 1914–1915* (London: Jane's Publishing, 1979).

Till, Geoffrey (ed.), *Seapower: Theory and Practice* (London: Frank Cass, 1994).

Till, Geoffrey, 'Luxury fleet? The sea power of (Soviet) Russia', in Rodger, N.A.M. (ed.), *Naval Power in the Twentieth Century* (Basingstoke: Macmillan Press Ltd, 1996).

Till, Geoffrey (ed.), *Seapower at the Millenium* (Stroud, UK: Sutton's Publishing, 2001).

Till, Geoffrey, *Naval Transformation, Ground Forces and the Expeditionary Impulse: The Sea-Basing Debate* (Carlisle, PA: SSI Letorte Papers, December 2006a).

Till, Geoffrey, *The Development of British Naval Thinking* (London: Routledge, 2006b).

Tracey, Nicholas, *Attack on Maritime Trade* (Basingstoke: Macmillan, 1991).

Tracey, Nicholas, 'Canada's naval strategy: the record and the prospects', in Griffiths, Ann L. and Haydon, Peter T., *Maritime Forces in Global Security* (Halifax NS: Dalhousie University, Centre for Foreign Policy Studies, 1995).

Tritten, Dr James J. and Barnett, R.W., 'Are naval operations unique?' *Naval Forces*, Vol. 7, November 1986.

Tritten, Dr James J. and Barnett, R.W., 'Is naval warfare unique?' *Journal of Strategic Studies*, December 1989.

Tritten, Dr James J., *Naval Perspectives For Military Doctrine Developments* (Norfolk VA: Naval Doctrine Command, September 1994).

Tritten, Dr James J., 'Development issues for multinational navy doctrine', in Haydon, Peter T. and Griffiths, Ann L. (eds), *Multinational Naval Forces* (Halifax, NS: Dalhousie University, Centre for Foreign Policy Studies, 1995).

Tritten, Dr James J., *A Doctrine Reader: The Navies of United States, Great Britain, France, Italy and Spain* (Newport, RI: Naval War College, 1995).

Tritten, Dr James J., *Navy Combat Leadership for Tomorrow: When Will We Get Such Men and Women?* (Norfolk, VA: Naval Doctrine Command, 1–00–001, 1996).

Tsamenyi, Martin, 'Analysis of contemporary and emerging navigational issues in the law of the sea', University of Woollongong, Australia, Working Paper No. 8, November 2001.

Tunander, Ole, *The Secret War Against Sweden* (London: Frank Cass, 2003).

Tunstall, Brian, *Naval Warfare in the Age of Sail: The Evolution of Fighting Tactics 1650–1815* (edited by Nicholas Tracey) (London: Conway, 1990).

Tyushkevich, S.A., *The Soviet Armed Forces: A History of their Organisational Development* (Moscow: Military Publishing House, 1978).

Tzalel, Moshe, *From Ice Breaker to Missile Boat: The Evolution of Israel's Naval Strategy* (Westport, CT: Greenwood Press, 2000).

Ullman, Harlan K., *In Harm's Way: American Seapower and the 21st Century* (Silver Spring, MD: Bartleby Press, 1991).

Ullman, H., 'When is a revolution in military affairs, a real revolution?' *World Defence Systems* (London: Royal United Services Institute, 2001).

Van Dyke, Jon M. *et al.* (eds), *Freedom for the Seas in the 21st Century: Ocean Governance and Environmental Harmony* (Washington, DC: Island Press, 1993).

Vidigal, Armando, *EvolucÂo do Pensamento Naval Brasileiro* (Rio de Janeiro: Biblioteca do Exercito, 1985).

Ward, Iain, *Mariners: The Hong Kong Marine Police 1948–97* (Wivenhoe, Exeter: IEW Publications, 1999).

Warner, Oliver, *The Glorious First of June* (London: Batsford, 1961).

Waters, Lt Cdr D.W., *A Study of the Philosophy and Conduct of Maritime Warfare 1815–1945* (London: MoD, Naval Historical Branch, 1957).

Wathen, J., *Humanitarian Operations: The Dilemma of Intervention* (Camberley, UK: Strategic and Combat Studies Institute, Occasional Papers, No. 42, July 2001).

Weatherford, Jack, *Genghiz Khan and the Making of the Modern World* (New York: Three Rivers Press, 2004).

Weeks, Stanley B., *US Naval Forward Presence in the Cold War: Perceptions of Former Soviet Elites* (Washington, DC: SAIC Research Memorandum, 1994).

Weir, Gary E., *An Ocean in Common* (College Station, TX: Texas A&M University Press, 2001).

West, Capt. A.J.W., 'The operational level of command in the Royal Navy', Paper, Camberley, UK, Higher Command and Staff Course, February 1993.

Westcott, A. (ed.), *Mahan on Naval Warfare* (Boston: Little, Brown & Co, 1919).

Wilson, Andrew R., 'Chinese seapower in the twenty-first century: aspirations and limitations' in Till, Geoffrey (ed.), *Seapower at the Millenium* (Stroud, UK: Sutton's Publishing, 2001).

Wilson, C., *Profit and Power: A Study of England and the Dutch Wars* (London: Longmans, 1957).

Wilson, David (ed.), *Maritime War in the 21st Century: The Medium and Small Navy Perspective* (Canberra: Royal Australian Navy Sea Power Centre, 2001).

Wilson, G.C., 'Wartime rules of engagement: a postwar history of the British experience, II', *Naval Review*, April 1998, pp. 121–127.

Wong, J.Y., *Deadly Dreams: Opium, Imperialism and the Arrow War (1856–1860) in China* (Cambridge: Cambridge University Press, 1998).

Woodman, Richard, *The Victory of Seapower: Winning the Napoleonic War 1806–1814* (London: Chatham Publishing, 1998).

Woodward, David, *The Russians at Sea* (London: Kimber, 1965).

Woodward, Adm. Sandy, *One Hundred Days: The Memoirs of the Falklands Battle Group Commander* (London: Harper Collins, 1992).

Wright, A., *Australian Carrier Decisions: The Acquisition of HMA Ships Allatron, Sydney and Melbourne* (Canberra: Canberra Maritime Studies Programme, Department of Defence (Navy), June 1998).

Yerxa, Donald A., *Admirals and Empire: The United States Navy and the Caribbean 1898–1945* (Columbia, SC: University of South Carolina, 1991).

You, Ji, 'The Chinese navy and national interest', in McCaffrie, Jack and Hinge, Alan (eds), *Sea Power in the New Century* (Canberra: Australian Defence Studies Centre, 1998).

Young, Oran R., *The Politics of Force: Bargaining During International Crises* (Princeton, NJ: Princeton University Press, 1968).

Zelikow, Philip D., 'Force without war, 1975–1982', *Journal of Strategic Studies*, March 1984.

Zimmerman, T., 'The American bombing of Libya: a screen for coercive diplomacy?' *Survival*, May/June 1987.

Index